LPIC-2
Study Guide

Second Edition

LPIC-2:
Linux Professional Institute Certification

Study Guide
Exam 201 and Exam 202

Second Edition

Christine Bresnahan

Richard Blum

Senior Acquisitions Editor: Kenyon Brown
Development Editor: Gary Schwartz
Technical Editor: Kevin Ryan
Production Editor: Christine O'Connor
Copy Editor: Linda Rectenwald
Editorial Manager: Mary Beth Wakefield
Production Manager: Kathleen Wisor
Executive Publisher: Jim Minatel
Book Designers: Judy Fung and Bill Gibson
Proofreader: Rebecca Rider
Indexer: John Sleeva
Project Coordinator, Cover: Brent Savage
Cover Designer: Wiley
Cover Image: Getty Images Inc./Jeremy Woodhouse

Copyright © 2016 by John Wiley & Sons, Inc., Indianapolis, Indiana

Published simultaneously in Canada

ISBN: 978-1-119-15079-4

ISBN: 978-1-119-15081-7 (ebk.)

ISBN: 978-1-119-15080-0 (ebk.)

Manufactured in the United States of America

To those looking to further their knowledge of Linux. "A wise man is full of strength, and a man of knowledge enhances his might." Prov 24:5 (ESV)

Acknowledgments

First, all glory and praise go to God, who through His Son, Jesus Christ, makes all things possible and gives us the gift of eternal life.

Many thanks go to the fantastic team of people at Sybex for their outstanding work on this project. Thanks to Kenyon Brown, the senior acquisitions editor, for offering us the opportunity to work on this book. Also thanks to Gary Schwartz, the development editor, for keeping things on track and making the book more presentable. Thanks, Gary, for all your hard work and diligence. The technical editor, Kevin E. Ryan, did a wonderful job of double-checking all of the work in the book in addition to making suggestions to improve the content. Thanks also goes to the young and talented Daniel Anez (theanez.com) for his illustration work. We would like to thank Carole Jelen at Waterside Productions, Inc., for arranging this opportunity for us and for helping us out in our writing careers.

Christine would particularly like to thank her husband, Timothy, for his encouragement, patience, and willingness to listen, even when he has no idea what she is talking about.

Rich would particularly like to thank his wife, Barbara, for enduring his grouchy attitude during this project and helping to keep up his spirits with baked goods.

About the Authors

Christine Bresnahan started working with computers more than 25 years ago in the IT industry as a systems administrator. Christine is an adjunct professor at Ivy Tech Community College, where she teaches Linux certification and Python programming classes. She also writes books and produces instructional resources for the classroom.

Richard Blum has worked in the IT industry for more than 25 years as both a system and network administrator, and he has published numerous Linux and open source books. Rich is an online instructor for Linux and web programming courses that are used by colleges and universities across the United States. When he is not being a computer nerd, Rich enjoys spending time with his wife, Barbara, and his two daughters, Katie and Jessica.

Contents at a Glance

Contents

Table of Exercises

Introduction

Welcome to the *LPIC-2: Linux Professional Institute Certification Study Guide*. If you used our *LPIC-1: Linux Professional Institute Certification Study Guide* to study for your LPIC-1 exam, welcome back! We're glad that you decided to stay with us for your LPIC-2 study resources.

Just like our LPIC-1 Study Guide, this book contains detailed explanations for all of the LPIC-2 exam objectives, along with example questions, flashcards for self-study, and practice questions. The purpose of this book is to help you pass both of the LPIC-2 exams, 201 and 202. These exams cover more advanced topics than the LPIC-1 exam, such as the Linux kernel, system startup, filesystems, network operations, DNS servers, web servers, file servers, email servers, network client management, and security. This book will walk you through all of these topics, helping prepare you for the LPIC-2 exam questions.

LPI's Certification Program

The purpose of the Linux Professional Institute's (LPI) LPIC-2 program is to define the basic knowledge required to administer small to medium-sized mixed (Microsoft and Linux) networks, focusing on the Linux operating system. The program guides professionals wishing to build on knowledge gained from the LPIC-1 program.

It is expected that you have already passed the LPI Linux Essentials (optional) exam and the LPIC-1 (or CompTIA Linux+) exam and have at least five years' experience in administering a Linux server(s) in a mixed network environment.

The successful LPIC-2 candidate should have at a minimum knowledge and experience concerning the following topics:

- Administering multiple Linux servers
- Advising management on computerization and purchasing
- Planning and managing a small, mixed-network environment, which includes the following:
    - LAN server:
        - Client management
        - DHCP
        - DNS
        - NFS
        - Samba
    - Internet gateway:
        - Firewall
        - Mail

- OpenSSH
- VPN
- Web cache/proxy
  - Internet server:
    - FTP server
    - Web server
    - Web server with a reverse proxy
- Team supervision skills

If you've already passed the LPIC-1 exam, you've proven to the world that you're proficient with the basic operation of Linux, along with the basic Linux commands. But don't stop there. When you pass the LPIC-2 exam, that will demonstrate that you have the skills that companies look for when hiring Linux administrators. Having the LPIC-2 certification validates your skills, and it helps prepare you for working with Linux servers in a commercial environment.

How to Become Certified

The LPIC-2 certification is available to anyone who has an active LPIC-1 certification and who passes the two required exams: 201 and 202.

To take an LPI exam, you must first register with LPI to obtain an LPI ID number (if you already did this for the LPIC-1 exam, you must use your existing LPI ID number for the LPIC-2 exam). If you need to register, you can do this online at https://cs.lpi.org/caf/Xamman/register. LPI will email your LPI ID number to you. With that you can log into the LPI Marketplace to purchase an exam voucher.

The exams are administered by Pearson VUE. The exam can be taken at any Pearson VUE testing center. If you pass, you will get a certificate in the mail saying that you have passed. Call (877) 619-2096 for Pearson VUE contact information.

To register for the exam with Pearson VUE, go to http://www.vue.com. Enter the exam voucher number that you received from the LPI Marketplace, and schedule the time and place to take the exam.

Who Should Buy This Book

Anyone who wants to pass the LPIC-2 certification exams may benefit from this book. You should already have a basic knowledge of Linux, as covered by the LPIC-1 exam material. If not, you should start with our *LPIC-1: Linux Professional Institute Study Guide* book and then move on to this book. This book focuses on the more advanced Linux topics covered by the LPIC-2 201 and 202 exams. Once you obtain your certification, this book will continue to be useful by serving as a handy resource for information on installing and maintaining Linux servers.

Even if you don't plan to take the LPIC-2 exams, this book makes an excellent resource for understanding advanced Linux server topics. It covers topics such as creating your own web server, email server, and file server. These skills are required by Linux administrators in small and medium-sized network environments.

This book is written with the assumption that you have a basic knowledge of Linux. You should be familiar with how Linux works and be able to work in the Linux command line, including the core commands such as `ls`, `cp`, `mv`, `cat`, `less`, `ps`, `free`, and `uptime`. You should also already know how to install a default Linux distribution environment, because that is not covered in this book.

 You'll need a Linux system with which to practice and perform the chapter activities. Any Linux desktop or server distribution will work for the activities in this book; however, we focus on the Ubuntu and CentOS Linux desktop distributions for our examples.

How This Book Is Organized

This book consists of 12 chapters plus supplementary information: an online glossary, this introduction, and the assessment test after the introduction.

Part I of the book, Chapters 1 through 6, covers the LPIC-2 201 exam topics. Part II, Chapters 7 through 12, covers the 202 exam topics. Each chapter begins with a list of the exam objectives that are covered in that chapter. However, the book doesn't cover the objectives in order.

Part I: The LPI 201 Exam

Chapter 1: Starting a System   This chapter covers how Linux boots from the system BIOS. It discusses the Linux bootloader program and how to create a dual-boot Linux environment.

Chapter 2: Maintaining the System   This chapter describes how to install and manage resources on a Linux system. It also covers how to back up Linux systems and communicate with system users to warn of system issues or downtime.

Chapter 3: Mastering the Kernel   This chapter focuses on the core of the Linux system—the kernel. It walks you through how to install a custom kernel, as well as how to create and maintain kernel modules required to support the hardware on your Linux system.

Chapter 4: Managing the Filesystem   This chapter explores the different Linux filesystems and how to manage and maintain them, as well as how to troubleshoot them when problems occur.

Chapter 5: Administering Advanced Storage Devices   This chapter takes a look at two of the more advanced storage methods used in Linux environments. It focuses on how to use RAID devices in Linux, either as hardware devices or using a software RAID emulator. It also demonstrates how to implement a Logical Volume Manager in a Linux environment.

Chapter 6: Navigating Network Services   This chapter takes a deeper look at how Linux interacts in a network environment. It covers how to use the Linux command-line commands to set up a network interface and how to troubleshoot basic network problems.

Part II: The LPI 202 Exam

Chapter 7: Organizing Email Services   This chapter examines how to run an Internet email server using Linux. It covers the two most popular email servers—sendmail and Postfix, as well as walking you through how to use the most popular Linux email client packages—Courier and Dovecot.

Chapter 8: Directing DNS   This chapter covers the basics of the DNS system and how to configure your Linux server to offer DNS services on your network.

Chapter 9: Offering Web Services   This chapter covers how to run your own web server using a Linux server. It discusses how to install and manage the Apache web server—the most popular web server on the Internet. It also covers the nginx web server, a newer up-and-coming web server that's quickly gaining in popularity. Also, this chapter dives into the basics of Squid, a popular web proxy server used by many companies as a web firewall to block users from accessing inappropriate websites.

Chapter 10: Sharing Files   This chapter discusses how to use your Linux server as a file server in a local network. It covers using both FTP and NFS to serve files, as well as the popular Samba package to serve files to Microsoft Windows clients on a network.

Chapter 11: Managing Network Clients   This chapter explores how to use a Linux server to provide basic network services to clients on a local network. It shows how to create a DHCP server for serving dynamic IP addresses, how to create an LDAP server for providing simple network directory services, and how to use PAM to provide authentication services to local applications.

Chapter 12: Setting Up System Security   This chapter explores some ways to use your Linux server security in a network environment. It covers using the `iptables` program as a firewall, OpenSSH for remote communication with clients, and OpenVPN to provide a secure tunnel for remote clients to get to your network.

At the end of each chapter, you'll find a couple of elements that you can use to prepare for the exam:

Exam Essentials   This section summarizes important information that was covered in the chapter. You should be able to perform each of the tasks or convey the information requested.

Review Questions   Each chapter concludes with 20 review questions. You should answer these questions and check your answers against the ones provided after the questions. If you can't answer at least 80 percent of these questions correctly, go back and review the chapter, or at least those sections that seem to be giving you difficulty.

> The review questions, assessment test, and other testing elements included with this book are *not* derived from the actual exam questions, so don't memorize the answers to these questions and assume that doing so will enable you to pass the exam. You should learn the underlying topic, as described in the text of the book. This will let you answer the questions provided with this book *and* pass the exam. Learning the underlying topic is also the approach that will serve you best in the workplace—the ultimate goal of a certification.

To get the most out of this book, you should read each chapter from start to finish and then check your memory and understanding with the end-of-chapter elements. Even if you're already familiar with a topic, you should skim the chapter; Linux is complex enough that there are often multiple ways to accomplish a task, so you may learn something even if you're already competent in an area.

Interactive Online Learning Environment and Test Bank

The authors have worked hard to provide some really great tools to help you with your certification process. The interactive online learning environment that accompanies the *LPIC-2: Linux Professional Institute Certification Study Guide: Exam 201 and Exam 202* provides a test bank with study tools to help you prepare for the certification exams—and increase your chances of passing them the first time! The test bank includes the following:

Sample Tests   All of the questions in this book are included, including the assessment test at the end of this introduction and the 240 questions from the review sections at the end of each chapter. In addition, there are two 72-question practice exams. Use these questions to test your knowledge of the study guide material. The online test bank runs on multiple devices.

Electronic Flashcards   The online text bank includes over 300 flashcards specifically written to hit you hard, so don't get discouraged if you don't ace your way through them at first. They're there to ensure that you're really ready for the exams. And no worries—armed with the review questions, practice exams, and flashcards, you'll be more than prepared when exam day comes. Questions are provided in digital flashcard format (a question followed by a single correct answer). You can use the flashcards to reinforce your learning and provide last-minute test prep before the exam.

Glossary   In addition, a glossary of key terms from this book is available as a fully searchable PDF.

Readers can access these tools by visiting `http://www.wiley.com/go/` `sybextestprep`.

Conventions Used in This Book

This book uses certain typographic styles in order to help you quickly identify important information and to avoid confusion over the meaning of words such as on-screen prompts. In particular, look for the following styles:

- *Italicized text* indicates key terms that are described at length the first time they are used in a chapter. (Italics are also used for emphasis.)

- A `monospaced` font indicates the contents of configuration files, messages displayed at a text-mode Linux shell prompt, filenames, text-mode command names, and Internet URLs.

- *`Italicized monospaced text`* indicates a variable—information that differs from one system or command run to another, such as the name of a client computer or a process ID number.

- **Bold monospaced text** is information that you're to type into the computer, usually at a Linux shell prompt. This text can also be italicized to indicate that you should substitute an appropriate value for your system. (When isolated on their own lines, commands are preceded by non-bold monospaced $ or # command prompts, denoting regular user or system administrator use, respectively.)

In addition to these text conventions, which can apply to individual words or entire paragraphs, a few conventions highlight segments of text:

A note indicates information that's useful or interesting but that's somewhat peripheral to the main text. A note might be relevant to a small number of networks, for instance, or it may refer to an outdated feature.

A tip provides information that can save you time or frustration and that may not be entirely obvious. A tip might describe how to get around a limitation or how to use a feature to perform an unusual task.

Warnings describe potential pitfalls or dangers. If you fail to heed a warning, you may end up spending a lot of time recovering from a bug, or you may even end up restoring your entire system from scratch.

Sidebar

A sidebar is like a note but longer. The information in a sidebar is useful, but it doesn't fit into the main flow of the text.

 Real World Scenario

Real World Scenario

A real world scenario is a type of sidebar that describes a task or example that's particularly grounded in the real world. This may be a situation the authors or someone the authors know has encountered, or it may be advice on how to work around problems that are common in real, working Linux environments.

EXERCISE

An exercise is a procedure that you should try on your own computer to help you learn about the material in the chapter. Don't limit yourself to the procedures described in the exercises, though! Try other commands and procedures to really learn about Linux.

The Exam Objectives

Behind every computer industry exam, you can be sure to find exam objectives—the broad topics in which exam developers want to ensure your competency. The official exam objectives are listed here. (They're also printed at the start of the chapters in which they're covered.)

 Exam objectives are subject to change at any time without prior notice and at LPI's sole discretion. Please visit LPI's website (http://www.lpi.org) for the most current listing of exam objectives.

Exam 201 Objectives

The following are the areas in which you must be proficient in order to pass the 201 exam. This exam is broken into seven topics (200–206), each of which has two or three objectives. Each objective has an associated weight that reflects its importance to the exam as a whole. The seven main topics are listed here:

Subject Area

---

200 Capacity Planning

201 Linux Kernel

202 System Startup

203 Filesystem and Devices

204 Advanced Storage Device Administration

205 Networking Configuration

206 System Maintenance

---

200 Capacity Planning

200.1 Measure and Troubleshoot Resource Usage

- Measure CPU usage.
- Measure memory usage.
- Measure disk I/O.
- Measure network I/O.
- Measure firewalling and routing throughput.
- Map client bandwidth usage.
- Match/correlate system symptoms with likely problems.
- Estimate throughput and identify bottlenecks in a system including networking.

200.2 Predict Future Resource Needs

- Use monitoring and measurement tools to monitor IT infrastructure usage.
- Predict capacity break point of a configuration.
- Observe growth rate of capacity usage.

- Graph the trend of capacity usage.
- Awareness of monitoring solutions such as Icinga2, Nagios, collectd, MRTG, and Cacti

201 Linux Kernel

201.1 Kernel Components

- Kernel 2.6.x, 3.x and 4.x documentation
- The /usr/src/linux/ kernel directory
- Creating a kernel using zImage
- Creating a kernel using bzImage
- Using xz compression to compress the kernel

201.2 Compiling a Linux Kernel

- The /usr/src/linux/ directory
- Kernel Makefiles
- Kernel 2.6.x, 3.x, and 4.x make targets
- Customize the current kernel configuration.
- Build a new kernel and appropriate kernel modules.
- Install a new kernel and any modules.
- Ensure that the boot manager can locate the new kernel and associated files.
- Module configuration files
- Use DKMS to compile kernel modules.
- Awareness of dracut

201.3 Kernel Runtime Management and Troubleshooting

- Use command-line utilities to get information about the currently running kernel and kernel modules.
- Manually load and unload kernel modules.
- Determine when modules can be unloaded.
- Determine what parameters a module accepts.
- Configure the system to load modules by names other than their file name.
- /proc filesystem
- Content of /, /boot/, and /lib/modules/
- Tools and utilities to analyze information about the available hardware
- udev rules

202 System Startup

202.1 Customizing System Startup

- Systemd
- SysV init
- Linux Standard Base Specification (LSB)

202.2 System Recovery

- BIOS and UEFI
- NVMe booting
- GRUB version 2 and Legacy
- Grub shell
- Boot loader start and handoff to kernel
- Kernel loading
- Hardware initialization and setup
- Daemon/service initialization and setup
- Know the different bootloader install locations on a hard disk or removable device.
- Overwrite standard bootloader options and using boot loader shells.
- Use systemd rescue and emergency modes.

202.3 Alternate Bootloaders

- SYSLINUX, ISOLINUX, PXELINUX
- Understanding of PXE for both BIOS and UEFI
- Awareness of systemd-boot and U-Boot

203 Filesystem and Devices

203.1 Operating the Linux Filesystem

- The concept of the fstab configuration
- Tools and utilities for handling swap partitions and files
- Use of UUIDs for identifying and mounting file systems
- Understanding of systemd mount units

203.2 Maintaining a Linux Filesystem

- Tools and utilities to manipulate an ext2, ext3, and ext4 filesystem
- Tools and utilities to perform basic Btrfs operations, including subvolumes and snapshots

- Tools and utilities to manipulate XFS
- Awareness of ZFS

203.3 Creating and Configuring Filesystem Options

- autofs configuration files
- Understanding of automount units
- UDF and ISO9660 tools and utilities
- Awareness of other CD-ROM filesystems (HFS)
- Awareness of CD-ROM filesystem extensions (Joliet, Rock Ridge, El Torito)
- Basic feature knowledge of data encryption (dm-crypt / LUKS)

204 Advanced Storage Device Administration

204.1 Configuring RAID

- Software RAID configuration files and utilities
- The mdadm program
- The `mdadm.conf` configuration file
- The `/proc/mdstat` file
- Using partition type 0xFD

204.2 Adjusting Storage Device Access

- Tools and utilities to configure DMA for IDE devices including ATAPI and SATA
- Tools and utilities to configure Solid State Drives including AHCI and NVMe
- Tools and utilities to manipulate or analyze system resources (e.g., interrupts)
- Awareness of sdparm command and its uses
- Tools and utilities for iSCSI
- Awareness of SAN, including relevant protocols (AoE, FCoE)

204.3 Logical Volume Manager

- Tools in the LVM suite
- Resizing, renaming, creating, and removing logical volumes, volume groups, and physical volumes
- Creating and maintaining snapshots
- Activating volume groups

205 Networking Configuration

205.1 Basic Networking Configuration

- Utilities to configure and manipulate ethernet network interfaces
- Configuring basic access to wireless networks

205.2 Advanced Network Configuration

- Utilities to manipulate routing tables
- Utilities to configure and manipulate ethernet network interfaces
- Utilities to analyze the status of the network devices
- Utilities to monitor and analyze the TCP/IP traffic

205.3 Troubleshooting Network Issues

- Location and content of access restriction files
- Utilities to configure and manipulate ethernet network interfaces
- Utilities to manage routing tables
- Utilities to list network states
- Utilities to gain information about the network configuration
- Methods of information about the recognized and used hardware devices
- System initialization files and their contents (Systemd and SysV init)
- Awareness of NetworkManager and its impact on network configuration

206 System Maintenance

206.1 Make and Install Programs from Source

- Unpack source code using common compression and archive utilities.
- Understand basics of invoking make to compile programs.
- Apply parameters to a configure script.
- Know where sources are stored by default.

206.2 Backup Operations

- Knowledge about directories that have to be include in backups
- Awareness of network backup solutions such as Amanda, Bacula, Bareos, and BackupPC
- Knowledge of the benefits and drawbacks of tapes, CDR, disk, or other backup media
- Perform partial and manual backups.

- Verify the integrity of backup files.
- Partially or fully restore backups.

206.3 Notify Users on System-Related Issues

- Automate communication with users through logon messages.
- Inform active users of system maintenance.

Exam 202 Objectives

The 202 exam comprises six topics (207–212), each of which contains two to five objectives. The six major topics are these:

Subject Area
207 Domain Name Server
208 HTTP Services
209 File Sharing
210 Network Client Management
211 E-Mail Services
212 System Security

207 Domain Name Server

207.1 Basic DNS Server Configuration

- BIND 9.x configuration files, terms and utilities
- Defining the location of the BIND zone files in BIND configuration files
- Reloading modified configuration and zone files
- Awareness of dnsmasq, djbdns, and PowerDNS as alternate name servers

207.2 Create and Maintain DNS Zones

- BIND 9 configuration files, terms, and utilities
- Utilities to request information from the DNS server

- Layout, content and file location of the BIND zone files
- Various methods to add a new host in the zone files, including reverse zones

207.3 Securing a DNS Server

- BIND 9 configuration files
- Configuring BIND to run in a chroot jail
- Split configuration of BIND using the forwarders statement
- Configuring and using transaction signatures (TSIG)
- Awareness of DNSSEC and basic tools
- Awareness of DANE and related records

208 HTTP Services

208.1 Basic Apache Configuration

- Apache 2.4 configuration files, terms, and utilities
- Apache log files configuration and content
- Access restriction methods and files
- mod_perl and PHP configuration
- Client user authentication files and utilities
- Configuration of maximum requests, minimum and maximum servers and clients
- Apache 2.4 virtual host implementation (with and without dedicated IP addresses)
- Using redirect statements in Apache's configuration files to customize file access

208.2 Apache Configuration for HTTPS

- SSL configuration files, tools, and utilities
- Generate a server private key and CSR for a commercial CA
- Generate a self-signed certificate
- Install the key and certificate, including intermediate CAs
- Configure Virtual Hosting using SNI
- Awareness of the issues with Virtual Hosting and use of SSL
- Security issues in SSL use, disable insecure protocols and ciphers

208.3 Implementing Squid as a Caching Proxy

- Squid 3.x configuration files, terms, and utilities
- Access restriction methods

- Client user authentication methods
- Layout and content of ACL in the Squid configuration files

208.4 Implementing Nginx as a Web Server and a Reverse Proxy

- Nginx installation and configuration
- Using Nginx as a reverse proxy
- Basic Web server

209 File Sharing

209.1 Samba Server Configuration

- Samba 4 documentation
- Samba 4 configuration files
- Samba 4 tools and utilities and daemons
- Mounting CIFS shares on Linux
- Mapping Windows usernames to Linux usernames
- User-Level Share-Level and AD security

209.2 NFS Server Configuration

- NFS version 3 configuration files
- NFS tools and utilities
- Access restrictions to certain hosts and/or subnets
- Mount options on server and client
- TCP Wrappers
- Awareness of NFSv4

210 Network Client Management

210.1 DHCP Configuration

- DHCP configuration files, terms, and utilities
- Subnet and dynamically-allocated range setup

210.2 PAM authentication

- PAM configuration files, terms, and utilities
- passwd and shadow passwords

210.3 LDAP Client Usage

- LDAP utilities for data management and queries
- Change user passwords
- Querying the LDAP directory

210.4 Configuring an OpenLDAP Server

- OpenLDAP
- Directory based configuration
- Access Control
- Distinguished Names
- Changetype Operations
- Schemas and Whitepages
- Directories
- Object IDs, Attributes and Classes

211 E-mail Services

211.1 Using E-mail Servers

- Configuration files for postfix
- Basic TLS configuration for postfix
- Basic knowledge of the SMTP protocol
- Awareness of sendmail and exim

211.2 Managing E-Mail Delivery

- Understanding of Sieve functionality, syntax, and operators
- Use Sieve to filter and sort mail with respect to sender, recipient(s), headers, and size
- Awareness of procmail

211.3 Managing Mailbox Access

- Dovecot IMAP and POP3 configuration and administration
- Basic TLS configuration for Dovecot
- Awareness of Courier

212 System Security

212.1 Configuring a Router

- iptables and ip6tables configuration files, tools, and utilities
- Tools, commands, and utilities to manage routing tables
- Private address ranges (IPv4) and Unique Local Addresses as well as Link Local Addresses (IPv6)
- Port redirection and IP forwarding
- List and write filtering and rules that accept or block IP packets based on source or destination protocol, port and address.
- Save and reload filtering configurations.

212.2 Managing FTP Servers

- Configuration files, tools, and utilities for Pure-FTPd and vsftpd
- Awareness of ProFTPd
- Understanding of passive vs. active FTP connections

212.3 Secure Shell (SSH)

- OpenSSH configuration files, tools, and utilities
- Login restrictions for the superuser and the normal users
- Managing and using server and client keys to login with and without password
- Usage of multiple connections from multiple hosts to guard against loss of connection to remote host following configuration changes

212.4 Security Tasks

- Tools and utilities to scan and test ports on a server
- Locations and organizations that report security alerts as Bugtraq, CERT, or other sources
- Tools and utilities to implement an intrusion detection system (IDS)
- Awareness of OpenVAS and Snort

212.5 OpenVPN

- OpenVPN installation and configuration
- Connecting to OpenVPN with network clients

Certification Objectives Map

Table OM.1 and Table OM.2 provide objective mappings for the LPIC-2 certification exams. They identify the chapters where the exam objectives are primarily covered.

TABLE OM.1   LPI LPIC-2 Exam 201 Objectives Map

Objectives	Chapter
Topic 200: Capacity Planning	
200.1 Measure and Troubleshoot Resource Usage	2
200.2 Predict Future Resource Needs	2
Topic 201: Linux Kernel	
201.1 Kernel Components	3
201.2 Compiling a Linux Kernel	3
201.3 Kernel Runtime Management and Troubleshooting	3
Topic 202: System Startup	
202.1 Customizing System Startup	1
202.2 System Recovery	1
202.3 Alternate Bootloaders	1
Topic 203: Filesystem and Devices	
203.1 Operating the Linux Filesystem	4
203.2 Maintaining a Linux Filesystem	4
203.3 Creating and Configuring Filesystem Options	4
Topic 204: Advanced Storage Device Administration	
204.1 Configuring RAID	5
204.2 Adjusting Storage Device Access	5
204.3 Logical Volume Manager	5

TABLE OM.2   LPI LPIC-2 Exam 202 Objectives Map

Objectives	Chapter
Topic 210: Network Client Management	
210.1 DHCP Configuration	11
210.2 PAM Authentication	11
210.3 LDAP Client Usage	11
210.4 Configuring an OpenLDAP Server	11
Topic 211: E-Mail Services	
211.1 Using E-mail Servers	7
211.2 Managing E-Mail Delivery	7
211.3 Managing Mailbox Access	7
Topic 212: System Security	
212.1 Configuring a Router	12
212.2 Managing FTP Servers	10
212.3 Secure Shell (SSH)	12
212.4 Security Tasks	12
212.5 OpenVPN	12

13. To apply a simulated data transfer across a network using both a server and a client, use the
_____ utility. (Choose the best answer.)

    A. tcpdump

    B. ping or ping6

    C. traceroute or traceroute6

    D. nmap

    E. nc

14. You just installed a new NIC and set up a wired network interface (eth2) on your server.
However, it has no network connectivity (no packets are being sent or received through the
interface). What should you do? (Choose all that apply.)

    A. Check the interface settings via the ifconfig eth2 command.

    B. Check the interface from another system using the ping or ping6 command.

    C. Check the packets coming to and from the interface by using the tcpdump utility.

    D. Check the kernel ring buffer using the dmesg utility.

    E. Check kernel messages in either of the /var/log/ directory's dmesg, messages, or
syslog files.

15. You need to use a rewinding tape device to create an archive. Which device could you use
on your Linux system? (Choose all that apply.)

    A. /dev/st0

    B. /dev/ht1

    C. /dev/sdt1

    D. /dev/nst0

    E. /dev/nht0

16. Which of the following statements are true about the rndc utility? (Choose all that apply.)

    A. You can start the BIND daemon using it.

    B. You can stop the BIND daemon using it.

    C. You can reload BIND configuration files with it.

    D. You can reload BIND zone files with it.

    E. The rndc utility does not deal with BIND.

17. The type directive in a BIND zone configuration file can be set to which of the following?
(Choose all that apply.)

    A. hint

    B. primary

    C. secondary

    D. forward

    E. stub

18. Which of the following are commands used with the `apache2ctl` utility? (Choose all that apply.)

　　A. force-stop

　　B. restart

　　C. graceful

　　D. fullstatus

　　E. status

19. Which of the following statements are true concerning Nginx? (Choose all that apply.)

　　A. Nginx uses separate program threads to handle each client.

　　B. Nginx uses an asynchronous architecture that allows it to spawn client threads within the main program as needed.

　　C. Nginx uses TCP port 80.

　　D. Nginx is deprecated and is being replaced by Apache.

　　E. Nginx can have multiple backend web servers to implement reverse proxy features.

20. Samba user account records can be stored in the _____ database. (Choose all that apply.)

　　A. smbpasswd

　　B. tdbsam

　　C. net

　　D. smbclient

　　E. ldapsam

21. Which of the following commands can display all current NFS exports and also reads the NFS export table when the NFS service starts? (Choose the best answer.)

　　A. rpcinfo

　　B. nfsstat

　　C. showmount

　　D. exportfs

　　E. mountstats

22. Where does DHCPd typically log DHCP events? (Choose all that apply.)

　　A. pump log file

　　B. messages log file

　　C. BOOTP journal

　　D. dhcpd.log file

　　E. systemd journal

23. Which PAM authentication module uses the Security Services Daemon for authenticating users? (Choose the best answer.)

   A. pam_sss.so

   B. pam_unix.so

   C. pam_nis.so

   D. pam_krb5.so

   E. pam_ldap.so

24. Which of the following OpenLDAP client utilities will allow you to add objects, such as user objects, to an LDAP database? (Choose all that apply.)

   A. ldappasswd

   B. ldapmodify

   C. ldapadd

   D. ldapsearch

   E. ldapobject

25. Which methods, supported by OpenLDAP, will allow you to configure an LDAP environment, using a single text configuration file? (Choose all that apply.)

   A. /etc/ldap.conf

   B. slapd-conf

   C. LDIF

   D. slapd.conf

   E. /etc/ldap

26. When using Postfix as your email server, which of the following sendmail emulation commands are available? (Choose all that apply.)

   A. sendmail

   B. procmail

   C. mailq

   D. mbox

   E. newaliases

27. Which of the following directories contains pseudo-files, which control router functions? (Choose the best answer.)

   A. /proc/sys/vm/

   B. /proc/sys/net/

   C. /proc/sys/dev/

   D. /srv/

   E. /proc/sys/iptables/

28. The Very Secure FTP package's primary configuration file is the _____ file. (Fill in the filename only with no directory references.)

29. Which of the following OpenSSH configuration options sets the supported level? (Choose the best answer.)

    A. `PermitRootLogin`

    B. `PubKeyAuthentication`

    C. `AllowUsers`

    D. `PasswordAuthentication`

    E. `Protocol`

30. Which of the following utilities, by default, will update firewall rules when it perceives a threat? (Choose all that apply.)

    A. `fail2ban`

    B. Snort

    C. Bugtraq

    D. `nmap`

    E. `nc`

Answers to Assessment Test

1. A, C, D, E. Option A is correct, because lsof shows open files and network connections by process. The pstree command shows current processes in a tree format, so it also is a correct choice. While its focus is primarily on network and routing information, you can determine which process (via its PID) is listening on a particular port using the netstat utility. Thus option D is also a correct answer. Option E is correct, because the pmap command shows a processes map for the designated PID. The iostat utility displays device I/O loading summary broken down per device, so option B is the only incorrect choice.

2. modules. Programmers developed the concept of kernel *modules* to allow you to insert device driver code into a running kernel without having to recompile the kernel. A module is a self-contained driver library file that can be dynamically linked and unlinked with the kernel. This means that a kernel module can be removed from the kernel when the device is finished being used, something that can't be done with compiled kernel drivers.

3. E. Option E is correct, because the Linux kernel configuration is stored in the /usr/src/linux/.config file. Option A is a directory that holds the final kernel binary, bzImage, after a compilation process, so it is an incorrect choice. Option B is a made-up filename, so it is wrong. The /boot/grub/grub.conf file is a GRUB Legacy configuration file, so option C is an incorrect choice. Option D's /etc/modules.conf file is a configuration file for kernel modules, so it is also a wrong choice.

4. B. The /proc/sys/kernel is a directory that contains the version file. This file contains Linux kernel version information, so option B is the correct choice. Option A is made up, so it is an incorrect choice. Option C's /proc/ioports is a file containing hardware I/O port information, so it is also an incorrect choice. The /proc/dma file contains Direct Memory Access (DMA) channel information, so option C is a wrong choice. Finally, /etc/sysctl.d is a directory that contains multiple kernel parameter setting files, so it also is an incorrect choice.

5. C. There is only one correct answer and that is option C. The update-rc.d command is an equivalent command to the chkconfig command. However, it is typically available on Debian-based distributions, while chkconfig is available on Red Hat–based distros. Option A's inittab (/etc/inittab) does define which applications start at which run level; however, it is a file and not a command, so it is a wrong choice. The rc in option B is a script (/etc/rc.d/rc) that runs all the scripts with a specified run level, so it is an incorrect choice. The init (option D) and telinit (option E) commands are essentially equivalent commands but to each other (you can change the current run level of your Linux system using either of them), so they are incorrect choices.

6. B, C, D. GRUB Legacy uses both a menu interface and an interactive shell (grub shell), so options B and C are correct. Option D is also correct, because within the GRUB Legacy configuration file, the initrd command is employed to define a file that's mounted by the kernel at boot time as a RAM disk. Option A is incorrect, because although LILO does not work with UEFI systems, GRUB Legacy was created in 1999 to provide a more robust and configurable bootloader than LILO, not due to UEFI. Also, option E is incorrect, because the /boot/grub/grub.cfg is a GRUB2 configuration file, not a GRUB Legacy file.

7.   A, B, C, D. Options A, B, C, and D are all alternative Linux bootloaders, so they are correct answers. Option E is Trivial File Transfer Protocol (TFTP), which is employed by the PXELINUX bootloader to transfer the boot image file to the workstation over the network. However, TFTP is not a bootloader, so option E is incorrect.

8.   B. There is only one correct choice. When used with no options or parameters, the mount command pulls data from the /etc/mtab file, which has a list of all currently mounted filesystems, and displays it. Thus, option B is correct. Option A is incorrect, because the /etc/fstab is the Filesystem Table, and it has a record for each filesystem to be mounted at either system boot time or when the mount -a command is issued. While the data in the /etc/mtab and /proc/mounts files is nearly identical, the mount command does not pull its data from the /proc/mounts file, so option C is wrong. Option D's /proc/filesystems file is incorrect, because this file contains filesystems support by the system's Linux kernel. Option E is also wrong, because blkid is not a file but a command, which displays various block devices and their attributes.

9.   smartd.conf. The smartd daemon's configuration file is either /etc/smartd.conf or /etc/smartmontools/smartd.conf (depending on your distribution).

10. A, B, D. Options A and B are the same command (the --misc option does not need to be included in the command) and they both show details on the specified RAID array, so those options are correct. Option D is also correct, because the /proc/mdstat file contains any running RAID array's current status. Option C is an incorrect choice, because /etc/mdadm.conf is the mdadm configuration file (though it may be located in /etc/mdadm/, depending on your distribution). Option E is a wrong choice, because there is no -show option for the mdadm command.

11. B, D. A logical volume storage pool (volume group) can be created using the vgcreate command, so option D is correct. The volume group can be increased in size via the vgextend command, so option B is also correct. The mdadm utility is used for managing RAID arrays and not logical volumes (though logical volumes can be RAID array members), so option A is a wrong choice. Option C's pvcreate command is used for designating filesystem partitions as physical volumes that can be placed into a volume group, but it does not increase a volume group's size or create it, so it is also an incorrect choice. The lvcreate command takes storage (logical extents) from a volume group and creates a logical volume, not a volume group, so option E is a wrong choice as well.

12. C. There is only one correct choice. The arp command will display ARP table information, so option C is the right choice. Option A is an incorrect choice, because this ifconfig command allows you to toggle on/off ARP for the designated network interface, not view the ARP table. The command in option B is made up, though close to a real command (ip addr show) that will display network interface information. Since it does not display ARP table information, option B is wrong. Option D's command will display the routing table but not the ARP table, so it is an incorrect choice. Finally, option E is also wrong, because the iwlist command in this option allows you to scan and find a local wireless connection's name, but you must specify the wireless device's name (e.g., wlan0) and not arp.

13. E. The nc utility allows you to simulate a server and a client, sending and receiving data on the network, by specifying command-line options. Therefore, option E is the best answer.

Option A's `tcpdump` command captures all packets that it sees on the network interface and displays a rough packet description, but it does not simulate data transfers, so it is an incorrect choice. The `ping` or `ping6` utility allows you to send ICMP packets and test connectivity between a server and client system, but it doesn't provide a true data transfer simulation, so option B is not the best answer. Also, option C's `traceroute` or `traceroute6` utility attempts to send ICMP packets to a specified destination and list the router "hops" that the packets traverse to get to the destination. However, they don't provide a true data transfer simulation (and may be blocked by many routers), so this option is also not the best choice. Finally, option D is not the best answer, because the `nmap` utility can determine what applications are listening to which network ports on your Linux system but not simulate data transfers to another system.

14. A, D, E. Option A is a correct choice, because you can double-check all of the various wired network interface settings and view such things as whether an IP address has been assigned. Options D and E are also correct choices, because it's possible that the appropriate network card hardware module was not loaded. You can find this information in either the kernel ring buffer or, if the buffer has been flushed to disk, in one of option E's files (depending on your distribution). Option B is not a correct choice, because if you already know that packets are not being sent or received through the interface, using `ping` or `ping6` will not give you any additional information. The same is true with option C, so it also is an incorrect choice.

15. A, B. Options A and B are correct, because the `/dev/st*` (SCSI) and `/dev/ht*` (PATA) tape devices automatically rewind. Option C is incorrect, because the `/dev/sdt1` device file does not represent a tape device but a filesystem partition. Options D and E are wrong, because the `/dev/nst*` (SCSI) and `/dev/nht*` (PATA) tape devices do *not* automatically rewind.

16. B, C, D. Options B, C, and D are true and therefore correct choices. You cannot start the BIND daemon using the `rndc` utility, so option A is an incorrect answer. Also, the `rndc` utility *does* deal with BIND, so option E is also a wrong choice.

17. A, D, E. A `type hint` directive specifies the Hint Zone, which is a list of current root name servers, so option A is a correct choice. The `type forward` directive indicates that this is a forwarding server for the zone, so option D is also a correct choice. A `type stub` directive is used to set a stub zone, so option E is a correct choice. There is no `type primary` directive. You would use `type master` to indicate a zone's primary name server, so option B is a wrong choice. Also, there is no `type secondary` directive. You would use `type slave` to set a zone's secondary name server. Therefore, option C is also an incorrect answer.

18. B, C, D, E. The `apache2ctl restart` command will send a SIGHUP signal to the Apache server, causing it to close any existing connections and restart. Therefore, option B is a correct answer. The `apache2ctl graceful` command restarts the Apache server, but existing connections are not closed, so option C is also a correct choice. Option D's `apache2ctl` command, `fullstatus`, will display a full Apache server status report, so it is a correct answer. Also, option E is a correct choice, because `apache2ctl status` will display a short Apache server status report. Option A is a made-up `apache2ctl` command, so it is the only incorrect answer.

19. B, C, E. Options B, C, and E are all truthful statements and are therefore correct answers. Option A is wrong, because Nginx does not use separate program threads for each client but instead deals with spawned client threads described in option B. Option D is also an incorrect choice, because Nginx is not deprecated and, instead, may end up someday replacing Apache.

20. A, B, E. Options A, B, and E are correct, because Samba user account information can be kept in the smbpasswd, tdbsam, or ldapsam databases. net is a command (not a database), which is similar to the Windows/DOS net utility and is used when a Samba server needs to join a domain or Active Directory as a member. Therefore, option C is a wrong answer. The smbclient in option D is either a command that connects, lists shares, and allows FTP-like services for a file share or a Samba package filename. Therefore, option D is also an incorrect choice.

21. D. Option D is the correct choice, because when used with no options, the exportfs command displays all of the current exports, and when the NFS service starts, it reads the /etc/exports file (the NFS export table) and performs the needed share exporting. Option A is an incorrect choice, because the rpcinfo command displays various RPC service data (including what ports are involved, if you add the -p option). The nfsstat utility displays NFS client and server activity statistics from the /proc/net/rpc/nfsd, /proc/net/rpc/nfs, and /proc/mounts files, so option B is an incorrect choice. Option C's showmount command displays NFS server information, such as its state and NFS clients mounting its provided exports, but it does not read the NFS export table when the service is started, so it is a wrong choice as well. The mountstats utility displays NFS client per-mount statistics from the /proc/self/mountstats file, so option E is an incorrect answer.

22. B, E. DHCPd logs all DHCP events to the standard log file for your Linux system. For distributions that still use the syslog facility that's typically the /var/log/messages file (option B). However, some current distributions use the systemd journal instead (option E). Option A's pump log file is not a log file. Instead, pump is a Linux DHCP client package and thus is an incorrect choice. Option C's BOOTP journal is an incorrect choice, because it is a protocol, Bootstrap Protocol (BOOTP), and not a journal. BOOTP allows a diskless workstation to send out a broadcast message on the network looking for a server to send it the operating system file to use to boot the workstation. The dhcpd.log file (option D) is also a wrong choice. This file does not exist. However, there is the dhcpd.conf configuration file as well as the dhcpd.leases file (for logging server-leased IP addresses) used in association with DHCP.

23. A. The pam_sss.so module uses the Security Services Daemon for authenticating users, and thus option A is the correct answer. The pam_unix.so module (option B) uses the standard /etc/passwd and /etc/shadow files, so it is an incorrect choice. Option C's pam_nis.so module is a wrong answer, because it uses an NIS server for authentication. The pam_krb5.so module (option D) is an incorrect choice, because this PAM module uses the Kerberos 5 authentication system. Option E's pam_ldap.so is also a wrong answer, because it uses a LDAP server for authentication and not the Security Services Daemon.

24. B, C. The ldapmodify (option B) utility allows you to add objects, such as user objects, to an LDAP database, and it also allows you to modify those objects, so it is a correct answer. The ldapadd utility (option C) is a link to the ldapmodify utility, and its primary purpose is to add objects defined in an LDIF file to the LDAP database. Therefore, option C is also a correct answer. Option A's ldappasswd utility allows you to generate an encrypted value from a text value in order to change the password assigned to the LDAP account you logged in with, and therefore it is a wrong choice. The ldapsearch utility (option D) is also an incorrect answer, because this utility allows you to create and customize queries in order to search an LDAP database. Option E's ldapobject is a made-up utility name and is therefore an incorrect choice.

25. D. This is a bit of a trick question, because there is only one correct answer, the slapd .conf method (option D), which uses a single text configuration file to configure an LDAP environment. The /etc/ldap.conf file (option A) *is* the single text configuration file, so therefore it is an incorrect answer. The slapd-conf method (option B) uses LDIF (option C) files to define the base LDAP directory tree, so those two choices are wrong. Option E's /etc/ldap is a directory used in the slapd-conf method, so it also is an incorrect choice.

26. A, C, E. Postfix provides similar commands that emulate common sendmail features: sendmail (option A) mimics the sendmail executable program and command options but redirects to the Postfix program, mailq (option C) lists the messages in the outgoing mail queue, and newaliases (option E) initializes the aliases database. Therefore, options A, C, and E are all correct choices. Option B's procmail is not a sendmail command but instead a popular email program that allows user-configured recipes that let each individual user direct how their email is received and processed. Therefore, it is an incorrect choice. Option D's mbox is also a wrong answer, because it is an email mailbox type that uses a single file for each user account and is usually stored in the /var/spool/mail directory or the individual user directories.

27. B. The /proc/sys/net/ directory (option B) contains pseudo-files with control router functions, especially in the ipv4 and ipv6 subdirectories, so it is the correct choice. The /proc/sys/vm/ directory (option A) contains pseudo-files, but they relate to the Linux kernel's virtual memory (VM) subsystem configuration, so it is a wrong choice. The /proc/sys/dev/ directory (option C) also contains pseudo-files. However, these files provide device parameters for certain system devices, so it is an incorrect choice. Not only does the /srv/ directory not contain pseudo-files, but it typically contains data served by the system, such as Samba shares and web pages. Therefore, option D is a wrong answer as well. The /proc/sys/iptables/ directory (option E) is a made-up directory and an incorrect choice.

28. vsftpd.conf. The primary configuration file is the vsftpd.conf, and it is located in the /etc/ directory or the /etc/vsftpd/ directory (depending on your distribution). It is internally documented, and there is also a vsftpd.conf man page.

29. E. The Protocol option (option E) sets the support level (more specifically called the *protocol level*) supported by the OpenSSH configuration, and thus it is the correct choice. Option A's PermitRootLogin option enables/disables direct logins by the root user, so it is a wrong answer. The PubKeyAuthentication option (option B) enables/disables public key authentication, so it is an incorrect choice. Option C's AllowUsers configuration option sets an allowed user list, which permits users on this list to log into the system using OpenSSH. Therefore, option C is also a wrong answer. Option D is an incorrect choice, because the PasswordAuthentication option enables/disables authentication via passwords.

30. A. This is a tricky question. Option A is the only correct choice. The `fail2ban` utility peruses certain log files for login attempts, and if it sees a particular IP address with multiple login failures, it updates firewall rules to reject (ban) the offending IP address. While Snort (option B), which is a powerful network sniffer, can be configured to kick off shell scripts (which could update firewall rules), *by default* it only sends alerts for suspected malicious activity, so it is an incorrect choice. Option C's Bugtraq is not a utility but instead a computer security mailing list, so it is a wrong answer. Option D's `nmap` utility can be used to audit network ports to determine what services are seen listening on particular ports (inside and outside a firewall), but it does no firewall modification, so it is also a wrong answer. Finally, option E's `nc` (or `netcat`) is a utility that is also useful for auditing your network's security, but it does not modify firewalls on the fly, so it is an incorrect choice.

The LPI 201 Exam

PART
I

Chapter

1

Starting a System

THE FOLLOWING EXAM OBJECTIVES ARE COVERED IN THIS CHAPTER:

- ✓ **202.1: Customizing SysV-init system startup**
- ✓ **202.2: System Recovery**
- ✓ **202.3: Alternate Bootloaders**

Before you can log in and start using your Linux system, a complicated process of booting the operating system must take place. A lot happens behind the scenes in the Linux boot process. It helps to know all of what is going on just in case something goes wrong.

This chapter examines the boot and startup processes in Linux systems. First, it looks at the role the computer firmware plays in getting the process started. After that, it discusses Linux bootloaders and examines how to configure them. Next, the chapter discusses the Linux initialization process, showing how Linux decides which background applications to start at bootup. The chapter ends by looking at some system recovery options that you have available to help salvage a system that won't boot.

The Linux Boot Process

When you turn on the power to your Linux system, it triggers a series of events that eventually leads to the login prompt. Normally, you don't worry about what happens behind the scenes of those events; you just log in and start using your applications.

However, there may be times when your Linux system doesn't boot quite correctly, or perhaps an application that you expected to be running in background mode isn't running. In those cases, it helps to have a basic understanding of how Linux boots the operating system and starts programs so that you can troubleshoot the problem.

This section walks through the steps of the boot process and shows how you can watch it to see which steps failed.

Following the Boot Process

The Linux boot process can be split into three main steps:

1. The workstation firmware starts, performing a quick check of the hardware, called a *Power-On Self Test (POST)*, and then it looks for a bootloader program to run from a bootable device.

2. The bootloader runs and determines what Linux kernel program to load.

3. The kernel program loads into memory and starts the necessary background programs required for the system to operate (such as a graphical desktop manager for desktops or web and database servers for servers).

While these three steps may seem simple on the surface, a somewhat complicated ballet of operations happens behind the scenes to keep the boot process working. Each step performs several actions as it prepares your system to run Linux.

Viewing the Boot Process

You can monitor the Linux boot process by watching the system console screen as the system boots. You'll see lots of informative messages scroll by as the system detects hardware and loads the software.

 Some graphical desktop Linux distributions hide the boot messages on a separate console window when they start up. Often, you can hit either the Esc key or the Ctrl+Alt+F1 key combination to view those messages.

Usually the boot messages scroll by somewhat quickly, and it's hard to see just what's happening. If you need to troubleshoot boot problems, you can review the boot-time messages using the dmesg command. Most Linux distributions copy the boot kernel messages into a special ring buffer in memory called the *kernel ring buffer*. The buffer is circular and set to a predetermined size. As new messages are logged into the buffer, older messages are rotated out.

The dmesg command displays the most recent boot messages that are currently stored in the kernel ring buffer, as shown in Listing 1.1.

Listing 1.1: The dmesg command output

```
$ dmesg
[    0.000000] Initializing cgroup subsys cpuset
[    0.000000] Initializing cgroup subsys cpu
[    0.000000] Initializing cgroup subsys cpuacct
[    0.000000] Linux version 3.13.0-37-generic (buildd@kapok) (gcc version 4.8.2
 (Ubuntu 4.8.2-19ubuntu1) ) #64-Ubuntu SMP Mon Sep 22 21:28:38 UTC 2014 (Ubuntu
3.13.0-37.64-generic 3.13.11.7)
[    0.000000] Command line: BOOT_IMAGE=/boot/vmlinuz-3.13.0-37-generic root=UUI
D=09007318-c158-4f3e-b519-e90bc538fb3a ro quiet splash vt.handoff=7
[    0.000000] KERNEL supported cpus:
[    0.000000]   Intel GenuineIntel
[    0.000000]   AMD AuthenticAMD
[    0.000000]   Centaur CentaurHauls
[    0.000000] e820: BIOS-provided physical RAM map:
[    0.000000] BIOS-e820: [mem 0x0000000000000000-0x000000000009fbff] usable
[    0.000000] BIOS-e820: [mem 0x000000000009fc00-0x000000000009ffff] reserved
[    0.000000] BIOS-e820: [mem 0x00000000000f0000-0x00000000000fffff] reserved
```

```
[    0.000000] BIOS-e820: [mem 0x0000000000100000-0x000000006edefffff] usable
[    0.000000] BIOS-e820: [mem 0x000000006edf0000-0x000000006edfffff] ACPI data
[    0.000000] BIOS-e820: [mem 0x00000000fffc0000-0x00000000ffffffff] reserved
[    0.000000] NX (Execute Disable) protection: active
[    0.000000] SMBIOS 2.5 present.
[    0.000000] DMI: innotek GmbH VirtualBox/VirtualBox, BIOS VirtualBox
12/01/2006
```

Most Linux distributions also store the boot messages in a log file, usually in the /var/log folder. For Debian-based systems, the file is usually /var/log/boot, while for Red Hat–based systems, the file is /var/log/boot.log.

Although it helps to be able to see the different messages generated during boot time, it is also helpful to know just what generates those messages. This chapter discusses each of these three boot steps, and it goes through some examples showing how they work.

The Firmware Startup

All IBM-compatible workstations and servers utilize some type of built-in firmware to control how the installed operating system starts. On older workstations and servers, this firmware was called the *Basic Input/Output System (BIOS)*. On newer workstations and servers, a new method, called the *Unified Extensible Firmware Interface (UEFI)*, is responsible for maintaining the system hardware status and launching an installed operating system.

Both methods eventually launch the main operating system program, however, and each method uses different ways of doing that. This section walks you through the basics of the BIOS and UEFI methods, showing you how they participate in the Linux boot process.

The BIOS Startup

The BIOS firmware found in older workstations and servers was somewhat limited in what it could do. The BIOS firmware had a simplistic menu interface that allowed you to change some settings to control how the system found hardware and define what device the BIOS should use to start the operating system.

One of the limitations of the original BIOS firmware was that it could read only one sector's worth of data from a hard drive into memory in order to run. As you can probably guess, that's not enough space to load an entire operating system. To get around that limitation, most operating systems (including Linux and Microsoft Windows) split the boot process into two parts.

First, the BIOS runs a bootloader program. The *bootloader* is a small program that initializes the necessary hardware to find and run the full operating system, which is usually found at another location on the same hard drive but sometimes situated on a separate internal or external storage device.

The bootloader program usually has a configuration file, so you can tell it where to find the actual operating system file to run or even to produce a small menu allowing the user to boot between multiple operating systems.

To get things started, the BIOS must know where to find the bootloader program on an installed storage device. Most BIOS setups allow you to load the bootloader program from several locations:

- An internal hard drive
- An external hard drive
- A CD/DVD drive
- A USB memory stick
- A network server

When booting from a hard drive, you must designate which hard drive, and which partition on the hard drive, the BIOS should load the bootloader program from. This is done by defining a *Master Boot Record (MBR)*.

The MBR is the first sector on the first hard drive partition on the system. There is only one MBR for the computer system. The BIOS looks for the MBR and reads the program stored there into memory. Since the bootloader program must fit in one sector, it must be very small—so it can't do much. The bootloader program mainly points to the location of the actual operating system kernel file, which is stored in a boot sector of a separate partition on the system. There are no size limitations on the kernel boot file.

 The bootloader program isn't required to point directly to an operating system kernel file—it can point to any type of program, including another bootloader program. You can create a primary bootloader program that points to a secondary bootloader program, which provides options to load multiple operating systems. This process is called *chainloading*.

The UEFI Startup

While there were plenty of limitations with BIOS, computer manufacturers learned to live with them, and BIOS was the default standard for IBM-compatible systems for many years. However, as operating systems became more complicated, it eventually became clear that a new boot method needed to be developed.

Intel created the *Extensible Firmware Interface (EFI)* in 1998 to address some of the limitations of BIOS. The adoption of EFI was somewhat of a slow process, but by 2005 the idea caught on with other vendors, and the *Universal EFI (UEFI)* specification was adopted as a standard. These days, just about all IBM-compatible desktop and server systems utilize the UEFI firmware standard.

Instead of relying on a single boot sector on a hard drive to hold the bootloader program, UEFI specifies a special disk partition, called the *EFI System Partition (ESP)* to store bootloader programs. This allows for any size of bootloader program, plus the ability to store multiple bootloader programs for multiple operating systems.

The ESP setup utilizes the old Microsoft File Allocation Table (FAT) filesystem to store the bootloader programs. On Linux systems, the ESP is typically mounted in the /boot/efi folder, and the bootloader files are typically stored using the .efi filename extension.

The UEFI firmware utilizes a built-in mini bootloader (sometimes referred to as a *boot manager*), which allows you to configure just which bootloader program file to launch.

Not all Linux distributions support the UEFI firmware. If you're using a UEFI system, make sure that the Linux distribution you select supports it.

With UEFI, you need to register each individual bootloader file that you want to appear at boot time in the boot manager interface menu. The `efibootmgr` Linux application allows you to create and remove boot entries or change the boot order. The UEFI interface includes a shell environment, allowing you to enter commands to alter boot settings, or select the bootloader to run each time you boot the system.

Once the firmware finds and runs the bootloader, its job is done. The bootloader step in the boot process can be somewhat complicated. The next section dives into covering this step.

Another popular new technology commonly found on UEFI systems is the use of solid state drives (SSDs) to replace legacy hard drives. SSD hardware doesn't use legacy hard drive controllers, but instead, utilizes the *Non-Volatile Memory Express (NVMe)* standard. The Linux kernel has supported NVMe systems since kernel version 3.3, and the UEFI boot process works just fine when using SSD hardware in Linux systems.

Linux Bootloaders

The bootloader program helps bridge the gap between the system firmware and the full Linux operating system kernel. In Linux, you have several choices of bootloaders. The most popular ones that you'll run across are these:

- Linux Loader (LILO)
- Grand Unified Bootloader (GRUB) Legacy
- GRUB2

In the original versions of Linux, the *Linux Loader (LILO)* bootloader was the only one available. It was extremely limited in what it could do, but it accomplished its purpose, that is, loading the Linux kernel from the BIOS startup. LILO became the default bootloader used by Linux distributions in the 1990s. The LILO configuration file is stored in a single file, `/etc/lilo.conf`, which defines the systems to boot. Unfortunately, LILO doesn't work with UEFI systems, so it has limited use on modern systems and is quickly fading into history.

The first version of the GRUB bootloader (now called *GRUB Legacy*) was created in 1999 to provide a more robust and configurable bootloader to replace LILO. GRUB quickly became the default bootloader for all Linux distributions, whether they were run on BIOS or UEFI systems.

GRUB2 was created in 2005 as a total rewrite of the GRUB Legacy system. It supports advanced features, such as the ability to load hardware driver modules and use logic statements to alter the boot menu options dynamically, depending on conditions detected on the system (such as if an external hard drive is connected).

> Since UEFI can load any size of bootloader program, it's now possible to load a Linux operating system kernel directly without a special bootloader program. This feature was incorporated in the Linux kernel starting with version 3.3.0. However, this method isn't common, because bootloader programs can provide more versatility in booting, especially when working with multiple operating systems.

This section walks through the basics of both the GRUB Legacy and GRUB2 bootloaders, which should cover just about every Linux distribution that you'll run into these days.

GRUB Legacy

The GRUB Legacy bootloader was designed to simplify the process of creating boot menus and passing options to kernels. GRUB Legacy allows you to select multiple kernels and/or operating systems using a menu interface as well as an interactive shell. You configure the menu interface to provide options for each kernel or operating system you wish to boot. The interactive shell provides a way for you to customize boot commands on the fly.

Both the menu and the interactive shell utilize a set of commands that control features of the bootloader. This section walks you through how to configure the GRUB Legacy bootloader, how to install it, and how to interact with it at boot time.

Configuring GRUB Legacy

When you use the GRUB Legacy interactive menu, you need to tell it what options to show. You do that using special GRUB *menu commands*.

The GRUB Legacy system stores the menu commands in a standard text configuration file. The configuration file used by GRUB Legacy is menu.lst, and it is stored in the /boot/ grub folder. (While not a requirement, some Linux distributions create a separate /boot partition on the hard drive.) Red Hat–derived Linux distributions (such as CentOS and Fedora) use grub.conf instead of menu.lst for the configuration file.

The GRUB Legacy configuration file consists of two sections:

- Global definitions
- Operating system boot definitions

The global definitions section defines commands that control the overall operation of the GRUB Legacy boot menu. The global definitions must appear first in the configuration file. There are only a handful of global settings. Table 1.1 shows these settings.

TABLE 1.1   GRUB Legacy global commands

Setting	Description
color	Specifies the foreground and background colors to use in the boot menu
default	Defines the default menu option to select
fallback	A secondary menu selection to use if the default menu option fails
hiddenmenu	Don't display the menu selection options
splashimage	Points to an image file to use as the background for the boot menu
timeout	Specifies the amount of time to wait for a menu selection before using the default

For GRUB Legacy, to define a value for a command you just list the value as a command-line parameter:

```
default 0
timeout 10
color white/blue yellow/blue
```

The color command defines the color scheme for the menu. The first pair of values defines the foreground/background colors for normal menu entries, while the second pair defines the foreground/background colors for the selected menu entry.

After the global definitions, you place definitions for the individual operating systems that are installed on the system. Each operating system should have its own definition section. You can use many boot definition settings to customize how the bootloader finds the operating system kernel file. Fortunately, just a few commands are required to define the operating system. The ones to remember are as follows:

- title—The first line for each boot definition section, this is what appears in the boot menu.
- root—Defines the disk and partition where the GRUB /boot folder partition is located on the system.
- kernel—Defines the kernel image file stored in the /boot folder to load.
- initrd—Defines the initial RAM disk file, which contains drivers necessary for the kernel to interact with the system hardware.
- rootnoverify—Defines non-Linux boot partitions, such as Windows.

The root command defines the hard drive and partition that contain the /boot folder for GRUB Legacy. Unfortunately, GRUB Legacy uses a somewhat odd way of referencing those values:

```
(hddrive, partition)
```

Also unfortunately, GRUB Legacy doesn't refer to hard drives the way Linux does: it uses a numbering system to reference both disks and partitions, starting at 0 instead of at 1. For example, to reference the first partition on the first hard drive of the system, you'd use (hd0,0). To reference the second partition on the first hard drive, you'd use (hd0,1).

The initrd command is another important feature in GRUB Legacy. It helps solve a problem that arises when using specialized hardware or filesystems as the root drive. The initrd command defines a file that's mounted by the kernel at boot time as a RAM disk. The kernel can then load modules from the RAM disk, which then allows it to access hardware or filesystems not compiled into the kernel itself. (Chapter 3, "Mastering the Kernel," discusses how to create the initrd image, as well as the initramfs image, used by Debian systems).

Listing 1.2 shows a sample GRUB Legacy configuration file that defines both a Windows partition and a Linux partition for booting.

Listing 1.2: Sample GRUB Legacy configuration file

```
default 0
timeout 10
color white/blue yellow/blue

title CentOS Linux
root (hd1,0)
kernel (hd1,0)/boot/vmlinuz
initrd /boot/initrd

title Windows
rootnoverify (hd0,0)
```

This example shows two boot options: one for a CentOS Linux system and one for a Windows system. The CentOS system is installed on the first partition of the second hard drive, while the Windows system is installed on the first partition of the first hard drive. The Linux boot selection specifies the kernel file to load, as well as the initrd image file to load into memory.

Installing GRUB Legacy

Once you build the GRUB Legacy configuration file, you must install the GRUB Legacy program in the MBR. The command to do this is grub-install.

The grub-install command uses a single parameter that indicates the partition on which to install GRUB. You can specify the partition using either the Linux or GRUB Legacy format. For example, to use the Linux format, you'd write

```
# grub-install /dev/sda
```

to install GRUB on the MBR of the first hard drive. To use the GRUB Legacy format, you must enclose the hard drive format in quotes:

```
# grub-install '(hd0)'
```

If you're using the chainloading method and prefer to install a copy of GRUB Legacy on the boot sector of a partition instead of to the MBR of a hard drive, you must specify the partition, again using either the Linux or GRUB format:

```
# grub-install /dev/sda1
# grub-install 'hd(0,0)'
```

You don't need to reinstall GRUB Legacy in the MBR after making changes to the configuration file, because GRUB Legacy reads the configuration file each time it runs.

Interacting with GRUB Legacy

When you boot a system that uses the GRUB Legacy bootloader, you'll see a menu that shows the boot options that you defined in the configuration file. If you wait for the time-out to expire, the default boot option will process. Alternatively, you can use the arrow keys to select one of the boot options and then press the Enter key to select it.

You can also edit boot options on the fly from the GRUB menu. First, arrow to the boot option that you want to modify, and then press the E key. Use the arrow key to move the cursor to the line that you need to modify, and then press the E key to edit it. Press the B key to boot the system using the new values. You can also press the C key at any time to enter an interactive shell mode, allowing you to submit commands on the fly.

GRUB 2

Since the GRUB2 system was intended as an improvement over GRUB Legacy, many of the features are the same, with just a few twists. For example, the GRUB2 system changes the configuration filename to grub.cfg, and it stores it in the /boot/grub/ folder. (This allows you to have both GRUB Legacy and GRUB2 installed at the same time.)

Configuring GRUB2

There are also a few changes to the commands used in GRUB2. For example, instead of the title command, GRUB uses the menuentry command, and you must also enclose each individual boot section within braces immediately following the menuentry command. Here's an example of a GRUB2 configuration file:

```
menuentry "CentOS Linux" {
    set root=(hd1,1)
    linux /boot/vmlinuz
    initrd /initrd
}
menuentry "Windows" {
    set root=(hd0,1)
}
```

Notice that GRUB2 uses the set command to assign values to the root keyword, and it uses an equal sign to assign the device. GRUB2 utilizes environment variables to configure settings instead of commands.

To make things more confusing, GRUB2 changes the numbering system for partitions. While it still uses 0 for the first hard drive, the first partition is set to 1. So to define the /boot folder on the first partition of the first hard drive, you now need to use

```
set root=hd(0,1)
```

Also, notice that the rootnoverify and kernel commands are not used in GRUB2. Non-Linux boot options are now defined the same as Linux boot options using the root environment variable, and you define the kernel location using the linux command.

The configuration process for GRUB2 is also somewhat different. While GRUB2 uses the /boot/grub/grub.cfg file as the configuration file, you should never modify that file. Instead, there are separate configuration files stored in the /etc/grub.d folder. This allows you (or the system) to create individual configuration files for each boot option installed on your system (for example, one configuration file for booting Linux and another for booting Windows).

For global commands, use the /etc/default/grub configuration file. The format for some of the global commands has changed from the GRUB Legacy commands so it is GRUB_TIMEOUT instead of just timeout.

Most Linux distributions generate the new grub.cfg configuration file automatically after certain events, such as when upgrading the kernel. Usually, the distribution will keep a boot option pointing to the old kernel file just in case the new one fails.

Installing GRUB2

Unlike GRUB Legacy, you don't need to install GRUB2. All you need to do is to rebuild the main installation file by running the grub-mkconfig program.

The grub-mkconfig program reads configuration files stored in the /etc/grub.d folder and assembles the commands into the single grub.cfg configuration file.

You can update the configuration file manually by running the grub-mkconfig command:

```
# grub-mkconfig > /boot/grub/grub.cfg
```

Notice that you must either redirect the output of the grub-mkconfig program to the grub.cfg configuration file or use the -o option to specify the output file. By default, the grub-mkconfig program just outputs the new configuration file commands to standard output.

Interacting with GRUB2

The GRUB2 bootloader produces a boot menu similar to the GRUB Legacy method. You can use arrow keys to switch between boot options, the E key to edit a boot entry, or the C key to bring up the GRUB2 command line to submit interactive boot commands. Figure 1.1 illustrates the editing of an entry in the GRUB2 boot menu on an Ubuntu system.

FIGURE 1.1   Editing an Ubuntu GRUB2 menu entry

```
                GNU GRUB  version 2.02~beta2-9ubuntu1.3

┌──────────────────────────────────────────────────────────────────┐
│setparams 'Ubuntu'                                                  │
│                                                                    │
│        recordfail                                                  │
│        load_video                                                  │
│        gfxmode $linux_gfx_mode                                     │
│        insmod gzio                                                 │
│        insmod part_msdos                                           │
│        insmod ext2                                                 │
│        set root='hd0,msdos1'                                       │
│        if [ x$feature_platform_search_hint = xy ]; then            │
│           search --no-floppy --fs-uuid --set=root --hint-bios=hd0,msdos1\
│--hint-efi=hd0,msdos1 --hint-baremetal=ahci0,msdos1  e1812834-910f-4de2\
│-962b-f77434be85a5                                                  │
│        else                                                        │
│           search --no-floppy --fs-uuid --set=root e1812834-910f-4de2-962\
└──────────────────────────────────────────────────────────────────┘

    Minimum Emacs-like screen editing is supported. TAB lists
    completions. Press Ctrl-x or F10 to boot, Ctrl-c or F2 for a
    command-line or ESC to discard edits and return to the GRUB
    menu.
```

 Some graphical desktops (such as Ubuntu) hide the GRUB boot menu
behind a graphical interface. Usually, if you hold down the Shift key when
the system first boots, this will display the GRUB boot menu.

Alternative Bootloaders

While GRUB Legacy and GRUB2 are the most popular Linux bootloader programs, you
may run into a few others, depending on which Linux distributions you are using.

The *Systemd-boot* bootloader program is starting to gain popularity in Linux distributions that use the systemd init method (see the next section). The systemd-boot bootloader
generates a menu of boot image options, and can load any EFI boot image.

The *U-Boot* bootloader program can boot from any type of disk, and load any type of
boot image.

The *Syslinux project* includes five separate bootloader programs that have special uses in
Linux:

- SYSLINUX—A bootloader for systems that use the Microsoft FAT filesystem (popular
  for booting from USB memory sticks)

- EXTLINUX—A mini bootloader for booting from an ext2, ext3, ext4, or btrfs filesystem

- ISOLINUX—A bootloader for booting from a LiveCD or LiveDVD

- PXELINUX—A bootloader for booting from a network server

- MEMDISK—A utility to boot older DOS operating systems from the other Syslinux
  bootloaders

The ISOLINUX bootloader is popular for use in distributions that release a LiveDVD version. The bootloader requires two files: `isolinux.bin`, which contains the bootloader program image, and `isolinux.cfg`, which contains the configuration settings.

> Newer systems also allow booting an iso image from a USB flash drive. To do this you'll need an additional file, `isodhpfx.bin`, which is a hybrid bootloader program image that can be loaded onto a hard drive or USB flash drive. This file is generated by the `xorriso` program.

The PXELINUX bootloader is somewhat complicated. It uses the *Pre-boot Execution Environment (PXE)* standard, which defines how a network workstation can boot and load an operating system from a central network server. PXE uses DHCP to assign a network address to the workstation and BOOTP to load the bootloader image from the server. The network server must support the Trivial File Transfer Protocol (TFTP) to transfer the boot image file to the workstation.

To utilize PXELINUX, the TFTP server needs to have the PXELINUX bootloader program stored as `/tftpboot/pxelinux.0` available for the workstations to download. Each workstation must also have a configuration file available in the `/tftpboot/pxelinux.cfg` directory. The files are named based on the MAC address of the workstation, and they contain specific configuration settings required for that workstation.

Secure Bootloaders

There's one other feature new to the UEFI boot method that can cause heartburn for Linux administrators. UEFI supports a feature called *secure boot*. In secure boot, the UEFI boot manager only loads bootloader images that are digitally signed to ensure their safety. This is a great feature to prevent a virus or malware program from taking over your system, but does add an additional layer of complexity to the Linux boot process.

There are generally three ways to run Linux in a secure boot environment:

- Disable secure booting in the UEFI boot manager
- Purchase your own digital signature key to sign your bootloader images
- Use a bootloader image signed by someone else

The first method is most often the easiest, as long as your system UEFI boot manager allows you to disable the secure boot feature. However, that can leave your Linux system vulnerable to attack, and not all systems allow you to disable secure boot.

Purchasing your own digital signature key can be expensive, and somewhat cumbersome if you change bootloader images frequently. Each time you change the bootloader image you need to re-sign the file, which means getting an external signing agent involved.

There is, however, a relatively simple solution. A few Linux organizations produce signed mini-bootloader images for public use. The mini-bootloader acts as a middleman in the boot process. The UEFI boot manager boots the mini-bootloader, then, in turn, it boots the standard Linux bootloader image.

Currently the two most popular mini-bootloader image methods are from the Linux Foundation (called preloader), and Fedora (called shim). The shim mini-bootloader file is named `shim.efi`, and is stored in the uefi folder on the system. When it boots, it automatically looks for a GRUB 2 bootloader image file named `grubx64.efi`, also in the uefi folder on the system. That way you can still change the GRUB 2 bootloader image without having to worry about the digitally signed `shim.efi` file.

Process Initialization

A Linux system comprises many programs running in background to provide services for the system. The `init` program starts all of those programs when the Linux system starts up. This is called the *initialization process*.

When the kernel finishes loading, it looks for the `init` program in one of three locations:

- `/sbin/init`
- `/etc/init`
- `/bin/init`

If none of these files exist, the kernel attempts to start a generic shell session using the `/bin/sh` program. If that fails as well, the kernel enters *panic mode* and stops processing.

The main job of the `init` program is to start other programs. The programs that start are based on the features that you want running in your Linux system. For example, a Linux server doesn't necessarily need to start a graphical desktop environment, or a Linux desktop doesn't necessarily need to start the Apache web server service.

Currently three popular initialization process methods are used in Linux distributions:

- Unix System V (also called SysV)
- systemd
- Upstart

The original Linux `init` program was based on the Unix System V `init` program, and it became commonly called *SysV* (or sometimes *SysV-init*). The SysV `init` program uses a series of shell scripts divided into separate *runlevels* in order to determine which programs run at what times. A runlevel groups common applications that must all start or stop together into a common group. Each program uses a separate shell script to start and stop the individual program, but the system can run all of the scripts at the same time.

The system administrator sets the runlevel in which the Linux system starts. This in turn determines which set of programs is running. The system administrator can also change the runlevel at any time while the system is running.

The SysV `init` program had served the Linux community well for many years, but as Linux systems became more complicated and required more services, the runlevel shell scripts became more complicated. This caused Linux developers to look for other solutions.

The *systemd* program was developed by the Red Hat Linux group to handle starting and stopping programs in dynamic Linux environments. Instead of runlevels, it uses targets and units to control what applications run at any time on the system. It uses separate configuration files that determine this behavior.

The *Upstart* version of the init program was developed as part of the Ubuntu Linux distribution. Its main goal was to handle the dynamic environment that hot-pluggable devices cause in Linux. The Upstart method uses separate configuration files for each service, and each service configuration file sets in which runlevel the service should start. That way, you have just one service file that's used for multiple runlevels.

The following sections take a closer look at each of these initialization process methods to help you get comfortable in any Linux environment.

The SysV Method

The key to the SysV initialization process is runlevels. The init program determines which programs to start based on the runlevel of the system.

Runlevels are numbered from 0 to 6, and each one is assigned a set of programs that should be running for that runlevel. When the Linux kernel starts, it determines which runlevel to start by a configuration file. It's important to know how to manage runlevels and how to determine when each runlevel is used by the kernel. The following sections show you how to do that.

Runlevels

While each Linux distribution defines applications that should be running at specific runlevels, there are some general guidelines that you can use. Table 1.2 shows the general usage of the Linux runlevels.

TABLE 1.2   Linux runlevels

Runlevel	Description
0	Shut down the system.
1	Single-user mode, used for system maintenance.
2	On Debian-based systems, multiuser graphical mode.
3	On Red Hat–based systems, multiuser text mode.
4	Undefined.
5	On Red Hat–based systems, multiuser graphical mode.
6	Reboot the system.

Most Linux distributions use the Red Hat runlevel method of using runlevel 3 for multiuser text mode and runlevel 5 for multiuser graphical mode. However, Debian-based systems use runlevel 2 for all multiuser modes.

Starting Applications in a Runlevel

There are two ways to start applications in runlevels:

- Using the /etc/inittab file
- Using startup scripts

The /etc/inittab file defines what applications start at which runlevel. Each line in the /etc/inittab file defines an application and uses the following format:

```
id:runlevels:action:process
```

The id field contains one to four characters that uniquely define the process. The runlevels field contains a list of runlevels in which the application should be running. The list is not comma separated, so the value 345 indicates that the application should be started in runlevels 3, 4, and 5.

The action field contains a keyword that tells the kernel what to do with the application for that runlevel. Possible values are shown in Table 1.3.

TABLE 1.3   The SysV inittab action values

Action	Description
boot	The process is started at boot time.
bootwait	The process is started at boot time, and the system will wait for it to finish.
initdefault	Specifies the runlevel to enter after the system boots.
kbrequest	The process is started after a special key combination is pressed.
once	The process is started once when the runlevel is entered.
powerfail	The process is started when the system is powered down.
powerwait	The process is started when the system is powered down, and the system will wait for it to finish.
respawn	The process is started when the runlevel is entered and restarted whenever it terminates.
sysinit	The process is started at boot time before any boot or bootwait items.
wait	The process is started once, and the system will wait for it to finish.

The `initdefault` line specifies the runlevel in which the system normally runs after boot:

```
id:3:initdefault:
```

Besides the runlevels, the SysV `init` method also specifies startup scripts to control how applications start and stop. The `/etc/init.d/rc` or `/etc/rc.d/rc` script runs all scripts with a specified runlevel. The scripts themselves are stored in the `/etc/init.d/rcx.d` or `/etc/rcx.d` folder, where *x* is the runlevel number.

Scripts are stored with a specific filename that indicates whether they start or stop at the runlevel. Scripts that start with an S start the programs, and scripts that start with a K stop the programs. The script filenames also contain a number, which indicates the order in which the `rc` program runs the scripts. This allows you to specify which scripts get started before others in order to control any dependency issues.

Modifying Program Runlevels

Working through all of the script files stored to start and stop individual programs can be somewhat of a hassle. To make life easier, Linux distributions include a couple of utilities to assign a runlevel easily for any program that you need to start or stop:

- `chkconfig`
- `update-rc.d`

The `chkconfig` command is used in most Red Hat–based Linux distributions. It's a very versatile command that allows you to list at what runlevels the application starts and also to change the runlevels in which a specific application starts.

When used with the `--list` parameter, the `chkconfig` command displays all of the applications defined, along with the runlevels in which they start. Alternatively, you can list a specific application to see how it is configured:

```
$ chkconfig --list network
network    0:off  1:off  2:on  3:on  4:on  5:on  6:off
$
```

In this example, the `network` application is configured to start in runlevels 2, 3, 4, and 5. You can then use the `--levels` parameter to modify the runlevels:

```
# chkconfig --levels 12345 network on
```

This sets the `network` program to start on runlevels 1, 2, 3, 4, and 5.

Table 1.4 shows the different formats that you can use with the `chkconfig` command.

TABLE 1.4   The chkconfig formats

Format	Description
chkconfig *program*	Check if the program is set to start at the current runlevel.

TABLE 1.4   The chkconfig formats *(continued)*

Format	Description
chkconfig *program* on	Start the program at the default runlevel.
chkconfig *program* off	Don't start the program at the default runlevel.
chkconfig --add *program*	Add the program to start at boot.
chkconfig --del *program*	Remove the program from starting at boot.
chkconfig --levels [*levels*] *program* on	Set the program to start at the specified runlevels.
chkconfig --list *program*	Display the current runlevel settings for the program.

For Debian-based Linux distributions, you'll need to use the update-rc.d command to control application runlevels. To start a program at the default runlevel, just use the following format:

```
update-rc.d program defaults
```

To remove the program from starting at the default runlevel, use the following format:

```
update-rc.d program remove
```

If you want to specify what runlevels the program starts and stops at, you'll need to use the following format:

```
update-rc.d -f program start 40 2 3 4 5 . stop 80 0 1 6 .
```

The 40 and 80 specify the relative order within the runlevel when the program should start or stop (from 0 to 99). This allows you to customize exactly when specific programs are started or stopped during the boot sequence.

Checking the System Runlevel

You've seen that the /etc/inittab file indicates the default runlevel with the initdefault action, but there's no guarantee that's the runlevel at which your Linux system is currently running. The runlevel command displays both the current runlevel and the previous runlevel for the system:

```
$ runlevel
N 2
$
```

The first character is the previous runlevel. The N character means the system is in the original boot runlevel. The second character is the current runlevel.

Changing Runlevels

You can change the current runlevel of your Linux system using either the init or telinit command. Just specify the runlevel number as the command-line parameter. For example, to reboot your system you can enter this command:

```
# init 6
```

The downside to using the init command is that it immediately changes the system to the specified runlevel. That may not be an issue if you're the only person on your Linux system, but in a multiuser Linux environment, this can have adverse effects for the other users.

A kinder way to change the runlevel on multiuser systems is to use one of a handful of special commands designed for that purpose:

- shutdown—Gracefully changes the runlevel to 1, or single-user mode
- halt—Gracefully changes the runlevel to 0 to stop the system
- poweroff—Gracefully changes the runlevel to 0 to stop the system
- reboot—Gracefully changes the runlevel to 6 to restart the system

Each of these commands also allows you to specify a message to send to any other users on the system before it changes the runlevel. You can also specify a time for the change, such as +15 for 15 minutes.

The systemd Method

The systemd initialization process method is quickly gaining in popularity in the Linux world. It's currently the default initialization process used in the Fedora, CentOS, and Red Hat Linux distributions.

The systemd initialization process introduced a major paradigm shift in how Linux systems handle services. This has also caused some controversy in the Linux world. Instead of lots of small initialization shell scripts, the systemd method employs one monolithic program that uses individual configuration files for each service. This is somewhat of a departure from the earlier Linux philosophy.

This section walks you through the basics of how the systemd initialization process works.

Units and Targets

Instead of using shell scripts and runlevels, the systemd method uses units and targets. A *unit* defines a service or action on the system. It consists of a name, a type, and a configuration file. There are currently eight different types of systemd units:

- automount
- device

- mount
- path
- service
- snapshot
- socket
- target

The systemd program identifies units by their name and type using the format name.type. You use the systemctl command to list the units currently loaded in your Linux system:

```
# systemctl list-units
UNIT                     LOAD   ACTIVE SUB      DESCRIPTION
...
crond.service            loaded active running Command Scheduler
cups.service             loaded active running CUPS Printing Service
dbus.service             loaded active running D-Bus System Message
...
multi-user.target        loaded active active  Multi-User System
network.target           loaded active active  Network
paths.target             loaded active active  Paths
remote-fs.target         loaded active active  Remote File Systems
slices.target            loaded active active  Slices
sockets.target           loaded active active  Sockets
...
#
```

Linux distributions can have hundreds of different units loaded and active. We just selected a few from the output to show you what they look like. The systemd method uses service type units to manage the daemons on the Linux system. The target type units are important in that they group multiple units together so that they can be started at the same time. For example, the network.target unit groups all of the units required to start the network interfaces for the system.

The systemd initialization process uses targets similar to the way SysV uses runlevels. A *target* represents a different group of services that should be running on the system. Instead of changing runlevels to alter what's running on the system, you just change targets.

To make the transition from SysV to systemd smoother, there are targets that mimic the standard 0 through 6 SysV runlevels, called runlevel0.target through runlevel6 .target.

Configuring Units

Each unit requires a configuration file that defines what program it starts and how it should start the program. The systemd system stores unit configuration files in the /lib/

systemd/system folder. Here's an example of the sshd.service unit configuration file used in CentOS:

```
# cat sshd.service
[Unit]
Description=OpenSSH server daemon
After=syslog.target network.target auditd.service

[Service]
EnvironmentFile=/etc/sysconfig/sshd
ExecStartPre=/usr/sbin/sshd-keygen
ExecStart=/usr/sbin/sshd -D $OPTIONS
ExecReload=/bin/kill -HUP $MAINPID
KillMode=process
Restart=on-failure
RestartSec=42s

[Install]
WantedBy=multi-user.target
#
```

The sshd.service configuration file defines the program to start (/usr/sbin/sshd), along with some other features, such as what services should run before the sshd service starts (the After line), what target level the system should be in (the WantedBy line), and how to reload the program (the Restart line).

Target units also use configuration files. They don't define programs, but instead they define which service units to start. Here's an example of the graphical.target unit configuration file used in CentOS:

```
# cat graphical.target
#  This file is part of systemd.
#
# systemd is free software; you can redistribute it and/or modify it
# under the terms of the GNU Lesser General Public License as published by
#  the Free Software Foundation; either version 2.1 of the License, or
#  (at your option) any later version.
[Unit]
Description=Graphical Interface
Documentation=man:systemd.special(7)
Requires=multi-user.target
After=multi-user.target
Conflicts=rescue.target
Wants=display-manager.service
AllowIsolate=yes
```

```
[Install]
Alias=default.target
#
```

The target configuration defines what targets should be loaded first (the After line), what targets are required for this target to start (the Requires line), what targets conflict with this target (the Conflicts line), and what targets or services the target requires to be running (the Wants line).

Setting the Default Target

The default target used when the Linux system boots is defined in the /etc/systemd/ system folder as the file default.target. This is the file the systemd program looks for when it starts up. This file is normally set as a link to a standard target file in the /lib/ systemd/system folder:

```
# ls -al default.target
lrwxrwxrwx. 1 root root 36 Oct  1 09:14 default.target ->
 /lib/systemd/system/graphical.target
#
```

On this CentOS system, the default target is set to the graphical.target unit.

The systemctl Program

In the systemd method, you use the systemctl program to control services and targets. The systemctl program uses options to define what action to take, as shown in Table 1.5.

TABLE 1.5 The systemctl commands

Command name	Explanation
list-units	Displays the current status of all configured units
default	Changes to the default target unit
isolate	Starts the named unit and stops all others
start name	Starts the named unit
stop name	Stops the named unit
reload name	Causes the named unit to reload its configuration file
restart name	Causes the named unit to shut down and restart
status name	Displays the status of the named unit (You can pass a PID value rather than a name, if you like.)

Command name	Explanation
enable name	Configures the unit to start when the computer next boots
disable name	Configures the unit not to start when the computer next boots

Instead of using shell scripts to start and stop services, you use the start and stop commands:

```
# systemctl stop sshd.service
# systemctl status sshd.service
sshd.service - OpenSSH server daemon
Loaded: loaded (/usr/lib/systemd/system/sshd.service; disabled)
Active: inactive (dead)

Oct 04 10:33:33 localhost.localdomain systemd[1]: Stopped OpenSSH server
 daemon.

# systemctl start sshd.service
# systemctl status sshd.service
sshd.service - OpenSSH server daemon
Loaded: loaded (/usr/lib/systemd/system/sshd.service; disabled)
Active: active (running) since Thu 2014-10-04 10:34:08 EDT; 4s ago
Process: 3882
ExecStartPre=/usr/sbin/sshd-keygen (code=exited, status=0/SUCCESS)
Main PID: 3889 (sshd)
CGroup: /system.slice/sshd.service
          3889 /usr/sbin/sshd -D

Oct 04 10:34:08 localhost.localdomain sshd-keygen[3882]: Generating SSH2 RSA
host key: [  OK  ]
Oct 04 10:34:08 localhost.localdomain systemd[1]: Started OpenSSH server daemon.
Oct 04 10:34:08 localhost.localdomain sshd[3889]: Server listening on
 0.0.0.0 port 22.
Oct 04 10:34:08 localhost.localdomain sshd[3889]: Server listening on ::
 port 22.
#
```

To change the target that is currently running, you must use the isolate command. For example, to enter single-user mode, you'd use the following:

```
# systemctl isolate rescue.target
```

To go back to the default target for the system, you just use the default command.

There's also a systemd-delta command that allows you to identify when multiple configuration files exist and overwrite each other.

One of the more controversial features of the systemd initialization process is that it doesn't use the standard Linux syslogd log file system. Instead, it has its own log files, and those log files are not stored in text format. To view the systemd log files, you need to use the journalctl program.

The Upstart Method

The Ubuntu Linux distribution created the Upstart initialization process as a replacement for the SysV initialization process. The goal was to create an initialization process that could better handle hot-pluggable devices that are commonly found on systems today.

The Upstart method replaces the /etc/inittab file and all of the /etc/init.d startup scripts with a single /etc/init folder. The /etc/init folder contains configuration files for each system service and program that needs to start, usually in the format name.conf, where name is the program name.

An example of an Upstart configuration file looks like this:

```
# tty1 - getty
#
# This service maintains a getty on tty1 from the point the system is
# started until it is shut down again.

start on stopped rc RUNLEVEL=[2345] and (
          not-container or
          container CONTAINER=lxc or
          container CONTAINER=lxc-libvirt)

stop on runlevel [!2345]

respawn
exec /sbin/getty -8 38400 tty1
$
```

The tty1.conf configuration file specifies when the tty1 console port should be enabled. Notice that the configuration file specifies the runlevels when it should start (2, 3, 4, and 5).

One of the great features of Upstart is that it can trigger a script to run not only at a specific runlevel but also when a device is connected to the system.

To change the runlevel or event that starts or stops a program, you just modify the program's configuration file in the /etc/init folder.

To stop a program or service using Upstart, you just use the stop command-line command, along with the program or service name:

```
$ sudo stop bluetooth
bluetooth stop/waiting
$
```

Likewise, to start up a program or service, you use the start command:

```
$ sudo start bluetooth
bluetooth start/running, process 2635
$
```

The Upstart initialization method provides a simpler way of managing programs and services running on the Linux system.

 The *Linux Standard Base (LSB)* is a specification supported by some Linux distributions in order to attempt to create a standard experience between Linux systems. Part of the LSB defines how systems use commands in init scripts. Standard init commands such as start, stop, and restart are defined by the LSB, and they should be supported by all Linux distributions that follow the LSB. Unfortunately, some major Linux distributions (such as Debian) have recently dropped out of the LSB group, making it seem less likely that there will be a standard Linux initialization method anytime soon.

System Recovery

There's nothing worse than starting up your Linux system and not getting a login prompt. Plenty of things can go wrong in the Linux startup process, but most of the issues come down to two categories:

- Kernel failures
- Drive failures

Fortunately, there are ways to help recover your Linux system from many of these errors. The following sections walk you through some standard troubleshooting practices that you can follow to attempt to recover a Linux system that fails to boot.

Kernel Failures

Kernel failures occur when the Linux kernel stops running in memory, causing the Linux system to crash. They are often a result of a software change, such as installing a new kernel without the appropriate module or library changes or starting (or stopping) a program at a new runlevel. Often these types of boot errors can be fixed by starting the system using an alternative method and editing the necessary files to change the system. This section describes the techniques that you can use to alter the system setup after a failed boot.

Selecting Previous Kernels at Boot

One of the biggest culprits for a failed boot is upgrading the Linux kernel, either on your own or from a packaged distribution upgrade. When you install a new kernel file, it's always a good idea to leave the old kernel file in place and create an additional entry in the GRUB boot menu to point to the new kernel.

By creating multiple kernel entries in the GRUB boot menu, you can select which kernel version to boot. If the new kernel fails to boot properly, you can reboot and select the older kernel version.

Most Linux distributions do this automatically when adding a new kernel, keeping the most recent older kernel available in the boot menu, as shown in Figure 1.2.

FIGURE 1.2 The CentOS Grub boot menu with multiple kernel options

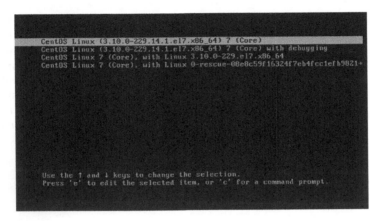

Single-User Mode

At times, you may need to perform some type of system maintenance, such as adding a new hardware module or library file to get the system to boot properly. In these situations, you will want the system to boot up without allowing multiple users to connect, especially in a server environment. This is called *single-user mode*.

The GRUB menu allows you to start the system in single-user mode by adding the single command to the linux line in the boot menu commands. To get there, press the e key on the boot option in the GRUB boot menu.

When you add the single command, the system will boot into runlevel 1, which creates a single login for the root user account. Once you log in as the root user account, you can modify the appropriate modules, init scripts, or GRUB boot menu options necessary to get your system started correctly.

Passing Kernel Parameters

Besides the single-user mode trick, you can add other kernel parameters to the linux command in the GRUB boot menu. The kernel accepts lots of parameters that alter the hardware modules that it activates or the hardware settings that it looks for with specific devices. (This is especially true for sound and network cards.) You can specify the different hardware settings as additional parameters to the kernel in the linux command and then boot from that entry in the GRUB menu.

Root Drive Failure

Perhaps the worst feeling a Linux system administrator can experience is seeing that the bootloader can't read the root drive device. This type of error may not be fatal, however, because it is sometimes possible to recover from a corrupt root drive. This section walks through the steps that you can take to attempt to recover a corrupt root drive and possibly save your Linux system.

Using a Rescue Disk

Many Linux distributions provide what's called a *rescue disk* to be used when fatal disk errors occur. The rescue disk usually boots either from the CD/DVD drive or as a USB stick, and it loads a small Linux system into memory. Since the Linux system runs entirely in memory, it can leave all of the workstation hard drives free for examination and repair. From the system command-line prompt, you can perform some diagnostic and repair tasks on your system hard drives.

The tool of choice for checking and fixing hard drive errors is the fsck command. The fsck command isn't a program. Rather, it is an alias for a family of commands that are specific to different types of filesystems (such as ext2, ext3, and ext4). You need to run the fsck command against the device name of the partition that contains the root directory of your Linux system. For example, if the root directory is on the /dev/sda1 partition, you'd run this command:

```
# fsck /dev/sda1
```

The fsck command will examine the inode table, along with the file blocks stored on the hard drive, and attempt to reconcile them. If any errors occur, you will be prompted whether to repair them or not. If there are many errors on the partition, you can add the -y parameter to answer yes automatically to all of the repair questions. After a successful repair, it's a good idea to run the fsck command one more time to ensure that all of the errors have been found and corrected. Continue running the fsck command until you get a clean run with no errors.

Mounting a Root Drive

When the fsck repair is complete, you can test the repaired partition by mounting it into the virtual directory created in memory. Just use the mount command to mount it to an available mount directory:

```
# mount /dev/sda1 /media
```

You can examine the filesystem stored in the partition to ensure that it's not corrupt. Before rebooting, you should unmount the partition using the umount command:

```
# umount /dev/sda1
```

After successfully unmounting the partition, you can reboot your Linux system using the standard bootloader and attempt to boot using the standard kernel and runlevels.

EXERCISE 1.1

Using Rescue Mode

This exercise demonstrates how to start your Linux distribution in single-user mode to examine filesystems and configurations without performing a complete bootup. To use single-user mode, follow these steps:

1. First, start your Linux distribution as normal, and log in at the standard login prompt (either the graphical desktop or the command-line login) as your normal user account.

2. Type **runlevel** to determine the default runlevel for your system. The first character returned refers to the previous runlevel (N denotes no previous runlevel since the system booted). The second character is the current runlevel. This is likely to be 2 on Debian-based systems, 3 on command-line Red Hat–based systems, or 5 on graphical desktop Red Hat–based systems.

3. Now reboot your system, and hit an arrow key when the GRUB menu appears to stop the countdown timer. If you're using a Linux distribution that hides the GRUB menu (such as Ubuntu), hold down the Shift key when the system boots to display the GRUB menu.

4. At the GRUB menu, use the arrow keys to go to the default menu entry (usually the first entry in the list), then press the e key. This takes GRUB into edit mode.

5. Look for either the linux or linux16 menu command lines. These define the kernel used to start the session.

6. Go to the end of the linux or linux16 line, and add the word **single**. Press **Ctrl-x** to save the change temporarily and start your system using that menu entry.

7. The Linux system will boot into single-user mode. Depending on your Linux distribution, it may prompt you to enter the root user account or to press Ctrl+D to continue on with the normal boot. Enter the root user account password to enter single-user mode.

8. Now you are at the root user command prompt. Enter the command **runlevel** to view the current runlevel. It should show runlevel 1. From here you can modify configuration files, check filesystems, and change user accounts.

9. Reboot the system by typing **reboot**.

10. You should return to the standard boot process and GRUB menu options as before. Select the standard GRUB menu option to boot your system and then log in.

11. At a command line prompt, type **runlevel** to ensure that you are back to the normal default runlevel for your Linux system.

Summary

Although Linux distributions are designed to boot without any user intervention, it helps to know the Linux boot process in case anything does go wrong. Most Linux systems use either the GRUB Legacy or GRUB2 bootloader program. These programs both reside in the BIOS Master Boot Record or in the ESP partition on UEFI systems. The bootloader loads the Linux kernel program, which then runs the init program to start individual background programs required for the Linux system.

There are several different types of initialization scripts used by Linux distributions. The SysV method is the oldest, derived from the original Unix system. The systemd method is a more modern replacement, and it is becoming more popular in many Linux distributions. The Ubuntu Linux distribution has also created the Upstart method, which is an advanced initialization method to the SysV method, allowing more dynamic control over which programs start based on what hardware devices are detected at boot time.

Finally, no discussion on Linux startup is complete without examining system recovery methods. If your Linux system fails to boot, the most likely cause is either a kernel issue or a root device issue. For kernel issues, you can often modify the GRUB menu to add additional kernel parameters or even to boot from an older version of the kernel. For root drive issues, you can try to boot from a rescue mode into a version of Linux running in memory and then use the fsck command to repair a damaged root drive.

Exam Essentials

Describe the Linux boot process. The BIOS or UEFI starts a bootloader program from the Master Boot Record, which is usually the Linux GRUB Legacy or GRUB2 program. The bootloader program loads the Linux kernel into memory, which in turn looks for the init program to run. The init program starts individual application programs and starts either the command-line terminals or the graphical desktop manager.

Describe the Linux GRUB Legacy and GRUB2 bootloaders. The GRUB Legacy bootloader stores files in the /boot/grub folder, and it uses the menu.lst or grub.conf configuration file to define commands used at boot time. The commands can create a boot menu, allowing you to select between multiple boot locations, options, or features. You must use the grub-install program to install the GRUB Legacy bootloader program into the

Master Boot Record. The GRUB2 bootloader also stores files in the /boot/grub folder, but it uses the grub.cfg configuration file to define the menu commands. You don't edit the grub.cfg file directly, but instead you store files in the /etc/default/grub file or individual configuration files in the /etc/grub.d folder. Run the update-grub program to generate the grub.cfg file from the configuration files.

Describe alternative Linux bootloaders.   The LILO bootloader is used on older Linux systems. It uses the /etc/lilo.conf configuration file to define the boot options. The Syslinux project has created the most popular alternative Linux bootloaders. The SYSLINUX bootloader runs on FAT filesystems, such as USB memory sticks. The ISOLINUX bootloader is popular on LiveCD distributions, because it can boot from a CD or DVD. It stores the bootloader program in the isolinux.bin file and configuration settings in the isolinux.cfg file. The PXELINUX bootloader program allows a network workstation to boot from a network server. The server must contain the pxelinux.0 image file along with the pxelinux.cfg directory, which contains separate configuration files for each workstation. EXTLINUX is a small bootloader program that can be used on smaller embedded Linux systems.

Describe Linux runlevels and the init structure.   The init program starts applications based on a default runlevel. Runlevels from 0 to 6 are defined, with each runlevel containing scripts that start and stop specific programs. The /etc/inittab configuration file defines the default runlevel for the Linux system, along with which programs start at what runlevel. Init scripts are stored in the /etc/init.d and /etc/rc.d folders and run as needed.

Explain the SysV initialization system.   The SysV init system uses a default runlevel specified by the line id:2:initdefault: in the /etc/inittab file. You use either the chkconfig, update-rc.d, or systemctl command to change which services are started when switching to specific runlevels. Runlevels 0, 1, and 6 are reserved for shutdown, single-user mode, and rebooting, respectively. Runlevels 3, 4, and 5 are the common user runlevels on Red Hat and most other distributions, and runlevel 2 is the normal user runlevel on Debian systems.

Describe how to change SysV init runlevels.   The programs init and telinit can be used to change to other runlevels. shutdown, halt, poweroff, and reboot are also useful when shutting down, rebooting, or switching to single-user mode.

Explain the systemd initialization system.   The systemd system uses units and targets to control services. The default target is specified by the file /etc/systemd/system/default .target, and it is a link to a target file in the /lib/systemd/system folder.

Describe how to change systemd init targets.   You use the systemctl program to start and stop services, as well as to change the target level of the system.

Describe how to recover from a failed boot.   The GRUB bootloaders provide you with options that can help if your Linux system fails to boot. You can press the e key at the GRUB boot menu to edit any boot menu entry and then add any additional kernel parameters, such as placing the system in single-user mode. You can also use a rescue disk to boot Linux into memory, then use the fsck command to repair any corrupt hard drives, and then use the mount command to mount them to examine the files.

Review Questions

You can find the answers in the Appendix.

1. What program does the workstation firmware start at boot time?
   - **A.** A bootloader
   - **B.** The init program
   - **C.** The Windows OS
   - **D.** The mount command
   - **E.** The telinit program

2. Where does the firmware first look for a Linux bootloader program?
   - **A.** The /boot/grub folder
   - **B.** The Master Boot Record (MBR)
   - **C.** The /var/log folder
   - **D.** A boot partition
   - **E.** The /etc folder

3. What Linux command lets you examine the most recent boot messages?
   - **A.** fsck
   - **B.** init
   - **C.** mount
   - **D.** dmesg
   - **E.** chkconfig

4. What folder do most Linux distributions use to store boot logs?
   - **A.** /etc
   - **B.** /var/messages
   - **C.** /var/log
   - **D.** /boot
   - **E.** /proc

5. Where does the workstation BIOS attempt to find a bootloader program? (Select all that apply.)
   - **A.** An internal hard drive
   - **B.** An external hard drive
   - **C.** A DVD drive
   - **D.** A USB memory stick
   - **E.** A network server

6. Where is the Master Boot Record located?

    A. The first sector of the first hard drive on the system

    B. The boot partition of any hard drive on the system

    C. The last sector of the first hard drive on the system

    D. Any sector on any hard drive on the system

    E. The first sector of the second hard drive on the system

7. Where is the EFI System Partition (ESP) stored on Linux systems?

    A. /boot

    B. /etc

    C. /var

    D. /boot/efi

    E. /boot/grub

8. What file extension do UEFI bootloader files use?

    A. .cfg

    B. .uefi

    C. .lst

    D. .conf

    E. .efi

9. Which was the first bootloader program used in Linux?

    A. GRUB Legacy

    B. LILO

    C. GRUB2

    D. SYSLINUX

    E. ISOLINUX

10. Where are the GRUB Legacy configuration files stored?

    A. /boot/grub

    B. /boot/efi

    C. /etc

    D. /var

    E. /proc

11. Where are GRUB2 configuration files stored? (Select all that apply.)

    A. /proc

    B. /etc/grub.d

    C. /boot/grub

    D. /boot/efi

    E. /var

12. What command must you run to generate the GRUB2 grub.cfg configuration file?

    A. chkconfig

    B. update-rc.d

    C. grub-mkconfig

    D. grub-install

    E. init

13. What program does the kernel use to start other programs?

    A. GRUB2

    B. systemctl

    C. telinit

    D. init

    E. BIOS

14. Which configuration file contains the SysV default runlevel?

    A. /etc/init.d

    B. /etc/inittab

    C. /etc/grub.d

    D. /etc/rc.d

    E. /boot/grub.cfg

15. What runlevel is the default for Debian-based systems?

    A. 0

    B. 1

    C. 6

    D. 5

    E. 2

16. What command would you use to change the current runlevel? (Select all that apply.)

    A. telinit

    B. chkconfig

    C. update-rc.d

    D. init

    E. dmesg

17. What command displays the runlevels in which a program will be started?

    A. chkconfig

    B. init

    C. dmesg

    D. update-rc.d

    E. telinit

18. What command do Debian systems use to set the runlevels for programs?

    A. chkconfig

    B. update-rc.d

    C. init

    D. telinit

    E. dmesg

19. What program allows you to fix corrupt hard drive partitions?

    A. mount

    B. umount

    C. fsck

    D. init

    E. telinit

20. Which command allows you to append a partition to the virtual directory on a running Linux system?

    A. mount

    B. umount

    C. fsck

    D. dmesg

    E. init

Chapter

2

Maintaining the System

THE FOLLOWING EXAM OBJECTIVES ARE COVERED IN THIS CHAPTER:

- ✓ 200.1 Measure and troubleshoot resource usage
- ✓ 200.2 Predict future resource needs
- ✓ 206.1 Make and install programs from source
- ✓ 206.2 Backup operations
- ✓ 206.3 Notify users on system-related issues

Keeping a Linux system up and running involves many important basic maintenance tasks, such as backing up data and capacity planning. Included in this task group is installing software as well as keeping the system user community informed.

This chapter begins by exploring the means and methods for notifying users about current system issues. Next, it covers backup topics, focusing on the various standard tools available to accomplish this task. It then touches on compiling and installing an application from source code, followed by the sometimes-tricky job of capacity planning and troubleshooting resource usage.

Keeping Users Informed

Proper communication with system users, whether they are fellow system administrators, programmers, clients, and so on, can go a long way in establishing good relations. Hopefully, your company has established standard policies for keeping system users informed. If so, you can use those policies to guide your manual and automated end-user communication methods.

Besides the old standbys of email, automated text messaging, and company intranet web pages, a Linux system offers the following additional utilities and files to help with communication:

- `/etc/issue`
- `/etc/issue.net`
- `/etc/motd`
- `/sbin/shutdown`
- `/bin/usr/notify-send (/usr/bin/notify-send)`
- `/bin/wall (/usr/bin/wall)`

In this section, we'll explore each method in detail. This information will help you to choose which utilities best meet your company's communication policies.

Looking at Fluid Messaging

Fluid messaging involves informing active system users of current events, such as a system shutdown, as they are happening. These methods are intended to be used either for emergency purposes or as supplemental communication for a planned situation.

Using the *wall* Command

The /usr/bin/wall command sends simple messages to certain system users. Only users who meet the following conditions will receive these messages:

- Users who are currently logged into a terminal (tty#) or a terminal-emulator (pts/#)
- Users who have their message status set to "yes"

The /bin/mesg or /usr/bin/mesg command allows you to view and set your message status. The mesg command is demonstrated here:

```
$ mesg
is n
$
$ mesg y
$
$ mesg
is y
$
$ mesg n
$
$ mesg
is n
$
```

Notice from the previous example, the mesg command used by itself simply shows the current message status. Issuing the mesg y command turns on messaging, and issuing mesg n turns it off.

What's happening behind the scenes with mesg is that you are granting (y) or revoking (n) write access to your terminal device. If write access is granted, other users can use programs such as /bin/write or /usr/bin/write to send messages to the terminal.

The general write command syntax is shown here:

```
write username terminal_id
```

An example of the write command in use is shown in Figure 2.1 and Figure 2.2.

FIGURE 2.1   Issuing the **write** command

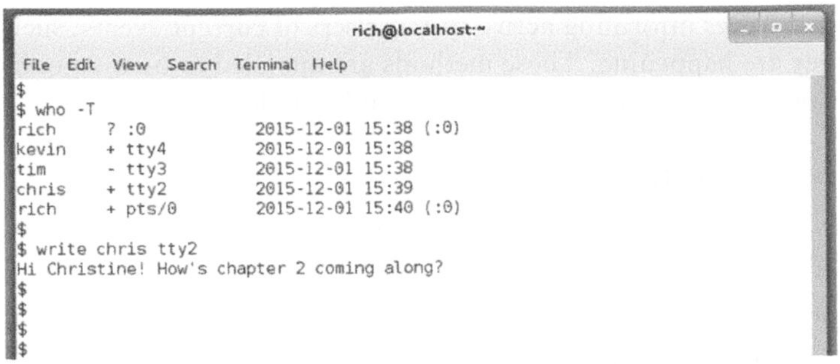

Notice in Figure 2.1 that the who -T command is used first. This command shows the current write access status of each logged-in user. A plus sign (+) between the username and terminal id indicates that write access is granted, while a minus sign (-) indicates that no write access has been granted. A question mark (?) indicates a user who is logged into the GUI. For a GUI user to receive a write command message, a GUI terminal emulator must be opened, designated by a pts/# terminal type, and write access must be granted. The pts/0 terminal id in Figure 2.1 indicates that the user, rich, has a terminal emulator application running in his GUI. However, the terminal must still have write access granted (+) in order to receive write command messages, which it does.

In Figure 2.1, after the who -T command is used, the write command is employed. To use the write command, two options must be included: the user's *username*, who is to receive the message, and that user's *terminal id*. In Figure 2.1, the user's *username* is chris, and the *terminal id* is tty2. Once the write command is issued, it waits for your message via standard input. However, there is no prompt to indicate this. Just type in your message, and press Ctrl+D when you are finished. The message is automatically sent, and it displays on the receiving user's terminal, as shown in Figure 2.2.

FIGURE 2.2   Receiving **write** command output

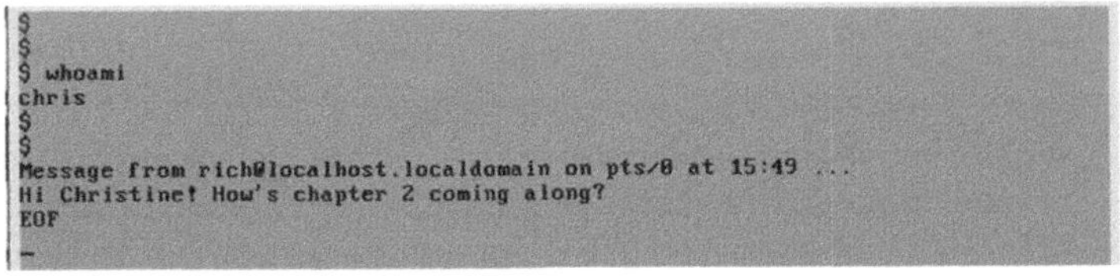

You can use the /bin/wall or /usr/bin/wall utility to broadcast a message to *all* terminals with write access granted. Thus, it can be a handy utility to use for standard communication.

The general wall command syntax is

wall *message*

Figure 2.3 and Figure 2.4 show the `wall` command in action. Notice in Figure 2.3 that the message is written *after* the `wall` command is issued. The `wall` command is similar to the `write` command in that it can accept the message via standard input. In Figure 2.3, the message is typed in and Ctrl+D is pressed to send the message.

FIGURE 2.3   Issuing the **wall** command

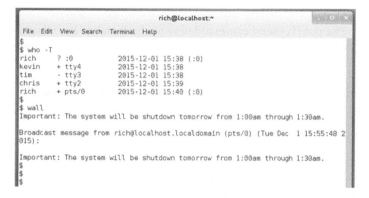

 By default, the `systemctl` utility (covered in Chapter 1) will send a wall message when any of its following commands are issued: `emergency`, `halt`, `kexec`, `power-off`, `reboot`, or `rescue`. To prevent a wall message from being sent while using `systemctl`, include the `--no-wall` option in its command line.

The `wall` message is disruptive in that it will display in the middle of whatever the user is currently doing in the terminal, as shown in Figure 2.4. However, the user receiving the message can simply press Enter to receive the $ prompt back.

FIGURE 2.4   Receiving **wall** command output

 On some distributions, anyone can use the wall command, not just those with super user privileges. This may cause some undesirable consequences in your particular work environment. To avoid problems, you may want to turn off terminal write access by default (if you haven't done so already), which you can set via login environment files, or block general access to the wall command.

Using the *notify-send* Command

The `wall` command is useful, but if a user is not logged into a console terminal or does not have a GUI terminal emulator open, you cannot send messages to that user. The `/bin/notify-send` or `/usr/bin/notify-send` utility can remedy this situation, and it is a good tool to use alongside the `wall` command.

> The `notify-send` command may not be installed by default. If it is not and you wish to install it, you can find the `notify-send` utility in the `libnotify-bin` package.

You can try out the `notify-send` command by sending yourself messages in the GUI. The general `notify-send` syntax looks like this:

```
notify-send "Title" "Message"
```

Figure 2.5 shows the `notify-send` command in action on a CentOS distribution. The command is issued within a GUI terminal emulator. Notice that the message is displayed at the desktop's bottom. Different Linux desktop environments will display these notification messages in different desktop display locations.

FIGURE 2.5   Trying out the **notify-send** command

> Be aware that users can turn off these notification messages via simple desktop environment settings. That can be problematic if you are solely dependent on the `notify-send` command for GUI user communication purposes.

To send notify-send messages to GUI users besides yourself, you need super user privileges. Additionally, you need certain environment variables, depending upon how you are implementing the notify-send utility and which distribution you are using.

In Figure 2.6, the notify-send is employed by a user with super user privileges who is logged into an Ubuntu distribution virtual console terminal. Notice that the DISPLAY environment variable is needed.

FIGURE 2.6   Issuing the **notify-send** command to another user

```
$
$
$ w
 16:45:01 up 25 min,  2 users,  load average: 0.00, 0.23, 0.31
USER     TTY      FROM           LOGIN@   IDLE   JCPU   PCPU WHAT
christin tty2                    15:31    5.00s  0.98s  0.02s w
kevin    :0       :0             15:36    ?xdm?  52.26s 0.83s init --user
$
$
$ DISPLAY=:0 sudo su -c "notify-send \"Test\" \"Test from Christine\" " kevin
$
```

The DISPLAY environment variable in Figure 2.6 is set to the w command's tty column value for the user kevin. This is necessary for the notify-send utility to know where to send its output. Notice that the sudo command is also used. It is needed so that the su -c command can be employed to issue the notify-send command as the user logged into the GUI; in this case, that's kevin. The backslashes (\) in front of the quotation marks (") surrounding both the notify-send command's message title and message are also necessary. Because the command, sent as an option with su -c, must be surrounded by its own quotation marks, the backslashes allow the notify-send options to have their necessary double quotation marks (") and not interfere with the su -c command's operation. The very last parameter in Figure 2.6's long command is the username kevin. This is an option to the su -c command, so that the user kevin will execute the notify-send command. The results of all of this work are shown in Figure 2.7.

FIGURE 2.7   Receiving **notify-send** command output

Figure 2.7 shows the sent test message. On this Ubuntu distribution, the received notify-send message displays near the upper-left area of the Unity desktop.

On other distributions, such as CentOS, when sending messages to other GUI users, even more environment variables are needed. In Figure 2.8, notice that prior to using the notify-send command, the DBUS_SESSION_BUS_ADDRESS environment variable must be set to the GUI user's current setting for that variable and then exported. This environment variable is often needed when you create a cron job to automate such communication.

FIGURE 2.8 Issuing the **notify-send** command to another user on CentOS

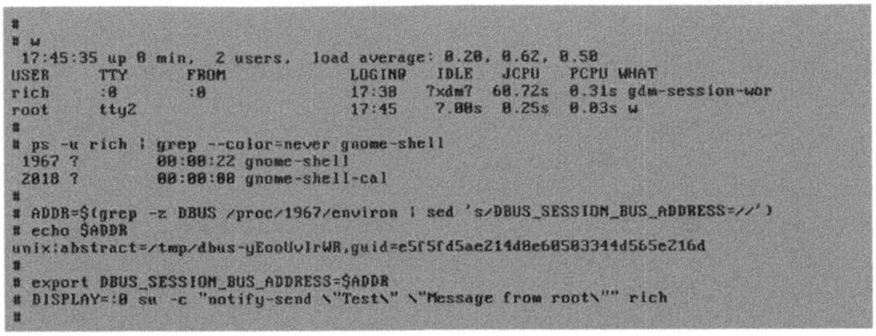

```
#
# w
  17:45:35 up 0 min,  2 users,  load average: 0.20, 0.62, 0.50
USER     TTY      FROM             LOGIN@   IDLE   JCPU   PCPU WHAT
rich     :0       :0               17:38   7xdm?  60.72s  0.31s gdm-session-wor
root     tty2                      17:45    7.00s  0.25s  0.03s w

# ps -u rich | grep --color=never gnome-shell
 1967 ?        00:00:22 gnome-shell
 2018 ?        00:00:00 gnome-shell-cal
# ADDR=$(grep -z DBUS /proc/1967/environ | sed 's/DBUS_SESSION_BUS_ADDRESS=//')
# echo $ADDR
unix:abstract=/tmp/dbus-yEooUvlrWR,guid=e5f5fd5ae214d8e60503344d565e216d
#
# export DBUS_SESSION_BUS_ADDRESS=$ADDR
# DISPLAY=:0 su -c "notify-send \"Test\" \"Message from root\"" rich
#
```

Figure 2.8 uses the grep and sed commands to pull out the needed current DBUS_SESSION_BUS_ADDRESS environment variable setting from the /proc/*proc_ID*/environ file. *proc_ID* is the process ID for the user's gnome-shell process.

> Using the notify-send utility as a global GUI user communication tool begs for a shell script. You should already have basic bash shell scripting experience. However, some advanced commands, such as the sed utility, may require you to seek additional help. Consult a resource, such as the *Linux Command Line and Shell Scripting Bible* (Wiley, 2015), to help you create your own notify-send script, or use your favorite search engine to find some shell script examples to modify.

The notify-send command has several additional options that can be useful. Unfortunately, on some distributions, the man pages for this particular utility are either nonexistent or sparse at best. If you need more information, use your favorite search engine to look up additional notify-send documentation.

Using the */sbin/shutdown* Command

The /sbin/shutdown command allows you to halt, reboot, or power down your system as well as to communicate with your system users while doing so. More likely than not, you are already familiar with this command.

As you would suspect, the shutdown command requires super user privileges for its use. The general syntax for the shutdown command is

shutdown [*options*] *time* [*wall message*]

The [*options*] include options to halt the system (-H), power off the system (-P), and reboot the system (-r), as well as several other useful selections. Once you've started a shutdown process, you can typically cancel it by using the shutdown -c command. See the man pages for additional shutdown options that you may wish to use.

> If no [options] are used, the shutdown command performs differently depending on the distribution that you are using. It may take the system to single-user mode, although a *time* must be specified, or it may immediately power off the system.

The *time* parameter allows you to specify a time to enact the shutdown options. It takes many formats, such as a military time layout specified as *hh:mm*. You can indicate the number of minutes from the current system time using a *+n* or *n* format. The shutdown command allows the now time parameter to indicate 0 minutes from now (immediately). On some distributions, if *time* is not specified, a +1 is assumed. See the man pages for all of the *time* specifications available on your distribution.

The [*wall message*] parameter lets you modify the shutdown command message sent to any logged-in users. This parameter operates in a similar manner as the wall command, with one major difference: it ignores the mesg setting on a terminal. Therefore, the message can be written on any terminal whether write access is granted or not.

> Keep in mind that, like the wall command, the [*wall message*] parameter will only broadcast the designated message to users logged into a terminal or using a terminal emulator. You will need another communication form to warn other users of the impending system shutdown.

An example of using the shutdown command is shown in Figure 2.9. Both the *time* and [*wall message*] parameters are included. This particular example is from an Ubuntu distribution.

FIGURE 2.9   Using the **shutdown** command with a message

```
$
$ sudo shutdown -P +5 "System shutdown pending. Please log off."

Broadcast message from christine@server01
        (/dev/tty2) at 7:54 ...

The system is going down for power off in 5 minutes!
System shutdown pending. Please log off.
```

Notice in Figure 2.9 that the [*wall message*] parameter is displayed under the system's shutdown communication message, "The system is going down for power-off in 5 minutes!" The various distributions display different standard shutdown communication messages, and your [*wall message*] may appear above or below the standard message. Even if you do not include a [*wall message*] parameter, the system's standard message is still broadcast to terminal users.

For the distribution shown in Figure 2.9, the user issuing the `shutdown` command does not receive a command prompt back. Therefore, in this case, instead of entering the `shutdown -c` command to cancel the shutdown, the Ctrl+C key combination is needed for cancelation. When using this method to cancel a shutdown, no messages are sent. When using the `shutdown -c` command, a wall message is broadcast to terminal users. A snipped version is shown here:

```
# shutdown -c

Broadcast message from root@localhost.localdomain ...
The system shutdown has been canceled at Wed ...
```

It's obviously important to know just how your Linux distribution handles the `/sbin/shutdown` command before you start using it on a live system. It would be a good practice not only to read your distribution's man pages but also to try out the `shutdown` command on a test system.

To ensure that all of your system users receive important fluid communications, you can look outside the command line for help. Many companies provide phone call, text, and email message broadcasting services, which may be useful for your various needs. Use your favorite search engine to locate such service companies. Before you do, check to see if your own company or organization already has internal services that it can use for these types of fluid communication methods.

There are some additional `shutdown [options]` that can be useful relating to the [*wall message*] parameter. The `-k` option will disable logins and send out warning messages, but it will not bring down the system. A snipped example of this is shown here:

```
$ sudo shutdown -k +20 "Please log out..."
$
Broadcast message from christine@server01
        (/dev/tty2) at 8:43 ...

The system is going down for maintenance in 20 minutes!
Please log out...
$
```

Notice that when using the `-k` option, the shutdown [*wall message*] looks no different from a regular shutdown message. Keep in mind that this option does not force anyone to log out.

Some distributions offer the `--no-wall` option. It allows a shutdown to proceed with no wall messages to the terminal users. Only the super user issuing the command will receive one message, similar to what is shown here:

```
# shutdown --no-wall +5
```

```
Shutdown scheduled for Wed 2016-12-02 09:02:48 EST,
use 'shutdown -c' to cancel.
```

Be aware that if you decide to cancel the shutdown after using the --no-wall option, the terminal users will still receive the cancelation message. Therefore, if you used this option on the original shutdown command and need to cancel the shutdown, be sure to suppress the cancelation message like this:

```
# shutdown -c --no-wall
```

Fluid messaging, such as using the /sbin/shutdown command's [*wall message*] parameter, involves informing active system users concerning events that are currently happening. There are also useful tools that allow communication automation for future events.

Looking at Static Messaging

Static messaging involves communicating with system users using files that are changed only when the message needs to change. They can contain serious information, such as company system access policies, or light-hearted announcements, such as when the next company picnic is scheduled.

The system users see these messages when they log into the system. Thus this static messaging form is specifically called *logon messaging*. These techniques are intended to be used as primary communication methods for planned situations. There are several Linux files that can help employ this automated communication style:

- /etc/issue
- /etc/issue.net
- /etc/motd

Each file serves a slightly different purpose and may not be available for all user types or on all distributions. As with most options, its best to explore them and then decide which logon messaging file to implement on your system(s).

Using the */etc/issue* File

The /etc/issue file allows text to be displayed on the tty terminal login screens. It typically holds a company's system access policy, and it rarely changes. It may also contain planned upcoming system outages. When unmodified, the /etc/issue file usually simply holds system information, such as what Linux kernel version is running. An example of this unmodified file from a CentOS distribution is shown here:

```
$ cat /etc/issue
\S
Kernel \r on an \m

$
```

Notice that a few special characters are used in the file. You can use @*character* and *character* arrangements as long as they are supported by your distribution's getty program (the program responsible for managing tty terminals).

With super user privileges, you can modify the file, for example, if system users need to be informed of an upcoming outage:

```
# cat /etc/issue
\S
Kernel \r on an \m


########################################################
                        NOTICE

        System will be down for maintenance
        When:   December 26 1:00am through 1:30am


########################################################


#
```

The modified /etc/issue file causes the tty login display to look like the one shown in Figure 2.10. Notice how the special characters are now formatted in the display.

FIGURE 2.10   Using a modified **/etc/issue** file

```
CentOS Linux 7 (Core)
Kernel 3.10.0-229.20.1.el7.x86_64 on an x86_64

#########################################################
                        NOTICE

        System will be down for maintenance
        When:   December 26 1:00am through 1:30am

#########################################################

localhost login: _
```

The /etc/issue file will *not* contain helpful comments for you to peruse, because all of its contents are displayed on the login screen. You can typically type in **man issue** to get help on modifying this file.

You will often need to provide your GUI users with logon messages too. If you use the GNOME Display Manager (GDM), you can easily accomplish this by modifying the GUI login banner. Use your GUI help application to locate "changing the login banner" documentation. It is typically located within any system administration guide provided. If you are using LightDM Greeter, be aware that while changing the background image is easy, adding and modifying logon greeter messages may be more difficult. Use your favorite search engine to explore the various options currently available.

Using the */etc/issue.net* File

The /etc/issue.net file is very similar to the /etc/issue file. Its primary purpose is to display logon messages for remote logins. By default, it is typically enabled only for Telnet connections. Here is an example of a default /etc/issue.net file on an Ubuntu distribution:

```
$ cat /etc/issue.net
Ubuntu 14.04.3 LTS
```

Nothing too exciting exists in this file. It simply contains the distribution's current version.

 You may want to check with your legal department and computer security team on what should be displayed within your company or organization's login messages. For security purposes, it's usually not a good idea to show the Linux distribution, its version, or kernel information. Legally, it is wise to include some message warning that unauthorized system use is prohibited.

To enable OpenSSH to use the /etc/issue.net file, you need to make a small configuration file change. Edit the /etc/ssh/sshd_config file on your system. (This configuration file will not exist if you do not have OpenSSH installed on your system.) You should find a line similar to the following:

```
#Banner   /etc/issue.net
```

Remove the hash mark (#) from the line. If the word none is listed, instead of the issue .net file, change it to /etc/issue.net. You will need to reboot your OpenSSH server for the change to take effect.

The following is a modified /etc/issue.net file:

```
$ cat /etc/issue.net

*******************************
        WARNING
Authorized access only
Violators will be prosecuted

*******************************


$
```

When OpenSSH has been configured to use the modified /etc/issue.net file, any ssh logins should look similar to Figure 2.11.

FIGURE 2.11   Using a modified **/etc/issue.net** file with OpenSSH

```
$
$ ssh christine@10.0.2.15

xxxxxxxxxxxxxxxxxxxxxxxxxxxxxx
            WARNING
Authorized access only
Violators will be prosecuted

xxxxxxxxxxxxxxxxxxxxxxxxxxxxxx

christine@10.0.2.15's password: _
```

Using the *ic/motd* File

The /etc/motd file (Message of the Day file) provides an additional logon communication method only for tty terminal users. The /etc/motd file contents are displayed after the user has logged into the system but before a command-line prompt is displayed.

Traditionally, the file contained more light-hearted messages, such as upcoming company events or sayings. It now typically contains upcoming system event information, often because the /etc/issue and /etc/issue.net files are needed for displaying legal logon messages.

On some distributions, the file pre-exists but is empty. On others, it is not installed by default but is easily created. As you would expect, you must have super user privileges to create or modify it. Here is a modified /etc/motd file located on a CentOS distribution:

```
# cat /etc/motd

Hello, I'm a modified MOTD file.

#
```

Figure 2.12 shows how the file is displayed after a user has logged into the system. Notice that the /etc/motd file's contents display after the user has logged in but before a shell prompt is received.

FIGURE 2.12   Using a modified **/etc/motd** file

```
CentOS Linux 7 (Core)
Kernel 3.10.0-229.20.1.el7.x86_64 on an x86_64

localhost login: chris
Password:
Last login: Wed Dec  2 16:15:58 on tty3

Hello, I'm a modified MOTD file.


[chris@localhost ~]$ _
```

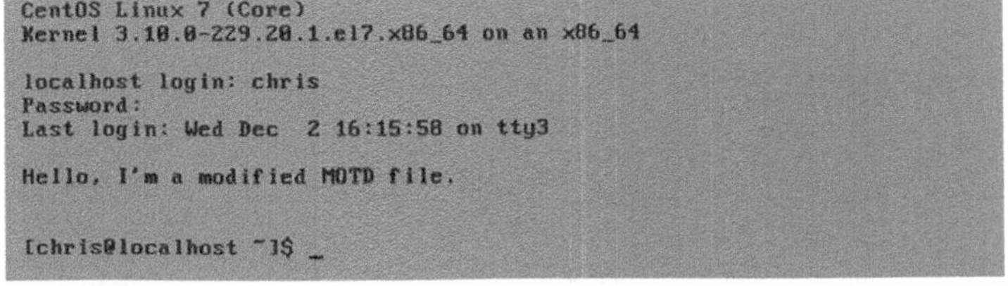

You can find out more about your distribution's /etc/motd file by entering **man motd** at the command line.

On some distributions, more files are involved than just /etc/motd. For example, on Ubuntu, a file called /run/motd.dynamic is displayed at login. It is automatically created by /etc/init.d/motd and contains items such as currently needed software package updates.

Static messaging using logon messages is just one of the many ways that you can communicate with system users. Fluid messaging methods also provide many helpful communication tools. There are many ways to keep Linux system users informed as part of your basic system maintenance process.

Backing Up the System

One of the most important system maintenance tasks that you handle is protecting system data via a backup process. All too often, companies and organizations treat this task with little thought and planning, which can lead to financial disaster. In addition, just having backups is useless if there are no plans in place for recovering the data.

We'll explore developing a backup strategy in this section. We'll also cover looking at different backup media that can be used in your strategy and various Linux utilities associated with data backups. Hopefully, the information provided here will help you start to develop a rigorous data backup plan, successfully implement it, and be ready to recover data if needed.

Developing a Backup Strategy

Developing a well-thought-out backup plan is key to protecting company data. Consider starting the data backup planning process with this question to company leaders, "Just how valuable is your data?"

Determining the data's value is just the first step, but it does help to guide your backup strategy. Keep in mind that there is no single backup solution. Your plan will depend entirely on your company's individual data protection needs.

Because they are often used interchangeably, confusion may exist between the terms *backup* and *archive*. When you design your backup and archival strategy, be sure to use these terms in your plan properly. A *backup* is a copy of the data that is used for safeguarding the original data. An *archive* is either a copy of the data or the actual data itself, typically put on less-expensive media and moved into long-term storage, which is often environmentally controlled and in a different physical location. Your data backup plan(s) may differ greatly from your data archival plan(s).

When developing a data backup plan, you should consider several important items. These items will allow you to determine a budget and make decisions on what methods to include in your backup plan. Typically, these important items include the following:

- Data categories
- Value of each data category
- Maximum acceptable data inaccessibility time

Data categories involve cataloging your data into groups in order to determine value. For example, you will have a system data category that covers data necessary for system operation. You may also have data categories such as customer payment information.

Once data has been categorized and a value determined, you need to decide on the maximum acceptable amount of time that data can be inaccessible. Typically, measurements such as recovery time objective (RTO) are used. RTO states the maximum tolerable length of time that data (or a computer) can be unreachable.

 Keep in mind that whole books have been written on creating backup and recovery strategies. Please use the information here as a simple starting point for your particular implementation.

When the previous key items have been determined, research and decisions on the following backup and recovery topics can take place:

- Backup media
- Backup storage and rotation solutions
- Backup types
- Data recovery
- Directories to backup
- Software solutions (network and local)

When you are developing this plan, none of these topics can be viewed in isolation. For example, the backup media that you select will affect your software and storage solution decisions. And, of course, the best backup plan is one that is reviewed and tested.

Looking at Backup Media

There are many factors to consider when you are looking at the media available for your backup strategy, such as portability, longevity, and cost. In this section, we'll explore different media, focusing on these important factors:

Magnetic Tape One of the oldest media used for backup, magnetic tape is still around and in use. It's known for its reliability and longevity. However, to achieve its optimal longevity, tapes should be stored in a location with regulated temperature and humidity controls. This is especially important if you are using them for data archival purposes. Magnetic tape is cheap, averaging around 1 cent per gigabyte. Even though it is inexpensive, technology companies are still working to improve it. Back in 2014, a company developed a single magnetic tape capable of holding at least 2.5 terabytes.

Though magnetic tape has several benefits, it also has disadvantages that keep many from using it in their backup schemes. For example, the data stored on tape can only be accessed sequentially, which causes data restoration to take a lot longer than data stored on media that can be randomly accessed. Also, tape is not multiuser; that is, only one process at a time can access it.

Overall, magnetic tape is not the most popular medium for periodic data backup purposes, but it does have its niche. It is extremely useful for data archival purposes due to its low cost. In fact, many film studios use magnetic tape to store their various necessary individual film formats.

 When considering a data archival plan, be sure to look at a media type's potential obsolescence. For example, Zip disks were used for a very short period of time. Tape has been around forever, and it may be just what you need for archival purposes.

Optical Discs   Optical discs include CDs, DVDs, and Blu-ray discs, and they became popular as backup media because of their low cost. In addition, their small size and portability make them easy to transport to offsite backup storage locations and/or easily store within a company onsite vault.

For some organizations, optical media do not work as backup media due to their relative small size. For a CD, you are limited to 700 MB of data. DVDs are typically limited to 4.7 GB. A Blu-ray disc's capacity often falls between 25 and 50 GB, though technology companies are working to increase Blu-ray's data storage capabilities. Another potential limitation for use in backups is that optical disks can be slower to write to and read from than other backup media, such as a local hard disk drive (HDD).

HDDs   HDDs are also an old and proven backup medium. You can use them for backups, whether their technology is IDE, SCSI, SATA, and so on. You just need to make sure that they are partitioned and that a filesystem has been placed on them. In view of their data capacity, HDDs are an inexpensive backup medium and they are faster to write to and read from than some other media, such as optical disks.

The biggest problem comes if you are using a local HDD, instead of a remote one, as your backup media. Since it is attached to your Linux system, any disaster that occurs to the system typically occurs to the backup HDD as well. However, they can be very convenient for smaller backup schemes, such as a production environment, which needs hourly backups that are later backed up to an offsite location and can survive losing a day's worth of work.

Solid State Drives   Solid state drives (SSDs) can be connected either locally or remotely, or they can be removable. Often popular for use as a disk for an operating system, their biggest advantage for backups is their writing and reading speed. Though not as portable as optical media, they still are relatively easy to transport and store.

SSDs can be prohibitive to use in a backup plan because of their cost. They are, at present, more expensive than optical media or HDDs. In addition, their data storage durability is unproven. It's thought that if an SSD is not used and left without power for a long period of time, it could potentially lose portions of its data.

It's not just the media type that is a factor but also the media's location during and after a backup. If you conduct your backups locally, then you may need to transport the backup media to another location for disaster recovery purposes. We explore this topic next.

Exploring Backup Storage and Rotation Solutions

Whether you choose a local or a remote backup solution, it may be necessary to come up with a media storage and rotation solution. Any removable media, local or remote, will need to be stored in a location that will protect its data. For example, if you choose optical discs as your backup medium and store the discs in the same building as the original data, a local fire may destroy both your original data and its backups.

 Companies often store their backup media in a fireproof safe. Keep in mind that *fireproof* does not guarantee that the media will not be destroyed in a fire. The term *fireproof* means that an object is fire resistant up to a certain temperature. Check any storage facilities that you use for their fire-resistance capabilities before choosing them as a place to store your backup media.

Depending on the backup or archive media that you have chosen, items to consider for media storage may include the following:

- Temperature control
- Humidity control
- Fire resistance
- Security

Temperature and humidity controls are especially important for data archives on tape. Security is also important for any media type. However your data is secured on the system, it should have equal or higher security on its backup media. Also consider who has access to the media storage location.

Not only should locally created backups have a media storage solution, but a rotation schedule is important too. If media is stored off site, you need to determine how often and when backup media will be returned locally for reuse.

Data restoration convenience can also be an issue for media stored off site. Often companies address this issue by creating multiple data backups. Therefore, some media can be stored off site in case of a big disaster, while other media can be stored carefully on site to restore data quickly when needed.

If you are rotating backup media on and off site, don't forget transportation security issues. Determine how the media should be protected while in transit to the storage facility. Some companies employ the use of an armored truck, because their data is essentially money.

If you choose a remote backup solution, your storage issues are greatly reduced and rotation typically becomes a non-issue. A storage area network (SAN) or network-attached storage (NAS) can be a handy solution for backing up data remotely. You can use these as local backup solutions, but for our purposes here, they are being treated as remote solutions.

A SAN provides block-level storage, and a NAS provides file-level storage. The primary difference between these two, for backup purposes, is that a NAS must be on the local area network (LAN), while a SAN can be physically miles away connected over a fast Fibre Channel network solution. It's easy to see right away that SAN storage has backup advantages over NAS, but cost can be a factor. In addition, data encryption as the data travels over the network should be part of your plan.

Again, the data value drives how much money you want to spend to back up, rotate, and store your data. Keep this in mind as you review these various topics.

 Real World Scenario

Cloud Storage Backup

Backing up data to the cloud may be the right solution for your company's data. Cloud backup and storage services, such as Amazon S3 (Simple Storage Service) and Google Cloud Storage, offer varied and affordable cloud backup solutions.

One problem they solve right away is the need for media rotation. Many offer quick and easy data recovery and have reasonably priced options. Some cloud services offer tools available in Linux package repositories that can allow you to integrate their cloud storage solutions easily into your current backup and archival scheme.

Nevertheless, cloud backup solutions may not be the right fit for your particular organization. Data limits may be prohibitive. Encryption of the data as it travels over their network may not be offered. Still their options are definitely worth investigating as a potential part of your backup plan.

Looking at Backup Types

For our purposes here, *backup types* refer to the different methods for backing up data that has been modified. The four most common types are these:

- Full
- Incremental
- Differential
- Snapshot

Each of these backup types is explored in this section. Their advantages and disadvantages are included:

Full Backup   A *full backup* is a copy of all data, ignoring its modification date, to another set of media. This backup type's primary advantage is that it takes a lot less time than other types to restore a system's data. However, not only does it take longer to create a full backup compared to the other types, but it also requires more storage. It requires no other backup types in order to restore a system fully.

Incremental Backup   An *incremental backup* makes a copy of only data that has been modified since the last backup operation (any backup operation type). Typically, a file's modified time stamp is compared to the last backup type's time stamp. This backup type takes a lot less time to create than the other types, and it requires a lot less storage space. However, the data restoration time for this backup type can be significant, because you first have to restore the full backup and then restore each incremental backup. For optimization purposes, you must complete a full backup periodically.

Differential Backup   A *differential backup* makes a copy of all data that has changed since the last full backup. It could be considered the happy medium between full and incremental backups. This backup type takes less time than a full backup but potentially more time than an incremental backup. It requires less storage space than a full backup but more space than a plain incremental backup. Also, restoration takes a lot less time using differential backups than incremental backups, because only the full backup and the latest differential backup are needed. For optimization purposes, you must complete a full backup periodically.

Snapshot Backup   A *snapshot backup* is considered a hybrid approach, and it is a slightly different flavor of backup. First, the backup software makes a full data copy to backup media, such as a SAN, and then the software uses pointers, such as hard links, to create a reference table linking the backup data with the original data. The next time you make a backup, instead of a full backup the backup software performs an incremental backup (only modified or new files are copied to the backup media), and the software copies and updates the pointer reference table. This saves space, because only modified files and the updated pointer reference table need to be stored for each additional backup.

 The snapshot backup type described here is a copy-on-write snapshot. There is another snapshot flavor called a *split-mirror snapshot*, where the data is kept on a mirrored storage device. When a backup is run, a copy of all the data is created, not just new or modified data.

With a snapshot backup, you end up with the ability to go back to any point in time and do a full system restore from that point. It also uses a lot less space than the other backup types. In essence, snapshots simulate multiple full backups per day without taking up the same space or requiring the same processing power as a full backup type would. The rsync utility (described later in this chapter) uses this method.

As you can see, you have a lot to choose from as to how best to implement your backup plan. But wait! There are even more issues to consider before you start creating a backup plan.

Looking at Data Recovery

The time comes when data needs to be restored. No one really likes to think about it, but it does happen. Files are accidently deleted, disk drives fail, and grand disasters happen. Like death and taxes, data recovery is inevitable.

Data restoration needs to be an integral part of your backup plan. The specific details are heavily dependent on the other plan choices you make. However, you need to plan for each one of the following data-restoration scenarios:

Single or Multiple Data File Recovery   This is the most common data-recovery scenario that occurs on a system. Users accidently delete their files. Other users ruin data within their files. It's convenient if you can provide a solution that allows users to recover these files themselves and provide up-front education on how to avoid these types of scenarios.

Full Partition or Disk Recovery   Hopefully, you have proper structures in place, such as RAID disks, to avoid these kinds of problems, but they still can happen. Your RTO measurements will play a big factor in the recovery plan for this scenario.

System Recovery   This is typically your worst-case situation. The entire system and all its data must be restored. There are two flavors of this restore: you can do a full system restore, which involves booting the OS from a live distribution and then restoring all of the files needed for the Linux OS to work (all of the system configuration files and all the data files). Another flavor is the configuration/data restore. This entails first reinstalling Linux and then restoring the system configuration files and all of the data files.

Planning for each data-restoration scenario will make the actual restoration event go much smoother. In addition to planning for data recovery, be sure to evaluate and test your plans regularly to ensure that they meet your company's current needs.

Exploring Directories to Back Up

When you categorize your data, one item to consider is where that data resides in your Linux directory structure. This will help you to determine which directories to include in the various backups. Also, the directories that you choose to back up are dependent on your planned recovery schemes.

It's a good idea to periodically document all of the packages installed on the system. You can create this documentation using package utilities, such as rpm or dpkg. This documentation is primarily for your own reference, just in case you need to know what packages were installed due to a data recovery failure or some other terrible data disaster. It's always better to have too much documentation instead of too little.

Table 2.1 contains important directories to consider including in your backup scheme. Your choices will vary depending on your restoration needs as well as your system's configuration. The Backup Consideration column makes suggestions based on the two system recovery options (full system restore and configuration/data restore) covered previously.

TABLE 2.1   Directories to consider for backup plans

Directory	Contents	Backup Consideration
/bin	User utility programs. Some distributions store many of these programs in /usr/bin.	Full system restore: yes Configuration/data restore: no
/boot	Holds configuration files used during the system boot process.	Full system restore: only for documentation purposes (for example, comparing boot files to restored boot files) Configuration/data restore: no
/dev	Contains device files for the hardware devices system.	Full system restore: only if distro is configured to use static /dev files. Configuration/data restore: no
/etc	System configuration files.	Yes
/home	Typically, the user's home directory. However, depending on your system's configuration, others may exist (example: /home2).	Yes
/lib	Stores kernel modules and shared libraries.	Full system restore: yes Configuration/data restore: no
/lost+found	Files saved during unplanned system shutdowns.	No
/media	Temporary mount directory for removable media devices.	No
/mnt	Temporary mount directory for removable media devices.	No
/opt	Third-party application software.	Yes
/proc	Virtual filesystem for running processes and kernel information.	No

Directory	Contents	Backup Consideration
/root	The root user's home directory.	Yes
/run	A tmpfs filesystem mounted early during the boot process and used by various tools.	No
/sbin	System administrator utility programs.	Full system restore: yes Configuration/data restore: no
/srv	System-specific files for various services.	Yes
/sys	Virtual filesystem stores information concerning and allows modification of connected hardware devices.	No
/tmp	Temporary files.	No
/usr	Stores binaries, documentation, source code, libraries, and so on.	Yes
/var	Contains log, lock, spool, mail, and temp files.	Yes (Some subdirectories, such as /var/run, can be excluded.)

Some of these directories may not appear in older Linux distributions. Also, be aware that some distributions are moving away from the File Hierarchy Standard (FHS), http://www.pathname.com/fhs/, or don't fully follow it. Therefore, be sure to understand all of the directories your particular distribution uses and what is stored in them before you create a backup plan.

Reviewing Backup Software Solutions

Reviewing the various software solutions to use in your backup plan is best done last. Once you have gathered and reviewed your backup and restore requirements, you'll have a clearer picture of what software will meet your needs.

You can group the backup software solutions into two primary categories: GUI and/or web-based solutions and command-line solutions. Both categories offer local and network backups. The first group to explore is the GUI and/or web-based solutions.

Amanda   Amanda (also called Amanda Network Backup) is an open-source software backup solution that runs on a Linux host machine. At its core are command-line utilities, such as dump and tar. It provides the ability to back up data from multiple-OS platforms to a variety of media that include disk and tape, as well as to the cloud. Amanda offers several editions, including a free downloadable Community Edition and an Enterprise Edition, which includes a nice GUI interface called Zmanda Management Console. Find out more about this solution at www.zmanda.com/.

Bacula   Bacula is also an open-source software backup solution that is released under the AGPL v3 license. It has five primary components (Director, Console, File, Storage, and Monitor services), which allow flexibility in how you manage your network backups, including web, GUI, and text-based interfaces. It provides the ability to back up data from multiple-OS platforms to a variety of media that include disk and tape, as well as to the cloud. However, the Bacula project doesn't recommend that you use its product if you are not experienced at using command-line options, such as tar and dump, due to its difficulty in setup. Nevertheless, there are many tutorials on the Web. Also, an enterprise version (closed-source) is available called Bacula Systems, which offers all of the various backup types and support. Find out more about this solution at http://blog.bacula.org/ and http://www.baculasystems.com/.

Bareos   Bareos is a fork of the Bacula backup software. It is open-source and also released under the AGPL v3 license. The Bareos backup solution is nearly a clone of Bacula. It has the same primary components as well as the various interfaces. Bareos does have a few additional features, including the ability to install the Director component on a Windows system. In addition, the Bareos developers have created their backup solution to protect your backup data following user-specified rules. This feature may make it difficult to reuse backup tapes with Bareos, and therefore the project developers recommend using another solution for this particular situation. Find out more about this solution at www.bareos.org.

Duplicity   Another popular backup solution is Duplicity. It can be used from the command line or via a GUI front end called deja-dup. It typically comes preinstalled on Ubuntu, and it is the core behind the Unity Backups icon. It is primarily targeted at Linux/Unix clients, but with some work you can get it to run on a Windows machine. It provides the ability to back up data to a variety of media, as well as to the cloud. It allows you to encrypt your backups using GNU Privacy Guard (GPG). Find out more about this solution at http://duplicity.nongnu.org/.

BackupPC   BackupPC is another open-source software backup solution, which is released under the GNU GPL. It can back up Linux, Unix, Mac OS X, and Windows machines, and it supports disk backup media. BackupPC has a web-based front end and uses rsync and tar at its core. Find out more about this solution at http://backuppc.sourceforge.net.

You may not need something as comprehensive as the GUI and/or web-based software solutions that are offered. Fortunately, the command-line solutions listed here are still viable alternatives:

- cpio
- dd
- dump/restore
- rsync

- star (tar with SELinux)

- tar

Keep in mind that some utilities used for data backups can also be used for other purposes. For example, tar can be used for backups or for distributing source code, as covered later in this chapter. In fact, several command-line backup solutions are covered in detail in the upcoming sections.

Once you have developed and reviewed your backup strategy, be sure to test it. Also, put into place a periodic backup plan review to ensure that it is meeting your company's data protection needs.

Performing Backups

If you have planned properly, backing up your data will occur on a regular and potentially automated basis. But occasionally you will need to conduct unscheduled data backups. For example, your organization may have a special project whose data protection needs to fall outside the company's normal backup plan. Whether the backup is planned or unplanned, several command-line utilities are available for you to use in data backups.

This chapter section takes a more in-depth look at a few utilities that you can employ in data backups (and archival). In addition, it covers verifying the backup, an important part in any backup process.

Using *tar* to Conduct Backups

The tar utility has been around for quite a while. Its name is an acronym for "tape archiver," which shows its age. Though it's old, it is still a very popular tool, and it is often used at the core of various software backup solutions because of its flexibility and stability.

Using the tar command, you start out with several files that need to be backed up. You end up with a copy of those files, stored in a single file, called an *archive* file. If the archive file is compressed using a data compression utility, the compressed archive file is called a *tarball*.

It may be a little confusing that the tar utility's resulting data backup files are called archive files. However, other than that small issue, the utility is fairly straightforward in its use.

The tar utility's resulting archive files can be stored on any filesystem media type, not just tapes. You can also move these archive files anywhere you choose, such as to the cloud, but encryption is recommended first.

One reason for the tar command's popularity is its straightforward command-line options. For example, to create a tar archive file, you use the -c option (*c* as in *create*) as opposed to something non-inherent like -F.

Table 2.2 lists several, but certainly not all, tar command options that you can use for creating a data backup. For a bigger list of various tar options, be sure to consult its man pages. In addition, you can find out a great deal more by typing **info tar** at the command line.

TABLE 2.2 `tar` command options for creating data backups

Long Style Option	Short Style Option	Option Description
--create	-c	Create a tar archive file (full or incremental, depending on other given options).
--update	-u	Append files to a pre-created tar archive file but only those files modified since the original archive file was created (cannot be used with tape media).
--listed-incremental=*file*	-g *file*	Create an incremental or full archive based on metadata stored in *file*.
--level=#		Force a level # archive.
--gzip	-z	Compress tar archive file into a tarball using `gzip` compression.
--bzip2	-j	Compress tar archive file into a tarball using `bzip2` compression.
--xz	-J	Compress tar archive file into a tarball using `xz` compression.

More than likely, you have already created tarballs using the `tar` command. However, a little review may be in order. Here is an example:

```
$ ls
Project42.dat    ProjectFileA.dat    ProjectFileB.dat
$
$ tar -Jcvf Project42.tar.xz *.dat
Project42.dat
ProjectFileA.dat
ProjectFileB.dat
$
```

In the previous `tar` command, four options are used. The -J option is used so that a tarball will be created using xz compression. The c option is used to create the tar archive. The v option allows the filenames to be displayed as standard output as they are placed into the tar archive. Finally, the f option designates the tar archive filename, `Project42.tar.xz`. The `*.dat` parameter asks for all of the files with a `.dat` file extension in the current working directory to be included in this archive.

> You can also use the "old style" tar command options. For this style, you remove the single dash in front of the tar option. For example, -c becomes c. Keep in mind that additional "old style" tar command options must be "squished" together. Thus, tar cvf is valid, but tar c v f is not.

You can use a variation of this command to create both full and incremental backups. A simple example helps to explain this concept. Here is the process for creating a full backup:

```
$ ls *.dat
Project42.dat    ProjectFileA.dat    ProjectFileB.dat
$
$ tar -g Archive1.snar -Jcvf Project42_Full.tar.xz *.dat
Project42.dat
ProjectFileA.dat
ProjectFileB.dat
$
```

Notice the -g option in the preceding full backup example. The -g option creates a file, called a snapshot file, named Archive1.snar. This snapshot file can have any name that you desire, and it can be located anywhere within the filesystem. The .snar file extension indicates that it is a tar archive snapshot file. A tar archive snapshot file contains metadata used in association with tar commands for creating full and incremental backups. The snapshot file uses file time stamps, so the tar command can determine if a file has been modified since it was last backed up. The snapshot file is also used to determine any files that are new or if files have been deleted since the last backup.

The previous example created a full backup of the designated files along with the metadata snapshot file, Archive1.snar. Now the same snapshot file will be used to help determine if any files have been modified, are new, or have been deleted to create an incremental backup:

```
$ echo "Answer to everything" >> ProjectFileC.dat
$
$ tar -g Archive1.snar -Jcvf Project42_Incremental.tar.xz *.dat
ProjectFileC.dat
$
```

In the example, a new file, ProjectFileC.dat, is created. Again, the tar command uses the -g option pointing to the previously created Archive1.snar snapshot file. This time, the metadata within Archive1.snar lets the tar command know that the ProjectFileC.dat file is a new file and that it was not included in a previous backup. Therefore, the new tarball contains only the ProjectFileC.dat file, and it is effectively an incremental backup.

The tar command views full and incremental backups in levels. A full backup is a one that includes all of the files indicated, and it is considered a level 0 backup. The first tar incremental backup after a full backup is considered a level 1 backup. The second tar incremental backup is considered a level 2 backup, and so on. You can force the tar command to do a full backup with a level *n* snapshot file via the --level=0 option.

You can continue to create additional incremental backups using the same snapshot file:

```
$ echo "42 is the answer to everything" >> ProjectFileD.dat
$
$ tar -g Archive1.snar -Jcvf Project42_Incremental_2.tar.xz *.dat
ProjectFileD.dat
$
```

Using these various tar options allow you to create a myriad of various backups for small projects or entire systems. However, whenever you create data backups, it is a good practice to verify them. Table 2.3 provides some tar command options for viewing and verifying data backups.

TABLE 2.3   **tar** command options for verifying/viewing data backups

Long Style Option	Short Style Option	Option Description
--compare --diff	-d	Compare a tar archive file's members with external files and list the differences.
--list	-t	Display a tar archive file's contents.
--verbose	-v	Display the files as they are processed (typically used when creating or restoring data backups).
--verify	-W	Verify the tar archive as it is being processed (cannot be used with compression).

Backup verification can take several different forms. You might ensure that the desired files are included in your backup by using the -v option on the tar command in order to watch the files being listed as they are included in the tar archive.

You can also verify that desired files are included in your backup after the fact. Use the -t option to list out tarball or tar archive file contents:

```
$ tar -tf Project42_Full.tar.xz
Project42.dat
ProjectFileA.dat
ProjectFileB.dat
```

```
$ tar -tf Project42_Incremental.tar.xz
ProjectFileC.dat
$ tar -tf Project42_Incremental_2.tar.xz
ProjectFileD.dat
$
```

 If you move a backup file to a new location over a network, it may get corrupted during the transfer. Verify that it arrived unaltered by using a checksum utility, such as md5sum, before and after the transfer.

You can verify files (sometimes called *members*) within an archive file by comparing them against the current files. The option to accomplish this task is -d. In this first example, no differences are found:

```
$ tar -df  Project42.tar.xz
$
```

However, when a file included in this tarball is altered in the current directory and the -d option is used again, the tar command lists the file's differences:

```
$ mv ProjectFileB.dat ../
$ cp ProjectFileA.dat ProjectFileB.dat
$
$ tar -df Project42.tar.xz
ProjectFileB.dat: Mode differs
ProjectFileB.dat: Mod time differs
ProjectFileB.dat: Size differs
$
$ rm ProjectFileB.dat
$ cp ../ProjectFileB.dat ProjectFileB.dat
$ tar -df Project42.tar.xz
ProjectFileB.dat: Mod time differs
$
```

Another good method for verifying your backup is to verify it automatically immediately after the tar archive is created. You can easily accomplish this by tacking on the -W option, as shown in this snippet:

```
$ tar -Wcvf Project_Verify.tar *.dat
Project42.dat
ProjectFileA.dat
[...]
Verify Project42.dat
Verify ProjectFileA.dat
[...]
$
```

You cannot use the -W option if you employ compression to create a tarball. However, you could create and verify the tar archive first and then compress it in a separate step.

You can also use the -W option when you extract files from a tar archive. This is handy for instantly verifying files restored from backups.

Table 2.4 lists some of the options that you can use with the tar command to restore data from a tar archive file or tarball. Be aware that several options used to create the backup, such as -g and -v, can also be used when restoring data.

TABLE 2.4 **tar** command options for restoring data from backups

Long Style Option	Short Style Option	Option Description
--extract --get	-x	Extract files from a tar archive file.
--gunzip	-z	Uncompress the tar archive file from a tarball using the gunzip command.
--bunzip2	-j	Uncompress the tar archive file from a tarball using the bunzip2 command.
--unxz	-J	Uncompress the tar archive file from a tarball using the unxz command.

You have most likely extracted files from tar archives and tarballs. However, a little review may be helpful. Here is an example where the incremental backup files, created earlier in this chapter, are restored to a new directory:

```
$ mkdir test
$ cd test
$ tar -Jxvf ../Project42_Incremental.tar.xz
ProjectFileC.dat
$
$ tar -Jxvf ../Project42_Incremental_2.tar.xz
ProjectFileD.dat
$
```

Unfortunately, chapter space is limited. We've only scratched the surface of all of the tar command capabilities that can be used for backups, such as using tar backup parameters and/or creating backup and restore shell scripts using the tar command. Be sure to take a look at GNU tar website, https://www.gnu.org/software/tar/manual/, to learn more about this popular command-line backup utility.

Working with Magnetic Tape

As covered earlier in this chapter, magnetic tape is still useful for storing data because it is inexpensive: measured in price per byte (or terabyte) ratios. It is often used for data archival purposes because of this low cost.

Each magnetic tape can contain several backups, one after the other. However, a tape is a sequential access medium, not a random access device like a hard drive. Think of a series of tar archive files lined up on a long, narrow road. To reach a tar archive file near the road's end, you must walk down that road, past the other tar archive files, to locate that particular file. If after you locate that file you need a tar archive file that's near the road's beginning, you must walk back down the road in the opposite direction (rewind) to reach that archive file. This paints a fair picture of magnetic tape access.

A magnetic tape contains special markers, such as tape beginning, tape end, and file mark (used between the backup files), as shown in Figure 2.13. These markers help the programs using the tape.

FIGURE 2.13 Depiction of magnetic tape files

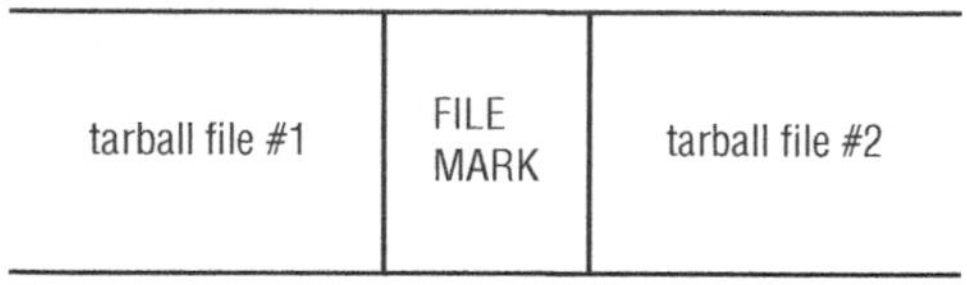

tarball file #1	FILE MARK	tarball file #2

For creating archives and backups, SCSI tape drives are popular because they are considered the most reliable. Linux interfaces SCSI tape devices to the system via two primary device files, /dev/st* and /dev/nst*, as shown in a snipped listing here:

```
$ ls -ld /dev/st[0-7]
crw-rw----. 1 root tape 9, 0 Dec   5   08:38 /dev/st0
crw-rw----. 1 root tape 9, 1 Dec   5   08:38 /dev/st1
[...]
crw-rw----. 1 root tape 9, 1 Dec   7   08:38 /dev/st7
$ ls -ld /dev/nst[0-7]
crw-rw----. 1 root tape 9, 128 Dec   5   08:38 /dev/nst0
crw-rw----. 1 root tape 9, 129 Dec   5   08:38 /dev/nst1
[...]
crw-rw----. 1 root tape 9, 135 Dec   7   08:38 /dev/nst7
$
```

The primary difference between a /dev/st* tape device file and a /dev/nst* device file is that the st SCSI device is an automatically rewinding tape device and the nst SCSI device is not. In other words, when the program you are using with the tape device is done, it will automatically rewind the tape back to its beginning or not. Automatically rewinding a tape at an operation's end was more popular when magnetic tapes were used in daily backup situations.

Though rarely used nowadays, a /dev/ht* device file refers to an automatically rewinding PATA-attached tape device. Also, a /dev/nht* device file refers to a PATA-attached tape device that will not automatically rewind.

You can find out more about SCSI magnetic tape devices by typing **man st** at the command line. In addition, the lsscsi command (if installed on your system) will display information about all of your SCSI devices, including SCSI magnetic tapes.

To control a tape and use it with an archive/backup program, employ the mt command. You need either super user privileges or tape group membership to use the mt program. The general syntax for this command is

mt [-f *device*] *operation* [*count*] [*arguments*]

The -f *device* specifies the tape drive device that you are controlling. You can substitute -t *device*. Also, if you have the environment variable TAPE defined, you can leave it off, which is why -f *device* is considered optional.

 Often the mt command is not installed by default. If you find this to be the case on your distribution, you can locate it in the mt-st software package.

A few of the more relevant tape device *operation* choices are listed in Table 2.5. Not all *operation* choices are valid for all tape drive types. For a more complete list, see the mt command's man page.

TABLE 2.5   **mt** operations for managing tape devices

Operation	Operation Description
status	Display tape status information.
load	Load tape (most tapes are automatically loaded when inserted into a tape drive).
erase	Erase all current data on tape.
fsf *count*	Skip *count* files on tape (go forward), and position tape head on the next file's first block.
bsf *count*	Skip *count* files on tape (rewind), and position tape head on the previous file's last block.
tell	Get current tape head position.
eod	Go to end of current data on tape.
rewind	Rewind tape.
eject	Rewind and unload tape (if needed).
offline	Rewind and unload tape (if needed).

Here is a simple snipped example of using the mt command. A tape is loaded within a SCSI tape drive, represented by device file /dev/st0, and the mt command is used to check its status:

```
# mt -f  /dev/st0 status
SCSI 2 tape drive:
File number=0, block number=0, partition=0.
[...]
 BOT  ONLINE  IM_REP_EN
#
```

The ONLINE status code shown indicates that the tape drive has a tape loaded and that it's ready for operation. The BOT status code indicates that the tape is positioned at the beginning of the first file. (In this case, no files have been loaded to the tape yet, so the tape head is positioned at the tape's beginning.)

Now that a tape is loaded and ready, you can use the tar command to back up files to the tape. What is actually happening is that a tarball file is placed on the tape, as shown in this snipped example:

```
# tar -Jcvf  /dev/st0  /home/chris/Project
tar: Removing leading '/' from member names
/home/chris/Project/
/home/chris/Project/ProjectFileA.dat
[...]

/home/chris/Project/Project_Verify.tar
#
```

Since this is an automatically rewinding tape device, /dev/st0, the tape will rewind when the backup operation is complete.

> If you have single- or multi-drive SCSI media changer devices, you'll use the mtx command to load and unload the tapes and not the mt command.

The files can later be restored, if desired, from the tape also using the tar command. Of course, you first have to load the appropriate tape into the tape drive. Here is a snipped example of restoring the files to a different directory from tape:

```
# mkdir temp
# cd temp
```

```
# tar -Jxvf  /dev/st0
/home/chris/Project/
/home/chris/Project/ProjectFileA.dat
[...]

/home/chris/Project/Project_Verify.tar
#
```

It's possible that you may never have to deal with magnetic tapes. But if you do, the `tar` and `mt` commands are worthy utilities to employ.

Using *rsync* to Conduct Backups

The rsync is a nice utility that allows you to perform backups to disk drives locally or to those connected over a network. Not only it is lightning fast, but you can easily encrypt your file transfers tunneling through OpenSSH.

It's fairly simple to conduct an rsync backup locally. Popular option combinations such as either -av or -ah, allow you to back up files to a local location quickly, as shown in Figure 2.14.

FIGURE 2.14   Using **rsync** locally

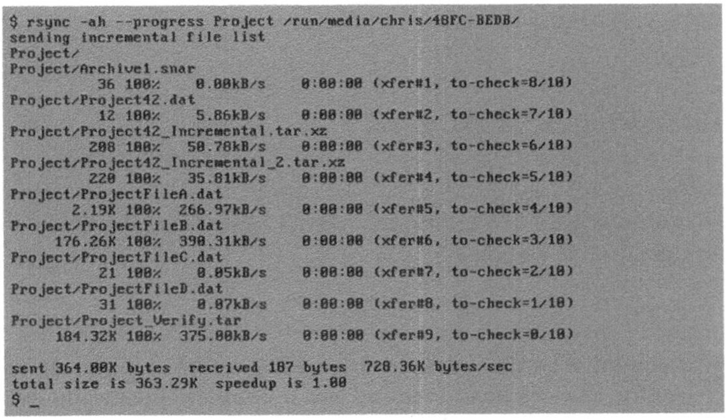

The -a option is called the archive option, and it is equivalent to using the -rlptgoD options. As you might suspect, adding -v increases the output's verbosity, while -h makes the output more human readable. The --progress option is nice if you like to see a progress report as the files are being backed up. For other rsync options, see the man pages.

To use rsync over a network and have the transfer be encrypted, both local and remote machines must have rsync and OpenSSH installed. Figure 2.15 shows a snipped example of using this method.

FIGURE 2.15   Using **rsync** over a network

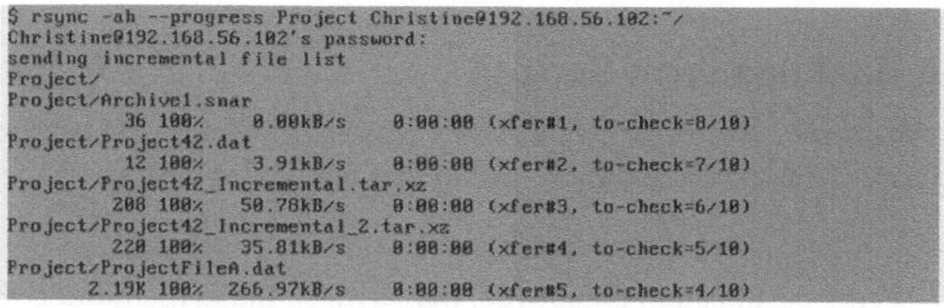

```
$ rsync -ah --progress Project Christine@192.168.56.102:~/
Christine@192.168.56.102's password:
sending incremental file list
Project/
Project/Archive1.snar
         36 100%    0.00kB/s    0:00:00 (xfer#1, to-check=8/10)
Project/Project42.dat
         12 100%    3.91kB/s    0:00:00 (xfer#2, to-check=7/10)
Project/Project42_Incremental.tar.xz
        208 100%   50.78kB/s    0:00:00 (xfer#3, to-check=6/10)
Project/Project42_Incremental_2.tar.xz
        220 100%   35.81kB/s    0:00:00 (xfer#4, to-check=5/10)
Project/ProjectFileA.dat
       2.19K 100%  266.97kB/s    0:00:00 (xfer#5, to-check=4/10)
```

If you specify your remote host destination via rsync://*host*:/, you are *not* using encryption. Be sure to use *host*:/ or *user*@*host*:/ to transfer files through OpenSSH.

You can do much more with rsync than just partial file backups. You can also set up full backups. In addition, employing hard links lets you use rsync for incremental backups as well. (Use your favorite search engine to find articles on using rsync and hard links to create incremental backups for your data.)

Using *dd* to Copy Data

Another command-line utility that you can use for data backups is the dd command. It's primarily used to create a low-level copy of a hard drive, and it is often used in digital forensics.

Don't use dd to back up or restore a disk that is currently mounted to a Linux system. Doing so could cause corruption.

The command itself is fairly straightforward. It is a handy utility for copying damaged disks. Its general syntax is as follows:

dd of=*output-device* if=*input-device*

The *output-device* is either an entire drive or a partition. The *input-device* is the same. Just make sure that you get the right device for out and the right one for in; otherwise, you may unintentionally wipe data!

If you are getting rid of a disk, you can also use the dd command to zero-out the disk, as shown here:

```
# dd of=/dev/sdc if=/dev/zero count=10
```

The if=/dev/zero uses the zero device file to write zeros to the disk. The count option is added so that this action is completed 10 times in order to zero-out the disk thoroughly. This particular task will take a long time to run, and it's still better to shred any disks that will no longer be used by your company.

For various additional options that may be useful for many other applications, see the man pages.

Automating Backups with Scripts

With anything repetitious, like backups, it makes sense to automate the activity as much as possible. Shell scripts can be very handy to use in this particular case.

In the certification objectives, the /bin/sh file is mentioned. Be careful in using this file in your shell scripts' hashpling. It may simply be a pointer to /bin/bash, but on some distributions it points to /bin/dash. It's best to check the /bin/sh file's long listing before using it in scripts or avoid it altogether by using your desired shell in the script's hashpling.

Once you have your backup scripts working and tested, consider running them with cron (or anacron) to ensure that backups are never forgotten. Since backups are a popular shell script, use your favorite search engine to find various examples located on the Internet. You may be able to find something that will meet your needs with only a few modifications.

Installing Programs from Source

There will be times when you need or want to install a program from source. It may be that the program is not available in a repository, or that you would like to view the source code before installing the program, or that you are considering writing a new program based on this one, and so on. When that time comes, it's handy to know the basic steps required:

1. Download the installation file.
2. Unpack the installation file.
3. Read the installation's documentation.
4. Prepare for compiling.
5. Compile the program.
6. Move the binaries to appropriate locations.

Programs you run, sometimes called binaries or machine code, were originally *source code* programs, written in a programming language "easy" for humans to understand. A source code program is compiled and/or interpreted into machine code, and it becomes an executable program. To modify an executable program, you need its source code version.

These steps are fairly straightforward, and they are typically required by most programs obtained in this manner. However, be aware that it is ultimately up to the program's creator as to how the installation takes place, so you may have to modify your actions to install a particular program successfully. And, of course, you need super user privileges to install programs this way.

Obtaining the Installation Files

There are many different ways to obtain the installation files for a particular program. Installation files typically come packaged in a tarball format. Often, the program's creator maintains a web presence that will direct you to the program's tarball download source.

 It's usually a good idea to get all of your system's software up to date prior to installing a new program. For example, on a RHEL-based system, use yum update, and on a Debian-based system, use sudo apt-get update and then sudo apt-get dist-upgrade.

Once you locate the program's tarball download source, use your choice of methods to download the file. You can use a direct HTTP or HTTPS download via your favorite web browser, or, if available, you can download via a torrent client, or you can use the wget command-line utility, and so on.

 The proper final location for original source code is in a /usr/src/ subdirectory. However, during the installation process, the source code should temporarily reside in a home or temporary directory.

Unpacking the Installation Files

To unpack the installation files, you simply extract them from the program's tarball file. For program distribution purposes, the compression method typically used is gzip compression, as indicated by a tarball file having a .tgz or .tar.gz extension. However, it is not unheard of for other compression methods, such as bzip2 or xz, to be used.

For demonstration purposes in this chapter, we'll install the curl program (http://curl .haxx.se) from source. Its tarball uses gzip compression, and it is shown here:

```
# ls
curl-7.46.0.tar.gz
```

To decompress and unpack the installation files from the tarball, use the tar command with the appropriate extraction and decompression options. If you don't remember the appropriate tar command extraction and decompression options, consult the man pages.

 Tab key command completion of the tarball filename can be very helpful here. Often these installation file tarballs have long names with version numbers attached.

Here is a snipped example of extracting the installation files from the `curl` program's tarball:

```
# tar -zxvf curl-7.46.0.tar.gz
curl-7.46.0/
curl-7.46.0/projects
[...]
curl-7.46.0/Makefile.in
#
```

Once the installation files are extracted, you should see a directory created within your current working directory. This directory contains the installation files that you need to complete this program's installation on your system.

```
# ls -F
curl-7.46.0/ curl-7.46.0.tar.gz
#
```

Once you change your present working directory into this new directory, you should see several files, such as README or README.txt, configure, Makefile.in, and so on. Every program's installation files will be slightly different.

Reading Installation Documentation

It's fairly clear what you should do with the README or README.txt file...read it! This is the general documentation file, and it will often have installation instructions within it (though installation instructions are sometimes located in a file called INSTALL). The most important reason for reading the README and INSTALL files is that the program author may have chosen to pursue a non-standard installation course. Hopefully, the author will document the course you should pursue in order to be successful.

Table 2.6 provides a brief description of files that you should consider reading before installing the software. Be aware that not all programs will have all of these files. Also, there may be additional files included or files with slightly different names.

TABLE 2.6   Installation files to read prior to installing a program

Typical Filename	Purpose
README	General documentation and installation instructions
INSTALL	Installation instructions
COPYING	Software license

Typical Filename	Purpose
RELEASE-NOTES	Features and bug fixes included in the program version
NEWS	Features and bug fixes included in the program version
AUTHORS	Program creator(s) and contact information

Another reason to read these files is that a program author will often document any needed dependencies. Unlike installing with utilities like yum or apt-get, software dependencies are not automatically obtained and installed as part of this process. You have to do it manually.

 You'll need the correct compilers (software that compiles programs) installed on your system for the source code installation to work properly. It's typically helpful to go ahead and install these potentially needed development tools ahead of time. On a Red Hat–based system, type **yum groupinstall "Development Tools"**, and on a Debian-based system, type **sudo apt-get install build-essential** at the command line.

Compiling Preparation

In this next basic step, you run a standard script that checks the system's configuration and sets up preparations for the compiling step. The script that you run is configure, and it should be one of the files within the program's installation file directory.

 For a security fix to a source-code installed program, you may need to employ the patch command and compile the program again. A patch file is created using the diff command on the new source code file and the original source code file. Afterward, this patch file is applied to the original source code using the patch utility before recompilation. For more information, type **man patch** at the command line.

Typically, when you run the configure script, it will look for both optional and mandatory dependencies and settings. The script will check to see if you have the proper compiler(s) installed, check for any necessary program dependencies, check for any optional dependencies, and create a file called Makefile. It can do some other checking and setup as well.

The Makefile is created (or updated) by the configure script using what it finds on your system as well as the contents of the Makefile.in file stored within the program's installation file directory.

Many configure scripts have a help utility that provides a list of options that you can use with the script. Type **./configure --help** at the command line to view these options.

Because a configure script can produce a great deal of output, it's a good idea to pipe it into a file, using tee, as well as to watch its display on the terminal screen. Using the curl program's configure script as an example, here is a snipped listing of its execution:

```
# cd curl-7.46.0
# ./configure | tee  ../curl_configure.log
checking whether to enable maintainer-specific por[...]
checking whether make supports nested variables... yes
[...]
HTTP2 support:   disabled (—with-nghttp2)
Protocols:             DICT FILE FTP GOPHER HTTP IMAP POP3 [...]
#
```

Typically, if the configure script finds what it needs, it ends successfully. If it runs into any serious problems, such as not finding a particular required library or compiler installed (mandatory requirements), tackle those problems first and then rerun the configure script.

Compiling the Program

At this point, you are ready to compile the source code into binary. The command to do so is make. The make command uses the Makefile file, which was either created or modified in the previous step, as a guide.

The following is a snipped example of compiling the curl program. Notice again that the output is preserved by piping it into the tee utility.

```
# make | tee  ../curl_make.log
Making all in lib
make[1]: Entering directory '/root/curl-7.46.0/lib'
make all-am
[...]
make[1]: Leaving directory '/root/curl-7.46.0'
#
```

Now that the program's source code is compiled, all that is left to do is to finish the installation process.

Completing the Installation

To complete the installation, you just need to run the make install command. It typically creates any needed program directories, moves the program binaries and any supporting files, such as documentation and program libraries, to their proper locations, and sets proper permissions settings for the files.

Using the curl example, here is a snipped example of using make install. Notice again, it is piped through the tee program to preserve its output if needed:

```
# make install | tee ../curl_make_install.log
Making install in lib
make[1]: Entering directory '/root/curl-7.46.0/lib'
[...]
make[1]: Leaving directory '/root/curl-7.46.0'
#
```

 NOTE   Once the program is installed, you can remove the installation files' directory and its contents. But you may want to hang onto the program's tarball, because an uninstall program that may prove useful is often included if you need to uninstall this program. Also, consider storing the unpacked source code in a /usr/src subdirectory.

Once everything is moved to its appropriate location, try out your new program! Here the curl program is used with its version option as a test:

```
# curl --version
curl 7.46.0 (x86_64-pc-linux-gnu) libcurl/7.46.0
[...]
#
```

In Exercise 2.1, you'll install a popular integrated development environment called Geany from source code.

EXERCISE 2.1

Installing the Geany IDE from Source Code

To install the Geany integrated development environment, follow these steps:

1. Log in as an ordinary user to a Linux system connected to the Internet, and open your favorite web browser.

2. Go to http://www.geany.org, and find the installation tarball to download. It will have a name similar to geany-#.#.tar.gz, where # is a version or release number.

3. Using your favorite method, download the Geany installation tarball.

4. Once the tarball is downloaded, log onto a user account that has super user privileges.

EXERCISE 2.1 *(continued)*

5. You will need to install compilers and a few other items. If you are on a Red Hat–based system, such as CentOS or Fedora, type **yum groupinstall "Development Tools"** and press Enter. If you are on a Debian-based distribution, such as Ubuntu, type **sudo apt-get install build-essential**, press Enter, and input the appropriate password. Answer appropriately any questions that arise during the installation to install these tools.

6. Copy the downloaded Geany tarball to your current directory.

7. Type **tar -zxvf geany-#.#.tar.gz** to unpack the tarball, where # is the version or release number of the Geany tarball. (Keep in mind that if the file does *not* end in .tar.gz, you will not only need to change the file extension in your command, but you may also need to change your tar command options in order to use the correct decompression method.)

8. Type **ls -F** to view the name of the Geany directory that contains the installation files.

9. Type **cd geany-#.#** and enter the correct numbers in place of # to move your present working directory into the newly created Geany directory.

10. Read the README and INSTALL files. You may find that additional packages need to be installed in the next step besides the ones listed.

11. Install the needed GTK2 library and, on a Debian system, install the intltool package as well. If you are on a Red Hat–based system, type **yum install gtk2-devel** and press Enter. If you are on a Debian-based system, type **sudo apt-get install gtk+2.0 intltool** and press Enter. Answer appropriately any questions that arise during the installation to get these packages installed.

12. Prepare for compilation by typing **./configure** and pressing Enter. If you receive any missing dependency errors, install any missing dependencies and run the configure script again.

13. Compile the Geany program by typing **make** and pressing Enter.

14. Use super user privileges to move the binaries and other files to their appropriate locations by typing **make install** or **sudo make install** (whichever command is appropriate for your super user situation) and pressing Enter.

15. Check the Geany program's version by typing **geany -V** and press Enter. If all is well, you should get a response.

16. Try out your Geany IDE by logging into the GUI as an ordinary user. Open a terminal emulator, type **geany**, and press Enter. If your program was successfully installed, you should see the Geany IDE window.

Managing Resource Usage

Managing your system's resource usage involves troubleshooting resource problems as they occur. However, measuring via monitoring and predicting future resource usage can help minimize resource problems ahead of time. Unfortunately, too many system administrators spend more time on troubleshooting and less time on monitoring/predicting.

This section provides a look at the various tools that you can use for all three activities. It also addresses when these tools should be used. In addition, it covers resource usage troubleshooting and capacity planning.

Measuring Resource Usage

There is an old saying that states, "You can't manage what you can't measure." This saying is appropriate for measuring resource usage. You must measure resources often, accurately, and thoroughly to gather the necessary data to manage these resources properly. In addition, you must measure accurately before you can begin to troubleshoot or capacity plan resource usage.

Resource measuring via monitoring comes in a couple of different forms. Sometimes you just need to keep an eye on things. At other times, you are monitoring data to find out why certain problems are occurring. Also, you may need to be regularly collecting data for system capacity planning.

 Entire books have been written on the subjects of resource troubleshooting, capacity planning, and monitoring resource usage. This section will get you started in the right direction, but you may need to explore other resources to complete your education.

It can be a little overwhelming trying to track all of the various system resource data statistics. Here are a few key items for which you should be measuring and collecting data on each system/network you manage:

- System uptime
- CPU usage and load statistics
- Memory usage and swap statistics
- Disk I/O and load statistics
- Network I/O and load statistics
- Firewall throughput
- Router throughput
- Network bandwidth usage

There will be times, however, when you many need to monitor special items on your system for troubleshooting, specific application growth, or special capacity planning. For example, you may need to determine if the `irqbalance` utility (which distributes interrupt requests among the system's multiple processors) helps to improve your system's performance. In this case, tracking each processor core's interrupt request load is necessary both before and after installing the `irqbalance` utility.

Fortunately, on a Linux system, you can employ many measurement command-line tools. Table 2.7 lists a few along with a general description of each.

TABLE 2.7 Command-line utilities for resource utilization monitoring and recording

Utility	Description	Display Type	Monitors
free	Shows the amount of free/used physical and swap memory.	Static	Memory
htop	Enhancement of the top utility, which allows horizontal as well as vertical scrolling, and uses function keys for process control.	Dynamic	CPU Memory Process States Uptime
iftop	Similar to the top utility, it shows current network traffic information, including DNS.	Dynamic	Network
iostat	Shows device I/O loading summary broken down per device.	Static or Dynamic	CPU Device I/O
iotop	Similar to the top utility, it shows current I/O usage by processes (or threads).	Dynamic	Device I/O
ip	The -s link option and route option will display network and routing statistics. (Replaces the netstat command.)	Static	Network Routing
iptraf	Shows network information, and it is menu driven.	Dynamic	Network
lsof	Shows open files and network connections by process.	Static	Network Process map
mpstat	Shows multiple processor statistics.	Static or Dynamic	CPU
mtr	Shows routing information for the URL parameter.	Dynamic	Routing
netstat	The netstat -i option and -r option will display network and routing statistics. This command is considered obsolete. Use ip instead.	Static	Network Routing

Utility	Description	Display Type	Monitors
ntop	Gathers network statistics that can be viewed via a web browser via port 3000.	Dynamic	Network
pmap	Shows a processes map for the PID parameter.	Static	Process map
ps	Shows current process information, including CPU consumption.	Static	CPU Process states
pstree	Shows current processes in a tree format.	Static	Process map
sar	Acronym for System Activity Reporter: a multiple resource monitoring utility that collects and displays a wide variety of resource usage information.	Static or Dynamic	CPU Memory Network Device I/O
ss	Displays socket statistics directly from kernel space. Provides more information than the netstat utility.	Static	Network
tcpdump	A packet analyzer/sniffer that shows designated network interface captured packet content descriptions.	Dynamic	Network
top	Multiple display panels that show various resource usage data such as processes consuming the most CPU. Display can easily be changed on the fly. The atop and htop utilities are enhancements of the top command.	Dynamic	CPU Memory Process states Uptime
uptime	Shows how long the system has gone without a reboot, load averages, and current number of users.	Static	Uptime
vmstat	Shows swap (virtual memory) performance.	Static or Dynamic	Memory
w	Shows current user information, including CPU consumption.	Static	CPU Process states

Your distribution may have additional utilities installed than those listed in Table 2.7, which you can employ for resource monitoring and system performance activities. A quick way to find these utilities is by typing **man -k monitor** and **man -k performance** at the command line.

Not every utility in Table 2.7 is installed by default on every distribution. Also, keep in mind that several full-resource-monitoring software solutions are available and are covered later in this chapter.

Several utilities in Table 2.7 have additional resources that they monitor other than the abbreviated types listed in the Monitors column. See the man pages for a full description of these various utilities. Be aware that there are many more monitoring command-line utilities available to install. Open your favorite web browser, and type in the search words **Linux monitoring** for additional monitor utility lists.

> You can turn any static display utility listed in Table 2.7 into a dynamic display via the watch command. The watch command will rerun the utility every two seconds (by default), but you can modify this interval. For example, to rerun the iostat command every five seconds, type **watch -n 5 iostat** and press Enter. The iostat command will rerun every five seconds until you press Ctrl+C. Find out more about watch by viewing its man pages.

The sar (acronym for System Activity Reporter) utility is a special one in that it can collect data over a long period of time and provide a great deal of it. Because of its ease of use, it's also a good tool for those new to resource monitoring. It's typically installed by default on most distributions, but if for some reason you don't find it on yours, it is located in the sysstat package.

The sar utility uses data stored by the sadc utility in /var/log/sa/ and, by default, displays data from the current file, though you can change this behavior via certain command options. Used without any options, the sar command will display today's stored CPU usage information in 10-minute intervals, as shown in this snipped example:

```
$ sar
[...]
12:20:01 PM  CPU   %user   %nice   %system   %iowait   %steal[...]
12:20:01 PM  all   1.97    0.00    1.84      0.22      0.00[...]
12:30:01 PM  all   0.29    0.00    1.37      0.16      0.00[...]
[...]
```

You can show current CPU information and change the displayed intervals as well. In this snipped example, CPU usage is shown by sar four times and is spaced one second apart:

```
$ sar 1 4
[...]
06:49:50 PM  CPU   %user   %nice   %system   %iowait   %steal[...]
06:49:51 PM  all   1.05    0.00    6.32      0.00      0.00[...]
06:49:52 PM  all   1.02    0.00    2.04      0.00      0.00[...]
```

```
06:49:53 PM    all    0.00       0.00       1.03       0.00       0.00[...]
06:49:54 PM    all    0.00       0.00       4.08       0.00       0.00[...]
Average:       all    0.52       0.00       3.35       0.00       0.00[...]
$
```

The sadc (acronym for System Activity Data Collector) utility collects various system resource usage data for sar. It stores the data in the /var/log/sa/ directory in the file sa*dd*, where *dd* is equal to the day of the month, by default.

> If you run sar with a particular option, such as networking or disk informa-
> tion, and you get the response "requested activities not available in
> file," you will need to modify your sadc configuration. On Red Hat–based
> systems, modify the file /etc/sysconfig/sysstat and add the desired
> option to the SADC_OPTIONS line. On a Debian-based distribution, modify
> the file /etc/default/sysstat and, within the sadc section, either add the
> option to the SA1_OPTIONS line or make sure that ENABLE="true" is set.

The sa1 utility stores system activities in binary data files. The sa2 creates a daily summary of sa1's collected data. Both sa1 and sa2 are typically run via cron.

Keep in mind that these utilities work together to process and display only local system information. To find out more information on sar, sadc, sa1, and sa2, take a look at their man pages.

Predicting Resource Usage

Predicting resource usage is formally called *capacity planning*. Capacity planning involves the following steps:

1. Understanding the system users' current needs
2. Monitoring the current system's usage of resources
3. Gathering future direction and anticipated needs of the system users and applications
4. Making predictions and decisions based on the information gathered

Capacity planning predictions need to have documented proof of both current resource usage and the current resource usage growth rate through time. Without this data, the projected resource usage growth and anticipated capacity break point of a configuration will be grossly inaccurate.

There are several full-resource-monitoring software solutions that you can use to collect data and produce the needed graphs. Generally, these solutions are divided into presentation software, which produces useful charts and/or graphs, and collector software (also called a *data logger*), which gathers resource usage data. You'll find that many of these software products have the ability to work together. A few of these are covered here:

Cacti   Cacti is a resource usage presentation software solution, which provides the ability to produce usage graphs from templates. It is a front end to RRDTool. Cacti stores its data in a MySQL database, and its front end is handled via PHP. It is often used for monitoring network traffic because it can handle rather complex networks. Also, it allows this gathered data to be used in MRTG graphs. Find out more about Cacti at `http://www.cacti.net`.

collectd   `collectd` is a daemon that allows you to monitor IT infrastructure usage. Written in C for portability, it collects local (and remote with a network plugin) system statistics. The `collectd` daemon is fairly easy to configure. You configure the data gathered and how it is gathered via plugins and a few other settings within the `collectd.conf` configuration file located in `/etc/` or `/etc/collectd/`, depending on your distribution. The configuration file's `LoadPlugin` options determine which plugins to use in `collectd`.

Other utilities are needed to display gathered statistics. If a utility is not installed by default on your Linux distribution, it is in the `collectd` package. You can get additional details on `collectd` at `https://collectd.org/`.

MRTG   This software solution's name is an acronym for Multi Router Traffic Grapher, which nearly says it all. It collects and graphs network traffic data. Written in Perl for portability, it can graph just about any network device's statistics. MRTG produces HTML pages that deliver a dynamic network traffic graph. It can be used in conjunction with RRDTool as well. Find out more about this solution at `http://oss.oetiker.ch/mrtg/`.

Nagios   This very popular software solution suite comes in two flavors: FOSS and proprietary. You'll have to pay for the Nagios XI software solution, but the Nagios Core product is free. Nagios Core provides monitoring of systems, network devices, and various services. It uses a plugin that allows you to create customized service checks if desired.

Nagios Core provides a centralized view for all monitored items throughout your company. There is a web interface for viewing current and collected data and logs of previous outages, events, alerts, and so on. Nagios Core is primarily a data collector, and it doesn't provide usage or performance graphing. However, the collected data can be used with third-party graphing tools, such as PNP4Nagios and nagiosgraph.

One of Nagios Core's best features is that it can send out problem alerts via email or text messaging. You can even incorporate your own custom alert script. Find out more about Nagios Core and the other Nagios products at `http://www.nagios.com`.

There is also a Nagios community that provides an ISO-certified CD-ROM for CentOS, including the tools most often used in Nagios. This allows you to install and set up Nagios quickly for monitoring. The Nagios community website is `http://www.fullyautomatednagios.org/`.

Icinga   Icinga started as a Nagios (described earlier) fork. It is now split into two different products, Icinga1 (the original Nagios fork) and Icinga2 (a total rewrite). Icinga is compatible and similar to Nagios, but incorporates a different (some feel it is better) user interface, and a quicker development cycle. Find out more about Icinga products at `www.icinga.org`.

RRDTool   An industry standard, RRDTool stands for Round-Robin Database Tool, because its collected resource usage data is stored in a round-robin database. This database's size doesn't change because the oldest data is deleted whenever newer data is stored in it. It does provide tools on how to use this data in order to produce resource usage graphs. However, it is often used in other utilities, such as Cacti, MRTG, and Nagios. Additional information on RRDTool can be found on its official website at http://www.rrdtool.org.

By using one or more of these full-resource monitoring software solutions, you can predict growth and avoid problems with resource exhaustion. In addition, these programs, as well as the command-line tools covered earlier, allow you to find current performance bottlenecks and diagnose resource usage problems, as covered next.

Troubleshooting Resource Usage

Once you have monitoring resource usage and capacity planning in place, you will minimize having to troubleshoot resource usage. However, when troubles do come, they will be much easier to solve.

Besides monitoring your resources, you should understand how these resource-monitoring software solutions interact. A particular resource symptom may be directly related to a problem with another resource. Therefore, it's important to correlate system symptoms with the likely cause of the problem. The following are a few items to consider as you troubleshoot resource usage:

Memory   Memory (also called RAM) is divided into 4 Kb chunks called *pages*. When the system needs more memory, using a memory management scheme, it takes an idle process's memory pages and copies them to disk. This disk location is a special partition called *swap space* or *swap* or *virtual memory*. If the idle process is no longer idle, its memory pages are copied back into memory. This process of copying memory pages to and from the disk swap space is called *swapping*.

You can view memory statistics on a system using command-line tools such as free, sar, and vmstat. If your system does not have properly sized memory, you should see high RAM usage. In addition, due to these memory issues, the system will increase swapping and result in increased disk I/O. The vmstat tool is handy in this case, because it allows you to view disk I/O specific to swapping as well as total blocks in and blocks out to the device.

 N⊘TE   Be aware that RAM bottlenecks keep processor(s) usage artificially low. If you increase the RAM on your system, your processor(s) loads will also increase.

Processes   It is crucial to identify what processes are using what resources, especially if a particular resource is having problems. You may need to determine if resource problems are causing the process problems or vice versa. The ps, psmap, and pstree utilities can be useful in correlating particular processes with particular resource problems.

For example, if a disk is experiencing unusually high I/O, it may be due to a particular process and it may be causing a group of processes performance troubles. This is called *I/O blocking*. In this particular example, you would find these processes in what is called an uninterruptible sleep. The vmstat utility's b column displays how many processes are in this state. To determine the actual processes, use the ps utility and look for a D process state.

Don't forget that the /proc directory has lots of useful information concerning a running system and its processes.

CPU   For troubleshooting and monitoring purposes, you need to understand your CPU's hardware. First, determine how many CPUs are on your system. For each CPU, you need to know the number of processor cores, whether or not hyper-threading is used, cache sizes, and so on. The /proc/cpuinfo file and the lscpu commands can be helpful here.

The various CPU items to watch include idle time, average use loads, queue length, interrupt request loads, and so on. The uptime, top, sar, and mpstat are a few of the utilities to help you here.

Device I/O   For device I/O, which is usually focused on disks, you need to understand your hardware. Is it NAS, iSCSI, or SAN? Are you using LVM, and what is the filesystem type employed? Once you understand your system's underlying disk hardware, then you will be better able to interpret monitoring software and utilities data.

The command-line utilities useful here include iostat, iotop, lsof, and sar. If your disks are accessed through your network, don't forget to include network monitors as part of your device I/O troubleshooting toolkit.

Network Throughput   Network package throughput and bottlenecks can be a constant worry in a system administrator's life. Understanding your network's hardware and topology is the first step in troubleshooting. Without a clear picture, you'll be chasing rabbits instead of solving problems.

Your network's size, hardware, and topology will also determine what tools will work best for your troubleshooting purposes. The command-line utilities iftop, ip, iptraf, and ntop can be helpful. If set up to capture network traffic, the sar utility can also be used. Also, lsof can display what network services, such as FTP, are in use on your system, and tcpdump can provide network packet analysis. And let's not forget those humble little helpful utilities such as ping, traceroute, and ifconfig.

Keep in mind that if you manage a large network, the various full-resource-monitoring software solutions, such as MRTG, may be more useful for troubleshooting. Their graphics capabilities might prove necessary for locating bottlenecks.

As you've probably noticed, the various resources can all directly affect one another. Thus, using a variety of command-line and resource-monitoring tools will help you in managing your system's resource usage.

Summary

The non-glamorous job of keeping a Linux system up and humming along involves many important basic maintenance tasks. Everyday maintenance tasks include routine ones such as backing up data. Without extra data copies, any disaster, large or small, could be ruinous. Monitoring the system resource usage is another basic and continual job that is necessary for a system's overall health.

Some non-standard jobs are also required, which are not conducted on a daily basis, such as installing a program from its source code. Data restores may also be needed occasionally, such as when a user accidentally deletes an important file.

Keeping system users happy is part of the maintenance job. Monitoring a system's current resource usage and planning for its future needs will lessen outages and poor performance. These tasks help to avoid "The computer is slow today" refrain from users. Of course, keeping your system users informed allows you to set expectations. Nothing causes frustration more than unmet expectations. A nice Linux feature is that there are many built-in communication tools that you can employ for notification purposes.

Exam Essentials

Summarize fluid system notification utilities.   The wall, mesg, notify-send, and shutdown utilities all can provide messages to system users. The wall command can send messages to all system users who are logged into a terminal and whose terminal has write access granted. The notify-send command can send notifications to GUI users. The shutdown command not only can shut down the system, but it can also send messages to system users while doing so.

Describe logon notification files.   The files /etc/issue, /etc/issue.net, and /etc/motd have different uses for static logon system notifications. All have content that can be displayed at some point during the terminal login process. For GUI users, logon notification must be set up via the display manager.

Explain the pros and cons of backup media.   Magnetic tape is inexpensive and useful for data archival purposes. Optical discs are portable, but their capacity is limited. HDDs are inexpensive, though not as cheap as tape, and they are faster for reading/writing than some other media. If local HDDs are used, a disaster could wipe out the backups. SSDs are the fastest medium, but they are also the most expensive.

Summarize different backup types.   A full backup is one where all data is copied to another medium. An incremental backup copies only the data that has been modified or added since the last backup. The differential backup type is similar to an incremental one, except that only data that has been modified or added since the last full backup is copied. For snapshots, a full backup is made and a pointer reference table is created. After that, an incremental backup is done along with the pointer reference table, which is copied and updated, saving space compared to other backup types.

Describe the different backup utilities.   The tar utility is an old but useful tool. It allows you to create backup files, called tar archive files. You can also use tar to compress the backup files on the fly, turning them into tarballs. If you are using magnetic tape as a backup medium, the mt command can assist in controlling the tape for backup purposes. The dd utility is useful for creating low-level bit-by-bit copies of a partition or an entire drive. It is often used in digital forensic applications. For a fast and reliable system backup utility, the rsync command is useful. It also allows file transfer encryption through OpenSSH.

Explain the steps to install a program from source.   To install a program from its source, you must first obtain the installation files, typically packed into a tarball. Once you unpack the tarball, it is important to read through the provided documentation and obtain any additional needed software. You then run the configure script in order to check the system and prepare for compilation. At that time, you also run the make command so that the program can be compiled. The final step is to use the make install command to move program files to their proper location.

Summarize the resource-monitoring utilities.   The command-line utilities included in Table 2.7 such as top, vmstat, and sar allow various system resources to be monitored, which provides data for troubleshooting and capacity planning. Full-resource products, such as MRGT and Nagios, provide data collection for all system resources. They also offer graphs for analysis.

Review Questions

You can find the answers in the Appendix.

1. Which of the following commands will allow a message to be sent to any tty terminals with write access allowed? (Choose all that apply.)

   A. mesg

   B. write

   C. echo

   D. mail

   E. wall

2. To shut down your system without sending a message to users, use which of the following /sbin/shutdown options?

   A. -c

   B. -k

   C. --no-wall

   D. --wall

   E. None of the above

3. Your company's legal department has decided that a login notification is needed on a Linux system that you manage, warning that unauthorized system use is prohibited. Which method is the best one for deploying this legal notification?

   A. Edit the /etc/issue file, and place the notification there.

   B. Edit the /etc/motd file, and place the notification there.

   C. Use the notify-send command to send the notification to users.

   D. Edit the ~./bashrc file, and place the notification there.

   E. None of the above.

4. Assume that money is plentiful, and you want the fastest media to use for your company's backups. Based on that information, which is the best backup media choice?

   A. Magnetic tapes

   B. Optical discs

   C. HDD

   D. SSD

   E. NAS

5. Your co-worker, also a system administrator, hands you an SSD and says, "This has all the files on it that were created and/or modified since the system's last full backup." Which of the following backup types can this backup be? (Choose all that apply.)

   A. Full

   B. Incremental

C. Differential

D. None of the above

E. All of the above

6. Which of the following Linux directories should be included in a backup when you plan on using the backup data in full system restores? (Choose all that apply.)

A. /bin/

B. /home/

C. /run/

D. /tmp/

E. All of the above

7. Which of the following software packages are GUI and/or web-based backup solutions? (Choose all that apply.)

A. Amanda

B. Duplicity

C. Nagios

D. Bacula

E. connectd

8. Which of the following tar command options would employ gzip compression for creating a backup tarball? (Choose all that apply.)

A. -g

B. --gzip

C. -z

D. g

E. z

9. When using the tar command for an incremental backup, a snapshot file is created. This snapshot file should have which of the following file extensions as part of its name?

A. .tar

B. .tgz

C. .tar.snap

D. .snap

E. .snar

10. To verify a tar backup immediately after it is created, you use which of the following tar command options? (Choose all that apply.)

A. --compare

B. --diff

    C. -d

    D. -W

    E. -J

11. Which of the following indicates a tape device that automatically rewinds? (Choose all that apply.)

    A. /dev/st0

    B. /dev/nst0

    C. /dev/ht1

    D. /dev/nht1

    E. /dev/nht0

12. To control a magnetic tape for backups, use the _____ program.

    A. tar

    B. star

    C. mt

    D. rsync

    E. dd

13. Which of the following rsync commands is the proper way to send a backup over the network to the remote host, ServerA, while having the transfer encrypted using OpenSSH?

    A. rsync -av Project /run/media/ServerA

    B. rsync -av Project ServerA

    C. rsync -av ServerA Project

    D. rsync -av Project ServerA:~/

    E. rsync -av Project rsync://ServerA:/

14. Which of the following are true about the dd command? (Choose all that apply.)

    A. The dd command can be used to create a low-level copy of a hard drive.

    B. The dd command is popular for daily incremental backups.

    C. The dd command can be safely used to back up a disk mounted at /.

    D. The dd command can be used for managing tapes.

    E. The dd command can be used to zero-out a hard disk.

15. When installing a program from source code, which of the following installation files typically can provide you with additional installation information? (Choose all that apply.)

    A. README

    B. INSTALL

    C. COPYING

    D. RELEASE-NOTES

    E. NEWS

16. During the process of installing a program from source, which of the following creates or updates the `Makefile` with the `Makefile.in` file's contents and what it finds on your system?

   A. `INSTALL`

   B. `configure`

   C. `make`

   D. `make install`

   E. `cp`

17. Which of the following monitoring commands allow you to view system memory information? (Choose all that apply.)

   A. `free`

   B. `mpstat`

   C. `mtr`

   D. `top`

   E. `vmstat`

18. Which of the following will show CPU usage information 20 times in 2-second intervals?

   A. `uptime 20 2`

   B. `uptime 2 20`

   C. `sar 20 2`

   D. `sar 2 20`

   E. None of the above

19. Which of the following are considered to be system resource-monitoring solutions? (Choose all that apply.)

   A. `collectd`

   B. Duplicity

   C. MRTG

   D. Nagios

   E. All of the above

20. Which of the following are true about Linux system memory? (Choose all that apply.)

   A. Memory is divided into sheets.

   B. Memory for an idle process can be swapped out to swap space.

   C. Swap can also be called virtual memory.

   D. Swapping is the memory management scheme, where idle processes swap memory.

   E. Memory-swapping statistics can be viewed using the `psmap` utility.

Chapter

3

Mastering the Kernel

THE FOLLOWING EXAM OBJECTIVES ARE COVERED IN THIS CHAPTER:

✓ **201.1: Kernel Components**

✓ **201.2: Compiling a Linux kernel**

✓ **201.3: Kernel runtime management and troubleshooting**

While we usually refer to the Linux operating system as just Linux, in reality, quite a few parts make up a complete Linux system. The Linux kernel is the main component that keeps things together and running on your system. It is the heart of the Linux system, controlling hardware, memory, and the running applications.

This chapter looks first at the different parts of the Linux kernel and how they fit together to control the computer. Next, the chapter examines how the Linux kernel is installed in different Linux distributions and where to find the different parts of it. After that, the chapter discusses how to create a new kernel in order to support new hardware or just to update your Linux system to the latest features. Finally, the chapter examines how to manage the kernel and kernel modules, along with how to troubleshoot the kernel if anything goes wrong.

What Is the Kernel?

A complete Linux system consists of four main parts:

- The Linux kernel
- The GNU utilities
- A graphical desktop environment
- Application software

Each of these four parts has a specific job in the Linux system. While each of the parts by itself isn't very useful, taken together, they create what we call Linux. Figure 3.1 shows a basic diagram of how these parts fit together to create the overall Linux system.

The core of the Linux system is the *kernel*. The kernel controls all of the hardware and software on the computer system, allocating hardware when necessary and executing software when required. This section walks through exactly what the kernel is, and then it covers the different parts of the kernel.

The Kernel Features

If you've been following the Linux world at all, no doubt you've heard the name *Linus Torvalds*. Linus is the person responsible for creating the first Linux kernel software while he was a student at the University of Helsinki. He intended it to be a copy of the Unix system, which was a popular operating system used by many universities at the time.

FIGURE 3.1 The Linux system

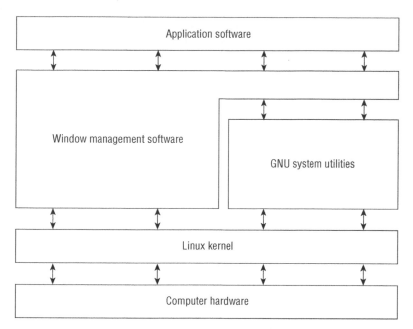

After developing the Linux kernel, Linus released it to the Internet community and solicited suggestions for improving it. This simple process started a revolution in the world of computer operating systems. Soon Linus was receiving suggestions from students as well as professional programmers from around the world.

Allowing anyone to change programming code in the kernel would result in complete chaos. To simplify things, Linus acted as a central point for all improvement suggestions. It was ultimately Linus's decision whether or not to incorporate suggested code in the kernel. This same concept is still in place with the Linux kernel code, except that instead of just Linus controlling the kernel code, a team of developers called the Linux Foundation has taken on the task.

The kernel is primarily responsible for four main functions:

- System memory management
- Software program management
- Hardware management
- Filesystem management

The following sections explore each of these functions in more detail.

System Memory Management

One of the primary functions of the operating system kernel is *memory management*. Memory management is the ability to control how programs and utilities run within the memory restrictions of the system. Not only does the kernel manage the physical memory available on the server, but it can also create and manage *virtual memory*, or memory that does not actually exist but is created on the hard drive and treated as real memory.

It does this by using space on the hard disk, called the *swap space*. The kernel swaps the contents of virtual memory locations back and forth from the swap space to the actual physical memory. This allows the system to think that there is more memory available than what physically exists, as shown in Figure 3.2.

FIGURE 3.2   The Linux system memory map

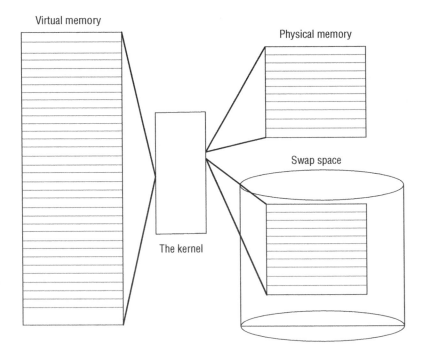

The memory locations are grouped into blocks called *memory pages*. The kernel locates each page of memory in either the physical memory or the swap space. The kernel then maintains a table of the memory pages that indicates which pages are in physical memory and which pages are swapped out to disk.

The kernel keeps track of which memory pages are in use and automatically copies memory pages that have not been accessed for a period of time to the swap space area (this is called *swapping out*), even if there's other memory available. When a program wants to access a memory page that has been swapped out, the kernel must make room for it in physical memory by swapping out a different memory page and swapping in the required page from the swap space. Obviously this process takes time, and it can slow down a running process. The process of swapping out memory pages for running applications continues for as long as the Linux system is running.

You can see the current status of the virtual memory on your Linux system by viewing the special /proc/meminfo file. Listing 3.1 shows an example of a sample /proc/meminfo entry.

Listing 3.1: The */proc/meminfo* file output

```
$ cat /proc/meminfo
MemTotal:        1908188 kB
MemFree:          408188 kB
MemAvailable:     855432 kB
Buffers:           32544 kB
Cached:           514140 kB
SwapCached:            0 kB
Active:          1033464 kB
Inactive:         341712 kB
Active(anon):     829016 kB
Inactive(anon):     1120 kB
Active(file):     204448 kB
Inactive(file):   340592 kB
Unevictable:          16 kB
Mlocked:              16 kB
SwapTotal:       1165308 kB
SwapFree:        1165308 kB
Dirty:              2112 kB
Writeback:             0 kB
AnonPages:        828536 kB
Mapped:           199596 kB
Shmem:              1660 kB
Slab:              61352 kB
SReclaimable:      29656 kB
SUnreclaim:        31696 kB
KernelStack:        5680 kB
PageTables:        31972 kB
NFS_Unstable:          0 kB
Bounce:                0 kB
WritebackTmp:          0 kB
CommitLimit:     2119400 kB
Committed_AS:    2673804 kB
VmallocTotal:   34359738367 kB
VmallocUsed:       30256 kB
VmallocChunk:   34359699448 kB
HardwareCorrupted:     0 kB
```

```
AnonHugePages:            0 kB
HugePages_Total:          0
HugePages_Free:           0
HugePages_Rsvd:           0
HugePages_Surp:           0
Hugepagesize:          2048 kB
DirectMap4k:          58748 kB
DirectMap2M:        1894400 kB
$
```

The MemTotal and MemFree lines show that this Linux server has 2 GB of physical memory, but that only about 408 MB is not currently being used (free). The output also shows that about 1 GB of swap space memory is available on this system.

By default, each process running on the Linux system has its own private memory pages. One process cannot access memory pages being used by another process. The kernel maintains its own memory areas. For security purposes, no processes can access memory used by the kernel processes.

To facilitate data sharing, you can create *shared memory pages*. Multiple processes can read and write to and from a common shared memory area. The kernel maintains and administers the shared memory areas, and it allows individual processes access to the shared area.

The special ipcs command allows you to view the current shared memory pages on the system. Here's the output from a sample ipcs command:

```
$ ipcs -m


—Shared Memory Segments—
key          shmid    owner    perms    bytes      nattch    status
0xcf124bdc 0          root     600      1000       6
0x0b234bfc 32769      root     600      8          6
0x07021999 65538      root     644      1704       2
0x00000000 163843     rich     600      4194304    2         dest
0x00000000 262148     rich     600      1048576    2         dest
$
```

Each shared memory segment has an owner that created the segment. Each segment also has a standard Linux permissions setting that sets the availability of the segment for other users. The key value is used to allow other users to gain access to the shared memory segment.

Software Program Management

The Linux operating system calls a running program a *process*. A process can run in the foreground, displaying output on a display, or it can run in background behind the scenes. The kernel controls how the Linux system manages all of the processes running on the system.

The kernel creates the first process, called the *init process*, to start all other processes on the system. When the kernel starts, it loads the init process into virtual memory. As the kernel starts each additional process, it gives it a unique area in virtual memory to store the data and code that the process uses.

Some Linux implementations contain a table of processes to start automatically upon bootup. On Linux systems, this table is usually located in the special file /etc/inittab.

As discussed in Chapter 1, "Starting a System," the Linux operating system uses an init system that utilizes either runlevel (for the SysV init method) or targets (for the systemd method) that determine which processes start. There are seven init run levels in the Linux operating system.

At run level 1, only the basic system processes are started, along with one console terminal process. This is called *single-user mode*. Single-user mode is most often used for emergency filesystem maintenance when something is broken. Obviously, in this mode only one person (usually the administrator) can log into the system to manipulate data.

For most Linux distributions, the standard init run level is 3. At this run level, most application software, such as network support software, is started. Another popular run level in Linux is run level 5. This is the run level where the system starts the graphical X Window software, and it allows you to log in using a graphical desktop window.

Debian-based Linux distributions (such as Ubuntu) use run level 2 as the standard run level for both console-based and graphical desktop environments.

The Linux system can control the overall system functionality by controlling the init run level. For example, by changing the run level from 3 to 5, the system can change from a console-based system to an advanced, graphical X Window System.

The ps command allows you to view the processes currently running on the Linux system. Listing 3.2 shows an example of what you'll see using the ps command.

Listing 3.2: The *ps* command output

```
$ ps ax
  PID TTY      STAT   TIME COMMAND
    1 ?        S      0:03 init
    2 ?        SW     0:00 [kflushd]
    3 ?        SW     0:00 [kupdate]
    4 ?        SW     0:00 [kpiod]
    5 ?        SW     0:00 [kswapd]
  243 ?        SW     0:00 [portmap]
  295 ?        S      0:00 syslogd
  305 ?        S      0:00 klogd
  320 ?        S      0:00 /usr/sbin/atd
  335 ?        S      0:00 crond
  350 ?        S      0:00 inetd
```

```
365 ?        SW      0:00 [lpd]
403 ttyS0    S       0:00 gpm -t ms
418 ?        S       0:00 httpd
423 ?        S       0:00 httpd
424 ?        SW      0:00 [httpd]
425 ?        SW      0:00 [httpd]
426 ?        SW      0:00 [httpd]
427 ?        SW      0:00 [httpd]
428 ?        SW      0:00 [httpd]
429 ?        SW      0:00 [httpd]
430 ?        SW      0:00 [httpd]
436 ?        SW      0:00 [httpd]
437 ?        SW      0:00 [httpd]
438 ?        SW      0:00 [httpd]
470 ?        S       0:02 xfs -port -1
485 ?        SW      0:00 [smbd]
495 ?        S       0:00 nmbd -D
533 ?        SW      0:00 [postmaster]
538 tty1     SW      0:00 [mingetty]
539 tty2     SW      0:00 [mingetty]
540 tty3     SW      0:00 [mingetty]
541 tty4     SW      0:00 [mingetty]
542 tty5     SW      0:00 [mingetty]
543 tty6     SW      0:00 [mingetty]
544 ?        SW      0:00 [prefdm]
549 ?        SW      0:00 [prefdm]
559 ?        S       0:02 [kwm]
585 ?        S       0:06 kikbd
594 ?        S       0:00 kwmsound
595 ?        S       0:03 kpanel
596 ?        S       0:02 kfm
597 ?        S       0:00 krootwm
598 ?        S       0:01 kbgndwm
611 ?        S       0:00 kcmlaptop -daemon
666 ?        S       0:00 /usr/libexec/postfix/master
668 ?        S       0:00 qmgr -l -t fifo -u
787 ?        S       0:00 pickup -l -t fifo
790 ?        S       0:00 telnetd: 192.168.1.2 [vt100]
791 pts/0    S       0:00 login—rich
792 pts/0    S       0:00 -bash
805 pts/0    R       0:00 ps ax
$
```

The first column in the output shows the process ID (PID) of the process. Notice that the first process is our friend the init process, and it is assigned PID 1 by the Linux system. All other processes that start after the init process are assigned PIDs in numerical order. No two processes can have the same PID.

The third column shows the current status of the process (S for sleeping, SW for sleeping and waiting, and R for running). The process name is shown in the last column. Processes that are in brackets have been swapped out of memory to the disk swap space due to inactivity. You can see that some of the processes have been swapped out, but most of the running processes have not.

Hardware Management

Still another responsibility of the kernel is *hardware management*. Any device with which the Linux system must communicate needs driver code inserted inside the kernel code. The driver code allows the kernel to pass data back and forth to the device, acting as a go-between for the applications and the hardware. There are two methods used for inserting device driver code into the Linux kernel:

- Drivers compiled in the kernel
- Driver modules added to the kernel

Previously, the only way to insert device driver code was to recompile the kernel. Each time you added a new device to the system, you had to recompile the kernel code. This process became even more inefficient as Linux kernels supported more hardware. Fortunately, Linux developers devised a better method to insert driver code into the running kernel.

Programmers developed the concept of kernel *modules* to allow you to insert device driver code into a running kernel without having to recompile the kernel. A module is a self-contained driver library file that can be dynamically linked and unlinked with the kernel. This means that you can remove a kernel module from the kernel when you've finished using the device, something you can't do with compiled kernel drivers. This greatly simplified and expanded using hardware with Linux.

The Linux system identifies hardware devices as special files, called *device files*. There are three classifications of device files:

- Character
- Block
- Network

Character device files are for devices that can handle data only one character at a time. Most types of modems and terminals are created as character files. *Block device files* are for devices that can handle data in large blocks at a time, such as disk drives.

The *network device file* types are used for devices that use packets to send and receive data. These include network cards and a special loopback device that allows the Linux system to communicate with itself using common network programming protocols.

Linux creates special files, called *nodes*, for each device on the system. All communication with the device is performed through the device node. Each node has a unique number pair that identifies it to the Linux kernel. The number pair includes a major and a minor device number. Similar devices are grouped into the same major device number. The minor device number is used to identify a specific device within the major device group. Listing 3.3 shows an example of a few device files on a Linux server.

Listing 3.3: Displaying device nodes on a Linux system

```
$ cd /dev
$ ls -al sda* ttyS*
brw-rw----. 1 root    disk    8,    0   Sep 10 16:27   sda
brw-rw----. 1 root    disk    8,    1   Sep 10 16:27   sda1
brw-rw----. 1 root    disk    8,    2   Sep 10 16:27   sda2
brw-rw----. 1 root    disk    8,    3   Sep 10 16:27   sda3
brw-rw----. 1 root    disk    8,    4   Sep 10 16:27   sda4
crw-rw----. 1 root    dialout 4,   64   Sep 10 16:27   ttyS0
crw-rw----. 1 root    dialout 4,   65   Sep 10 16:27   ttyS1
crw-rw----. 1 root    dialout 4,   66   Sep 10 16:27   ttyS2
crw-rw----. 1 root    dialout 4,   67   Sep 10 16:27   ttyS3
$
```

Different Linux distributions handle devices using different device names. In this distribution, the sda device is the first SCSI hard drive, and the ttyS devices are the standard IBM PC COM ports. Listing 3.3 shows all of the sda devices that were created on the sample Linux system. Not all are actually used, but they are created in case the administrator needs them. Similarly, the listing shows all of the ttyS devices created.

The fifth column is the major device node number. Notice that all of the sda devices have the same major device node, 8, while all of the ttyS devices use 4. The sixth column is the minor device node number. Each device within a major number has its own unique minor device node number.

The first column indicates the permissions for the device file. The first character of the permissions indicates the type of file. Notice that the SCSI hard drive files are all marked as block (b) devices, while the COM port device files are marked as character (c) devices.

Filesystem Management

A *filesystem* defines how the operating system stores data on storage devices. Unlike some other operating systems, the Linux kernel can support different types of filesystems to read and write data to and from hard drives, CD or DVD devices, and USB flash drives. Besides having over a dozen filesystems of its own, Linux can read and write to and from filesystems used by other operating systems, such as Microsoft Windows. The kernel must be compiled with support for all types of filesystems that the system will use. Table 3.1 lists the standard filesystems that a Linux system can use to read and write data.

TABLE 3.1   Linux filesystems

Filesystem	Description
ext	Extended filesystem—the original Linux filesystem
ext2	Second extended filesystem, provided advanced features over ext
ext3	Third extended filesystem, supports journaling
ext4	Fourth extended filesystem, supports advanced journaling
HPFS	OS/2 high-performance filesystem
JFS	IBM's journaling filesystem
ISO 9660	ISO 9660 filesystem (CD-ROMs)
MINIX	MINIX filesystem
msdos	Microsoft FAT16
NCP	NetWare filesystem
NFS	Network File System
NTFS	Microsoft NT filesystem
procfs	Access to system information
ReiserFS	Advanced Linux filesystem for better performance and disk recovery
SMB	Samba SMB filesystem for network access
sysv	Older Unix filesystem
UFS	BSD filesystem
umsdos	Unix-like filesystem that resides on top of MS-DOS
VFAT	Windows 95 filesystem (FAT32)
XFS	High-performance 64-bit journaling filesystem

Any hard drive that a Linux server accesses must be formatted using one of the filesystem types listed in Table 3.1.

The Linux kernel interfaces with each filesystem using the *Virtual File System (VFS)*. This provides a standard interface for the kernel to communicate with any type of filesystem. VFS caches information in memory as each filesystem is mounted and used.

Parts of the Kernel

When installing a new kernel (or updating an existing kernel) various components are available to install. This section walks through each of these components, and it describes what they contribute to the kernel environment on your Linux system.

Kernel Binary

The *kernel binary* file is the actual kernel program itself. This is what the bootloader program loads into memory, so it must be present on the Linux system for the system to boot and start.

The kernel binary file can be somewhat large, depending on how many drivers are compiled into the kernel by default. Because of that, the kernel binary file is usually compressed to save space in memory when the kernel is loaded. The name of the kernel file depends on how the kernel binary file was compressed. Table 3.2 lists the different kernel binary filenames that are used in Linux distributions.

TABLE 3.2   Linux kernel binary filenames

Filename	Description
bzImage	A larger kernel binary file compressed using the GNU zip utility
kernel	A generic name for an uncompressed kernel binary file
vmlinux	An uncompressed kernel binary file, not usually used as the final boot version
vmlinuz	A generic compressed kernel binary filename
zImage	A small kernel binary file compressed using the GNU zip utility

The bzImage file format is the most popular one used. However, many Linux distributions copy that file to the vmlinuz filename. When looking for the kernel binary file on your Linux system, you'll often see the main binary filename with the kernel version appended, such as vmlinuz-4.3.3. This method allows you to maintain more than one kernel on your system and boot using a different kernel version for different situations.

The kernel binary file must be accessible by the bootloader program, which is what loads the kernel in memory at boot time. Because of that, the kernel binary files are normally stored under the /boot directory structure in the filesystem, although some Linux distributions keep the kernel binary files directly under the root directory (/).

Most Linux distributions bundle the kernel binary file as a package that you can easily install using a common package management system (such as Debian `apt-get` or Red Hat yum). The package installs the kernel binary file in the correct location and makes the necessary modifications to the GRUB bootloader menu to boot using the new kernel. This makes installing a new kernel almost painless.

Kernel Modules

The Linux kernel needs device drivers to communicate with the hardware devices installed on your Linux system. However, compiling device drivers for all known hardware devices into the kernel would make for an extremely large kernel binary file.

To avoid that situation, the Linux kernel uses kernel modules, which are individual hardware driver files that can be linked into the kernel at runtime. That way the system can link only the modules that are needed for the hardware that's present on your system.

If the kernel is configured to load hardware device modules, the individual module files must be available on the system as well. If you're compiling a new Linux kernel, you'll also need to compile any hardware modules along with the new kernel.

Module files may be distributed either as source code that needs to be compiled or as binary object files on the Linux system that are ready to be dynamically linked to the main kernel binary program. If the module files are distributed as source code files, you must compile them to create the binary object file. The `.ko` file extension is used to identify the module object files.

The standard location for storing module object files is in the `/lib/modules` directory. This is where the Linux module utilities (such as `insmod` and `modprobe`) look for module object library files by default. (See the "Maintaining the Kernel" section later in this chapter.)

Some hardware vendors release only module object files for their hardware modules without releasing the source code. This helps them protect the proprietary features of their hardware while still allowing their hardware products to be used in an open source environment. While this arrangement violates the core idea of open source code, it has become a common ground between companies trying to protect their product secrets and Linux enthusiasts who want to use the latest hardware on their systems.

Kernel Source

If you plan to recompile the kernel binary file yourself, you'll need to have the original source code files for the Linux kernel. You can obtain the Linux kernel source code files using two different methods:

- Download the kernel source code from the main Linux kernel development repository.
- Install the kernel source code from the software repository for your specific Linux distribution.

The www.kernel.org website maintains the official repository for Linux kernel releases. The repository maintains the current stable release of the kernel, which is recommended for production use, plus the latest development release. If you're looking for the most recent kernel source code, this is the place to go.

As part of the open source requirements, individual Linux distributions also release the Linux kernel source code as distribution packages, available for installation from their individual software repository sites. This is the safest way to install the Linux kernel, because each Linux distribution makes available only the Linux kernel source code that is known to work correctly in the distribution's environment.

Whether you download a Linux source code bundle from the www.kernel.org website or install it from your distribution's repository, you should extract the source code files into the /usr/src/linux directory. This is where utilities look for the source code files.

Usually, it's a good idea to install the Linux kernel source code into a separate directory that identifies the kernel version, such as /usr/src/linux-4.3.3. That way, you can maintain multiple versions of the kernel source code at the same time. Just create a link from that directory to the /usr/src/linux directory for the kernel version with which you want to work. Also, the Red Hat–based Linux distributions use the /usr/src/kernels folder instead of /usr/src/linux, so be careful when working in those environments.

Kernel Patches

Linux kernel versions have incremental releases for bug fixes and security patches (such as going from version 4.3.0 to 4.3.1). While you can recompile a new kernel by downloading the full source code for the incremental release, if you already have the source code for the original release, there's an easier way to upgrade to the new version.

A *patch release* is a special source code package that contains only the changes applied to the major kernel source code release to get to the incremental release (for example, upgrading from kernel version 4.3.0 to patch release 4.3.1). You just download the patch source code package, use the Linux patch command to apply the patch updates to the existing kernel source code files on your system, and then recompile the kernel.

When working with patches for later incremental releases (such as upgrading 4.3.1 to 4.3.2), you must first uninstall the previous patch (4.3.1) to go back to the original release (4.3.0) and then apply the patch for the 4.3.2 incremental release, because each patch release is based on updating the original release code. Uninstalling patches is also handled by the patch command using the -R option.

Kernel Headers

The Linux kernel is written mostly using the C programming language. Part of the C programming language is a feature called *header files*. The header files tell the C compiler what library files are required to compile the kernel source code. These same library files are also vital for compiling any module source code files.

If you need to just compile modules from source code, you don't need to download the full Linux kernel source code files, just the kernel header files. Fortunately, most Linux distributions include packages for just the kernel header files related to the installed kernel version. This makes it easier to compile modules if you're experimenting with new hardware.

The kernel header files are normally installed in the /usr/src/linux/ directory structure in Debian-based distributions or the /usr/src/kernels directory structure in Red Hat–based distributions, and they use the .h file extension.

Kernel Documentation

Another important piece of the Linux kernel files is the *kernel documentation*. The kernel documentation is split into lots of separate text files, detailing just what each source code file does within the kernel structure. If you plan on doing any work with the Linux kernel source code, it's a good idea to have the kernel documentation files handy.

Because of the size of the files, the kernel documentation files are often installed separately from the kernel source code package in distribution releases, but if you download the kernel source code from the www.kernel.org website, they are included. The kernel documentation files are usually installed in the /usr/src/linux/Documentation directory structure but may be in the /usr/src/kernels directory structure for Red Hat–based systems.

Kernel Versions

One of the more confusing parts of working with the Linux kernel is the versioning system. Throughout the history of the Linux kernel, six different system versions have been implemented. This section walks through the different kernel version numbers, and it describes how to interpret what each one means.

The Original Kernel Releases

When Linus released the original Linux kernel in September 1991, he assigned it version 0.01. By starting with version 0, he indicated that it was mainly for testing and not intended to be used as any type of production system for handling important data.

As the Linux system became popular and new additions were made, the updated versions still kept the 0 main version number and incremented the part after the period to indicate each newer version (such as 0.01, 0.02, and so on). This version method remained in use up until version 0.95, which was released in March 1992.

The Linux Version 1 Series

In March 1994, Linus released the first production version of Linux as version 1.0. This release started a standard versioning system that followed the format 1.*x.y.*

In this format, the *x* represents the major version release number. Odd-numbered major version releases indicate a test (or development) release, while even-numbered version releases indicate a production release. The *y* indicates incremental minor patch release levels within the major releases. This version method was in use until version 1.3, released in May 1995.

The Linux Version 2 Series

After version 1.3, Linus determined that the next release version contained enough changes to warrant a new major version number, and version 2.0 was released in June 1996. The version 2 series kernels maintained the 2.x.y format just like the version 1 series, with odd-numbered major releases indicating test releases and even-numbered major releases indicating production releases. This method was in use until version 2.4, released in January 2001.

The Linux Version 2.6 Series

In December 2003, Linus released version 2.6.0 of the Linux kernel and started yet another new versioning system. He felt that the main Linux kernel was fairly stable, and he decided to keep the 2.6 version number and start a new numbering format. Newer versions of the Linux kernel used the format 2.6.x.y.

The 2.6 remained constant, shifting the major release number down a level to the third number (the x) and the incremental minor patch number as the fourth number (the y).

Another thing that changed with the 2.6 version was that all releases were production releases. Development releases used an -rc designation after the end of the kernel version (for release candidate). When a release was deemed stable for production, the -rc was removed. This method stayed in use until release 2.6.39 in May 2011.

The Linux Version 3 Series

In July 2011, Linus celebrated the 20th anniversary of the Linux kernel by starting the version 3 series with version 3.0. The new version release reverted to using the three-digit 3.x.y release system, with x representing major releases and y incremental minor patch releases. However, the version 3 series maintained the -rc designation for development releases started in the 2.6 version series. This method stayed in use until release 3.19 in February 2015.

 The version 3 series also introduced a fourth digit, .z, as in 3.x.y.z, which represented occasional special patch releases, mostly related to emergency security fixes.

The Linux Version 4 Series

In April 2015, Linus determined that it was time for another major release version change, and thus the version 4 series began with version 4.0. The version 4 series maintains the 4.x.y release system, and it also uses the -rc designation for test releases. This is the current Linux kernel version used at the time of this writing.

Compiling a Kernel

Under most normal Linux environments, you'll never need to worry about compiling a new kernel. All of the major Linux distributions do that for you and release the new kernels as software packages in their repositories. Updating the kernel is often automatic, handled by the automatic software update process for the distribution.

However, there may be times when you want to experiment with a new kernel, such as when implementing new hardware or testing new kernel features. If you decide to undertake the task of compiling your own Linux kernel, there are five steps involved with the process:

1. Obtaining the source code
2. Creating a configuration file based on the system hardware
3. Compiling the source code
4. Compiling and installing module files
5. Installing the new kernel binary file

Each of these steps can get somewhat complicated, and compiling a new Linux kernel is not for the faint of heart. That said, if you do decide to compile a new kernel, the process is outlined in the following sections.

> With most Linux distributions, if you compile your own custom kernel, you won't be able to request support from the standard help infrastructure for the distribution (such as support forums). You may find help in other Linux forums available for kernel development, such as the vger.kernel.org mailing list, but be prepared to provide lots of detailed information about your exact environment and issue.

Obtaining Source Code

As mentioned in the "Kernel Source" section, there are two ways to obtain the Linux kernel source code. You can download the most recent version directly from the official www.kernel.org website, or you can obtain it with most Linux distributions, which include a software package that contains the kernel source code for the most recently installed kernel version.

If you're just experimenting with different kernel features in your specific Linux distribution, we recommend that you install just the kernel software package from your distribution's repository. This ensures that you're working with a kernel that you know works in your Linux environment. However, most Linux distributions are somewhat behind in keeping up with the latest kernel releases. If you're trying to work with the latest hardware or kernel features, you may need to download and install the current stable or development source code directly from the www.kernel.org website.

When you go to the www.kernel.org website, you'll see a matrix of different kernel versions available, along with different download options (such as downloading just the incremental patch or the full source code). The most recent production version of the kernel is labeled *stable*. Previous versions of the kernel are labeled *longterm*, while the most recent development version is labeled *mainline*.

Source code packages are bundled using the tar archive utility and compressed using the xz compression utility. You'll need both of these utilities installed on your system to be able to extract the source code files.

To download a full kernel source code package, click the `tar.xz` link for the version that you need. The download filename will be in the format

`linux-version.tar.xz`

where *version* is the kernel version. To extract the source code file, use the following command:

`# tar xvf linux-version.tar.xz`

The `tar` command will extract all of the source code files into a folder named `linux-version`, creating the necessary subfolders contained within the package automatically.

 As you can probably guess, the Linux kernel source code creates many files, and it takes up a lot of disk space. Make sure that you have at least 1 GB of disk space available on your system to extract the files.

You can extract the kernel source code files into a folder under your home directory if you just want to peruse the files and documentation. However, if you plan on compiling and installing the kernel on your Linux system, it's best to extract the source code files into the `/usr/src/` folder structure. Don't place the new source code files in the `/usr/src/linux` folder directly; instead, create a link between the `/usr/src/linux` folder and the source code folder that you created when extracting the files:

`# ln /usr/src/linux-4.3.3 /usr/src/linux`

Creating the Configuration File

Before you can compile the new kernel from the source code, you need to determine just which kernel features you want to include in your new kernel binary file. This is done using a *kernel configuration file*.

The kernel configuration file is a text file that contains separate lines for each kernel feature, showing the feature name and its setting. The kernel configuration file is stored in the `/usr/src/linux/.config` file. If you already have the kernel source code installed, you can look at this file to see what features are available for configuration. Listing 3.4 shows a small snippet of a `.config` file from an Ubuntu system.

Listing 3.4: The kernel .config configuration file

```
CONFIG_64BIT=y
CONFIG_X86_64=y
CONFIG_X86=y
CONFIG_INSTRUCTION_DECODER=y
```

```
CONFIG_PERF_EVENTS_INTEL_UNCORE=y
CONFIG_OUTPUT_FORMAT="elf64-x86-64"
CONFIG_ARCH_DEFCONFIG="arch/x86/configs/x86_64_defconfig"
CONFIG_LOCKDEP_SUPPORT=y
CONFIG_STACKTRACE_SUPPORT=y
CONFIG_HAVE_LATENCYTOP_SUPPORT=y
CONFIG_MMU=y
CONFIG_NEED_DMA_MAP_STATE=y
CONFIG_NEED_SG_DMA_LENGTH=y
CONFIG_GENERIC_ISA_DMA=y
CONFIG_GENERIC_BUG=y
CONFIG_GENERIC_BUG_RELATIVE_POINTERS=y
CONFIG_GENERIC_HWEIGHT=y
CONFIG_ARCH_MAY_HAVE_PC_FDC=y
CONFIG_RWSEM_XCHGADD_ALGORITHM=y
...
```

You need to set many configuration options for the kernel. To create the .config file, you don't need to run through each line manually. Instead, you can use an automated script that asks questions for each feature and creates the .config file for you based on your answers to the questions.

The make utility runs the script contained in the source code. The make utility uses *make targets* to determine just what script to run. There are lots of different targets that you can use.

The make config target is the basic script to run to create the configuration file. It asks many questions regarding every feature that you can include in the kernel. Listing 3.5 shows some of the questions that are asked.

Listing 3.5: The make config output

```
$ make config
...
*
* Linux/x86 4.3.3 Kernel Configuration
*
64-bit kernel (64BIT) [Y/n/?] y
*
* General setup
*
Cross-compiler tool prefix (CROSS_COMPILE) []
Compile also drivers which will not load (COMPILE_TEST) [N/y/?]
```

```
Local version—append to kernel release (LOCALVERSION) []
Automatically append version information to the version string (LOCALVERSION_
AUTO) [N/y/?]
Kernel compression mode
> 1. Gzip (KERNEL_GZIP)
  2. Bzip2 (KERNEL_BZIP2)
  3. LZMA (KERNEL_LZMA)
  4. XZ (KERNEL_XZ)
  5. LZO (KERNEL_LZO)
  6. LZ4 (KERNEL_LZ4)
choice[1-6?]:
Default hostname (DEFAULT_HOSTNAME) [(none)]
Support for paging of anonymous memory (swap) (SWAP) [Y/n/?]
System V IPC (SYSVIPC) [Y/n/?]
POSIX Message Queues (POSIX_MQUEUE) [Y/n/?]
Enable process_vm_readv/writev syscalls (CROSS_MEMORY_ATTACH) [Y/n/?]
open by fhandle syscalls (FHANDLE) [Y/n/?]
uselib syscall (USELIB) [Y/n/?] (NEW)
Auditing support (AUDIT) [Y/?] y
Enable system-call auditing support (AUDITSYSCALL) [Y/n/?]
  ...
```

While most of the questions have default answers that you can usually use, going through so many questions isn't an efficient way to create the configuration file. Fortunately, you can use some additional shortcut scripts by specifying different targets:

- defconfig—Creates a default configuration file based on the system type detected
- oldconfig—Updates an existing configuration file with only the new features
- menuconfig—Uses a text-based menu system allowing you to select which features to include
- xconfig—Creates a graphical menu allowing you to select which features to include
- gconfig—Uses the GTK graphical menu allowing you to select which features to include

The xconfig target produces an easy-to-use menu for either the GNOME or KDE desktop system, as shown in Figure 3.3.

The graphical configuration menus are handy in that they divide the multitude of questions into categories to help make the changes more manageable. The left panel shows the main categories of configuration settings, such as memory, filesystem, and network features. When you click a main category topic, the top-right panel shows the sub-options available within the category. When you click a sub-option, an explanation of the option appears in the lower-right panel.

FIGURE 3.3   The *make xconfig* menu options

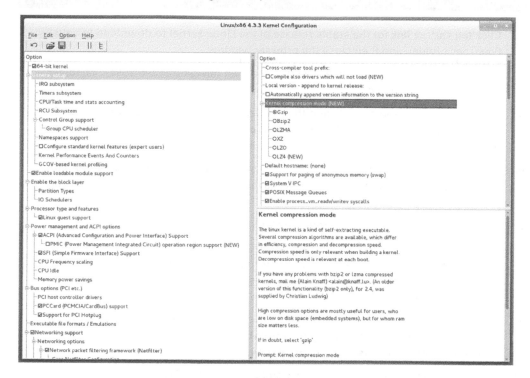

If you've created a configuration before but want to start over, use the mrproper target. The mrproper target clears out all previous configuration settings from the configuration file and removes all previously compiled object files. However, it might be a good idea to copy the old configuration file before using this target, just in case something goes wrong!

When you've completed filling out the category and sub-option settings, save the configuration by clicking the disk icon in the toolbar at the top of the window. Once you've created the /usr/src/linux/.config file, you're ready to start compiling the new kernel.

EXERCISE 3.1

Creating a Kernel Configuration File

In this exercise, you'll download the latest Linux kernel code and take a look at the different kernel features available for use when creating the kernel configuration file.

1. Log in as a normal user on your Linux system.

2. Open a browser window, and navigate to the www.kernel.org website.

3. Click the tar.xz link for the stable release of the Linux kernel to download to your Downloads folder, and then close the browser window.

4. Open a terminal session on your desktop, and then navigate to the /usr/src folder by typing **cd /usr/src**.

5. Expand the kernel source code into the /usr/src folder by typing **sudo tar xvf /home/*userid*/Downloads/linux-*version*.tar.xz**, where *userid* is your user name and *version* is the version of the Linux kernel that you downloaded.

6. Link the new source code folder to the /usr/src/linux folder by typing **sudo ln linux-*version* linux**, where *version* is the version of the Linux kernel that you downloaded.

7. Change to the /usr/src/linux folder by typing **cd /usr/src/linux**.

8. Make sure that your Linux distribution has the appropriate C and C++ compiler packages installed. For RPM-based systems, type **sudo yum groupinstall "Development Tools"**. For DEB-based systems, type **sudo apt-get install pkg-config g++**.

9. Make sure that your Linux distribution has the Qt development package installed. For RPM-based systems, type **sudo yum install qt-devel**. For DEB-based systems, type **sudo apt-get install libqt4-dev**.

10. Run the xconfig make target by typing **sudo make xconfig**.

11. Look through the categories in the left panel. Select a few categories, and observe what sub-options appear for each category.

12. Click the Disk icon in the toolbar to create a .config file from the configuration settings.

13. Exit the xconfig utility.

14. Use a text editor to view the /usr/src/linux/.config file that you generated to see how the configuration settings match what you had set in the xconfig utility. Alternatively, you can list the file from the command line by typing **cat .config | less**.

Compiling and Installing the Kernel

After you've created the configuration file for the kernel, you're ready to start the compiling process. Thanks to the make utility, this step is a breeze.

First, if you made any previous attempts to compile the kernel, you'll want to remove the old object files created by using the clean target:

```
# make clean
```

Then, if you want to create an uncompressed kernel binary file, just enter the command

```
# make
```

The script will then take over, compiling all of the kernel code to produce the new kernel. (Be prepared; this process will take a very long time.) If you prefer to create a compressed kernel file, just use the bzImage target:

```
# make bzImage
```

As the compile process works, you'll see lots of messages scroll past the console, such as these:

```
CC      lib/list_sort.o
CC      lib/uuid.o
CC      lib/flex_array.o
CC      lib/iov_iter.o
CC      lib/clz_ctz.o
CC      lib/bsearch.o
CC      lib/find_bit.o
CC      lib/llist.o
CC      lib/memweight.o
```

The CC lines indicate object code files that are being created. The LD lines indicate object code files that are being linked to create the executable file. When the process completes, the final kernel binary file should be in the /usr/src/linux/arch/x86/boot folder as bzImage.

After the compile process completes, you're ready to install the new kernel binary file. You can manually install the kernel binary file by simply copying the bzImage file to the /boot folder on your system. You'll want to add the version number to the file so that you can distinguish it from the other kernel binary files. Name it using the vmlinuz filename, which is recognized by most Linux distributions:

```
# cp /usr/src/linux/arch/x86/boot/bzImage /boot/vmlinuz-4.3.3
```

Besides the kernel binary file, there's also a System.map file in the /usr/src/linux folder associated with the generated kernel binary file. The System.map file is used for debugging the kernel, so it's not required, but it can help to copy it into the /boot folder as well. As with the kernel binary file, you'll want to add the kernel version to the end of the System.map filename:

```
# cp /usr/src/linux/System.map /boot/System.map-4.3.3
```

As you can probably guess, there is also a make script target for installing the kernel binary and System.map files automatically:

```
# make install
```

This automatically copies the new kernel binary from the /usr/src/linux folder to the appropriate location in the /boot folder for your bootloader. However, you will still need to rename the new kernel binary file to add the kernel version to it, making it separate from the older kernel files installed.

Compiling and Installing Modules

After you compile and install the kernel, you'll want to compile and install the newer version of the modules required for your system. Just as with the kernel compile, you use the make utility to create and install the new module object library files.

First, you'll need to create the module object library files by using the modules target:

```
# make modules
```

After that completes, you can install them using the make_modules install target:

```
# make modules_install
```

This script installs the modules into the /lib/modules/kernel-*version*/ folder, where *version* matches the kernel version. The kernel will look in this folder by default when it needs to load modules. This also applies to any command-line commands used to load modules manually. (This is discussed in the "Working with Module Files" section later in this chapter.)

Creating an Initial RAM Disk

One downside to using kernel modules is that the kernel must load each of the modules at boot time to access the hardware devices. However, if there are modules that control how the kernel reads the hard drive (such as with a RAID system) or modules for reading a specific filesystem (such as ReiserFS), that situation will cause a problem. (How can the kernel load a module that's required to read the filesystem on which the the module is stored?)

To solve that problem, Linux developers created the idea of an *initial RAM disk* (also called *initrd*). The initial RAM disk is a filesystem contained in a file that the kernel loads into memory at boot time as a disk. The kernel can read and load any files contained within the initial RAM disk as it boots. All you need to do is to create an initial RAM disk file that contains the required module files needed to boot the system. Once the system boots, the initial RAM disk is removed from memory to free up memory space.

There are two common utilities used to create an initial RAM disk file, depending on the Linux distribution you use. This section discusses both of them.

The *mkinitrd* Utility

Red Hat–based Linux distributions (such as Red Hat Enterprise Linux, Fedora, and CentOS) use the mkinitrd utility to generate an initial RAM disk file and copy the module's files into it. The general format for the command is

```
# mkinitrd outputfile version
```

where *outputfile* is the name of the initial RAM disk file to create, and *version* is the kernel version for which the file is created. There are a few command-line options that you can use for the mkinitrd command. They are shown in Table 3.3.

TABLE 3.3   The **mkinitrd** command options

Option	Description
--builtin=*module*	Assume the module is built into the kernel, even if it's not.
--force	Allow the output file to be overwritten if it already exists.
--fstab=*filename*	Determine what filesystem support is required to read the specified filename.
--image-*version*	Add the kernel version to the generated initial RAM disk image file.
--nocompress	Force the image file to be uncompressed. The default is to create a compressed image file.
--omit-lvm-modules	Omit logical volume manager modules from the image.
--omit-raid-modules	Omit RAID disk modules from the image.
--omit-scsi-modules	Omit SCSI disk modules from the image.
--preload=*module*	Load the specified module before the SCSI modules are loaded.
--verbose	Display verbose information as each module is loaded.
--version	Display the version of the mkinitrd program.
--with=*module*	Load the specified module before the SCSI modules are loaded.

In most situations, you can run the mkinitrd command without any options to generate the initial RAM disk image file:

```
# mkinitrd /boot/initrd.img-4.3.3 4.3.3
```

Because the initial RAM disk file is used at boot time, most Linux distributions store it in the same folder where the kernel binary file is located, usually the /boot folder.

The *mkinitramfs* Utility

Debian-based Linux distributions (such as Debian and Ubuntu) use the mkinitramfs utility to generate the initial RAM disk file. The general format for the command is

```
# mkinitramfs -o outputfile version
```

where *outputfile* is the image file to create and *version* is the kernel version. Table 3.4 lists the options that are available.

TABLE 3.4   The *mkinitramfs* command options

Option	Description
-c	Create a compressed image file.
-d confdir	Set the configuration directory.
-k	Retain the temporary directory created to build the initial RAM disk file.
-o outputfile	Define the output image filename.
-r root	Set the root partition used by the bootloader.
--supported-host-*version*=hversion	Determine if it can create an image for the specified running kernel version.
--supported-target-*version*=tversion	Determine if it can create an image for the specified kernel version.

In most situations, you can just use the -o option to specify the output image file:

```
# mkinitramfs -o /boot/initramfs-4.3.3.img 4.3.3
```

Most Debian Linux distributions also store the initial RAM disk file in the same folder as the kernel binary file, the /boot folder.

Booting the New Kernel

Once you have compiled and installed the kernel binary and initial RAM disk image files, you're ready to use them to boot your Linux system. These days, most Linux distributions use either the GRUB Legacy or GRUB2 bootloader program to boot the system. If your Linux distribution uses the GRUB Legacy bootloader, you must manually update the GRUB configuration file /boot/grub/menu.lst or /boot/grub/grub.conf to add a new boot section for the new kernel. The new boot section should start with a title and include the new kernel binary file and initial RAM disk image files:

```
title Test (4.3.3)
   root (hd0,0)
   kernel /vmlinuz-4.3.3 ro root=/dev/sda1
   initrd /initrd.img-4.3.3
```

If your Linux distribution uses the GRUB2 bootloader, after you install the new kernel binary into the boot menu, you just need to run the update-grub command:

```
# update-grub
```

The update-grub command scans the /boot folder and adds the new kernel binary to the GRUB boot menu automatically. It also updates the grub.cfg configuration file to include the new initial RAM disk file that you created and installed.

If for some reason the update-grub command doesn't automatically detect the new kernel binary file, you'll have to add an entry manually to one of the boot option files in the /etc/grub.d folder. You can pick one of the custom boot option files, such as *the* 40_custom file. Just add the new entry pointing to the new kernel to the bottom of the existing entries:

```
menuentry "Test (4.3.3)"
    set root=(hd0,1)
    linux /vmlinuz-4.3.3 ro root=/dev/sda1
    initrd /initrd-4.3.3
```

After you add the new entry, save the file and then run the update-grub command. It should add the new kernel option to the /boot/grub/grub.cfg configuration file.

When you reboot your Linux system, you should see the new kernel binary option listed in the boot options. If you're using a Linux distribution that hides the GRUB boot menu by default, hold down the Shift key when you boot and it should appear. In the Ubuntu Linux distribution, you'll also need to select the Advanced options for Ubuntu menu entry to see the list of available kernels to boot with; then just select your new kernel option.

 WARNING   Always add the new kernel binary as a new boot option and leave the old kernel binary in the menu as a secondary boot option. That way, if the new kernel binary doesn't work, you can still boot from the old kernel binary file.

Creating a Kernel Package

If you're in an environment that supports lots of Linux workstations, trying to compile and copy a new kernel binary to all of the workstations can be somewhat tedious. Fortunately, the kernel source code provides a few make targets that can help:

- rpm-pkg—Creates both source and binary RPM packages
- binrpm-pkg—Creates a binary RPM package
- deb-pkg—Creates a binary DEB package

After you run the make command with the appropriate target, the kernel binary file will be included as part of the package generated. You can then use the standard software package management tool (rpm for Red Hat or dpkg for Debian) to install the new kernel binary package on each workstation.

Maintaining the Kernel

Once you have a Linux kernel installed, there are a few steps you can take to make sure things are operating properly. This section walks you through the command-line commands that you should know to monitor the kernel operation, including tracking installed modules, detecting hardware devices, and troubleshooting kernel issues.

Working with Module Files

You should be familiar with a few different files when working with modules. You've already seen that the modules required to support a kernel are stored in the /lib/modules folder. Each kernel has its own folder for its own modules (such as /lib/modules/4.3.3), allowing you to create separate modules for each kernel version on the system if needed.

The modules that the kernel will load at boot time are listed in the /etc/modules file in Debian systems or in separate text files in the /etc/modules-load.d folder for Red Hat–based systems. Most hardware modules can be loaded dynamically, because the system automatically detects hardware devices, so this file may not contain very many modules.

If needed, you can customize a kernel module to define unique parameters required, such as hardware settings required for the device to operate. The kernel module configurations are stored in the /etc/conf.modules configuration file.

Finally, some modules may depend on other modules being loaded first in order to operate properly. These relationships are defined in the modules.dep file and stored in the /lib/modules/*version*/ folder, where *version* is the kernel version. The format for each entry is

```
modulefilename: dependencyfilename1 dependencyfilename2 ...
```

When you use the modules_install target to install the modules, it calls the depmod utility, which determines the module dependencies and generates the modules.dep file automatically. If you modify or add any modules after that, you must manually run the depmod command to update the modules.dep file.

If you compile your own modules outside of the standard kernel modules, you have another problem to consider. Since the modules are compiled for a specific kernel, each time the system upgrades the kernel, you need to recompile your custom modules.

A solution to this problem is *Dynamic Kernel Module Support (DKMS)*. The DKMS system provides a way for you to register your custom modules and provide instructions on how to compile and install them each time a new kernel is installed. The dkms program monitors the kernel version and automatically runs scripts to recompile and install modules when the kernel version changes.

Module Commands

You can use a host of command-line commands to help you troubleshoot and fix kernel module issues. This section walks you through the different module commands that are available to help with any module issues you might run into.

Listing Modules

The first command is `lsmod`, which lists all of the modules installed on your system. Listing 3.6 shows an example of using the `lsmod` command on an Ubuntu system.

Listing 3.6: The *lsmod* command output

```
$ lsmod
Module                  Size  Used by
vboxsf                 39706  1
snd_intel8x0           38153  2
snd_ac97_codec        130285  1 snd_intel8x0
ac97_bus               12730  1 snd_ac97_codec
snd_pcm               102099  2 snd_ac97_codec,snd_intel8x0
snd_page_alloc         18710  2 snd_intel8x0,snd_pcm
snd_seq_midi           13324  0
snd_seq_midi_event     14899  1 snd_seq_midi
snd_rawmidi            30144   1 snd_seq_midi
snd_seq                61560  2 snd_seq_midi_event,snd_seq_midi
snd_seq_device         14497  3 snd_seq,snd_rawmidi,snd_seq_midi
snd_timer              29482  2 snd_pcm,snd_seq
rfcomm                 69160  0
hid_multitouch         17407  0
joydev                 17381  0
snd                    69322  12
snd_ac97_codec,snd_intel8x0,snd_timer,snd_pcm,snd_seq,snd_rawmidi,snd_seq_
device,snd_seq_midi
bnep                   19624  2
bluetooth             391136  10 bnep,rfcomm
serio_raw              13462  0
vboxvideo              12658  1
drm                   303102  2 vboxvideo
vboxguest             276728  7 vboxsf
i2c_piix4              22155  0
soundcore              12680  1 snd
video                  19476  0
mac_hid                13205  0
parport_pc             32701  0
ppdev                  17671  0
lp                     17759  0
parport                42348  3 lp,ppdev,parport_pc
hid_generic            12548  0
```

```
usbhid                    52659  0
hid                      106148  3 hid_multitouch,hid_generic,usbhid
psmouse                  106692  0
ahci                      34091  3
libahci                   32716  1 ahci
e1000                    145227  0
pata_acpi                 13038  0
$
```

Notice that the lsmod command also shows which modules are used by other modules. This can be crucial information when trying to troubleshoot hardware issues.

Getting Module Information

If you need more information about a specific module, use the modinfo command, as shown in Listing 3.7.

Listing 3.7: The modinfo command output

```
$ modinfo bluetooth
filename:       /lib/modules/3.13.0-63-generic/kernel/net/bluetooth/bluetooth.ko
alias:          net-pf-31
license:        GPL
version:        2.17
description:    Bluetooth Core ver 2.17
author:         Marcel Holtmann <marcel@holtmann.org>
srcversion:     071210642A004CFE1860F30
depends:
intree:         Y
vermagic:       3.13.0-63-generic SMP mod_unload modversions
signer:         Magrathea: Glacier signing key
sig_key:        E2:53:28:1F:E2:65:EE:3C:EA:FC:AA:3F:29:2E:21:2B:95:F0:35:9A
sig_hashalgo:   sha512
parm:           disable_esco:Disable eSCO connection creation (bool)
parm:           disable_ertm:Disable enhanced retransmission mode (bool)
$
```

The modinfo command shows you exactly which module file is used to support the module, along with detailed information about where the module came from.

Installing New Modules

If you need to install a new module manually, there are two commands to help with that:

- insmod
- modprobe

The insmod command is the most basic, requiring you to specify the exact module file to load. As you've seen, the kernel module files are stored in the /lib/modules folder structure, with each kernel version having its own folder. If you look in that folder on your Linux system, you'll see a folder tree structure for the different types of hardware.

For example, Ubuntu Linux desktop systems have the following folder for Bluetooth hardware drivers:

```
/lib/modules/3.13.0-63-generic/kernel/drivers/bluetooth
```

This folder is for the currently installed Linux kernel on the system—3.13.0–63. Inside that folder are many different device driver module files for various types of Bluetooth systems:

```
$ ls -l
total 420
-rw-r--r--1 root root 23220 Aug 14 19:07 ath3k.ko
-rw-r--r--1 root root 14028 Aug 14 19:07 bcm203x.ko
-rw-r--r--1 root root 26332 Aug 14 19:07 bfusb.ko
-rw-r--r--1 root root 18404 Aug 14 19:07 bluecard_cs.ko
-rw-r--r--1 root root 19124 Aug 14 19:07 bpa10x.ko
-rw-r--r--1 root root 16964 Aug 14 19:07 bt3c_cs.ko
-rw-r--r--1 root root 38148 Aug 14 19:07 btmrvl.ko
-rw-r--r--1 root root 34204 Aug 14 19:07 btmrvl_sdio.ko
-rw-r--r--1 root root 17524 Aug 14 19:07 btsdio.ko
-rw-r--r--1 root root 14524 Aug 14 19:07 btuart_cs.ko
-rw-r--r--1 root root 53964 Aug 14 19:07 btusb.ko
-rw-r--r--1 root root 14188 Aug 14 19:07 btwilink.ko
-rw-r--r--1 root root 15572 Aug 14 19:07 dtl1_cs.ko
-rw-r--r--1 root root 74772 Aug 14 19:07 hci_uart.ko
-rw-r--r--1 root root 15156 Aug 14 19:07 hci_vhci.ko
$
```

Each .ko file is a separate device driver module file that you can install into the 3.13.0–63 kernel. To install the module, just specify the filename on the insmod command line. Some modules also require parameters, which you must specify on the command line as well:

```
$ sudo insmod /lib/modules/3.13.0-49-generic/kernel/drivers/bluetooth/
btusb.ko
password:
$
```

The downside to using the insmod program is that you may run into modules that depend on other modules, and the insmod program will fail if those other modules aren't already installed. To make the process easier, the modprobe command helps resolve module dependencies for you.

Another nice feature of the modprobe command is that it understands module names, and it will search the module library for the module file that provides the driver for the module name.

Because of this versatility, many options are available for the modprobe command. Table 3.5 shows the command-line options that you can use.

TABLE 3.5 The **modprobe** command options

Option	Description
-a	Insert all modules listed on the command line.
-b	Apply a blacklist command specified in the configuration file.
-C	Specify a configuration file other than the default.
-c	Display the current configuration used.
-d	Specify the root directory to use for installing modules. The default is /.
-f	Force the module installation even if there are version issues.
-i	Ignore the install and remove commands specified in the configuration file for the module.
-n	Perform a dry run of the module install to see if it will work without actually installing it.
-q	Quiet mode; don't display any error messages if the module installation or removal fails.
-r	Remove the module listed.
-s	Send any error messages to the syslog facility on the system.
-V	Display the program version and exit.
-v	Provide additional information (verbose) as the module is processed.

As you can see, the modprobe command is a fully featured tool all by itself. Perhaps the handiest feature is that it allows you to install modules based on the module name and not have to list the full module filename:

```
$ sudo modprobe -iv btusb
insmod /lib/modules/3.13.0-63-generic/kernel/drivers/bluetooth/btusb.ko
$
```

Notice that by adding the -v option for verbose mode, the output shows the `insmod` command automatically generated by the `modprobe` command. The `insmod` command shows the specific module file used to install the module.

Removing Modules

Normally, it does no harm to install a module in the system if the hardware device is not present. The kernel just ignores unused modules. However, some Linux administrators prefer to keep the kernel as lightweight as possible. Thus, the Linux developers created a method for removing unnecessary modules—the `rmmod` command. The `rmmod` command removes a module by specifying the module name.

However, your friend the `modprobe` command can also remove modules for you, so you don't really need to memorize another command. Instead, just use the -r option with the modprobe command:

```
$ sudo modprobe -rv btusb
rmmod btusb
$
```

The `modprobe` -r command invokes the `rmmod` command automatically, removing the module by name. You can verify that the module has been removed by using the `lsmod` command.

Working with Hardware

Of course, modules work only when there's hardware connected to the system. Sometimes, you may run into an issue with matching the correct module with the correct hardware device. There are a few commands that you can use to query the hardware devices on your Linux system. These are discussed in this section.

Working with PCI Cards

The *Peripheral Component Interface (PCI)* is an old IBM-compatible PC standard for connecting hardware boards to PC motherboards. The standard has been updated a few times to accommodate faster interface speeds, as well as increase data bus sizes on motherboards. The *PCI Express (PCIe)* standard is currently used on most servers and desktop workstations to provide a common interface for external hardware cards, such as fast Ethernet and external SCSI drive support.

The Linux kernel supports the PCI and PCIe standards, and it can usually detect and interact with a PCI or PCIe board when the appropriate driver module is loaded.

The `lspci` command allows you to view the currently installed and recognized PCI and PCIe cards on the Linux system. You can include several command-line options with the `lspci` command to display various information about the PCI and PCIe cards installed on the system. Table 3.6 shows the more common options that come in handy.

TABLE 3.6   The `lspci` command-line options

Option	Description
-A	Define the method to access the PCI information.
-b	Display connection information from the card point of view.
-k	Display the kernel driver modules for each installed PCI card.
-m	Display information in machine-readable format.
-n	Display vendor and device information as numbers instead of text.
-q	Query the centralized PCI database for information about the installed PCI cards.
-t	Display a tree diagram that shows the connections between cards and buses.
-v	Display additional information (verbose) about the cards.
-x	Display a hexadecimal output dump of the card information.

The output from the lspci command without any options shows all of the devices connected to the system, as shown in Listing 3.8.

Listing 3.8: The lspci command output

```
$ lspci
00:00.0 Host bridge: Intel Corporation 440FX–82441FX PMC [Natoma] (rev 02)
00:01.0 ISA bridge: Intel Corporation 82371SB PIIX3 ISA [Natoma/Triton II]
00:01.1 IDE interface: Intel Corporation 82371AB/EB/MB PIIX4 IDE (rev 01)
00:02.0 VGA compatible controller: InnoTek Systemberatung GmbH VirtualBox
Graphics Adapter
00:03.0 Ethernet controller: Intel Corporation 82540EM Gigabit Ethernet
Controller (rev 02)
00:04.0 System peripheral: InnoTek Systemberatung GmbH VirtualBox Guest Service
00:05.0 Multimedia audio controller: Intel Corporation 82801AA AC'97 Audio
Controller (rev 01)
00:06.0 USB controller: Apple Inc. KeyLargo/Intrepid USB
00:07.0 Bridge: Intel Corporation 82371AB/EB/MB PIIX4 ACPI (rev 08)
00:0d.0 SATA controller: Intel Corporation 82801HM/HEM (ICH8M/ICH8M-E) SATA
Controller [AHCI mode] (rev 02)
$
```

You can use the output from the lspci command to troubleshoot PCI card issues, such as if a card isn't recognized by the PnP system.

Working with USB Devices

By far the most popular standard used for devices today is the *Universal Serial Bus (USB)*. USB is both a protocol and a hardware standard for transferring data between hardware devices. The original USB 1.0 standard provided for up to 127 hardware devices to share the same communication channel and transfer at speeds up to 12 Mbps. All types of hardware vendors rushed to implement the USB interface for their devices. Everything from keyboards, mice, printers, and even external storage devices uses the USB standard.

While the original USB standard was a major breakthrough in hardware communications, it wasn't long before the slower speeds started causing problems. The updated USB 2.0 standard provided for transfer speeds up to 480 Mbps, a significant increase in speed. The current USB 3.0 standard provides an incredible 4.8 Gbps transfer speed, but unfortunately it uses a different type of interface port, making it incompatible with older USB devices.

You can view the basic information about USB devices connected to your Linux system by using the lsusb command. Table 3.7 shows the options that are available with that command.

TABLE 3.7   The **lsusb** command options

Option	Description
-d	Display only devices from the specified vendor ID.
-D	Display information only from devices with the specified device file.
-s	Display information only from devices that use the specified bus.
-t	Display information in a tree format, showing related devices.
-v	Display additional information about the devices (verbose mode).
-V	Display the version of the lsusb program.

The basic lsusb output is shown in Listing 3.9.

Listing 3.9: The lsusb command output

```
$ lsusb
Bus 001 Device 004: ID 1908:1320 GEMBIRD PhotoFrame PF-15-1
Bus 001 Device 003: ID 80ee:0022 VirtualBox
Bus 001 Device 002: ID 80ee:0021 VirtualBox USB Tablet
Bus 001 Device 001: ID 1d6b:0001 Linux Foundation 1.1 root hub
$
```

Once you see the list of USB devices, you can obtain more information for a specific device by using the -d and -v options.

Automatically Detecting Hardware

Computer hardware is generally categorized into two types:

- Coldplug devices
- Hotplug devices

Coldplug devices are hardware that can be connected to the system only when it is completely powered down. These usually include things commonly found inside the computer case, such as memory, PCI cards, and hard drives. You can't remove any of these things while the system is running.

Conversely, you can usually add and remove *hotplug* devices at any time. These are often external components, such as network connections, monitors, and USB devices. The trick with hotplug devices is that somehow the Linux kernel needs to know when a hotplug device is connected and automatically load the correct device driver module to support the device.

The *udev device manager* is a program that runs in the background on Linux systems, listening to kernel notifications about hardware devices. As new hardware devices are plugged into the running system, or existing hardware devices are removed, the kernel sends out notification event messages.

The udevd program runs in the background and listens to these notification messages. The overall operation of the udevd program is controlled by settings in the /etc/udev/ udev.conf configuration file.

The udevd program matches the kernel messages against rules defined in a set of configuration files, normally stored under the /etc/udev/rules.d and /lib/udev/rules.d folders. If a device matches a defined rule, udevd acts on the event notification as defined by the rule. Device rules define which kernel module to load to support the device and what device name to assign to the device.

Each Linux distribution defines a standard set of rules for udevd to follow. Rules define actions such as mounting USB memory sticks under the /media folder or assigning a USB network card to the /dev/eth0 device.

You can modify the default rules defined by your Linux distribution, but it's usually not necessary.

Some Linux distributions include the udevmonitor program, which allows you to display kernel device events to the standard output. This lets you watch kernel events as you plug in new devices to help troubleshoot issues. In some Linux distributions, this feature is part of the udevadmin application, which allows you to control settings of the udevd program dynamically and monitor the kernel messages it detects.

Troubleshooting the Kernel

If things do go wrong with the kernel, a few tools are available to help you troubleshoot things. This section goes through two of the more common tools that you'll want to know about.

Displaying the Kernel Version

Before you can do much troubleshooting, you'll want to know just which kernel version your system is booting. The uname command can provide quite a bit of useful information here.

By default, the uname command displays a string that isn't overly useful:

```
$ uname
Linux
$
```

This is actually the name of the kernel that is running. For lots more information, use the -a option:

```
$ uname -a
Linux ubuntu02 3.13.0-63-generic #103-Ubuntu SMP Fri Aug 14 21:42:59 UTC
2015 x86_64 x86_64 x86_64 GNU/Linux
$
```

Now that's more useful. The information provided by the uname command is as follows:

- The kernel name (Linux)
- The system network hostname (ubuntu02)
- The kernel release (3.13.0–63-generic)
- The kernel version (#103 Ubuntu SMP Fri Aug 14 21:42:59 UTC 2015)
- The machine hardware name (x86_64)
- The processor type (x86_64)
- The operating system (GNU/Linux)

You can also display each value individually by using other command-line options, as shown in Table 3.8.

TABLE 3.8   The **uname** command options

Option	Description
-a	Display all values.
-s	Display the kernel name.

TABLE 3.8   The **uname** command options *(continued)*

Option	Description
-n	Display the network hostname.
-r	Display the kernel release.
-v	Display the kernel version.
-m	Display the machine hardware name.
-p	Display the processor type.
-o	Display the operating system.

The uname command is the first place to go to when you need to check which kernel loaded at boot time, especially if you have multiple kernels configured on your system.

The */proc* Filesystem

The Linux kernel creates a dynamic pseudo directory named /proc that allows you to peek at configuration and performance information related to the kernel while it's running. The /proc filesystem contains information on hardware, such as assigned interrupt requests (/proc/interrupts), I/O ports (/proc/ioports), and direct memory access (DMA) channels (/proc/dma). Viewing this information is as easy as using the cat command to display the file contents. Listing 3.10 shows the output from the /proc/interrupts file.

Listing 3.10: The /proc/interrupts file contents

```
$ cat /proc/interrupts
          CPU0
   0:       129    XT-PIC-XT-PIC    timer
   1:       986    XT-PIC-XT-PIC    i8042
   2:         0    XT-PIC-XT-PIC    cascade
   8:         0    XT-PIC-XT-PIC    rtc0
   9:      4808    XT-PIC-XT-PIC    acpi, vboxguest
  10:      9827    XT-PIC-XT-PIC    eth0
  11:     32914    XT-PIC-XT-PIC    ohci_hcd:usb1, ahci, snd_intel8x0
  12:       505    XT-PIC-XT-PIC    i8042
  14:      2440    XT-PIC-XT-PIC    ata_piix
  15:         0    XT-PIC-XT-PIC    ata_piix
 NMI:         0    Non-maskable interrupts
 LOC:    119411    Local timer interrupts
```

```
SPU:           0    Spurious interrupts
PMI:           0    Performance monitoring interrupts
IWI:       19157    IRQ work interrupts
RTR:           0    APIC ICR read retries
RES:           0    Rescheduling interrupts
CAL:           0    Function call interrupts
TLB:           0    TLB shootdowns
TRM:           0    Thermal event interrupts
THR:           0    Threshold APIC interrupts
MCE:           0    Machine check exceptions
MCP:           9    Machine check polls
ERR:           0
MIS:           0
$
```

You can use the lsdev command to display hardware information found in the /proc filesystem in one easy table, as shown in Listing 3.11. You may have to install the command since many Linux distributions don't install it by default.

Listing 3.11: The lsdev command output

```
$ lsdev
Device            DMA   IRQ   I/O Ports
────────────────────────────
0000:00:01.1                 0170-0177 01f0-01f7 0376-0376 03f6-03f6
0000:00:03.0                 d010-d017
0000:00:04.0                 d020-d03f
0000:00:05.0                 d100-d1ff d200-d23f
0000:00:0d.0                 d240-d247 d250-d257 d260-d26f
ACPI                         4000-4003 4004-4005 4008-400b 4020-4021
ahci                         d240-d247   d250-d257   d260-d26f
ata_piix          14    15   0170-0177 01f0-01f7 0376-0376 03f6-03f6
cascade            4     2
dma                          0080-008f
dma1                         0000-001f
dma2                         00c0-00df
e1000                        d010-d017
eth0                    10
fpu                          00f0-00ff
i8042              1    12
Intel                        d100-d1ff   d200-d23f
keyboard                     0060-0060 0064-0064
```

```
PCI                         0cf8-0cff
pic1                        0020-0021
pic2                        00a0-00a1
rtc0                     8  0070-0071
rtc_cmos                    0070-0071
snd_intel8x0            11
timer                    0
timer0                      0040-0043
timer1                      0050-0053
vboxguest                9
vesafb                      03c0-03df
$
```

You'll find kernel information in the /proc/sys/kernel folder, which contains files that you can read to obtain kernel information and write to set kernel parameters. Reading kernel parameters is as easy as using the cat command:

```
$ cat /proc/sys/kernel/version
#103-Ubuntu SMP Fri Aug 14 21:42:59 UTC 2015
$
```

You can set kernel parameters either by writing to the /proc filesystem file directly or by using the sysctl command. You can specify either the kernel parameter and value on the sysctl command line, or you can specify a group of parameters and values in the /etc/sysctl.conf configuration file, which the sysctl command will read and process. Most Linux distributions also utilize a /etc/sysctl.d folder, which contains multiple files of kernel parameter settings. This helps organize the settings based on the applications that require them.

Summary

The Linux system consists of several layers of software. At the center of the Linux system is the Linux kernel, which manages the system hardware, memory, and running applications. The kernel is key to having a properly running Linux system.

The kernel consists of several parts—the actual kernel binary file, kernel modules for managing hardware, the kernel source code, kernel patches for upgrading existing systems, kernel headers used for compiling modules, and the kernel documentation. At a bare minimum, your Linux system must have the kernel binary and module files installed. If you want to experiment with creating a customized kernel, you'll need the kernel source code files.

You can either download the kernel source code files from your Linux distribution repository or get the latest production and development versions from the www.kernel.org website. Once you download and extract the kernel source code, you must create a configuration file, which sets the kernel features that you need for your system. There are automated scripts available to help with this process, including graphical menus for selecting which features to include.

After configuring the kernel features, the next step is to compile the source code to create a kernel binary file. The kernel binary file that is created is often a compressed file named bzImage. You must copy this file to the bootloader folder (usually /boot), then compile the module files included for the kernel, and create an initial RAM disk so that the kernel can access the modules at boot time.

After you get the new kernel running, you'll want to be able to monitor and troubleshoot the kernel. Linux includes commands to display the hardware devices detected at boot time and dynamically added as the system is running. There are also commands to work with kernel modules, listing the modules installed and installing or removing modules as necessary.

Finally, you can use the /proc filesystem to monitor hardware and kernel features, as well as change kernel parameters while the system is running.

Exam Essentials

Describe the parts of the Linux kernel and where to find them. The kernel binary file is the program that runs at boot time. It's normally stored in the /boot folder with the filename bzImage or vmlinuz. The kernel also uses module files, which are stored in the /lib/ modules folder. The kernel source code and documentation files are stored in the /usr/src/ linux folder structure (or are linked from another location to this folder).

Explain the different types of kernel images. The vmlinux image is a non-compressed image that's not normally used for booting. The zImage image file is a small, compressed image file, while the bzImage image file format creates a larger compressed image file. The bzImage file format is the most popular, but it is often renamed to vmlinuz by most Linux distributions.

Identify the kernel stable and development releases. Kernels in the version 1 and 2 series used an odd/even format of version numbering, where odd-numbered releases were development and even number releases were stable. Kernels in the version 3 and 4 series append an -rc to the end of the version number to indicate development releases.

Describe kernel modules. Kernel modules allow you to load device drivers separately from the main kernel executable file. This allows you to run a small kernel and load only the modules required for the system devices. The module files are object files that can be either loaded or unloaded during runtime. Kernel modules are found in the /lib/modules folder structure.

Describe how to configure a kernel. Once you download the kernel source code, you can use the make utility with the config, menuconfig, xconfig, or gconfig target. The config target asks questions to allow you to select the configuration and settings for the kernel.

The menuconfig target produces a text-based menu system for selecting configuration settings. Both the xconfig and gconfig targets generate a graphical menu that allows you to set configuration settings.

Explain how to compile a new kernel.   Once you download the kernel source code and generate a configuration file, you can compile the kernel using the make utility. If you don't specify a target, the make utility will create an uncompressed kernel binary file. You can specify the zImage or bzImage target to create a compressed kernel binary file. After you compile the kernel, you'll need to compile the associated modules by using the make utility with the modules target.

Explain how to create an initrd image.   After you compile the kernel modules, you can create an initial RAM disk image with the compiled module files. For Red Hat–based systems, you should use the mkinitrd command, while for Debian-based systems, you should use the mkinitramfs command.

Describe how to install a new kernel.   You can manually copy the bzImage kernel binary file to the /boot folder, along with the System.map file generated for the binary file and the initial RAM disk created with the kernel modules. After you copy the files to the /boot folder, you must either manually add a new entry to the GRUB Legacy boot menu or, for GRUB2 systems, run the update-grub command to add the new kernel automatically to the boot menu.

Explain how to query the kernel settings.   The /proc filesystem provides an interface to the kernel settings and performance statistics. The /proc/sys/kernel folder contains files for kernel settings that you can modify during runtime. You can also use the sysctl command to modify kernel settings at any time. The /etc/sysctl.conf configuration file allows you to specify multiple settings that can be applied when the sysctl program runs.

Explain how to work with modules for a kernel.   The lsmod command lets you view the modules currently loaded into the kernel. The modinfo command provides detailed information about the module and the module file with which it's associated. The insmod and modprobe commands allow you to insert new modules into the running kernel. The rmmod command lets you remove a module from the running kernel.

Explain how Linux detects hardware and loads modules.   The udev system uses the udevd program running in the background to listen to kernel hardware events. It matches the kernel events against rules defined in the /etc/udev folder. When a kernel event matches a rule, the rule specifies what module should be loaded and the device name to which the device is assigned.

Review Questions

You can find the answers in the Appendix.

1. Which part of a Linux system manages system memory?
   A. GNU utilities
   B. Kernel
   C. Graphical desktop
   D. Application software

2. What is the area on the hard disk called that is used as memory storage?
   A. Swap space
   B. Virtual memory
   C. Filesystem
   D. Physical memory

3. What method does Linux use to load device drivers into the kernel?
   A. DLL files
   B. Virtual memory
   C. Modules
   D. Bootloader

4. Which kernel file type is used to boot the Linux system?
   A. Binary file
   B. Modules
   C. Patch file
   D. Source code

5. What type of release can you use to upgrade an existing kernel to a newer version?
   A. Patch release
   B. Modules
   C. Binary files
   D. Development release

6. Which make utility target uses text-based questions to configure the kernel?
   A. xconfig
   B. mrproper
   C. clean
   D. config

7. Which make utility target uses a graphical interface to configure the kernel?

   A. config

   B. mrproper

   C. gconfig

   D. clean

8. Which make utility target should you use to remove any old object files from a previous compile?

   A. gconfig

   B. mrproper

   C. bzImage

   D. oldconfig

9. Which make utility target is commonly used to generate a compressed kernel binary file?

   A. bzImage

   B. kernel

   C. config

   D. clean

10. Which program should you use to create an initial RAM disk for a Debian-based system?

   A. mkinitrd

   B. make bzImage

   C. mkinitramfs

   D. make initrd

11. Which command should you use to list all of the installed modules?

   A. modinfo

   B. insmod

   C. rmmod

   D. lsmod

12. Which command should you use to install a module if you don't know its filename?

   A. insmod

   B. rmmod

   C. modprobe

   D. lsmod

13. Which command should you use to display information about USB devices installed on the system?

   A. lsusb

   B. lspci

   C. lsmod

   D. lsdev

14. Which option in the lsusb command displays detailed information about the USB devices?

   A. -d

   B. -s

   C. -t

   D. -v

15. Which type of hardware devices can you connect to the Linux system as it's running?

   A. Coldplug

   B. Hotplug

   C. PCI

   D. PCIe

16. What program does Linux use to detect hotplug devices and load the appropriate modules?

   A. lsusb

   B. udevd

   C. modprobe

   D. insmod

17. Where are the udevd configuration settings stored?

   A. /lib/modules

   B. /boot

   C. /etc/udev/rules.d

   D. /etc/udev/udev.conf

18. Where are the udevd rules stored?

   A. /etc/udev/udevd.conf

   B. /etc/udev/rules.d

   C. /boot

   D. /lib/modules

19. Where is the dynamic pseudo-directory the kernel creates to peek at kernel settings and performance statistics located?

   A. `/etc/kernel`

   B. `/boot/kernel`

   C. `/proc`

   D. `/usr/src/linux`

20. What command allows you to change kernel settings during runtime?

   A. `sysctl`

   B. `lsmod`

   C. `modprobe`

   D. `lsdev`

Chapter

4

Managing the Filesystem

THE FOLLOWING EXAM OBJECTIVES ARE COVERED IN THIS CHAPTER:

✓ 203.1 Operating the Linux filesystem

✓ 203.2 Maintaining a Linux filesystem

✓ 203.3 Creating and configuring filesystem options

Data is kept as ones and zeros on storage media, such as disk drives and DVDs. A *filesystem* bridges the gap between the ones and zeros stored on the media and the files you work with in your applications. Managing a filesystem includes providing access to the stored data as well as tuning, monitoring, and repairing filesystems in order to improve access times and protect the data. This chapter covers all of these topics so that you can properly manage your Linux filesystems.

Operating the Linux Filesystem

To manage and control a Linux filesystem, you need to know more than a general filesystem definition. You should be aware of basic filesystem structures. It's also important to understand the various filesystem types that determine how the files are handled on storage media. We cover several filesystem types and their descriptions in this chapter section. Understanding these filesystem types and their schemes will assist you in picking the right filesystem type for your data needs.

Be aware that some documentation spells the word *filesystem* as *file system*.

Besides understanding the filesystem types, you must know how to attach a filesystem to the Linux directory structure. Filesystems can be temporarily or persistently attached to the directory structure. How to accomplish these tasks is also covered in this section.

Understanding Filesystem Structures

Hard disk drives and other storage media typically come with manufacturer low-level formatting applied. However, for many non-optical storage media devices, such as disks, partitioning and high-level formatting are still required.

Partitioning storage media, addressed in the LPIC-1 certification, is necessary prior to high-level formatting. Typically, *partitioning* is logically dividing a storage media device into individual sections called *partitions*. Be aware, however, that a single partition can span a whole device, as well as multiple devices. Logical volume management, covered in Chapter 5, allows multiple partitions to be logically grouped together into one partition, called a *volume*. Partitioning is accomplished via either GUI or command-line utilities, such as parted, fdisk, and gdisk.

High-level formatting is often just called *formatting* or *making the filesystem*. This formatting is accomplished using utilities such as mkfs and was addressed in the LPIC-1 certification. It is also covered later in this chapter.

When a partition or volume is formatted, several structures are put into place, depending on the filesystem type selected. One partition area holds the actual file data. The other area(s) hold structures containing items such as filesystem metadata, file metadata, journal files (described later in this chapter), and so on.

File metadata is stored in an *inode table*. When a file is created on the partition or volume, a new entry in the inode table is created. The inode table is a table of index numbers, called *inodes*. Typically, an inode is a number uniquely assigned to a file when it is created. (There are exceptions to this, such as when a hard link is created to a file. The hard link file and the original file share an inode number.) The inode and its assigned file's metadata, such as permissions, ownership, and pointers to the various file data locations, are stored in the inode table.

A file's name is not stored in the inode table. A file's name is stored in its directory. A directory is actually a file that contains a table. The table has metadata on each file stored in that directory. Each file's name and its associated inode number are listed within the directory table.

Every partition or volume can have a different filesystem type. This allows a great deal of flexibility for addressing your particular data needs.

Understanding Filesystem Types

A filesystem determines how the files are handled on physical media. Each type has its own unique methods for accessing, updating, and protecting data integrity. Thus, your filesystem type choice is an important selection.

The term *filesystem* is sometimes used to refer to the Linux directory structure's layout. For example, the Filesystem Hierarchy Standard provides a standard for key system file locations within the Linux directory structure. Also, you will often read about two important filesystems in the Linux directory structure, root (/) and /boot, which are required for a Linux installation. The term *filesystem* in this chapter does *not* refer to directories within the Linux virtual directory structure.

Filesystems can be categorized in many different ways, such as to how they protect data integrity, the physical medium on which they can be used, their original target operating system, and so on. For our purposes here, they are split into native Linux filesystems and non-native filesystems. Later in this chapter, we'll cover network-based and optical filesystems.

Looking at Native Linux Filesystems

A native Linux filesystem is one that was originally designed to be used on Linux. Table 4.1 shows filesystems, in alphabetical order, that fall into this category.

TABLE 4.1   Native Linux filesystem types

Name	Max File Size	Max Filesystem Size	Journaling	Description
btrfs	16 EiB	16 EiB	COW	Newer, high-performance filesystem that supports large file and filesystem sizes. Performs its own form of Redundant Array of Independent Disks (RAID) as well as volume management. Additional features include built-in snapshots, improved fault-tolerance, compression on the fly, and so on.
ext2	2 TiB	16 TiB	No	One of the original Linux filesystems. Deprecated.
ext3	2 TiB	16 TiB	Yes	Created as an improvement to ext2 with journaling added; quicker startup and recovery.
ext4	16 TiB	1 EiB	Yes	Created as an improvement to ext3 with larger file and filesystem sizes supported as well as performance enhancements.
reiserFS	1 EiB	16 TiB	Yes	Created before ext3. Also called *Reiser3*. Newer version, Reiser4, not incorporated into Linux kernel.

You'll notice in Table 4.1 that most modern filesystems use journaling, while Btrfs uses COW instead. The difference between these two data integrity features is as follows. *Journaling* is a method that tracks uncommitted (file metadata not yet updated) data changes in a log file, called a journal. If the data commitment process is interrupted, say by a system crash, the journal is used to commit the intended data changes. This method provides effective data protection in a system interruption event.

The ext filesystem types are sometimes written with "fs" added to their name to indicate that they are a filesystem type. For example, ext3 can be written as ext3fs.

COW stands for Copy-On-Write, and it is another method used to protect data. To understand it, you first need to understand how files are handled in non-COW filesystems. When a file is created, it is written on the storage medium's free space and the metadata is created pointing to the file's data location. In a non-COW filesystem, when that file's data is modified, the old data is overwritten with the new data.

On a COW filesystem, file creation is handled similarly. However, file data modification is handled differently. For a COW filesystem, when a file's data is modified, the new data is written on the storage medium's free space; the file's metadata is updated to point to the new data. Thus, if the data commitment process is interrupted, say by a system crash, the original data still exists and is not lost.

 On a COW filesystem, when a file is created, its metadata is not created exactly as on a non-COW filesystem. For a COW filesystem, the filesystem's metadata's new data is written on the storage medium's free space. Then pointers are updated to point to the new filesystem metadata. This adds an extra layer of protection.

Looking at Non-native Linux Filesystems

There are additional filesystems to consider besides native Linux filesystems. These are non-native filesystems, which are filesystems not originally created for Linux but which can be handled by Linux. Table 4.2 shows several filesystems, in alphabetical order, that fall into this category.

TABLE 4.2 Non-native Linux filesystem types

Name	Max File Size	Max Filesystem Size	Journaling	Description/Features
ntfs	2 TiB	256 TiB	Yes	Read access is supported on Linux, but software to do so may not be installed by default. For write access, additional software may also be needed. Developed by Microsoft.
vfat	4 GiB	2 TiB	No	Typically used on USB flash drives. Developed by Microsoft.

TABLE 4.2   Non-native Linux filesystem types *(continued)*

Name	Max File Size	Max Filesystem Size	Journaling	Description/Features
XFS	8 EiB	8 EiB	Yes	High-performance filesystem that supports large file and filesystem sizes. Developed by Silicon Graphics.
ZFS	16 EiB	256 ZiB	COW	ZFS on Linux (ZoL) is a high-performance filesystem often compared to Btrfs. Developed by Sun Microsystems (now part of Oracle).

As you can see from Table 4.1 and Table 4.2, you can choose from a wide variety of filesystems to use on your Linux system. Keep in mind that these two tables are not an exhaustive list. There are many more filesystems to consider. These are simply a few of the more popular ones. Use your favorite search engine or type **man filesystems** at the command line to find additional filesystems for Linux.

The maximum file and filesystem sizes are theoretical limits. In practice, you may find the filesystems to have lower thresholds than stated here.

A relatively new non-native filesystem created for Windows systems is ReFS (Resilient File System). It currently has limited deployment, but it may be supported on Linux sometime in the future.

Making a Filesystem

Once you have created a partition or volume and chosen a filesystem for it, you are ready to format (make) a filesystem. As mentioned earlier, this sets up various structures on the partition (volume) for proper data management.

The primary tool to format a filesystem is mkfs, and you need super user privileges to use it. The mkfs utility is actually a front end to various other utilities used for each filesystem type.

The desired filesystem type can be chosen via the command mkfs.*fstype* or mkfs -t *fstype*. The *fstype* is a special code that represents the filesystem type being selected. For example, ext4 is the type code to select an ext4 (ext4fs) filesystem type.

Another command that you can use to make ext2, ext3, or ext4 filesystems is mke2fs. It is simply a pointer to the mkfs.ext2 utility, which will create an ext2 filesystem. Used with the -t *fstype* option, you can make an ext3 or ext4 filesystem, depending on which *fstype* you select.

The following is an example of using the mkfs utility to format a partition to the ext4 filesystem type. It was completed on an Ubuntu distribution. Therefore, sudo is used to gain the necessary super user privileges.

```
$ sudo mkfs.ext4 /dev/sdb1
[sudo] password for christine:
mke2fs 1.42.9 (4-Feb-2014)
Filesystem label=
OS type: Linux
Block size=4096 (log=2)
Fragment size=4096 (log=2)
Stride=0 blocks, Stripe width=0 blocks
131072 inodes, 524288 blocks
26214 blocks (5.00%) reserved for the super user
First data block=0
Maximum filesystem blocks=536870912
16 block groups
32768 blocks per group, 32768 fragments per group
8192 inodes per group
Superblock backups stored on blocks:
    32768, 98304, 163840, 229376, 294912

Allocating group tables: done
Writing inode tables: done
Creating journal (16384 blocks): done
Writing superblocks and filesystem accounting information:  0/1done

$
```

Notice from the preceding example's output that several structures were set up as the /dev/sdb1 partition formatting was processing. These structures include inodes, inode tables, and a journal. Recall from earlier in this chapter that each filesystem type will have both common and unique structures created during formatting in order to manage the filesystem. Each filesystem type has its own unique methods for accessing, updating, and protecting data integrity.

Using the command mkfs -t ext4 /dev/sdb1 in the preceding example would have accomplished the exact same result.

You can check the filesystem type created using the parted utility and super user privileges, as shown in this snipped example on an Ubuntu system:

```
$ sudo parted -l
[...]
Model: ATA VBOX HARDDISK (scsi)
Disk /dev/sdb: 4295MB
Sector size (logical/physical): 512B/512B
Partition Table: msdos

Number  Start    End      Size     Type      File system  Flags
 1      1049kB   2149MB   2147MB   primary   ext4
$
```

The filesystem on /dev/sdb1 is indeed an ext4 filesystem. This is a handy way to double-check your mkfs formatting.

You can also use the blkid utility to check the filesystem type, as shown in this snipped example from an Ubuntu system:

```
$ sudo blkid
/dev/sda1: [...] TYPE="ext4"
/dev/sda5: [...] TYPE="swap"
/dev/sdb1: [...] TYPE="ext4"
$
```

This output also shows that the filesystem on /dev/sdb1 is an ext4 filesystem. Neither the blkid nor the parted utility requires the partition to be attached to the Linux directory system in order to display its filesystem type.

Attaching a Filesystem

Once you make your filesystem, it's important to know how to attach the filesystem to the Linux directory structure. Linux uses a method to store files within a single directory structure called a *virtual directory*. At the base of this virtual directory is the root directory (/), and directories and files beneath the root directory are listed based on the directory path. You can attach filesystems to the virtual directory structure either temporarily or persistently, depending on your present needs. After you've attached a filesystem to the virtual directory structure, you can store and access data on that filesystem.

Attaching a Filesystem Temporarily

Attaching a filesystem to the Linux virtual directory is called *mounting*, and temporary mounting is done via the mount command. To mount a filesystem, you must have super user privileges (though there are exceptions, as you'll read about later.) The basic command for mounting a filesystem is

```
mount -t fstype device mount_point
```

The *fstype* is the filesystem type that you are mounting. The same *fstype* codes used in the mkfs command are used here, such as xfs. The fstype must be supported by the Linux kernel on your distribution in order to be mounted.

You can easily determine the filesystem types supported by your Linux distribution's kernel by viewing the /proc/filesystems file.

The *device* is an absolute path name to the partition or volume holding this filesystem, such as /dev/sdb1. (Later in this chapter, you will read how other items besides device can be used instead.)

The *mount_point* in the mount command is the location within the virtual directory where the filesystem will reside, such as /home/christine/Temp. The following example demonstrates mounting a filesystem on an Ubuntu distribution:

```
$ mkdir /home/christine/Temp
$
$ sudo mount -t ext4 /dev/sdb1 /home/christine/Temp
[sudo] password for christine:
$
$ ls -F /home/christine/Temp
lost+found/
$
```

Once the filesystem is mounted, you can store, modify, and access data using the mount_point as a reference. Here is an example using the previously mounted filesystem:

```
$ touch /home/christine/Temp/a_file.txt
$
$ ls -F /home/christine/Temp
a_file.txt   lost+found/
$
```

Notice that when the filesystem was mounted, a lost+found directory already existed in the *mount_point* directory. The lost+found directory is used for recovering files on ext2, ext3, and ext4 filesystems. If a file residing on this filesystem is not closed properly, such as when a system crash occurs or a software bug is encountered, it is stored in this directory. Also, the fsck command, covered later in this chapter, stores recovered files in the lost+found directory. Keep in mind that a file located here may not be fully intact, depending on the problem encountered by the file.

If any files exist in the *mount_point* prior to mounting the filesystem, they will no longer be accessible after the filesystem is mounted.

The mount command, when used with no options or parameters, pulls the data it displays directly from the /etc/mtab file. The /etc/mtab file contains a list of all of the currently mounted filesystems. Thus, you can easily check that your filesystem was properly mounted to the desired location using the mount command. Here is an example with snipped output shown on the Ubuntu distribution used previously:

```
$ mount
/dev/sda1 on / type ext4 (rw,errors=remount-ro)
[...]
/dev/sdb1 on /home/christine/Temp type ext4 (rw)
$
```

The example's output shows that the /dev/sdb1 partition is mounted at the /home/christine/Temp mount point. It also shows that the filesystem type is ext4.

> The data in the files /etc/mtab and /proc/mounts is nearly identical, with a few exceptions. First, if a filesystem was attached with mount using the -n option, the /etc/mtab file will *not* contain information on that filesystem. Also, the /proc/mounts file is typically more up to date than /etc/mtab.

The mount command has several useful options. A few are listed in Table 4.3.

TABLE 4.3   mount command options

Parameter	Description
-a	Mounts all of the filesystems specified in the /etc/fstab file.
-F	Used with the -a option. Mounts all of the filesystems at the same time.
-f	Simulates mounting a filesystem but does not mount it.
-L label	Mounts the filesystem with the specified label.
-l	Adds filesystem labels automatically. Only for ext2, ext3, or XFS filesystems.
-n	Mounts the filesystem without registering it in the /etc/mtab file.
-o opts	Adds specified opts string to the filesystem.
-r	Mounts the filesystem as read-only.

Parameter	Description
-s	Ignores mount options not supported by the filesystem.
-t *fstype*	Mounts the filesystem as the filesystem type, *fstype*.
-U *uuid*	Mounts the filesystem with the specified *uuid*.
-v	Explains all of the steps required to mount the filesystem (verbose).
-w	Mounts the filesystem as read/write.

The -o option allows you to mount the filesystem with one or more comma-separated *opts*. A few of the more popular *opts* selections are listed here:

check=none: Mounts the filesystem without performing an integrity check.

exec: Permits binary file execution.

group: Allows a non–super user to mount the filesystem, if the user belongs to the specified group.

owner: Allows a specified non–super user to mount the filesystem.

ro: Mounts the filesystem as read-only.

rw: Mounts the filesystem as read-write.

sync: Forces filesystem buffers to write from memory to the media for every write to the filesystem. No effect on XFS.

user: Allows a specified non–super user to mount the filesystem.

users: Allows all users to mount the filesystem.

To see all of the various mount command options and the -o option's opts selections available, type **man mount** at the command line.

For a ZFS on a Linux (ZoL) filesystem, no mount command is needed. It is automatically mounted. Find out more about ZoL at http://zfsonlinux.org/.

Detaching a Filesystem

You can detach a filesystem from the Linux virtual directory structure with the umount command. Be careful here! There is no "n" in the umount command, and you'll need super user privileges to use it, as shown on this Ubuntu system:

```
$ ls -F /home/christine/Temp
a_file.txt  lost+found/
```

```
$
$ sudo umount /home/christine/Temp
[sudo] password for christine:
$
$ ls -F /home/christine/Temp
$
```

Notice in the previous directory that the directory mount point, /home/christine/Temp, is used with the umount command instead of the device filename, /dev/sdb1. While you could use the device filename, it's a best practice to use the directory mount point in case the device is mounted in multiple locations.

> Non–super users cannot detach a filesystem from the directory structure unless the filesystem was mounted with special options. Those special options include group, owner, user, and users.

Be aware that if the filesystem that you wish to unmount is being used by a process or has open files on it, you cannot detach it from the directory structure. The following example shows a filesystem mounted on an Ubuntu system that cannot be unmounted because the filesystem is in use:

```
$ sudo mount -t ext4 /dev/sdb1 Temp
[sudo] password for christine:
$
$ sudo umount Temp
umount: /home/christine/Temp: device is busy.
        (In some cases useful info about processes that use
         the device is found by lsof(8) or fuser(1))
$
```

Fortunately, the umount command gives some helpful tips. You can use the lsof or fuser command to determine what is keeping the filesystem busy, as shown here:

```
$ lsof Temp
COMMAND PID USER        FD   TYPE DEVICE SIZE/OFF NODE NAME
bash    1580 christine  cwd  DIR  8,17   4096     2    Temp
nano    5008 christine  cwd  DIR  8,17   4096     2    Temp
$
$ fuser Temp
/home/christine/Temp:  1580c   5008c
```

In the preceding example, the lsof command shows the details of the processes currently using the Temp directory. The details indicate that the user christine is using the nano text editor on a file within the Temp directory. The fuser has a brief output displaying the process PIDs and a code (c) indicating that the processes' current directory is /home/ christine/Temp. You can find a complete description of various fuser codes by typing **man fuser** at the command line. Once these processes are no longer keeping the directory busy, the filesystem can be successfully detached from the Temp directory.

Attaching Removable Media Manually

Many distributions detect and automatically mount removable media. (See this chapter's "Understanding Auto-mounting" section for details on how this occurs.) There are times, however, when either the system does not automatically mount removable media or you do not want the media mounted at default mount points. In these cases, you can manually mount the removable media.

Keep in mind, if the system *does* automatically mount the media, you will need to use umount to detach it from the virtual directory structure *before* you manually mount it to your desired location.

To mount removable media manually, the command is no different from the command that you use for temporarily mounting a filesystem. Just be sure that the mount point pre-exists, and use the correct filesystem type as shown here:

```
$ sudo mount -t vfat /dev/sdd1 Temp
[sudo] password for christine:
$
$ ls Temp
AAA_Work_ToDo            peazip-5.9.0.LINUX.GTK2.tgz
curl-7.46.0.tar.gz       Shell_Scripts
[...]
$
```

Depending on your distribution, you may be able to unmount the removable media, which was automatically mounted *without* using super user privileges. However, you might find that you *must use* super user privileges to mount and unmount the device manually.

Flash drives are often formatted as vfat or ntfs. The ext2 filesystem is also popular for flash drives. Optical storage has different filesystems, as covered later in this chapter.

If you don't know the filesystem type or the device name for your removable media, you can use either the dmesg or the blkid command (or both). A snipped example of these two commands in action is shown here:

```
$ dmesg
[...]
[ 3882.584572]  sdd: sdd1
```

```
[ 3882.635207] sd 6:0:0:0: [sdd] No Caching mode page found
[ 3882.635211] sd 6:0:0:0: [sdd] Assuming drive cache: write through
[ 3882.635213] sd 6:0:0:0: [sdd] Attached SCSI removable disk
[...]
$
$ sudo blkid
[...]
/dev/sdd1: SEC_TYPE="msdos" LABEL="TRAVELDRIVE" UUID="65AA-9655"
 TYPE="vfat"
$
```

Using these commands allows you to find that the flash drive device filename is /dev/sdd1 and that it is formatted as a vfat filesystem type. Notice that the blkid command also provides UUID and label information for the removable media.

A handy utility to use with removable media is the sync command. The sync command allows you to "flush" the filesystem buffers. In other words, any filesystem metadata updates residing in memory are written to the filesystem structures on the media. The sync utility forces the data commitment process to take place immediately. This allows you to detach removable media safely from the directory structure without worrying about corruption. An example of using sync is shown here:

```
$ cp Documents/Listing_c04_Ubuntu_mount-t.odt Temp/
$
$ sync
$ echo $?
0
$ sudo umount Temp
[sudo] password for christine:
$
```

In the preceding example, a file is copied to the manually mounted USB flash drive at Temp. The sync command is used to flush filesystem buffers. The sync utility provides an exit status, which you can view using the echo $? command. A zero (0) indicates all is well, whereas a one (1) indicates that a problem has occurred. Because there were no errors reported by sync, the flash drive was safely unmounted using the umount command.

In Exercise 4.1, you'll experiment with manually attaching a USB flash drive to your Linux system.

EXERCISE 4.1

Manually Mount a USB Flash Drive

To experiment with temporarily attaching and detaching a filesystem, follow these steps:

1. Log in as an ordinary user, and open a command-line terminal.

2. If it doesn't already exist, create a temporary directory in your home directory by typing **mkdir Temp** at the command line and pressing Enter.

3. Attach a USB flash drive to the Linux system by plugging it into one of the USB ports. (If you are using a virtualized system, you may have additional steps here.)

4. Determine the USB flash drive device name by typing **dmesg** and pressing Enter. Look for the key phrase Attached SCSI removable disk or something similar.

5. Determine the exact device name and the USB flash drive's filesystem by using super user privileges (this may require that you precede the command with sudo or log into a super user account), typing **blkid**, and pressing Enter.

6. Record your USB flash drive's name. It will be something similar to /dev/sdb1, depending on its formatting and your Linux system.

7. Record your USB flash drive's filesystem. It will be something similar to vfat, nfts, or ext2, depending on its formatting.

8. Type **mount** and press Enter. If your USB flash drive was automatically mounted, you will see it listed here. If you see it listed, record its mount point. If you *do not* see it listed, skip to step 10.

9. Because the system automatically mounted your USB flash drive, you will need to detach it from the directory structure before you try to mount the flash drive manually. Type **umount** ***mount-point***, where ***mount-point*** is the USB flash drive's mount point that you recorded in the previous step. (If you receive a permissions error, retry the command using super user privileges).

10. Now attempt to mount your USB flash drive manually. Type **mount -t** ***fstype*** ***drive-name* Temp**, where ***fstype*** is the filesystem type that you recorded in step 7 and ***drive-name*** is the drive name that you recorded in step 6. (If you receive a permissions error, retry the command using super user privileges). Be aware that if it is an NTFS-formatted drive, your distribution may not have the software installed to handle this type of drive format.

11. Once you have the USB flash drive successfully mounted, type **ls -F Temp** and press Enter. Do you see your flash drive files? If you mounted the USB flash drive correctly, you should see them.

12. Type **mount** and press Enter. See if you can find your manually mounted USB flash drive in the command's output. You should be able to find it.

13. Type **mountpoint Temp** and press Enter. You should receive the message Temp is a mountpoint.

14. Flush the filesystem buffers by typing **sync** and pressing Enter. (Although you didn't write anything to the USB flash drive, syncing the drive before you detach it is still a good habit.)

15. Detach the USB flash drive by typing the command **umount Temp** and pressing Enter. (If you receive a permissions error, retry the command using super user privileges. If you get a command not found message, double-check that you typed the umount command and not "unmount.")

EXERCISE 4.1 *(continued)*

16. Type **mount** and press Enter. See if you can find your manually mounted USB flash drive in the command's output. You should not be able to find it because you unmounted it from the system.

17. Type **ls -F Temp** and press Enter. If you created this directory as part of this exercise, you should not see any files and get only a prompt back. If it was previously created, you should see any files originally stored there.

Attaching a Filesystem Persistently

Instead of manually attaching your filesystems after every system reboot, you can have them attached by the system when it boots. This is done via a record placed in the /etc/fstab file, which is appropriately named the Filesystem Table.

Generally speaking, each /etc/fstab record consists of six fields. Any record preceded by a hash mark (#) is considered a comment line. The following items describe these fields.

Partition or Volume   A device partition, such as /dev/sda1, is usually listed here. A logical volume (covered in Chapter 5) could be listed here as well. Logical volumes start with /dev/mapper/.

Another method for identifying a device partition or volume is by using a label. The labels can be set to user-friendly names, such as TmpDir, on partitions whose device filename may be easy to forget, such as /dev/sdf3. A label is assigned when the partition or volume is formatted using mkfs. You can possibly determine a filesystem's label using the e2label command.

Instead of a device partition or volume, a *Universally Unique IDentifier (UUID)* may be used, and they are becoming the preferred method for partition identification within /etc/fstab. A UUID, as its name implies, is a unique identification number. This number is assigned when the partition or volume is formatted using mkfs. You can determine a filesystem's UUID using the blkid command. This number is persistent, and it is especially useful if you have a large number of partitions attached to your system.

Mount Point   The *mount point* is the absolute directory reference for where the partition or volume is to be attached to the Linux directory structure. This is the same *mount_point* you would use with the mount command, if you were to mount the filesystem temporarily. For a swap filesystem, you will see the keyword swap here. Swap filesystems are covered in more detail later in this chapter.

Filesystem Type   The filesystem type is the filesystem type code used to identify the partition or volume's filesystem format. It is the same *fstype* that you would use with the mount command if you were to mount the filesystem temporarily.

For a swap filesystem, you will see the keyword swap here. Swap filesystems are covered in more detail later in this chapter.

Mount Options   The comma-separated keywords listed here are the various mount options that you can set on the filesystem. They are the same *opts* that you would use with the mount -o command if you were to mount the filesystem temporarily. To see the more popular mount options, look back to the "Attaching a Filesystem Temporarily" section, and to see all the various mount options, type **man mount** at the command line.

Backup Selection   This field is a Boolean field in that it can be set to either 0 (false) or 1 (true). A 0 indicates that the dump utility will not conduct a backup on this filesystem. A 1 indicates that the dump utility will conduct a backup. If the dump backup utility is not used on the system, this setting is ignored. It has no effect on other backup utilities.

Integrity Check Order   This field can be set to a blank, 0, 1, or 2, and it is used by the fsck utility (covered later in this chapter) at system boot. A blank or 0 indicates that fsck should never be run on the filesystem at system boot.

A 1 indicates that this filesystem takes priority, and it should be checked, if needed, before any other filesystems. Typically, the filesystem mounted at root (/) is the only filesystem set with this indicator.

A 2 indicates that this filesystem should be checked, if needed, at system boot. However, it and any other filesystem due for a check and set to 2 will be checked *after* the filesystem(s) set to 1 is checked.

Should you need to mount any filesystems recently added to the /etc/ fstab manually, you can simply type **mount -a** at the command line using super user privileges. The command mounts all of the filesystems listed in /etc/fstab that are not currently attached to the virtual directory structure.

A sample /etc/fstab file is shown in Listing 4.1. This sample file is not from any particular distribution, but instead it was created for educational purposes only.

Listing 4.1: Sample **/etc/fstab** file

```
#partition              mount point fs type  options         dump  fsck
/dev/sda1               /           ext4     defaults        0     1
UUID=7e32f35e-[...]     /boot       xfs      defaults        0     0
Label=Temp             /home/temp   ext4     users, noauto   0     0
/dev/sdb3               /var        ext4     defaults        0     2
server01:/nfsshare      /tmp/share  nfs      users           0     0
/dev/mapper/a-swap      swap        swap     defaults        0     0
```

Let's look at the sample /etc/fstab file line by line.

Line 1   Any line preceded by a hash mark (#) in this file is a comment line. You'll typically find the column headers listed as a comment, which is handy.

Line 2   The partition, /dev/sda1, is to be mounted at root (/) in the virtual directory structure. It is an ext4 filesystem, and all of the default mount options (rw, suid, dev, exec, auto, nouser, and async) are to be used. The dump backup utility is not used on this system, and therefore a zero (0) is listed in the dump column for this filesystem. Since this is the root directory, this filesystem takes priority and should be checked, if needed, before any other filesystems. Thus, a one (1) is listed in the fsck column.

Line 3   This partition is identified in the /etc/fstab by its UUID number. The number is snipped in the listing, and the full UUID for this partition is 7e32f35e -c9e1-4aa9-8bab-df362221d706. A UUID number is long, because it is a unique identification number. Even with their long length, UUIDs are becoming the preferred method for partition identification within /etc/fstab. This partition is an xfs filesystem type, and it is mounted at the /boot mount point. The fsck utility does not run on XFS filesystems, and therefore a zero (0) is listed in the fsck column for this filesystem.

Line 4   This particular partition uses a label for identification, Label=Temp. Also, notice that it has a few options set, users and noauto. The users option allows any user authorized to use this system, not just those with super user privileges, to mount or unmount this labeled partition. Also, the noauto option keeps the partition from being mounted at boot time or when a mount -a command is issued.

Line 5   The /dev/sdb3 partition is mounted at /var. Note that in its fsck column, a number two (2) is used. This means that this filesystem should be checked, if needed, at system boot. However, if /dev/sda1 is due for a check, /dev/sdb3 will be checked *after* /dev/sda1 has been checked.

Line 6   The server01:/nfsshare is a Network File System (NFS) share. NFS is discussed in detail in Chapter 10. However, it is briefly covered later in this chapter as well. For the first LPIC-2 exam, be aware of what an NFS share partition looks like within the /etc/fstab file.

Line 7   The last line in the sample /etc/fstab listing, /dev/mapper/a-swap, is a logical volume. Logical volumes are covered in detail in Chapter 5. This particular volume is mounted as the swap filesystem. The swap filesystem is covered later in this chapter.

When the system reboots, it will issue the mount -a command. Every filesystem listed in /etc/fstab, which does not have the noauto option set, will be mounted to its designated mount point in the system's virtual directory structure.

In recent years, a few /etc/fstab alternatives have been considered. One alternative was the /etc/fstab.d/ directory. It was proposed in January 2012, and then after many concerns were raised, the proposal was dropped.

Looking at systemd Mount Units

Distributions using systemd have additional options for persistently attaching filesystems. Filesystems can be specified either within the /etc/fstab file (covered earlier) or within a mount unit file. A mount unit file provides configuration information for systemd (covered in Chapter 1) to mount and control designated filesystems.

 On Linux servers using **systemd**, if you only use the **/etc/fstab** file, **systemd** still manages these filesystems. The mount points listed in **/etc/fstab** are converted into native units when either the server is rebooted or **systemd** is reloaded. In fact, using /etc/fstab for persistent filesystems is the preferred method over manually creating a mount unit file. For more information on this process, type **man systemd-fstab-generator** at the command-line.

A single mount unit file is created for *each* mount point, and the file name contains the mount point's absolute directory reference. However, the absolute directory reference has its preceding forward slash (/) removed; subsequent forward slashes are converted to dashes (-); and any trailing forward slash is removed. Mount unit file names also have a .mount extension. For example, the mount point, /home/temp/, would have a mount unit file named home-temp.mount.

A mount unit file's contents mimic other systemd unit files, with a few special sections and options. Using the /home/temp/ mount point, here is an example mount unit file for it:

```
# cat /etc/systemd/system/home-temp.mount
[Unit]
Description=Test Mount Units

[Mount]
What=/dev/sdo1
Where=/home/temp
Type=ext4
Options=defaults
SloppyOptions=on
TimeOutSec=4

[Install]
WantedBy=multi-user.target
#
```

There are three sections needed at a minimum for this particular mount point: [Unit], [Mount], and [Install]. The What option within the [Mount] section can use the device file name or a UUID, such as /dev/disk/by-uuid/*UUID*.

The SloppyOptions is helpful, in that if set to on, it ignores any mount options not supported by a particular filesystem type. By default, it is set to off. Another helpful option is the TimeOutSec. If the mount command does not complete by the number of designated seconds, the mount is considered a failed operation.

Be sure to include the [Install] section and set either the WantedBy or the RequiredBy options. If you do not do this, the filesystem will not be mounted upon a server reboot.

Any newly configured mount unit file should be tested, especially prior to conducting a system reboot. First test a manual mounting of the file system as shown snipped here:

```
# blkid | grep /dev/sdo1
/dev/sdo1: UUID="474c1322-[...] TYPE="ext4"
#
# mkdir /home/temp
#
# touch /home/temp/test_mount_units.txt
#
# ls /home/temp
test_mount_units.txt
#
# mount -t ext4 /dev/sdo1 /home/temp
#
# ls /home/temp
lost+found
#
# umount /home/temp
#
# ls /home/temp
test_mount_units.txt
#
```

Once you have tested the new filesystem via manually mounting and unmounting it, the mount unit file is tested. Using the example mount unit file, the following demonstrates testing it on a CentOS distribution:

```
# systemctl daemon-reload
#
# systemctl start home-temp.mount
#
# ls /home/temp
lost+found
#
```

In the preceding example, the first command reloads systemd and the second command has systemd mount the filesystem using the home-temp.mount mount unit file. The second systemctl command is similar to how a service is started, in that it uses the start command.

Next make sure that the filesystem is properly mounted. The mount command works in this situation, and so does the systemctl command. Like a service, you use the systemctl command to obtain a mounted filesystem's status as shown snipped here:

```
# mount | grep /home/temp
/dev/sdo1 on /home/temp type ext4 (rw,relatime,data=ordered)
#
# systemctl status home-temp.mount
● home-temp.mount - Test Mount Units
   Loaded: loaded (/etc/systemd/system/home-temp.mount; [...]
   Active: active (mounted) since Sat 2017-06-11 16:34:2[...]
    Where: /home/temp
     What: /dev/sdo1
  Process: 3990 ExecMount=/bin/mount /dev/sdo1 /home/temp[...]
[...]
#
```

There is one additional step required. To ensure systemd will mount the filesystem persistently, the mount unit file must be enabled as shown here:

```
# systemctl enable home-temp.mount
Created symlink from
/etc/systemd/system/multi-user.target.wants/home-temp.mount to
/etc/systemd/system/home-temp.mount.
#
```

Keep in mind that you should only use mount unit files if you need to tweak the persistent filesystem configuration. If you do not, it's best to use a /etc/fstab record to mount the filesystem persistently. For more mount unit file information, see the systemd.mount man pages.

Viewing Attached Filesystems

If you want to view your system's current filesystem attachment structure or view various block device's attributes, several handy tools are available. Each provides a different viewpoint of the virtual directory structure and its underlying storage media.

A simple command to start with is the mountpoint command. It requires no super user privileges. Just type in **mountpoint *directory_reference*** at the command line, and if you receive the message is a mount point, then a filesystem has been mounted at that particular directory location, as shown on the Ubuntu distribution here:

```
$ mountpoint  /
/ is a mountpoint
$
$ mountpoint /home
/home is not a mountpoint
```

Another nice command is blkid. With the blkid command, you can view the various block devices and their attributes. Super user privileges are not required to see some of the information; however, accounts without super user privileges receive unverified cached information or none at all. Here is a snipped example of using the blkid command on an Ubuntu distribution:

```
$ blkid
$
$ sudo blkid
[sudo] password for christine:
/dev/sda1: UUID="0dc214d2-[...] TYPE="ext4"
/dev/sda5: UUID="1b0f22a2-[...] TYPE="swap"
/dev/sdb1: UUID="06c41b8c-[...] TYPE="ext4"
/dev/sdc1: UUID="14ca54ba-[...] TYPE="ext4"
/dev/sdc2: LABEL="Extra" UUID="82558d44-[...] TYPE="ext4"
$
$ sudo blkid -L Extra
/dev/sdc2
$
$ sudo blkid -U 14ca54ba-ee44-4588-a32c-dee848a0435f
/dev/sdc1
$
```

Notice in the previous example that using super user privileges with the blkid command typically gives more thorough information (and therefore it's a good idea to use it with super user privileges). Also notice that you can display information concerning a particular block device using either its label (-L option) or its UUID (-U option). If desired, you can specify a single device file name with the blkid command, as shown here on a CentOS distribution:

```
# blkid /dev/sda1
/dev/sda1: UUID="7e32f35e-[...] TYPE="xfs"
#
```

When temporarily mounting a partition or volume, which was covered earlier in this chapter, you can use the mount command with the -L option to specify the device's label, instead of using its partition or volume designation.

You can also use the -U option with the mount command to specify the device's UUID, instead of using its partition or volume designation. The UUID may need to be encased in a set of double quotation marks. Also, because it is easy to mistype the UUID number, be sure to use the shell's tab command completion feature when entering it.

The lsblk command can also be a helpful utility. It works in a similar manner to the blkid command in that it also displays block device information. Since some of its options pull information from the blkid command, it's best to have super user privileges when employing it. Here are two snipped lsblk command examples on a CentOS distribution:

```
# lsblk
NAME             MAJ:MIN RM   SIZE RO TYPE MOUNTPOINT
sda                  8:0   0    8G  0 disk
├─sda1               8:1   0  500M  0 part /boot
└─sda2               8:2   0  7.5G  0 part
  ├─centos-root 253:0   0  6.7G  0 lvm  /
  └─centos-swap 253:1   0  820M  0 lvm  [SWAP]
[...]
#
# lsblk -f
NAME            FSTYPE      LABEL UUID            MOUNTPOINT
sda
├─sda1          xfs               7e32f35e-[...]  /boot
└─sda2          LVM2_member       YlVA3C-[...]
  ├─centos-root
                xfs               1ea0c68f-[...]  /
  └─centos-swap
                swap              09502922-[...]  [SWAP]
[...]
#
```

The -f option used with lsblk will display the block device's UUIDs and labels, if used. Note that not all distributions display block device UUIDs with the lsblk -f command and option.

Another utility that you may find helpful is the e2label command. With this utility, you can view any filesystem label for an ext2, ext3, or ext4 filesystem, as shown here on an Ubuntu distribution:

```
$ sudo e2label /dev/sdc2
[sudo] password for christine:
Extra
```

Notice that super user privileges are required to use the e2label command. You can also change the label by passing a new label name after the device name in this command string.

 You can also change the label as well as the UUID of a filesystem by using the tune2fs command. This utility is covered later in this chapter.

The findfs utility can also be helpful in managing your filesystems. It allows you to view the block device associated with a particular UUID or label, as shown on an Ubuntu system here:

```
$ findfs LABEL=Extra
/dev/sdc2
$
$ findfs UUID="82558d44-16af-4f2c-8670-6f54732bb31b"
/dev/sdc2
$
```

The `findfs` command does not require super user privileges. However, unfortunately, when typing in a filesystem UUID for the `findfs` command, the shell's tab command completion is not available.

Besides the utilities mentioned thus far, other utilities can be useful, including these:

`findmnt`: Displays mounted filesystems in a tree format.

`df`: Displays mounted filesystem disk space usage, and it includes the filesystem's mount point.

`mount`: Displays mounted filesystems, and it includes the filesystem's mount point.

You can use the `-l` option on the `mount` command to show labels and you can use the `-t` `fstype` command to narrow your list to only certain filesystem types, as shown in this snip from a CentOS distribution:

```
$ mount -t xfs
/dev/mapper/centos-root on / type xfs [...]
/dev/sda1 on /boot type xfs [...]
$
```

All of these utilities are very helpful in managing your filesystems. You may not need them in every situation, but they are handy to know for the various circumstances that you may encounter on your Linux systems.

Exploring Additional Filesystem Topics

Certain filesystem topics require additional discussion. These include looking at filesystems, such as memory-based, swap, Btrfs, and so on. Also, filesystems that can be automatically mounted (outside the /etc/fstab file) are a special topic that requires additional detail.

Looking at Memory-Based Linux Filesystems

When covering filesystems, a topic that deserves some special attention is virtual or memory-based Linux filesystems. These filesystems are unique in that their data resides within system memory, but you can view their data using their mount points.

You'll often find these memory-based filesystems mounted at /dev, /proc, /sys, and /run or one of their subdirectories. A few memory-based filesystem examples are devpts, proc, sysfs, and tmpfs.

To understand this a little better, let's look at proc files. Files in the proc filesystem are memory based (virtual), typically contain system information, and are continually updated, though they show no size information in their file listings. A virtual proc file's long listing on a CentOS system example is shown here:

```
$ ls -l /proc/cpuinfo
-r--r--r--. 1 root root 0 Jan 13 13:12 /proc/cpuinfo
```

Even though the /proc/cpuinfo file resides in memory, by using the filesystem's mount point, the data can be accessed or viewed. Here is a snipped example of displaying the /proc/cpuinfo file's data, which resides in memory:

```
$ cat /proc/cpuinfo
processor       : 0
vendor_id       : GenuineIntel
[...]
power management:

$
```

These filesystems are created when the system boots and are often automatically mounted by the system. However, if special options are needed for these memory-based filesystems, you'll see them listed in the /etc/fstab file.

Because these filesystems are memory based, when a system shuts down, all of the data residing in these filesystems is deleted. Therefore, they are a great means for storing system, process, and other temporary information.

Looking at the Btrfs Filesystem

The Btrfs filesystem takes a unique approach to how high-level formatting and mounting is accomplished. It deserves some special attention.

A relatively newer filesystem, Btrfs was created to handle large file and filesystem sizes as well as the needed scalability. The Btrfs filesystem uses a B-tree data structure, thus its name. This data structure provides a proficient method for accessing and updating large data blocks stored on the filesystem. This method can also stay proficient as the filesystem size grows.

The Btrfs filesystem provides data integrity through COW (described earlier in this chapter). This COW implementation, in addition to protecting metadata, provides snapshots, allowing you to move the filesystem back to a previous snapshot should a disaster occur. The term *snapshot*, as used here, refers to a distinct unit. It shares the data and metadata with the original snapshot partition, but it acts as its own partition by allowing files to be added (which won't appear on the original partition), and it can be mounted independently.

Btrfs also provides data integrity via a checksum feature and its own integrated RAID functionality. You can set up RAID 0, RAID 1, or RAID 10 configurations using Btrfs.

Performance and scalability attributes of Btrfs include its own integrated logical volume management (logical volumes are covered in detail within Chapter 5). It also provides data compression and defragmentation.

A few simple examples will help in your understanding of the Btrfs filesystem. All of the examples shown in this section were performed on a CentOS distribution using super user privileges.

 Before you attempt any of these commands on your system, determine if the Btrfs filesystem type is supported by your Linux distribution's kernel by typing **grep btrfs /proc/filesystems** at the command line. If nothing displays, Btrfs is not supported. If you get the word btrfs back, then the Btrfs filesystem is supported by your system.

First, formatting partitions with the Btrfs filesystem is similar to doing other high-level formatting using the mkfs command. The example shown here is done on two partitions, because you will need at least two partitions to implement Btrfs RAID:

```
# mkfs -t btrfs  /dev/sdb  /dev/sdc
Btrfs v3.16.2
See http://btrfs.wiki.kernel.org for more information.

Turning ON incompat feature 'extref':
increased hardlink limit per file to 65536
adding device /dev/sdc id 2
fs created label (null) on /dev/sdb
  nodesize 16384 leafsize 16384 sectorsize 4096 size 8.00GiB
#
```

In the preceding example, because no options besides -t btrfs were used and two partitions were included, Btrfs is set up to use RAID 0 (disk striping) for data and RAID 1 (mirroring) for its metadata. Other options will allow you to set up different RAID types. Also, you can include more than two partitions.

You can then mount the Btrfs filesystem. However, you only need to mount one of the partitions in order to mount the Btrfs filesystem RAID volume, as shown here:

```
# mkdir BTrial
#
# mount /dev/sdb BTrial
#
# ls BTrial
#
# touch BTrial/file_b.txt
#
# ls BTrial
file_b.txt
#
```

Once the Btrfs filesystem volume is mounted, you can use it like any other filesystem, as shown in the preceding example. Notice, though, that there is no lost+found directory as you would see on an ext4 filesystem mount point.

A handy command to help you with your Btrfs filesystem is the `btrfs filesystem show` command. An example of this command is shown here:

```
# btrfs filesystem show
Label: none  uuid: 5125431c-37c3-4d70-aa85-42b8b4fea161
        Total devices 2 FS bytes used 384.00KiB
        devid    1 size 4.00GiB used 847.12MiB path /dev/sdb
        devid    2 size 4.00GiB used 827.12MiB path /dev/sdc
Btrfs v3.16.2
#
```

Exploring Btrfs Subvolumes

Another interesting Btrfs feature is subvolumes. Btrfs subvolumes can act like subdirectories of a mounted Btrfs filesystem. They are not true subdirectories in that they can be mounted separately from their parent volume. Even though a Btrfs subvolume can be mounted, it is not a block device. A *Btrfs subvolume* is an organizational structure.

A Btrfs subvolume structure is similar to a POSIX namespace. This namespace type is used in programming, and it is sometimes called a *naming system*. The structure uses names to refer to particular resources. These names are organized in a manner to avoid collisions. Name collision has many illustrations. For example, when referring to a city, if we refer to a city named Carmel, a collision occurs, because there are many cities named Carmel. To avoid collisions, often the city and an additional name (such as a state and/or country name) is used to avoid confusion (collisions). For example, in the United States of America, Carmel, Indiana is a different city from Carmel, New York, and they are both different from Carmel, California. Namespace structures often employ such methods to avoid resource name collisions.

Btrfs subvolumes are useful in certain situations. For example, you can maintain a pool of subvolumes, mounting them as the data they contain is needed.

To create a subvolume, the parent Btrfs volume must first be mounted. The basic syntax to create a subvolume is as follows.

```
btrfs subvolume create Mount_Point/Subvolume_Name
```

The *Mount_Point* is the current parent Btrfs volume's mount point. The Subvolume_Name is the subvolume's name.

To demonstrate creating a subvolume, we'll use the Btrfs filesystem created earlier. Before creating a subvolume, the Btrfs filesystem (parent volume) must be mounted as shown here on a CentOS distribution using super user privileges:

```
# mount /dev/sdb BTrial
#
# ls BTrial/
file_b.txt
#
# btrfs subvolume create BTrial/subvolume_1
Create subvolume 'BTrial/subvolume_1'
#
```

Once the subvolume is created, named `subvolume_1` in the preceding example, the subvolume is accessed via a directory reference. You can create additional files, subdirectories, and even additional subvolumes within the subvolume.

You check subvolumes via the `subvolume list` command along with the parent volume's mount point. The -t option is handy in that it displays the information in table format as shown here:

```
# btrfs subvolume list  BTrial
ID 258 gen 13 top level 5 path subvolume_1
#
# btrfs subvolume list -t BTrial
ID    gen   top level    path
--    ---   ---------    ----
258   13    5            subvolume_1
#
```

To access the subvolume, you use a directory reference that includes its parent volume's mount point and the subvolume name. In essence, the subvolume is accessed as a subdirectory of the parent volume's mount point. Here is an example:

```
# cd BTrial/subvolume_1
#
# pwd
/root/BTrial/subvolume_1
#
# touch file_b_subvol.txt
#
# ls
file_b_subvol.txt
#
# cd
#
```

```
# pwd
/root
#
# ls -R BTrial/
BTrial:
file_b.txt  subvolume_1

BTrial/subvolume_1:
file_b_subvol.txt
#
```

By default, to mount a Btrfs parent volume and subvolume, you only need to mount the parent volume:

```
# umount BTrial
#
# mount /dev/sdb BTrial
#
# btrfs subvolume list -t BTrial
ID   gen   top level   path
--   ---   ---------   ----
258  14    5           subvolume_1
#
```

Once the parent volume is mounted, any mounted subvolumes can be checked. This is done via the subvolume list command, as shown in the preceding example.

If you have either an ext2, ext3, or ext4 filesystem, you can convert it to a Btrfs filesystem without losing any data! Just employ the btrfs-convert utility. Once converted, the original filesystem image is stored in a subvolume named ext2_subvol by default. For more details, enter **man btrfs-convert** at the command line.

Access to Btrfs parent volumes and subvolumes are via an entry point. This entry point is called the *default level*, and it is typically set to the top level (sometimes called the *top level subvolume*). The standard top level has an ID number of 5, as shown in the preceding example.

You can determine a subvolume's default level via the subvolume get-default command. The example shown here confirms that the current default level is the top level (ID 5):

```
# btrfs subvolume get-default BTrial
ID 5 (FS_TREE)
```

A subvolume can be mounted independently of its parent volume. However, if the subvolume's default level is set to ID 5 (top level), data in the parent volume can still be accessed. Remember that Btrfs subvolumes are not true block devices.

There are two methods to mount a subvolume and *not* allow access to the parent volume. For the first method, you must modify your mount command options. In the following example, the parent and subvolume are unmounted, and then the subvolume is mounted in a manner to prevent access to the parent volume:

```
# umount BTrial
#
# mkdir BTrial_subvol
#
# mount -o subvol=subvolume_1 /dev/sdb BTrial_subvol
#
# ls BTrial_subvol/
file_b_subvol.txt
#
# umount BTrial_subvol
#
```

After the parent volume is unmounted, a new directory (mount point) is created, BTrial_subvol. Next, the subvolume is mounted using a special mounting option -o subvol=*subvolume_name*, where *subvolume_name* is subvolume_1, the name of the example subvolume. A directory listing shows only the subvolume's data, and there is no access provided to the parent volume.

The second method for mounting a subvolume and blocking parent volume access is to change the subvolume's default level ID number. The default level ID number is changed from 5 to the subvolume's ID number. The subvolume must be mounted, because the mount point is used in the command that changes this ID number. The subvolume set-default command is used to accomplish this task, as shown here:

```
# mount /dev/sdb BTrial
#
# btrfs subvolume list -t BTrial
ID    gen   top level    path
--    ---   ---------    ----
258   14    5            subvolume_1
#
# btrfs subvolume get-default BTrial/subvolume_1
ID 5 (FS_TREE)
#
```

```
# btrfs subvolume set-default 258 BTrial/subvolume_1
#
# btrfs subvolume get-default BTrial/subvolume_1
ID 258 gen 14 top level 5 path subvolume_1
#
# umount BTrial
#
```

Once the subvolume's default level is changed, only a simple mount command is used. No access is granted to the parent volume. An example of this is shown here:

```
# mount /dev/sdb BTrial_subvol
#
# ls BTrial_subvol/
file_b_subvol.txt
#
# btrfs subvolume get-default BTrial_subvol
ID 258 gen 14 top level 5 path subvolume_1
#
# btrfs subvolume list -t BTrial_subvol
ID    gen   top level    path
--    ---   ---------    ----
258   14    5            subvolume_1
#
# umount BTrial_subvol
#
```

 If you need to remove a subvolume, it must be mounted. The command to remove the subvolume after it is mounted is `btrfs subvolume delete` *Mount_Point*.

Exploring Btrfs Snapshots

Once you understand Btrfs subvolumes, you can further explore Btrfs snapshots, because snapshots are also subvolumes. Snapshots are fairly easy to create and manage (once you understand Btrfs subvolume concepts).

To create a snapshot, the parent volume or subvolume must be mounted. The `btrfs` command to use is `subvolume snapshot`. The basic syntax for this command is as follows:

```
btrfs subvolume snapshot Volume_Mount_Point Snapshot_Name
```

The *Volume_Mount_Point* in the subvolume snapshot command designates what mounted volume or subvolume to snapshot. The *Snapshot_Name* in the command designates the snapshot subvolume mount point.

Building on the previous Btrfs examples, a snapshot is created of the subvolume mounted at BTrial_subvol. The snapshot command is broken onto two lines for clarity and shown in the example here:

```
# mount /dev/sdb BTrial_subvol
#
# ls BTrial_subvol/
file_b_subvol.txt
#
# btrfs subvolume snapshot BTrial_subvol \
> BTrial_subvol/my_snapshot
Create a snapshot of 'BTrial_subvol' in 'BTrial_subvol/my_snapshot'
#
# ls -RF BTrial_subvol/
BTrial_subvol/:
file_b_subvol.txt   my_snapshot/

BTrial_subvol/my_snapshot:
file_b_subvol.txt
#
```

 NOTE   Recall that the Btrfs filesystem has its own integrated RAID functionality. Therefore, even though the snapshot is a subvolume, the data can be protected via the chosen RAID structure.

Because a snapshot is a subvolume, you can view its details via the subvolume list command. An example is shown here, using the previously created snapshot:

```
# btrfs subvolume list BTrial_subvol
ID 258 gen 27 top level 5 path subvolume_1
ID 259 gen 26 top level 258 path my_snapshot
#
```

Just like regular subvolumes, snapshot subvolumes can be mounted with or separately from their parent volume. Also, it is fairly simple to create a system snapshot subvolume. Creating a snapshot subvolume prior to software upgrade allows an easy rollback to the earlier software version, should the need arise.

Obviously, there is a lot to the Btrfs filesystem. If you desire further information, type **man btrfs-filesystem** at the command line or use your favorite web search engine. You may see Btrfs listed as experimental, which is no longer true.

Looking at Optical Filesystems

Optical filesystems are typically used for CD-ROM and DVD storage media. Besides the popular ISO-9660 filesystem, there are several others used on Linux systems, as shown in Table 4.4.

TABLE 4.4   Optical filesystem types

Name	Description/Features
El Torito	An ISO-9660 extension that allows a system to boot from optical media with an ISO-9660 filesystem and this extension. Up to 63 different El Torito boot images can be stored on a single optical disk. This extension is recognized by Linux.
HFS	Hierarchical File System (HFS) created by Apple for use on its Mac OS devices. It can be used on partitions as well as optical media. As of Mac OS X v10.6, HFS filesystems are read-only and cannot be created or updated. On Linux, HFS filesystems are read-only.
HFS+	An extended HFS version created by Apple for use on its Mac OS devices. It can be used on partitions as well as optical media. HFS+ filesystems are read/write on Mac OS. On Linux, HFS+ filesystems are read-only, unless HFS+ journaling is disabled; then writing is allowed.
ISO-9660	A cross-platform filesystem standard published by the International Organization for Standardization (ISO) for optical media. Many CDs and DVDs have traditionally been formatted with this filesystem. It does have some limitations, which can be overcome by various extensions.
Joliet	A series of ISO-9660 extensions created by Microsoft, which enable the support of longer filenames and allow the use of Unicode for internationalization purposes. These extensions are recognized by Linux.
Rock Ridge	A series of ISO-9660 extensions (sometimes called attributes), which enable the support of longer filenames (up to 255 bytes), symbolic links, more than eight levels of directory hierarchy, and so on. These extensions are recognized by Linux.
UDF	Universal Disk Format (UDF) is a cross-platform specification ISO/IEC 13346 standard primarily for DVDs. On Linux, it is considered an alpha product, and it is part of the UDFtools package.

Often, you'll have preformatted optical media that automatically mounts when loaded onto a Linux system. However, if you need to mount it manually, similar to manually mounting USB flash drives covered earlier in this chapter, you'll need to know its device name.

Typically, optical media can be accessed via the /dev/cdrom device name. Older distributions may also use the /dev/dvd device name. In addition, your system may use device names such as /dev/cdrw and /dev/dvdrw to indicate a read/write optical media device.

An example of automatically mounting a DVD on an Ubuntu distribution, then unmounting it, and then manually mounting it to a subdirectory is shown here:

```
$ mount
[...]
/dev/sr0 on /media/christine/STAR_TREK__INTO_DARKNESS type udf
(ro,nosuid,nodev,uid=1001,gid=1001,iocharset=utf8,umask=0077,
uhelper=udisks2)
$
$ ls -l /dev/cdrom
lrwxrwxrwx 1 root root 3 Jan 19 15:29 /dev/cdrom -> sr0
$
$ sudo umount /media/christine/STAR_TREK__INTO_DARKNESS
[sudo] password for christine:
$
$ sudo mount -t udf /dev/cdrom Temp
mount: block device /dev/sr0 is write-protected,
mounting read-only
$
$ ls -F Temp
VIDEO_TS/
$
$ blkid
/dev/sr0: LABEL="STAR_TREK__INTO_DARKNESS" TYPE="udf"
$
$ mount | grep udf
/dev/sr0 on /home/christine/Temp type udf (ro)
$
$ sudo umount Temp
$
$ ls Temp
$
```

In the preceding example, notice that the /dev/cdrom device file is symbolically linked to the /dev/sr0 device file. The mount command was used with the -t udf filesystem type option to mount the video DVD manually to the Temp subdirectory. Besides that slightly different mount command, the same commands that you use to mount and unmount a USB flash drive manually are used on the video DVD.

A handy utility for use with optical media and an ISO image file, known as an *ISO image*, is the mkisofs command. An ISO image (ISO for short) is a single file that contains all of a CD/DVD device's files. ISOs are often used to create bootable optical disks for operating system installation.

The mkisofs utility has been replaced on recent distributions by the gen-isoimage utility. Not to worry. The genisoimage utility is an exact duplicate of mkisofs. However, you may find that mkisofs does not exist on your system or within its man pages. Simply substitute **genisoimage** in place of mkisofs. Keep in mind that the certification objectives mention mkisofs and not the genisoimage utility.

You can create an ISO from a directory of files using mkisofs. You can also copy files from an optical disk to create an ISO image on your system. An example of creating an ISO image file from a bootable optical disk's files on a CentOS distribution is shown here:

```
# mount -t iso9660 /dev/cdrom Temp
mount: /dev/sr0 is write-protected, mounting read-only
#
# ls Temp
AUTORUN.INF        initrd.trk     memdisk       syslinux.cfg
boot.cat           isolinux.bin   memtest.x86   trinity.ico
bootlogo.jpg       isolinux.cfg   pxelinux.0    trk3
disableautorun.exe kernel.trk     pxelinux.cfg  vesamenu.c32
#
# mkisofs -o my.iso Temp/
I: -input-charset not specified, using utf-8 [...]
Using TRSRU000.EXE;1 for  Temp/trk3/t[...]
  6.47% done, estimate finish Tue Jan 19 10:35:05 2017
[...]
Total translation table size: 0
Total rockridge attributes bytes: 0
Total directory bytes: 10240
Path table size(bytes): 82
Max brk space used 1b000
77335 extents written (151 MB)
#
# ls my.iso
my.iso
#
```

```
# file my.iso
my.iso: # ISO 9660 CD-ROM filesystem data 'CDROM [...]
#
# eject /dev/cdrom
#
```

There are a great many options and a good deal of flexibility associated with the mkisofs command. If used without any other options besides -o, the mkisofs utility will make a pure and unbootable ISO-9660 ISO file. Table 4.5 shows a few of the more relevant options associated with the topic covered here. However, to review all of the various mkisofs options, type either **man mkisofs** or **man genisoimage**, depending on your distribution.

TABLE 4.5   A few mkisofs command options

Option	Description
-b *ISO_file*	Enables the El Torito extension to make the resulting ISO bootable. The bootable ISO file is passed to mkisofs via this option.
-boot-info-table	Option used with El Torito bootable ISO files. Inserts a boot information table in the ISO file.
-boot-load-size *size*	Specifies how many 512-byte virtual sectors to load when using the -no-emul-boot option. Best to set to 4 (or a multiple of 4), because some BIOSes may have problems if it is not.
-c *catalog*	Required for an El Torito bootable CD. It specifies a boot catalog file (catalog). If not in the local directory, the pathname must be relative to the source path specified.
-hfs	Makes an ISO9660/HFS hybrid ISO file. Best to use with either the -map or -magic option.
-J	Enables Joliet extensions, which allows support for other OSs. If another OS does not handle Joliet extensions, the disk can still be read by the OS.
-magic *file*	Indicates the magic file (*file*) to set creator and type information needed for various Apple/Unix encoded files. Necessary with -hfs option if -map option is not used.
-map *file*	Indicates the map file (*file*) to set creator and type information needed for various Apple/Unix encoded files. Necessary with -hfs option if -magic option is not used.

Option	Description
-no-emul-boot	Used for an El Torito bootable CD. It specifies that the boot image used is a "no emulation" image, so when the system loads and executes this ISO, it will do so without executing any disk emulation.
-o *filename*	Specifies the ISO file (*filename*) to be created.
-R	Enables Rock Ridge extensions, which allows support for other OSs. It does not change file ownership or file permissions.
-r	Enables Rock Ridge extensions, which allows support for other OSs. It also changes file ownership to root, enables read access to all users, and removes write permissions.
-udf	Enables support for the UDF filesystems. Typically used on video DVDs.

You'll often see combinations of extension support given to ISO images. For example, to create an ISO image to be shared with a Windows OS, you might use the -JR options with your mkisofs command.

Making a bootable ISO image copy takes a little more work than the previous mkisofs example. As shown in the following CentOS distribution example, using super user privileges you must first unmount the disk if it is automatically mounted and then mount it as a loopback device using the -o loop option, which will allow the system to access the files more readily:

```
# umount /run/media/chris/TRK_3.4/
#
# blkid
[...]
/dev/sr0: UUID="20[...]" LABEL="TRK_3.4" TYPE="iso9660"
#
# mount -o loop /dev/cdrom Temp
#
```

Once it is mounted as a loopback device, you can then employ the tar command (covered in Chapter 2) to carry out a recursive copy of the files to a newly created directory, DiskCopy, without creating an intermediate tar file, as shown here:

```
# mkdir DiskCopy
#
# tar -cvf - Temp | (cd DiskCopy && tar -xvf -)
```

```
Temp/
[...]
#
```

You can certainly use other methods besides tar to copy the files to a new directory. Once the files are copied, the mkisofs command can be put to use with several options. This will create a bootable ISO file called myBoot.iso and place it two directories above where the copied files are located (DiskCopy/Temp), as shown here:

```
# cd DiskCopy/Temp
#
# ls
AUTORUN.INF        initrd.trk    memdisk      syslinux.cfg
boot.cat           isolinux.bin  memtest.x86  trinity.ico
[...]
#
# mkisofs -b isolinux.bin -c boot.cat -no-emul-boot \
> -boot-load-size 4 -boot-info-table -JR \
> -o ../../myBoot.iso ../Temp
I: -input-charset not specified, using utf-8
(detected in locale settings)
Using TRSRU000.EXE;1 for  ../Temp/trk3/trsrun-1_0-nq.exe
 (trsrun-1_0.exe)
Size of boot image is 4 sectors -> No emulation
  6.47% done, estimate finish Tue Jan 19 11:36:06 2017
[...]
Total translation table size: 2048
Total rockridge attributes bytes: 3217
Total directory bytes: 10240
Path table size(bytes): 82
Max brk space used 1c000
77349 extents written (151 MB)
#
```

Notice in the preceding example that the -JR options were used with the mkisofs command, which enables both Joliet and Rock Ridge extensions on this ISO file. You can see in the mkisofs command's output that the total Rock Ridge attribute bytes are displayed (3217). Refer back to Table 4.5 if you need a refresher on all of the mkisofs options and parameters used.

You can double-check that the ISO file is bootable by using the file command, as shown here:

```
# cd
# file myBoot.iso
```

```
myBoot.iso: # ISO 9660 CD-ROM filesystem data
'CDROM                           ' (bootable)
#
```

Now that the ISO file is ready to go, you can record it onto another optical device using the cdrecord utility. Here is a snipped example of using the cdrecord utility to record the ISO file onto a CD:

```
# umount Temp
#
# cdrecord -tao speed=0 dev=/dev/cdrom myBoot.iso
Device type   : Removable CD-ROM
Version       : 5
[...]
Device seems to be: Generic mmc2 DVD-R/DVD-RW.
Using generic SCSI-3/mmc   CD-R/CD-RW driver (mmc_cdr).
Driver flags  : MMC-3 SWABAUDIO BURNFREE
[...]
Track 01: Total bytes read/written:
158410752/158410752 (77349 sectors).
[...]
#
```

 If the cdrecord utility is not available on your system, you can install it via the CDRTools package.

The options used with the cdrecord utility include the -tao option, which sets the Track At Once (TAO) writing mode that is required here, and the speed=0 option, which allows the lowest possible speed for an MMC-compliant driver's optical drive and media. Now that these steps are complete, a bootable image, which can be used on various OSs, resides on the CD.

There are many ways to use optical media and various optical media utilities available on Linux. Hopefully, this section ignited some useful ideas that you can explore on your Linux system.

Looking at Swap Filesystems

The term *swap filesystem* is really inaccurate. A swap partition doesn't hold a filesystem, but instead it is a special location on the disk that acts as the system's swap space (also called virtual memory). Understanding swap space was covered in Chapter 2.

Typically, a swap partition is created, formatted, and added to the /etc/fstab configuration file at system installation. However, you may need to create and manage additional swap partitions, for example, if you increase your system's RAM.

You aren't limited to swap disk partitions. You can set up your swap space on a logical volume (covered in Chapter 5) and increase the size as needed using logical volume resizing tools. You can also create a file using the dd command to make it the proper size and then turn it into a swap file to be used as swap space.

A couple of useful utilities are available for checking your current swap space. Most likely, you're already familiar with the free command. But you may not be familiar with using the swapon command for swap space statistics, as shown here on a CentOS distribution:

```
# free -m
        total   used    free    shared   buff/cache   available
Mem:    993     467     136     7        390          365
Swap:   819     0       819
#
# swapon -s
Filename    Type        Size      Used   Priority
/dev/dm-1   partition   839676    0      -1
#
```

In the preceding example, the -m option is used with the free command in order to show the memory statistics in megabytes. Notice that this is a pretty quiet system, memory-wise. Also, the -s option is used with the swapon command to show swap space statistics. On some distributions, you can get the same information from the /proc/swaps file.

The Priority column within the preceding example's swap space statistics is shown as a negative one (-1). The priority number determines which swap space is used first (if there are multiple swap spaces). If you do not set the priority number, it is created by the Linux kernel, and it will be set to a negative number. You can set the priority yourself and, if you do, it must be a positive number. Higher numbers get higher use preference.

You can have more than one system swap space. In fact, in many cases, it is desirable to do so. The Web has some great discussions on this performance issue. Open your favorite search engine, and type in **purpose of multiple Linux swap partitions** to find a few.

Once you've created a new disk partition, the mkswap command is used to "format" the partition into a swap partition. An example on a CentOS system, using super user privileges, is shown here:

```
# mkswap /dev/sdd1
Setting up swapspace version 1, size = 838652 KiB
no label, UUID=3297cded-69e9-4d35-b29f-c50cf263fb8b
#
```

```
# blkid
[...]
/dev/sdd1: UUID="3297cded-[...]-c50cf263fb8b" TYPE="swap"
#
```

Now that the swap partition has been properly prepared, you can activate it using the swapon command, as shown here:

```
# swapon /dev/sdd1
#
# swapon -s
Filename        Type        Size      Used    Priority
/dev/dm-1       partition   839676    0       -1
/dev/sdd1       partition   838652    0       -2
#
# free -m
        total   used    free    shared    buff/cache    available
Mem:    993     581     66      8         345           249
Swap:   1638    0       1638
#
```

You can see that the swap space size has increased significantly due to adding a second swap partition. If desired, the new swap partition's use priority can be changed from its current negative two (-2) to a higher priority using the swapon command, as shown here:

```
# swapoff /dev/sdd1
#
# swapon -p 0 /dev/sdd1
#
# swapon -s
Filename        Type        Size      Used    Priority
/dev/dm-1       partition   839676    4       -1
/dev/sdd1       partition   838652    0       0
#
```

You must first use the swapoff command on the swap partition before changing its priority and then use the swapon -p *priority* command to change the preference priority. You can set *priority* to any number between 0 and 32767. For the various options available with the swapon command, type **man swapon** at the command line.

WARNING   If you want to move your system to a new swap space, do not use the swapoff command on the current swap space until your new swap partition is set up and ready to go. Otherwise, you may end up with a hung system.

If all is well with your new swap partition, you should add it to the /etc/fstab file so that it will be persistent. You can closely mimic the current swap partition's record settings, but be sure to change the partition name to your new swap partition.

Looking at Network-Based Filesystems

Some filesystems are not locally attached, but instead they physically reside on network-attached storage media. These network-based filesystems are shared across the network.

Filesystems that can be included in this category are NFS (covered in Chapter 10) and Common Internet File System (CIFS), which is implemented via Samba (also covered in Chapter 10) and is called SMBFS on older systems.

You can stretch the filesystem definition a bit to include Network Attached Storage (NAS), which has entire Linux distributions available to implement it, such as OpenMediaVault (http://www.openmediavault.org/). NAS typically uses NFS or CIFS at its core. While we're stretching definitions, let's include Storage Attached Networks (SANs). You can implement a SAN with the iSCSI protocol on Linux.

You need a brief introduction to network-based storage because, even though NFS and Samba are handled in Chapter 10 and are part of the second certification exam objectives, the first certification exam objectives require you to know AutoFS. The AutoFS service is covered in the next section.

Understanding Auto-Mounting

Many distributions automatically mount removable media, such as USB flash drives and DVDs, to a Linux virtual directory. Typically, on various current distributions, removable media are automatically mounted to the /run or /media directory. Dynamic device management (udev, covered in Chapter 3) is responsible for handling these devices' auto-mounting functions. Older Linux distributions used the Hardware Abstraction Layer Daemon (HALd), and they often mounted removable media to the /mnt directory.

Exploring AutoFS

Another type of auto-mounting is geared to network-based filesystems. For example, the automounter service, AutoFS, can manage NFS filesystems' auto-mounting functions, as well as those of other network-based filesystems. You can put NFS filesystems in the/etc/fstab configuration file so that they are automatically mounted upon system boot. However, in some cases, the system can experience performance problems using this arrangement. By allowing AutoFS to manage mounting NFS filesystems, you avoid these problems. For example, one way that AutoFS helps with system performance is that NFS filesystems are mounted when they are accessed instead of at system boot time. This makes the boot process much faster.

If not currently installed on your system, the AutoFS service and various required files are in the autofs package. Also, if you'd like to follow along with the commands, it's suggested that you read about NFS in Chapter 10 and set up a simple NFS filesystem that you can use with AutoFS.

AutoFS uses the /etc/auto.master file, also called the *master map*, as its primary configuration file for managing automatically attached network storage. The master map file gives the AutoFS service information concerning network-based filesystems, including where they are currently located, where they are to be mounted, and options to use.

 You can define a different master map in the AutoFS configuration file, /etc/sysconfig/autofs or /etc/default/autofs (depending on your distribution). The configuration file also contains other settings, such as how long a mounted filesystem can be inactive before it is detached (time-out value). However, the currently defined master map file works in most cases, so there is rarely a need to change it.

Except for comment lines that are preceded with a hash mark (#), each master map entry has this basic format:

```
mount-point map-name [mount-options]
```

Entries in the master map are one of three different map types. Each map type determines the exact syntax of the master map entry. These maps are described here:

Built-in Map   The built-in map file is triggered by having -hosts in a master map's map-name field. It has AutoFS mount all of the NFS filesystems available from any NFS server listed within a special directory, /net. (This is sometimes called *lazy mounting*, but built-in mapping sounds better.)

For example, if you wanted the NFS filesystem from the NFS server, Server01, to be mounted, you would need the directory, /net/Server01, along with the built-in map entry in the master map file. The NFS filesystem from Server01 would be automatically mounted at /net/Server01. Thus, the directories not only serve as a trigger for the built-in map, but they also serve as a mount point. You can have multiple directories under /net, one for each NFS server. For example, if you also have NFS filesystems on Server02 and Server03, the /net/Server02 and /net/Server03 directories would act as triggers for the built-in map and mount points too.

A typical built-in map entry in the master map file looks like this:

```
/net    -hosts
```

Direct Map   A direct map entry is simply a pointer to another file. The other file is /etc/auto.direct. This entry is typically not in the master map by default, so if you desire it, you will have to add it. A typical direct map entry in the master map file looks like this:

```
/-  /etc/auto.direct
```

Within the /etc/auto.direct file, absolute directory path names are listed for the mount points as well as options and their associated servers. Two typical entries in the direct map file may look like this:

```
/home/bucket   server01.acme.com:/home/bucket
/mnt/nfs/var/nfsshare   192.168.56.101:/var/nfsshare
```

Indirect Maps   An indirect map entry is also a pointer to another file. The other file is
/etc/auto.*directory* (listed in the certification objectives as /etc/auto.[dir]), where
directory matches the mount point. For example, the typical default indirect map entry in
the master map file looks like this:

```
/misc   /etc/auto.misc
```

The /etc/auto.misc file is typically used for mounting removable media, such as optical
filesystems or USB flash drives. It also has several entries available for you to use if they
include no preceding hash mark, such as this one:

```
cd   -fstype=iso9660,ro,nosuid,nodev :/dev/cdrom
```

Because this file is an indirect map, this entry will cause any CDs to mount under the
/misc directory, specifically using the mount point /misc/cd. Thus, the term *indirect map*
is applied here. Whereas a direct map file indicates an absolute directory reference, such as
/home/bucket, an indirect map file only lists a relative map point, such as cd, which will be
mounted under the directory listed in its master map entry, such as /misc.

You can have additional indirect map files as needed. For example, if your company had
special projects called ProjectX and ProjectY, which required temporary (but not backed
up) work space under the /tmp directory for several systems, you could set up two NFS
filesystems and then add an entry as such in your master map:

```
/tmp   /etc/auto.tmp
```

Continuing this example, you would then create the file /etc/auto.tmp. This indirect map
file could contain the following two entries:

```
projectx   -fstype=nfs4,rw :/tmp/projectx
projecty   -fstype=nfs4,rw :/tmp/projecty
```

 An older version of a map file, which is often still found on some systems,
is the /etc/autofs.net file. However, this file is a script and not a true
map file. It has been replaced within AutoFS by the built-in map within the
master map file.

Additional sub-master maps can also be included, which are handy if you have a large-
scale network-based filesystem deployment. This entry in the master map includes any maps
(whose entries must follow the same formatting as those in the master map file) located in
the /etc/auto.master.d/ directory:

```
+dir:/etc/auto.master.d
```

When you modify the AutoFS configuration and map files, you will need to restart your AutoFS service. Also, remember that you will need to access the directory to be automatically mounted via AutoFS (an ls command will suffice) to trigger the auto-mount of that directory. You can check that the directory is mounted using the df command. If the directory is not mounting, check the /var/log/messages file for any pertinent error messages.

 If you are using AutoFS for NFS filesystems and get an error similar to unable to read auto.master, then you may need to comment out the +auto.master line, by putting a hash mark (#) in front of it.

AutoFS and its maps allow a great deal of flexibility for auto-mounting network-based filesystems. If you decide to set up AutoFS and add any network-based filesystems to it that currently are mounted via the /etc/fstab file, be sure to remove them from /etc/fstab or you'll have some interesting situations during your next system reboot!

Exploring Automount Units

If your Linux server has systemd, you can configure on-demand mounting as well as mounting in parallel using automount units. In addition, you can set filesystems to unmount automatically upon lack of activity.

An automount unit configuration file operates very similarly to a mount unit file (covered earlier in this chapter). The naming convention is the same, except that the file extension is .automount.

Within an automount unit configuration file, there are only three options available. The Where option is a required option, and it is configured the exact same way as it is in mount unit files.

The DirectoryMode option is not a required option. The option's setting determines the permissions placed on any automatically created mount point and parent directories. By default, it is set to the 0755 octal code.

The TimeOutIdleSec option is also not required. This particular option allows you to configure the amount of time (in seconds) a mounted filesystem has been idle. Once the time limit is reached, the filesystem is unmounted. By default this option is disabled.

Looking at Encrypted Filesystems

One more filesystem group that deserves a look is the encrypted filesystems. *Encryption* is the process of turning text that a human or machine can read (plaintext) into text that a human or machine cannot read (cipher text) and vice versa, using an algorithm (cipher). Decryption reverses the process, allowing you to access/read the text and it usually requires a key (or set of keys) by the algorithm. The key(s) is often a passphrase, which is similar to a password.

A couple of Linux-encrypted filesystems can be used on Linux and include the following:

dm-crypt   The dm-crypt encryption can be implemented using the cryptsetup utility. This type can be a little confusing, because the software behind cryptsetup is called dm-crypt, and it's very basic encryption type is also called dm-crypt.

The dm-crypt encrypted filesystems use Device Mapper (which is also used in LVM and covered in Chapter 5). This allows plaintext to be used by applications, while any writes to the volume are encrypted.

Unless you have a good grasp on encryption, it is not recommended that you use the dm-crypt type. It uses an unsalted passphrase hash for its single key, and it maintains no metadata on the volume.

eCryptfs   A newer encrypted filesystem type, eCryptfs, is actually a pseudo-filesystem in that it is layered on top of a current filesystem. The layer provides encryption capabilities, which include picking which cipher algorithm to use, such as AES, Blowfish, des3_ede, and so on.

One of the nicest things about eCryptfs is that there are no new utility commands to learn. As long as you have the software package `ecryptfs-utils` on your system, you simply use the `mount` command with eCryptfs as follows:

```
# mount -t ext4 /dev/sdd1 /home
# mount -t eCryptfs /home /home
```

The first mount command attaches the partition to the Linux virtual directory structure. The second mount command layers the eCryptfs filesystem on top of it. It's that easy!

The eCryptfs filesystem encrypts a partition or volume on a file-by-file basis. Also, encrypted files can be copied between various systems, because eCryptfs metadata is stored in each file's header.

You can add options such as key byte size, cipher choice, file name encryption, and so on via the mount command's -o option. In addition, eCryptfs volumes can be automatically mounted at system boot via entries in the `/etc/fstab` file.

You may not be able to find eCryptfs documentation in your system's man pages. To explore the various eCryptfs options and additional details, see `http://linux.die.net/man/7/ecryptfs`.

Linux Unified Key Setup (LUKS)   LUKS is an improved dm-crypt encrypted filesystem type. It also can be implemented using the `cryptsetup` utility and uses the Device Mapper. It is the preferred method over the basic dm-crypt type.

LUKS uses a master key and multiple user keys. It maintains metadata on the volume, and it provides improved anti-forensic features.

Keep in mind that encryption does not mean protection from hardware disasters. It only helps to protect data from those who should not have access to it. You still need to employ all of the other important items and methods in order to protect your data's integrity.

Certification objectives may refer to the LUKS encrypted filesystem type as `dm-crypt/LUKS`.

Maintaining Linux Filesystems

Part of managing a Linux system includes properly maintaining its filesystems via various system utilities available for this purpose. Filesystem maintenance comprises manipulating standard filesystems via utilities such as tune2fs, monitoring a filesystem's health, and repairing filesystems when problems are encountered.

The monitoring of SMART devices is also included in this section. We cover various utilities that can assist in this necessary task.

Adjusting a Filesystem

Adjusting a filesystem may be required for various reasons, and these can include many different items. For example, you may decide to change a filesystem's label because it no longer reflects the filesystem's purpose.

Utilities for adjusting filesystems are often specific to a certain filesystem or group of filesystems. For the extended filesystems ext2, ext3, and ext4, you can use the utilities shown in Table 4.6 to modify them.

TABLE 4.6   Adjustment utilities for ext2, ext3, ext4 filesystems

Utility	Description
debugfs	An interactive utility that can be used to modify metadata
e2label	Modifies a filesystem label
resize2fs	Enlarges or shrinks an unmounted filesystem
tune2fs	Tunes filesystem attributes, including UUIDs and labels

The tune2fs command is a very versatile utility. Here is an example on an Ubuntu distribution of changing an unmounted disk partition's UUID with super user privileges:

```
$ sudo blkid /dev/sdc1
[sudo] password for christine:
/dev/sdc1: UUID="14ca54ba-ee44-4588-a32c-dee848a0435f" TYPE="ext4"
$
$ uuidgen
b77a195a-e5a8-4810-932e-5d9adb97adc6
$
$ sudo tune2fs /dev/sdc1 \
> -U b77a195a-e5a8-4810-932e-5d9adb97adc6
tune2fs 1.42.9 (4-Feb-2014)
```

```
$
$ sudo blkid /dev/sdc1
/dev/sdc1: UUID="b77a195a-e5a8-4810-932e-5d9adb97adc6"
TYPE="ext4"
$
```

Notice that in the preceding example, the uuidgen command was used to generate a new UUID. It's a good idea to generate a UUID with this utility because the UUID needs to be unique, and this utility can produce a reasonably unique number. The tune2fs command was then used to change the /dev/sdc1 partition's UUID via the -U option. The tune2fs command in the previous code snippet was split into two lines so it would display properly in the example, but you can put it all on one line if desired.

With some distributions moving to XFS as their default filesystem, understanding the various XFS utilities has become even more important. Utilities used to modify the XFS filesystem are shown in Table 4.7.

TABLE 4.7   Adjustment utilities for an XFS filesystem

Utility	Description
xfs_admin	Tunes filesystem attributes, including UUIDs and labels
xfs_fsr	Improves filesystem file layout
xfs_growfs	Expands filesystem size

The newer Btrfs filesystem is likely to show up on a distribution that you are managing. Therefore, we've included utilities to modify the Btrfs filesystem in Table 4.8.

TABLE 4.8   Adjustment utilities for a Btrfs filesystem

Utility	Description
btrfs balance	Reallocates and balances data across the filesystem. (It often has the side benefit of reducing the filesystem reserved for metadata.)
btrfs-convert	Converts an extended filesystem (ext2, ext3, or ext4) into a Btrfs filesystem and vice versa.
btrfstune	Tunes filesystem attributes and enables/disables extended features.
btrfs property set	Sets various filesystem properties, such as the label.

The format of the Btrfs commands varies in where you place options and parameters. Therefore, it's always a good idea to check their man pages prior to using them. However, that can be tricky too. For example, to view the man pages for the btrfs balance command, you must type in **man btrfs-balance** at the command line. If you can't find what you are looking for, then try typing in **man -k btrfs** to view the various Btrfs man pages available.

Keep in mind that you can also adjust a filesystem's behavior via its mount options. The man pages for the mount command have a special section, called FILESYSTEM SPECIFIC MOUNT OPTIONS, which contains rather useful information concerning this topic.

Checking and Repairing a Filesystem

Protecting, monitoring, and repairing a filesystem all go hand in hand. Fortunately, there are many tools in this category that you can employ.

> You'll notice that some utilities listed in an earlier section in the chapter are also listed in the tables provided here. This is because many of these utilities serve the multiple purposes of checking and repairing a filesystem as well as adjusting it in some way.

For extended filesystems, the utilities shown in Table 4.9 can be used to check and repair the filesystems.

TABLE 4.9   Check/repair utilities for ext2, ext3, and ext4 filesystems

Utility	Description
fsck.*	Checks and optionally repairs Linux filesystems. Replace the * with the filesystem type that you wish to check, such as fsck.ext4.
debugfs	An interactive utility that can be used to extract data in order to move it to a new location.
dumpe2fs	Displays filesystem information.
tune2fs	Displays filesystem attributes with the -l option.

The fsck.* utilities use the lost+found directories, covered earlier in the chapter. If fsck is used to repair a filesystem and it finds files that are not complete (such as a data-filled file that has an inode number but has no name in any directory table), it will attempt to restore these files and place them in the lost+found directory for that filesystem.

The fsck command is a just a front end for all of the various fsck filesystem check utilities, such as fsck.*fstype*, where *fstype* is ext4, xfs, brtfs, and so on. However, the fsck.xfs and fsck.btrfs utilities do nothing. Because the XFS and Btrfs filesystems have their own repair utilities and do not operate in the same fashion as extended filesystems, these fsck utilities are just stubs.

You can check all of the filesystems listed within the /etc/fstab file by issuing the fsck command using super user privileges at the command line. Be aware, though, this is of no value for certain filesystems, such as XFS and Btrfs.

Utilities used to check and repair the XFS filesystem are shown in Table 4.10.

TABLE 4.10   Check/repair utilities for an XFS filesystem

Utility	Description
xfs_check	Checks filesystem's consistency but does no repairs. Considered the "dry run" of an xfs_repair. No longer included in many current distributions.
xfsdump	Creates a backup (dump) of the filesystem's data and its attributes, which can be directed to either storage media, a file, or standard output.
xfs_info	Displays and checks filesystem information. Equivalent to running xfs_grow -n.
xfs_metadump	Copies filesystem metadata to a file.
xfs_repair	Checks filesystem's consistency and does any needed repairs. If the xfs_check command is not on your system, use xfs_repair -n to perform a "dry run" instead.
xfsrestore	Restores filesystem's data and its attributes from a backup dump created by the xfsdump utility.

The XFS filesystem has many wonderful utilities to assist you in keeping it up and running. At the command line, type **man -k xfs** to see a list of XFS utility man pages on your system.

The Btrfs filesystem has several utilities for checking and repairing a filesystem. A few are shown in Table 4.11.

TABLE 4.11   Check/repair utilities for a Btrfs filesystem

Utility	Description
btrfs check	Checks and optionally repairs an unmounted (offline) filesystem.
btrfs get property	Gets various filesystem properties, such as the label.
btrfs rescue	Recovers a damaged filesystem.

Utility	Description
`btrfs restore`	Restores files from a damaged filesystem. This is the most powerful of the three repair utilities (check, rescue, and restore).
`btrfs scrub`	Reads all data from disk and checks for consistency. Can adversely affect system load when running.
`btrfsck`	Replaced by the `btrfs check` utility, but may call it on some distributions.

A Btrfs filesystem also has the `btrfs filesystem` utility, which has useful subcommands such as show and df. These subcommands provide filesystem information, such as device UUIDs and disk usage information.

 Real World Scenario

When Filesystems Go Bad

It's not a case of *if* it will happen. It's a case of *when* it will happen. Filesystems will have problems and, more than likely, it will be up to you to fix things.

It's a mistake to handle filesystem repairs on the fly or look up utility information as a problem is occurring. Properly maintaining a filesystem includes implementing plans for these minor calamities, so that they don't turn into major disasters. In addition, these recorded plans should be reviewed and tested on a regular basis, just like any other disaster plans.

Of course, data backups (covered in Chapter 2) and disaster plans are vitally important, but you need planned preventive practices as well. These should include regularly scheduled maintenance for all of your filesystems, along with continual filesystem health monitoring. The filesystem utilities covered in this section can be of assistance to you as you implement these practices.

Using SMART

The acronym SMART stands for "Self-Monitoring Analysis and Reporting Technology." SMART devices are typically hard or solid-state disk drives. However, they can also be SCSI attached tape drives.

A SMART device has a built-in system that allows the device to communicate with software on your system. This communication includes providing disk health information—potentially looming disk failure warnings and self-test results.

 On Linux, the software for communicating with SMART devices comes from the `smartmontools` package. This package may not be installed on your system by default.

The smartd daemon enables monitoring on any attached SMART devices that have SMART capability. It can check the devices every so many minutes and log errors via its configured log file, by default either /var/log/smartd.log, /var/log/messages, or /var/log/syslog, depending on your distribution.

You can configure smartd using its configuration file. Depending on your distribution, the file is either /etc/smartd.conf or /etc/smartmontools/smartd.conf.

You can directly interact with SMART devices using the smartctl command. To view an individual device's information, you can use the smartctl -i *device* command, where *device* is the device's filename. Here's a snipped example of using this command on a Debian-based distribution, showing a USB-attached drive without SMART capabilities:

```
$ sudo smartctl -i /dev/sda1
[...]
Vendor:             Maxtor
Product:            OneTouch II
[...]
Device does not support SMART
$
```

The device does not have to be mounted on the system in order to obtain its SMART information. It only needs to be attached to the system, which can be handy.

Many hard drives have SMART capabilities. Here's a snipped example of using the smartctl command on an Ubuntu distribution, showing an older hard drive that has SMART capabilities:

```
$ sudo smartctl -i /dev/sda6
[...]
=== START OF INFORMATION SECTION ===
Model Family:      Seagate Momentus 5400.6
[...]
SMART support is: Available—device has SMART capability.
SMART support is: Enabled
```

Notice in the preceding example not only that the drive has SMART capabilities but also that SMART support is enabled. If your disk does not have SMART support enabled, you can enable it using the smartctl -s on *device* command.

Even if your device does have SMART capabilities, it may not be supported by the smartctl command. To see what device types are supported, type **smartctl -P showall | less** at the command line. This is a long list, so you do need to pipe (|) the output into the less utility if you desire to peruse the information. You can also visit the website https://www.smartmontools.org/wiki/Supported_USB-Devices to see what USB devices are supported by the smartctl command.

You can conduct a number of tests on your hard drive via the -t option on the smartctl command. The option takes different arguments to determine which test type to conduct. For instance, you can conduct a selftest, short, or long test. Both the selftest and short test options are fairly quick. The long test option can be rather lengthy, as shown in this snipped example:

```
$ sudo smartctl -t long /dev/sda6
[...]
=== START OF OFFLINE IMMEDIATE AND SELF-TEST SECTION ===
[...]
Testing has begun.
Please wait 74 minutes for test to complete.
Test will complete after Fri Jan 22 12:44:10 2017

Use smartctl -X to abort test.
```

In the preceding example, you can see that the test will take 74 minutes to complete. Some drives can take even longer! No output will be shown on your terminal when the test is complete. However, you can check on the test's progress, as shown here:

```
$ sudo smartctl -a /dev/sda6 | grep -A1 "Self-test execution"
Self-test execution status:  ( 249)Self-test routine in progress
                                90% of test remaining.
$
```

Don't let the term Self-test routine in the preceding listing confuse you. All of the tests are self-tests, and the long test is an extended self-test.

Once the test is done, you can see the results by using the smartctl -a *device* command. In fact, you can use this command at any time to determine the current overall health of your drive. The smartctl -a option shows a great deal of information. Therefore, it may be a good idea to redirect the output to a file or pipe it into the less utility. A snipped example of this command on an Ubuntu distribution is shown here:

```
$ sudo smartctl -a /dev/sda6
[...]
Self-test execution status: (   0) The previous self-test routine
                                completed without error or
                                no self-test has ever been run.
[...]
$
```

You can get a summary of the SMART device's health by asking for its health status. The status information is derived from various tests. Here's a snipped example of a drive's summary health status:

```
$ sudo smartctl -H /dev/sda6
[...]
SMART overall-health self-assessment test result: PASSED
$
```

In the preceding example, the status of PASSED means that all is well with the drive. If for some reason a failing status is reported, this means that the drive has already failed or will fail shortly. You can view the device's error logs by typing in **smartctl -l error** *device*, using super user privileges.

A SMART device is not smart. Be aware that any strange error rates provided from a SMART device may indicate a looming disk failure. This is true even though a SMART device does not indicate a future drive failure may occur in its health status.

Using smartctl and smartd to assess various devices' health are helpful additions to the utilities used in maintaining filesystem health. Of course, like many other things in life, if you don't use them, they're of no benefit.

Summary

Filesystems provide a link between your system's data and its various applications. Understanding how different filesystems work and are managed is critical to protecting data and its integrity. In addition, you need to understand the different utilities used to maintain the various filesystems. You must avoid disasters by tuning and monitoring filesystem health. However, when problems do occur, it's important to know just how to repair or restore a filesystem.

Exam Essentials

Describe /etc/fstab configuration file entries. The /etc/fstab configuration file, also called the Filesystem Table, is the primary configuration file for mounting filesystems at system boot time. File entries contain the filesystem identification, which may be a device's partition filename, volume, UUID, label, network-based filesystem id, or swap filesystem. Mount points are included along with various mount options, filesystem types, and indicators for dump backups and filesystem checks. No filesystems handled by AutoFS should have entries in this file.

Explain how to handle swap partitions and files. While a swap partition is typically created, formatted, and added to the /etc/fstab configuration file at system installation, you may need to create and manage additional swap space. Swap space can be set up on a disk partition, logical volume, and even a file. Once a new disk partition (or file) is created, the mkswap command is used to enable the partition to be used as swap space. It is then activated using the swapon command. The swap space status can be checked via the swapon -s command or cat /proc/swaps. The swapoff command deactivates the designated swap space.

Summarize the use of filesystem UUIDs.   A UUID is a unique identification number assigned when the partition or volume is formatted using mkfs. You can determine a filesystem's UUID using either the blkid or the lsblk -f command. Filesystems can be mounted either persistently in the /etc/fstab file using their UUID or temporarily using the -U *uuid* option on the mount command. An unmounted filesystem's UUID can be changed using the tune2fs -U *new-uuid* command. Be sure to obtain the *new-uuid* from the uuidgen command.

Describe the AutoFS configuration files.   Used for the automatic mounting of network-based filesystems, the AutoFS service uses several configuration files. The primary AutoFS configuration file, which controls its behavior, is either /etc/sysconfig/autofs or /etc/default/autofs, depending on the distribution being used. AutoFS uses the /etc/auto .master file, called the master map, for managing automatically attached network storage. Within the master map are records that either activate automatic mounting of filesystems or call other configuration files (maps). A direct map entry points to the file /etc/auto .direct, which directs AutoFS to mount the designated network-based filesystems to mount points via absolute directory references. An indirect map points to various files, /etc/auto.*directory*, where *directory* matches the mount point. These maps designate network-based filesystems to mount points via relative directory references under the *directory*.

Explain UDF and ISO9660 tools.   A utility used with optical media is the mkisofs command that can create an ISO image. It is often used to create bootable optical disks for operating system installation. The mkisofs utility has been replaced on recent distributions by the genisoimage utility. You can create a bootable ISO from a directory of files using mkisofs and check that the ISO file is bootable using the file command. The ISO image can be burned onto another optical device using the cdrecord utility.

Summarize the Linux encrypted filesystems.   A very basic encryption type, dm-crypt encryption, can be implemented using the cryptsetup utility. It uses an unsalted passphrase hash for its single key and maintains no metadata on the volume. LUKS is an improved dm-crypt encrypted filesystem type, which can also be implemented using cryptsetup. It is preferred over the basic dm-crypt type. LUKS uses a master key and multiple user keys, and it maintains metadata on the volume.

A newer encrypted filesystem type, eCryptfs, is layered on top of a current filesystem. The layer provides the encryption capabilities and provides various cipher algorithm choices to use. It requires two mounts. The first mount command attaches a partition or volume to the Linux virtual directory structure, and the second layers the eCryptfs filesystem on top of it. The eCryptfs filesystem encrypts on a file-by-file basis, and it stores metadata in each file's header.

Describe the various extended filesystem utilities.   Tools that are used to modify the extended filesystems, ext2, ext3, and ext4, include debugfs, e2label, resize2fs, and tune2fs. Utilities that can check on, report on, repair, or back up extended filesystems include the debugfs, dumpe2fs, and tune2fs -l commands. Also, the fsck utility is a front end that checks and optionally repairs extended filesystem types. The command format is fsck.*fstype*, where *fstype* is ext2, ext3, or ext4.

Explain the XFS filesystem tools.   Some distributions now use XFS as their default filesystem. Therefore, understanding the various XFS utilities has become even more important. Utilities that are used to check on, display information concerning, and repair XFS filesystems include the xfs_check, xfsdump, xfs_info, xfs_metadump, xfs_repair, and xfsrestore commands. The tools that modify XFS filesystem attributes or increase its size include the xfs_admin, xfs_fsr, and xfs_growfs utilities.

Summarize the Btrfs filesystem.   The newer Btrfs filesystem provides data integrity through COW, which, in addition to protecting metadata, provides snapshots, allowing you to move the filesystem back to a previous snapshot. Data integrity is also provided via a checksum feature and an integrated RAID feature, which allows RAID 0, RAID 1, or RAID 10 configurations.

Review Questions

You can find the answers in the Appendix.

1. Assuming that you have or can obtain super user privileges, which of the following commands would allow you to make an ext2 filesystem on the /dev/sdd2 partition? (Choose all that apply.)

    A. `mkfs -t ext2 /dev/sdd2`

    B. `mkfs -t extended2 /dev/sdd2`

    C. `mkfs.ext2 /dev/sdd2`

    D. `mke2fs.ext2 /dev/sdd2`

    E. `mke2fs /dev/sdd2`

2. Which one of the following files contains a list of all of the filesystems your system supports?

    A. `/proc/filesystems`

    B. `/etc/mtab`

    C. `/proc/mounts`

    D. `/proc/swaps`

    E. `/proc/cpuinfo`

3. Assuming that you have (or have access to) super user privileges to temporarily attach a formatted filesystem to the Linux virtual directory structure, which of the following should you do? (Choose the best answer.)

    A. Issue the `mkfs` command, using super user privileges, on the filesystem.

    B. Run the `e2label` utility on the filesystem.

    C. Nothing. The AutoFS service will automatically attach it.

    D. Add an entry for this filesystem in the /etc/fstab configuration file.

    E. Use the `mount` command with the proper options and parameters.

4. The number c344d0f9–6d54–4a92-ad4d-c5a44fac2eeb identifies a filesystem that needs to be temporarily mounted. Which option for the needed command should you choose? (Choose the best answer.)

    A. `-o`

    B. `-L`

    C. `-U`

    D. `-a`

    E. `-n`

5. Which command should be used to force filesystems to write metadata residing in memory to the filesystem media structures? (Choose the best answer.)

    A. `unmount`

    B. `fuser`

    C. `lsof`

    D. `sync`

    E. `dmesg`

6. Each entry in the /etc/fstab has several required fields. Which of the following could describe one of the fields? (Choose all that apply.)

   A. Mount point

   B. Filesystem type

   C. cpio backup option

   D. Filesystem check priority

   E. AutoFS identifier

7. You need to determine a filesystem's UUID. Which utility can help you do this? (Choose the best answer.)

   A. findmnt

   B. blkid

   C. e2label

   D. findfs

   E. mount

8. Using a Btrfs filesystem, which RAID configurations can be implemented? (Choose all that apply.)

   A. RAID 0

   B. RAID 1

   C. RAID 5

   D. RAID 6

   E. RAID 10

9. Which of the following are considered extensions of the ISO9660 standard? (Choose all that apply.)

   A. UDF

   B. btrfs

   C. El Torito

   D. Joliet

   E. Rock Ridge

10. Which command should be used to create an ISO? (Choose the best answer.)

   A. mkfs

   B. mkfs -t iso

   C. mkisofs

   D. cdrecord

   E. mount -t iso9660

11. You've just created a new disk partition, /dev/sde3, and want to prepare it as swap space. Which command do you use? (Choose the best answer.)

    A. `mkfs -t swapon /dev/sde3`

    B. `mkswap /dev/sde3`

    C. `swapon /dev/sde3`

    D. `swapoff /dev/sde3`

    E. `swapon -s`

12. Which of the following map types can be found in the /etc/auto.master file? (Choose all that apply.)

    A. Built-in

    B. Direct

    C. Indirect

    D. SMART

    E. Road

13. You want to change the AutoFS service's master map to a different configuration file than the /etc/auto.master file. Which configuration file might you edit to accomplish this, depending on your distribution? (Choose the best answer.)

    A. `/etc/auto.direct`

    B. `/etc/auto.misc`

    C. `/etc/autofs.net`

    D. `/etc/auto.tmp`

    E. `/etc/sysconfig/autofs`

14. Which of the following encrypted filesystems is a layered filesystem? (Choose the best answer.)

    A. XFS

    B. dm-crypt

    C. eCryptfs

    D. LUKS

    E. Btrfs

15. Which of the following is *not* a utility for adjusting the ext2, ext3, and ext4 filesystems? (Choose the best answer.)

    A. `debugfs`

    B. `e2label`

    C. `resize2fs`

    D. `uuidgen`

    E. `tune2fs`

16. You have generated a new UUID and want to assign it to an unmounted ext4 filesystem. Which utility do you use? (Choose the best answer.)

    A. debugfs

    B. e2label

    C. resize2fs

    D. blkid

    E. tune2fs

17. You have super user privileges, and you type the command `fsck.xfs` to run a filesystem check on an XFS filesystem. What will happen? (Choose the best answer.)

    A. You corrupt the filesystem, because you did not unmount it first.

    B. You only receive a report on filesystem health.

    C. No information is displayed, but if errors are found, you are asked if you would like to attempt a repair.

    D. You only receive a report on filesystem health, and if errors are found, you are asked if you would like to attempt a repair.

    E. Nothing.

18. You have a Btrfs filesystem that has performed well for a long time. However, for some reason, it has suffered a catastrophic problem and you need to restore files. Which utility should you use? (Choose the best answer.)

    A. btrfs check

    B. btrfs get property

    C. btrfs rescue

    D. btrfs restore

    E. btrfs scrub

19. Which of the following commands checks for inconsistencies but does not conduct any repairs for an XFS filesystem? (Choose the best answer.)

    A. xfs_check

    B. xfsdump

    C. xfs_info

    D. xfs_metadump

    E. xfsrestore

20. You have a disk drive partition /dev/sdc3 that supports SMART and has it enabled. Assuming that you have super user privileges, which command will show you a quick summary status, including whether or not it has passed the overall health self-assessment test? (Choose the best answer.)

    A. smartctl -t short /dev/sdc3

    B. smartctl -H /dev/sdc3

    C. smartctl -i /dev/sdc3

    D. smartctl -a /dev/sdc3

    E. smartctl -t long /dev/sdc3

Chapter 5

Administering Advanced Storage Devices

THE FOLLOWING EXAM OBJECTIVES ARE COVERED IN THIS CHAPTER:

- ✓ 204.1 Configuring RAID
- ✓ 204.2 Adjusting Storage Device Access
- ✓ 204.3 Logical Volume Manager

RAID and logical volumes are considered advanced storage device configurations, because of their complicated structures and the many confusing terms surrounding them. These configurations can assist in protecting your data as well as improving your overall data access speeds. In addition, as your data's storage needs increase, these storage structures offer rather seamless storage media progression. Various utilities can help in setting up kernel options to support and configure these advanced devices. Some of these utilities are also helpful in monitoring the devices. Understanding these devices and their configuration and administration is important for your data's management. All of these topics are covered in this chapter.

Configuring RAID

For system data protection and performance reasons, many companies and individuals turn to RAID. *Redundant Array of Independent Disks (RAID)* is a set of multiple physical disk partitions combined in a virtual single drive. Depending on the chosen RAID structure, this logical drive can achieve improved access performance, increased data protection, and reduced down time.

 The RAID acronym used to stand for Redundant Array of Inexpensive Disks.

In this section, the various RAID structures are explored. Picking the correct structure is critical for achieving your desired results. In addition, getting a drive ready for RAID membership, setting up a RAID array, and managing that array are covered so that you are ready to implement RAID on your Linux server(s).

Understanding RAID

RAID arrays come in various structures (sometimes called *RAID levels*). Each structure is denoted by a number, and it provides particular benefits. While not a substitute for backups, some RAID structures can improve data protection. Other structures may improve read times. First, determine your particular data needs for each system and application. Once you have those requirements in hand, review these various RAID structures to choose the best ones for meeting your data needs.

RAID 0   This RAID structure is also called *disk striping*. Each data file is spread across multiple disks in the array. For example, if you have two disks, then a file's data is broken into chunks between the two disks. A two-disk RAID 0 diagrammed example is shown in Figure 5.1.

FIGURE 5.1   RAID 0 diagram

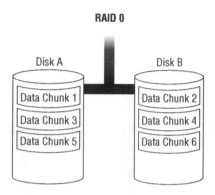

Reading and writing to the different file chunks can occur in parallel, which can potentially speed up reads and writes to the file. This RAID structure is typically used for swap space or graphics applications. The downside is that there is no fault tolerance. If any drives in the RAID array go bad, you lose the whole array.

RAID 1   *Disk mirroring* is the other name for this RAID structure type. The same data is written to two different disks, which provides an original and a mirrored backup copy. The structure requires a minimum of two disks, and the disks must always be in multiples of two: one disk for the data and one disk for the data copy (mirror). A two-disk RAID 1 example is shown in Figure 5.2.

FIGURE 5.2   RAID 1 diagram

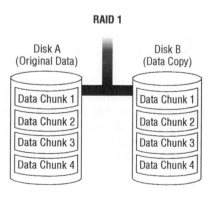

This RAID structure provides high fault tolerance. If you lose a disk, you have a backup copy that is immediately accessible. The main problem with this RAID structure is its cost. You must purchase a duplicate drive for every drive to be included in the array.

RAID 10   Also called *disk mirroring and striping* or *RAID 1+0*, this RAID structure is a combination of RAID 1 (mirroring) and RAID 0 (striping). It needs a minimum of four disks: two disks for striping and two disks to mirror the striping disks. A four-disk RAID 10 example is shown in Figure 5.3.

FIGURE 5.3   RAID 10 diagram

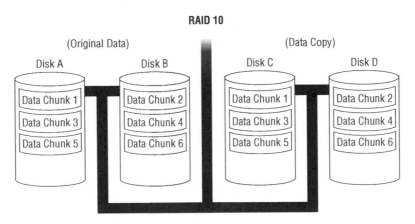

While this array structure provides fault tolerance, including very fast regeneration of any failed disk, the cost is high. You need to have double capacity for the mirroring structure portion.

RAID 2, 3, 4   These three RAID structures are typically no longer used, though you may find a few RAID 4 arrays still around. RAID 2 is a form of RAID 0, which provided specialized error checking that is now handled by the disk drives themselves.

RAID 3 is also a form of RAID 0, but it adds parity data and uses a minimum of three disks. The parity data is stored on a designated disk, called the *parity disk*. Other data, such as file data, is stored on the other two disks. A minimum of three disks is required. If a single data disk fails, the data can be regenerated using the other data disk and the parity disk. However, there is no regeneration if the parity disk fails.

RAID parity is a special checksum. A *checksum* is produced when a certain mathematical algorithm is used on data. You can try out a cyclic redundancy check (CRC) checksum algorithm using the cksum utility on Linux. The RAID parity process uses regular data on the drives, and it runs it through the designated mathematical algorithm to produce parity data. This produced parity data is also stored on the drives. Where the parity is stored depends on the RAID array structure. If a drive fails, by using the data on the good drive(s) and its corresponding parity, the original data can be rebuilt.

The RAID 4 structure is a form of RAID 3, and it also requires a three-disk minimum. The difference is that it provides faster access than RAID 3, because RAID 3 processes bytes of data, while RAID 4 processes blocks of data. The RAID 4 structure still has the fatal flaw of no original data regeneration if the parity disk fails.

RAID can be implemented via software, hardware, and even firmware. The certification focuses on the utilities used for software-controlled RAID.

RAID 5   This RAID structure is also called *disk striping with parity*, because it stripes both data and parity. The parity data is not written to a single drive, as in RAID 3 or RAID 4, but it is instead spread across the disks. A three-disk RAID 5 example is shown in Figure 5.4.

FIGURE 5.4   RAID 5 diagram

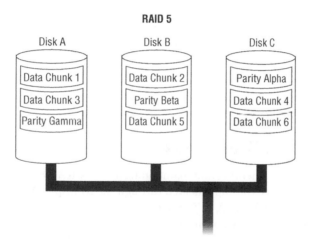

RAID 5 can be implemented either by software or hardware controllers, but hardware controllers are typically recommended for large RAID 5 implementations. With a hardware controller, write performance can be improved by adding extra cache memory.

For RAID 5, a minimum of three disks is required. With parity spread among the drives, there is improved fault tolerance over RAID 3 and RAID 4, and it achieves better data read times. However, if a single drive fails, it takes time to rebuild the lost drive's data. In that time, if another drive fails (and it can) you've lost the entire RAID array. For this reason, many companies with large data installations do not recommend a RAID 5 structure.

RAID 6   This RAID array structure is also called *disk striping with double parity*. It stripes both data and parity, like RAID 5, except the same parity data chunk is written two times, each on a different disk. This allows two drives to fail with no problems, and it increases its fault tolerance. A four-disk RAID 6 example is shown in Figure 5.5.

FIGURE 5.5 RAID 6 diagram

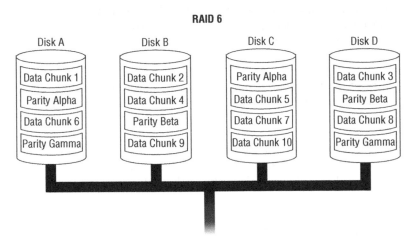

There is a four-disk minimum requirement for RAID 6, which makes it a little more expensive than RAID 5. Also, writes are slightly slower due to the double parity. However, this structure provides faster reads, so it's useful for large data applications.

It's nice to have choices, and the various RAID array structures provide several. With an understanding of these RAID varieties and your particular data requirements, you can choose the most applicable structure to meet your systems' needs.

Implementing RAID on Linux

This section focuses on implementing and maintaining a Linux RAID structure via software. Linux software RAID arrays are implemented through the Multiple Devices (md) device driver, and it supports RAID 0, 1, 10, 4, 5, and 6.

Before you set up a RAID array on Linux, you need to check some things on your system. In addition, you must get any needed drives ready for RAID array membership. Once you've handled these preliminaries, you can create your RAID array. After the RAID array is created, several utilities are involved in managing it. We cover each item involved in this process in this section.

Checking Your System

The first item to check on your system is whether the kernel supports RAID. The Linux kernel v2.6 and up can support all RAID levels. You can check your kernel version using the uname -r command, as shown here on an Ubuntu distribution:

```
$ uname -r
3.13.0-71-generic
$
```

In addition, check to see if your system has the /proc/mdstat file. This useful file provides current system RAID status information. Just its presence is another positive indicator that RAID is supported on your system:

```
$ ls /proc/mdstat
/proc/mdstat
$
```

Another check uses the modprobe command to see if you can load various RAID kernel modules. Using super user privileges, type **modprobe raid6** at the command line, as shown here:

```
$ sudo modprobe raid6
[sudo] password for christine:
$
```

No error message after issuing this modprobe command is a good sign. However, double-check that it worked by displaying the current contents of the /proc/mdstat file:

```
$ cat /proc/mdstat
Personalities: [raid6] [raid5] [raid4]
unused devices: <none>
$
```

Notice that the Personalities line in this Ubuntu distribution's /proc/mdstat file shows three different RAID levels: 6, 5, and 4. This indicates that this system supports those RAID levels.

We'll cover the /proc/mdstat file in greater depth later in this chapter. For now, it's useful for checking your system.

At this point, you can check additionally supported RAID levels by continuing to issue **modprobe raid#**, where # is the RAID level that you want to check. Typically, you will find that RAID levels 0, 1, 10, 4, 5, and 6 are supported on current Linux distributions without any modifications. If a level is not presently supported, you'll get an error message similar to the following:

```
$ sudo modprobe raid3
[sudo] password for christine:
modprobe: FATAL: Module raid3 not found.
$
```

Once you know that your Linux system can support the desired RAID level, you need to see if your system has the Multiple Disk or Device Administration (mdadm) utility installed. On this Ubuntu distribution, it is not installed by default:

```
$ dpkg -s mdadm
dpkg-query: package 'mdadm' is not installed and
 no information is available
[...]
$
```

However, on this CentOS system, the mdadm utility is installed by default:

```
# rpm -qa | grep mdadm
mdadm-3.3.2-2.el7_1.1.x86_64
#
```

If you do not have the mdadm utility and need to install it, its package is conveniently named mdadm. So, for example, on an Ubuntu system you can install it via the sudo apt-get install mdadm command, assuming that you have super user privileges.

You may have heard of managing RAID on a Linux system using an old utility called raidtools2, which has an even older version named raidtools. Current distributions use the mdadm utility. It is a single program, as opposed to the raidtools2 program collection.

Once these system checks are completed and any needed changes are made, you can continue toward implementing a RAID array. The next step involves disk drives.

Getting a Drive Ready for RAID Membership

Before creating a RAID array, you need to partition the various drives that will have membership in the array. But before you start partitioning, you need to think through a few important issues, such as the partition type code to use as well as the partition size and how much disk space you will leave unpartitioned.

Some individuals create the RAID array and then perform partitioning. However, this can cause problems, especially when recovering data due to a failed disk. It is best to partition the drives first and to create the RAID array afterward.

A regular data drive partition typically has a partition type code of 83 (for MBR partitions) or 8300 (for GPT partitions). For a RAID array member, the partition type code can be set either to da (MBR partitions only) or fd.

Partition type codes are sometimes written using their hex code equivalent. The hex value for partition type code fd is 0xFD (MBR partitions) or 0xFD00 (GPT partitions). The certification lists the 0xFD hex value in its objectives.

You will need to choose the correct type code based on the partition table and the *md superblock*, sometimes called *metadata*. When a RAID array is created, by default the md superblock is written to a particular location on all disks in the array. Currently, Linux recognizes two md superblock version groups, v0.90 and v1.0 and up. The primary difference between these two version groups is the superblock's location on the disk. They also help to determine what partition type code to use.

If you are using a GPT partition table, then the fd type code (0xFD00) is recommended, because the Linux system can automatically detect RAID. If your system is using md superblock v1.0 or higher (which it typically is, if you have not created a RAID array using this partition) and it's an MBR partition, use the da partition type code (0xDA).

Optimally, all of your RAID array drives and spare drives will be the same size, but this isn't always the case. In situations where your drives are not equally sized, it may be a good idea to leave some space unpartitioned. This can be helpful if your spare disks are slightly smaller than the RAID array drive members and you need to use them to replace a failed array drive.

A *spare drive* is one that is not currently an active RAID array member, but instead it is added to the RAID array as a spare. Typically, this spare drive is automatically moved into full RAID array membership should a drive member fail. A spare drive can also be automatically moved from one array in the same spare group or domain to another array that needs a spare due to a failed drive.

For drives that will be used in the same RAID array (members and spares), make them all the same partition size. The md device driver can deal with different partition sizes in a RAID array by ignoring the excess. However, you will be wasting that mismatched space.

Now with your partition type code and size determined, you are ready to partition your drives. Use the appropriate partition tool, such as fdisk or parted, to create your needed partitions. (The LPIC-1 certification focused on partitioning storage media.) In the snipped example here, five drives are partitioned on a CentOS distribution using super user privileges to prepare them for RAID array membership:

```
# lsblk
NAME       MAJ:MIN RM  SIZE RO TYPE MOUNTPOINT
sda        8:0     0    8G  0 disk
├─sda1     8:1     0  500M  0 part /boot
└─sda2     8:2     0  7.5G  0 part
[...]
```

```
sde          8:64   0    1G  0 disk
sdf          8:80   0    1G  0 disk
sdg          8:96   0    1G  0 disk
sdh          8:112  0    1G  0 disk
sdi          8:128  0    1G  0 disk
[...]
#
# fdisk /dev/sde
[...]
Command (m for help): n
Partition type:
   p   primary (0 primary, 0 extended, 4 free)
   e   extended
Select (default p): p
Partition number (1-4, default 1): 1
First sector (2048-2097151, default 2048):
Using default value 2048
[...]
Command (m for help): t
Selected partition 1
Hex code (type L to list all codes): da
Changed type of partition 'Linux' to 'Non-FS data'

Command (m for help): w
[...]
# fdisk /dev/sdf
[...]
# fdisk /dev/sdg
[...]
# fdisk /dev/sdh
[...]
# fdisk /dev/sdi
[...]
#
# lsblk
NAME        MAJ:MIN RM   SIZE RO TYPE MOUNTPOINT
sda          8:0    0     8G  0 disk
├─sda1       8:1    0   500M  0 part /boot
└─sda2       8:2    0   7.5G  0 part
[...]
```

```
sde          8:64   0    1G  0 disk
└─sde1       8:65   0 1023M  0 part
sdf          8:80   0    1G  0 disk
└─sdf1       8:81   0 1023M  0 part
sdg          8:96   0    1G  0 disk
└─sdg1       8:97   0 1023M  0 part
sdh          8:112  0    1G  0 disk
└─sdh1       8:113  0 1023M  0 part
sdi          8:128  0    1G  0 disk
└─sdi1       8:129  0 1023M  0 part
[...]
#
```

In this example, the lsblk command is used to display all of the various block devices currently attached to the system. The fdisk utility is employed to make whole disk partitions on five drives. (These rather small disks are being used for example purposes only.) Notice that the partition type code used is da (0xDA).

Once you have checked your system for RAID support, installed any needed packages, and prepared the needed drives for RAID array membership, you are ready for the next task: creating a RAID array.

Creating a RAID Array

To set up a RAID array, you need to employ the Multiple Disk or Device Administration (mdadm) utility. The basic syntax of this flexible tool is

mdadm [--mode] raid-device [options] component-devices

The mdadm utility is a single program that conducts many jobs related to RAID arrays. It requires super user privileges and has several operating modes. Each operating mode is designed for a particular function, such as creating a RAID array. Also, each mode has its own specific mdadm command options. You can choose the operating mode with the --mode option, and the mode choices are shown in Table 5.1.

TABLE 5.1 The mdadm utility's modes

Mode (long option)	Mode (short option)	Description
--assemble	-A	Assemble mode: Assembles previously created RAID array members into an active array.

TABLE 5.1   The mdadm utility's modes *(continued)*

Mode (long option)	Mode (short option)	Description
--auto-detect	none	*Auto-detect mode*: Asks the Linux kernel to activate any auto-detected RAID arrays. Several requirements must be met for this to work properly, such as RAID array members must have a v0.90 superblock.
--build	-B	*Build mode*: Builds a RAID array of drives that have no superblocks.
--create	-C	*Create mode*: Creates a new RAID array by adding superblocks to each drive member and then assembling the members into an active array.
--follow	-F	*Follow mode*: Monitors md drives and, if an event or alert occurs, performs a designated action, such as sending an email or running a program. Useless for a RAID 0 array.
--grow	-G	*Grow mode*: Grows (or shrinks) or reshapes a RAID array.
--incremental	-I	*Incremental assembly mode*: Adds a single drive to designated RAID array, and if the added drive allows the array to be activated, the array is automatically activated. Similar to assemble mode but for one drive at a time.
--manage	none	*Manage mode*: Manages RAID array members, such as adding a new spare drive to a RAID array.
--misc	none	*Miscellaneous mode*: Includes RAID array operations that do not fall into any other mode category, such as deleting a drive's superblock.
--monitor	-F	*Monitor mode*: Operates exactly like follow mode.

The focus here is on the mdadm create mode. Because the drives partitioned earlier did not have superblocks, the superblocks need to be created on them. After that is completed, the drives are assembled into the desired RAID configuration.

 The mdadm utility has an excellent man page, and it is worth taking the time to peruse all of the information contained within it. Access the man page by typing **man mdadm** at the command line. Also, you can view some good examples from the mdadm -h command. There are numerous examples, so you should pipe the command's output into the less pager utility.

In following snipped example, four (-n 4) of the disks previously partitioned are created (-C) into a sample RAID level 6 array (-l 6), designated by /dev/md0, on a CentOS distribution. The example command here is broken onto multiple lines for clarity:

```
# mdadm -C /dev/md0 -l 6 -n 4 \
> /dev/sdf1 /dev/sdg1 /dev/sdh1 /dev/sdi1
mdadm: Defaulting to version 1.2 metadata
mdadm: array /dev/md0 started.
#
```

If the utility finds anything on the partitions that is a potential problem, it displays a message about the potential problem along with the question, Continue creating array?. If you encounter any problem messages from the mdadm utility, thoroughly investigate them prior to proceeding with creating the RAID array.

 Make a grievous mistake creating your RAID array? No need to worry. You can essentially erase it and start over. See the "Removing a RAID Array" section later in this chapter.

Notice that in the preceding example, when the mdadm utility creates a superblock on the new RAID array members, it defaults to version 1.2 metadata (superblock). Also, once a superblock is written to the partitions, the new RAID array, /dev/md0, is started.

 If your partitions already have a superblock created on them by the mdadm utility, you'll use the --assemble or -A option to select assemble mode instead of using create mode.

When the RAID level 6 array was created in the previous example, short options were used on the mdadm command. You can use the long options, if desired.

Earlier, we mentioned that each mdadm utility mode has its own set of options. You can quickly view these options at the command line by entering the mode and then typing **--help**, as shown here:

```
# mdadm --create --help
Usage:  mdadm --create device -chunk=X --level=Y --raid-devices=Z devices
[...]
Options that are valid with --create (-C) are:
 --bitmap=            : Create a bitmap for the array with the given filename
                        or an internal bitmap is 'internal' is given
 --chunk=         -c  : chunk size in kibibytes
 --rounding=          : rounding factor for linear array (==chunk size)
 --level=         -l  : raid level: 0,1,4,5,6,10,linear,multipath and synonyms
 --parity=        -p  : raid5/6 parity algorithm: {left,right}-{,a}symmetric
 --layout=            : same as --parity, for RAID10: [fno]NN
 --raid-devices=  -n  : number of active devices in array
 --spare-devices= -x  : number of spare (eXtra) devices in initial array
 --size=          -z  : Size (in K) of each drive in RAID1/4/5/6/10 - optional
 --data-offset=       : Space to leave between start of device and start
                        of array data.
 --force          -f  : Honour devices as listed on command line.  Don't
                        insert a missing drive for RAID5.
 --run            -R  : insist of running the array even if not all
                        devices are present or some look odd.
 --readonly       -o  : start the array readonly - not supported yet.
 --name=          -N  : Textual name for array - max 32 characters
 --bitmap-chunk=      : bitmap chunksize in Kilobytes.
 --delay=         -d  : bitmap update delay in seconds.


#
```

This --help option is handy if you need to recall quickly a particular mode's option syntax. Be aware that the auto-detect mode has no options, so using --help with it will display only general mdadm help information.

 Several long options need an equals sign between themselves and their setting, while short options often need a space. For example, --raid-devices=6 is equivalent to -n 6.

Checking a RAID Array

Once you create a RAID array, you should immediately check to make sure that all is well. The /proc/mdstat file is helpful here, because it contains any running RAID array's current status. In this example, the sample /dev/md0 RAID level 6 array's current status information is shown:

```
# cat /proc/mdstat
Personalities: [raid6] [raid5] [raid4]
md0: active raid6 sdi1[3] sdh1[2] sdg1[1] sdf1[0]
      2093056 blocks super 1.2 level 6, 512k chunk, [...]

unused devices: <none>
#
```

The /dev/md0 RAID array's status looks good. The four partitions are actively participating. You can also see information concerning the array's RAID level (level 6) and its chunk size (512k).

Data is broken up over the RAID array drives into stripes, and those stripes are further broken into chunks. The mdadm utility typically sets these chunks' size to 512 KiB each by default.

Another good check requires the use of the mdadm utility's miscellaneous mode. Here is an example of checking the sample /dev/md0 RAID array:

```
# mdadm --misc --detail  /dev/md0
/dev/md0:
         Version: 1.2
   Creation Time: Tue Feb  9 14:05:42 2017
      Raid Level: raid6
      Array Size: 2093056 (2044.34 MiB 2143.29 MB)
   Used Dev Size: 1046528 (1022.17 MiB 1071.64 MB)
    Raid Devices: 4
   Total Devices: 4
     Persistence: Superblock is persistent

     Update Time: Tue Feb  9 14:05:54 2017
           State: clean
  Active Devices: 4
 Working Devices: 4
  Failed Devices: 0
   Spare Devices: 0

          Layout: left-symmetric
      Chunk Size: 512K
```

```
       Name: localhost.localdomain: [...]
       UUID: 38edfd0d:45092996:954b269a:9e919b3a
     Events: 17

Number   Major   Minor   RaidDevice State
    0       8       81          0     active sync   /dev/sdf1
    1       8       97          1     active sync   /dev/sdg1
    2       8      113          2     active sync   /dev/sdh1
    3       8      129          3     active sync   /dev/sdi1
#
```

This command provides a large amount of helpful information. Notice in the preceding example that not only is state information given, but identification information, such as the UUID, is displayed as well. This data can help you diagnose any problems that occurred during the RAID array's creation.

When using the mdadm utility for miscellaneous mode, you do not have to include the --misc option. The utility automatically recognizes miscellaneous mode options.

Format and Mount the RAID Array

Once a RAID array has been created (or assembled) and checked, it can be treated like any other partition: formatting it with a filesystem and mounting it. In the snipped example here, you can see that the sample RAID 6 array, /dev/md0, is formatted with an ext4 filesystem and then mounted to a temporary directory:

```
# mkfs -t ext4 /dev/md0
mke2fs 1.42.9 (28-Dec-2013)
Filesystem label=
OS type: Linux
Block size=4096 (log=2)
[...]
#
# mount -t ext4 /dev/md0 Temp
# ls Temp
lost+found
#
# touch Temp/My_RAID_File.txt
#
# ls Temp
lost+found   My_RAID_File.txt
#
```

In the previous example, notice that the lost+found directory is on the /dev/md0 filesystem, as you would see on a non-RAID partition formatted with the ext4 filesystem. Once you have mounted your RAID array to its desired permanent location, just like with other filesystems, you add a record to the /etc/fstab file, so the RAID array is automatically mounted at system boot time.

Save RAID Array Configuration

Because the kernel, the md driver, and mdadm can read each RAID member's superblock, a configuration file is not absolutely necessary. Also, when creating a RAID array, a configuration file is not created. If a RAID configuration file does exist, it is not automatically updated by the mdadm utility.

However, it's a good idea to create and maintain a RAID configuration file. This mdadm utility file is useful for a potential RAID array recovery situation, and some Linux distributions produce errors when you attempt to assemble an array if no configuration file is present.

 On your Linux distribution, you may find the opposite to be true in that, with an mdadm configuration, file errors are produced and/or more RAID problems occur when assembling a RAID array. In this case, still maintain a RAID configuration file, but keep it offline on a flash drive should it be needed for recovery purposes.

The mdadm configuration file, mdadm.conf, should be stored either in the /etc/ directory or in the /etc/mdadm/ directory, depending on your distribution. Since it is not created when the mdadm utility is installed, you will need to check which configuration file location your distribution uses. You can find this out by typing **man mdadm.conf** at the command line. Of course, you must have the mdadm utility installed before issuing this command.

Once the proper location is determined for your configuration file, you can create it. The best way to create this file is using the mdadm utility's --scan option. First, just do a simple scan to see what the command will produce, as shown here in this snipped example:

```
# mdadm --verbose --detail --scan /dev/md0
ARRAY /dev/md0 level=raid6 num-devices=4 metadata=1.2
name=localhost.localdomain:0 UUID=38edfd0d:45092996:954[...]
   devices=/dev/sdf1,/dev/sdg1,/dev/sdh1,/dev/sdi1
#
```

This is the information that needs to be stored within your configuration file for this particular RAID array. Notice the keyword ARRAY is output with the information. This keyword can be used in the mdadm.conf file to identify a RAID array.

Instead of typing in this information, which could introduce typographical errors, redirect the command's standard output into the proper configuration filename, as shown here on this CentOS distribution:

```
# ls /etc/mdadm.conf
ls: cannot access /etc/mdadm.conf: No such file or directory
```

```
#
# mdadm --verbose --detail --scan /dev/md0 >> /etc/mdadm.conf
#
# cat /etc/mdadm.conf
ARRAY /dev/md0 level=raid6 num-devices=4 metadata=1.2 name=localhost
.localdomain:0 UUID=38edfd0d:45092996:954[...]
   devices=/dev/sdf1,/dev/sdg1,/dev/sdh1,/dev/sdi1
#
```

If the mdadm.conf configuration file pre-exists, be sure to make a backup copy prior to adding the new RAID array's information to it.

Once you have this configuration file created and/or new RAID array information stored in it, you have completed the RAID array's implementation phase. However, you can tweak the file to add some additional configuration information for monitoring purposes. There are many ways to monitor and manage your RAID array properly, some of which include modifying this configuration file. These topics are more appropriately covered in a RAID array's management phase.

Managing a RAID Array

Once you have your RAID array in production, you move into the management phase. Managing RAID arrays involves monitoring them for problems, handling any difficulties, fine-tuning their configuration if warranted, and so on. These important management tasks are covered in this section.

Monitoring Your RAID Array

One of the most important RAID array management tasks is monitoring (also called *following*). Monitoring allows you to take quick action when problems occur, improve data access performance, and reduce outages.

The mdadm utility has a monitor mode, which is central to monitoring your software-controlled RAID array. With this mode, you can monitor your RAID array(s) for certain events (also called *alerts*). These events are shown in Table 5.2.

TABLE 5.2   The mdadm monitor mode events

Event/Alert Name	Description
DeviceDisappeared	An entire array that was created or assembled has left array configuration status.
RebuildStarted	An array has started to rebuild.

Event/Alert Name	Description
Rebuild*NN*	An array that is rebuilding is *NN*% done.
RebuildFinished	An array that is rebuilding is either completely done or was aborted.
Fail	An active array member has been designated faulty.
FailSpare	An array spare drive, which was currently being added into full array membership to replace a failed drive, has been designated faulty.
SpareActive	An array spare drive, which was currently being added into active array membership to replace a failed drive, has been successfully added as an active array member.
NewArray	A new array has been added in the /proc/mdstat file.
DegradedArray	A new array appears to have an array member missing.
MoveSpare	A spare drive has been moved from one array in the same spare group or domain to another array that needs a spare due to a failed drive.
SparesMissing	The configuration file indicates that an array should have *n* spare drives, but it is detected that fewer than *n* spare drives exist in the array.
TestMessage	At startup, an array is detected with the --test option used for monitor mode.

The monitoring process can be started manually at the command line. The basic mdadm utility syntax for kicking off monitoring is

mdadm --monitor *options devices*

You can substitute --follow for --monitor in the command. This command starts mdadm in monitor mode, where it will screen the RAID arrays every 60 seconds (by default) and report any events.

Be aware that when the mdadm utility starts its monitoring mode and finds arrays to monitor, it will not exit. Therefore, it's a good idea to tack an ampersand (&) onto the command's end and run it in background mode.

RAID 0 arrays are not monitored by mdadm. Because there is no fault tolerance in a RAID level 0 array, this array structure falls outside the mdadm utility's monitoring mode's scope. If you attempt to monitor a RAID 0 array with mdadm, you will instantaneously receive a DeviceDisappeared event message.

You can set various options with monitor mode to meet your system's needs. A list of the mdadm monitor options on a CentOS distribution is shown here:

```
# mdadm --monitor --help
[...]
Options that are valid with the monitor (-F --follow) mode are:
  --mail=       -m  : Address to mail alerts of failure to
  --program=    -p  : Program to run when an event is detected
  --alert=          : same as --program
  --syslog      -y  : Report alerts via syslog
  --increment=  -r  : Report RebuildNN events in the given
                      increment. default=20
  --delay=      -d  : seconds of delay between polling state.
                      default=60
  --config=     -c  : specify a different config file
  --scan        -s  : find mail-address/program in config file
  --daemonise   -f  : Fork and continue in child, parent exits
  --pid-file=   -i  : In daemon mode write pid to specified file
                      instead of stdout
  --oneshot     -1  : Check for degraded arrays, then exit
  --test        -t  : Generate a TestMessage event against each
                      array at startup
#
```

The --mail option allows you to designate a single email address to receive event notifications. The --program option designates a program to run upon an event notification. As an alternative to using these options, you can use the --scan option, which will cause the mdadm utility to look inside the mdadm.conf configuration file for these settings. Within the configuration file, you add the keyword MAILADDR followed by a single email address. Also, you may add the keyword PROGRAM followed by the name of a program or shell script to run, should an alert occur. If you use the --scan option and the mdadm.conf file has no program or email keywords, or if you start monitor mode without the --mail or --program options, event notifications are sent to standard output.

Having odd problems with your RAID array? Put a watch on it. Type **watch cat /proc/mdstat** at the command line, and view what is happening every few seconds to the RAID array's status. This may help in your problem-discovery process.

Another interesting option is `--daemonise`. This allows you to start `mdadm` in monitor mode as a daemon. This useful option can be put into a system startup script.

Adding a Spare Disk to a RAID Array

You can add a spare disk to a RAID array when you create it. However, if you didn't add one (or more) at creation time, or your spare disk has become an active RAID member due to another drive failing, you may want to add a spare to an active RAID array.

When you need to add a spare drive to a RAID array, you should first ensure that it is not already a RAID array member. This may not be needed for a single RAID array system, but if you have a large array installment, it's worth the extra few minutes. A snipped example of checking a drive for array membership is shown here:

```
# mdadm --misc --examine /dev/sde1
mdadm: No md superblock detected on /dev/sde1.
#
# mdadm --misc --examine /dev/sdf1
/dev/sdf1:
          Magic: a92b4efc
        Version: 1.2
[...]
#
```

This preceding example shows the output that you receive for both a non-RAID member as well as an active RAID member. The /dev/sde1 partition *is not* part of a RAID array, but the /dev/sdf1 partition *is* a RAID array member. Note that if the drive is not already partitioned, you would pass the whole drive name, /dev/sde in this case, to the `mdadm` utility instead of the partition name to check for RAID membership.

> When partitioning new drives to serve as RAID array spares, make their partition size and type the same as current RAID members. You cannot add spares to a RAID array that have a smaller size than current members have.

Prior to adding a spare to your RAID array, check the array's current number of spares by using the grep command, along with the `mdadm` utility's miscellaneous mode's `--detail` option. An example is shown here:

```
# mdadm --misc --detail /dev/md0 | grep Spare
  Spare Devices: 0
#
```

The /dev/md0 RAID array currently has no spare drives. To fix this situation, the /dev/sde1 partition is hot-added here using the `mdadm` utility's manage mode:

```
# mdadm --manage --add /dev/md0 /dev/sde1
mdadm: added /dev/sde1
```

```
#
# mdadm --misc --detail /dev/md0 | grep Spare
  Spare Devices: 1
#
```

Notice that once the partition was added, the Spare Devices count went up by one. You can add more than one device at a time, if desired.

If you add a spare device to a RAID array and are using the mdadm.conf configuration file, be sure to update it.

Growing the RAID Array

You can change the size or shape of your RAID array using the mdadm utility. *Size* or *shape* refers to the ability to change RAID array configuration items such as chunk size and the number of active RAID array members. You can even do conversions, such as changing a RAID level 5 array into a RAID level 6 array.

The mdadm utility's grow mode handles these various changes. Be aware that changing the size and shape of your RAID array is a time-consuming (from hours to days) and potentially data-dangerous activity. Always make sure that you have backups completed prior to any grow mode activities. To see all of the various grow mode options, type **mdadm --grow --help** at the command line.

To prepare for a recovery after an unexpected grow mode problem, you should specify a special backup file for the mdadm utility to use in the resizing or reshaping process. This backup file is specified by the --backup-file option. The backup file should reside on a different disk or RAID array than the one you are growing.

Removing a RAID Array

If desired, you can remove an entire RAID array. To do so, you must first stop the array using the mdadm utility's manage mode.

Just as you should do when employing the mdadm utility's grow mode, make a backup of any data that you wish to preserve prior to removing a RAID array.

The sample /dev/md0 RAID array is stopped in this example here:

```
# mdadm --manage --stop /dev/md0
mdadm: stopped /dev/md0
#
```

Once a RAID array is stopped, its members and spare drives can be removed by deleting their superblock. You can either do this one drive at a time or remove the superblocks for all drives at the same time, as shown here:

```
# mdadm --zero-superblock  /dev/sde1
#
# mdadm --zero-superblock  /dev/sdf1 /dev/sdg1 /dev/sdh1
#
```

Once the superblock is removed from the drives, they can be either employed in other RAID arrays or used for other purposes. Be sure to update the mdadm.conf configuration file when removing any RAID arrays.

Adjusting Storage Devices

Nowadays, you typically don't need to adjust your storage devices. However, it is important to understand these concepts and their associated utilities. This is especially true if you end up with a unique situation that requires modifying a storage device's attributes. In addition, the utilities covered in this section can be used for monitoring and testing, which is always useful. Also in this section, we cover understanding and managing iSCSI drives.

Looking at Drive Interface Concepts

When looking at adjusting various storage devices, it makes sense to review some basic drive interface concepts. The following terms and concepts will help as you learn how to use the Linux utilities created to adjust them.

PATION   *Parallel Advanced Technology Attachment (PATA)*, also called simply ATA or IDE (which here stands for Integrated Drive Electronics), is drive interface technology that started with the ATA-1 standard in 1988. It depends on parallel ribbon cables and provides transfer speeds of up to 133 MiB/second in burst mode.

Historically on Linux, PATA disk drives were denoted by the /dev/hd* device files. Currently, most PATA drivers treat PATA disks as if they are SCSI disks, so the drives are denoted by /dev/sd* device files.

SATA   *Serial Advanced Technology Attachment (SATA)* is also a drive interface technology. It is considered an advancement over the PATA interface because of its use of serial cables, which aren't hampered by cable length limits like ribbon cables are. SATA is self-configuring, allows Plug and Play (PnP), and provides transfer speeds of up to 6 Gbits/second. On Linux, SATA disk drives are denoted by /dev/sd* device files.

ATAPI   *Advanced Technology Attachment Packet Interface (ATAPI)* is an optical media and tape interface protocol, which uses PATA or SATA disk interfaces. Introduced in 1997, it was part of the Enhanced IDE (EIDE) disk interface standard, which is heavily associated with the ATA-2 disk interface standard released around the same time.

SCSI   *Small Computer System Interface (SCSI)* is an older drive interface technology that got its start in the early 1980s. SCSI devices use a parallel interface and are platform independent. SCSIs can transfer up to 80 MB/second and can support fiber cable. On Linux, SCSI disk drives, like SATA drives, are denoted by /dev/sd* device files.

SAS   A newer version of SCSI is *Serial Attached SCSI (SAS)*, and it is becoming very popular. It uses a Synchronous Serial Port (SSP) controller that supports the Serial Peripheral Interface (SPI) protocol. SAS devices come at a lower cost than traditional SCSI devices and provide higher reliability as well as faster serial transfer speeds. On Linux, SAS disk drives, like traditional SCSI drives, are denoted by /dev/sd* device files.

iSCSI   *Internet Small Computer System Interface (iSCSI)* is a storage network transport protocol. SCSI commands, using the iSCSI protocol, can be sent to remote storage devices on local or wide area networks and even over the Internet. When configured, a SCSI storage server's disk appears as a locally attached client-side disk. On Linux, iSCSI disk drives, like traditional SCSI drives, are denoted by /dev/sd* device files.

AHCI   The Advanced Host Controller Interface (ACHI) is a legacy specification implemented in hardware, which allows software communication with SATA devices. This technology provides advanced SATA standard features, such as hot-plugging. It also allows TRIM (covered later in this chapter) to be used on Solid State Drives (SSD). The Linux kernel has supported the AHCI standard since version 2.6.19.

If your SSD is not being recognized by your system, it may be a BIOS or UEFI configuration problem. Check your system's BIOS or UEFI configuration menu for SATA mode. If your SATA mode is set to IDE mode, switch it instead to AHCI.

NVMe   Introduced in March 2011, Non-Volatile Memory Express (NVMe) is a standard that was originally created by an association of over 90 companies. It is currently directed by a promoter group of 13 companies. Specifically, the NVMe is a logical device interface and command set standard for SSDs attached via the PCI Express bus. The Linux kernel has contained an NVMe standard interface driver since version 3.3.

On Linux, NVMe-interfaced SSDs are represented by the /dev/nvme* device files. However, the /dev/nvme* device file naming convention is slightly different than the naming convention for SATA and SCSI drives. The NVMe standard uses a namespace (described in Chapter 4) architecture, which is an additional top layer available for subdividing into partitions. For example, here is an NVMe device file reference:

/dev/nmve0n1p1

The nmve denotes that the drive is an NVMe standard SSD. The 0 in the device file name indicates that this is the first NVMe drive. The n1 denotes that this is the drive's namespace one. The p1 denotes that this is partition 1 within this drive's namespace one.

Therefore, the NVMe drive is listed first; the namespace is subdivision of the drive; and the partition is a subdivision of the namespace. If you want to refer to a second NMVe drive's third namespace and second partition, use the /dev/nvme1n3p2 device file name.

It is important to understand just how the Linux kernel views the various drive interfaces as well as the device files used to access them. The next issue is how to test and adjust these various interfaces.

You can determine whether your system is treating a disk as an ATA drive or a SCSI drive by using the lshw command, if it is available on your distribution. Using super user privileges, type **lshw --class disk**. Also, you can typically determine drive types by looking in the /proc/ide and /proc/scsi directories.

Testing and Tuning Drives

The topic of tuning a filesystem was briefly explored in Chapter 4, "Managing the Filesystem." In this section, we cover testing and tuning kernel drive interfaces.

One item that you can tune is *direct memory access (DMA)*. DMA allows data to be sent directly to/from an attached device to/from the system's memory. This allows the processors to be freed from dealing with data transfer issues, which in turn can speed up the system. To enable this feature, DMA support from the system's motherboard, BIOS, and drive is required.

Another item to tune is write-back caching. When using write-back caching, a drive stores data to be written in a cache buffer prior to writing it physically on the drive. Once data is in the cache, the system is told that the data has been committed to disk. In certain large data volume scenarios with write-back caching enabled, the drive can accept data much faster than before and improves its write speed. The downside is that a system crash can cause uncommitted data in the cache to be lost. However, since most filesystems are journaled, the risk is minimal.

Using *hdparm*

The hdparm utility was originally designed for PATA drives and ATAPI optical media interfaced devices. However, it can also handle SATA storage. In addition, if your SCSI devices support SCSI/ATA command Translation (SAT), some options within the hdparm utility can be used on them as well.

Check to see if your system has the hdparm utility installed. On Ubuntu, try the **dpkg -s hdparm** command. On a Red Hat system, such as CentOS, using super user privileges, enter the command **rpm -qa | grep hdparm** at the command line. If your distribution does not have the hdparm utility installed, you can obtain it from the hdparm package.

By using hdparm, you can view, test, and, if needed, modify various drive settings. Be aware that most drives come with their optimum configuration already set.

In the unlikely event that you change any drive settings, you'll need to modify or create the /etc/udev/rules.d/50-hdparm.rules file to make them permanent.

For demonstration purposes here, on an Ubuntu distribution, we've set up two small sample drives. One is a SATA drive, and it is represented by the device file /dev/sde. The other is a PATA (IDE) drive. It is being treated as a SCSI device, and it is represented by the device file /dev/sda.

Using hdparm with the -I option on the SATA drive, /dev/sde, you can get a lot of good information, as shown in the snipped listing here:

```
$ sudo hdparm -I /dev/sde
[sudo] password for christine:

/dev/sde:

ATA device, with non-removable media
[..]
...Serial Number:       VB3c70fec6-fd2c80f3
...Firmware Revision:   1.0
Standards:
...Used: ATA/ATAPI-6 published, ANSI INCITS 361-2002
...Supported: 6 5 4
Configuration:
[...]
Capabilities:
[...]
   DMA: mdma0 mdma1 mdma2 udma0 udma1 udma2 udma3 udma4
udma5 *udma6
[...]
control=120ns
Commands/features:
   Enabled   Supported:
      *       Power Management feature set
      *       Write cache
[...]
Checksum: correct
$
```

Notice that write cache is enabled. The asterisk (*) next to udma6 indicates that this DMA form is enabled as well. This also works fine with the PATA drive, /dev/sda, which is being treated as a SCSI disk by Linux, as shown here:

```
$ sudo hdparm -I /dev/sda
[sudo] password for christine:
```

```
/dev/sda:

ATA device, with non-removable media
[...]
    DMA: mdma0 mdma1 mdma2 udma0 udma1 *udma2 udma3 udma4
udma5 udma6
[...]
    Enabled    Supported:
       *       Power Management feature set
       *       Write cache
[...]
$
```

This drive uses a different DMA form, udma2. However, it does have write cache enabled, just like the /dev/sde drive.

The hdparm utility's various features may or may not work with SCSI drives. In these cases, the sdparm utility (covered in the next section) may help.

 WARNING   Many hdparm utility features and options can cause harm to your drives. Be sure to peruse the hdparm man pages carefully prior to using the utility. Also, try out the various options first on non-production disks.

Several hdparm options allow you to view whether a single feature is set. An example of checking the write cache back setting on the /dev/sda drive is shown here:

```
$ sudo hdparm -W /dev/sde
[sudo] password for christine:

/dev/sde:
 write-caching =  1 (on)
$
$ sudo hdparm -W /dev/sda

/dev/sda:
 write-caching =  1 (on)
$
```

If for some reason you want to turn off write caching, you can easily do so. Just use the -W option again as such: **hdparm -W 0 /dev/*device***. Many of the hdparm utility's options used by themselves show current settings, and if used with an option parameter, they change that setting.

Several options are available with the hdparm utility to view and set various drive settings. Table 5.3 lists just a few that you may be able to try out.

TABLE 5.3 A few hdparm utility options

Option	Description
-i	Displays drive information taken by kernel drivers at the system's boot time. This information is likely to be less current and accurate than when using the -I option.
-I	Displays drive information taken directly from the drive itself. This information is likely to be more current and accurate than when using the -i option.
-t	Performs and displays device read timings. Use for benchmark and comparison purposes.
-T	Performs and displays device cache read timings. Use for benchmark and comparison purposes.
-W	When used without a parameter, it displays the drives' write-caching features.
-X	Sets the DMA. This option is dangerous. Most drives already have their DMA set properly.

One of the more interesting features of the hdparm utility is its security controls. You can secure your drives using some of these options, though they are considered dangerous. Quickly view the various security options available by typing **hdparm --security-help** at the command line.

One of the more useful (and not dangerous) hdparm options is for testing drive performance. It's best to use these tests when the drive is inactive. Here an Ubuntu distribution drive is tested for both its device and cache reads:

```
$ sudo hdparm -tT /dev/sde
[sudo] password for christine:

/dev/sde:
Timing cached reads:    11810 MB in 2.00 seconds=5916.78 MB/sec
Timing buffered disk reads: 1024 MB in 2.69 seconds=380.94 MB/sec
$
$ sudo hdparm -tT /dev/sda

/dev/sda:
Timing cached reads:    10996 MB in 2.00 seconds=5504.82 MB/sec
Timing buffered disk reads: 992 MB in 3.00 seconds=330.43 MB/sec
$
```

Of course, just one test is not going to give you accurate data. You may want to perform these tests several times and average your results.

Using *sdparm*

The sdparm utility is sometimes referred to as the "hdparm for SCSI," but that is not the case. The sdparm utility is very different from hdparm in how it acquires information and sets various parameters.

 Typically, the sdparm utility is not installed by default. If your distribution does not have sdparm installed, you can obtain it from the sdparm package.

The sdparm utility pulls information from a SCSI device's Vital Product Data (VPD) tables. VPD information includes items such as part numbers, serial numbers, and code sets.

You can also use the sdparm utility to control a SCSI device's behavior. For example, you can spin down a SCSI drive and alter its write-back caching.

Many options are available with the sdparm utility to view and set various drive settings. Table 5.4 lists just a few that you may want to try out.

TABLE 5.4   A few sdparm utility options

Option	Description
none	Displays all of the common mode parameters for the device.
--all	Displays all recognized field information for the device type.
--command *cmd*	Executes the command (cmd) passed. Valid cmd parameters include stop, sync, start, load, and so on.
--hex	Displays VPD pages in hex instead of trying to decode them, which is useful if sdparm is having trouble interpreting the pages.
--page	Displays the hex code associated with each VPD. Try passing the option the page (*nn*) with the specified device to derive page information needed.
--vendor	Displays the hex code associated with each device vendor. Try passing the option the vendor code (*nn*) associated with the specified device to derive information if needed.

Be sure to read through the sdparm utility's man pages. It can be a tricky utility to use. Also, a good website describing sdparm in detail is http://sg.danny.cz/sg/sdparm.html.

Using *sysctl*

The sysctl utility is used to modify kernel parameters while a system is running. Included in these parameters are those associated with storage devices.

To see a list of kernel parameters that can be modified, type **sysctl -a** at the command line, using super user privileges. Because the list is long (there are several kernel parameters), you may want to pipe the output into a pager, such as less. To view individual parameters, pass the parameter as an option to the sysctl command.

Any file listed in /proc/sys/ directories and subdirectories is also a kernel parameter that can be modified. Here is an example on an Ubuntu distribution using sysctl as well as the /proc/sys/ file to view the kernel parameter settings for automatically ejecting optical disks when they have been unmounted:

```
$ sudo sysctl dev.cdrom.autoeject
[sudo] password for christine:
dev.cdrom.autoeject = 0
$
$ ls /proc/sys/dev/cdrom/autoeject
/proc/sys/dev/cdrom/autoeject
$
$ cat /proc/sys/dev/cdrom/autoeject
0
$
```

Many kernel parameters are Boolean values, meaning that 0 indicates that the feature is off and 1 indicates that the feature is on. In the preceding example, the dev.cdrom.autoeject parameter is Boolean, and it is currently turned off.

WARNING   Some parameters, such as scsi_logging_level, do not have a Boolean setting, and if it is set to 0, it means that SCSI logging is turned off. The SCSI logging-level parameter is a rather complicated one to set. To set this parameter, it is strongly recommended that you use the scsi_logging_level utility, which is not typically installed by default. It is available in the sg3-utils or sg3_utils package, depending on your distribution.

To change a kernel parameter setting, you can use the sysctl utility. In this example, the dev.cdrom.autoeject parameter is turned on, thus causing optical devices to eject automatically when they are unmounted:

```
$ sudo sysctl -w dev.cdrom.autoeject=1
[sudo] password for christine:
dev.cdrom.autoeject = 1
$
```

```
$ sudo sysctl dev.cdrom.autoeject
dev.cdrom.autoeject = 1
$
$ cat /proc/sys/dev/cdrom/autoeject
1
$
```

You can see that the associated /proc/sys/ file is instantly updated when the sysctl utility is used to modify the kernel parameter. However, this modification is not persistent. To make the modification persistent, you must modify the /etc/sysctl.conf configuration file. The following is a snipped file listing on an Ubuntu distribution:

```
$ cat /etc/sysctl.conf
#
#/etc/sysctl.conf-Configuration file for setting system variables
#See /etc/sysctl.d/ for additional system variables.
#See sysctl.conf (5) for information.
#
[...]
# Do not accept ICMP redirects (prevent MITM attacks)
#net.ipv4.conf.all.accept_redirects = 0
[...]
$
```

Once you have made configuration changes to this file, you can test it by issuing the command **sysctl -p** and then viewing the modified parameters.

 On some distributions, if you customize /etc/sysctl.conf, you will need to move it to /etc/sysctl.d/99-sysctl.conf. Additional kernel parameter configuration files are found in the /etc/sysctl.d/ directory. To test these files, you will need to issue the command **sysctl -p** *filename*.

Relatively few kernel parameters should be modified for tuning disk access and use. However, these two particular RAID parameters may be useful to tune:

```
$ sudo sysctl -a | grep raid
dev.raid.speed_limit_max = 200000
dev.raid.speed_limit_min = 1000
```

These two kernel parameters control RAID speed. Increasing the limits could increase the speed of any rebuilding or reshaping of a RAID array.

Using *smartctl* and *smartd*

You cannot reset or modify a drive's SMART attributes, because they are set in a drive's protected area. You can only enable/disable SMART using the smartctl utility:

```
sudo smartctl -s on /dev/sda
```

However, besides the manual tests, checks, and analysis shown in Chapter 4 with the smartctl utility and SMART devices, you can set up scheduled device tests with the smartd daemon and its accompanying configuration file. Depending on your distribution, the file is either /etc/smartd.conf or /etc/smartmontools/smartd.conf.

If smartd is started at system initialization (see your distribution's documentation on how to check for this and set this up if needed), it will enable SMART monitoring on any ATA devices that have this capability. After that, it will check the SMART devices (including SCSI drives) every 30 minutes, sending any warnings, error messages, and changes in SMART elements to the system logger.

You change polling times, tests that are conducted, and who receives any messages via the configuration file. The DEVICESCAN keyword can be set with various options. For example, to run a long test on all of your system's SMART devices on Sundays from 1 a.m. to 2 a.m., you would enter the following record into the configuration file:

```
DEVICESCAN -s L/../../7/01
```

> The first DEVICESCAN keyword record encountered in the configuration file that does not start with a hash mark (#) is the record used. Any others below it are ignored.

A great deal of excellent documentation exists on the smartd configuration file. See the man pages for your distribution's smartd configuration file, or just look in the file itself. The smartd configuration file is typically heavily documented with many good examples.

> For filesystems such as ext3 and ext4, the tune2fs utility can also tune a few items. Be sure to review the tune2fs utility covered in Chapter 4.

Using *nvme*

To tune and view logs for NVMe-interfaced SSDs, you must use NVMe standard compliant commands. The nvme utility provides these commands through a command-line interface. It is provided along with documentation via the nvme-cli package.

The nvme-cli package is typically not installed by default on most distributions, and it is often *not* included in standard repositories. However, you can access the latest nvme-cli source at https://github.com/linux-nvme/nvme-cli. The general guidelines from Chapter 1 on installing a program from source can be helpful when installing the nvme-cli package.

Once installed, view all of the various commands available to tune your NVMe-interfaced SSDs by typing in **nvme help** at the command line. A snipped example on an Ubuntu distribution is shown here:

```
$ nvme help
[...]The following are all implemented sub-commands:
  list            List all NVMe devices and namespaces on machine
  id-ctrl         Send NVMe Identify Controller
  id-ns           Send NVMe Identify Namespace, display structure
  list-ns         Send NVMe Identify List, display structure
  create-ns       Creates a namespace with the provided parameters
  delete-ns       Deletes a namespace from the controller
  attach-ns       Attaches a namespace to requested controller(s)
  detach-ns       Detaches a namespace from requested controller(s)
  list-ctrl       Send NVMe Identify Controller List, display structure
  get-ns-id       Retrieve the namespace ID of opened block device
  get-log         Generic NVMe get log, returns log in raw format
  fw-log          Retrieve FW Log, show it
  smart-log       Retrieve SMART Log, show it
  smart-log-add   Retrieve additional SMART Log, show it
  error-log       Retrieve Error Log, show it
  get-feature     Get feature and show the resulting value
  set-feature     Set a feature and show the resulting value
  format          Format namespace with new block format
  fw-activate     Activate new firmware slot
  fw-download     Download new firmware
  admin-passthru  Submit arbitrary admin command, return results
  io-passthru     Submit an arbitrary IO command, return results
  security-send   Submit a Security Send command, return results
  security-recv   Submit a Security Receive command, return results
  resv-acquire    Submit a Reservation Acquire, return results
  resv-register   Submit a Reservation Register, return results
  resv-release    Submit a Reservation Release, return results
  resv-report     Submit a Reservation Report, return results
  dsm             Submit a Data Set Management command, return results
```

```
flush          Submit a Flush command, return results
compare        Submit a Comapre command, return results
read           Submit a read command, return results
write          Submit a write command, return results
show-regs      Shows the controller registers. Requires admin character device
version        Shows the program version
help           Display this help

See 'nvme help <command>' for more information on a specific command.
$
```

Notice in the example that the term *controller* is used. The NVMe standard is also called the NVM Host Controller Interface (NVMHCI) standard. An NVMe controller is a PCI Express function that implements NVMe (or NVMHCI) specifications. You may have one or more controllers managing a particular NVMe-interfaced SSD's namespace(s). Described earlier in this chapter, an NVMe namespace is another drive division layer, which can consist of one or more partitions. The nvme utility makes managing, tuning, and reviewing drive logs fairly easy.

Also notice in the preceding example that the nvme utility allows the retrieval of SMART logs (covered in Chapter 4). Because the NVMe standard does not come with either an AHCI or a SCSI-capable interface, if an SSD has SMART capability, there is no current way to retrieve SMART information via the standard SMART utility (smartctl).

The nvme utility is very handy. It allows you to perform any necessary tuning or management of your NVMe-interfaced SSDs.

 Real World Scenario

SSD Unique Problems

An SSD stores data in blocks, which are further subdivided into pages. Data is written at the lower page level, but is erased at the higher block level. This configuration overtime causes severe internal fragmentation.

In addition, when existing SSD data needs to be modified, it cannot be overwritten. Instead, the old data is moved into a buffer, deleted (at the block level), and then the old buffered data is written along with any new or modified data (at the page level). Therefore, more data is erased and rewritten on an SSD filesystem than each modification requested. This phenomenon is called *write amplification*, and it is often written as an equation:

write amplification = *data written to the SSD / data written by the host*.

Internal fragmentation in combination with write amplification can adversely impact performance. *Wear leveling*, a formula used by an SSD controller to distribute data evenly writes across an SSD's blocks to avoid wearing out a particular block, is also adversely affected.

To help with internal SSD block fragmentation, the TRIM command (sometimes called *discard*) is used. This command lets the SSD know which blocks are free and in turn, the SSD controller defragments the blocks. The TRIM command may be implemented in various ways on your system. On Linux, the mount option, discard, will issue the TRIM command after a file is deleted and only operates on the file's previously-consumed data blocks. This is called an *automatic trim*. A *manual trim* is performed using the fstrim command, which defragments all of the free blocks within the designated filesystem.

Using fstrim

The fstrim command can be used periodically to avoid performance problems on SSDs due to internal fragmentation. However, before you attempt to use the fstrim command, you should check to ensure that your SSD does support TRIM. You can use the hdparm command (covered earlier) and grep to check your drive, as shown on an Ubuntu distribution here:

```
$ sudo hdparm -I /dev/sda  | grep TRIM
$
```

No response from the command means that TRIM is *not* supported. If TRIM is supported, you can employ the fstrim to enact TRIM commands upon your SSD. The fstrim command's general syntax is as follows:

fstrim [*options*] *mountpoint*

The *mountpoint* is where the SSD partition is currently mounted. The various *options* available are shown in Table 5.5.

TABLE 5.5 fstrim Command Options

Short Option	Long Option	Description
-l	--length	Start searching for free blocks at the designated number of bytes past the starting point.
-m	--minimum	TRIM only the minimum (or above) contiguous free block ranges, designated in bytes. Causes the operation to finish faster for badly internally fragmented filesystems.
-o	--offset	Set the starting point, in bytes, to begin searching for free blocks to TRIM.
-v	--verbose	Displays the number of filesystem bytes that may receive a TRIM.

You can also get help on the fstrim utility by typing **fstrim** and using either the -h or --help option.

You need to use super user privileges, and the SSD must be mounted. In this example, the fstrim command is issued using the verbose option on a CentOS distribution:

```
# fstrim -v /home
/home: 1503238553 bytes were trimmed
#
```

The fstrim command's output can be a little misleading. The bytes shown did not necessarily have the TRIM command enacted upon them. Instead, these bytes were audited and if found to need defragging, they were defragged.

> Some distributions run the fstrim utility on a regular basis via a cron job. Other distributions may perform the fstrim operation regularly as well, but include it within startup scripts. Take a look at your particular distribution and determine what will work best for your SSD needs. If your system is not rebooted on a regular basis, you may want to ensure fstrim is run via a cron job.

Most drives, except SSDs, will never need to be tuned. However, many of the utilities in this section can be also be used for either monitoring or testing.

Implementing iSCSI

Internet Small Computer System Interface (iSCSI) is a networking protocol (RFC 3720) that allows the transport of SCSI commands over TCP/IP. In essence, it allows remotely located drives (over a company's intranet or even over the Internet) to appear as if they are local SCSI drives.

To understand iSCSI (described briefly earlier in this chapter), it's important to understand a few basic *storage area network (SAN)* concepts. A SAN consists of network attached storage devices, where various systems and the storage devices communicate with each over a network. A SAN network's primary purpose is to enable that communication, and it is typically a high-speed network dedicated only to SAN communications.

There are three popular SAN protocols besides iSCSI to explore. The following descriptions will help you understand various iSCSI alternatives.

Fibre Channel Protocol   A *Fibre Channel SAN* is a high-speed, highly-reliable SAN, which typically runs on optical fiber cables and offers speeds of up to 32-gigabits per second. This expensive-to-implement SAN uses the Fibre Channel Protocol (FCP) to transport SCSI commands over the dedicated network.

ATA over Ethernet Protocol   *ATA over Ethernet AoE* is a network transport protocol that does not use the Internet protocol, but instead runs on a network's layer 2. Using this protocol,

ATA commands are transported over an Ethernet network. The network can be shared with other TCP/IP packets, which makes AoE lower in cost to implement. Because it is a non-routable protocol, it provides inherit security and ease of SAN implementation.

Fibre Channel over Ethernet Protocol For those who cannot afford the expense of a dedicated optical fiber network, the *Fibre Channel over Ethernet (FCoE) protocol* provides a lower cost alternative. FCoE encapsulates Fibre Channel protocol frames for traveling over Ethernet networks.

Like AoE and FCoE, an iSCSI SAN implementation's network is not dedicated to the iSCSI SAN, but it can be shared with other TCP/IP communications.

An iSCSI SAN is inexpensive compared to Fibre Channel SAN and much simpler to set up. However, because iSCSI shares its network with other TCP/IP protocols, depending on how it is implemented, it may not achieve the same data transfer rates as a Fibre Channel SAN.

When looking at the various available SAN protocols, you might ask, "Which is the best SAN protocol?." The answer to this question is, "It depends upon your network environment and SAN requirements." For example, if you have data access requirements that demand high-speed and reliability, most likely FCP will work best for you. However, if you have a reliable high-speed Ethernet network already in place and need an inexpensive solution, iSCSI, AoE, or FCoE may fit perfectly.

You may find that iSCSI is right for your SAN needs. But before you begin an iSCSI implementation, you need to understand the protocol's important terms and concepts.

Understanding iSCSI

In an iSCSI SAN, the remote system offering up an iSCSI disk is called the *target*. The local system desiring to use the offered iSCSI disk is called the *initiator*. Thus, a client (initiator) server (target) relationship exists in offering and accessing iSCSI drives.

A *logical unit number (LUN)* is a number used to identify a unique logical SCSI device on the target system. LUN numbering starts at zero, so the first SCSI device to be offered via iSCSI is typically assigned lun0. An iSCSI LUN can have an alias name up to 255 characters in length, which makes a particular LUN drive easier to identify.

You can create a truly unique ID for a SCSI device on your system using the scsi_id command. The command uses a SCSI device's own VPD 0x80 or 0x83 page data (if those VPD pages are supported by the SCSI device) to generate this ID. To use this command on some distributions, you must enter **/lib/udev/scsi_id** instead of scsi_id at the command line. Depending on your distribution, you can get help on scsi_id by typing **/lib/udev/scsi_id --help** or **man scsi_id** at the command line.

An *iSCSI Qualified Name (IQN)* is a unique address that identifies the iSCSI target server along with its offered iSCSI drive. An IQN has the following basic format:

`iqn.domain-date.domain:unique-scsi-name`

The *domain-date* is the date when your organization officially registered its domain. The format is *year-month*. The *domain* is the organization's domain. The *unique-scsi-id* is a unique name given to the SCSI drive. It is your choice how to identify each SCSI drive uniquely, as long as the names are unique for each SCSI drive on the target server. For example, an IQN might look like this:

`iqn.2016-02.com.example.server07:iscsidisk1`

In the previous example, the *domain-date* is February 2016 written in reverse order: `2016-02`. The *domain* is `server07.example.com`, but notice that it also is written in reverse order. Finally, the *unique-scsi-name* is `iscsidisk1`. Alternatively, you could use the SCSI drive's LUN within the unique SCSI name, such as `iscsilun0`.

Real World Scenario

World Wide Identification

A *World Wide Identifier (WWID)*, also called a *World Wide Name (WWN)*, is a unique identifier defined by the Institute of Electrical and Electronics Engineers (IEEE) standards body. This hexadecimal identifier is unique for each device, and it is hard-coded into a device by its manufacturer. The WWID contains a unique code to identify the manufacturing company as well.

Linux uses the WWID for identifying certain drives, such as iSCSI drives. It creates a symbolic link between the WWID and its associated drive. On an iSCSI target system, type **ls -l /dev/disk/by-id** at the command line to see any attached iSCSI disks along with their WWID. This works equally well for locally attached SCSI drives.

The advantage of using a WWID to identify particular SCSI drives is that if you add additional drives to a system, their device names may change, whereas their WWIDs will never change. Thus, instead of using a SCSI drive's /dev/*device* in the /etc/fstab, you can use its WWID instead. For iSCSI drives, using their WWID assists in creating a *unique-scsi-name* for their IQN.

An iSCSI's drive IQN is important, because it is used in many of the iSCSI configuration files and settings for identifying the target server's offered SCSI drive. Thus, you will want to take some time in determining a *unique-scsi-name* for the IQN. If you have a large iSCSI SAN installment, you should use the `scsi_id` command's output, or the SCSI's WWID/WWN, to identify the drive uniquely. For smaller installments, a made-up name or the SCSI's LUN should suffice.

Setting Up a Target iSCSI Disk

The primary tool for setting up an iSCSI disk on a target server is the targetcli utility. It is a shell interface that allows you to manage the kernel's target subsystem, Linux IO (LIO). The LIO has been around since Linux kernel v2.6, and it is a subsystem that supports storage fabrics. A *storage fabric* is any hardware that connects SAN storage devices to systems. LIO supports storage fabrics, such as Fibre Channels and iSCSI.

The certification objectives do not specifically state that setting up the target server iSCSI configuration or using targetcli to offer iSCSI disks for initiator clients is covered on the exam. However, if you desire to set up an iSCSI target server for practicing with initiator clients, then this chapter section will get you headed in the right direction.

First, on your system, you need to ensure that the target subsystem will start at boot time and the service is running. Here is an example of enabling the target subsystem on a CentOS distribution to start at reboot:

```
# systemctl enable target
ln -s '/usr/lib/systemd/system/target.service'
'/etc/systemd/system/multi-user.target.wants/target.service'
#
```

Once you ensure the target subsystem is running, using super user privileges, enter the targetcli utility. You will receive a /> prompt when you have entered the utility. An example is shown here:

```
# targetcli
Warning: Could not load preferences file /root/.targetcli/prefs.bin.
targetcli shell version 2.1.fb37
Copyright 2011-2013 by Datera, Inc and others.
For help on commands, type 'help'.

/>
```

If you do not have the targetcli utility on your system, you can install it via the targetcli package. Be aware that on some older distributions the tgtd service was used along with the tgtadm utility for managing target server iSCSI devices.

Now that you are within the targetcli utility, you can create a backstore. A *backstore* is a data accessing method that points to and allows access to a physical storage medium (a whole drive, disk partition, or even a plain file) in a storage fabric SAN. In the targetcli, you change your present working directory using a cd command and then issue a create command, as shown in the example here:

```
/> cd /backstores/block
/backstores/block> create iscsidisk1 dev=/dev/sde
Created block storage object iscsidisk1 using /dev/sde.
/backstores/block> ls
o- block ............ [Storage Objects: 1]
  o- iscsidisk1 ...... [/dev/sde (1.0GiB) write-thru deactivated]
```

In this example, the SCSI backstore was created, given the unique SCSI ID iscsidisk1, and it was then assigned to the sample drive, /dev/sde. Notice that you can use the ls command to confirm the newly created backstore.

 If you are creating your own unique SCSI ID and including any alphabetic characters, be sure to make the characters lowercase. If you use uppercase characters, the targetcli utility will flip-flop between using uppercase and lowercase characters for the ID within its interface. This can lead to confusion.

Once a backstore is created, you must create the IQN for the target iSCSI. However, it's best first to change your present working directory into the iscsi directory within targetcli, as shown here:

```
/backstores/block> cd /iscsi
/iscsi> create iqn.2016-02.com.example.server07:iscsidisk1
Created target iqn.2016-02.com.example.server07:iscsidisk1.
Created TPG 1.
Global pref auto_add_default_portal=true
Created default portal listening on all IPs (0.0.0.0), port 3260.
```

Notice that once the IQN is created, the service is listening on port 3260. The only problem is that by the 0.0.0.0 designation, the service is open to all IP networks, which can be a security risk. This is easily fixed, as follows:

```
/iscsi> cd iqn.2016-02.com.example.server07:iscsidisk1/tpg1
/iscsi/iqn.20...csidisk1/tpg1> cd portals
/iscsi/iqn.20.../tpg1/portals> delete 0.0.0.0 3260
Deleted network portal 0.0.0.0:3260
/iscsi/iqn.20.../tpg1/portals> create 192.168.56.103
Using default IP port 3260
Created network portal 192.168.56.103:3260.
```

Now only the designated initiator client node (192.168.56.103) may use this port (3260) to access the offered iSCSI device. If needed, you can use the ls command again to check your configuration thus far.

Once the IQN is properly set up, you must create a LUN to refer to the iSCSI drive. Again, you will need to change directories and use the `create` command, as shown in this example:

```
/iscsi/iqn.20.../tpg1/portals> cd ..
/iscsi/iqn.20...csidisk1/tpg1> cd luns
/iscsi/iqn.20...sk1/tpg1/luns> create /backstores/block/iscsidisk1
Created LUN 0.
/iscsi/iqn.20...sk1/tpg1/luns> ls
o- luns ......................................... [LUNs: 1]
  o- lun0 ................... [block/iscsidisk1 (/dev/sde)]
/iscsi/iqn.20...sk1/tpg1/luns>
```

For testing purposes, you can turn off any authentication, as shown in the following example. However, should you be using this in a production environment, review both the `get auth` and `set auth` commands.

```
/iscsi/iqn.20...sk1/tpg1/luns> cd ..
/iscsi/iqn.20...csidisk1/tpg1> set attribute authentication=0
Parameter authentication is now '0'.
/iscsi/iqn.20...csidisk1/tpg1> set attribute demo_mode_write_protect=0
Parameter demo_mode_write_protect is now '0'.
/iscsi/iqn.20...csidisk1/tpg1> set attribute generate_node_acls=1
Parameter generate_node_acls is now '1'.
```

Once the target server's iSCSI drive is set up, you can double-check the settings, as shown here:

```
/iscsi/iqn.20...csidisk1/tpg1> cd /
/> ls
o- / .................................................. [...]
  o- backstores ..................................... [...]
  | o- block ......................... [Storage Objects: 1]
  | | o- iscsidisk1 [/dev/sde (1.0GiB) write-thru activated]
  | o- fileio ........................ [Storage Objects: 0]
  | o- pscsi ......................... [Storage Objects: 0]
  | o- ramdisk ....................... [Storage Objects: 0]
  o- iscsi .............................. .... [Targets: 1]
  | o- iqn.2016-02.com.example.server07:iscsidisk1 [TPGs: 1]
  |   o- tpg1 ........................ [gen-acls, no-auth]
  |     o- acls .............................. [ACLs: 0]
  |     o- luns .............................. [LUNs: 1]
  |     | o- lun0 ........... [block/iscsidisk1 (/dev/sde)]
```

```
    |     o- portals ......................... [Portals: 1]
    |       o- 192.168.56.103:3260 ..................... [OK]
    o- loopback ............................... [Targets: 0]
/> exit
Global pref auto_save_on_exit=true
Last 10 configs saved in /etc/target/backup.
Configuration saved to /etc/target/saveconfig.json
#
```

When you have completed your iSCSI target's setup, leave the targetcli utility using the exit command.

If you are in a production environment, you will need to add the appropriate rules to your firewall utility, such as firewalld, ufw, or iptables. For testing purposes, you can just lower the firewall as needed.

Setting Up an Initiator iSCSI Disk

The primary tool for managing an iSCSI disk on an initiator client is the iscsiadm utility. This utility is used to discover and log into iSCSI target servers. It is also used for managing the open-iscsi database files, which are located in the /var/log/iscsi/ directory.

> If you do not have the iscsiadm utility on your system, you can install it via the iscsi-initiator-utils or open-iscsi package, depending on your distribution.

For many operations, the iscsiadm utility needs the iscsi daemon, iscsid, to be up and running. The iscsid interfaces with the kernel and implements the open-iSCSI protocol.

The iscsid daemon is configured via the /etc/iscsi/iscsid.conf file. This file also controls several of the iscsiadm utility's operations. iSCSI can use the Challenge-Handshake Authentication Protocol (CHAP) for establishing a secure connection between an iSCSI target server and an initiator client. This configuration file is where you would place the necessary CHAP settings. A snipped version of the configuration file is shown here:

```
# cat /etc/iscsi/iscsid.conf
[...]
node.startup = automatic
node.leading_login = No
[...]
discovery.sendtargets.iscsi.MaxRecvDataSegmentLength = 32768
[...]#
```

On the initiator client, the process of finding an iSCSI disk on a target server is called *target discovery*. When target discovery first occurs, the configuration file's discovery.*

settings are used. The /etc/iscsi/iscsid.conf file is very well documented. To determine any needed settings for your particular iSCSI configuration, peruse the file with a pager utility.

Enabling the iscsid daemon to start at reboot on a CentOS initiator client is shown here:

```
# systemctl enable iscsid
ln -s '/usr/lib/systemd/system/iscsid.service'
'/etc/systemd/system/multi-user.target.wants/iscsid.service'
```

 You don't have to start the iscsid daemon at this point. It is typically configured to start automatically whenever the iscsiadm utility is used. However, if your system is configured differently, you may need to go ahead and use the appropriate command to start the daemon.

To begin the target discovery process, you must use the iscsiadm command. In this example, the iscsiadm utility's discovery mode (-m discovery) is used to locate any SendTargets. A SendTarget is a target type, designated by -t st, which tells the iSCSI target server to reply to the request with an iSCSI devices available list. The iSCSI target server is designated by the -p option. In the following example, the target server is at 192.168.56.103:

```
# iscsiadm -m discovery -t st -p 192.168.56.103
192.168.56.103:3260,1 iqn.2016-02.com.example.server07:iscsidisk1
#
```

When the target was discovered in the preceding example, the iscsiadm tool also created two records. One was a discovery record stored in the /var/lib/iscsi/send_targets database file for the SendTarget type. (Different target type records are stored in their appropriate database file.) An example send_targets file is shown here:

```
# cat /var/lib/iscsi/send_targets
192.168.56.103,3260
#
```

The other record created by the iscsiadm tool during the discovery process was a discovered node record. The node record is stored in the /var/lib/iscsi/nodes database file, and it contains the target server's available iSCSI device's IQN, as shown here:

```
# cat /var/lib/iscsi/nodes
iqn.2016-02.com.example.server07:iscsidisk1
#
```

These iSCSI database records are persistent (unless you delete them). The database filenames can be a little confusing. Keep in mind that the IQNs are in the nodes file, while the target server's IP address is in the send_targets file. These records complete the discovery process.

Once the discovery process is complete, a session between the target server and the initiator client must be established. The iscsiadm command is used to log into the target in order to create this connection. The example command here is broken onto multiple lines for clarity:

```
# iscsiadm -m node \
> -T iqn.2016-02.com.example.server07:iscsidisk1 \
> -p 192.168.56.103 -l
Logging in to [iface: default,
target: iqn.2016-02.com.example.server07:iscsidisk1,
portal: 192.168.56.103,3260] (multiple)
Login to [iface: default, target:
iqn.2016-02.com.example.server07:iscsidisk1,
portal: 192.168.56.103,3260] successful.
#
```

For this command, the node mode is used (-m node). The target iSCSI disk is designated by the -T option and its IQN. The target server is selected by the -p option and its IP address (192.168.56.103). Finally, a login session is requested by the -l option. Now the session is established, and the attached iSCSI drive can be used.

There are various ways to configure your iSCSI target clients using the iscsiadm utility. Type **man iscsiadm** at the command line to view its various options.

Using an iSCSI Disk

It's a good idea to check your attached iSCSI drive prior to using it. The iscsiadm utility has a nice output capability. It allows you to display a great deal of information via its -P# option, as shown in this snipped output:

```
# iscsiadm -m session -P3
iSCSI Transport Class version 2.0-870
version 6.2.0.873-28
Target: iqn.2016-02.com.example.server07:iscsidisk1 (non-flash)
   Current Portal: 192.168.56.103:3260,1
   Persistent Portal: 192.168.56.103:3260,1
[...]
     Attached SCSI devices:
     ************************
```

```
      Host Number: 11    State: running
      scsi11 Channel 00 Id 0 Lun: 0
         Attached scsi disk sdj        State: running
#
```

Notice in the output that the attached iSCSI drive is designated by the sdj device file-name. You can now use utilities on the initiator client, as you would do for locally attached SCSI devices. For example, the lsblk utility allows information to be displayed concerning the iSCSI device, as shown here:

```
# lsblk
NAME              MAJ:MIN RM  SIZE RO TYPE MOUNTPOINT
sda                   8:0   0    8G  0 disk
├─sda1                8:1   0  500M  0 part /boot
└─sda2                8:2   0  7.5G  0 part
  ├─centos-root 253:0   0  6.7G  0 lvm  /
  └─centos-swap 253:1   0  820M  0 lvm  [SWAP]
[...]
sdj                   8:144 0    1G  0 disk
sr0                  11:0   1 1024M  0 rom
#
```

 The dmesg utility can be helpful when viewing iSCSI disk information as well. Look for messages such as iSCSI Initiator over TCP/IP and Direct-Access LIO-ORG along with your iSCSI device's unique SCSI ID.

Once you have checked your iSCSI drive, you can partition it, format it, and mount it, just as you would do with a locally attached drive. An example of doing this on a CentOS distribution is shown in the snipped listing here:

```
# parted /dev/sdj mklabel msdos
Information: You may need to update /etc/fstab.

# parted /dev/sdj mkpart primary 8192s 100%
Information: You may need to update /etc/fstab.

# parted -l
[...]
Model: LIO-ORG iscsidisk1 (scsi)
Disk /dev/sdj: 1074MB
[...]
```

```
#
# mkfs -t ext4 /dev/sdj1
mke2fs 1.42.9 (28-Dec-2013)
[...]
Writing inode tables: done
Creating journal (4096 blocks): done
Writing superblocks and filesystem accounting information: done

# mount -t ext4 /dev/sdj1 Temp
#
# ls Temp
lost+found
#
# touch Temp/My_iSCSI_file.dat
#
# ls Temp
lost+found  My_iSCSI_file.dat
#
```

Last, you should update two configuration files. Of course, be sure to include your new iSCSI drive into the initiator client's /etc/fstab file. The other configuration file is the /etc/iscsi/initiatorname.iscsi file. It should be updated to contain the discovered node (iSCSI devices available on a target server and denoted by their IQN) that you are now using on the initiator client. Here is an example:

```
# cat /etc/iscsi/initiatorname.iscsi
InitiatorName=iqn.2016.02.com.example.server07:iscsidisk1
#
```

The keyword InitiatorName needs to precede the IQN. However, you can also create an alias using the InitiatorAlias keyword. An example of an alias in this configuration file is shown here:

```
InitiatorAlias="LUN0 Test iSCSI Drive"
```

Once the configuration files are updated, your iSCSI drive is ready for use. Keep an eye on its performance, and make any necessary changes using the various utilities covered in this chapter section.

The utilities covered in this section are useful for reviewing, monitoring, testing, and occasionally modifying storage media parameters or those associated with storage media. Also, if you find that iSCSI is right for your SAN needs, the terms and concepts covered will help you employ an iSCSI SAN.

Managing Logical Volumes

Data has a habit of increasing. While you may be able to predict accurately your data's growth within a short timeframe, it is much more difficult to predict data growth accurately over longer periods. Fortunately, logical volumes are handy for those times when your predictions are less than accurate.

It's good to understand this storage media scheme and have it in place prior to actually needing it. This section covers logical volumes, their various terms, and gives practical steps on setting them up.

Understanding LVM

Logical volume management or *logical volume manager (LVM)* allows multiple partitions to be grouped together and used as a single partition for formatting, mounting on the Linux virtual directory structure, storing data, and so on. This grouping is accomplished through an abstraction layer so that the multiple partitions are referred to as a single volume. You can also add additional partitions to a logical volume as your data needs grow.

LVM has three primary parts. Each part plays an important role in creating and maintaining logical volumes.

Physical Volume   A *physical volume (PV)* is created using the LVM's /sbin/pvcreate command. This utility designates an unused disk partition (or whole drive) to be used by LVM. The LVM structures, a volume label, and metadata are added to the partition during this process.

Volume Group   A *volume group (VG)* is created using the LVM's /sbin/vgcreate command, which adds PVs to a storage pool. This storage pool is used in turn to build various logical volumes.

You can have multiple volume groups. When using the command to add a PV(s) to a VG, volume group metadata is added to the PV during this process. This metadata includes name, unique VG name, physical extent size, and so on.

A disk's partition, designated as a PV, can belong to only a single VG. However, a disk's other partitions, also designated as PVs, can belong to other VGs.

Logical Volume   A *logical volume (LV)* is created using the LVM's /sbin/lvcreate command. This is the final object in logical volume creation. A LV consists of storage space chunks (logical extents) from a VG pool. It can be formatted with a filesystem, mounted, and used just like a typical disk partition.

While you can have multiple VGs, each LV is created from only one designated VG. However, you can have multiple LVs sharing a single VG. You can resize (grow or reduce) an LV using the appropriate LVM commands. This feature adds a great deal of flexibility to your data storage management.

You can see that there are many ways to divide and manage your data storage media using LVM. Like with many other data management structures, you should determine your company's data management needs prior to determining an LVM scheme.

Besides knowing about PVs, VGs, and LVs, there are some additional terms to understand. These terms are helpful to know as you start creating LVs.

A *physical extent (PE)* is the smallest block size that can be allocated on a PV. This size is set during the process of adding a PV to a VG. By default, the vgcreate command chooses 4 MiB. However, you can choose a different setting using the -s or --physicalextentsize option. The typical size range is 8 KiB to 16 GiB. For example, if you have a 2 TiB PV and use the default 4 MiB PE size, approximately 500,000 PEs will be added to the volume group. After the initial PV, any PV added to the VB will have the same PE size set.

LVs are made up of *logical extents (LE)*. Logical extents are mapped to VG physical extents. The mapping provides a way to access the data without concern about where a physical extent is located.

There are many acronyms involved with LVM. If this is your first time through LVM concepts, make a cheat sheet for the various acronyms and their meaning. This will help you as you read through the next few sections.

Creating Logical Volumes

The lvm utility is an interactive utility for creating and managing LVs. If it's not installed, you can install it via the lvm2 package. Using super user privileges, you can enter the utility and view the various tools available for LVM, as shown on this CentOS distribution here:

```
# lvm
lvm> help
Available lvm commands:
Use 'lvm help <command>' for more information

devtypes     Display recognised built-in block device types
dumpconfig   Dump configuration
formats      List available metadata formats
help         Display help for commands
lvchange     Change the attributes of logical volume(s)
lvconvert    Change logical volume layout
lvcreate     Create a logical volume
lvdisplay    Display information about a logical volume
lvextend     Add space to a logical volume
lvmchange    With the device mapper, this is obsolete and
             does nothing.
```

lvmdiskscan	List devices that may be used as physical volumes
lvmsadc	Collect activity data
lvmsar	Create activity report
lvreduce	Reduce the size of a logical volume
lvremove	Remove logical volume(s) from the system
lvrename	Rename a logical volume
lvresize	Resize a logical volume
lvs	Display information about logical volumes
lvscan	List all logical volumes in all volume groups
pvchange	Change attributes of physical volume(s)
pvresize	Resize physical volume(s)
pvck	Check the consistency of physical volume(s)
pvcreate	Initialize physical volume(s) for use by LVM
pvdata	Display the on-disk metadata for physical volume(s)
pvdisplay	Display various attributes of physical volume(s)
pvmove	Move extents from one physical volume to another
pvremove	Remove LVM label(s) from physical volume(s)
pvs	Display information about physical volumes
pvscan	List all physical volumes
segtypes	List available segment types
tags	List tags defined on this host
vgcfgbackup	Backup volume group configuration(s)
vgcfgrestore	Restore volume group configuration
vgchange	Change volume group attributes
vgck	Check the consistency of volume group(s)
vgconvert	Change volume group metadata format
vgcreate	Create a volume group
vgdisplay	Display volume group information
vgexport	Unregister volume group(s) from the system
vgextend	Add physical volumes to a volume group
vgimport	Register exported volume group with system
vgmerge	Merge volume groups
vgmknodes	Create the special files for volume group devices in /dev
vgreduce	Remove physical volume(s) from a volume group
vgremove	Remove volume group(s)
vgrename	Rename a volume group
vgs	Display information about volume groups
vgscan	Search for all volume groups
vgsplit	Move physical volumes into a new or existing volume group

```
version     Display software and driver version information
lvm> quit
Exiting.
#
```

In this example, you can see all of the various tools available to create and manage LVs. Generally, any tool that starts with pv is for PVs, any tool that starts with vg is for VGs, and any tool that begins with lv is for LVs.

 Occasionally, you'll see references to lvm2 or LVM2 in LVM documentation. This refers to a new version of LVM, version 2, which was introduced back in Linux kernel v2.6. It added some features and improved on design over LVM version 1 (lvm1). This chapter uses LVM2.

Be aware that you do not need to enter the lvm utility to access these tools. For example, the pvcreate tool is available straight from the command line:

```
# which pvcreate
/sbin/pvcreate
#
```

The five steps required to set up your first LV are as follows:

1. Create your PVs.
2. Create your VG.
3. Create your LV.
4. Format your LV.
5. Mount your LV.

There are important considerations in the first three steps. Each decision you make in the early steps will determine how flexible and easy it is to manage your LVs.

Creating the PVs

Before designating drives as PVs, they should be partitioned. Afterward, you can designate the partitions as a PV using the pvcreate command.

In the following example on a CentOS distribution, four partitions are designated as PVs using the pvcreate command. These four partitions are small sample partitions created for demonstration purposes:

```
# lsblk
NAME           MAJ:MIN RM  SIZE RO TYPE  MOUNTPOINT
[...]
```

```
sdj                8:144   0    1G   0 disk
└─sdj1             8:145   0 1023M   0 part
sdk                8:160   0    1G   0 disk
└─sdk1             8:161   0 1023M   0 part
sdl                8:176   0    1G   0 disk
└─sdl1             8:177   0 1023M   0 part
sdm                8:192   0    1G   0 disk
└─sdm1             8:193   0 1023M   0 part
[...]
#
```

pvcreate /dev/sdj1
```
  Physical volume "/dev/sdj1" successfully created
#
```
pvcreate /dev/sdk1
```
  Physical volume "/dev/sdk1" successfully created
#
```
pvcreate /dev/sdl1
```
  Physical volume "/dev/sdl1" successfully created
#
```
pvcreate /dev/sdm1
```
  Physical volume "/dev/sdm1" successfully created
#
```

The pvcreate command designates the specified disk partition to be used by LVM and adds LVM structures, a volume label, and metadata to the partition. The specified disk partition must be unused.

To see the information on your PVs, you can use the pvdisplay command. You can specify a PV to see information only on that particular PV, or you can simply enter the pvdisplay command to see all of your PVs' information, as shown in the snippet here:

pvdisplay
```
[...]
  "/dev/sdk1" is a new physical volume of "1023.00 MiB"
  --- NEW Physical volume ---
  PV Name               /dev/sdk1
  VG Name
  PV Size               1023.00 MiB
  Allocatable           NO
  PE Size               0
  Total PE              0
  Free PE               0
  Allocated PE          0
```

```
PV UUID                   8vzvRi-8XZI-98tu-FW82-wwwX-os83-Z2a76L

"/dev/sdj1" is a new physical volume of "1023.00 MiB"
[...]
Allocated PE              0
PV UUID                   uFBQqx-OVD6-Vb68-6mjC-P9LR-iND6-ooFdkc

#
```

Notice that a unique PV UUID is created for each PV. This UUID is generated by the pvcreate command, and it can be overwritten using the --uuid option when using pvcreate.

> The various LVM commands have extensive man pages along with many options that allow you to modify their default behavior. Peruse each LVM tool's man page, as needed, to learn more.

Be sure to set up more than one PV. The whole point of LVM is having additional storage media to add on the fly to your LVs. Once you have PVs set up, you can begin the next step—creating a VG.

Creating a VG

Any PV can be added to a VG. The command to use is vgcreate, and its basic syntax is as follows:

```
vgcreate  VG_name  PV
```

You can designate more than one PV during the VG creation process. If you need to add PVs at a later time to a VG, you should use the vgextend command.

> It's important to choose your PE size prior to creating your VG pool. Once set, it can be difficult to change, if current VG members need to have the new PE size. The -s option sets the PE size when you use the vgcreate command.

Common practice names the first VG vg00, the next one vg01, and so on. However, it's your choice what to name your volume group. Because many distributions on installation set up LVM for the virtual directory structure's root (/) and other directories, it's a good idea to check for any current VGs on your system using the vgdisplay command, as shown here:

```
# vgdisplay | grep Name
  VG Name                   centos
#
```

The preceding example was conducted on a CentOS distribution. Notice that a VG is already set up named centos. Therefore, to create a new VG on this system, the centos name should *not* be used. Here is an example of creating a VG on a CentOS distribution, named vg00, using four PVs:

```
# vgcreate vg00 /dev/sdj1 /dev/sdk1 /dev/sdl1 /dev/sdm1
  Volume group "vg00" successfully created
#
```

Once you have successfully created a VG, it makes sense to check it. You can do so with the vgdisplay command, which operates similarly to the pvdisplay command, as shown here:

```
# vgdisplay vg00
  --- Volume group ---
  VG Name                vg00
  System ID
  Format                 lvm2
  Metadata Areas         4
  Metadata Sequence No   1
  VG Access              read/write
  VG Status              resizable
  MAX LV                 0
  Cur LV                 0
  Open LV                0
  Max PV                 0
  Cur PV                 4
  Act PV                 4
  VG Size                3.98 GiB
  PE Size                4.00 MiB
  Total PE               1020
  Alloc PE / Size        0 / 0
  Free  PE / Size        1020 / 3.98 GiB
  VG UUID                2n3wGF-xPSE-r13R-V5kX-I0pV-LDie-bZBQ5f

#
```

Notice in the preceding example that a unique VG UUID was created. Also notice the default PE size was set. You can override many of these defaults by adding various options to the vgcreate command to create a VG with your needed settings.

Once your VG storage pool contains at least one PV, you can move on to creating a LV. The next section covers this task.

Creating an LV

To create an LV from a VG storage pool, the lvcreate command is employed. Its basic syntax is as follows:

lvcreate -L *size VG_name*

With the lvcreate command, the volume's size is designated using the -L option and the VG from which to pull logical extents (LE)s is designated by *VG_name*.

If for some reason a VG does not have enough LEs to give to the LV for the designated size, then it will not be able to create the LV. Here is an example, where the LV size requested is 6 GiB (-L 6g), but only 3.98 GiB are available from the designated VG:

```
# lvcreate -L 6g vg00
  Volume group "vg00" has insufficient free space (1020 extents):
1536 required.
#
```

The minimum size that you can specify for an LV is the VG's PE size. Thus, if you use the default PE size when creating your VG, the smallest size LV is 4 MiB.

Here is an example of using the lvcreate command to create an LV. Many default options are accepted, but remember that you can view the lvcreate command's man pages to see the various non-default settings available for your use. In this example, the -v (verbose) option is used to display more information during the LV creation process:

```
# lvcreate -L 2g -v vg00
  Finding volume group "vg00"
  Archiving volume group "vg00" metadata (seqno 1).
  Creating logical volume lvol0
  Creating volume group backup "/etc/lvm/backup/vg00" (seqno 2).
  Activating logical volume "lvol0".
  activation/volume_list configuration setting not defined:
Checking only host tags for vg00/lvol0
  Creating vg00-lvol0
  Loading vg00-lvol0 table (253:2)
  Resuming vg00-lvol0 (253:2)
  Wiping known signatures on logical volume "vg00/lvol0"
  Initializing 4.00 KiB of logical volume "vg00/lvol0"
with value 0.
  Logical volume "lvol0" created.
#
```

Notice that the first LV from this VG's default name is lvol0. However, you must now use its full path name for displaying this LV's information, /dev/vg00/lvol0. Later on in this chapter, you'll learn how to use its Device Mapper name too. Here is a snipped example of using the lvdisplay command to show the LV's information:

```
# lvdisplay /dev/vg00/lvol0
 --- Logical volume ---
  LV Path                /dev/vg00/lvol0
  LV Name                lvol0
  VG Name                vg00
  LV UUID                rvdLvZ-Mk1r-8CCO-prnv-B82H-LdGI-SgGPxZ
  LV Write Access        read/write
[...]
  Block device           253:2

#
```

Notice that it too has been assigned an LV UUID. You can designate a non-default LV name using the lvcreate command's -n option.

Besides the lvdisplay command, you can use the lvs and the lvscan commands to display information on all of your system's LVs, as shown in this snipped example here:

```
# lvscan
  ACTIVE                '/dev/centos/swap' [820.00 MiB] inherit
  ACTIVE                '/dev/centos/root' [6.67 GiB] inherit
  ACTIVE                '/dev/vg00/lvol0' [2.00 GiB] inherit
#
# lvs
  LV    VG     Attr      LSize   Pool Origin [...]
  root  centos -wi-ao----   6.67g              [...]
  swap  centos -wi-ao---- 820.00m              [...]
  lvol0 vg00   -wi-a-----   2.00g              [...]
#
```

Once you have your LV created, you can treat it as if it is a regular partition. Of course, it is different in that you can grow or shrink this partition on the fly as needed.

Formatting and Mounting an LV

You don't have to do anything special with your LV in order to make a filesystem on it and then mount it to the virtual directory structure. The system views it as a normal partition, as shown in this snipped example here:

```
# mkfs -t ext4 /dev/vg00/lvol0
[...]
Creating journal (16384 blocks): done
```

```
Writing superblocks and filesystem accounting information: done

#
# mount -t ext4 /dev/vg00/lvol0 Temp
#
# ls Temp
lost+found
#
# touch Temp/My_LVM_File
#
# ls Temp
lost+found  My_LVM_File
#
```

Now that you have all of the various LVM parts created and an LV attached to your virtual directory structure, you still must maintain and manage it. The next section covers this topic.

Supporting Logical Volumes

Managing your system's LVs includes resizing them, which typically means increasing their size. However, sometimes you need to reduce an LV's size. Also, LVM includes creating LV snapshots, renaming them, removing an LV, and so on.

Growing Your VGs and LVs

The time comes when you need to increase an LV's size. It may be due to increasing data on the volume or it could be a new application being installed. In any case, growing an LV is fairly easy.

Before increasing an LV's size, it's worthwhile to look at increasing a VG's size with more PVs. You can't increase an LV beyond what its VG has to offer.

Once you've added or located additional storage, be sure that it is designated as a PV prior to attempting to add it to a VG pool. In this example, the new partition /dev/sdn1 is located via the lsblk command and then designated as a PV using the pvcreate utility:

```
# lsblk
NAME            MAJ:MIN RM  SIZE RO TYPE  MOUNTPOINT
[...]
sdk              8:160  0    1G  0 disk
└─sdk1           8:161  0 1023M  0 part
  └─vg00-lvol0 253:2    0    2G  0 lvm
[...]
```

```
sdn                  8:208  0    1G  0 disk
└─sdn1               8:209  0 1023M  0 part
[...]
#
# pvcreate -v /dev/sdn1
    Set up physical volume for "/dev/sdn1" with 2095104[...]
    Zeroing start of device /dev/sdn1
    Writing physical volume data to disk "/dev/sdn1"
  Physical volume "/dev/sdn1" successfully created
#
```

Notice here that some of the partitions, such as sdk1, are already shown to be part of an LV. The -v (verbose) option was used with the pvcreate utility to display more information because the partition is designated as a PV.

NOTE   If you have two oversized VGs, you can merge them with the vgmerge command. This can be useful if you have no additional partitions to use and need to increase an LV's size immediately.

Besides the pvdisplay command, you can use the pvscan utility to check the system for all available PVs. A snipped example of both is shown here:

```
# pvscan
[...]
  PV /dev/sdj1   VG vg00   lvm2 [1020.00 MiB / 0     free]
  PV /dev/sdk1   VG vg00   lvm2 [1020.00 MiB / 0     free]
  PV /dev/sdl1   VG vg00   lvm2 [1020.00 MiB / 1012.00 MiB free]
  PV /dev/sdm1   VG vg00   lvm2 [1020.00 MiB / 1020.00 MiB free]
  PV /dev/sdn1             lvm2 [1023.00 MiB]
  Total: 6 [12.49 GiB] / in use: 5 [11.49 GiB] /
   in no VG: 1 [1023.00 MiB]
#
# pvdisplay /dev/sdn1
  "/dev/sdn1" is a new physical volume of "1023.00 MiB"
  --- NEW Physical volume ---
  PV Name               /dev/sdn1
  VG Name
  PV Size               1023.00 MiB
  Allocatable           NO
  PE Size               0
  Total PE              0
  Free PE               0
```

```
    Allocated PE          0
    PV UUID               Gx679x-c59d-C0pS-2L7a-8yz9-addf-QBtw3Y
#
```

With the additional needed PV(s) designated, the VG can be extended. To increase the size of a VG pool, use the vgextend command, designating your additional PV(s) as shown here:

```
# vgextend vg00 /dev/sdn1
    Volume group "vg00" successfully extended
#
```

Once you have enough storage space in a VG, then you can go about growing your LV. To grow an LV, use the lvextend command. The -L option is used to set the new desired size of the LV. In this example, the LV, /dev/vg00/lvol0, is increased from 2 GiB to 4 GiB:

```
# lvextend -L 4g -v /dev/vg00/lvol0
    Finding volume group vg00
    Archiving volume group "vg00" metadata (seqno 3).
    Extending logical volume vg00/lvol0 to 4.00 GiB
  Size of logical volume vg00/lvol0 changed from
  2.00 GiB (512 extents) to 4.00 GiB (1024 extents).
    Loading vg00-lvol0 table (253:2)
    Suspending vg00-lvol0 (253:2) with device flush
    Resuming vg00-lvol0 (253:2)
    Creating volume group backup "/etc/lvm/backup/vg00"[...]
  Logical volume lvol0 successfully resized
#
```

Notice that a volume group backup is created. These backups are VG metadata only, and they do not contain any user or system LV data. They are often automatically created when using utilities like lvextend. However, it may be useful to create a VG metadata backup manually using the vgcfgbackup utility. You can restore the metadata using the vgcfgrestore command.

A helpful way to check your extended LV is using the --maps option. This option allows you to see the LV's logical extents mapped to PV physical extents. You can see in this snipped example that the newly grown /dev/vg00/lvol0 has a few physical extents assigned to it from the newly added /dev/sdn1 PV:

```
# lvdisplay --maps /dev/vg00/lvol0
  --- Logical volume ---
  LV Path              /dev/vg00/lvol0
[...]
```

```
  LV Size                4.00 GiB
[...]
 --- Segments ---
  Logical extents 0 to 254:
    Type          linear
    Physical volume     /dev/sdj1
    Physical extents    0 to 254
[...]
  Logical extents 1020 to 1023:
    Type          linear
    Physical volume     /dev/sdn1
    Physical extents    0 to 3
[...]
#
```

> **NOTE** If you need to shrink an LV's size, you can do so with the lvreduce command. However, this command can destroy data, so use it with caution, and be sure to review its man pages prior to using the command.

If you need to grow an LV that has swap space on it, some extra steps are involved. You must first enable alternative swap space, if you do not have a secondary swap space filesystem already in use. (See Chapter 4 for more information on managing your system's swap space.) After that, disable that swap space on the LV using the swapoff command. Once the LV swap space is disabled, you can use the normal methods for growing the LV. At this point, use the mkswap command to make the swap filesystem on the enlarged LV. Finally, re-enable the swap space using the swapon command.

Creating and Maintaining an LV Snapshot

An LV snapshot (sometimes called an LVM snapshot) deserves some special attention. It is more of an active data copy as opposed to a stagnant backup copy.

An LV snapshot is a copy-on-write, or COW, snapshot. When an LV COW snapshot is initially created, a location (snapshot LV) to store the snapshot is set up. At that time, no user or system LV data is copied to the snapshot location. Only metadata (concerning the user and system data's location) is copied. Thus, when a snapshot is created, it happens very quickly and does not cause any LV service interruptions.

After the initial snapshot creation, whenever any original LV data is to be changed, that data is first copied to the snapshot's location, which is known as copy-on-write behavior. Due to the need to copy any data from the original LV to the snapshot location prior to modification, an LV snapshot slightly slows down an LV's write performance.

Snapshots should not be considered data backups. They serve a different purpose.

Since only metadata and data that has been modified on the LV since the snapshot was created are physically stored on the LV snapshot, these snapshots hold virtual data copies. Also, they take up less room than the original LV.

LV snapshots are readable and writeable, and they can be mounted to the Linux virtual directory structure. Thus, they serve a few rather useful purposes. For example, you can use them to back up the original LV's data to another storage medium without stopping any applications using the original LV. You can also conduct new or modified program tests using production data. Any data writes that occur on the snapshot, but not on the original LV, are not automatically merged with original LV data. This allows you to write test data to the snapshot without adversely affecting production data. However, you can merge modified snapshot data with original LV data using the lvconvert command with the --merge option, if needed.

To create an LV snapshot, use the lvcreate command. Here is a snipped example of creating and activating an LV snapshot on a CentOS distribution:

```
# lvcreate -v -L 500m -s -n backup_snapshot /dev/vg00/lvol0
    Setting chunksize to 4.00 KiB.
    Finding volume group "vg00"
    Archiving volume group "vg00" metadata (seqno 32).
    Creating logical volume backup_snapshot
[...]
  Logical volume "backup_snapshot" created.
#
```

The -s option denotes that an LV snapshot should be created. The name of the snapshot is indicated by the -n option and in this case is backup_snapshot. The LV for which to create this snapshot is the last command item, /dev/vg00/lvol0.

The -L option sets the snapshot's size. For temporary LV snapshots, which will be used for items such as backups, the size can be fairly small, as in the preceding example. However, if this is a long-term snapshot, size it at a minimum to the original LV. This will allow it plenty of room to grow over time. If a snapshot's volume becomes full, the snapshot is unusable, so you may need to grow the volume size at some point in the future or remove this snapshot and create a new one. You can monitor an LV snapshot's size using the lvs utility.

 When you create an LV snapshot, it derives its LEs from the same VG as the original LV's VG. If for some reason a VG does not have enough LEs to give to the LV snapshot for its designated size, then it will not be able to create the snapshot.

Because the LV snapshot is actually an LV itself, you can view it using the `lvdisplay` command. Also, if you view the original LV, you will see that it has an active snapshot set for it, as shown in this snipped example here:

```
# lvdisplay /dev/vg00/lvol0
[...]
  LV snapshot status      source of
                          backup_snapshot [active]
[...]
#
# lvdisplay /dev/vg00/backup_snapshot
 --- Logical volume ---
  LV Path                 /dev/vg00/backup_snapshot
  LV Name                 backup_snapshot
  VG Name                 vg00
[...]
  LV snapshot status      active destination for lvol0
  LV Status               available
  # open                  0
  LV Size                 4.00 GiB
  Current LE              1024
  COW-table size          500.00 MiB
  COW-table LE            125
  Allocated to snapshot   0.00%
  Snapshot chunk size     4.00 KiB
  Segments                1
  Allocation              inherit
  Read ahead sectors      auto
  - currently set to      8192
  Block device            253:5

#
```

This particular sample LV snapshot was created for backup purposes. Therefore, the next thing to do is to mount the LV snapshot as read-only to a temporary location, as shown here:

```
# mount -o ro -t ext4 /dev/vg00/backup_snapshot Temp
#
# ls Temp
lost+found  My_LVM_File
#
```

At this point, you can perform a backup of the LV snapshot's data. Once your backup is complete, remove the LV snapshot. If you don't unmount the LV snapshot prior to removing it, you can get the following error:

```
# lvremove /dev/vg00/backup_snapshot
  Logical volume vg00/backup_snapshot contains a filesystem in use.
#
```

> An LV snapshot for backups should be thought of as a temporary structure. Once it has served its purpose, remove it from your system. A snapshot slows an LV's write performance, and if it is needed only for backups or testing purposes, it should be removed.

To avoid errors, simply unmount the LV snapshot prior to attempting to remove it using the `lvremove` command:

```
# umount /dev/vg00/backup_snapshot
#
# lvremove /dev/vg00/backup_snapshot
Do you really want to remove active logical volume
backup_snapshot? [y/n]: y
  Logical volume "backup_snapshot" successfully removed
#
```

The `lvremove` command can be used to remove other LVs besides just snapshots. It works the same for other LV types.

Renaming Your LV

Renaming an LV is simple using the `lvrename` utility. This is especially handy if you named your LV incorrectly when you originally created it.

Here's an example of renaming the `/dev/vg00/lvol0` LV to `/dev/vg00/new_name` on a CentOS distribution:

```
# lvrename /dev/vg00/lvol0 /dev/vg00/new_name
  Renamed "lvol0" to "new_name" in volume group "vg00"
#
```

You can also use a slightly different format for renaming a volume, as shown here:

```
# lvrename vg00 new_name lvol0
  Renamed "new_name" to "lvol0" in volume group "vg00"
#
```

This example designates the `vg00` VG and renames the `new_name` LV back to `lvol0`.

Employ the LVM Configuration File

When using the various LVM utilities, each utility uses a central configuration file to govern its behavior. This configuration file is the /etc/lvm/lvm.conf file. The file has wonderful internal documentation and additional assistance is provided when you type **man lvm.conf** at the command line.

The lvm.conf file's existence is not required, because the LVM utilities will use default settings. However, if the file does exist and has not been modified, it most likely will contain these default settings. The lvm.conf configuration file is considered a global file, and it may load additional local configuration files to refine its settings. LVM uses timestamps in association with this global file and any local configuration files. If the global (or local) configuration file has been modified, LVM reloads them.

Here an lvm.conf file is displayed, snipped, on a CentOS distribution:

```
# cat /etc/lvm/lvm.conf
# This is an example configuration file for the LVM2 system.
# It contains the default settings that would be used if there was no
# /etc/lvm/lvm.conf file.
#
# Refer to 'man lvm.conf' for further information including the file layout.
#
# To put this file in a different directory and override /etc/lvm set
# the environment variable LVM_SYSTEM_DIR before running the tools.
[...]
    # By default we accept every block device:
    # filter = [ "a/.*/" ]
[...]
#
```

Though you may never need to modify the lvm.conf file, there are some cases where it may be useful for your particular environment. For example, you can modify the lvm.conf configuration file to use filters, which are regular expressions. (A filter is shown in the preceding example and starts with filter =.) These filters in turn will limit what the various LVM *scan utilities can view. This is useful for speeding up scans should you have a large mixed storage environment.

You can employ the lvm dumpconfig utility to display lvm.conf settings. Here is a snipped example of this:

```
# lvm dumpconfig --type default
config {
        checks=1
        abort_on_errors=0
        profile_dir="/etc/lvm/profile"
}
```

```
[...]
tags {
        hosttags=0
#       tag {
#               host_list=""
#       }
}
#
```

There is a lot of information displayed by the `lvm dumpconfig` commands. It is worth piping the output into a pager utility for easy viewing.

A full description can be added to each configuration item displayed by the `lvm dumpconfig` command. Just simply tack on the **--withcomments** option to the end of any --type options. To see all of the various items that you can view and do with `lvm dumpconfig`, type **man lvm-dumpconfig** at the command line.

On earlier distributions, the `lvmconf` command was used to display `lvm.conf` settings instead of the `lvm dumpconfig` command.

In Exercise 5.1, you'll experiment with adding and removing LVs on your Linux system.

EXERCISE 5.1

Adding and Removing Logical Volumes

To experiment with creating and removing LVs, follow these steps:

1. If needed, add a drive with at least 4 GB virtually (if using a virtualized system) or physically to your system.

2. Log in as an ordinary user and use super user privileges throughout this exercise, or log in as a super user.

3. Create at least four new partitions on your new drives, and make them around 1 GB each. Record the partition names for your partitions.

4. Using the recorded partition names from the previous step, designate each partition as a PV by typing **pvcreate /dev/*partition*** and pressing Enter, where *partition* is the recorded partition name. Do this for each partition that you created in step 3. You should have four PVs at this step's end.

5. Create a VG using three of the four PVs from the previous step by typing **vgcreate vgex0 /dev/*partition1* /dev/*partition2* /dev/*partition3*** and pressing Enter. Be

sure to use three partition names that you designated as PVs in step 4. You should have a VG named vgex0 at this step's end.

6. Check your new VG by typing **vgdisplay vgex0** and pressing Enter.

7. Create a small LV from your newly created VG pool, named exvol0, by typing **lvcreate -L 500m -n exvol0 vgex0** and pressing Enter. You should have a new LV named exvol0 at this step's end.

8. View your new LV by typing **lvdisplay exvol0** and pressing Enter.

9. Create a second small LV from your newly created VG pool, named exvol2, by typing **lvcreate -L 500m -n exvol2 vgex0** and pressing Enter. You should have a new LV named exvol2 at this step's end.

10. View your second new LV by typing **lvdisplay exvol2** and pressing Enter.

11. Type in **lvscan** and press Enter to view all of your system's LVs.

12. Remove your first LV by typing **lvremove exvol0** and pressing Enter.

13. Type **lvscan** and press Enter to view all of your system's LVs.

14. Try various LVM commands discussed in this chapter that will allow you to do things such as resize your VG, vgex0, or mount the LV to a temporary directory in the Linux directory structure. The more you play with the various LVM commands, the more comfortable you will be when dealing with a production system.

Understanding the Device Mapper

LVs are assisted by the Device Mapper. The *Device Mapper* is a kernel driver, and it provides the ability to create mapped devices. It maps physical storage blocks to virtual storage blocks, creating a framework for LVM and RAID.

You can interact with the Device Mapper directory via the dmsetup utility. For example, to see the various LVs on your system, type **dmsetup info**. To see information for only one LV, pass its name along to the utility, as shown in the snippet here:

```
# dmsetup info /dev/vg00/lvol0
Name:              vg00-lvol0
State:             ACTIVE
[...]
UUID: LVM-2n3wGFxPSEr13RV5kXI0pVLDiebzB[...]
#
```

You can get help on the utility by entering **dmsetup help** at the command line. It's unlikely that you will need to modify any Device Mapper settings. However, you do need to be aware of the mapper. When you create an LV using the lvcreate command, not only can you reference it via its /dev name, such as /dev/vg00/lvol0 in earlier examples, but you can also reference it via /dev/mapper/*LV_name*. Here is a snipped example of using the dmsetup info command with the lvol0 LV's Device Mapper name:

```
# dmsetup info /dev/mapper/vg00-lvol0
Name:              vg00-lvol0
State:             ACTIVE
[...]
UUID: LVM-2n3wGFxPSEr13RV5kXI0pVLDiebZB[...]
#
```

You'll often see Device Mapper names being used in the /etc/fstab configuration file. Here is a snipped example from a CentOS distribution:

```
# cat /etc/fstab
[...]#
/dev/mapper/centos-root /     xfs     defaults     0 0
[...]
/dev/mapper/centos-swap swap  swap    defaults     0 0
[...]
#
```

As you can see, there are /dev/mapper names in the /etc/fstab file. On some distributions, /dev/mapper names must be used instead of /dev names for LVs so that the system will invoke LVM at system boot. Therefore, best practice recommends using /dev/mapper names within the /etc/fstab file for mounting LVs at system boot.

Though fairly easy to set up, logical volume management can be very complex to use. Hopefully, this section has helped you on your path to becoming an LVM expert.

Summary

Advanced devices, such as RAID and logical volumes, can assist in protecting your data and the access to it. Various utilities can help in setting kernel options to support and configure these devices. Additionally, some of these utilities are helpful in monitoring advanced storage devices as well as configuring them. Understanding these devices, the terminology surrounding them, how to configure and provide access to them, as well as continually managing their use are all important in data system administration.

Exam Essentials

Determine if software RAID is supported.   You can check if your system supports software RAID by determining if the /proc/mdstat file exists on it. This file provides current system RAID status information. Also, using the modprobe command, you can attempt to load various RAID kernel modules, such as raid6. Afterward, check the Personalities line in the /proc/mdstat file to see if any RAID levels are present, which indicates that the system supports those RAID levels.

Describe software RAID configuration files and utilities. The Multiple Disk or Device Administration (mdadm) utility is the primary utility for managing RAID arrays. RAID arrays are typically represented by device files /dev/md#, but they can also be represented by the Device Mapper. RAID arrays to be mounted at boot should have a record in the /etc/fstab file. The mdadm configuration file, mdadm.conf, is stored in either the /etc/ directory or the /etc/mdadm/ directory. RAID array information should be put into this configuration file, not by hand, but instead via redirected mdadm command scan output of a particular RAID array, using the --verbose, --detail, and --scan options.

Know Non-Volatile Memory Express (NVMe) Basics. NVMe is a logical device interface and command set standard for SSDs attached via the PCI Express bus. The Linux kernel has contained an NVMe standard interface driver since version 3.3. On Linux, NVMe interfaced SSDs are represented by the /dev/nvme* device files. The NVMe standard uses a namespace architecture, which is an additional top layer available for subdividing into partitions. Therefore, if you want to refer to a third NMVe drive's fourth namespace and first partition, use the /dev/nvme2n4p1 device.

Explain how to tune and test drives. The hdparm utility allows you to view, test, and, if needed, modify various drive settings, even though most drives come with their optimum configuration already set. The -I option shows all of the various drive settings, while the -W option shows or sets the drive setting, such as write-caching, listed. The hdparm options -t and -T conduct various performance tests, which should be done when the drive is inactive.

The sdparm utility gathers information from a SCSI device's Vital Product Data (VPD) tables, which includes data items such as part numbers, serial numbers, and code sets. The sdparm utility can be used to control a SCSI device's behavior, such as spinning down the drive or altering its write-back caching.

The sysctl utility modifies kernel parameters while a system is running. These parameters include those associated with storage devices. Use the -a option to view all of the various modifiable kernel parameters, or view the files in the /proc/sys/ directory. Several kernel parameters are Boolean values, and relatively few kernel parameters should be modified for tuning disk access and use.

Summarize iSCSI and its management. For an iSCSI SAN, the remote system serving an iSCSI disk is the target, and the client desiring to use an iSCSI disk is the initiator. A logical unit number (LUN) is one method used to identify a unique logical SCSI device on the target system. However, a World Wide Identifier (WWID), also called a World Wide Name (WWN), can be used. In addition, a unique ID for a SCSI device can be created using the scsi_id command. An iSCSI Qualified Name (IQN) is a unique address that identifies both the iSCSI target server and its offered iSCSI drive. The primary tool for setting up a target iSCSI disk is the targetcli utility, and the primary tool for managing an iSCSI disk on the initiator client is the iscsiadm utility. The iscsiadm utility discovers and logs into iSCSI targets, and it is used for managing the open-iscsi database files located in the /var/log/iscsi/ directory. New initiator iSCSI drives should have a record put into the initiator's /etc/fstab file and their IQN put into the /etc/iscsi/initiatorname.iscsi file.

Describe Logical Volume Management.   Multiple partitions collected and used as a single partition are at the core of logical volume management or Logical Volume Manager (LVM). The collection is accomplished through an abstraction layer so that the multiple partitions are referred to as a single volume. LVM has three primary parts. The first is the physical volume (PV), which is created using the LVM's pvcreate command. The utility designates an unused disk partition (or whole drive) to be used by LVM. Next, a volume group (VG), created by the LVM's vgcreate command, adds one or more PVs to a storage pool. This storage pool is used in turn to build the last item, a logical volume (LV). An LV is created using the LVM's lvcreate command and consists of storage space chunks. A physical extent (PE), set during the process of adding a PV to a VG, is the smallest block size that can be allocated on a PV, and logical extents (LEs) are mapped to VG physical extents and used on LVs. This mapping provides a way to access the data without concern about where a physical extent is located. LVs are also assisted by the Device Mapper, which is a kernel driver that provides the ability to create mapped devices. It maps physical storage blocks to virtual storage blocks, creating a framework for both LVM and RAID.

Explain how to resize, rename, and remove LVs.   To resize an LV, first increase the VG pool size if needed by adding additional PV(s) and afterward using the vgextend command. Once that's completed, grow an LV using the lvextend command, with the -L option set to the new desired LV size. To rename an LV, use the lvrename utility, designating both the old name and the desired new name. Prior to removing an LV, unmount the LV. Once it's unmounted, use the lvremove utility to remove the LV.

Review Questions

You can find the answers in the Appendix.

1. Which of the following RAID array structures are considered fault tolerant? (Choose all that apply.)

    A. RAID 0

    B. RAID 1

    C. RAID 10

    D. RAID 5

    E. RAID 6

2. Which one of the following RAID structures is also called disk striping with double parity? (Choose the best answer.)

    A. RAID 0

    B. RAID 1

    C. RAID 10

    D. RAID 5

    E. RAID 6

3. After you issue the `modprobe raid6` command using super user privileges on your system, which file should you check to determine if software RAID is supported on your system? (Choose the best answer.)

    A. `/proc/mdstat`

    B. `/dev/md0`

    C. `/etc/fstab`

    D. `/etc/mdadm/mdadm.conf`

    E. `/dev/mapper`

4. Which of the following is *not* an mdadm command mode? (Choose the best answer.)

    A. Grow mode

    B. `--follow`

    C. Delete mode

    D. `--manage`

    E. Miscellaneous mode

5. Which of the following mdadm command options chooses the mode to make a RAID array? (Choose the best answer.)

    A. `--grow`

    B. `-F`

    C. `--make`

    D. `-C`

    E. `--misc`

6. Current RAID array status is held in what file? (Choose the best answer.)

    A. `/etc/mdadm/mdadm.conf`

    B. `/etc/mdadm.conf`

    C. `/etc/fstab`

    D. `/proc/mdstat`

    E. `/etc/sysctl.conf`

7. Which of the following `mdadm` options would show in the RAID array in which the `/dev/sdc1` drive has membership? (Choose the best answer.)

    A. `--misc --detail  /dev/md0`

    B. `--misc --examine /dev/sdc1`

    C. `--detail --scan /dev/md0`

    D. `--monitor --help`

    E. None of the above

8. To delete an unmounted RAID array, you must do which of the following? (Choose all that apply.)

    A. Stop the RAID array.

    B. Shrink the RAID array.

    C. Monitor the RAID array.

    D. Delete RAID array drives' superblocks.

    E. Delete RAID array drives' data and superblocks.

9. On which of the following drive types can the `hdparm` utility be used? (Choose all that apply.)

    A. PATA

    B. ATAPI

    C. SATA

    D. SCSI

    E. All of the above

10. Which of the following `sdparm` command options will show all of the common mode parameters for a designated device? (Choose the best answer.)

    A. `--all`

    B. `--command show`

    C. `--hex`

    D. `--page`

    E. None of the above

11. What number designates both an iSCSI target server and an iSCSI disk being offered by that target? (Choose the best answer.)

    A. WWID

    B. WWN

    C. IQN

    D. LUN

    E. scsi_id

12. Where are iSCSI discovery records stored? (Choose all that apply.)

    A. /etc/iscsi/iscsid.conf

    B. /lib/udev/scsi_id

    C. /var/lib/iscsi/nodes

    D. /var/lib/iscsi/send_targets

    E. /var/log/iscsi.conf

13. Which of the following allows multiple partitions or whole disks to be grouped together and used as a single drive? (Choose all that apply.)

    A. PATA

    B. RAID

    C. iSCSI

    D. Logical volume management

    E. Storage fabric

14. Which is a designated unused disk partition or drive that can be used by LVM? (Choose the best answer.)

    A. PV

    B. VG

    C. LV

    D. SATA

    E. Backstore

15. Which of the following is *not* true concerning PEs? (Choose the best answer.)

    A. PE stands for "physical extent."

    B. A PE is the smallest block size that can be allocated on a PV.

    C. PE block size is set during the process of designating a PV.

    D. The default PE block size is 4 MiB.

    E. A PE block size setting can be chosen.

16. Which of the following is true concerning LEs? (Choose the best answer.)

    A. LEs are made up of LVs.

    B. LEs are mapped to VG physical extents.

    C. LE mapping provides a way to block data access.

    D. LE mappings occur during PV designation.

    E. None of the above.

17. Which of the following LVM utilities will designate a partition as a PV? (Choose the best answer.)

    A. pvdisplay

    B. vgcreate

    C. lvcreate

    D. pvcreate

    E. pvscan

18. You've just finished creating vg01. What utility would be the best one to check it? (Choose the best answer.)

    A. pvdisplay

    B. vgcreate

    C. pvscan

    D. vgdisplay

    E. lvdisplay

19. Which of the following are true about LV snapshots? (Choose all that apply.)

    A. LV snapshots are LVs themselves.

    B. LV snapshots are read-only.

    C. LV snapshots can be mounted to the directory.

    D. LV snapshots contain copies of the original LV data.

    E. LV snapshots are created using the vgcreate command.

20. To rename an LV, which utility should you use? (Choose the best answer.)

    A. lvrename

    B. lvremove

    C. lvconvert

    D. lvs

    E. lvmchange

Chapter

6

Navigating Network Services

THE FOLLOWING EXAM OBJECTIVES ARE COVERED IN THIS CHAPTER:

✓ **205.1 Basic network configuration**

✓ **205.2 Advanced Network Configuration**

✓ **205.3 Troubleshooting network issues**

These days, it's a necessity to have your Linux system connected to some type of network. Whether it's because of the need to share files and printers on a local network or because of the need to connect to the Internet to download updates and security patches, most Linux systems have some type of network connection.

This chapter looks at how to configure your Linux system to connect to a network, as well as how to troubleshoot network connections if things go wrong. First, it covers the basics of networking to make sure that you're familiar with all of the terms and configuration pieces necessary to talk with other devices on the network. Next, the chapter examines how to set those configuration values in both wired and wireless network environments. After that, the chapter shows some simple troubleshooting techniques that you can use to help find the problem if anything goes wrong.

Networking Basics

Before we look at how Linux handles network connectivity, it'll help to go through the basics of computer networking. *Computer networking* is how we get data from one computer system to another. To help simplify things, computer networks are often described as a *layered* system. Different layers play different roles in the process of getting the data from one network device to another.

There's much debate, though, on just how best to split up the networking layers. While the standard OSI network model uses seven layers, we'll use a simplified four-layer approach to describing the network functions:

- The physical layer
- The network layer
- The transport layer
- The application layer

The following sections detail the parts contained in each of these four layers.

The Physical Layer

The physical layer consists of the hardware required to connect your Linux system to the network. If you've ever connected a computer to either a home or an office network, you're already familiar with the two main methods used to connect network devices—wired and wireless network connections.

Wired network connections use a series of network switches to connect network devices using special Ethernet cables. The network switch accepts data packets from the network device and then sends the data packets to the correct destination device on the network. For large office network installations, switches are usually connected in a cascade design to help reduce traffic load on the network. Switches can be interconnected to help segment the network traffic into smaller areas. Figure 6.1 demonstrates a common layout for a wired network.

FIGURE 6.1   A wired office network infrastructure

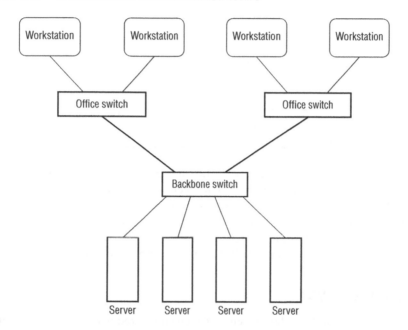

While the term *wired* may make you think of copper cables, it can also apply to network connections that use *fiber-optic cables*. Fiber-optic cables use light to transmit data down a thin glass strand, achieving faster speeds and covering longer distances than conventional copper connections. Although wired networking can be cumbersome, it does provide the fastest network speeds (currently up to 100 gigabits per second). For that reason, wired networking is still popular in Linux server environments where high throughput is a must.

Nowadays though, most small office and home networks utilize *wireless networking*. Instead of using physical wires or fiber cables to connect devices, wireless networking uses radio signals to transmit the data between the network device and a *network access point*. The access point works in a similar manner as the switch, in that it controls how data is sent to each network device communicating with it.

Each access point uses a unique *Service Set Identifier (SSID)* to identify it from other access points, which can be a name or number. You just tell your Linux system to which access point it should connect by specifying the correct SSID value. Figure 6.2 demonstrates a common wireless network layout.

FIGURE 6.2   A wireless network infrastructure

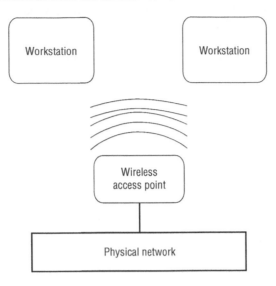

The downside to wireless networking is that you can't control where the radio signals travel. It's possible that someone outside your home will intercept your access point signals and try to connect with them. Because of that, it's important to implement some type of encryption security on your access point. Only devices using the correct encryption key can connect to the wireless access point. Common wireless encryption techniques are Wired Equivalent Privacy (WEP), Wi-Fi Protected Access (WPA), and Wi-Fi Protected Access version 2 (WPA2).

The Network Layer

The *network layer* controls how data is sent between connected network devices, both in your local network and across the Internet. For data to get to the correct destination device, there must be some type of network addressing scheme to identify each network device uniquely. The most common method for doing that is the *Internet Protocol (IP or IPv4)*.

While the IP network protocol is by far the most popular in use, it's not the only network protocol available. Apple formerly used a proprietary protocol called AppleTalk to allow Apple computers to communicate with each other on a local network, and Novell used the IPX/SPX protocol for communication between Novell network servers and clients. These network protocols, however, have faded from standard use and aren't covered in the LPIC-2 exam.

To connect your Linux system to an IP network, you'll need four pieces of information:

- An IP address
- A hostname

- A default router
- A netmask value

The following sections walk through what each of these values represents.

The IP Address

In an IP network, each network device is assigned a unique 32-bit address. Network layer software embeds the source and destination IP addresses into the data packet so that networking devices know how to handle the data packet and the Linux system knows which packets to read and which to ignore.

To make it easier for humans to recognize the address, IP addresses are split into four 8-bit values, represented by decimal numbers, with a period between each value. This format is called *dotted-decimal notation*. For example, a standard IP address in dotted-decimal notation looks like 192.168.1.10.

IP addresses are split into two sections. One part of the IP address represents the *network address*. All devices on the same physical network have the same network address portion of their IP address. For example, if your home network is assigned the network address 192.168.1.0, all of the network devices must start with the IP address 192.168.1.

The second part represents the *host address*. Each device on the same network must have a unique host address. Figure 6.3 demonstrates assigning unique IP addresses to devices on a local network.

FIGURE 6.3   Network addressing on a local network

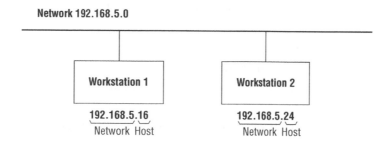

To complicate things even further, a newer IP network protocol called *Internet Protocol version 6* (IPv6) has become popular. The IPv6 networking scheme uses 128-bit addresses instead of the 32-bit addresses used by IP, which allows many more network devices to be identified uniquely on the Internet.

The IPv6 method uses hexadecimal numbers to identify addresses. The 128-bit address is split into eight groups of four hexadecimal digits separated by colons, such as this:

```
fed1:0000:0000:08d3:1319:8a2e:0370:7334
```

If one or more groups of four digits are 0000, that group or those groups may be omitted, leaving two colons:

`fed1::08d3:1319:8a2e:0370:7334`

However, only one set of consecutive zeroes can be compressed this way. IPv6 also provides for two different types of host addresses:

- Link local addresses
- Global addresses

The IPv6 software on a host device automatically assigns the *link local address*. The link local address uses a default network address of `fe80::`; then it derives the host part of the address from the media access control (MAC) address built into the network card. This ensures that any IPv6 device can automatically communicate with any other IPv6 device on a local network without any configuration.

The IPv6 global address works in a similar manner as the original IP version: each network is assigned a unique network address, and each host on the network must have a unique host address.

Default Router

With IP and IPv6, devices can only communicate directly with other devices on the same physical network. To connect different physical networks together, you use a *router*. A router passes data from one network to another network. Devices that need to send packets to hosts on remote networks must use the router as a go-between. Usually, a network will contain a single router to forward packets to an upper-level network. This is called a *default router* (or sometimes a *default gateway*).

Thus, for a device to communicate in an IP network, it must know three separate pieces of information:

- Its own host address on the network
- The network address of the local physical network
- The address of a local router used to send packets to remote networks

You've already seen how to specify host addresses using the dotted-decimal notation (such as 192.168.1.10). You specify the network address using a *netmask* address, which is covered in the next section.

Netmask Address

The netmask address distinguishes between the network and host address portions in the IP address by using 1 bit to show which bits of the 32-bit IP address are used by the network and 0 bits to show which bits represent the host address. Since most people don't like working with binary numbers, the netmask address is usually shown in dotted-decimal format. For example, the netmask address 255.255.255.0 indicates that the first three decimal numbers in the IP address represent the network address and the last decimal number represents the host address.

There's another way to represent netmask addresses called the Classless Inter-Domain Routing (CIDR) notation. CIDR notation represents the netmask as just the number of masked bits in the IP address. CIDR notation is usually shown with a slash between the network address and the CIDR value. Thus, the network 192.168.1.0 and netmask 255.255.255.0 would have the CIDR notation of 192.168.1.0/24. While CIDR notation is becoming popular in the networking world, Linux configuration files still use the netmask value to define the network.

As mentioned, to connect your Linux system to a network, you need to specify three values. Here's an example of what you would need:

- Host address: 192.168.20.5
- Netmask address: 255.255.255.0
- Default gateway: 192.168.20.1

With these three values in hand, you're almost ready to configure your Linux system to work on the Internet. There's just one more piece of the puzzle that you'll need to worry about, and we'll look at that in the next section.

Hostnames

With all of these IP addresses, it can be impossible to remember just what servers have what addresses. Fortunately for us, there's yet another network standard that can help out. The *Domain Name System (DNS)* assigns a name to hosts on the network.

With DNS, each network address is assigned a *domain name* (such as linux.org) that uniquely identifies the network, and each host in that network is assigned a *hostname*, which is added to the domain name to uniquely identify the host on the network.

Thus, to find the host shadrach on the domain example.org, you'd use the DNS name shadrach.example.org. The DNS system uses servers to map host and domain names to the specific network addresses required to communicate with that server. Servers responsible for defining the network and hostnames for a local network interoperate with upper-level DNS servers to resolve remote hostnames.

To use DNS in your network applications, all you need to configure is the address of the DNS server that services your local network. From there, your local DNS server can find the address of any hostname anywhere on the Internet.

Dynamic Host Configuration Protocol

We need to discuss one more network layer feature before we move on to configuring the Linux system. Trying to keep track of host addresses for all of the devices on a large network can be cumbersome. Keeping individual IP address assignments straight can be a challenge, and often you'll run into the situation where two or more devices are accidentally assigned the same IP address.

The *Dynamic Host Configuration Protocol (DHCP)* was created to make it easier to configure client workstations, which don't necessarily need to use the same IP address all the time. With DHCP, the client communicates with a DHCP server on the network using a temporary address. The DHCP server then tells the client exactly which IP address, netmask address, default gateway, and even DNS server to use. Each time the client reboots, it may receive a different IP address, but that doesn't matter as long as it's unique on the network.

Most home network routers include a DHCP server function, so all you need to do is to set your Linux client to use DHCP and you're finished. You don't need to know any of the "behind the scenes" details of the network addresses.

While DHCP is great for clients, it's not a good idea to use it for servers. Servers need to have a fixed IP address so that the clients can always find them. Although it's possible to configure static IP addresses in DHCP, usually it's safest to configure the network information manually for servers. This is called a *static host address*.

The Transport Layer

The *transport layer* can often be the most confusing part of the network. While the network layer helps get data to a specific host on the network, the transport layer helps get the data to the correct application contained on the host. It does that by using *ports*.

Ports are sort of like apartment numbers. Each application that's running on a network server is assigned its own port number, just as each apartment in the same apartment building is assigned a unique apartment number. To send data to a specific application on a server, the client software needs to know both the server IP address (just like the apartment building address) and the transport layer port number (just like the apartment number).

There are two common transport protocols used in the IP networking world:

- Transmission Control Protocol
- User Datagram Protocol

The *Transmission Control Protocol (TCP)* sends data using a guaranteed delivery method. It ensures that the server receives each portion of data that the client computer sends and vice versa. The downside to this is that a lot of overhead is required to track and verify all of the data sent, which can slow the data transfer speed.

For data that's sensitive to transfer speed (such as real-time data like voice and video), this can cause unwanted delays. The alternative to this is the *User Datagram Protocol (UDP)*. UDP doesn't bother to ensure delivery of each portion of the data; it just sends the data out on the network and hopes it gets to the server!

While losing data may sound like a bad thing, for some applications (such as voice and video) it's perfectly acceptable. Missing audio or video packets just show up as blips and breaks in the final audio or video result. As long as most of the data packets arrive, the audio and video are understandable.

The Application Layer

The application layer is where all of the action happens. This is where the network programs process the data sent across the network and then return a result. Most network applications behave using the *client/server paradigm*. With the client/server paradigm, one network device acts as the server, offering some type of service to multiple network clients (such as a web server offering content via web pages). The server listens for incoming connections on specific transport layer ports assigned to the application. The clients must know what transport layer port to use to send requests to the server application.

To simplify that process, both TCP and UDP use *well-known ports* to represent common applications. These port numbers are reserved so that network clients know to use them when looking for specific application hosts on the network. Table 6.1 shows some of the more common well-known application ports.

TABLE 6.1 TCP and UDP well-known ports

Port	Protocol	Application
22	TCP	Secure Shell Protocol (SSH)
23	TCP	Telnet (interactive command lines)
25	TCP	SMTP (Simple Mail Transport Protocol)
53	UDP	DNS (Dynamic Name System)
80	TCP	HTTP (Hypertext Transport Protocol)
143	TCP	IMAP (Internet Message Access Protocol)
443	TCP	HTTPS (Secure HTTP)

Now that you've seen the basics of how Linux uses networking to transfer data between systems, the next section dives into the details on how to configure these features in your Linux system.

Configuring Network Features

As you saw in the previous section, you'll need to configure five main pieces of information in your Linux system to interact on a network:

- The host address
- The network address

- The default router (sometimes called the gateway)
- The system hostname
- A DNS server address for resolving hostnames

  There are three different ways to configure this information in Linux systems:

- Manually editing network configuration files
- Using a graphical tool
- Using command-line tools

  The following sections walk you through each of these methods.

Network Configuration Files

Every Linux distribution uses network configuration files to define the network settings required to communicate on the network. Unfortunately, though, there's no single standard configuration file that all distributions use. Instead, different distributions use different configuration files to define the network settings. Table 6.2 shows the most common network configuration files that you'll run into.

TABLE 6.2   Linux network configuration files

Distribution	Network Configuration Location
Debian-based	`/etc/network/interfaces` file
Red Hat–based	`/etc/sysconfig/network-scripts` directory
OpenSUSE	`/etc/sysconfig/network` file

While each of the Linux distributions uses a different method of defining the network settings, they all have similar features. Most configuration files define each of the required network settings as separate values in the configuration file. Listing 6.1 shows an example from a Debian-based Linux system.

Listing 6.1: Sample Debian network static configuration settings

```
auto eth0
iface eth0 inet static
    address 192.168.1.77
    netmask 255.255.255.0
    gateway 192.168.1.254
```

```
iface eth0 inet6 static
   address 2003:aef0::23d1::0a10:00a1
   netmask 64
   gateway 2003:aef0::23d1::0a10:0001
```

The example shown in Listing 6.1 assigns both an IP address and an IPv6 address to the wired network interface designated as eth0.

Listing 6.2 shows how to define the IP network settings automatically using a DHCP server on the network.

Listing 6.2: Sample Debian network DHCP configuration settings

```
auto eth0
iface eth0 inet dhcp
iface eth0 inet6 dhcp
```

If you just want to assign an IPv6 link local address and not retrieve an IPv6 address from a DHCP server, replace the inet6 line with this:

```
iface eth0 inet6 auto
```

The auto attribute tells Linux to assign the link local address, which allows the Linux system to communicate with any other IPv6 device on the local network but not with a global address.

For Red Hat–based systems, you'll need to set the network settings in two separate files. The first file defines the network and netmask addresses in a file named after the network interface name (such as ifcfg-eth0). Listing 6.3 shows an example from a CentOS Linux system.

Listing 6.3: Sample CentOS ifcfg-eth0 file configuration settings

```
DEVICE="eth0"
NM_CONTROLLED="no"
ONBOOT=yes
TYPE=Ethernet
BOOTPROTO=static
NAME="System eth0"
IPADDR=192.168.1.77
NETMASK=255.255.255.0
IPV6INIT=yes
IPV6ADDR=2003:aef0::23d1::0a10:00a1/64
```

The second file required on Red Hat–based systems is the network file, which defines the hostname and default gateway, as shown in Listing 6.4.

Listing 6.4: Sample CentOS network file configuration settings

```
NETWORKING=yes
HOSTNAME=mysystem
GATEWAY=192.168.1.254
IPV6FORWARDING=yes
IPV6_AUTOCONF=no
IPV6_AUTOTUNNEL=no
IPV6_DEFAULTGW=2003:aef0::23d1::0a10:0001
IPV6_DEFAULTDEV=eth0
```

Notice that the Red Hat network configuration file also defines the hostname assigned to the Linux system. For other types of Linux systems, storing the hostname in the /etc/ hostname file has become somewhat of a de facto standard. However, some Linux distributions use /etc/HOSTNAME instead.

You will also need to define a DNS server so that the system can use DNS hostnames. Fortunately, all Linux systems follow this standard, and it is handled in the /etc/resolv .conf configuration file:

```
domain mydomain.com
search mytest.com
nameserver 192.168.1.1
```

The domain entry defines the domain name assigned to the network. By default, the system will append this domain name to any hostnames that you specify. The search entry defines any additional domains used to search for hostnames. The nameserver entry is where you specify the DNS server assigned to your network. Some networks can have more than one DNS server; just add multiple nameserver entries in the file.

> To help speed up connections to commonly used hosts, you can manually enter their hostnames and IP addresses into the /etc/hosts file on your Linux system. Linux will check this file before using DNS to look up the hostname.

Graphical Tools

The *Network Manager* tool is a popular program used by many Linux distributions to provide a graphical interface for defining network connections. Network Manager starts automatically at boot time, and it appears in the system tray area of the desktop as an icon.

If your system detects a wired network connection, the icon appears as two arrows pointing in opposite directions. If your system detects a wireless network connection, the icon appears as an empty radio signal. When you click the icon, you'll see a list of the available wireless networks detected by the network card, as shown in Figure 6.4.

FIGURE 6.4   Network Manager showing a wireless network

Click your access point to select it from the list. If your access point is encrypted, you'll be prompted to enter the password to gain access to the network.

Once your system is connected to a wireless access point, the icon appears as a radio signal. Click the icon, and then select Edit Connections to edit the network connection settings for the system, as shown in Figure 6.5.

FIGURE 6.5   The Network Connections window

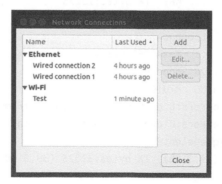

You can select the network connection to configure (either wireless or wired) and then click the Edit button to change the current configuration. Network Manager allows you to specify all four of the network configuration values by using the manual configuration option, or you can set the configuration to use DHCP to determine the settings. Network

Manager automatically updates the appropriate network configuration files with the updated settings.

Command-Line Tools

If you're not working with a graphical desktop client environment, you'll need to use the Linux command-line tools to set the network configuration information. You'll need to know three main commands to do that:

ifconfig—This command sets the IP address and netmask values for a network interface.

iwconfig—This command sets the SSID and encryption key for a wireless interface.

route—This command sets the default router address.

Before you can get very far, you'll need to know the device name that Linux assigns to your network card. The easiest way to do that is to use the ifconfig command by itself, without any parameters, as shown in Listing 6.5.

Listing 6.5: The ifconfig output

```
$ ifconfig
eth0      Link encap:Ethernet  HWaddr 08:00:27:b0:e3:02
          inet addr:192.168.1.67  Bcast:192.168.1.255  Mask:255.255.255.0
          inet6 addr: fe80::a00:27ff:feb0:e302/64 Scope:Link
          UP BROADCAST RUNNING MULTICAST  MTU:1500  Metric:1
          RX packets:677 errors:0 dropped:0 overruns:0 frame:0
          TX packets:118 errors:0 dropped:0 overruns:0 carrier:0
          collisions:0 txqueuelen:1000
          RX bytes:97003 (97.0 KB)  TX bytes:15225 (15.2 KB)

lo        Link encap:Local Loopback
          inet addr:127.0.0.1  Mask:255.0.0.0
          inet6 addr: ::1/128 Scope:Host
          UP LOOPBACK RUNNING  MTU:65536  Metric:1
          RX packets:171 errors:0 dropped:0 overruns:0 frame:0
          TX packets:171 errors:0 dropped:0 overruns:0 carrier:0
          collisions:0 txqueuelen:0
          RX bytes:39325 (39.3 KB)  TX bytes:39325 (39.3 KB)

$
```

This example shows two network interfaces on the Linux system:

eth0—The wired Ethernet interface

lo—The local loopback interface

The *local loopback interface* is a special virtual network interface. Any local program can use it to communicate with other programs just as if they were across a network. That can simplify transferring data between programs.

The eth0 network interface is the wired network connection for the Linux system. The ifconfig command shows the IP address assigned to the interface (both an IP address and an IPv6 link local address are assigned), the netmask value, and some basic statistics about the packets on the interface.

If the output doesn't show a network address assigned to the interface, you can use the ifconfig command to specify the host address and netmask values for the interface. The options for the ifconfig program are shown in Table 6.3.

TABLE 6.3   The ifconfig command options

Option	Description
-a	Display all interfaces.
-s	Display a short listing.
-v	Display more information about errors.
interface	Specify the interface name.
up	Enable the interface.
down	Disable the interface.
[-]arp	Enable or disable the Address Resolution Protocol (ARP) on the interface.
[-]promisc	Enable or disable promiscuous mode on the interface.
[-]allmulti	Enable or disable the ability to receive multicast packets.
metric N	Set the interface metric.
mtu N	Set the maximum transmission unit (MTU) size.
netmask addr	Set the network mask for the interface.
add addr	Add an IPv6 address to the interface.
del addr	Remove an IPv6 address from the interface.
tunnel ::aa.bb.cc.dd	Create an IPv6-in-IPv4 tunnel to the specified destination.
irq addr	Specify the IRQ interrupt for the interface.

TABLE 6.3 *The* ifconfig *command options (continued)*

Option	Description
io_addr addr	Specify the IO address for the interface.
mem_start addr	Specify the start address for the interface shared memory.
media type	Specify the media type for the interface.
[-]broadcast addr	Set the broadcast address for the interface.
[-]pointtopoint addr	Create a point-to-point connection to a remote device.
hw class address	Specify the hardware address for the interface.
multicast	Allow multicast packets for the interface.
address	Specify an IPv4 address for the interface.
txqueuelen len	Specify the length of the transmit queue for the interface.

This long list of options allows you to customize lots of features of the network interface. Usually, though, you just need to use a couple of options to define the basic network settings. For example, to set the address and netmask values and then activate the eth0 interface, you'd use the following command:

```
# ifconfig eth0 up 192.168.1.67 netmask 255.255.255.0
```

The up parameter tells the Linux system to activate the interface after configuring it. You can also assign an address to an interface and leave it deactivated by using the down parameter.

There are also two shortcut commands, ifup and ifdown, that you can use to quickly bring a specific interface that's already configured up or down.

If your Linux system uses a wireless network connection, you'll most likely see a wlan0 interface listed in the ifconfig output:

```
wlan0   Link encap:Ethernet  HWaddr 00:23:15:a6:1b:dc
        inet addr:192.168.1.65  Bcast:192.168.1.255  Mask:255.255.255.0
        inet6 addr:fe80::223:15ff:fea6:1bdc/64 Scope:Link
        UP BROADCAST RUNNING MULTICAST  MTU:1500  Metric:1
        RX packets:13513 errors:0 dropped:0 overruns:0 frame:0
```

```
TX packets:6894 errors:0 dropped:0 overruns:0 carrier:0
collisions:0 txqueuelen:1000
RX bytes:20016644 (20.0 MB)  TX bytes:608292 (608.2 KB)
```

Before you can use the ifconfig command to assign an address to a wireless interface, you must assign the wireless SSID and encryption key values using the iwconfig command:

```
# iwconfig wlan0 essid "MyNetwork" key s:mypassword
```

The essid parameter specifies the access point SSID name, and the key parameter specifies the encryption key required to connect to it. Notice that the encryption key is preceded by an s:. That allows you to specify the encryption key in ASCII text characters; otherwise, you'll need to specify the key using hexadecimal values.

If you don't know the name of a local wireless connection, you can use the iwlist command to display all of the wireless signals that your wireless card detects. Just specify the name of the wireless device, and use the scan option:

```
$ iwlist wlan0 scan
```

To specify the default router for your network, you must use the route command:

```
# route add default gw 192.168.1.1
```

You can also use the route command by itself to view the current default router configured for the system.

```
$ route
Kernel IP routing table
Destination     Gateway         Genmask         Flags Metric Ref Use Iface
default         192.168.1.254   0.0.0.0         UG    0      0   0   eth0
192.168.1.0     *               255.255.255.0   U     1      0   0   eth0
$
```

The default router defined for the Linux system is 192.168.1.254, and it is available from the eth0 network interface. The output also shows that to get to the 192.168.1.0 network you don't need a gateway, since that's the local network to which the Linux system is connected.

If your network is connected to multiple networks via multiple routers, you can manually create the routing table in the system by using the add or del command-line option for the route command. The format for that is

```
route [add] [del] target gw gateway
```

where target is the target host or network and gateway is the router address.

If your network uses DHCP, you'll need to ensure that a proper DHCP client program is running on your Linux system. The DHCP client program communicates with the network DHCP server in the background, and it assigns the necessary IP address settings as directed by the DHCP server. Three common DHCP programs are available for Linux systems:

- dhcpcd

- dhclient

- pump

The dhcpcd program is becoming the most popular of the three, but you'll still see the other two used in some Linux distributions.

When you use your Linux system's software package manager utility to install the DHCP client program, it sets the program to launch automatically at boot time and handle the IP address configuration needed to interact on the network.

 While the ifconfig and iwconfig commands are by far the most popular methods for retrieving and setting IP and wireless information, a newer set of programs is starting to appear in the Linux world. Simply called ip and iw, these programs allow "one-stop shopping" for all of your IP and wireless configuration needs. With the ip command, you can list the IP address, network mask, and router information with just a couple of commands:

```
ip addr show
ip route show
```

Similarly, with the iw command, you can display all of the wireless statistics (such as which frequencies your wireless card is listening on) and select which bands your wireless card uses. If you find that the ifconfig or iwconfig commands don't work in your particular Linux distribution, try using the ip and iw commands instead.

Basic Network Troubleshooting

Once you have a Linux network interface installed, there are a few things that you can do to make sure it's operating properly. This section walks you through the commands that you should know to monitor the network interface and troubleshoot it if things aren't working correctly.

Checking the Log Files

One primary reason for a lack of network connectivity is that something went wrong with the kernel loading the appropriate module for the network card hardware. The way to troubleshoot this is to look at the kernel boot messages.

One way to do that is with the dmesg command, which displays the contents of the kernel ring buffer. The kernel ring buffer contains kernel messages, but it cycles old messages out as new messages are received. If you recently booted the Linux system, the boot messages may still be in the buffer. Here's an example of the kernel boot messages for a properly loaded wired network connection:

```
[2.06] e1000 0000:00:03.0 eth0: (PCI:33MHz:32-bit) 08:00:27:b0:e3:02
[2.06] e1000 0000:00:03.0 eth0: Intel(R) PRO/1000 Network Connection
[21.89] e1000: eth0 NIC Link is Up 1000 Mbps Full Duplex, Flow Control: RX
[21.90] IPv6: ADDRCONF(NETDEV_UP): eth0: link is not ready
[21.90] IPv6: ADDRCONF(NETDEV_CHANGE): eth0: link becomes ready
```

If it's been awhile since you booted the Linux system, the kernel boot messages may have rolled out of the kernel ring buffer. In that case, you'll need to check the log files in the /var/log directory. Depending on your Linux distribution, the kernel boot messages may be in the dmesg, syslog, or messages file.

Viewing the ARP Cache

Each Linux system on the network has two unique addresses assigned to it. You've seen that it requires a unique IP (or IPv6) address, but it also has a unique hardware address assigned to the network card itself. This is the *media access control (MAC)* address, and it is assigned by the network card manufacturer to identify each network card uniquely on the network.

As your Linux system communicates with other devices on the network, it maps the hardware MAC addresses associated with each system it talks with to the individual network IP addresses. It does this using the *Address Resolution Protocol (ARP)*. Linux maintains a cache of these addresses, called the *ARP table*. You can view the contents of the ARP table by using the arp command:

```
$ arp
Address          HWtype  HWaddress          Flags Mask      Iface
10.0.2.2         ether   52:54:00:12:35:02  C               enp0s3
$
```

This helps you map IP addresses to specific hardware devices on the network. Table 6.4 shows a few command-line options for the arp command that allow you to manipulate the ARP table if you run into problems.

TABLE 6.4   The *arp* command options

Option	Description
-a	Use BSD style output format.
-D	Use the interface name instead of the hardware address in the ARP table.

TABLE 6.4   *The* arp *command options (continued)*

Option	Description
`-d address`	Delete the specified ARP table entry.
`-e`	Use default Linux-style output.
`-f filename`	Create new ARP table entries from the data in the file.
`-H type`	Show only MAC addresses of the type specified.
`-i`	Display only addresses received on the specified address.
`-n`	Show numerical addresses instead of hostnames.
`-s address hw_addr`	Create a new ARP table entry.
`-v`	Use verbose mode.

By comparing the MAC addresses assigned to IP addresses, you may be able to detect duplicate IP addresses assigned to different devices on your local network.

Sending Test Packets

One way to test network connectivity is to send test packets to known hosts. Linux provides the ping and ping6 commands to do just that. The ping and ping6 commands send *Internet Control Message Protocol (ICMP)* packets to remote hosts using either IP (ping) or IPv6 (ping6). ICMP packets work behind the scenes to track connectivity and provide control messages between systems. If the remote host supports ICMP, it will send a reply packet back when it receives a ping packet.

The basic format for the ping command is just to specify the IP address of the remote host:

```
$ ping 10.0.2.2
PING 10.0.2.2 (10.0.2.2) 56(84) bytes of data.
64 bytes from 10.0.2.2: icmp_seq=1 ttl=63 time=14.6 ms
64 bytes from 10.0.2.2: icmp_seq=2 ttl=63 time=3.82 ms
64 bytes from 10.0.2.2: icmp_seq=3 ttl=63 time=2.05 ms
64 bytes from 10.0.2.2: icmp_seq=4 ttl=63 time=0.088 ms
64 bytes from 10.0.2.2: icmp_seq=5 ttl=63 time=3.54 ms
64 bytes from 10.0.2.2: icmp_seq=6 ttl=63 time=3.97 ms
64 bytes from 10.0.2.2: icmp_seq=7 ttl=63 time=0.040 ms
^C
```

```
--- 10.0.2.2 ping statistics ---
7 packets transmitted, 7 received, 0% packet loss, time 6020ms
rtt min/avg/max/mdev = 0.040/4.030/14.696/4.620 ms
$
```

The ping command continues sending packets until you press Ctrl+C. You can also use the -c command-line option to specify a set number of packets to send and then stop.

For the ping6 command, things get a little more complicated. If you're using an IPv6 link local address, you also need to tell the command which interface to send the packets out on:

```
$ ping6 -c 4 fe80::c418:2ed0:aead:cbce%eth0
PING fe80::c418:2ed0:aead:cbce%eth0(fe80::c418:2ed0:aead:cbce) 56 data bytes
64 bytes from fe80::c418:2ed0:aead:cbce: icmp_seq=1 ttl=128 time=1.47 ms
64 bytes from fe80::c418:2ed0:aead:cbce: icmp_seq=2 ttl=128 time=0.478 ms
64 bytes from fe80::c418:2ed0:aead:cbce: icmp_seq=3 ttl=128 time=0.777 ms
64 bytes from fe80::c418:2ed0:aead:cbce: icmp_seq=4 ttl=128 time=0.659 ms

--- fe80::c418:2ed0:aead:cbce%eth0 ping statistics ---
4 packets transmitted, 4 received, 0% packet loss, time 3003ms
rtt min/avg/max/mdev = 0.478/0.847/1.475/0.378 ms
$
```

The %eth0 part tells the system to send the ping packets out on the eth0 network interface for the link local address.

WARNING   Unfortunately, these days many hosts don't support ICMP packets because they can be used to create a denial-of-service (DOS) attack against the host. Don't be surprised if you try to ping a remote host and don't get any responses.

Testing Network Routes

The route command provides information about the default router on your local network, but it doesn't help you with determining just how your packets get to a remote destination outside your local network. The traceroute command can do that.

The traceroute command attempts to send ICMP packets to the specified destination, and it lists all the router hops that the packets traversed to get to the remote host, as well as the time it took for the packet to get to each intermediate route:

```
$ traceroute www.google.com
traceroute to www.google.com (74.125.21.103), 30 hops max, 60 byte packets
 1  10.0.2.2 (10.0.2.2)  1.398 ms  0.146 ms  0.134 ms
 2  192.168.1.254  3.442 ms  3.290 ms  3.044 ms
```

```
 3   162-194-188-3.lightspeed.iplsin.sbcglobal.net (162.194.188.3)  21.100 ms
20.891 ms  20.671 ms
 4   75.19.192.192 (75.19.192.192)  21.092 ms  21.280 ms  21.368 ms
 5   75.19.192.184 (75.19.192.184)  21.051 ms  20.887 ms  20.683 ms
 6   12.83.79.1 (12.83.79.1)  23.565 ms  20.763 ms  20.760 ms
 7   ggr6.cgcil.ip.att.net (12.122.132.189)  25.598 ms  24.118 ms  23.424 ms
 8   12.251.23.6 (12.251.23.6)  25.932 ms  26.039 ms  25.841 ms
 9   209.85.242.133 (209.85.242.133)  26.004 ms 209.85.242.217 (209.85.242.217)
28.107 ms 209.85.242.137 (209.85.242.137)  27.266 ms
10   72.14.237.130 (72.14.237.130)  31.427 ms 209.85.143.111 (209.85.143.111)
27.148 ms 209.85.241.47 (209.85.241.47)  30.260 ms
11   72.14.239.90 (72.14.239.90)  75.216 ms 72.14.239.190 (72.14.239.190)
47.397 ms 209.85.142.110 (209.85.142.110)  44.399 ms
12   216.239.56.164 (216.239.56.164)  66.881 ms 209.85.142.65 (209.85.142.65)
44.669 ms 216.239.56.166 (216.239.56.166)  68.130 ms
13   * * *
14   yv-in-f103.1e100.net (74.125.21.103)  57.001 ms  56.802 ms  56.696 ms
$
```

This output shows that it took 14 router hops to get from the Linux system to the www .google.com host. Notice that the times for each hop increase as the packets get closer to the destination host.

The mtr command (short for My Traceroute) is designed to provide real-time information about network performance. It combines the traceroute and ping commands into a single interface that continually updates in real-time:

```
# mtr www.google.com
                         My traceroute  [v0.85]
ubuntu02 (0.0.0.0)                                 Wed Jul 13 15:25:09 2016
Keys:  Help   Display mode   Restart statistics   Order of fields   quit
                          Packets                 Pings
Host                      Loss%   Snt   Last   Avg  Best  Wrst StDev
 1. 10.0.2.2              0.0%    24    7.0   1.5   0.0   7.0   1.7
 2. homeportal            0.0%    24    5.4   5.3   0.8  17.4   3.9
 3. 162-194-188-2.lightspeed.ip  8.3%  23  14.15 14.08 14.43 14.33  3.6
 4. 75.19.192.190         0.0%    23   22.5  20.6  12.8  29.9   4.0
 5. 12.83.79.1            0.0%    23   27.6  23.3  13.1  32.1   4.7
 6. ggr2.cgcil.ip.att.net 0.0%    23   35.4  57.6  20.9 160.2  44.7
 7. 12.250.102.18         0.0%    23   22.0  25.4  20.8  33.8   3.1
 8. 209.85.254.120        0.0%    23   34.6  26.9  21.5  35.8   4.2
 9. 209.85.254.238        0.0%    23   30.8  27.5  21.1  38.5   4.5
10. 72.14.239.90          0.0%    23   44.3  47.5  41.5  61.0   5.2
11. 209.85.248.53         0.0%    23   48.2  47.9  38.0  61.5   5.4
```

```
12. ???
13. yw-in-f106.1e100.net        0.0%   23  41.6  46.3  37.2  66.9   6.0
```

By continually sending ping packets to the remote routers, the mtr command can display a detailed hop-by-hop picture of what's happening to your network packets.

Testing Client/Server Connectivity

Just being able to push ping or traceroute packets to a remote host may not necessarily prove much; sometimes you need to simulate real data across the network. A great tool for doing that is the nc command (short for netcat).

The nc command allows you to simulate both a server and a client from the command line. You can use the nc command to send data out on the network, as well as receive data from the network by specifying command-line options, as shown in Table 6.5.

TABLE 6.5   The nc command-line options

Option	Description
-4	Force IPv4 addresses only.
-6	Force IPv6 addresses only.
-b	Allow broadcast packets.
-C	Send CRLF characters at the end of each line.
-D	Enable debugging.
-d	Don't read from the standard input.
-h	Display help.
-I len	Specify the size of the TCP receive buffer.
-i int	Specify the delay interval between sending and receiving.
-k	Force listening after a connection closes.
-l	Listen for an incoming connection.
-n	Do not try DNS hostname lookups for addresses.
-O len	Specify the size of the TCP output buffer.
-P user	Specify a proxy username.

TABLE 6.5   *The* nc *command-line options (continued)*

Option	Description
-p port	Specify the source port.
-q sec	Specify the number of seconds to wait after an EOF.
-r	Use random send and receive ports.
-S	Use the MD5 signature option.
-s addr	Specify the IP address of the sending interface.
-T tos	Specify the TCP Type of Service value.
-t	Allow scripted Telnet sessions.
-U	Use Unix domain sockets.
-u	Use UDP instead of TCP.
-V table	Specify the routing table to use.
-v	Display more verbose output.
-w sec	Specify the timeout value.
-X proto	Specify the proxy protocol.
-x addr	Specify the proxy address.
-Z	Use DCCP mode.
-z	Scan for listening applications but don't send data.

To use nc, you just need to set up a server on one system and a client on another system. To start a server, use the –l option to specify a port to listen on:

```
$ nc -l 8000
```

Then, on the client system, specify the server's IP address and the port to connect to:

```
$ nc 192.168.1.77 8000
```

The nc command will connect to the server, and then any text typed on one end will be sent to the other using TCP.

Finding Host Information

Sometimes the problem isn't with network connectivity but with the DNS hostname system. You can test a hostname using the host command:

```
$ host www.linux.org
www.linux.org is an alias for linux.org.
linux.org has address 107.170.40.56
linux.org mail is handled by 20 mx.iqemail.net.
$
```

The host command queries the DNS server to determine the IP addresses assigned to the specified hostname. By default, it returns all IP addresses associated with the hostname. Some hosts are supported by multiple servers in a load-balancing configuration. The host command will show all of the IP addresses associated with those servers:

```
$ host www.google.com
www.google.com has address 74.125.138.104
www.google.com has address 74.125.138.105
www.google.com has address 74.125.138.147
www.google.com has address 74.125.138.99
www.google.com has address 74.125.138.103
www.google.com has address 74.125.138.106
www.google.com has IPv6 address 2607:f8b0:4002:c0c::67
$
```

You can also specify an IP address for the host command, and it will attempt to find the hostname associated with it:

```
$ host 107.170.40.56
56.40.170.107.in-addr.arpa domain name pointer iqdig11.iqnection.com.
$
```

Notice, though, that often an IP address will resolve to a generic server hostname that hosts the website and not the website alias, as is the case here with the www.linux.org IP address.

Another great tool to use is the dig command. The dig command displays all of the DNS data records associated with a specific host or network. For example, you can look up the information for a specific hostname:

```
$ dig www.linux.org

; <<>> DiG 9.9.4-RedHat-9.9.4-18.el7_1.5 <<>> www.linux.org
;; global options: +cmd
;; Got answer:
```

```
;; ->>HEADER<<- opcode: QUERY, status: NOERROR, id: 45314
;; flags: qr rd ra; QUERY: 1, ANSWER: 2, AUTHORITY: 0, ADDITIONAL: 1

;; OPT PSEUDOSECTION:
; EDNS: version: 0, flags:; udp: 4096
;; QUESTION SECTION:
;www.linux.org.            IN     A

;; ANSWER SECTION:
www.linux.org.         14400     IN      CNAME linux.org.
linux.org.     3600     IN     A     107.170.40.56

;; Query time: 75 msec
;; SERVER: 192.168.1.254#53(192.168.1.254)
;; WHEN: Sat Feb 06 17:44:29 EST 2016
;; MSG SIZE  rcvd: 72

$
```

Or you can look up DNS data records associated with a specific network service, such as a mail server:

```
$ dig linux.org MX

; <<>> DiG 9.9.5-3ubuntu0.5-Ubuntu <<>> linux.org MX
;; global options: +cmd
;; Got answer:
;; ->>HEADER<<- opcode: QUERY, status: NOERROR, id: 16202
;; flags: qr rd ra; QUERY: 1, ANSWER: 1, AUTHORITY: 0, ADDITIONAL: 1

;; OPT PSEUDOSECTION:
; EDNS: version: 0, flags:; udp: 4096
;; QUESTION SECTION:
;linux.org.          IN     MX

;; ANSWER SECTION:
linux.org.         3600     IN     MX     20  mx.iqemail.net.

;; Query time: 75 msec
;; SERVER: 127.0.1.1#53(127.0.1.1)
;; WHEN: Tue Feb 09 12:35:43 EST 2016
```

```
;; MSG SIZE  rcvd: 68

$
```

The MX data record points to the server that accepts mail for the domain.

Network Security

If a client can't connect to a network service, you may need to look into the security restriction settings for the service. Many network applications provide network security by allowing only specific hosts to connect (called a whitelist) or by blocking problematic hosts (called a blacklist).

The tcp_wrappers program is a common Linux utility that allows you to create whitelists and blacklists for network applications. It does that by acting as a proxy for network applications defined in the /etc/inetd.conf configuration file. It intercepts all packets destined to the transport ports specified in the configuration file, compares the source IP address to a database list, and then passes allowed addresses to the specified application.

The access lists are contained in two files:

- /etc/hosts.allow
- /etc/hosts.deny

As you can probably guess, the hosts.allow file is the whitelist file. Client addresses specified in that file are allowed access to the applications. The hosts.deny file is the blacklist file. Client addresses specified in that file are denied access.

Advanced Network Troubleshooting

Besides the simple network tests shown in the previous section, Linux has some more advanced programs that can provide further information about the network environment. The following sections describe some of the more advanced features that you have available when doing your network troubleshooting.

Viewing Open Network Connections

Sometimes it helps to be able to see just what network connections are active on a Linux system. There are two ways to troubleshoot that issue: the lsof command and the netstat command.

The *lsof* Command

The lsof command provides a list of files that are currently open on the Linux system. Since Linux treats network connections as files, any open network session will appear in the lsof output list.

The lsof command will produce lots of output. To limit the output to only network connections, use the –i command-line option:

```
# lsof -i
COMMAND     PID   USER    FD   TYPE DEVICE SIZE/OFF NODE NAME
avahi-dae   602   avahi   12u  IPv4 15753    0t0  UDP *:mdns
avahi-dae   602   avahi   13u  IPv4 15754    0t0  UDP *:39181
chronyd     613   chrony  1u   IPv4 14930    0t0  UDP *:ntp
chronyd     613   chrony  2u   IPv6 14931    0t0  UDP *:ntp
chronyd     613   chrony  3u   IPv4 14932    0t0  UDP localhost:323
chronyd     613   chrony  5u   IPv6 14933    0t0  UDP localhost:323
sshd        1052  root    3u   IPv4 17701    0t0  TCP *:ssh (LISTEN)
sshd        1052  root    4u   IPv6 17703    0t0  TCP *:ssh (LISTEN)
dhclient    1246  root    6u   IPv4 18831    0t0  UDP *:bootpc
dhclient    1246  root    20u  IPv4 18772    0t0  UDP *:7714
dhclient    1246  root    21u  IPv6 18773    0t0  UDP *:12082
master      1513  root    13u  IPv4 19506    0t0  TCP localhost:smtp (LISTEN)
master      1513  root    14u  IPv6 19507    0t0  TCP localhost:smtp (LISTEN)
cupsd       2981  root    11u  IPv6 24473    0t0  TCP localhost:ipp (LISTEN)
cupsd       2981  root    12u  IPv4 24474    0t0  TCP localhost:ipp (LISTEN)
#
```

Or, if you're interested in seeing IPv6 network connections, use the –i6 option:

```
# lsof -i6
COMMAND    PID   USER    FD   TYPE DEVICE SIZE/OFF NODE NAME
chronyd    613   chrony  2u   IPv6 14931    0t0  UDP *:ntp
chronyd    613   chrony  5u   IPv6 14933    0t0  UDP localhost:323
sshd       1052  root    4u   IPv6 17703    0t0  TCP *:ssh (LISTEN)
dhclient   1246  root    21u  IPv6 18773    0t0  UDP *:12082
master     1513  root    14u  IPv6 19507    0t0  TCP localhost:smtp (LISTEN)
cupsd      2981  root    11u  IPv6 24473    0t0  TCP localhost:ipp (LISTEN)
#
```

The *netstat* Command

The netstat command can provide a wealth of network information for you. By default, it lists all of the open network connections on the system:

```
# netstat
Active Internet connections (w/o servers)
Proto Recv-Q Send-Q Local Address        Foreign Address       State
Active UNIX domain sockets (w/o servers)
```

```
Proto RefCnt Flags      Type      State       I-Node   Path
unix  2       [ ]       DGRAM                 10825 @/org/freedesktop/
systemd1/notify
unix  2       [ ]       DGRAM                 10933    /run/systemd/
shutdownd
unix  6       [ ]       DGRAM                 6609     /run/systemd/journal/
socket
unix  25      [ ]       DGRAM                 6611     /dev/log
unix  3       [ ]       STREAM    CONNECTED   25693
unix  3       [ ]       STREAM    CONNECTED   20770    /var/run/dbus/system_
bus_socket
unix  3       [ ]       STREAM    CONNECTED   19556
unix  3       [ ]       STREAM    CONNECTED   19511
unix  2       [ ]       DGRAM                 24125
unix  3       [ ]       STREAM    CONNECTED   19535
unix  3       [ ]       STREAM    CONNECTED   18067    /var/run/dbus/system_
bus_socket
unix  3       [ ]       STREAM    CONNECTED   32358
unix  3       [ ]       STREAM    CONNECTED   24818    /var/run/dbus/system_
bus_socket
...
```

The netstat command produces considerable output, because normally many pro-grams use network services on Linux systems. You can limit the output to just TCP or UDP connections by using the –t command-line option for TCP connections or –u for UDP connections:

```
# netstat -t
Active Internet connections (w/o servers)
Proto Recv-Q Send-Q Local Address      Foreign Address        State
tcp   1      0 10.0.2.15:58630         productsearch.ubu:https CLOSE_WAIT
tcp6  1      0 ip6-localhost:57782     ip6-localhost:ipp       CLOSE_WAIT
#
```

You can also get a list of what applications are listening on which network ports by using the –l option:

```
# netstat -l
Active Internet connections (only servers)
Proto Recv-Q Send-Q Local Address          Foreign Address     State
tcp   0      0 ubuntu02:domain             *:*                 LISTEN
tcp   0      0 localhost:ipp               *:*                 LISTEN
tcp6  0      0 ip6-localhost:ipp           [::]:*              LISTEN
udp   0      0 *:ipp                       *:*
```

```
udp        0        0 *:mdns                  *:*
udp        0        0 *:36355                 *:*
udp        0        0 ubuntu02:domain         *:*
udp        0        0 *:bootpc                *:*
udp        0        0 *:12461                 *:*
udp6       0        0 [::]:64294              [::]:*
udp6       0        0 [::]:60259              [::]:*
udp6       0        0 [::]:mdns               [::]:*
...
```

As you can see, a standard Linux workstation still has numerous things happening in the background, waiting for connections.

Viewing Network Statistics

Yet another great feature of the netstat command is that the -s option displays statistics for the different types of packets that the system has used on the network:

```
# netstat -s
Ip:
    240762 total packets received
    0 forwarded
    0 incoming packets discarded
    240747 incoming packets delivered
    206940 requests sent out
    32 dropped because of missing route
Icmp:
    57 ICMP messages received
    0 input ICMP message failed.
    ICMP input histogram:
        destination unreachable: 12
        timeout in transit: 38
        echo replies: 7
    7 ICMP messages sent
    0 ICMP messages failed
    ICMP output histogram:
        echo request: 7
IcmpMsg:
        InType0: 7
        InType3: 12
        InType11: 38
        OutType8: 7
```

```
Tcp:
    286 active connections openings
    0 passive connection openings
    0 failed connection attempts
    0 connection resets received
    0 connections established
    239933 segments received
    206091 segments send out
    0 segments retransmited
    0 bad segments received.
    0 resets sent
Udp:
    757 packets received
    0 packets to unknown port received.
    0 packet receive errors
    840 packets sent
    0 receive buffer errors
    0 send buffer errors
UdpLite:
TcpExt:
    219 TCP sockets finished time wait in fast timer
    15 delayed acks sent
    26 delayed acks further delayed because of locked socket
    Quick ack mode was activated 1 times
    229343 packet headers predicted
    289 acknowledgments not containing data payload received
    301 predicted acknowledgments
    TCPRcvCoalesce: 72755
IpExt:
    InNoRoutes: 2
    InMcastPkts: 13
    OutMcastPkts: 15
    InOctets: 410722578
    OutOctets: 8363083
    InMcastOctets: 2746
    OutMcastOctets: 2826
#
```

The netstat statistics output can give you a rough idea of how busy your Linux system is on the network or if there's a specific issue with one of the protocols installed.

Another tool used to view network socket statistics is the ss command. The ss command works in a similar manner to the netstat command, but it can also display detailed socket information, such as the send and receive queues for the sockets:

```
# ss
Netid  State   Recv-Q  Send-Q    Local Address:Port        Peer Address:Port
u_str  ESTAB   0       0       @/tmp/dbus-IBMGoMLy3h 14063           * 14062
u_str  ESTAB   0       0       @/tmp/dbus-IBMGoMLy3h 13346           * 13345
u_str  ESTAB   0       0                         * 11993            * 11994
u_str  ESTAB   0       0                         * 10067            * 10068
u_str  ESTAB   0       0       @/tmp/.X11-unix/X0   13143           * 13142
u_str  ESTAB   0       0       @/tmp/.X11-unix/X0   12098           * 12097
u_str  ESTAB   0       0                         * 13794            * 13795
u_str  ESTAB   0       0       @/tmp/.X11-unix/X0   13568           * 13567
u_str  ESTAB   0       0       /var/run/dbus/system_bus_socket 12015 * 12014
u_str  ESTAB   0       0                         * 7509             * 7515
u_str  ESTAB   0       0                         * 12122            * 12124
u_str  ESTAB   0       0                         * 9463             * 9465
u_str  ESTAB   0       0       @/tmp/dbus-EMEzMtP8a8 13869           * 13868
u_str  ESTAB   0       0       @/tmp/dbus-EMEzMtP8a8 12432           * 12367
```

By examining the send and receive queues in the sockets, you can tell if an application is having trouble keeping up with the data it sends or receives.

Scanning the Network

While the netstat command is great for determining what applications are listening to which network posts on your Linux system, the nmap command takes that idea one step further and allows you to scan your local network to view what network ports other hosts have open.

The nmap command is somewhat powerful, so it's not usually installed by default in Linux distributions. However, you can usually install it directly from the software repository in most Linux distributions. For Ubuntu, you just use

```
$ sudo apt-get install nmap
```

The basic format for the nmap command is

```
nmap [scan type] [options] target
```

The nmap command provides different types of network scanning, from brute-force connection attempts to stealthy connections that can slip through firewalls. The target parameter allows you to scan a specific host on the network or a range of hosts on the network based on IP addresses.

Here's an example of the output from a simple scan:

```
$ nmap 10.0.2.2

Starting Nmap 6.40 ( http://nmap.org )
Nmap scan report for 10.0.2.2
Host is up (0.0026s latency).
Not shown: 988 closed ports
PORT      STATE    SERVICE
548/tcp   filtered afp
555/tcp   filtered dsf
631/tcp   open     ipp
1057/tcp  filtered startron
1079/tcp  filtered asprovatalk
1164/tcp  filtered qsm-proxy
2040/tcp  filtered lam
4224/tcp  filtered xtell
5100/tcp  filtered admd
5960/tcp  filtered unknown
27352/tcp filtered unknown
49175/tcp filtered unknown

Nmap done: 1 IP address (1 host up) scanned in 10.74 seconds
$
```

The nmap command found several TCP network ports that accepted connections on the destination system.

Be careful when running the nmap tool in a network environment. Ensure that you have permission from the administrator for each host that you scan. Because of its use by attackers, many organizations ban the use of nmap on their networks and prosecute anyone caught using it (even internal employees).

Capturing Network Traffic

When it comes to troubleshooting specific network applications, nothing can replace viewing the actual network packets that are sent between the systems on the network. Fortunately, Linux provides the tcpdump command just for doing that.

The tcpdump program places the network card in promiscuous mode, which enables it to capture all network traffic that it sees (not just traffic destined for the host). This allows you to sniff any type of network traffic and even use your Linux system as a crude network sniffer to troubleshoot other network issues.

By default, tcpdump captures all packets that it sees on the network interface and displays a rough description of each packet, as shown here:

```
# tcpdump
tcpdump: verbose output suppressed, use -v or -vv for full protocol decode
listening on enp0s3, link-type EN10MB (Ethernet), capture size 65535 bytes
18:10:04.782397 IP localhost.localdomain > 10.0.2.2: ICMP echo request, id
27838, seq 1, length 64
18:10:04.783052 IP 10.0.2.2 > localhost.localdomain: ICMP echo reply, id 27838,
seq 1, length 64
18:10:05.787166 IP localhost.localdomain > 10.0.2.2: ICMP echo request, id
27838, seq 2, length 64
18:10:05.792399 IP 10.0.2.2 > localhost.localdomain: ICMP echo reply, id 27838,
seq 2, length 64
18:10:06.789194 IP localhost.localdomain > 10.0.2.2: ICMP echo request, id
27838, seq 3, length 64
18:10:06.791284 IP 10.0.2.2 > localhost.localdomain: ICMP echo reply, id 27838,
seq 3, length 64
18:10:07.797694 IP localhost.localdomain > 10.0.2.2: ICMP echo request, id
27838, seq 4, length 64
18:10:07.805278 IP 10.0.2.2 > localhost.localdomain: ICMP echo reply, id 27838,
seq 4, length 64
#
```

In this example, the tcpdump command captured the ICMP request packets sent from the ping command to a remote host, as well as the reply packets returned by the remote host to the Linux system.

You can also specify command-line options that restrict what tcpdump captures and how it displays the data. Table 6.6 shows some of the more useful command-line options.

TABLE 6.6 Useful *tcpdump* command-line options

Option	Description
-A	Display the packet contents in ASCII.
-b	Display the AS number in BGP routing packets.
-B	Set the packet capture buffer size.
-c	Exit after receiving the specified number of packets.
-C	If writing the output to a file, check the file size and, if larger than specified, start a new capture file.
-d	Dump the packet-matching code in human-readable form.
-dd	Dump the packet-matching code as a C program fragment.

Option	Description
-ddd	Dump the packet-matching code as decimal numbers.
-D	Display the list of network interfaces.
-e	Display the link-level headers for each packet.
-E	Define the key used to decrypt encrypted packets.
-f	Display IP addresses numerically instead of using hostnames.
-F	Specify a file to read filters from.
-G	Rotate the dump file to a new file the specified number of seconds.
-h	Display the tcpdump version.
-H	Detect 802.11s headers.
-i	Specify the interface to listen for packets on.
-I	Place the interface in monitor mode (only for wireless interfaces).
-j	Specify the timestamp format.
-J	Display the supported timestamp formats for the interface.
-K	Don't verify packet checksum values.
-l	Make the output line buffered.
-L	Display the list of data link types for the interface.
-m	Load SMI MIB modules.
-M	Specify the shared secret key for validating TCP digests.
-n	Don't convert IP addresses to names.
-N	Don't display fully qualified domain names, only hostnames.
-O	Don't use the packet-capture optimizer.
-p	Don't place the interface in promiscuous mode.
-P	Select which packet direction to capture (in, out, or inout).
-q	Quick mode, display less packet detail.

TABLE 6.6   *Useful* tcpdump *command-line options (continued)*

Option	Description
-r	Read packets from the specified file.
-s	Capture only the specified number of bytes from each packet.
-S	Use absolute rather than relative TCP sequence numbers.
-t	Don't print the timestamp for each packet.
-tt	Display an unformatted timestamp.
-ttt	Use a delta timestamp from the previous line.
-tttt	Display the timestamp using the date and default format.
-ttttt	Use a delta timestamp from the first packet.
-T	Specify the type of packets to filter.
-u	Display undecoded NFS handles.
-v	Display slightly more verbose output.
-vv	Display even more verbose output.
-vvv	Display full verbose output.
-w	Write all packets to the specified file.
-W	Specify the number of capture files to generate.
-x	Display the packet data in hex.
-xx	Display the packet data and link-layer data in hex.
-X	Display the packet data in hex and ASCII.
-XX	Display the packet data and link-layer data in hex and ASCII.
-y	Specify the data link type to use.
-z	Run the specified command for each capture file generated.
-Z	Change to the specified userid before opening the capture file.

As you can see from Table 6.6, you have many ways to customize the tcpdump program to display and store network data captured from the network card. This is a great tool to use for troubleshooting network applications that don't work.

Determining the Network Environment

This exercise demonstrates how to quickly assess the network configuration and programs for your Linux system without having to dig through lots of configuration files. To document your system network information, follow these steps:

1. Log in as root, or acquire root privileges by using su or by using sudo with each of the following commands.

2. Type **ifconfig** to display the current network interfaces on your system. You will most likely see a loopback interface (named l0) and one or more network interfaces. Write down the IP (called inet) and IPv6 (called inet6) addresses assigned to each network interface, along with the hardware address and the network mask address.

3. If your system has a wireless network card that supports scanning, type **iwlist wlan0 scan** to view the wireless access points in your area.

4. If your system has a wireless network card, type **iwconfig** to display the current wireless settings for your network interface.

5. Type **route** to display the routes defined on your system. Note the default gateway address assigned to your system. It should be on the same network as the IP address assigned to the system.

6. Type **cat /etc/resolv.conf** to display the DNS settings for your system.

7. Type **netstat -l** to display the programs listening for incoming network connections. The entries marked as unix are using the loopback address to communicate with other programs internally on your system.

8. Install the tcpdump program on your system using either apt-get for Debian-based systems or yum for Red Hat–based systems.

9. Type **tcpdump** to start the tcpdump program listening on the default network interface for your system.

10. Open a second terminal session; then type **ping www.linux.org**. Press the Ctrl+C key combination after a few ping packets have processed.

11. Switch back to the tcpdump session window, and observe the packets detected and displayed.

Summary

Connecting Linux systems to networks can be painless if you have the correct tools. To connect the Linux system, you'll need an IP address, a netmask address, a default router, a hostname, and a DNS server. If you don't care what IP address is assigned to your Linux system, you can obtain these values automatically using DHCP. However, if you are running a Linux server that requires a static IP address, you may need to configure these values manually.

Linux stores network connection information in configuration files. You can either manually modify the files to store the appropriate network information or use a graphical or command-line tool to do that. Network Manager is the most popular graphical tool used by Linux distributions. It allows you to configure both wired and wireless network settings from a graphical window. The Network Manager icon in the Panel area shows network connectivity, as well as basic wireless information for wireless network cards.

If you must configure your network settings from the command line, you'll need to use a few different tools. For wireless connections, you'll need to use the `iwconfig` command to set the wireless access point and SSID key. For both wireless and wired connections, you'll need to use the `ifconfig` command to set the IP address and netmask values for the interface. You will also need to use the `route` command to define the default router for the local network.

To use hostnames instead of IP addresses, you'll need to define a DNS server for your network. You do that in the `/etc/resolv.conf` configuration file. You will also need to define the hostname for your Linux system in either the `/etc/hostname` or `/etc/HOSTNAME` file.

Once your network configuration is complete, you may have to do some additional troubleshooting for network problems. The `ping` and `traceroute` commands allow you to send ICMP packets to remote hosts to test basic connectivity and trace the path the packets take across the network. The `nc` command allows you to send any type of data across the network between two systems. If you suspect issues with hostnames, you can use the `host` and `dig` commands to query the DNS server for hostnames.

For more advanced network troubleshooting, you can use the `lsof` and `netstat` commands to display what applications are using which network ports on the system. The `nmap` command allows you to perform a complete scan of any system on the network to detect open ports and applications. Finally, the `tcpdump` command lets you peek at the network traffic as it crosses the network card on your system.

Exam Essentials

Describe the utilities required to configure and manipulate Ethernet network interfaces. To set the IP and netmask addresses on an Ethernet interface, you use the `ifconfig` command. To set the default router (or gateway) for a network, you use the `route` command. Some Linux distributions use the newer `ip` command, which can configure all three values.

Explain how to configure basic access to a wireless network. Linux uses the `iwlist` command to list all wireless access points detected by the wireless network card. You can configure the settings required to connect to a specific wireless network using the `iwconfig` command. At a minimum, you'll need to configure the access point SSID value and most likely specify the encryption key value to connect to the access point.

Describe how to manipulate the routing table on a Linux system. The `route` command is used to display the existing router table used by the Linux system. You can add a new route by using the `add` option or remove an existing route by using the `del` option. You can specify the default router (gateway) used by the network by adding the `default` keyword to the command.

Summarize the tools that you would need to analyze the status of network devices. The `ifconfig` command displays the current status of all network interfaces on the system. You can also use the `lsof` command to display all open network files or the `netstat` command to display statistics for all listening network ports. You can use the `nmap` command to scan the network status of remote systems on your network or use the `arp` command to display the hardware address associated with each IP address on the network.

Explain the utilities used to monitor and analyze TCP/IP traffic. The `netstat` command allows you to monitor what applications are listening for new network connections or what applications are connected to remote server applications. The `tcpdump` command allows you to capture and analyze specific network traffic.

Explain how Linux can restrict access to a network application. Linux network applications can utilize the `tcp_wrappers` application, which acts as a middleman, intercepting client connections to the application. The `/etc/hosts.allow` file lists clients that are allowed to connect to the network applications on the system, while the `/etc/hosts.deny` file lists clients that are blocked from accessing the network applications.

Describe how Linux initializes the network interfaces. Debian-based Linux systems use the `/etc/network/interfaces` file to configure the IP address, netmask, and default router. Red Hat–based Linux systems use files in the `/etc/sysconfig/network-scripts` folder. The `ifcfg-eth0` file contains the IP address and netmask settings, while the `network` file contains the default router settings. These files are examined at bootup to determine the network interface configuration. You can see the network interface initialization status by using the `dmesg` command, or look in the system log files, such as `/var/log/syslog` or `/var/log/messages`.

Explain how to test network connectivity. The `ping` command allows you to send ICMP messages to remote hosts, and it displays the response received. For more advanced testing, the `traceroute` command attempts to connect to a remote host and lists all network routers traversed to reach the remote system.

Describe one graphical tool used to configure network settings in Linux. The Network Manager tool provides a graphical interface for changing settings on the network interfaces. The Network Manager appears as an icon in the desktop Panel area. If your Linux system uses a wireless network card, the icon appears as a radio signal, while for wired network connections it appears as two arrows. When you click the icon, it shows the current network status, and for wireless interfaces, it shows a list of the access points detected. When you open the Network Manager interface, it allows you to either set static IP address information or configure the network to use a DHCP server to set the network configuration dynamically.

Review Questions

You can find the answers in the Appendix.

1. Which network layer uses the Wi-Fi Protected Access (WPA) encryption?
    - **A.** Network
    - **B.** Physical
    - **C.** Transport
    - **D.** Application

2. What network layer feature defines the network to which the system is connected?
    - **A.** IP address
    - **B.** Default router
    - **C.** Hostname
    - **D.** Netmask
    - **E.** DNS server

3. Which of the following is a correct netmask value?
    - **A.** 255.255.255.0
    - **B.** 255.255.0.255
    - **C.** 192.168.1.0
    - **D.** 192.168.0.1
    - **E.** 0.255.255.255

4. What two parts make up an IP address?
    - **A.** Host address and router
    - **B.** Netmask and host address
    - **C.** Netmask and router
    - **D.** Host address and hostname
    - **E.** Network address and host address

5. How many bits are used in an IPv6 address?
    - **A.** 32
    - **B.** 64
    - **C.** 128
    - **D.** 256
    - **E.** 8

6. What network setting defines the network device that routes packets intended for hosts on remote networks?
    - **A.** Default router
    - **B.** Netmask

C. Hostname

D. IP address

E. DNS server

7. What device setting defines a host that maps a hostname to an IP address?

A. Default router

B. Netmask

C. Hostname

D. IP address

E. DNS server

8. What is used to assign an IP address automatically to a client?

A. Default router

B. DHCP

C. ARP table

D. Netmask

E. `ifconfig`

9. What type of address is used so that local applications can use network protocols to communicate with each other?

A. Dynamic address

B. Loopback address

C. Static address

D. Hostname

E. MAC address

10. Which transport layer protocol guarantees packet delivery?

A. TCP

B. UDP

C. ICMP

D. DNS

E. DHCP

11. Which nc command format listens for incoming HTTP connections to simulate a web server?

A. `nc 192.168.1.77 80`

B. `nc -l 80`

C. `nc 192.168.1.77`

D. `nc 80 192.168.1.77`

E. `nc -l 22`

12. What folder do Red Hat–based systems use to store network configuration files?

    A. /etc/sysconfig/network-scripts

    B. /etc/network

    C. /etc/ifcfg-eth0

    D. /etc/ifconfig

    E. /etc/iwconfig

13. Which configuration line sets a dynamic IP address for a Debian system?

    A. iface eth0 inet static

    B. iface eth0 inet dhcp

    C. auto eth0

    D. iface eth0 inet6 auto

    E. BOOTPROTO=dynamic

14. Which file contains a list of DNS servers that the Linux system can use to resolve hostnames?

    A. /etc/hosts.allow

    B. /etc/resolv.conf

    C. /etc/inetd.conf

    D. /etc/network/interfaces

    E. /etc/host.deny

15. Which ifconfig format correctly assigns an IP address and netmask to the eth0 interface?

    A. ifconfig eth0 down 192.168.1.50 netmask 255.255.255.0

    B. ifconfig eth0 255.255.255.0 192.168.1.50

    C. ifconfig up 192.168.1.50 netmask 255.255.255.0

    D. ifconfig up

    E. ifconfig down

16. What command displays all of the available wireless networks in your area?

    A. iwlist

    B. iwconfig

    C. ifconfig

    D. ip

    E. arp

17. What option sets the wireless access point name in the iwconfig command?

    A. key

    B. netmask

   C. address

   D. essid

   E. channel

18. What command can you use both to display and to set the IP address, netmask, and default router values?

   A. ifconfig

   B. iwconfig

   C. router

   D. ifup

   E. ip

19. What tool allows you to send ICMP messages to a remote host to test network connectivity?

   A. netstat

   B. nmap

   C. ping

   D. nc

   E. tcpdump

20. Which command allows you to view network packets?

   A. dig

   B. tcpdump

   C. ping

   D. netstat

   E. nc

The LPI 202 Exam

PART

III

The LPI 202
Exam

Chapter

7

Organizing Email Services

THE FOLLOWING EXAM OBJECTIVES ARE COVERED IN THIS CHAPTER:

- ✓ 211.1 Using e-mail servers
- ✓ 211.2 Managing E-Mail Delivery
- ✓ 211.3 Managing Mailbox Access

Email is one of the most-used features of the Internet. Whether you're creating a small intra-office email system or a Linux email server to support thousands of users, knowing how to configure email services on a Linux system has become a necessity.

This chapter looks at how to configure your Linux system to interact with email servers and clients. First, it covers the basics of email, showing just how email services are implemented in a Linux environment. Next, the chapter examines the protocols with which you'll need to become familiar in order to work with email in Linux. Following that, the chapter discusses two of the most popular email server packages used in Linux—sendmail and Postfix. Finally, it shows you how to customize both local and remote email delivery packages to allow Linux users to read and send mail messages.

The Linux Mail System

Before we look at how to use email servers in Linux, let's examine how Linux handles email in general. Linux follows the Unix method of handling email. One of the main innovations of the Unix operating system was to make email processing software modular.

Instead of having one monolithic program that handles all of the pieces required for sending and receiving mail, Linux uses multiple small programs that work together in the processing of email messages. Each program handles a smaller piece of the system's total functionality. Email functions are broken into separate pieces and then assigned to separate programs running on the system. Figure 7.1 shows you how most open source email software modularizes email functions in a Linux environment.

As you can see, the Linux email server is normally divided into three separate functions:

- The mail transfer agent (MTA)
- The mail delivery agent (MDA)
- The mail user agent (MUA)

The lines between these three functions are often fuzzy. Some Linux email packages combine functionality for the MTA and MDA functions, while others combine the MDA and MUA functions. The following sections describe these basic email agents and explain in greater detail how they are implemented in Linux systems.

FIGURE 7.1   The Linux modular email environment

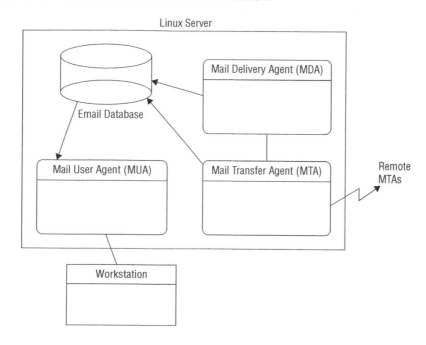

Mail Transfer Agent

The *mail transfer agent (MTA)* software is responsible for handling both incoming and outgoing email messages. For each outgoing email message, the MTA determines the destination host of the recipient address. If the destination host is the local machine, the MTA can either deliver the email message directly to the user's local mailbox or pass the message off to a local MDA program for delivery. If the destination host is a remote mail server, the MTA must establish a communication link with another MTA program on the remote host to transfer the message.

For incoming messages, the MTA must be able to accept connection requests from remote email servers and receive messages for local users. The most common protocol used for Internet mail transfer is the *Simple Mail Transfer Protocol (SMTP)*.

The Linux environment has many different types of open source MTA programs, and each type offers different features for the mail administrator. You should choose the MTA program that meets the most requirements of your particular email environment.

The LPIC-2 exam covers two popular MTA packages that are in wide use in the Linux world:

- sendmail
- Postfix

Besides these two packages, which are covered on the LPIC-2 exam, two other popular MTA packages that you'll find in Linux environments are Exim and qmail.

The following sections describe the sendmail and Postfix MTA programs in more depth.

Sendmail

Sendmail is one of the most popular Linux MTA programs available. Written by Eric Allman while at the University of California, Berkeley, sendmail is now maintained by the Sendmail Consortium (http://www.sendmail.org).

The sendmail program has gained popularity mainly due to its ability to be extremely versatile. Many of the standard features in sendmail have become synonymous with email systems—virtual domains, message forwarding, user aliases, mail lists, and host masquerading.

You can use sendmail for many types of email configurations, such as large corporate Internet email servers, small corporate servers that connect to ISPs, and even stand-alone workstations that forward mail through a mail hub. By simply changing a few lines in the sendmail configuration file, you can change its characteristics and behavior.

Sendmail can also parse and handle mail messages according to predefined rule sets. Mail administrators often need to filter messages depending on particular mail requirements. To do that, they can simply add new rules to the sendmail configuration file.

Unfortunately, with versatility comes complexity. The sendmail program's large configuration file is sometimes overwhelming for novice mail administrators to handle. Many books have been written to help the mail administrator determine the proper configuration file settings for a particular email server application.

Postfix

Wietse Venema wrote the Postfix program to be a complete MTA package replacement. Postfix is written as a modular program; it uses several different programs to implement the MTA functionality.

Postfix requires a separate user account to be added to the Linux server. It then runs each module as that common user account. If an attacker compromises a Postfix module, they only have access to files owned by that user account and won't be able to control the entire Linux server.

One of Postfix's best features is its simplicity. Instead of one large complex configuration file or multiple small configuration files, Postfix uses just two configuration files with plain-text parameter and value names to define functionality. Most of the parameters default to common values so that mail administrators can configure a complete mail server with minimum effort.

Exim

Yet another popular MTA package is the Experimental Internet Mailer (Exim) package, created by Philip Hazel for the University of Cambridge. Despite the "experimental" part of the name, Exim has become a stable and trustworthy mail delivery system.

Unlike Postfix, Exim sticks with the Sendmail model of using one large program to handle all of the email functions. It attempts to avoid queuing messages as much as possible, instead, relying on immediate delivery in most environments. It can handle thousands of emails per hour without queuing.

Exim uses one large configuration file, which is split into multiple sections. The access control section describes an access control list (ACL), which defines how the server handles incoming messages. The rewrite section allows you to define rules for changing the address of incoming messages to incorporate multiple host addresses on a single server. It also provides an authentication section, which allows you to define multiple authentication methods to handle SMTP authentication.

Mail Delivery Agent

Often, Linux email implementations rely on separate stand-alone *mail delivery agent (MDA)* programs to deliver messages to local users. Because these MDA programs concentrate only on delivering mail to local users, they can add bells and whistles that aren't available in MTA programs that include MDA functionality.

The MDA program concentrates on the message destined for a user on the local email server. It receives messages from the MTA program and then determines how those messages are to be delivered. Figure 7.2 demonstrates how the MDA program interacts with the MTA program.

FIGURE 7.2   Using an MDA program on an email server

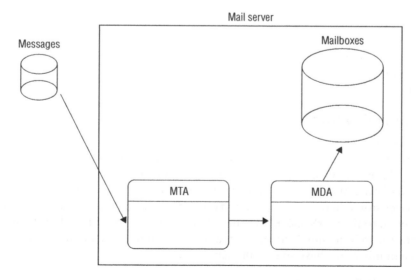

When the MTA program determines that a message is destined for a local user, it passes the message to the MDA program. At this point, the MDA program ensures that the message gets delivered to the proper location, either to the local user's mailbox or to an alternative location defined by the local user.

Currently three different types of user mailboxes are commonly used on Linux systems:

- /var/spool/mail files (called the mbox method)
- $HOME/mail files
- Maildir-style mailbox directories (called the maildir method)

Each mailbox type has features that make it attractive to use. The *mbox* mailbox method uses a single file for each user account to hold all of the email messages for that user. The individual mbox files are usually stored either altogether in the /var/spool/mail directory or in the individual user directories. This is the original method of storing email messages in Linux.

As you might guess, there's a performance issue with storing all of the email messages for a user in a single file. Parsing individual email messages in the file can take some time, especially if the user has numerous messages. The *maildir* mailbox method offers increased performance, security, and fault tolerance by storing each email message as an individual file within a protected directory structure.

With the maildir method, there is a separate directory for each user account, and the MDA program places individual email messages in those directories as separate files. In the past, many popular MDA and MUA programs were not able to use the maildir method, but that's slowly changing as the benefits of maildir-style mailboxes become more popular.

Different MDA programs combine various features that make them useful to the mail administrator. Some of the more popular features are these:

- Automatic mail filtering
- Automatic mail replying
- Automatic program initialization by mail

You can incorporate several open source MDA programs with the standard MTA email system. Two of the most popular MDA programs are binmail and procmail, which are described in the following sections.

The Binmail Program

Binmail is the most popular MDA program used on Linux systems. You might not recognize it by its official name, but you most likely have used it by its system name: mail. The name *binmail* comes from its normal location on the system, /bin/mail.

The binmail program has become popular because of its simplicity. By default, it can read email messages stored in the /var/spool/mail directory, or you can provide command-line options to point to the user's $HOME/mail file. No configuration is required for binmail to do its job. Unfortunately, its simplicity means that it is limited in its functions. Because of that, some mail administrators have sought alternative MDA programs.

The Procmail Program

Another popular MDA program is *procmail*, written by Stephen R. van den Berg. It has become so popular that many Linux implementations now install it by default, and many MTA programs use it in default configurations.

The popularity of the procmail program comes from its versatility in creating user-configured *recipes* that allow a user to direct how received email is processed. A user can create a personal `.procmailrc` file in their $HOME directory to direct messages based on regular expressions to separate mailbox files, forward messages to alternative email addresses, or even send messages directly to the /dev/null file to trash unwanted email automatically.

Mail User Agent

The Linux email model uses a local mailbox for each user to hold messages for that user. *Mail user agent (MUA)* programs became available as an interface for users to read messages stored in their mailboxes. MUAs do not receive messages; they only display messages that are already in the user's mailbox. Many MUA programs also offer the ability to create separate mailbox files or folders for the user to sort and store email.

Over the history of Internet email, two different philosophies have developed on where user email messages should be stored. Both philosophies have proponents and opponents, but in reality, each one can be beneficial given a particular email environment.

One philosophy is to download messages directly to the user's workstation, thus freeing up disk space on the mail server. This method makes the mail administrator's job easier, but it often leads to confusion for users who check their email from multiple workstations.

The second philosophy solves the problem of multiple workstations by keeping all of the messages on the email server. As the user reads each email message, only a copy of the message is sent to the workstation for display purposes. The actual message is still stored in a file or directory on the email server. No matter which workstation the user checks email from, the same messages are available for viewing.

Although this method makes life easier for the user, the mail administrator's life is more complicated, because disk space now becomes a crucial factor, since all messages are being stored on the email server.

With the advent of fancy graphical user interface (GUI) devices, MUA programs have become more sophisticated in how they can display messages. Linux command-line MUA programs still use text-mode graphics to display text messages. However, many graphical window-based systems now have the ability to display rich text and HTML-formatted documents.

To accommodate this feature, many email MUAs support the *Multipurpose Internet Mail Extensions (MIME)* format. MIME allows messages to contain multiple versions of the same message, each formatted using a different display method. The MUA's job is to determine which display method to use for the message. This allows text-based terminals to display the message in a text mode and GUI terminals to display the message in a more visually complex and sophisticated mode.

Although users often like the look of HTML-formatted messages, these messages quickly become troublesome for email administrators. A simple three-sentence message can turn into a large mail message because of added HTML formatting, complete with fancy background graphics and signature blocks that include pictures. It doesn't take long for these messages to clog up the email system.

MUA Programs

Linux supports both text-oriented and graphics-oriented MUA programs for reading email messages. The most common text-oriented command-line program is our friend binmail (yes, the same binmail that works as an MDA).

There isn't anything too fancy about binmail. If you run it by itself on a command line, you'll see a list of any email messages in your mailbox. The binmail program uses simple single-letter commands to navigate through the messages in your mailbox, as shown in Listing 7.1.

Listing 7.1: Sample mail program session

```
$ mail
"/var/spool/mail/rich": 4 messages 4 new
>N 1 barbara@shadrach.isp Sat Mar 12 18:47 12/417 "This is the first tes"
 N 2 katie@shadrach.ispl. Sat Mar 12 18:57 12/415 "Second test message"
 N 3 jessica@shadrach.isp Sat Mar 12 19:23 12/413 "Third test message"
 N 4 mike@shadrach.ispnet Sat Mar 12 19:42 12/423 "Fourth and final test"
& 1
Message 1:
From barbara@shadrach.ispl.net Sat Mar 12 18:47:05 2016
Date: 12 Mar 2016 23:47:05 -0000
From: barbara@shadrach.ispl.net
To: rich@shadrach.ispl.net
Subject: This is the first test message
Hi, This is a test message
& d
& 2
Message 2:
From katie@shadrach.ispl.net Sat Mar 12 18:57:32 2016
Date: 12 Mar 2016 23:57:32 -0000
From: katie@shadrach.ispl.net
To: rich@shadrach.ispl.net
Subject: Second test message
Hi, this is the second test message
& q
Saved 3 messages in mbox
$
```

Also, a few graphics-oriented MUA programs run in various Linux desktop environments. Most Linux distributions that use the GNOME desktop environment support the *Evolution* email client. Figure 7.3 shows an example of the Evolution main window.

FIGURE 7.3 The Evolution MUA program

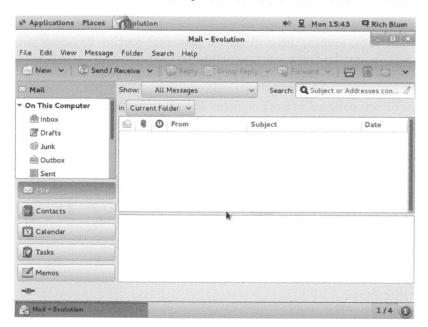

Another popular graphical MUA program is the *Thunderbird* email client, created by the same development team that created the Firefox browser (Mozilla). Thunderbird provides a simple setup that supports most common email servers (including Gmail and Yahoo) and interfaces with the local email system in Linux.

For KDE desktops, the *KMail* package provides basic email client services. It has similar features to Evolution but with the look and feel of the KDE desktop. All of these graphical MUA programs allow you to manage multiple mailboxes as well as create local mail folders for sorting your messages.

Email Protocols

Before diving into the email software setups, it helps to get a handle on the protocols used in Linux email handling. You'll need to become familiar with three different standard protocols when working with email in Linux:

- Simple Mail Transport Protocol (SMTP)
- Post Office Protocol (POP)
- Internet Message Access Protocol (IMAP)

The following sections detail these three protocols.

Simple Mail Transfer Protocol

The Simple Mail Transfer Protocol has been used since the early 1980s to relay email messages and attachments to many different types of computer systems. Its ease of use and portability made it the standard protocol used to transfer messages between computer systems on the Internet. To have an understanding of how email works, you need to get to know SMTP.

While SMTP was designed to work on many different types of transport media, the most common transport medium in which you'll find it is the Internet, using a TCP/IP connection on port 25. You can check if an email server is running an SMTP server by using the `telnet` program to connect to TCP port 25 on the remote host and then see if you get a response.

You can test this out on your own Linux server by connecting to hostname `localhost` using port 25. Listing 7.2 shows a sample Telnet session to a Linux server running the Postfix MTA package.

Listing 7.2: Sample SMTP session

```
$ telnet localhost 25
Trying 127.0.0.1...
Connected to localhost.
Escape character is '^]'.
220 myhost ESMTP Postfix (Ubuntu)
QUIT
221 Bye
Connection closed by foreign host.
$
```

The first line shows the `telnet` command format using host `localhost` and TCP port 25. If the server is running an SMTP server, you should see a response similar to the one shown in the listing. The first number is a three-digit response code. This code can be used for troubleshooting purposes if email is not being transferred properly.

Following the three-digit code is the hostname of the SMTP server, followed by a description of the SMTP software package that the server is using. In this example, the Ubuntu server is using the Postfix SMTP software package to accept incoming SMTP connections.

You can close the connection by typing the word QUIT and pressing the Enter key. The SMTP server should send you a closing message and kill the TCP connection.

As you can tell from this example, SMTP uses simple ASCII text commands, and it returns three-digit reply codes with optional ASCII text messages. SMTP was originally defined in Internet Request for Comments (RFC) document number 821 maintained by the Internet Engineering Task Force (IETF) and updated in RFC 2821. Several modifications have been made to SMTP over the years, but the basic protocol commands remain in use.

SMTP Basic Commands

When a TCP session has been established and the SMTP server acknowledges the client by sending a welcome banner (as shown in Listing 7.2), it's the client's responsibility to control the connection between the two computers. The client accomplishes this by sending special commands to the server. The server should respond accordingly to each command sent.

RFC 2821 defines the basic client commands that an SMTP server should recognize and to which it should respond. Since RFC 2821 was written, there have been several extensions to the SMTP protocol, which not all servers have implemented. This section documents the basic SMTP keywords that are defined in RFC 2821.

The format of an SMTP command is

command [parameter]

where *command* is a four-character SMTP command and *parameter* is optional qualifying data for the command. Table 7.1 shows the basic SMTP commands available. The following sections describe the commands in more detail.

TABLE 7.1   SMTP basic commands

Command	Description
HELO	Opening greeting from client
MAIL	Identifies sender of message
RCPT	Identifies recipients
DATA	Identifies start of message
SEND	Sends message to terminal
SOML	Send-or-Mail
SAML	Send-and-Mail
RSET	Resets SMTP connection
VRFY	Verifies username on system
EXPN	Queries for lists and aliases
HELP	Requests list of commands
NOOP	No operation—does nothing
QUIT	Stops the SMTP session
TURN	Reverses the SMTP roles

Much work has been done on the format of the actual DATA messages. Technically, there is no wrong way to send a message, although work has been done to standardize on a method. RFC 822 defines a standard method for defining the email message subject, recipients, sender, and the type of document. Listing 7.3 shows a sample session sending a short email message to a local user on an SMTP server.

Listing 7.3: Sample SMTP session

```
rich@myhost:~$ telnet localhost 25
Trying 127.0.0.1...
Connected to localhost.
Escape character is '^]'.
220 myhost ESMTP Postfix (Ubuntu)
HELO localhost
250 myhost
MAIL FROM:rich@localhost
250 2.1.0 Ok
RCPT TO:rich
250 2.1.5 Ok
DATA
354 End data with <CR><LF>.<CR><LF>
This is a short test of the SMTP email system.
.
250 2.0.0 Ok: queued as E67A820C0E
QUIT
221 2.0.0 Bye
Connection closed by foreign host.
rich@myhost:~$ mail
"/var/mail/rich": 1 message 1 new
>N   1 rich@localhost      Wed Mar 16 23:21   11/408
? 1
Return-Path: <rich@localhost>
X-Original-To: rich
Delivered-To: rich@myhost
Received: from localhost (localhost [127.0.0.1])
    by mthost (Postfix) with SMTP id E67A820C0E
    for <rich>; Wed, 16 Mar 2016 23:20:41 -0400 (EDT)
Message-Id: <20160317032053.E67A820C0E@myhost>
Date: Wed, 16 Mar 2016 23:20:41 -0400 (EDT)
```

```
From: rich@localhost

This is a short test of the SMTP email system.
? x
rich@myhost:~$
```

Listing 7.3 shows a typical SMTP exchange between two hosts. After entering the message header information, the client enters the `DATA` command and the server responses. Next, the client sends the email message. The terminating period follows the completed message, indicating the end of the message to the server. As you can see, the SMTP server transferred the message to the local user's mailbox account exactly as the server received it. Also note how the SMTP server included a timestamp and the return path information in the text of the email message.

SMTP Response Codes

For each command that the client sends to the SMTP server, the server must reply with a response message. As you can see from Listing 7.3, response messages are made up of two parts.

The first part is a three-digit code that is used by the SMTP software to identify whether the command was successful and, if not, why. The second part is a text string that helps humans understand the reply. Often, the text string is passed on by the SMTP software and displayed to the user as part of a response message.

Usually, a space separates the code from the text string. In the case of multiline responses (such as the `HELP` and `EXPN` commands), a dash (-) separates the code from the text on all but the last line, which conforms to the normal pattern of using a space. This helps the client host identify when to expect more lines from the server.

There are four different groups, or categories, of reply codes:

- Error response codes
- Informational response codes
- Service response codes
- Action response codes

SMTP error responses are not overly descriptive. They just give you a general idea of what might have gone wrong if there was an error in the SMTP process. Informational codes are used to display additional information about a command.

Service codes are used to mark the status of the SMTP service in the connection. Action codes are a result of the SMTP server trying to perform a function requested by the client, such as `MAIL`, `RCPT`, and `DATA` commands. They return the status of the requested action so that the client will know what actions to take next in the SMTP process. Table 7.2 shows the valid SMTP response codes.

TABLE 7.2 SMTP response codes

Code	Category	Description
500	Error	Syntax error, command not recognized
501	Error	Syntax error in parameters
502	Error	Command not implemented
503	Error	Bad sequence of commands
504	Error	Command parameter not implemented
211	Informational	System status or system help
214	Informational	Help message
220	Service	Service ready
221	Service	Service closing transmission channel
421	Service	Service not available
250	Action	Requested mail action OK, completed
251	Action	User not local, will forward to <forward-path>
354	Action	Start mail input: end with <CRLF>.<CRLF>
450	Action	Requested mail action not taken: mailbox unavailable
451	Action	Requested action aborted: error in processing
452	Action	Requested action not taken: insufficient system storage
550	Action	Requested action not taken: mailbox unavailable
551	Action	User not local: please try <forward-path>
552	Action	Requested mail action aborted: exceeded storage allocation
553	Action	Requested action not taken: mailbox name not allowed
554	Action	Transaction failed

Knowing the basic SMTP response codes can help with the troubleshooting process if things go wrong with email delivery. Often the exact response code received by the server is attached to an email message if it bounces back.

Extended SMTP

Since its invention, SMTP has performed well in transporting messages between computers across the Internet. As it got older, though, system administrators began to recognize its limitations. Instead of trying to replace a standard protocol that was in use all over the world, work was done to try to improve the basic SMTP by keeping the original specifications and adding new features.

Extended SMTP (ESMTP) adds extra commands for special features to the standard SMTP commands. The ESMTP commands are optional, so each client and server must negotiate which ones to use. ESMTP is implemented in a connection by replacing the original SMTP greeting (HELO) with a new greeting command, EHLO. When an SMTP server receives this command, it realizes that the client is capable of sending extended SMTP commands. It will return a list of the extended SMTP commands that it recognizes.

Listing 7.4 shows a sample EHLO session and the commands that are available.

Listing 7.4: Extended SMTP commands

```
rich@myhost:~$ telnet localhost 25
Trying 127.0.0.1...
Connected to localhost.
Escape character is '^]'.
220 myhost ESMTP Postfix (Ubuntu)
EHLO localhost
250-myhost
250-PIPELINING
250-SIZE 10240000
250-VRFY
250-ETRN
250-STARTTLS
250-ENHANCEDSTATUSCODES
250-8BITMIME
250 DSN
QUIT
221 2.0.0 Bye
Connection closed by foreign host.
rich@myhost:~$
```

Notice that the server indicates that more commands are available now that it is in extended mode. One of the new groups of commands is the *Enhanced Status Codes* options. These options can be used on the MAIL and RCPT commands to indicate the delivery status of a particular email message for the client. Two ESMTP commands that are extremely useful are the ETRN and STARTTLS commands. The ETRN command allows the client and server systems to reverse roles and transfer new messages from the server to the client, all within the same SMTP connection.

The STARTTLS command allows the client and server to negotiate an encrypted session instead of using plaintext to transfer the messages, providing a layer of protection against unwanted snooping.

Post Office Protocol

Back in the old days (the 1980s), mailbox users would have to sit at a dumb terminal, log into the host computer, and read their email messages via a character-based text email processor. Now things are different. Computer users have the freedom of reading their email from anywhere at any time and have fancy GUI interfaces to do that.

If users cannot be at the physical email server to view their email, the next best thing is for them is to use a software package that can connect to the email server via a network and to read their messages on their local workstation. One protocol that allows a client to read email messages that are on a remote server is defined in RFC 1939 and called the *Post Office Protocol (POP)*. Currently, POP is at version three, thus the new name POP3.

Description of the Post Office Protocol

Much like SMTP, POP3 is a command-based protocol. The POP3 server listens for connection requests on TCP port 110 and responds by issuing a banner line indicating that it is ready for commands. One method of determining if a host is running a POP3 server is to telnet to port 110 and see if you get a POP3 greeting banner. Listing 7.5 shows an example of this.

Listing 7.5: Sample POP3 client session

```
rich@myhost:~$ telnet localhost 110
Trying 127.0.0.1...
Connected to localhost.
Escape character is '^]'.
+OK Hello there.
QUIT
+OK Better luck next time.
Connection closed by foreign host.
rich@myhost:~$
```

When the connection to TCP port 110 is made, the POP3 server produces a response banner to identify itself. After receiving the response banner, the client sends a QUIT command to log off the server.

Authentication

In a POP3 session, the first step for the client would be to log into the server. There are several different methods to do this:

- USER/PASS commands: send a userid and password in plaintext format
- APOP command: sends the userid in plaintext but the password as an MD5 encrypted value
- AUTH command: negotiates a secure authentication method between the POP3 server and client

The AUTH command provides a mechanism for the server and client to use advanced authentication methods, which are harder to crack if anyone is snooping on the network connection. These days, it's recommended to use some type of encrypted authentication method, especially if you're connecting to a POP3 server on a remote network.

POP3 Client Commands

Once the POP3 client has successfully logged into the server, it enters transaction mode. It must issue commands to control the transfer of messages from the server to the client. Each command will solicit a specific POP3 action from the server. Table 7.3 shows the basic POP3 commands.

TABLE 7.3 POP3 client commands

Command	Description
STAT	Returns current status of the mailbox
LIST	Returns a brief list of mailbox messages
RETR	Returns a specific mailbox message
DELE	Deletes a specific mailbox message
UIDL	Provides a unique numeric identifier for each message
TOP	Returns a brief listing of the most recent mailbox messages
NOOP	Performs no operation
RSET	Resets the session back to the start
QUIT	Terminates the POP3 session

The LIST, RETR, and DELE commands use a generic message-numbering system, based on the order in which email messages are stored in the mailbox. As messages are deleted, the numbers assigned to the remaining messages change.

To avoid this confusion, the UIDL command displays the unique ID number associated with each email message. You can then use that identifier in the RETR and DELE commands instead of the generic numbers to ensure that no mistakes are made when referencing messages.

Internet Message Access Protocol

Although POP3 is easy to implement, it does have its drawbacks. Mainly, it lacks any serious message-handling capabilities. Messages are usually downloaded en masse from the email server and then deleted from the server. This technique is good for the ISP hosting the mail server, because it saves on required disk space, but for the email user, this could get confusing.

When messages are downloaded, they become tied to the workstation where the download was performed. If your users retrieve email from only a single workstation on the network, that may not be a problem. However, if they need to access their mailbox from a home workstation as well as from another workstation at work, this gets to be a big problem. This means that their mailbox messages get split between two workstations located in different areas.

To compensate for this situation, a new protocol was devised. The *Internet Message Access Protocol (IMAP)* was developed at the University of Washington so that email users can access their mailboxes from multiple locations without splitting their mail among workstations.

By maintaining the mailbox on the email server and allowing the client to manipulate the messages directly on the server, the IMAP program greatly simplifies email access. Of course, the downside to this scenario is that the email server must maintain all of the email messages on its own disk. This can lead to some scary disk space situations for the email administrator. You must take care when administering an IMAP server that the system does not max out on disk space and crash (with all of the mailboxes and messages on it).

Description of the Internet Message Access Protocol

Just like POP3, IMAP uses a client/server command method of transferring messages from the server to the client. The client establishes a TCP connection to port 143 of the server to initiate the connection. The server should respond with a greeting banner. Listing 7.6 shows a sample IMAP session.

Listing 7.6: Sample IMAP session

```
rich@myhost:~$ telnet localhost 143
Trying 127.0.0.1...
Connected to localhost.
```

```
Escape character is '^]'.
* OK [CAPABILITY IMAP4rev1 UIDPLUS CHILDREN NAMESPACE THREAD=ORDEREDSUBJECT
THREAD=REFERENCES SORT QUOTA IDLE ACL ACL2=UNION] Courier-IMAP ready. Copyright
1998-2011 Double Precision, Inc.  See COPYING for distribution information.
a001 LOGOUT
* BYE Courier-IMAP server shutting down
a001 OK LOGOUT completed
Connection closed by foreign host.
rich@myhost:~$
```

This example shows a Telnet session to the default IMAP port on the local server. After the connection is established, the IMAP server presents a greeting banner. The client sends the LOGOUT command to the server to close the IMAP session.

Each command from the client must start with a unique identifier that tags the command. The server can use this identifier when responding to the command so that the client will know to which command the server is responding in the case of multiple commands being processed.

The identifier is usually a short alphanumeric string generated by the client. The eighth line in Listing 7.6 shows that the client chose the tag a001 as the first command-line identifier. Usually, client command identifiers increment sequentially throughout the IMAP session to simplify things, but that's not a requirement.

When the client establishes a connection, it starts out in an unauthenticated state. For the client to be allowed to perform any operations with the mailbox, it must first authenticate itself with the server. Once the client has authenticated itself to the server, it can issue IMAP commands to manipulate mail messages. IMAP supports each user having multiple mailboxes on a server. The user can read, transfer, and delete messages to and from any mailbox to which they have access on the server. This is a vast improvement over POP3.

IMAP User Authentication

Similar to POP3, IMAP provides several methods to authenticate a client, some more secure than others. However, unlike POP3 clients, IMAP clients often keep established sessions open for an extended period of time while they process their messages. Thus, the username and password pair are not transferred across the network several times each hour as with POP3. Nonetheless, it is still beneficial to transmit username and password information using an encrypted method if possible. Two different authentication methods are available in IMAP:

- LOGIN: Allows the client to use plaintext usernames and passwords to log into the IMAP server.

- AUTHENTICATE: The client and server negotiate a common encrypted authentication method.

When the client issues a valid AUTHENTICATE command, the server responds with a challenge string. It is the responsibility of the client to respond to the challenge with the appropriate response. If the IMAP server does not support the authentication method proposed by the client, it will respond with a NO response message. The client must attempt to negotiate a common authentication method, falling back to the LOGIN method as a last resort. Listing 7.7 shows a sample AUTHENTICATE session.

Listing 7.7: Sample AUTHENTICATE session

```
$ telnet localhost 143
Trying 127.0.0.1...
Connected to localhost.
Escape character is '^]'.
* OK [CAPABILITY IMAP4rev1 UIDPLUS CHILDREN NAMESPACE THREAD=ORDEREDSUBJECT
THREAD=REFERENCES SORT QUOTA IDLE ACL ACL2=UNION] Courier-IMAP ready. Copyright
1998-2011 Double Precision, Inc.  See COPYING for distribution information.
a001 AUTHENTICATE
a001 BAD Missing required argument to AUTHENTICATE
a002 AUTHENTICATE KERBEROS
a002 NO AUTHENTICATE KERBEROS failed
a003 AUTHENTICATE LOGIN
+ VXNlciBOYW1lAA==
cmljaA==
+ UGFzc3dvcmQA
dGVzdA==
a003 OK AUTHENTICATE completed
a004 LOGOUT
* BYE test.ispnet.net IMAP4rev1 server terminating connection
a004 OK LOGOUT completed
Connection closed by foreign host.
$
```

This example shows a failed attempt by the client to negotiate the KERBEROS IMAP authentication method. Next, the client attempts to use the LOGIN authentication method. The server responds by issuing a base64-encoded challenge. The client responds with the appropriate encoded username and password.

IMAP Commands

Once the client is authenticated with the IMAP server, it can begin manipulating messages. IMAP provides a large number of commands used to read, move, and delete mail messages from within different mailboxes on the server. Table 7.4 shows the available commands.

TABLE 7.4   IMAP commands

Command	Description
APPEND	Appends a message to the end of a mailbox
CAPABILITY	Requests a list of capabilities of the IMAP server
CHECK	Creates a checkpoint for the mailbox
CLOSE	Closes the open mailbox
COPY	Copies messages between mailboxes
CREATE	Creates a new mailbox
DELETE	Deletes a mailbox
EXAMINE	Opens a mailbox in read-only mode
EXPUNGE	Removes all messages from a mailbox tagged for deleting
FETCH	Retrieves the text of a specified message
LIST	Retrieves a list of all mailboxes
LOGOUT	Logs out from the current server
LSUB	Retrieves a list of only active mailboxes
NOOP	Performs no operation
RENAME	Renames a mailbox
SEARCH	Searches messages in an active mailbox that match a search string
SELECT	Selects an active mailbox
STATUS	Requests the status of a mailbox
STORE	Alters information associated with a message
SUBSCRIBE	Adds a mailbox to the list of active mailboxes
UID	Sets message references to the UID number instead of the sequence number
UNSUBSCRIBE	Removes a mailbox from the list of active mailboxes

The default mailbox for a client is called the INBOX. All new messages appear in the INBOX. The client has the ability to create new mailboxes (sometimes called folders by email client software) to move messages from the INBOX to other areas to reduce clutter.

Using Email Servers

Now that you've seen how the email process in Linux works, we can turn our attention to the software packages required to set up a full-featured Linux email server. First, you'll want to install an MTA server. The two main MTA software packages used in the Linux world are these:

- sendmail
- Postfix

Just about every Linux distribution contains one or both of these packages in its software repository, so installing them is easy. Once you get an MTA server installed, you'll most likely need to tweak the configuration settings for your environment. This section walks through the parts involved with each package and how to set them up on your Linux system.

Using Sendmail

The *sendmail* MTA package comprises several different parts, each part performing a separate function of the MTA process.

Besides the main sendmail program, there is a configuration file and several tables that you can create to contain information used by sendmail while processing incoming and outgoing mail messages. Table 7.5 lists the parts used in a normal sendmail installation.

TABLE 7.5   Sendmail parts

Part	Description
sendmail	Executable program that receives messages from local and remote users and determines how to deliver them
sendmail.cf	Configuration file that controls the behavior of the sendmail program
sendmail.cw	Contains a list of domain names for which the sendmail program will receive messages
sendmail.ct	Contains a list of trusted users that can control the sendmail operations
aliases	Contains a list of valid local mail addresses that can redirect mail to another user, a file, or a program

Part	Description
`newaliases`	Creates a new aliases database file from a text file
`mailq`	Checks the mail queue and prints any messages
`mqueue`	The directory used to store messages waiting to be delivered
`mailertable`	Used to override routing for specific domains
`domaintable`	Used to map old domain names to new ones
`virtusertable`	Used to map users and domains to alternate addresses
`relay-domains`	Used to allow specific hosts to relay messages though the `sendmail` program
`access`	Used to allow or refuse messages from specific domains

While this list of files may seem intimidating, things really aren't all that bad. Fortunately, there are some tools to help with the sendmail configuration process.

Configuring Sendmail

The `sendmail` program needs to be told how to handle messages as the server receives them. As an MTA program, `sendmail` processes incoming mail and redirects it to the proper location, either on a remote system or on the local system. Usually, by default, the sendmail package is configured to process mail for local users but not for sending or receiving messages from remote users.

The configuration file is used to direct `sendmail` as to how to manipulate the destination mail addresses in order to determine where and how to forward messages. The default location for the configuration file is `/etc/mail/sendmail.cf`.

The `sendmail.cf` file consists of rule sets that parse the incoming mail message and determine what actions to take. Each rule set is used to identify certain mail formats and instruct `sendmail` on how to handle that message. As a message is received, its header is parsed and passed through the various rule sets to determine an action to take on the message.

Rules also have helper functions defined in the configuration file. You can define three different types of helper functions:

- Classes define common phrases that are used to help the rule sets identify certain types of messages.

- Macros are values that are set to simplify the typing of long strings in the configuration file.

- Options are defined to set parameters for the `sendmail` program's operation.

The configuration file is made up of a series of classes, macros, options, and rule sets. Each function is defined as a single text line in the configuration file. Each line begins with a single character that defines the action for that line. Lines that begin with a space or a tab are continuation lines from a previous action line. Lines that begin with a pound sign (#) indicate comments and are not processed by sendmail.

The action at the beginning of the text line defines what the line is used for. Table 7.6 shows the standard sendmail actions and what they represent.

TABLE 7.6 Sendmail configuration file lines

Configuration Line	Description
C	Defines classes of text
D	Defines a macro
F	Defines files containing classes of text
H	Defines header fields and actions
K	Defines databases that contain text to search
M	Defines mailers
O	Defines sendmail options
P	Defines sendmail precedence values
R	Defines rule sets to parse addresses
S	Defines rule set groups

Trying to get the right combination of configuration lines for a specific email environment is a tricky process—not for the faint of heart. Fortunately, there's an easier way to create a sendmail configuration file, so most likely you'll never have to touch the sendmail.cf configuration file directly.

Using the m4 Preprocessor

Most sendmail server configurations are a matter of setting common rules to implement common features, such as forwarding local messages to an MDA program or passing email destined for an alias address to the proper local user account. Because of this, developers created a simpler way of generating the monolithic sendmail.cf configuration file.

They used the GNU *m4 macro processor* to create the sendmail configuration file from a set of simple macro definitions. They created macro definitions to define common sendmail features, and the m4 macro processor generates the sendmail.cf configuration lines needed to implement those features. Some macro definitions are built into the m4 processor program. Other macro definitions are defined in the sendmail configuration distribution.

You can now use the m4 preprocessor to create configuration files by just defining a small set of macros that list the features that you need to be available in your email server. Table 7.7 lists some of the macros that are available for you to use in the sendmail configuration file.

TABLE 7.7 Sendmail macro definitions

Macro	Description
define	Defines specific option values in the configuration file.
divert(n)	Defines a buffer action for m4. When n = -1, the buffer is deleted. 0 starts a new buffer.
DOMAIN	Defines what domain(s) the MTA will be using to transfer messages.
FEATURE	Defines a special feature set that will be used in the configuration file.
MAILER	Defines a method of mail transport for sendmail.
MASQUERADE_AS	Defines an alternative hostname that sendmail will answer messages as.
OSTYPE	Defines the operating system on which the macro is used. This allows the m4 program to add operating system–specific macro files.

The entries in the macro definition file are expanded by the m4 preprocessor to create the complete configuration file. Listing 7.8 shows a sample macro file that can be used to create a standard sendmail configuration file.

Listing 7.8: Sample sendmail macro file

```
divert(-1)
divert(0)dnl
include(`/usr/lib/sendmail-cf/m4/cf.m4')dnl
OSTYPE(`linux')dnl

FEATURE(`allmasquerade')dnl
FEATURE(`masquerade_envelope')dnl
FEATURE(`always_add_domain')dnl
FEATURE(`virtusertable')dnl
FEATURE(`local_procmail')dnl
```

```
FEATURE(`access_db')dnl
FEATURE(`blacklist_recipients')dnl

MASQUERADE_AS(`ispnet1.net')dnl

MAILER(`smtp')dnl
MAILER(`procmail')dnl
```

As shown in this example, many different features can be defined with the FEATURE macro command. Each feature represents a separate set of action lines in the final configuration file. Note how each line ends with the text dnl. This represents the end of a line entry in the macro file.

WARNING   You may have noticed the odd way of quoting text strings in the m4 macro file. The m4 preprocessor uses the backtick (`) and the single tick (') to represent quote marks. If you do not use these characters properly, the m4 program will not create the final configuration file properly.

After you create the macro file, just use the m4 preprocessor program to create the sendmail configuration file:

```
# m4 < myserver.mc > /etc/mail/sendmail.cf
```

You must redirect the macro file into the m4 preprocessor and redirect the output to a file.

Running Sendmail

After creating a configuration file, you can start the sendmail program. The easiest method for using sendmail is as a background daemon process, having it check the mail queue for new messages on a regular basis. You can use the -b and -q options to accomplish this:

```
# sendmail -bd -q5m
```

The -bd option runs sendmail as a background process, and the -q5m option tells it to check the outgoing mail queues every 5 minutes for new messages to send. Remember to execute this command with root privileges. At this point, if your configuration file is correct, you should be able to send and receive messages using sendmail.

Using Postfix

The *Postfix* system is a bit different from sendmail in that instead of one program, Postfix consists of several small programs to process email messages. Postfix also uses several mail queue directories to store email messages as they progress through the programs. This helps to ensure that no messages are lost if the server should fail at any time during the email process. Figure 7.4 shows a block diagram of the core Postfix parts.

FIGURE 7.4   Block diagram of Postfix

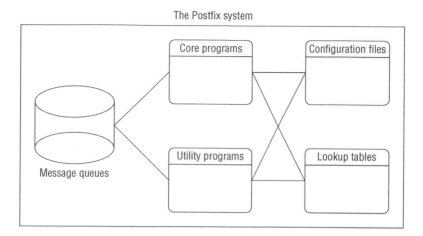

Each piece of the Postfix block diagram provides a different function for the whole email process. The following sections describe the different pieces of the Postfix block diagram in more detail.

Postfix Core Programs

The Postfix package utilizes a master program that runs as a background process at all times. The master program allows Postfix to spawn programs that scan the mail queues for new messages and send them to the proper destinations.

You can configure the core programs to remain running for set times after they are utilized. This allows the master program to reutilize a running helper program if necessary, saving processing time. However, after a set time limit, the helper program quietly stops itself. Listing 7.9 shows the Postfix processes that may be seen running on a normal Linux system.

Listing 7.9: Postfix background programs

```
$ ps ax
  232 con- I+  0:00.34 /usr/sbin/postfix/master
  236 con- I+  0:00.07 qmgr
  237 con- I+  0:00.05 pickup
$
```

These processes run continually in background to control mail delivery on the Postfix system. The master program is used to control the overall operation of Postfix. It is responsible for starting other Postfix processes as needed. The qmgr and pickup programs are configured to remain as background processes longer than other core programs. The pickup program determines when messages are available to be routed by the Postfix system. The qmgr program is responsible for the central message routing system for Postfix.

Besides the qmgr and pickup programs, Table 7.8 shows other core programs that Postfix uses to transfer mail messages.

TABLE 7.8   Core Postfix mail processing programs

Program	Description
bounce	Posts a log in the bounce message queue for bounced messages and returns the bounced message to the sender
cleanup	Processes incoming mail headers and places messages in the incoming queue
error	Processes message delivery requests from qmgr, forcing messages to bounce
flush	Processes messages waiting to be retrieved by a remote mail server
local	Delivers messages destined for local users
pickup	Waits for messages in the maildrop queue and sends them to the cleanup program to begin processing
pipe	Forwards messages from the queue manager program to external programs
postdrop	Moves an incoming message to the maildrop queue when that queue is not writable by normal users
qmgr	Processes messages in the incoming queue, determining where and how they should be delivered, and spawns programs to deliver them
sendmail	Provides a sendmail-compatible interface for programs to send messages to the maildrop queue
showq	Reports Postfix mail queue status
smtp	Forwards messages to external mail hosts using SMTP
smtpd	Receives messages from external mail hosts using SMTP
trivial-rewrite	Receives messages from the cleanup program to ensure that header addresses are in a standard format for the qmgr program, and is used by the qmgr program to resolve remote host addresses

Postfix Utility Programs

Besides the Postfix core programs, several utilities are used by both Postfix processes and local Postfix users to help manipulate and transfer messages. Table 7.9 shows the different Postfix utilities available on a Postfix system.

TABLE 7.9   Postfix utility programs

Program	Description
mailq	Checks the Postfix mail queues for messages and displays the results
postfix	Controls starting, stopping, and reloading the Postfix system
postalias	Creates, updates, or queries the Postfix alias database
postcat	Displays the contents of Postfix queue files
postconf	Displays and modifies parameter entries in the main.cf configuration file
postkick	Sends command requests to running Postfix services
postlock	Locks specified Postfix files and executes a specified command
postlog	Logs a message to the system-logging facility using Postfix-style log messages
postmap	Creates or queries a Postfix lookup table
postsuper	Performs maintenance on specified Postfix queue directories

Each Postfix utility program plays a different role in either processing mail messages or querying the Postfix system for status information. Postfix core programs utilize some of the utilities, while the Postfix administrator can use others to manipulate messages and obtain statistics about the running system.

Postfix Configuration Files

The next block in the diagram is the Postfix configuration files. The configuration files contain information that the Postfix programs use when processing messages. Unlike some other MTA programs, it is possible to change configuration information while the Postfix server is running and issue a command to have Postfix load the new information without completely downing the mail server.

The three Postfix configuration files are located in a common Postfix directory. The default location for this directory is /etc/postfix. Usually, all users have access to view the configuration files, while only the root user has the ability to change values within the files. Of course, you can modify this for your own security situation. Table 7.10 lists the Postfix configuration files.

TABLE 7.10 Postfix configuration files

File	Description
install.cf	Contains information from the install parameters used when Postfix was installed
main.cf	Contains parameters used by the Postfix programs when processing messages
master.cf	Contains parameters used by the Postfix master program when running core programs

The operation of the core Postfix programs can be controlled using the master.cf configuration file. Each program is listed in a separate line along with the parameters to control its operation. Listing 7.10 shows a sample master.cf file with default settings.

Listing 7.10: Sample master.cf configuration file

```
# ========================================================================
# service type  private unpriv chroot wakeup  maxproc command + args
#               (yes)   (yes)  (yes)  (never) (100)
# ========================================================================
smtp       inet  n       -      -      -       -       smtpd
pickup     unix  n       -      -      60      1       pickup
cleanup    unix  n       -      -      -       0       cleanup
qmgr       unix  n       -      n      300     1       qmgr
#qmgr      unix  n       -      n      300     1       oqmgr
tlsmgr     unix  -       -      -      1000    1       tlsmgr
rewrite    unix  -       -      -      -       -       trivial-rewrite
bounce     unix  -       -      -      -       0       bounce
defer      unix  -       -      -      -       0       bounce
trace      unix  -       -      -      -       0       bounce
verify     unix  -       -      -      -       1       verify
flush      unix  n       -      -      1000?   0       flush
proxymap   unix  -       -      n      -       -       proxymap
proxywrite unix  -       -      n      -       1       proxymap
smtp       unix  -       -      -      -       -       smtp
relay      unix  -       -      -      -       -       smtp
```

```
showq      unix  n      –      –      –      –      showq
error      unix  –      –      –      –      –      error
retry      unix  –      –      –      –      –      error
discard    unix  –      –      –      –      –      discard
local      unix  –      n      n      –      –      local
virtual    unix  –      n      n      –      –      virtual
lmtp       unix  –      –      –      –      –      lmtp
anvil      unix  –      –      –      –      1      anvil
scache     unix  –      –      –      –      1      scache
maildrop   unix  –      n      n      –      –      pipe
  flags=DRhu user=vmail argv=/usr/bin/maildrop -d ${recipient}
uucp       unix  –      n      n      –      –      pipe
  flags=Fqhu user=uucp argv=uux -r -n -z -a$sender–$nexthop!rmail ($recipient)
ifmail     unix  –      n      n      –      –      pipe
  flags=F user=ftn argv=/usr/lib/ifmail/ifmail -r $nexthop ($recipient)
bsmtp      unix  –      n      n      –      –      pipe
  flags=Fq. user=bsmtp argv=/usr/lib/bsmtp/bsmtp -t$nexthop -f$sender $recipient
scalemail-backend unix - n      n      -      2      pipe
  flags=R user=scalemail argv=/usr/lib/scalemail/bin/scalemail-store ${nexthop}
${user} ${extension}
mailman    unix  –      n      n      –      –      pipe
  flags=FR user=list argv=/usr/lib/mailman/bin/postfix-to-mailman.py
  ${nexthop} ${user}
```

The Postfix operational parameters are set in the main.cf configuration file. Postfix parameters have a default value that is implied within the Postfix system. If a parameter value is not present in the main.cf file, its value will be preset by Postfix. If a parameter value is present in the main.cf file, its contents override the default value.

Each Postfix parameter is listed on a separate line in the configuration file along with its value in the form

```
parameter = value
```

Both *parameter* and *value* are plain ASCII text strings that can be easily read by the mail administrator. The Postfix master program reads the parameter values in the main.cf file when Postfix is first started and again whenever a Postfix reload command is issued.

Two examples of this are the myhostname and mydomain parameters. If they are not specified in the main.cf configuration file, the myhostname parameter assumes the results of a gethostname() command, while the mydomain assumes the domain part of the default myhostname parameter. If you don't wish to use these values for the email server, you can specify different values in the configuration file using these parameters:

```
myhostname = mailserver.smallorg.org
mydomain = smallorg.org
```

When Postfix starts, it recognizes the local mail server as `mailserver.smallorg.org` and the local domain as `smallorg.org`, and it ignores any system set values. Table 7.11 shows some of the more common `main.cf` configuration settings that you may have to set for your email environment.

TABLE 7.11   Common Postfix settings

Setting	Description
myorigin	Specifies the domain or full hostname used for outgoing email messages
mydestination	Specifies the domain(s) for which Postfix will accept mail
relay_domains	Specifies allowed domains for forwarding mail
relayhost	Specifies points to an SMTP relay host for all outbound messages
virtual_alias_domains	Specifies a file that maps domain aliases to user accounts

Once you set the Postfix variable settings, you can use the `kill -HUP` command to stop and restart the `master` program. This forces Postfix to reread the configuration files and restart the SMTP server.

Sendmail Emulation Commands

With the popularity of the sendmail package, many email-oriented software packages expect the sendmail executable programs and utilities to be present to operate. Because of that, Postfix provides similar commands that emulate common sendmail features:

- `sendmail`: mimics the sendmail executable program and command options but redirects to the Postfix program
- `mailq`: lists the messages in the outgoing mail queue
- `newaliases`: initializes the aliases database

The `newaliases` command reads a text list of aliases and the real user accounts to which they point from the `/etc/aliases` file, and then it generates a binary database file read by Postfix for delivering mail sent to the aliases.

Postfix Lookup Tables

Postfix also uses several lookup tables that can be created by the mail administrator. Each lookup table defines parameters that control the delivery of mail within the Postfix system. Table 7.12 shows the different lookup tables that can be created for Postfix.

TABLE 7.12   Postfix lookup tables

Table	Description
access	Maps remote SMTP hosts to an accept/deny table for security
alias	Maps alternative recipients to local mailboxes
canonical	Maps alternative mailbox names to real mailboxes for message headers
relocated	Maps an old user mailbox name to a new mailbox name
transport	Maps domain names to delivery methods for remote host connectivity and delivery
virtual	Maps recipients and domains to local mailboxes for delivery

Each lookup table is a plain ASCII text file. Once the text file is created, you must create a binary database file by using the postmap command. Postfix uses the binary database file when searching the lookup tables. This helps speed up the lookup process for Postfix.

Postfix Security

Postfix supports secure SMTP using TLS encryption. By enabling TLS encryption Postfix has the ability to encrypt email messages, as well as authenticate remote SMTP servers and clients securely.

To use TLS security in Postfix, you'll need a certificate and private key. You can use the OpenSSL package to generate a self-signed certificate, or you can obtain a certificate signed by an authorized Certificate Authority (see Chapter 9, "Offering Web Services," for details on how to use self-signed certificates).

By default, TLS is disabled in Postfix. To enable it, you'll need to add a line to the main.cf configuration file:

```
smtpd_tls_security_level = may
```

The may option allows hosts still to connect without encrypting the session. To require that all hosts use encryption, you must use the encrypt option.

After you enable security on the Postfix server, you need to define where the server certificate and private key are located:

```
smtpd_tls_cert_file = /etc/postfix/cert.pem
smtpd_tls_key_file = /etc/postfix/key.pem
smtpd_tls_mandatory_ciphers = high
smtpd_tls_mandatory_exclude_ciphers = aNULL, MD5
smtpd_tls_security_level = encrypt
smtpd_tls_mandatory_protocols = TLSv1
```

Postfix provides a few other configuration options that allow you to customize how your security environment operates. Consult the official Postfix documentation to see the other configuration statements available.

Starting Postfix

To start the Postfix software, you must be logged in as the root user and use the command

```
# postfix start
```

The first time Postfix is started, it will check the /var/spool/postfix directory and create any message queue directories as needed:

```
postfix-script: warning: creating missing Postfix pid directory
postfix-script: warning: creating missing Postfix incoming directory
postfix-script: warning: creating missing Postfix active directory
postfix-script: warning: creating missing Postfix bounce directory
postfix-script: warning: creating missing Postfix defer directory
postfix-script: warning: creating missing Postfix deferred directory
postfix-script: warning: creating missing Postfix flush directory
postfix-script: warning: creating missing Postfix saved directory
postfix-script: warning: creating missing Postfix corrupt directory
postfix-script: warning: creating missing Postfix public directory
postfix-script: warning: creating missing Postfix private directory
```

These are the directories where Postfix stores messages as they are being processed. You should be able to check the log where your mail logs are kept (often the /var/log/maillog file) to see if Postfix started properly:

```
Mar  2 22:49:56 shadrach postfix-script: starting the Postfix mail system
Mar  2 22:49:56 shadrach postfix/master[864]: daemon started
```

You should not see any warning or error messages (other than the ones for creating the missing directories). If so, compare the messages with your configurations to determine what may possibly be wrong.

If Postfix started properly, you should see three new processes running in background mode on the mail server:

```
864 ?          S       0:00 /usr/libexec/postfix/master
865 ?          S       0:00 pickup -l -t unix -u -c
866 ?          S       0:00 qmgr -l -t unix -u
```

The first field is the process ID of the running program. The programs are shown in the last field. The master program should run at all times. The pickup and qmgr programs should be configured in the master.cf configuration file to wake up at predetermined intervals; thus, they should also remain running.

The Postfix program either creates or replaces the /usr/sbin/sendmail file with the Postfix version. If this was done, any messages sent should use the Postfix system to send the message. You can test this by sending a test message to a remote user and watching the Postfix processes:

```
864 ?          S          0:00 /usr/libexec/postfix/master
865 ?          S          0:00 pickup -l -t unix
866 ?          S          0:00 qmgr -l -t unix -u
885 ?          S          0:00 cleanup -t unix -u
886 ?          S          0:00 trivial-rewrite -n rewrite -t unix -u
896 ?          S          0:00 smtp -t unix -u -c
```

If Postfix is installed properly, it should call the cleanup, trivial-rewrite, and smtp programs to help it deliver the message to the final destination. These programs will stay active in background mode until they reach their timeout limit set in the master.cf file, and then they will quietly go away. Of course, the best way to determine if Postfix worked is to see if the message actually made it to the remote user.

Local Email Delivery

While most Linux MTA programs can perform local email delivery on their own, if you want any fancy features, you'll need to incorporate a specialized MDA program. Currently, the most popular MDA program for Linux is the procmail program. However, a standard is being developed that provides advanced email message filtering for any MDA or MTA application. The Sieve programming language can be added to any mail application, and it defines advanced methods for handing messages. This section walks you through both the procmail program and the Sieve language for filtering messages on your Linux system.

Procmail Basics

The procmail program has become so popular that many Linux distributions now install it by default, and many MTA programs utilize it in default configurations.

This section walks you through how to install procmail and write simple recipes to help redirect your incoming mail.

Installing Procmail

Most Linux distributions include procmail as a package in the software repositories. You can use the standard method of installing software to install the procmail package (apt-get for Debian-based systems or yum for Red Hat–based systems).

To run procmail on all email messages, you must configure the MTA program to pass incoming messages to procmail instead of storing the messages in the standard mailboxes.

For sendmail, that's as easy as adding a single line to the m4 macro file:

```
MAILER(`procmail')dnl
```

Similarly, for Postfix to use procmail, you just add a setting to the main.cf configuration file:

```
mailbox_command = /usr/bin/procmail -m /etc/procmailrc
```

This example allows the mail administrator to create a common procmailrc file that applies to all users. By default, procmail applies the recipes in the /etc/procmailrc file to all users but using the root username. The root user will own any folders created by this recipe. By specifying the -m option in the command line, procmail will run the recipes as the recipient username. This comes in handy when writing recipes that store messages in separate folders.

Procmail Recipes

Once procmail is installed, the most important part of procmail is the recipes created for mail filtering. The recipes control what procmail does with each incoming message. As the administrator, you can define recipes that apply to all incoming email in the /etc/procmailrc file. Also, each user can create their own recipes using the .procmailrc file located in their $HOME directory to specify how their messages are handled.

 Note that the .procmailrc file for each user account starts with a period. This indicates that the file is a hidden file. This file won't appear in a standard ls listing or in the display of graphical file manager programs unless you select the option to display hidden files.

Each recipe defines a matching expression value and an action for procmail to take when a message matches the expression. The format of a procmail recipe is

```
recipe header line
condition line(s)
action line
```

The recipe header line defines the basic action of the recipe. All recipe lines start with the heading

```
:0 [flags] [: locallockfile]
```

The flags identify the basic functions that the recipe will perform. Table 7.13 lists the flags that are available.

TABLE 7.13   Procmail recipe flags

Flag	Description
A	This recipe will not be executed unless the conditions of the preceding recipe are met.
a	This recipe will not be executed unless the conditions of the preceding A or a recipe are met.
B	Egreps the body of the message.
b	Feeds the body of the message to the destination (default).
c	Generates a copy of this message.
D	Distinguishes between uppercase and lowercase (default is to ignore case).
E	This recipe will not be executed unless the conditions of the preceding recipe were not met.
e	This recipe will not be executed unless the preceding E or e recipe failed.
f	Considers the pipe as a filter.
H	Egreps the message header (default).
h	Feeds the header of the message to the destination (default).
i	Ignores any write errors on the recipe.
r	Does not ensure that messages end with an empty line (raw mode).
W	Waits for the filter or program to finish and checks the exit code. Suppresses any "Program failure" messages.
w	Waits for the filter or program to finish and checks the exit code. Does not suppress any error messages.

The flags are listed in the recipe header line after the :0 header. More than one flag can be entered on the recipe header line.

After the flags, if a lock file is required, the mail administrator can either specify a lock file by name or omit the lock filename to allow procmail to use a default lock file. For example, the recipe header line

```
:0:
```

specifies procmail to use the default flags (Hhb) and to utilize the default lock file when processing the message.

Since mbox-style mailboxes store messages for a user in a single file, the lock file is required in procmail. If your MTA uses maildir-style mailboxes (such as Postfix), you don't need to use a lock file.

After the header line, one or more recipe condition lines must be defined. Each condition line must start with an asterisk (*). After the asterisk, a normal regular expression is used as the matching condition. Besides normal regular expressions, procmail defines seven special conditions. Table 7.14 lists the special conditions.

TABLE 7.14   Procmail special conditions

Condition	Description
!	Inverts the condition
$	Evaluates the condition according to shell substitution rules inside double quotes
?	Uses the exit code of the specified program
<	Checks if the total message length is less than the specified number of bytes (in decimal)
>	Checks if the total message length is greater than the specified number of bytes (in decimal)
variable ??	Matches the remainder of the condition against the environment variable specified
\	Quotes any of the special characters to use as normal characters

The easiest way to learn how to write condition lines is to see a few examples. This condition line checks to see if the message subject header field contains the word *guitars*:

```
* ^Subject:.*guitars
```

Any received messages with the word *guitars* in the message subject header field would match this condition. This condition line checks to see if the message subject header field contains the words *guitars* and *bass*:

```
* ^Subject:.*guitars.*bass
```

Received messages with both *guitars* and *bass* in the message subject header field would match this condition line. Finally, this condition line checks the entire message for the word *meeting*:

```
*meeting*
```

Any received message with the word *meeting* anywhere in the message would match this condition line.

After the condition lines are defined, the procmail action line must be defined. The action line defines the action that procmail will take if the condition line is matched with a message.

Much like the condition line, the action line starts with a special character that describes the basic action that will be taken. Table 7.15 describes the action line special characters.

TABLE 7.15   Procmail action line special characters

Character	Description
!	Forwards message to the specified addresses
|	Starts the specified program
{	Starts a block of recipes checked if the condition is matched
}	Ends a block of recipes checked if the condition is matched
text	Forwards message to the mailbox defined by *text*

Each recipe has only one action line. The action line defines what procmail will do with any messages that match the condition lines. Again, the easiest way to explain this is to show some examples.

```
:0 c
messages
```

This recipe places a copy of all messages received in the mailbox directory named messages.

```
:0
* ^From.*guitar-list
{
    :0 c
    ! rich@ispnet3.net
```

```
    :0
    guitars
}
```

This recipe demonstrates using a recipe inside a recipe. The main recipe checks if the message was received from the `guitar-list` user. If it is, both internal recipes are checked. The first one forwards a copy of the message to the `rich@ispnet3.net` email address, and the second saves the message in the `guitars` directory.

```
:0 hc
* !^FROM_DAEMON
* !^X-Loop: rich@ispnet1.net
| (formail -r -I"Precedence: junk" \
-A"X-Loop: rich@ispnet1.net"; \
echo "Thanks for your message, but I will be out of the office until 1/4") \
| $SENDMAIL -t
```

This recipe demonstrates both using an external program as well as creating an auto-reply. All messages that are not sent from either a daemon process or from the original user are forwarded to the `formail` program.

This program is included with the procmail distribution. It is used to help filter header information from messages. Two header fields are added: a `Precedence:` line and an `X-Loop` line to help prevent message loops. After that, a message is generated and sent to the local MTA process (Postfix, hopefully).

```
:0
* ^Subject.*work
/dev/null
```

The last recipe demonstrates filtering messages based on a `Subject` header line. Any message with a subject of `work` is placed in the mail folder `/dev/null`. Any information copied there is lost forever. Thus, this recipe deletes any messages with the subject `work`.

Each message is processed against each recipe. Any recipes whose condition line matches the message are processed. However, recipes that match a message but are not specifically set to copy the message redirect the message from the normal inbox.

Sieve

Sieve is a programming language created specifically for filtering email messages in either a client or server environment. Sieve is based on Internet Standard RFC5228, which defines the basic commands used in Sieve to process email messages. Several different MDA packages implement the Sieve programming language, including Dovecot and Cyrus.

This section walks through some of the basic commands that you can use in Sieve to customize email handling, as well as showing you a few simple examples on how to use them.

Sieve Commands

The Sieve programming language is divided into three types of commands:

- Action commands
- Control commands
- Test commands

Action commands define the action taken on an incoming email message. There are four actions that the filter can take:

keep—save the message in the default mailbox location for the user

fileinto—save a copy of the message to a specified location

redirect—forward the message

discard—silently ignore the message

> While not part of the base actions, the reject action has been added as an optional extension. It allows you to refuse an incoming email message but send a reason message back to the sender.

The control commands define conditional actions based on features of the incoming email messages, such as the sender, subject header, or message content. There are three types of control commands:

if—performs a conditional check on the message

require—adds external extensions to the script

stop—ends processing of the script

Finally, the test commands are used in the if commands to decide which part of the condition to execute. The test commands are what makes Sieve so versatile. You can test for many different features of an email message and act accordingly. The basic test commands are as follows:

address—compares the address of a sender or recipient

allof—combines multiple tests with a logical AND operation

anyof—combines multiple tests with a logical OR operation

envelope—evaluates parts of the SMTP commands, such as the From or Rcpt headers

exists—determines if a specific header exists in the message

false—always evaluates to a logical FALSE condition

header—determines if specific SMTP headers are present

not—inverts the result of a test condition

size—evaluates the size of an email message

true—always evaluates to a logical TRUE condition

The easiest way to examine how the Sieve programming language works is to see it in action. The following section walks you through some example Sieve scripts to demonstrate how it works.

Sieve Scripts

Sieve scripts work similarly to procmail recipes. The mail filter compares the incoming email message against the Sieve script, taking the actions specified. A simple Sieve script is as easy as

```
require ["fileinto"];
fileinto "saved";
```

This script moves all of the messages into the mailbox named saved. If you want to move only specific messages, you can add an if control command:

```
require ["fileinto"];
if header :is "Sender" "guitar-list.org"
   {
   Fileinto "guitars";
   }
else
   {
   fileinto "saved";
   }
```

This script uses the if control to check the message header for the sender of the message. If the message was sent by the guitar-list.org address, Sieve places the message in the guitars mailbox; otherwise, the message is placed in the saved mailbox.

With Sieve, you can easily filter out unwanted messages:

```
require ["fileinto", "reject"];
if header :contains "subject" "pills"
{
    reject "please stop spamming me"
}
elsif address :matches :domain "from" "badhost.com"
{
    discard;
}
```

The Sieve programming language provides lots of different options for creating filters. For a complete list of all of these features, refer to RFC5228.

Remote Email Delivery

While all of the user account mailboxes are located on the Linux server, most likely not all (if any) of your users will actually use the physical Linux server. Instead, most system users connect remotely to the Linux server using some type of client workstation. To read their email messages, they must use some type of email client package, such as Thunderbird for Linux workstations or one of the many Windows and Mac OS X email clients.

To support remote clients, the Linux server must have either a POP3 or IMAP package installed. There are several popular POP3 and IMAP packages available for Linux, and the LPIC-2 exam covers two of them:

- Courier

- Dovecot

This section walks you through how to use both of these packages in your Linux system.

Using Courier

The *Courier* email server package is actually categorized as an MTA package, because it contains full SMTP capabilities as well as the ability to support POP3 and IMAP. However, it's not commonly used as an MTA package; it's better known for its POP3 and IMAP capabilities. Often, you'll see the Courier package installed alongside the sendmail or Postfix MTA package to provide IMAP and POP3 support.

Once you install the Courier package for your Linux distribution, the configuration files are located in the /etc/courier directory. The authdaemonrc file contains the configuration settings required for authenticating user accounts for login. The imapd and pop3d files contain configuration settings for those specific servers. Table 7.16 shows the more common configuration settings that you may need to tweak for your specific environment.

TABLE 7.16   Courier configuration settings

Setting	Description
ADDRESS	Specifies the interface IP address to listen to for incoming requests. A value of 0 indicates to listen on all interfaces.
MAILDIRPATH	Specifies the directory where email messages are stored.
MAXDAEMONS	Specifies the maximum number of client connections allowed.
MAXPERIP	Specifies the maximum number of connections per client.
PORT	Specifies the TCP port to listen to for incoming requests.

By default, Courier uses the standard Linux authentication database to authenticate user logins. You can, however, create a separate login database using either MySQL or the Lightweight Directory Access Protocol (LDAP).

Using Dovecot

The *Dovecot* package was created primarily as an IMAP server, but it also supports POP3. Because of its popularity, most Linux distributions include the Dovecot package as part of the standard software repository.

Dovecot Configuration

Once you install Dovecot, the configuration file should be /etc/dovecot.conf, though some distributions create a separate /etc/dovecot directory to store the dovecot.conf file and a separate subdirectory under that to store separate configuration files for each Dovecot feature.

In the configuration file, you can change settings that control which servers start, what protocols they use, and what authentication methods the servers support. Some Linux distributions (such as Ubuntu) also include a subdirectory under the dovecot directory to create separate configuration files for each feature supported by Dovecot. Table 7.17 shows the configuration settings that you may need to tweak for your environment.

TABLE 7.17 Dovecot configuration settings

Setting	Description
auth	Specifies the login authentication method used
listen	Specifies the IP address and optional port to listen to for incoming requests
login_max_connections	Specifies the maximum number of connections
login_max_processes_count	Specifies the maximum number of logins
login_process_per_connection	Specifies whether each login creates its own process
mail_location	Defines the type and location of mailboxes on the system
mechanisms	Defines the authentication methods that the server supports
protocols	Specifies the protocols supported by the server

Dovecot also supports the Sieve programming language for handling incoming mail messages. This feature is called the "vacation extension" in Dovecot. It allows you to create code for handling things such as automatic replies or sending email messages directly to specific folders. You define the vacation settings in the plugin section of the configuration file:

```
sieve_vacation_min_period
sieve_vacation_max_period
sieve_vacation_default_period
sieve_vacation_use_original_recipient
sieve_vacation_dont_check_recipient
sieve_vacation_send_from_recipient
```

Time periods can be set using seconds (s), minutes (m), hours (h), or days (d), such as 7d for seven days.

Dovecot Administration

Once you have Dovecot configured for your environment, you use the doveadm command to control it. The doveadm command has several different options for managing the Dovecot application program, as well as for handling mailbox messages. There are two options that control the Dovecot master process:

reload—stops and restarts the Dovecot processes

stop—halts the Dovecot processes

Once Dovecot is running, there are several doveadm options that you use to control the Dovecot process:

director—manage Dovecot directors

exec—execute Dovecot commands

instance—manage the list of running instances

kick—disconnect users

log—locate, test, or reopen log files

penalty—show current penalties

proxy—manage Dovecot proxy connections

who—display current users

There are also doveadm options for managing mailboxes:

acl—manage access control lists

altmove—move messages to alternative storage

backup—synchronize mailboxes to a remote location

batch—execute multiple commands

copy—copy messages to another mailbox

deduplicate—remove duplicate messages

dump—dump the contents of a mailbox

expunge—remove messages based on query

fetch—retrieve messages based on query

flags—add, remove, or replace message flags

fts—manipulate the full text search index

force-resync—fix broken mailboxes

import—import messages into a mailbox

index—index messages in a mailbox

mailbox—mailbox handling commands

move—move messages between mailboxes

purge—remove messages from mailboxes

quota—set or show quota settings

replicator—manage a user's mail replication

search—show a list of mailboxes or messages

stats—display or reset mailbox statistics

sync—synchronize the mailbox with another location

The doveadm commands provide a full set of administration tools for managing the Dovecot mailbox environment.

EXERCISE 7.1

Setting Up and Testing an Email Server

This exercise demonstrates how to set up a simple email server on your Linux system. To do this, follow these steps:

1. Log in as root, or acquire root privileges by using su or by using sudo with each of the following commands.

2. Open a command prompt; then type **sudo apt-get install sendmail** or **yum install sendmail** to install the sendmail package on your system. You won't see any objects added to the menu when this program is installed.

3. Type **sudo apt-get install courier-imap courier-pop** or **yum install courier-imap** and **yum install courier-pop** to install the Courier IMAP and POP3 servers. Again, you won't see any objects added to the menu when these programs are installed.

4. Test the sendmail SMTP server by typing **telnet localhost 25** at a command line. If your system has the sendmail program running, you should be greeted by a welcome banner. Type **QUIT**, and then hit the Enter key to exit the SMTP session.

5. Test the Courier IMAP server by typing **telnet localhost** 143 at a command line. You should see the Courier IMAP welcome banner. Type **a01 LOGOUT**, and hit the Enter key to exit and return to the command prompt.

6. Test the Courier POP3 server by typing **telnet localhost** 110 at the command line. You should see the Courier POP3 welcome banner. Type **QUIT**, and hit the Enter key to exit and return to the command prompt.

7. Send a test email message to yourself by typing **telnet localhost** 25 at the command line. At the SMTP prompt, type **HELO localhost** then press the Enter key. Next, continue the SMTP session by entering the following commands:

```
MAIL FROM: rich@localhost
RCTP TO: rich
DATA
Subject: Test message
This is a test message.
.
QUIT
```

Substitute your username for the username in the RCPT TO line shown in this example.

8. At the command prompt, check your mailbox by typing the **mail** command at the command prompt. You should see at least one message waiting for you. Enter the message number as shown in the message listing to view the message. Type **d** to delete the message and then **x** to exit the mail program.

9. Exit from the command prompt to return to your desktop.

Summary

Linux uses several programs to implement email features in a server environment. The mail transfer agent (MTA) is responsible for sending mail messages to both local and remote users, as well as receiving mail messages from remote servers. The two most popular Linux MTA packages are sendmail and Postfix.

The mail delivery agent (MDA) can provide advanced features for processing mail destined for local user accounts. You can create systemwide rules (called recipes) for processing all mail messages. Individual users can also specify rules for processing their own mail. The procmail program is the most common MDA program used in Linux.

The mail user agent (MUA) provides an interface for users to access the email messages in their mailboxes. Both text-based as well as graphical MUA packages are available for Linux. The binmail program is the most common text-based package for the command line. The Evolution, Thunderbird, and KMail packages are commonly found in graphical desktop Linux environments.

The sendmail program uses a single configuration file to store all settings required to run the MTA server. The /etc/sendmail.cf file can be somewhat difficult to build, so the sendmail developers created macros using the m4 macro preprocessor to help make setting up a sendmail server easier. The sendmail program normally uses the /var/spool/mail directory for storing mail messages, with each user account mailbox being a separate file under that directory.

The Postfix program uses multiple configuration files and stores them all in the /etc/postfix folder. It creates system mailboxes in the /var/spool/postfix directory for processing email messages, and then it can use either the standard mbox mailbox format that sendmail uses for user messages, or it can use a more advanced directory structure called maildir.

The procmail program allows both the system administrator and individual users to create recipes for forwarding email messages to separate folders, to remote email addresses, or to the trash. The /etc/procmailrc file contains recipes that are applied to all email messages, while each user's $HOME/.procmailrc file contains recipes that apply only to email for that user.

The Sieve programming language provides a standard interface for handling incoming email messages. It allows you to define what type of messages to filter and how to handle the filtered messages.

The Courier and Dovecot programs provide IMAP and POP3 servers, which allow remote users to access their mailboxes. The Courier package stores configuration files in the /etc/courier directory, and Dovecot stores its configuration in the /etc/dovecot.conf file.

Exam Essentials

Describe the configuration files required for Postfix.   Postfix uses three configuration files, all located in the /etc/postfix directory. The install.cf file contains settings for managing the installation parameters when you install Postfix. The main.cf file contains settings for processing messages, and the master.cf file contains settings to control the running Postfix processes.

Describe how SMTP is used to transfer mail between two email users.   SMTP is a text-based protocol. Once you establish a connection to an SMTP server, the client program controls the connection by issuing four-character commands. The server responds with a three-digit response code, along with human-readable text. The client specifies the email message recipient, identifies the sender, and then sends the message text. SMTP servers can be configured to accept messages for non-local user accounts and then relay the message to the appropriate server for the user.

Summarize the common SMTP programs available for Linux.   The sendmail and Postfix programs are the most common SMTP programs for Linux. The sendmail program was the original SMTP program used in Unix systems, and it was ported to the Linux environment.

The Postfix program makes creating an email server easier by simplifying the configuration process. It also improves recovery from a server crash by splitting the email process into several programs, with each program having its own storage directory for processing email messages. Two other popular SMTP programs are Exim and qmail, each of which can be found in specialized email server installations.

Explain what the procmail program adds to the email process.   MTA programs have the ability to store incoming email messages in mailboxes for individual local users, but they don't normally do much else. The procmail MDA program provides advanced features for mail processing. The MTA program passes email messages for local users to the procmail program, which then compares each received message against recipes defined by the system administrator and each individual user. The recipes can sort email messages into separate directories, forward email to other user accounts (both local and remote), or automatically respond to email messages.

List where to define procmail recipes.   You can define procmail recipes in two locations. The /etc/procmailrc file contains recipes that procmail applies to all email messages that the server receives. This can come in handy if you need to store copies of all incoming email or if you need to redirect all incoming email temporarily to another server. Besides the main procmailrc configuration file, each user can create an individual .procmailrc file in their $HOME directory to process their own email messages.

Explain how remote users can access their email mailboxes.   You can install POP3 and/or IMAP server software on the Linux system to allow remote users to connect to the server to read their email messages. The POP3 server normally downloads user email messages directly to the client MUA software on the remote workstation, so no email messages are stored on the server. The IMAP server normally allows users to store their email messages on the server, as well as create separate directories for sorting messages. Most MUA client programs (such as Evolution, Thunderbird, and KMail) support both POP3 and IMAP connections to servers.

Describe how the Sieve programming language works.   The Sieve programming language is a standard for defining rules for processing incoming email messages. It can be implemented in any MDA or MTA application. Sieve defines controls for determining which email messages are handled and actions for defining what the server should do with the email messages that match the controls.

Describe how the Dovecot program works.   The Dovecot program also provides both POP3 and IMAP server capabilities for accessing user mailboxes remotely. It uses a single configuration file called /etc/dovecot.conf to control server features.

Review Questions

You can find the answers in the Appendix.

1. Where are the Postfix configuration files located?
    A. `/var/spool/postfix`
    B. `/etc/postfix`
    C. `/var/spool/mail`
    D. `/var/log`
    E. `/etc/mail`

2. What is the name of the main Postfix process?
    A. `qmgr`
    B. `pickup`
    C. `master`
    D. `cleanup`
    E. `smtp`

3. What is the Postfix configuration file that manages when Postfix processes start and stop?
    A. `master.cf`
    B. `main.cf`
    C. `install.cf`
    D. `/var/spool/postfix`
    E. `/var/log/maillog`

4. What is the Postfix configuration file that controls mail processing?
    A. `master.cf`
    B. `/etc/sendmail.cf`
    C. `/etc/aliases`
    D. `main.cf`
    E. `/var/log/maillog`

5. What directory does Postfix use for storing email messages as it processes them?
    A. `/var/spool/mail`
    B. `/var/spool/postfix`
    C. `/etc/postfix`
    D. `/etc/mail`

6. What sendmail emulation command in Postfix allows you to check on the number of messages waiting in the mail queue to be delivered?
    A. `newaliases`
    B. `master`

   C. pickup

   D. smtp

   E. mailq

7. Which sendmail emulation command converts the text alias entries into the binary `aliases` database file?

   A. newaliases

   B. master

   C. pickup

   D. smtp

   E. mailq

8. What text file does the `newaliases` command read to create the `aliases` database?

   A. /etc/aliases

   B. /etc/postfix/master.cf

   C. /etc/postfix/main.cf

   D. /etc/postfix/install.cf

9. What log file does Postfix use to store system messages?

   A. /var/spool/mail

   B. /var/log/maillog

   C. /var/spool/postfix

   D. /var/log/messages

10. Where do individual users store procmail recipes to apply to their own email messages?

   A. /etc/postfix

   B. /etc/procmailrc

   C. $HOME/.procmailrc

   D. /etc/aliases

   E. /users/.procmailrc

11. What files does the email administrator use to store recipes to apply to all incoming email messages?

   A. /etc/postfix

   B. /etc/procmailrc

   C. $HOME/.procmailrc

   D. /etc/aliases

   E. /users/.procmailrc

12. What does the following procmail recipe do to incoming email messages?

```
:0 c
messages
```

   A. The system rejects all incoming email messages.

   B. The system forwards all email messages to an alias account.

   C. The system copies all incoming email messages to the messages directory.

   D. The system moves all incoming email messages to the messages directory.

   E. The system deletes all incoming email messages.

13. What MDA program is commonly used to forward email messages to local mailboxes?

   A. Sendmail

   B. Procmail

   C. Postfix

   D. Courier

   E. Dovecot

14. What configuration setting in Postfix must you change to forward all incoming email messages to procmail?

   A. `mailbox_command`

   B. `mydestination`

   C. `myhost`

   D. `relayhost`

15. Which mailbox style stores all messages for a user in a single file?

   A. Sendmail

   B. Courier

   C. Maildir

   D. Mbox

   E. Exim

16. Which mailbox style uses separate files to store each message for each user?

   A. Sendmail

   B. Courier

   C. Maildir

   D. Mbox

   E. Exim

17. Where are the Courier configuration files located?

   A. `/var/spool/mail`

   B. `/var/spool/postfix`

    C. /etc/courier

    D. /etc/mail

    E. /var/log

18. What Courier configuration setting determines how many remote clients can connect at the same time?

    A. MAXDAEMONS

    B. MAILDIRPATH

    C. ADDRESS

    D. MAXPERIP

    E. PORT

19. Where does Dovecot store its configuration settings? (Select two.)

    A. /etc/dovecot

    B. /etc/postfix

    C. /var/spool/mail

    D. dovecot.conf

    E. /var/spool/postfix

20. What Dovecot setting specifies the authentication methods that the server supports?

    A. mail_location

    B. mechanisms

    C. listen

    D. login_max_connections

    E. protocols

Chapter

8

Directing DNS

THE FOLLOWING EXAM OBJECTIVES ARE COVERED IN THIS CHAPTER:

✓ 207.1 Basic DNS server configuration

✓ 207.2 Create and maintain DNS zones

✓ 207.3 Securing a DNS server

The *Domain Name System (DNS)* is a network protocol at the heart of many Internet activities. It provides IP addresses to various systems that provide services, and it uses a distributed database to do this.

For Linux systems, BIND is a popular package that provides DNS. Setting up DNS via BIND can be a complicated process, involving modifying configuration files and creating and maintaining zones, in addition to securing the DNS server and its various transactions. All of these topics (and more) are covered in this chapter.

Configuring a DNS Server

In part, you have DNS to thank for being able to type a web page's address, such as www.ivytech.edu (or a shortened version of that name, such as ivytech.edu) into a browser's address bar and having the browser reach the web site. In this section, you'll learn about how DNS works, how to install BIND software to implement DNS services, BIND's various configuration files, starting and stopping BIND, setting up BIND logging, and even implementing a local caching-only DNS server.

Understanding DNS and BIND

Before launching into how to install BIND and configure it, it's best to understand how DNS works. Designed in 1983, DNS is a complicated but rigorous structure that has survived the test of time.

Looking at DNS

Typically, when someone would like to visit a web page, they open a web browser and type in letters (or words), separated by dots, into the browser's address line, such as www.ivytech.edu. These dot-separated letters make up a *fully qualified domain name (FQDN)*, and they are the human-friendly addresses used by individuals to access various services, such as web pages, across a network.

Systems connected to a network, such as the Internet, do not use FQDNs. Instead, they use IP addresses to identify each other. Thus, there exists a need to translate FQDNs into IP addresses and vice versa. This need is typically fulfilled by DNS. The process of translating between a system's FQDN and its IP address is called *name resolution*. DNS is a network protocol that uses a distributed database to provide the needed name resolution.

Historically a system's local /etc/hosts file was used to provide name resolution. If desired, you can still use this file for that purpose on very small local networks that consist of a few systems.

If DNS used a single database in a sole location, the results would be disastrous. Large networks would bog down while waiting for name resolutions to complete. Fortunately, DNS has a database with a robust distributed structure, providing the needed name resolution performance levels.

The DNS database structure, also called the *Domain Name Space*, is an inverted or upside-down tree. This structure is somewhat similar to the Linux virtual directory structure. In DNS, a web host may be referred to by its host name and domains, separated by dots, such as www.example.com, whereas in the Linux virtual directory structure, the files and directory names are separated by forward slashes, such as /home/rich/filea.txt.

The Domain Name Space's hierarchical structure is rather vast. An artistic representation of a name space snippet is shown in Figure 8.1.

FIGURE 8.1   Domain Name Space depiction

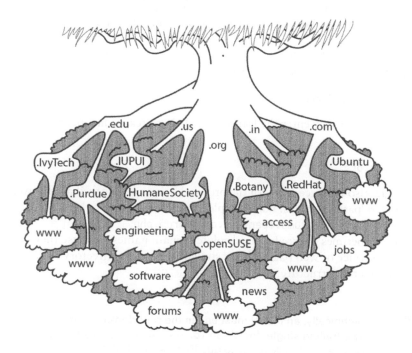

At the top of the domain namespace is the root domain, also called *null*. It is typically written in documentation either with two single quotes right next to each other (") or as a single dot (.).

Below the root domain are *Top-Level Domains (TLDs)*. These TLDs can be generic, such as .com, .edu, .gov, and so on. They can also be country codes, typically only two letters long, such as .IN for India and .US for the United States of America. In addition, there are infrastructure, restricted, sponsored, and test TLDs. The organizations that manage these TLDs are selected by the Internet Corporation for Assigned Names and Numbers (ICANN). ICANN is also responsible for managing the root domain area.

Below the TLDs are *first-level domains*, and they are considered to be TLD subdomains. Typically, first-level domains are for various companies, organizations, or individuals. For example, referring back to Figure 8.1, the first-level domains depicted include .Ubuntu, .RedHat, .openSUSE, and .IvyTech. Each first-level domain name must be unique and registered with ICANN through a domain name registrar.

Following the first-level domains on the domain name space tree are further subdomains that can either be actual systems (hosts, sometimes called *nodes*) or additional subdomains. These hosts and any subdomains are usually managed by the first-level domain owner. Typically, you see either www or a name for the host. In Figure 8.1, hosts (nodes) are shown as leaves on the tree.

While it is true that you can go to even deeper subdomain levels (up to 127 levels) and have a domain name like me.linux.cs.myorg.com, it's typically not a good idea. It is a better practice to use subfolders such as myorg .com/cs/linux/me instead of multilevel subdomains.

When a user types an FQDN into a web browser's address bar, they include many different information pieces, as shown here:

host_name.first-level_domain.TLD

For example, a user may enter the following FQDN to reach the openSUSE distribution's forums:

forums.opensuse.org

A FQDN can also be preceded with the protocol being used as well as followed by any needed subfolders/paths or ports. For example, to reach the same website as just shown, a user could enter https://forums.opensuse.org/forum.php.

FQDNs are sometimes referred to as absolute domain names, because they show the entire path to a service or web page. This is similar to absolute directory references in the Linux virtual directory structure.

Technically, an FQDN must end in the root domain name, which is indicated by a trailing single dot (.). So forums.opensuse.org should be written as forums.opensuse.org. to qualify as a true FQDN.

The name resolution process (translating an FQDN into an IP address that allows you to reach the desired host or service) is rather complicated. Several players are involved.

The first player is the *name server*. A name server can store information about a domain namespace portion, called a *zone*, which will provide the name resolution data. If a name server doesn't store zone information, it has software that can obtain the needed name resolution information.

Domain Name Space is broken up into different zones. For example, the root zone, shown in Figure 8.2, is managed by ICANN. The root zone manages authoritative information concerning the TLDs (also shown in Figure 8.2) on its name servers. Thus, these name servers store information about the root zone, and they are often referred to as the *root servers*.

FIGURE 8.2 Namespace root zone and TLDs

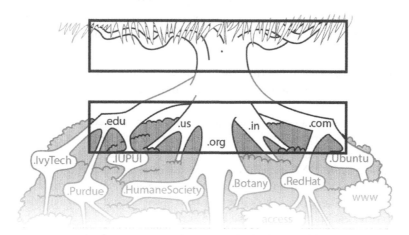

Thirteen named managers take care of the root servers handling the root zone. Some people mistakenly take that to mean that there are only 13 servers. Actually, there are hundreds of root servers managing the DNS root zone, and these servers are spread all over the world. You can find out more about these 13 designated managers and their root servers at https://www.iana.org/domains/root/servers.

Additional zones also exist, but they are not as clear-cut as the root zone. Once you get to the first-level domains, a zone may be the entire first-level domain and all it subdomains, or it may be the first-level domain and only a *portion* of its subdomains.

 A zone defines what a domain name server has authority over. It includes maintaining the zone's authoritative data files, called either *zone files* or *zone databases*, covered later in this chapter.

At the first-level domains and below, a domain name's owner is responsible for managing the zone(s) and the name servers. A minimum of two name servers are required per zone, as noted here:

Primary (Master) Server   This name server is required, and it is considered the *authoritative server*, because it has authority over the domain; the information it contains (such as the domain's name and what subdomains exist in that domain) is called *authoritative information*.

Secondary (Slave) Server   This name server is optional; it is considered an authoritative server, but it receives its information from the primary server and is often used for performance reasons to offload the primary server's burden.

Caching Server   Often used by ISPs, this name server receives its information from the primary (or secondary) server, and it stores the information locally in its own cache, which provides faster name resolution.

Forwarding Server   This specialized caching server also forwards queries to the other servers if it cannot find the needed query answer in its cache; it is often implemented for security reasons and can also be implemented on the DNS client side to improve name resolution performance.

A domain owner can have more than two name servers for a domain, depending on the domain's performance needs. However, at a minimum, there must be a primary server and one other of the listed servers.

DNS servers can also be a combination of the server types listed previously. For example, you could have a secondary server that is also acting as a caching server. These combo-DNS servers are sometimes called *Hybrid servers*.

There are also *Stealth DNS servers*, which are sometimes called *Hidden DNS servers*. These servers are typically behind firewalls. They can be either primary or secondary DNS servers, are used for an organization's internal DNS queries, and are often hybrids in that they may also offer caching and recursive DNS services.

As you probably have recognized, understanding what DNS server types your company or organization needs can be a large part of a DNS server implementation project. While there is great flexibility, there can also be terminology confusion. Whether you are implementing DNS servers or just studying for the certification, it is worthwhile to record the various server type definitions for study or use during implementation project meetings.

Another important player in name resolution is the *resolver*. The resolver is a program or library routine that forms a query (for example, "What is the IP address of www.example.com?") and needs to obtain the query answer. (A resolver can also refer to a DNS client.)

When a resolver creates its query, it first checks its own DNS cache, if available. If this query has been recently answered and the resolver's cache has the answer, the query process stops.

The various name resolutions that exist in the different DNS caches are often governed by a time to live (TTL) setting. Once that time has passed, the name resolution is flushed from the cache.

If the resolver's cache does not contain the answer, the resolver sends the query to an internal or external (typically an ISP) name server. This query is a single UDP request and the name server is typically called a *Recursive Name Server*. If previous name resolutions have been stored on this server (cached) or stored on a local caching server, the Recursive Name Server responds to the query, using a single UDP reply containing the appropriate IP address. If the name resolution has not been cached, the Recursive Name Server will start its own query process.

As an example, suppose a resolver is trying to determine the IP address of the www .example.com website. The name resolution process example is depicted in Figure 8.3.

FIGURE 8.3   DNS query process

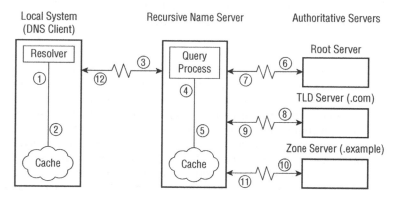

For Figure 8.3, each step the name resolution process takes in this example query is described here:

1. The resolver checks its own server's cache for www.example.com's IP address.

2. The resolver is informed that the name resolution data is not found in the local cache.

3. The resolver queries its ISP's Recursive Name Server, which starts a query process.

4. The Recursive Name Server query process checks its local cache for the www.example .com's IP address.

5. The Recursive Name Server is informed that the name resolution data is not found in the local cache.

6. The Recursive Name Server queries the authoritative root server for the .com TLD server location.

7. The root server responds with the authoritative information stating where a .com TLD server is located.

8. The Recursive Name Server queries the authoritative .com TLD server for the .example zone server location.

9. The .com TLD server responds with the authoritative information stating where an .example zone server is located.

10. The Recursive Name Server queries the authoritative .example zone server for the www host's IP address.

11. The .example zone server responds with the authoritative information stating the IP address of the www host.

12. The Recursive Name Server passes along the IP address of www.example.com to the resolver.

This entire name resolution process would move much more slowly if the DNS database was not distributed. In addition, providing caching of recent name resolutions is beneficial for performance.

On the client side of name resolution, different caching or forwarding server configurations are possible. Your particular DNS client-side setup will be dictated by the applications and data needs of your system(s) as well as their resources.

Sometimes confusion exists when it comes to name resolution concerning IP addresses and MAC addresses. Address Resolution Protocol (ARP) translates an IPv4 address into a system's NIC MAC address. Neighbor Discovery Protocol (NDP) translates IPv6 addresses into MAC addresses (though your IPv6 address may contain the system's MAC address, depending on its configuration). Typically, a system's MAC address is used from only one router *hop* to the next, and it does not go beyond a single router. Thus, your system's MAC address is used to send packets from the closest router to the system and does not go beyond that point, whereas a system's IP address does go beyond a single *hop.* Chapter 6 contains more details on network configuration.

There are additional finer details to the name resolution process. The DNS structure is extremely rigorous and whole books have been written on the topic. A book dedicated entirely to DNS is useful if you want to dig deeper into understanding its nuances.

Looking at BIND

Berkeley Internet Name Domain (BIND) provides DNS protocol implementation. BIND got its start more than 30 years ago at the University of California at Berkeley, and it is open source. It also is the most popular DNS software available.

Certification objectives cover BIND version 9.x, also called BIND 9. Though BIND was originally written by four Berkeley graduate students, it ended up being maintained by the Internet Systems Consortium (ISC). Around 2009, the ISC started on BIND 10. In 2014, BIND 10 was renamed Bundy, and it is no longer handled by the ISC. Bundy is currently maintained by the Bundy-Project at http://bundy-dns.de/. This chapter's and the certification objective's focus is on BIND 9, which is still maintained by the ISC.

The various details on configuring and maintaining DNS on Linux using BIND are covered later in this chapter. First, it is worth looking at a few BIND alternatives and companion tools.

Looking at BIND Alternatives

You have several alternatives to BIND. The following describes four alternatives, or companion tools, arranged in alphabetical order.

djbdns   The djbdns software was written by Daniel J. Bernstein (of qmail fame), thus the djb preceding dns in its name. This software is actually several DNS applications, including tinydns, which was very popular around the turn of the millennium. The djbdns software collection was released to the public domain in 2007 and resulted in several project forks, including the Debian project's dbndns and ndjbdns at http://pjp.dgplug.org/ndjbdns/.

dnsmasq   Often installed by default on various distributions (such as Ubuntu), the dnsmasq utility provides a lightweight combination of DNS and Dynamic Host Control Protocol (DHCP) services as well as a few others. (If it's not installed on your distribution, you can obtain it via the dnsmasq package.) The software is designed for small networks.

For DNS services, it acts as a DNS forwarding server and can maintain a small cache so that not all queries need to be forwarded to other servers. It is fairly easy to configure, and it includes the /etc/hosts file's contents in its configuration. Some turn off many of the dnsmasq utility features and configure it to act as only a local cache and forwarding server. This can greatly improve name resolution speeds.

pdnsd   pdnsd is not a full DNS server solution but instead is a utility that works alongside DNS to improve performance. This GPL-licensed proxy DNS server software has a permanent persistent cache for a small set of DNS name servers. The leading p in its name stands for *persistent*. Its primary function is to allow applications that use resolvers at system boot time to handle situations where the desired DNS name server is unreachable or down. Also, it can conduct parallel name server queries to speed up query processing.

PowerDNS   PowerDNS is a full-service DNS server implementation. It is free, is open source, and has the GPL license, but it also offers 24/7 support contracts. PowerDNS's maintaining company also provides training and consulting services.

The PowerDNS software has a modular approach in that one application provides an authoritative server, while a separate software application provides recursive server features. It also offers an application programming interface (API) for managing zone data, and the data can be stored either in plain-text files or in a third-party database, such as MySQL, PostgreSQL, or MariaDB. Find out more about PowerDNS by visiting their website at https://www.powerdns.com/.

Configuring DNS on Linux

How you configure BIND on your Linux system(s) depends on your DNS goals. If you are a domain owner, you'll need at least two name servers. On one name server, you will need to configure DNS via BIND as an authoritative primary server to handle DNS name resolution queries. Your second required server can be any of the other three types—authoritative secondary, caching, or forwarding—depending on your domain's performance needs.

If you're primarily configuring your system to be a DNS client (resolver), you may want to consider configuring your system to be a caching-only server (if it's not preconfigured this way). By caching name resolutions, resolver speeds can improve significantly.

Installing BIND on Linux

Whether you plan on setting up a name server or just following along in this chapter, you'll need the BIND 9 software package and utilities. The BIND 9 software is in the bind9 or bind package, depending on your distribution. Also, you'll need various utilities to troubleshoot and manage it, which are in the bindutils package.

Typically, on Red Hat–based distributions, you need to install the bind and bindutils, if not already installed. For an Ubuntu distribution, you will need to install bind9 and bind9utils, and it is also very helpful to install bind9-doc.

The following shows checking a CentOS distribution for the various bind packages and installing the missing software:

```
# rpm -qa | grep ^bind
bind-libs-9.9.4-18.el7_1.5.x86_64
bind-libs-lite-9.9.4-18.el7_1.5.x86_64
bind-license-9.9.4-18.el7_1.5.noarch
bind-utils-9.9.4-18.el7_1.5.x86_64
#
# yum install bind
[...]
Install  1 Package
Upgrade            ( 4 Dependent packages)

Total download size: 3.7 M
Is this ok [y/d/N]: y
Downloading packages:
[...]
Complete!
#
```

Both the CentOS and the Ubuntu distributions offer a nice set of BIND documentation. Ubuntu provides it via the bind9-doc package. Once installed, the documentation is located in the /usr/share/doc/bind9/ directory for review. The Ubuntu /etc/bind/ named.conf file strongly recommends that you do so prior to modifying it.

The CentOS distro documentation is provided by the bind package and is created in the /usr/share/doc/bind-version/ directory. It primarily consists of several .html files, including an Administrator Resource Manual (ARM).

Comparing BIND Services and Daemons

The BIND daemon provides DNS services, and it is typically located on a system in the /usr/sbin/ directory. There are several differences to note between the distributions. For example, the BIND daemon is fairly straightforward on a Red Hat distribution. The BIND package names start with the word bind, as shown here on CentOS:

```
# rpm -qa | grep ^bind
bind-libs-lite-9.9.4-29.el7_2.3.x86_64
bind-libs-9.9.4-29.el7_2.3.x86_64
bind-utils-9.9.4-29.el7_2.3.x86_64
bind-9.9.4-29.el7_2.3.x86_64
bind-license-9.9.4-29.el7_2.3.noarch
#
```

As you would expect, the service name and the daemon are both called named. The daemon runs under the named username, as shown here on CentOS:

```
# systemctl status named | grep -i active
   Active: active (running) since Thu 2016-03-17 11:23:48 EDT; 1min 20s ago
#
# ps -ef | grep ^named
named    2956    1  0 11:23 ?    00:00:00 /usr/sbin/named -u named
#
```

On Ubuntu, the BIND package name is only slightly different (bind9) than on a Red Hat–based distribution, as shown here:

```
$ sudo apt-cache show bind9 | grep -i status
[sudo] password for christine:
Status: install ok installed
$
```

To control the BIND DNS services on Ubuntu, the bind9 service name (instead of named) is used, as shown here:

```
$ service bind9 status
 * bind9 is running
$
```

Also, you can see that on an Ubuntu distribution, the /usr/sbin/named daemon is running, but it runs under the bind username (instead of named), as shown here:

```
$ sudo ps -ef | grep ^bind
[sudo] password for christine:
bind    1242    1  0 08:20 ?    00:00:00 /usr/sbin/named -u bind
```

```
$
$ grep bind /etc/passwd
bind:x:117:126::/var/cache/bind:/bin/false
$
```

Other distribution BIND differences exist in the configuration files and their locations, which is typical. We needed to specifically address these BIND package, service, and daemon name differences, prior to further review of BIND DNS implementation.

Exploring BIND's Files on Linux

The main configuration file for BIND is /etc/named.conf or /etc/bind/named.conf, depending on your distribution. Here is a snipped version of the /etc/named.conf file on a CentOS distribution:

```
# cat /etc/named.conf
//
// named.conf
//
// Provided by Red Hat bind package to configure ISC BIND [...]
[...]
options {
    listen-on port 53 { 127.0.0.1; };
    listen-on-v6 port 53 {::1; };
    directory       "/var/named";
    dump-file       "/var/named/data/cache_dump.db";
    statistics-file "/var/named/data/named_stats.txt";
    memstatistics-file "/var/named/data/named_mem_stats.txt";
    allow-query     { localhost; };
[...]
    recursion yes;

    dnssec-enable yes;
    dnssec-validation yes;

    /* Path to ISC DLV key */
    bindkeys-file "/etc/named.iscdlv.key";

    managed-keys-directory "/var/named/dynamic";

    pid-file "/run/named/named.pid";
    session-keyfile "/run/named/session.key";
};
```

```
logging {
        channel default_debug {
                file "data/named.run";
                severity dynamic;
        };
};

zone "." IN {
    type hint;
    file "named.ca";
};

include "/etc/named.rfc1912.zones";
include "/etc/named.root.key";


#
```

The named.conf file provides many different configuration settings. To understand the various settings, it is useful to break them down into groupings (also called clauses) as follows:

Comments   Comment fields within the named.conf file often provide very helpful configuration information or warnings. Comment lines either begin with // or they are encased by /* comment */. You can also add a comment at a line's end, as long as the comment is preceded by a hash mark (#). Because the named.conf file default structure can vary so greatly among the different distributions, it is worthwhile to review this file's comments as part of your BIND setup investigation process.

Options   Within the options section, global options are set. Individual zone options are set within the zone section(s) or files, and they override global options.

The listen-on and listen-on-v6 settings specify what port number to listen to for UDP and TCP traffic and which IP addresses (also called the *address match list*), including the local host address, will listen for any incoming queries.

The directory setting indicates the primary directory for the named daemon. This is the directory where the zone files are located, as well as other important files. The directory is typically set to /var/named/, and it is the default BIND configuration.

The dump-file directive defines where a cache and/or zone database is dumped. The database(s) is dumped only when the rndc dumpdb command is issued. (The rndc command is covered later in this chapter.)

Records within the named.conf file are either inert or active. Comments are inert (inactive). Any record that ends with a semicolon (;) is an active statement, which causes a BIND configuration directive to take effect.

When the `rndc stats` command is issued, it will write any server statistics to the file indicated by the `statistics-file` setting. If this global option is not set, the stats are written to the /*directory*/named.stats file, where *directory* is the defined directory option.

The `memstatistics-file` setting determines where DNS server memory usage statistics are recorded when the server exits. In older BIND versions, this occurred only when an additional setting (`deallocate-on-exit`) was set to yes. However, in BIND 9, these memory usage statistics are written by default.

The `allow-query` directive is an important setting concerning access and security. You can specify an IP address match list of systems allowed to make queries to this DNS server. The IP addresses are listed within the curly brackets ({}) and separated by a semicolon (;). The designation of `localhost` within an address match list means that the server's IP address and its loopback address, 127.0.0.1, are included in the match list and allowed to make queries.

> It's important to include the `allow-query` directive in your named.conf file's options section. If you do not include it, the default is set to allow-query{any;}, which effectively allows any system from anywhere to make queries to your DNS server. If your DNS server is a Recursive Name Server that has a public IP address, and you do not set the `allow-query` directive, your server could become involved in a DNS amplification attack.
>
> Also, as of BIND v9.4, there is a new directive, `allow-query-cache`, which has syntax similar to the `allow-query` directive and should be set to allow only designated systems access to this server's DNS cache.

The `recursion` setting, if set to yes, tells BIND that this DNS server is to act as a Recursive Name Server. This server type was covered earlier in the chapter. You should set `recursion` to no if you are configuring an authoritative server, such as a primary or secondary DNS server. These server types were also covered earlier in the chapter.

The `dnssec-enable` directive is set to yes by default (for BIND v9.5 and up). This enabling can be for securing zone transfers, for DNS Security Extensions (DNSSEC), for safeguarding DNS query responses, for securing DDNS updates, and so on. These important topics are covered later in this chapter.

Hand in hand with the `dnssec-enable` directive, the `dnssec-validation` directive is part of the DNSSEC process and is set to yes by default (for BIND v9.5 and up). However, either the `managed-keys` or `trusted-anchors` option must be set as well for this setting to be effective.

The `bindkeys-file` directive sets the location of a trusted keys repository for use with zone keys. Zone keys are covered later in this chapter.

The DNSSEC process uses keys. These keys are kept in the file designated by the `manage-keys` directive. If `dnssec-validation` is enabled (set to yes), this directive should be included for the global option.

The pid-file directive specifies a file to hold the BIND daemon's (named) process ID (PID). If the directive is not set, the file used is named.pid, and it is typically located in one of the following directories, /run/named/, /var/run/, or /etc/, depending on your distribution.

BIND allows dynamic updates to zones. A key used to update a zone is placed in the file designated by the session-keyfile setting.

Logging   Within the logging section, directives configure the BIND logging system. Logs can assist in troubleshooting DNS problems as well as tracking security and performance issues.

The various named channel settings determine where and what information is logged. In the preceding named.conf example, the file directive names the log file and its location. In this case, the location is a subdirectory (data) under the directory directive /var/named/ directory setting. The severity directive determines what possible information is logged. It can be set to very little information, critical (only critical errors), or to a great deal of information, dynamic (debugging data, notices, warnings, and so on). Some distributions have logging set in their configuration file by default while others do not.

Zones   Because a zone defines what a domain name server has authority over, BIND's focus is on zones instead of on domains. Thus, the zone directives are very important. Individual zone options override any global options.

If a zone is defined here, it is typically the root zone, as is the case in the preceding named .conf example. The zone "." (also called the *root zone* depicted earlier in Figure 8.2) directive sets the authoritative root server (depicted earlier in Figure 8.3) to query. Various root server addresses are normally stored in the named.ca file. The type hint setting denotes that the selected root server from this file can respond with the needed authoritative information. The root zone directive is needed so that any zone not defined within the local system's DNS configuration can have a query for it fulfilled. This root zone directive is often called a *Hint for Root Level Servers* and is noted as such in the certification objectives.

Additional zones can be defined in this file, but on most distributions they are not. Zone directives are often put into their own separate files and then included in the named.conf file via an include statement, as described next.

Include Files   Additional configuration settings can be stored in separate files and then included using an include statement. In the preceding named.conf example, there are two include statements. The first loads the default zone configuration file, /etc/named .rfc1912.zones. The second include statement loads the DNS root key for the root zone. Keys are covered later in this chapter.

Some distributions, such as Ubuntu, have all of the named.conf configuration settings stored in include files. For example, here are the only active statements in an Ubuntu /etc/ bind/named.conf file:

```
$ cat /etc/bind/named.conf
[...]
```

```
include "/etc/bind/named.conf.options";
include "/etc/bind/named.conf.local";
include "/etc/bind/named.conf.default-zones";
$
```

Several more groupings (clauses) and settings are available for the named.conf file. To see them all, type **man named.conf** at the command line.

 The /sbin/named-checkconf utility will conduct a syntax check on your named.conf file, which is helpful if you modify it. The utility does not check any configuration files loaded via the include statements, but you can check these files by passing their names to the utility. Learn more by typing **man named-checkconf** at the command line.

Zone configuration files are covered in depth later in this chapter. However, it's helpful to look at the default zone configuration file on a Linux DNS client where BIND has been installed.

On some distributions, this default zone configuration file is /etc/named.rfc1912.zones. On other distributions, the zone file is /etc/bind/named.default-zones. You can often find your distribution's default zone file name by looking through its named.conf file or one of the named.conf file's include files.

The default zone configuration contains only zone directives, and it is typically created when BIND is installed. Each zone directive points to zone files (also called databases) located in the /var/named or /etc/bind directory, depending on your distribution. Here is a snipped default zone configuration file example from a CentOS distribution:

```
# cat /etc/named.rfc1912.zones
// named.rfc1912.zones:
[...]

zone "localhost.localdomain" IN {
    type master;
    file "named.localhost";
    allow-update { none; };
};

zone "localhost" IN {
    type master;
    file "named.localhost";
    allow-update { none; };
};
  [...]
```

```
zone "0.in-addr.arpa" IN {
    type master;
    file "named.empty";
    allow-update { none; };
};


#
```

The directives look fairly similar to the root zone directive shown in the preceding `named.conf` file example. In fact, if your distribution does not include a root zone directive in its `named.conf` file, it's most likely here in the default zone configuration file.

The `type master` directive indicates that this zone file contains the primary (master) authoritative configuration for this particular zone. These zone configuration files (databases) are described in detail later in this chapter. For now, just be aware of these files.

Your distribution may not only have a different location for zone files (databases), but the files may have different naming conventions. For example, on a CentOS distribution, the zone files are called `/var/named/named.`*`label`*, as shown in one column here:

```
# ls -1 /var/named/named.*
/var/named/named.ca
/var/named/named.empty
/var/named/named.localhost
/var/named/named.loopback
#
```

On an Ubuntu distribution, these zone files are typically called `/etc/bind/db.`*`label`*. Here is a directory listing showing these files on an Ubuntu distro:

```
$ ls -1 /etc/bind/db.*
/etc/bind/db.0
/etc/bind/db.127
/etc/bind/db.255
/etc/bind/db.empty
/etc/bind/db.local
/etc/bind/db.root
$
```

Both the primary DNS configuration file, `named.conf`, and the default zone configuration file are loaded when BIND is started.

Configuring BIND on Linux

BIND provides DNS services via the named daemon. By default, the daemon listens for both UDP and TCP traffic on port 53.

> The certification objectives focus on configuring BIND to function as a caching-only DNS server. Thus, this section also focuses on only this DNS server type.

A caching-only DNS server is worth exploring. This type of server is sometimes called a *resolver*, and it is often set up locally to reduce query times for local systems. When a caching-only DNS server has an answer for an FQDN to IP address translation query, it saves it to file or memory (BIND saves it to memory). Other local systems can then have their queries answered by the local caching-only server, until the answer's TTL value is reached or BIND is restarted. Substantial improvements in query time can be achieved if the caching-only DNS server is physically close to the other systems it is serving.

> Keep in mind that many DNS terms thrown around, such as *resolver*, can cause confusion. Though a caching-only DNS server may sometimes be called a *resolver*, recall that a resolver is also a system's library routine or program that checks its own cache and/or files for an answer to the DNS query. If it can't find the answer, it forwards the query to another resolver on another system.

Before you can configure BIND on your system, you need to have the proper software installed. Even though you are only configuring a caching-only DNS server, it's still a good idea to have the various BIND tools and utilities from the bindutils package installed as well. Installing BIND and its utilities on a Linux system was covered earlier in this chapter.

On some distributions, the installed BIND configuration files come already configured to provide client-side caching-only DNS name services. So you may just need to make a few minor adjustments to meet your requirements. Other distributions require several BIND configuration file changes in order to get a caching-only server up and running.

> Be aware that some distributions, such as Ubuntu, come with dnsmasq pre-installed and set to run on boot. If you are installing and configuring BIND on such a distribution, some caching oddities may occur. The dnsmasq BIND alternative was covered earlier in the chapter.

Before making any configuration file changes, first decide what local servers will be allowed to query the caching-only DNS server. Once you have chosen those servers, using super user privileges, change the allow-query directive in either the named.conf or named.conf.options configuration file, depending on your distribution. Though you could just add the IP addresses of the chosen servers to the `allow-query` directive, it's better first to create an access control list using the `acl` (Access Control List) directive, as shown here:

```
acl chosen {
    192.168.52.0/24;
    localhost;
    localnets;
};
```

In the preceding example, the `acl` directive is given a name, chosen. You can pick any name for your server's `acl`. The local servers are listed between the curly brackets, with each designation ending in a semicolon (`;`). In the preceding example, any servers within the 192.168.52 subnet are allowed to query this DNS caching-only server via the `192.168.52.0/24` setting. Also, the keywords `localhost` and `localnets` are included. The `localhost` keyword indicates that the current server can access its own DNS caching from internal DNS queries. The `localnet` keyword indicates that any servers on the current subnet may use this server's DNS cache.

It is important to keep this DNS caching-only server private, behind a firewall, and allow only designated servers to use it. If you do not take these actions, your DNS caching-only server could be used in a DNS amplification attack, which allows malicious people to overwhelm other servers and thus deny access to them.

Once your `acl` list is created, you modify the `allow-query` directive within the options group (clause) in the same configuration file. Using the example `acl` list, named chosen, from the preceding example, here is how the modified `allow-query` directive would look:

```
allow-query    { chosen; };
```

You also may need to modify the `listen-on` directive. For testing purposes, you can set it to any, but once your caching-only DNS server has been tested, change the setting to your `acl` list's name, as shown here:

```
listen-on port 53 { chosen; };
```

Keep in mind that if you are using IPv6 instead of IPv4, not only will your `acl` list setting configuration need to be different than shown in the example, but you will also need to modify the `listen-on-v6` directive in the configuration file.

When you are first setting up your caching-only DNS server, put the keyword any in your `allow-query` and `listen-on` settings instead of an `acl` list name. You can then test your service, and once you have it working correctly, come back and replace any with your `acl` list's name.

By default, the recursion directive is already set to yes. If for some reason it is set to no in your named.conf or named.conf.options file, you will need to change it. No matter what access to the cache you have granted, no access will be granted if recursion is set to no.

After you complete the necessary changes, double-check the configuration file's syntax using the named-checkconf command. By default, it will check the /etc/named.conf file, so if you had to modify a different configuration file (due to your distribution's BIND implementation), tack on the configuration file's name as shown here:

```
# named-checkconf /etc/named.conf
#
```

No response from the utility means that the syntax is OK. If you did receive a response, it would tell you the configuration file line number, where the problem is located, and give you a brief indication of the syntax problem. It's typical to forget to put a semicolon (;) at a directive setting's end.

If needed, modify the system's firewall to allow access to port 53, or whatever port you have DNS using. Do this prior to starting up the BIND daemon. Firewalls are covered in Chapter 12.

Now you can start up the BIND service, called named or bind9 (depending on your distribution), which will load up the modified configuration files. Here's an example of starting up named on a CentOS distribution:

```
# systemctl start named
#
```

Here's an example of starting up bind9 on an Ubuntu distribution:

```
$ sudo service bind9 start
$
```

 You can use several methods for starting and stopping BIND, as well as reloading BIND configuration files. These various methods are explored later in this chapter.

Now that you have BIND up and running with the modified configuration, you can test your caching-only DNS server. On the caching-only server, use the nslookup command along with an FQDN to look up and the caching-only DNS server's IP address, as shown in this example:

```
# nslookup www.sybex.com 192.168.0.103
Server:         192.168.0.103
Address:        192.168.0.103#53

Non-authoritative answer:
Name:       www.sybex.com
```

```
Address: 208.215.179.132

#
```

In the preceding example, the FQDN to look up is www.sybex.com. The caching-only DNS server's IP address is 192.168.0.103. The response displaying a non-authoritative answer of an FQDN and its associated IP address indicates that the caching-only DNS name server is working.

To ensure that everything is functioning, it's worthwhile to perform nslookup tests on the various systems that you are allowing to use this caching-only DNS name server. In addition, for comparison purposes, use the time command along with the nslookup command to see any DNS query time improvements. Here's an example on another system, where the nslookup command was timed *without* using the local caching-only DNS server:

```
$ time nslookup www.sybex.com
Server:         8.8.8.8
Address:        8.8.8.8#53

Non-authoritative answer:
Name:      www.sybex.com
Address: 208.215.179.132


real     0m0.320s
user     0m0.013s
sys      0m0.018s
$
```

To test the local caching-only server and obtain a quick look at the time that you may be saving by employing this DNS type, try the same command as shown in the previous example, but direct the query to the local caching-only DNS server, as shown here:

```
$ time nslookup www.sybex.com 192.168.0.103
Server:          192.168.0.103
Address:     192.168.0.103#53

Non-authoritative answer:
Name:      www.sybex.com
Address: 208.215.179.132


real     0m0.192s
user     0m0.015s
```

```
sys      0m0.009s
$
```

The difference between the real time output and the time command output will help you to see if there is any improvement. In these previous two examples, there is a slight improvement. Of course, there are many potentially influencing factors on the time command's output for the nslookup command, but the output will give you a general idea.

 You may want to secure your caching-only DNS server using a chroot jail. This topic is covered later in this chapter.

On your caching-only DNS server, set the BIND daemon to start on system boot if it's not already configured to do so. The method you use depends on your particular system distribution. Here's an example of using systemd on a CentOS distribution to configure BIND to start at system initialization:

```
# systemctl enable named
ln -s '/usr/lib/systemd/system/named.service'
'/etc/systemd/system/multi-user.target.wants/named.service'
#
```

Once you have your caching-only DNS name server configured and tested, you will need to configure the other local systems to use this name server for their name resolution queries. Enter the caching-only DNS name server's IP address into the local system's /etc/resolv.conf file. Here a local Ubuntu distribution system has its file modified and tested:

```
$ grep nameserver /etc/resolv.conf
nameserver 127.0.1.1
$
$ sudo nano /etc/resolv.conf
[sudo] password for christine:
$
$ grep nameserver /etc/resolv.conf
nameserver 192.168.0.103
nameserver 127.0.1.1
$
$ dig +short +identify www.sybex.com
208.215.179.132 from server 192.168.0.103 in 3 ms.
$
```

First, the local caching-only DNS name server's IP address is added to the Ubuntu system's resolv.conf file. Next, the dig utility is used to test a name resolution query. With the +short and +identify options, a short listing of the name resolution along with the information source (192.168.0.103) is displayed. This shows that the caching-only DNS name server cache is successfully being used to answer the query.

For older distributions, modifying the resolv.conf file, as shown in the preceding example, is all that is needed. However, most current distributions reconfigure the /etc/resolv.conf file upon boot, and to persistently set the local caching-only DNS name server, you need to modify other files. The various distributions handle setting persistent name servers differently.

For a current Ubuntu distribution, the first file to modify is the /etc/network/interfaces file. Here is the file prior to the needed modification:

```
$ cat /etc/network/interfaces
# interfaces(5) file used by ifup(8) and ifdown(8)
auto lo
iface lo inet loopback
$
```

Here is the file after the needed modification:

```
$ cat /etc/network/interfaces
# interfaces(5) file used by ifup(8) and ifdown(8)
auto lo
iface lo inet loopback
auto eth0
iface eth0 inet dhcp
dns-nameservers 192.168.0.103 192.168.0.1
$
```

Keep in mind that if you are not using DHCP for a network interface but a static IP address instead, your configuration will look slightly different. The important part of this modification is the addition of the dns-nameservers directive. In this case, it directs a resolver query to go to the 192.168.0.103 system, which happens to be the local caching-only DNS name server.

Because the modification in the preceding example is using DHCP, another file modification is also needed. (You do not need to make this modification if you are using static IP addresses.) The dhclient.conf file in the /etc/dhcp/ directory should have any preceding hash marks (#) removed and then the desired name servers listed, as shown here:

```
$ grep prepend /etc/dhcp/dhclient.conf
prepend domain-name-servers 192.168.0.103;
$
```

Once you make the necessary changes, you can reboot the system. After a restart, check the resolv.conf file to see if it was properly updated by the system, as shown snipped here:

```
$ cat /etc/resolv.conf
[...]
```

```
nameserver 192.168.0.103
nameserver 192.168.0.1
$
```

The resolv.conf file looks correct with the desired name servers in the correct order. You can now test to see if the Ubuntu system is using your local caching-only DNS name server. An example using the dig utility on a configured Ubuntu system is shown here:

```
$ dig +short +identify www.sybex.com
208.215.179.132 from server 192.168.0.103 in 1 ms.
$
```

The dig command and its options show that the current system is using the local caching-only DNS server located at IP address 192.168.0.103. DNS query times should now improve for this system.

Current Ubuntu distributions typically use the dnsmasq utility for providing local caching and lightweight DHCP services. If you decide to use a local caching-only DNS server instead, you will need to disable the dnsmasq service. To do so, edit the NetworkManager.conf file located in the /etc/Network/Manager/ directory. Place a hash mark (#) in front of the dns=dnsmasq line, save the file, and restart your network manager.

For a CentOS distribution, the process is fairly similar. You update the DNS name server to use, denoted by the DNS1 directive, in the following file:

/etc/sysconfig/network-scripts/ifcfg-*interface*

If your configuration does not already have the DNS1 setting, you can add it using the example caching-only DNS server IP address used previously, as follows:

DNS1=192.168.0.103

You can also add a secondary DNS name server using the DNS2 directive, if needed. Once you restart the network services (or reboot the system), you can perform the tests shown for the Ubuntu distribution.

Your system may come with the /sbin/lwresd utility preinstalled. The lwresd is a simple caching-only DNS name server daemon. It listens for queries on the IPv4 loopback interface, 127.0.0.1. The lwresd daemon is installed as part of the bind9 package on Red Hat–based distributions. For an Ubuntu system, you can install it using the sudo apt-get install lwresd command. Once installed, you can find out more by typing **man lwresd** at the command line.

Now your local systems should see improved DNS query response times. Be sure to test the query response times periodically in order to ensure that all are still performing as expected.

Starting, Stopping, and Reloading BIND

Several methods are available for starting and stopping BIND as well as for reloading modified BIND configuration files without stopping the BIND service. Because there are so many methods, it's worthwhile to explore them so you can choose the right method for your server(s) needs.

Looking at Traditional Methods

The more traditional methods for starting and stopping the BIND service include using the system initialization daemons. In addition, you can send the BIND service signals via the `kill` command.

The various traditional methods are shown here. Because some methods are dependent on your system's initialization method (systemd or SysV), they may not work for your particular server:

- Starting BIND
    - systemd: `systemctl start` *BINDname*
    - SysV: `service` *BINDname* `start`
- Stopping BIND
    - systemd: `systemctl stop` *BINDname*
    - SysV: `service` *BINDname* `stop`
    - N/A: `kill -s SIGTERM` *BIND_PID*
    - N/A: `kill -s SIGINT` *BIND_PID*
- Restarting BIND
    - systemd: `systemctl restart` *BINDname*
    - SysV: `service` *BINDname* `restart`
- Reloading BIND configuration files
    - systemd: `systemctl reload` *BINDname*
    - SysV: `service` *BINDname* `reload`
    - N/A: `kill -s SIGHUP` *BIND_PID*

In the preceding commands, the *BINDname* variable is either `named` or `bind9`, depending on your distribution. Also, the *BIND_PID* is the BIND daemon's process ID (PID). The BIND daemon's PID is typically stored in the `/run/named/named.pid` or `/var/run/named.pid` file, depending on your distribution. Therefore, you can use the `kill` command to reload configuration files, as shown here:

```
# kill -s SIGHUP $(cat /run/named/named.pid)
#
```

Though the traditional methods work, they are not considered best practices. This is especially true with the kill command (even though it is mentioned in the certification objectives), because sending the wrong signal to the BIND daemon could have unintended consequences. The best way to control the BIND daemon is via the rndc utility, which is covered next.

Exploring *rndc*

The /usr/sbin/rndc tool is the primary utility for managing BIND. It has many features, including the ability to use a TCP connection to communicate with a remote name server and send it commands authenticated with digital signatures.

To see all of the various features of your rndc utility, just type **rndc** and press Enter, as shown snipped here:

```
# rndc
Usage: rndc [-b address] [-c config] [-s server] [-p port]
            [-k key-file ] [-y key] [-V] command

command is one of the following:

  reload   Reload configuration file and zones.
  reload zone [class [view]]
          Reload a single zone.
[...]
  reconfig Reload configuration file and new zones only.
[...]
  stop     Save pending updates to master files and stop the
           server.
  stop -p  Save pending updates to master files and stop the
           server reporting process id.
  halt     Stop the server without saving pending updates.
  halt -p  Stop the server without saving pending updates
           reporting process id.
  flush    Flushes all of the server's caches.
  flush [view]
          Flushes the server's cache for a view.
  flushname name [view]
          Flush the given name from the server's cache(s)
  flushtree name [view]
          Flush all names under the given name from the
          server's cache(s)
  status   Display status of the server.
```

```
[...]
  *restart Restart the server.

* == not yet implemented
[...]
#
```

Not all of the rndc features are shown in the preceding example! The utility provides several commands that offer finer control for stopping BIND and/or reloading configuration files.

You can get a quick and nicely formatted BIND daemon status using the rndc tool, as shown snipped here:

```
# rndc status
[...]
CPUs found: 1
worker threads: 1
UDP listeners per interface: 1
number of zones: 101
debug level: 0
xfers running: 0
xfers deferred: 0
soa queries in progress: 0
query logging is OFF
recursive clients: 0/0/1000
tcp clients: 0/100
server is up and running
#
```

The reload command, which reloads the configuration and zone files, is fairly simple as well:

```
# rndc reload
server reload successful
#
```

However, be aware that while you can stop the BIND daemon using rndc, you cannot start or restart it using the rndc utility. Here is an example:

```
# rndc stop
#
# rndc restart
rndc: 'restart' is not implemented
#
```

```
# systemctl start named
#
# rndc status
[...]
server is up and running
#
```

The systemctl command had to be used on this particular distribution in order to start the BIND daemon back up. Be aware that if the BIND daemon is not running, the rndc status command may produce an odd message, as shown here:

```
# rndc stop
#
# rndc status
rndc: connect failed: 127.0.0.1#953: connection refused
#
# systemctl start named
#
```

Because the rndc utility does not (yet) have every feature that you may need to control the BIND daemon, you should still know how to use the other methods (covered earlier) for controlling BIND.

Configuring BIND Logging

An important part of setting up your BIND configuration is determining how you want BIND messages to be logged as well as the desired message detail level. Though it was briefly covered earlier in this chapter, taking a more-in-depth look at configuring BIND logging is worthwhile. Logs can assist in troubleshooting DNS problems as well as tracking security and performance issues. Therefore, you may want to configure BIND to provide more complex logging than its default configuration provides.

Typically, BIND logging is configured in the named.conf file. The logging directives determine what is logged and where it is logged. Here is the general syntax for the BIND logging configuration:

```
logging {
  [ channel channel_name {
    ( file path/name
        [ versions ( number | unlimited ) ]
        [ size size_spec ]
      | syslog syslog_facility
      | stderr
      | null );
    [ severity (critical | error | warning | notice |
```

```
                info | debug [ level ] | dynamic ); ]
    [ print-category yes | no; ]
    [ print-severity yes | no; ]
    [ print-time yes | no; ]
  }; ]
  [ category category_name {
    channel_name; [ channel_name; ... ]
  }; ]
[...]
};
```

The `logging` directives can be broken up into two primary groupings: *channel* and *category*. A `channel` is either a predefined channel directive or it is a custom channel. It controls where messages are logged and filters what is logged. A `category` directive defines DNS message types to be logged.

Looking at Logging Channels

As an example, here is a snipped `named.conf` file from a CentOS distribution showing the logging configuration for this system:

```
# cat /etc/named.conf
[...]
logging {
        channel default_debug {
                file "data/named.run";
                severity dynamic;
        };
};
[...]
#
```

The default configuration shown has only one `channel` set, `default_debug`. This setting is a predefined channel directive. There are four predefined channel directives, briefly described here:

- `default_debug`: Write log messages to `named.run` in the specified directory, with the `severity` filter directive set to `dynamic`.

- `default_stderr`: Write log messages to `stderr` (while running BIND in the foreground for debugging) with the `severity` filter directive set to `info`.

- `default_syslog`: Write log messages to `syslog` or `rsyslog`, with the `severity` filter directive set to `info`.

- `null`: Write all log messages to `/dev/null` (do not keep log messages).

You can modify the default settings of these predefined channel directives. For example, the default_debug channel would normally send log messages to the named.run file in the *directory* (where *directory* is set earlier in the named.conf file or defaults to the /var/named/ directory). This default was overwritten in the preceding example, and log messages are sent to the *directory*/data/named.run file.

You are not stuck with the predefined channel directives. You can set up multiple custom channels to finely control your BIND logging. As long as each channel is uniquely named, you can set as many unique logging directives as desired for that channel.

Within a custom channel, you can set where the log messages are sent. These locations include a file, a syslog facility, standard error (stderr), or null, which essentially throws out log messages.

For the file directive, at a minimum, the file's name must be specified. To control the file's location, the *path* setting, you can do any one of the following:

- Accept the default location of the /var/named/ directory.

- Accept the location set by the directory directive (typically located earlier in the named.conf file).

- Set a path relative to the directory directive.

- Set a custom path via declaring an absolute directory path.

You can even control the log file's size through the size setting. The log file's version numbers are managed via the versions directive.

The severity directive is a filter that has seven levels. A message whose classified severity is equal to or higher than the specified severity level is logged through the declared channel. Going from the lowest severity to the highest, the levels that you can set are these:

- dynamic
- debug *level*
- info
- notice
- warning
- error
- critical

For the debug severity filter, you can specify a debug level. The higher the debug level number, the more information is logged. If no level is specified, it defaults to debug level 1. Debugging can be turned off by specifying level 0. The dynamic severity filter is similar to debug severity, but it uses any debugging level set when the named daemon is started.

The print- directives allow you to control additional information that is logged. If not set, they default to no. If set to yes, print-category logs the category (covered soon in this chapter), `print-severity` logs the actual severity level (as opposed to the set severity filter level), and `print-time` will log the date and time.

Once you have set where information will be logged and how that logging data will be filtered via the channels, you then set the category.

Looking at Logging Categories

Categories determine what DNS information will be logged, and categories are pointed to channels so that the log messages are filtered and recorded to the desired location. The category general syntax within a `logging` directive is shown snipped as follows:

```
logging {
[...]
  [ category category_name {
    channel_name; [ channel_name; ... ]
  }; ]
[...]
};
```

Each log message `category` can go into a single declared (or default) channel or into multiple channels. You have a lot of flexibility as to how to filter and record these various log message categories.

If no `category` is defined, it defaults to

```
category default { default_syslog; default_debug; };
```

The category's name is `default`, which essentially captures all of the various categories' messages that are normally captured without being declared. The `default` category does not capture a particular category if that category is also declared within the `named.conf` file. In the preceding example, the categories' messages are sent to two different channels: `default_syslog` and `default_debug`.

> Because of the rather confusing nature of DNS logging, it's a good idea to start out with a simple `logging` directive. Configure your DNS logging to capture all of the various categories, set a low `severity` filter (debug 3), and send the log messages to a single file. Over time, you will get an idea of what particular messages you want to log, what to filter out, and how to divide the log messages among the various logging facilities. Slowly change and test your `logging` settings as you make these discoveries.

There are several log message categories. A few category names to use within a `category` directive are shown in Table 8.1. You will notice that potentially a lot of overlap can occur among the various log message categories.

TABLE 8.1   DNS logging category names

Name	Log Message Description
client	Client request operations.
config	Configuration file analyzing and handling.
database	Internal zone and cache database operations.
default	All category messages normally captured without being declared. Does not include categories declared within the named.conf file.
delegation-only	Queries that receive a "domain not found" message (NXDOMAIN) in response to a delegation-only zone or a delegation-only in a hint or stub zone declaration.
dispatch	Incoming packet transmissions (dispatch) to server modules for processing.
dnssec	Packet operations via the DNSSEC and TSIG protocols. These protocols are covered later in this chapter.
edns-disabled	Queries in which a server fails to respond, because the query is not understood (typically, a query that is not following proper protocols) or packet loss has occurred.
general	DNS items that are not classified into a particular category. Also called the *catch-all.*
lame-servers	Remote server (lame server) misconfigurations discovered during a query process.
network	Network operations.
notify	NOTIFY (DNS zone change notification) operations.
queries	Query operations.
query-errors	Query operations that failed.
resolver	DNS name resolution operations.
RPZ	Response Policy Zone (RPZ) operations.
security	Request approval and denial operations.
update	Dynamic DNS (DDNS) update operations.

Name	Log Message Description
update-security	DDNS update request approval and denial operations.
xfer-in	Server receiving zone transfer(s) operations.
xfer-out	Server sending zone transfer(s) operations.

Once you have set what DNS BIND category messages are to go to what channels and how to filter them in the named.conf configuration file, you need to either restart BIND or reload the configuration file into BIND. This topic was covered earlier in the chapter.

 Some DNS managers set *each* individual category into its own channel, with that channel having a high severity filter (so few messages are filtered out) and recording the log messages to a file. While this may prove useful as you start exploring DNS logging, be aware that you will have numerous log files, which may quickly become rather large.

There are more categories than those listed in Table 8.1. Also, the BIND developers may add additional log message categories in the future. You can stay up to date on current BIND 9 logging category additions and other BIND enhancements by visiting the ISC's website at https://www.isc.org/.

Creating and Maintaining DNS Zones

Domain Name Space is broken up into different zones. A zone defines what a name server has authority over. It includes maintaining the zone's authoritative data files, called either zone files or zone databases. The various configuration files are explored in this section along with how to make needed modifications for your DNS needs.

Exploring BIND Zone Files

Zone files can be loosely broken into two categories: zone configuration files and zone databases. Each category is important to understand in order to maintain your zone(s) properly.

Looking at Zone Configuration Files

The default zone configuration files were briefly covered earlier in this chapter and are typically loaded via include statements within the BIND configuration file, named.conf, or another included configuration file. Here is a snipped Ubuntu distribution's /etc/bind/ named.conf file showing the include statements used to load the zone configuration files:

```
$ cat /etc/bind/named.conf
[...]
include "/etc/bind/named.conf.local";
include "/etc/bind/named.conf.default-zones";
$
```

Zone configuration files typically contain only zone directives. Each zone directive points to zone files (also called databases) located in the /var/named or /etc/bind directory, depending on your distribution. As an example, here is a snipped zone configuration file on an Ubuntu system:

```
$ cat /etc/bind/named.conf.default-zones
[...]
zone "localhost" {
    type master;
    file "/etc/bind/db.local";
};

zone "127.in-addr.arpa" {
    type master;
    file "/etc/bind/db.127";
};

zone "0.in-addr.arpa" {
    type master;
    file "/etc/bind/db.0";
};

zone "255.in-addr.arpa" {
    type master;
    file "/etc/bind/db.255";
};
$
```

Each zone statement in the zone configuration file contains the zone keyword followed by the zone's name in double quotation marks. The type directive determines the zone's type, which can be set to one of the following:

- master: Indicates this is the zone's primary name server.
- slave: Designates this as the zone's secondary name server.
- forward: Indicates that this is a forwarding server for this zone.

- `hint`: Specifies the *Hint Zone,* which is a list of current root name servers.
- `redirect`: Designates the redirect zone, which is used to answer queries when `domain not found` messages (`NXDOMAIN`) are received for the queries.
- `stub`: Sets this as a stub zone, which is like a secondary name server zone, except that it uses only the primary zone's transferred records and ignores the rest of a zone. (Stub zones are a limited supported BIND feature and are not part of the DNS standard.)
- `static-stub`: Indicates that this is a special stub zone, where the primary zone records are not transferred, but instead the zone records are statically configured.
- `delegation-only`: Specifies that this zone is to enforce a root zone's delegation-only status.

Zone statements differ depending on their set `type`. For a `master` type zone statement, there will be a `file` directive, indicating the name and, if needed, the location of the zone file (database). There may also be control statements that direct zone transfers and updates. For example, the `allow-update` directive can prevent a zone from being updated via

```
allow-update { none;};
```

or instead allow a zone to be updated by listing various servers allowed to provide dynamic updates between the curly brackets (in place of the none directive).

> **NOTE**   Many different control statements are available for defining a zone. To see all of the various control statements, look in the Administrator Resource Manual (ARM) located in the `/usr/share/doc/bind9/` or the `/usr/share/doc/bind-`*version*`/` directory, depending on your distribution.

For a `slave` type zone statement, the `file` directive is optional, but it is still often used to avoid zone transfers (discussed later in this chapter) when BIND is restarted. The filename is typically the same as the zone name. There may also be control statements specific to `slave` type servers. For example, the `allow-notify` directive determines which local server is allowed to send NOTIFY (DNS zone change notification) messages to this secondary server. Here is an example of a secondary name server zone statement:

```
zone "secondary.example.com" IN {
    type slave;
    file "/etc/bind/secondary.example.com";
    masters {192.168.0.104;};
    allow-notify {192.168.0.104;};
};
```

> **NOTE**   You will notice that some zone statements contain an IN. This indicates the statement's class. The class can be either IN (Internet), CH (Chaosnet network protocol), or HS (for the Hesiod network software). Typically, you see only the IN class listed in zone records.

The forward type zone statement has fewer possible settings than the other two types. Here is the basic syntax for this statement type:

```
zone zone_name [class] {
    type forward;
    [ forward (only|first); ]
    [ forwarders { [ ip_addr [port ip_port]; ... ] }; ]
};
```

The optional forward directive has two possible settings. If it is set to only, the server only forwards queries to the servers in the forwarders list. If it is set to first, the server will at first forward queries to the forwarders servers, and if no answer is found, the current server will attempt to answer the query.

Typically, a forwarding zone is used for security purposes. Your environment may have several servers that should not send queries beyond the firewall protecting its local network. In this environment, you would set up a designated forwarding and caching server, which is allowed to send queries past the firewall. This is sometimes called a *split* configuration.

For the forwarders setting, one or more server IP addresses are listed. These servers are queried one after the other for the name resolution answer, until an answer is found or all of the servers have been queried.

Here is a simple example of a forwarding name server zone statement:

```
zone "forward.example.com" IN {
    type forward;
    forwarders {192.168.64.106; 192.168.64.107;};
};
```

The hint type zone was covered earlier in this chapter. It may be included within the named.conf configuration file or a specific zone configuration file, depending on your distribution. Here is the hint type zone statement from a CentOS systems named.conf file:

```
# cat /etc/named.conf
[...]
zone "." IN {
    type hint;
    file "named.ca";
};
[...]
#
```

To find out information concerning the redirect, stub, static-stub, and delegation-only zone type statements, see the BIND Administrator Resource Manual (ARM). Aside from the one on your system, you can find a copy on the Internet Software Consortium's website at www.isc.org.

Looking at Zone Databases

Zone databases (also called zone files) contain information in plain text concerning zones. This information is called *authoritative data.*

Zone databases can be produced by the BIND installation, typically for default setups. Here is an example of an Ubuntu distribution's /etc/bind/db.0 zone file produced by installing BIND:

```
$ cat /etc/bind/db.0
;
; BIND reverse data file for broadcast zone
;
$TTL    604800
@   IN   SOA    localhost. root.localhost. (
                     1       ; Serial
                604800      ; Refresh
                 86400      ; Retry
               2419200      ; Expire
                604800 )   ; Negative Cache TTL
;
@   IN   NS    localhost.
$
```

You can also create the zone databases, such as when you need to set up primary (master) and secondary (slave) name servers for a zone you administer. In this case, your zone databases will reside on your primary name server.

Secondary name servers receive their authoritative zone information from the primary name server's zone databases. When this authoritative zone information is copied over to the secondary name server, it is called a *Zone Transfer.*

Zone transfers can occur for many different reasons. A few reasons are as follows:

- The secondary server's BIND daemon has started or restarted.
- The zone data's refresh time has expired (explained later in this section).
- The master server (designated by the named.conf file's allow-notify directive) has sent the secondary server a DNS zone change notification.
- A zone data refresh was requested manually via the rndc utility (explained later in this chapter).

On current BIND implementations, a secondary server will not read the zone database in its text form. The secondary server expects to receive zone database information from the primary server in raw binary form. This can pose problems if you are conducting name server tests. Fortunately, BIND provides a utility, /sbin/named-compilezone, which you can use to convert zone database data from plain text to raw binary form and vice versa.

You'll typically find your default zone databases located in either the /var/named/ directory or the /etc/bind/ directory, depending on your server's distribution. You should store any created zone databases in the appropriate directory, along with default BIND zone databases.

Zone authoritative data comes in two forms: directives and resource records. Zone database directives are optional, but they control some useful settings. Each directive is capitalized and preceded by a $ symbol. Here are the most common directives.

$ORIGIN   The $ORIGIN directive sets a domain name that is added to any file record's end that does not have a full domain name. The general syntax is

$ORIGIN domain-name. [comment]

Notice the dot (.) at the domain-name's end. This is an important part of the directive. To understand how this works, here is an example $ORIGIN directive:

$ORGIN example.com.

Now if a zone resource record contains just www, with this directive set, it will be read as www.example.com. In essence, it provides a handy shortcut method for dealing with domain names.

$INCLUDE   The $INCLUDE directive operates just like the include statement in a zone configuration file. It reads in the designated file and processes any directives or resource records in the file. The general syntax is as follows:

$INCLUDE filename [origin] [comment]

If the *origin* keyword is included in the directive, $ORIGIN is set to the *origin* value for the designated file's processing. If it is not included and $ORIGIN has been previously set, it is used instead.

$TTL   The $TTL directive sets the default time to live (TTL), which determines how long name server data for a particular resolution is held in cache. The general syntax is

$TTL seconds [comment]

The *seconds* can be designated anywhere from 0 to 2,147,483,647 (about 68 years). This setting is valid only if a resource record does not define its own TTL.

Resource records are not optional. These records provide the zone's authoritative name resolution information. There are several different resource record types. The most common ones are shown in Table 8.2. Each resource record type is described fully in a Request For Comment (RFC) document, which is also specified in the table.

TABLE 8.2   Resource record types

Type	Description
A	A host address record for IPv4 addresses. (RFC 1035)
AAAA	A host address record for IPv6 addresses. (RFC 1886)
CNAME	A canonical name record maps an alias name to a host name. (RFC 1035)
MX	A mail exchange record declares a preference value(s) followed by a mail exchange host name(s). (RFC 974 & 1035)
NS	A name server record specifies the zone's authoritative name server. (RFC 1035)
PTR	A pointer record points to another domain namespace location and is typically used in reverse lookups. (RFC 1035)
SOA	A start of authority record identifies the authority zone's start and includes the zone's authoritative data. Only one SOA record per zone should be created. (RFC 1035)
TXT	A text record holds free-form text enclosed in quotation marks, which can serve various purposes, such as domain name identification. (RFC 1035)

To explore the various resource record types and directives in a zone database, we'll use an example zone configuration. The example zone is for a made-up domain called `example.com`, and it consists of the following servers:

- `serv1.example.com`: The example zone's primary (master) name server
- `serv2.example.com`: The example zone's secondary (slave) name server
- `maila.example.com`: The example zone's primary mail server
- `mailb.example.com`: The example zone's secondary mail server
- `LPIC2.example.com`: An example.com subdomain that contains many other servers

For this example zone configuration, an example zone database has been created and is shown here:

```
$ cat /var/named/example.com.zone
;
```

```
; BIND data file for example.com
;
;       Zone Database Directives
;
$TTL    604800          ; TTL is 7 days
$ORIGIN example.com.
;
;       Zone Database Resource Records
;
@       IN      SOA     serv1.example.com. hostmaster.example.com. (
                        0    ; serial
                        2H   ; refresh
                        30M  ; retry
                        2W   ; expire
                        7D   ; minimum
                        )
;
@       IN      NS      serv1.example.com.
serv1 IN      A       192.168.64.110
;
@       IN      NS      serv2.example.com.
serv2 IN      A       192.168.64.111
;
@       IN      MX   0  maila.example.com.
maila IN      A       192.168.64.112
;
@       IN      MX   5  mailb.example.com.
mailb IN      A       192.168.64.113
;
LPIC2 IN      A       192.168.64.120
www     IN      CNAME   LPIC2
;
```

Let's dissect this example BIND zone data file. Notice the first five lines of this zone database, which are comment lines. Each comment is preceded by a semicolon (;), and it can take up an entire file line. Comments can also be included at a line's end, as long as the text is preceded by a semicolon.

After the comment lines, two directives are included in this database: $TTL and $ORIGIN. After the directives and a few more comment lines, the zone's resource records are listed.

 There should be no spaces or tabs in the beginning of a resource record.

The first resource record is a start of authority (SOA) record, and it should always be the first record. It essentially defines the zone as well as additional details concerning how this zone is to be managed. It has the following contents:

- `@`: Indicates the domain's name. (The at sign (`@`) is used as a shorthand reference to the domain's name, indicated in this example by the `$ORIGIN` directive.)

- `IN`: Designates that this is an Internet class record.

- `SOA`: Indicates that this is a SOA type record.

- `serv1.example.com.`: Specifies this server's name, with a required trailing dot(.), where this database is located.

- `hostmaster.example.com.`: Designates the username (`hostmaster`) as this server's email contact, with a required trailing dot (.).

- Authority values: Specified between the two parentheses, these values control the following settings:

  - `serial`: A manually incremented number, which starts at 0 (indicating no modifications have been made). It should be incremented by 1 every time a change is made to this file, so secondary servers know the file has been modified and they should copy it (an update is needed).

  - `refresh`: Sets how often a secondary server should check the master server file and see if an update is needed.

  - `retry`: If the secondary server checks the master server file for a needed update and a failure occurs, this sets how long the secondary server should wait before trying the check again.

  - `expire`: Sets the maximum time for a secondary server to use the authoritative zone data without a successful data refresh from the primary server. Once the time has passed, the zone data is considered non-authoritative.

  - `minimum`: Also called the TTL setting, this sets the time before the zone data is flushed from the server's cache.

Any authority values that are time values can be specified different ways. A plain number indicates the value is in seconds. For minutes, tack on an `M`; for hours use an `H`; for days use a `D`; and to indicate weeks, add a `W`.

 Use an email alias for your server's email contact. The hostmaster shown in the SOA record is a typical alias.

After the SOA resource record in the preceding example zone database, there are two resource records describing the primary (master) name server responsible for the `example .com.` domain. These records are shown here:

```
@      IN     NS     serv1.example.com.
serv1 IN     A      192.168.64.110
```

The first record starts with the shorthand reference (@) to the domain's name, and the NS states that this is an authoritative name server for the domain defined in the SOA record. The record ends with the name server's name.

The second record starts with the name server's host name (serv1), and the A declares this record to be an address resource record. At the record's end is the IP address for the primary server.

 Though an @ for the domain name is shown in these examples, you could actually type out the domain name (example.com. in this example zone database). In addition, you can leave it blank, and it will default to the last domain name specified.

After the primary name server resource records in the example zone database are two resource records describing the secondary name server responsible for the example.com. domain. Recall that for each zone, there must be a primary server and at least one other server type, such as a secondary (slave) or forwarding server. This server is defined by the records shown here:

```
@      IN     NS      serv2.example.com.
serv2 IN      A       192.168.64.111
```

After the secondary name server records are mail server records. These records, displayed here, are used to declare specific servers to act as mail servers for the domain:

```
@      IN     MX   0  maila.example.com.
maila IN      A       192.168.64.112
;
@      IN     MX   5  mailb.example.com.
mailb IN      A       192.168.64.113
```

In the preceding example, the MX indicates that these two servers are mail exchange servers. Notice that one record (maila.example.com) has a 0 listed in it, while the other record (mailb.example.com) has a 5 listed. These numbers indicate a preference ranking. In other words, the resource records indicate that the maila server (ranked 0) should be used before the mailb server (ranked 5).

The example zone database's last two active lines define a system's authoritative DNS record within this domain and set up an alias (also called a *Canonical Name*) for it:

```
LPIC2 IN      A       192.168.64.120
www   IN      CNAME   LPIC2
```

The CNAME in the second line declares that this resource record is a canonical name record. The record declares that www is an alias for LPIC2 and that www.example.com maps to the host address record for LPIC2.example.com.

Canonical names are a good idea to create if you have several hostnames that map to a single IP address or if you have changed a server's hostname. Be aware that SOA and MX resource record types should not point to a CNAME record. In addition, CNAME record types should not point to other CNAME record types but should point to host address (A) record types only.

Resource records are case insensitive, so you can use WWW.EXAMPLE.COM, www.example.com, or www.Example.com in your records. Traditionally, all lowercase is used.

Here is an actual zone database for the local loopback interface, which is located on an Ubuntu system:

```
$ cat /etc/bind/db.local
;
; BIND data file for local loopback interface
;
$TTL    604800
@   IN   SOA    localhost. root.localhost. (
                  2       ; Serial
             604800       ; Refresh
              86400       ; Retry
            2419200       ; Expire
             604800 )    ; Negative Cache TTL
;
@   IN   NS    localhost.
@   IN   A     127.0.0.1
@   IN   AAAA  ::1
$
```

As a review, consider using the preceding actual zone database, and go back through this section, its examples, and Table 8.2 to see if you can determine what each directive or resource record is declaring. The more zone database authoritative data you review, the more familiar you will start to feel with zone database syntax.

On Ubuntu, additional zones are typically added to the /etc/bind/named .conf.local file instead of being created in their own file. For a CentOS distribution, additional zones are typically added to their own files and stored in the /var/named/ directory. See your distribution's documentation for details.

Once you have created a zone database, you may need to take additional steps to have BIND load the zone database at startup. On this Ubuntu distribution, additional zones are added to the named.conf.local file, and it is already included in a file BIND loads upon startup, /etc/bind/named.conf, as shown here:

```
$ grep local /etc/bind/named.conf
[...]
include "/etc/bind/named.conf.local";
$
```

On a CentOS distribution, zone files are stored within the /var/named/ directory. A zone directive must be added to the /var/named/named.conf file so that a newly added zone database will be loaded at BIND startup as follows:

```
zone "example.com" IN {
    type master;
    file "example.com.zone";
    allow-update { none; };
};
```

As an alternative on a CentOS system, you could put the zone directive within its own external file and then use an include statement to pull the zone directive into the named.conf file.

Once you have the proper BIND configuration files modified, if needed, you can restart BIND or reload its configuration files. Look back to the "Starting, Stopping, and Reloading BIND" chapter section for how to do this if you need a reminder.

Looking at Reverse Zones

A *Reverse Zone* is a special zone that provides a mapping from an IP address to a FQDN (reverse of traditional DNS name server resolution). You need a named.conf reverse zone record and a reverse zone database to employ this special zone.

Continuing with the example.com.zone database created earlier for the example.com. domain (192.168.64.), here is the needed named.conf file record for a reverse zone:

```
zone "64.168.192.in-addr.arpa" IN {
    type master;
    file "example-reverse.com.zone";
    allow-update { none; };
};
```

Notice that it is slightly different from earlier named.conf zone entries in that a partial IP address (first three octets) is used instead of the server name. Also note that the partial IP address is backwards. Instead of 192.168.64, it is written as 64.168.192. In addition, you must tack on .in-addr.arpa to the backwards partial IP address.

Following along with this created example, here is the needed reverse zone database:

```
$ cat /var/named/example-reverse.com.zone
;
; BIND reverse zone data file for example.com
;
```

```
;      Zone Database Directives
;
$TTL   604800          ; TTL is 7 days
$ORIGIN 64.168.192.in-addr.arpa.
;
;      Zone Database Resource Records
;
@      IN      SOA     serv1.example.com. hostmaster.example.com. (
               0    ; serial
               2H   ; refresh
               30M  ; retry
               2W   ; expire
               7D   ; minimum
               )
;
@      IN      NS      serv1.example.com.
;
110    IN      PTR     serv1.example.com.
111    IN      PTR     serv2.example.com.
;
112    IN      PTR     maila.example.com.
113    IN      PTR     mailb.example.com.
;
120    IN      PTR     LPIC2.example.com.
;
```

The primary differences between this reverse zone file and other zone files are the $ORIGIN directive and the PTR resource records. The $ORIGIN directive uses the partial reverse IP address, followed by in-addr.arpa and a trailing dot (.). There are five PTR resource records, one for each system in the example zone. A PTR resource record starts with the host's final IP octet, includes the IN class and PTR type directives, and ends with the host's FQDN plus a trailing dot. With this zone file, a reverse DNS lookup for 192.168.64.120 will return the LPIC2.example.com FQDN.

 Watch your zone database file-naming conventions. Different distributions have different DNS zone file-naming conventions, and the zone filenames in these examples may not apply to your particular distribution. See your distribution's documentation for its zone file-naming conventions.

Checking Your Zone Files

Once you have your zone databases configured, you should check their syntax prior to loading the zones. This is fairly easy due to the handy /sbin/named-checkzone utility.

The basic named-checkzone utility syntax is as follows:

```
named-checkzone [options] domain-name zone-database
```

To make sure that you get the zone's *domain-name* correct, use grep to pull out the $ORIGIN directive (if it is used) from the zone database. Here is a named-checkzone demonstration using grep and the example reverse zone database from the preceding section. The named-checkzone command is broken between two lines for clarity:

```
# grep ORIGIN /var/named/example-reverse.com.zone
$ORIGIN 64.168.192.in-addr.arpa.
#
# named-checkzone 64.168.192.in-addr.arpa. \
> /var/named/example-reverse.com.zone
zone 64.168.192.in-addr.arpa/IN: loaded serial 0
OK
#
```

At the end of the preceding example's listing, you'll see the word OK. That means all is well with the zone database's syntax.

When running named-checkzone against a zone database, if you receive errors such as `ignoring out-of-zone` data and `has 0 SOA records`, you most likely have entered the wrong *domain-name* or your specified *domain-name* has a typographical error.

The name-checkzone utility does give you a little leeway in specifying the zone's *domain-name*. Here is an example showing the example zone file (from earlier in the chapter) being checked using the *domain-name* with the trailing dot (.) and again without the trailing dot:

```
# grep ORIGIN /var/named/example.com.zone
$ORIGIN example.com.
#
# named-checkzone example.com. /var/named/example.com.zone
zone example.com/IN: loaded serial 0
OK
#
# named-checkzone example.com /var/named/example.com.zone
zone example.com/IN: loaded serial 0
OK
#
```

Receiving the OK response means the example.com.zone file's syntax is in order. You can do this simple test prior to conducting more extensive tests on your zone configuration.

Managing BIND Zones on Linux

After configuring and checking your zone files, you must maintain them. This includes various items, such as delegating a zone if needed and troubleshooting problems when they arise. This section will help you get started managing your zone(s).

Delegating a Zone

By its tree structure, DNS already has and uses delegated zones. For example, a DNS query (that cannot be answered locally) that is asking for the www.example.com server's IP location will first go to the root zone, then to the .com TLD server location, and on to the .example name server, which will finally provide the desired IP number. This is DNS's inherent delegated nature.

Recall that a DNS zone defines what a domain name server has authority over, including maintaining the zone's authoritative data files. When you manage a zone, you are managing that zone's authoritative data. There may be times when a managed zone (or a portion of it) that you control needs to be delegated to another name server(s). Simply stated, *delegating a zone* means that a zone's authority data is put on another name server(s) and zone authority is given to that name server(s).

Be aware that some zone delegation terms apply to DNS's inherent delegated nature. Other zone delegation terms apply to delegating a zone. This section focuses on delegating a zone.

A zone (sometimes called a *parent zone*) often has zone subsections (sometimes called subdomains or *child zones*). For load and performance reasons, a parent zone may need to perform zone delegation to an active child zone.

Using the example zone created in the "Looking at Zone Databases" chapter section, imagine that the example.com zone has these additional servers in it:

- LinuxEssentials.example.com
- LPIC1.example.com
- education.LPIC2.example.com
- faq.LPIC2.example.com
- objectives.LPIC2.example.com
- partners.LPIC2.example.com
- practicetests.LPIC2.example.com

Also imagine that the LPIC2 child zone servers are rather heavily traveled, causing the example.com primary name server, serv1.example.com, to have performance issues. You could delegate a zone in this situation to ease the problem.

In this case, the child zone, LPIC2.example.com, would become the primary name server for the LPIC2.example.com child zone.

In order to accomplish this zone delegation, you need to do the following:

- Pick another server in the child zone to act as either a secondary server or a forwarding/caching server.
- Install BIND on LPIC2.example.com and the other chosen server.
- On the master LPIC2.example.com server
  - Configure the BIND named.conf file.
  - Configure the zone file(s).
  - Configure BIND to start as desired.
  - Configure the chosen server as appropriate for its role.

One more important issue in this zone delegation is how the zone parent configuration points to this delegated zone on the child zone's master server. To do this, on the parent zone name server, add a few records directly to the parent zone's database file's bottom or to the named.conf.local file's bottom, depending on your distribution. Here is a snipped example on a parent zone CentOS system:

```
$ cat /var/named/example.com.zone
[...]
;
; subdomain LPIC2.example.com
;
@      IN      NS      LPIC2.example.com.
LPIC2 IN      A       192.168.64.120
;
```

The last record in the preceding example is sometimes called the *glue record*. A glue record provides a child zone's master name server's IP address for zone delegation purposes. This avoids a deadlock situation, which can occur in DNS if glue records are not provided and which speeds up DNS queries involving the child zone.

Once you have added the glue records and have restarted BIND or reloaded its configuration files on the parent zone server, you have finished. The zone has been delegated.

Troubleshooting BIND

Whether you have set up a caching-only DNS server or are just trying to find a DNS query problem's root cause, several tools are available to help. Each one has its own merits. The following are the primary tools that you can use in troubleshooting efforts:

- host
- dig
- nslookup
- rndc

The first utility is a rather simple one. The host utility performs basic DNS name resolutions (also called *lookups*). An example is shown here:

```
$ host www.sybex.com
www.sybex.com has address 208.215.179.132
```

Not much information is provided, but the host command does allow you to see if name resolution is working. By default, the host command queries the name servers in the /etc/resolv.conf file.

In this example, the network cable was not properly connected. Thus, the host command provided an error message:

```
$ host www.sybex.com
;; connection timed out; no servers could be reached
$
```

It's a swift and useful test. It allows you to determine quickly if a serious problem is occurring or if DNS is humming along.

Consider checking your resolv.conf file, covered earlier in the chapter. If the name servers are not listed in this file, that may be the source of your server's DNS problem.

The dig utility is very handy in trying to determine what might be at a DNS problem's heart, and it can help you with auditing your name resolution process in order to improve it.

Depending on the options given, the dig utility will ask certain questions of DNS name servers and display any answers received. Here is a simple dig query/answer on a CentOS system example:

```
$ dig sybex.com

; <<>> DiG 9.9.4-RedHat-9.9.4-29.el7_2.3 <<>> sybex.com
;; global options: +cmd
;; Got answer:
;; ->>HEADER<<- opcode: QUERY, status: NOERROR, id: 21258
;; flags: qr rd ra;QUERY: 1,ANSWER: 1,AUTHORITY: 0, ADDITIONAL: 1

;; OPT PSEUDOSECTION:
; EDNS: version: 0, flags:; udp: 512
;; QUESTION SECTION:
;sybex.com.                 IN    A

;; ANSWER SECTION:
sybex.com.          900    IN    A    208.215.179.132
```

```
;; Query time: 60 msec
;; SERVER: 192.168.0.1#53(192.168.0.1)
;; WHEN: Thu Mar 31 11:45:01 EDT 2017
;; MSG SIZE  rcvd: 54

$
```

In the preceding example, a great deal of information is displayed. Generally, you'll only want to pull out some of the display. For example, status: NOERROR indicates that the server exists. Also notice the line beneath ANSWER SECTION. This line gives you the IP address for the server. Notice the A in the line as well. The dig command, by default, asks for A resource record types (look back at Table 8.2 for the resource record types list).

Another useful data tidbit in the returned information is the Query time result. This shows how quickly the answer was received to the dig utility's question. This is useful information in determining how well your name resolution is happening and can be especially helpful when you are setting up a local caching-only DNS name server (as covered earlier in this chapter).

The host command can produce somewhat similar (though briefer) output to the dig command's output. Type host -a *server* at the command line.

If you'd like a shorter answer to your dig query, you can use the +short option, or you can pipe the dig utility's answer into the grep command. These two methods are shown here:

```
$ dig +short sybex.com
208.215.179.132
$
$ dig sybex.com | grep sybex
; <<>> DiG 9.9.4-RedHat-9.9.4-29.el7_2.3 <<>> sybex.com
;sybex.com.   IN   A
sybex.com.   795   IN   A   208.215.179.132
$
```

By default, the dig command queries the name servers in the /etc/resolv.conf file. To direct a dig query to a different name server, add the @ option to the command followed by the IP address or the server's name. Here is an example:

```
$ dig @192.168.0.101 +short sybex.com
208.215.179.132
$
```

If you are just doing performance tests, then grep for the query time only, as shown here:

```
$ dig sybex.com | grep Query
;; Query time: 39 msec
$
```

The dig returned query status can be an initial step in tracking down DNS problems. Here is an example, where a bogus server name was used in the dig query:

```
$ dig sybex_fake.com | grep status
;; ->>HEADER<<- opcode: QUERY, status: NXDOMAIN, id: 351
$
```

Notice in the preceding example that the status NXDOMAIN was returned. This indicates that the name servers believe the sybex_fake.com server does not exist. If you receive a REFUSED status, the name servers are refusing the dig query for this server (typically because of set zone policies).

You may get an address returned for the sybex_fake.com website. This is typically due to people using FQDNs within published materials for malicious purposes. You may need to make up your own bogus server name to use in a dig query in order to receive the NXDOMAIN status.

You can also do reverse DNS lookups. Use the -x option and follow it with an IP address. You are likely to get a great deal of information back, as shown in this snipped example here:

```
$ dig -x 208.215.179.132
[...]
;; Got answer:
;; ->>HEADER<<- opcode: QUERY, status: NOERROR, id: 2197
[...]
;; QUESTION SECTION:
;132.179.215.208.in-addr.arpa.    IN    PTR

;; ANSWER SECTION:
[...]
132.179.215.208.in-addr.arpa. 900 IN    PTR    onewiley.net.
[...]
132.179.215.208.in-addr.arpa. 900 IN    PTR    onewiley.com.
[...]
132.179.215.208.in-addr.arpa. 900 IN    PTR    onewiley.org.
```

```
[...]
;; Query time: 97 msec
;; SERVER: 192.168.0.1#53(192.168.0.1)
;; WHEN: Thu Mar 31 11:53:20 EDT 2017
;; MSG SIZE  rcvd: 2861

$
```

Notice that in this case the PTR records are returned. This test can be useful when you have set up a new reverse zone and you want to ensure that it's working properly.

 Don't forget that you can use the dig +short +identify *server* command to see what name server or whose cache is providing answers to name server lookups. This is especially useful if you have just set up a local caching-only DNS server and wish to test it.

In your troubleshooting process, if you need to bypass a cache and follow the DNS name resolution path, the +trace option is useful. This option is shown snipped here because of the verbose output:

```
$ dig +trace sybex.com
[...]
.           447619   IN   NS   b.root-servers.net.
[...]
com.        172800   IN   NS   m.gtld-servers.net.
[...]
sybex.com.  172800   IN   NS   ns.wileypub.com.
[...]
sybex.com.  900      IN   A    208.215.179.132
[...]
$
```

In the dig +trace output, you should see a progression from root zone servers to the TLD servers and finally to name servers, which can provide an authoritative answer to the query. This option can be very helpful in troubleshooting when managing your own DNS zone.

If you have mail servers, you can check their name resolution by using the dig utility as well. Just pass the MX option as shown here:

```
$ dig MX +short ivytech.edu
0 ivytech-edu.mail.protection.outlook.com.
$
```

Besides mail servers, you can also determine a zone's name server(s). Instead of passing the MX option to dig, simply pass the NS option or the ANY option to get all of the various resource records types. Just remember that if you are trying to view *your* managed zone's name server(s), you'll need to add the @ option covered earlier.

> **NOTE** The host command will allow you to view mail servers as well. Type *host -t MX server* at the command line to see a zone's mail servers.

The dig utility is very flexible and zone managers are always coming up with new and creative ways to use this utility. Type **linux dig tutorial** in your favorite web browser. You'll find many sites that can provide various insights into using this tool.

The nslookup utility is a troubleshooting tool with an interesting history. Near the millennium's turn, it was decided to deprecate this utility. In 2004, the BIND developers changed their minds and decided to "un-deprecate" it. The nslookup utility has its detractors, but it is still a useful tool (and mentioned in the certification objectives).

What makes the nslookup utility unique is that it can operate in either an interactive or a non-interactive mode. For the non-interactive mode, you enter the server whose information you wish to view (and optionally a name server to query), as shown in the example here:

```
$ nslookup sybex.com
Server:        192.168.0.1
Address:       192.168.0.1#53

Non-authoritative answer:
Name:    sybex.com
Address: 208.215.179.132

$
```

Like host and dig, if you don't include a name server, by default the nslookup command queries the servers in the /etc/resolv.conf file. Here is an example where nslookup is directed to query a particular name server:

```
$ nslookup sybex.com 192.168.0.103
Server:        192.168.0.103
Address:       192.168.0.103#53

Non-authoritative answer:
Name:    sybex.com
Address: 208.215.179.132

$
```

Notice that in both of the preceding examples a non-authoritative answer is given. You can force nslookup to retrieve an authoritative answer, but first you must find an authoritative server via the -query=ns option, as shown snipped here:

```
$ nslookup -query=ns ivytech.edu
Server:        192.168.0.1
Address:    192.168.0.1#53

Non-authoritative answer:
ivytech.edu    nameserver = nsext4.ivytech.edu.
[...]
Authoritative answers can be found from:
nsext1.ivytech.edu    internet address = 168.91.17.181
[...]
$
```

Once you have an authoritative server's IP address, pass it along with nslookup query as is done here:

```
$ nslookup ivytech.edu 168.91.17.181
Server:        168.91.17.181
Address:    168.91.17.181#53

Name:   ivytech.edu
Address: 208.40.244.223

$
```

The preceding query does not show a non-authoritative answer line. This indicates that an authoritative answer was received.

You can enter into the nslookup utility's interactive mode by simply typing **nslookup** at the command line and pressing Enter. Here is an example of entering into interactive mode and conducting a query similar to earlier examples:

```
$ nslookup
>
> server 192.168.0.103
Default server: 192.168.0.103
Address: 192.168.0.103#53
>
> sybex.com
Server:        192.168.0.103
Address:    192.168.0.103#53

Non-authoritative answer:
```

```
Name:    sybex.com
Address: 208.215.179.132
>
> exit

$
```

In the preceding example, the server command is used to designate a name server to query. You simply type a server name, **sybex.com** in the example, and press Enter to get an answer. Finally, type **exit** to leave the nslookup utility's interactive mode.

 If you are experiencing DNS problems after a recent change to the BIND zone configuration or a zone database, remember that you have two important tools to help you resolve these problems. You can use the named-checkconf utility to check your named.conf and the named-checkzone tool to verify that your zone database file syntax is correct.

Troubleshooting BIND with *rndc*

Earlier we covered the /usr/sbin/rndc utility regarding stopping BIND and/or loading modified BIND configuration files. You can also do troubleshooting with the rndc utility.

Using rndc you can control troubleshooting items such as modifying the debugging level on the fly. A few rndc troubleshooting-related commands are shown snipped here:

```
# rndc
Usage: rndc [-b address] [-c config] [-s server] [-p port]
           [-k key-file ] [-y key] [-V] command
[...]
  stats    Write server statistics to the statistics file.
  querylog newstate
           Enable / disable query logging.
  dumpdb [-all|-cache|-zones] [view ...]
           Dump cache(s) to the dump file (named_dump.db).
[...]
  trace    Increment debugging level by one.
  trace level
           Change the debugging level.
  notrace  Set debugging level to 0.
[...]
  status   Display status of the server.
[...]
#
```

The cache and/or zone databases are dumped to a file (defined by the named.conf file's dump-file directive) when the rndc dumpdb command is issued. Name server statistics can be written to a file (defined by the named.conf file's statistics-file setting) when the rndc stats command is used. Looking through these various files can assist you in tracking down name server problems.

Don't forget your various logging options set in the named.conf file. These DNS logs can also be very helpful in troubleshooting BIND problems.

Recent BIND versions save secondary server zone files in a raw binary format. While this provides a performance improvement, it can make troubleshooting and debugging difficult. To help in troubleshooting, try using the named-compilezone utility to convert the zone files temporarily to text. As an alternative, you can change the secondary server zone files back to text for a while. Use the masterfile-format text directive in the named.conf files' secondary name server zone statement.

In Exercise 8.1, you will try out various troubleshooting tools on your Linux system.

EXERCISE 8.1

Trying Out Troubleshooting Tools

To experiment with DNS troubleshooting tools, follow these steps:

1. Start up a Linux Red Hat–based or a Debian-based distribution system (it can be a virtualized Linux system) that has Internet access.

2. Log in as an ordinary user.

3. If one is not already open, open a command-line terminal.

4. Pick your favorite college or university's primary website, and record the URL. (If you don't have a favorite college or university, use Purdue.edu instead.)

5. Perform a simple DNS lookup by typing **host purdue.edu** (or substitute the URL you recorded in step 4) and press Enter.

6. Record the IP address returned by the host command.

7. Perform a reverse DNS lookup by typing **dig -x IP-address**, where **IP-address** is the IP address you recorded in the previous step. In the resulting output, you should see the URL you entered in step 5 (though it may have www tacked onto the front of the URL).

8. Try a simple DNS lookup using the nslookup command. At the command line, type **nslookup purdue.edu** (or substitute the URL you recorded in step 4) and press Enter. You should receive the same IP address that you received in step 6. Also, you might see a Non-authoritative answer phrase.

9. Locate the name servers that have authority over this particular URL by typing **nslookup -query=ns purdue.edu** (or substitute the URL you recorded in step #4) and press Enter. You should see one or more hostnames, preceded by nameserver. Pick a name server, and record its hostname. (For example, you may pick ns1.rice.edu).

10. Request an authoritative answer using nslookup by typing at the command line **nslookup purdue.edu ns1.rice.edu** (or substitute the URL you recorded in step 4, followed by the hostname you recorded in step 9), and press Enter. You should receive the IP address but this time without the Non-authoritative answer phrase.

11. Trace through the various name servers by typing at the command line **dig +trace purdue.edu** (or substitute the URL you recorded in step 4) and press Enter. You'll see a great deal of information scroll by on your screen as it traces through domain namespace.

12. Experiment with the host, dig, and nslookup commands. View their man pages, and try out their different options.

Securing a DNS Server

Unfortunately, security is an ever-changing topic, because malicious attackers never seem to stop. This section attempts to help you get started in securing your DNS server(s). But don't rely on this information alone. You need to keep up to date on the latest security issues, enhancements, and lockdown tasks, which can change daily. The ISC keeps a website with current security information, called the Security Advisory. Use your favorite search engine, and type **Internet Systems Consortium Security Advisory** to locate the site.

Setting Up Basic Security

You can take some basic steps to ensure that your name servers or DNS clients are not compromised. These include keeping your BIND software current and not allowing too much name server information to be obtained.

Several of the basic items covered here can help prevent security problems:

Keep BIND software current.   BIND software security vulnerabilities may be uncovered via malicious hackers, security researches, BIND administrators, and so on. No matter who uncovers the vulnerability, it is important to keep BIND and its dependencies updated. Historically, the ISC is quick to release BIND security vulnerability patches, so be sure to check regularly for updates.

Hide BIND information.   Besides keeping BIND software current, you should hide your system's BIND version. That information can be fairly easy to obtain using the dig command and the Chaosnet network protocol class, as shown snipped here:

```
$ dig @192.168.0.103 chaos version.bind txt
[...]
```

```
;; ANSWER SECTION:
version.bind.       0   CH   TXT   "9.9.4-RedHat-9.9.4[...]
[...]
$
```

You can easily fix this by adding an additional clause to your `named.conf` file's options, as shown snipped here:

```
# cat /etc/named.conf
[...]
options {
[...]
    version "null";
[...]
#
```

The `version` directive will now answer any `version.bind` queries with `null`. You can put anything in the text you desire. Here is an example of the query's answer now:

```
$ dig @192.168.0.103 chaos version.bind txt
[...]
;; ANSWER SECTION:
version.bind.       0   CH   TXT   "null"
[...]
$
```

Consider various views.   Some security experts recommend setting up a different `view`. A `view` is an additional statement grouping (clause) within the `named.conf` file, which allows you to separate and isolate various zones. You can use the `view` clauses in conjunction with defined `named.conf` file access control lists (`acl`).

For example, you manage Zone A, which is accessed by external DNS clients as well as internal DNS clients. In this case, you may only want to block BIND version information for Zone A external clients. Therefore, you set up two `view` statements. One `view` offers functionality for Zone A's internal clients, which includes viewing BIND version information. The other `view` offers functionality for Zone A's external clients, which can include ignoring any Chaosnet network protocol class and other security-related settings.

A few items that you should consider including in managed Zone external clients' views (Internet and Chaosnet) are as follows. You should review these settings prior to implementation to see if they apply to your managed zone. Whether you need to implement them depends on the DNS service you intend to provide to the external world:

- Ignore `chaos` queries via setting `version` to `"null"` or throw out the queries via setting `file` to `"/dev/null"` in the root zone (zone `"."`) definition section.

- Set recursion to no in order to instruct BIND that external clients *cannot* use this DNS server as a Recursive Name Server. This prevents a DNS amplification attack (see US-CERT alert TA13–088A).

- Turn off any external client view queries by setting allow-query to {none;} (no one), which, in effect, turns off queries for the external views.

- Disallow external client access to this server's cache via setting allow-query-cache to {none;} (available only on BIND v9.4 and up).

- Turn off any external client access by setting allow-recursion to {none;} (no one).

Keep in mind that some of these settings are duplicates. For example, if recursion is set to no, then by default allow-query-cache is set to {none;}. However, it does not hurt to set these directives implicitly.

Split your DNS server.   "Split configuration of BIND" is mentioned in the certification objectives. A *Split DNS server* (also called a *Dual Horizon* or *Split Horizon server*) is one that is serving two different DNS purposes (think split personality). For example, you may have a DNS server for external clients as well as for internal clients. In other words, a single server is providing two different DNS services, each with different protection needs. Using the example, you want to limit what information external clients can get about internal clients.

Obviously, the best security solution is to set up the different DNS server functionalities on two different physical servers. However, this does increase administrative overhead, especially if you have the internal client server behind a firewall and internal clients that are physically separated over the Internet. Thus, should you decide to split a single DNS server, you have a few important configuration items to consider.

Using the preceding external and internal clients' example, the idea is to provide a different query answer, depending on who is sending the query. One answer is for external clients. A different answer is for internal clients.

First, on your primary (master) server, as covered previously, you need to set up two different views: one view for external clients and one view for internal clients. This sets up access control lists (acl) for each client type and essentially divides up the two groups.

Each view will get its own zone definition within the named.conf file. The only difference between the zone definitions will be the zone database to which the file directive points. In other words, you need *different* authoritative information stored in each zone database. One zone database is for external views and one zone database is for internal views.

After you have your primary server set up with its different external and internal views and answers, you need to set up your secondary (slave) server. Because the primary server sends zone updates (via a zone transfer) to the secondary server, you need to ensure that the right updates are sent (primary external zone database to secondary external zone database and primary internal zone database to secondary internal zone database). This can be tricky, because even though the different view zone databases have different filenames, they have the same zone name in their SOA resource records. To prevent mix-ups during zone transfers, you can set up TSIG communication, which is covered later in this chapter.

Run only BIND.   Any public DNS server you manage, which is outside your firewall, should run only BIND and not provide other services, such as hosting web pages. This lowers your attack surface, so there are fewer security risks. Less software and fewer services provide a reduced chance of security vulnerabilities. If you have an important internal DNS server, it's a good idea to do the same for it as well.

Run BIND as a non-root user.   Most current distributions already implement this. Here is a snipped example of a CentOS distribution showing that BIND is running as the user named, and it belongs to the group named:

```
# systemctl status named
[...]
  Process: 2812 ExecStart=/usr/sbin/named -u named [...]
[...]
   CGroup: /system.slice/named.service
           └─2815 /usr/sbin/named -u named
#
# groups named
named: named
#
```

On older distributions, you may need to do this manually. First, create a BIND username and group. Traditionally, the non-root username for BIND is either named or bind. Following that, modify startup files to make BIND run as a non-root user by adding -u *BIND_user* to where BIND is invoked (/usr/sbin/named) in the script. Double-check that any files that BIND needs to access, such as zone files and dump files, have write or read access granted to the BIND username and/or group. Here are the settings on the /var/named/ directory on the previous CentOS system:

```
# ls -l /var/named
total 16
drwxrwx---. 2 named named  103 Mar 20 03:11 data
drwxrwx---. 2 named named   58 Apr  3 18:08 dynamic
-rw-rw----. 1 root  named 2076 Jan 28  2013 named.ca
-rw-rw----. 1 root  named  152 Dec 15  2009 named.empty
-rw-rw----. 1 root  named  152 Jun 21  2007 named.localhost
-rw-rw----. 1 root  named  168 Dec 15  2009 named.loopback
drwxrwx---. 2 named named    6 Mar 16 09:40 slaves
#
```

Control zone updates.   To keep zones from being updated by malicious attackers, it's best to lock down your zone dynamic updates. Some security researchers recommend not using dynamic updates at all but instead implementing scripts to update zone databases as needed.

Within each zone configuration file in the zone directive, restrict needed zone dynamic updates via the `allow-update` directive. Set the directive to `none` to eliminate any dynamic updates, or set it to an IP servers list, with servers that are allowed to dynamically update the zone. If you have external and internal `views` set up, be sure to disallow any updates in the external `views`. Here is an example of eliminating any updates:

```
allow-update { none;};
```

In addition, you should consider locking down the `allow-update-forwarding` directive per `view` and per zone. This directive determines which servers are allowed to submit dynamic updates to a secondary server. In this case, the secondary server then dynamically updates the primary server.

The `allow-notify` directive determines which server is allowed to send NOTIFY (DNS zone change notification) messages to a secondary server. By default, the primary server is the only one that can send a NOTIFY message to a secondary server. However, it's a good idea to implicitly list the master server's IP address.

To help prevent malicious attacks associated with dynamic updates and update notifications, it's a good idea to secure the communication concerning these items. This is done via TSIG, covered later in this chapter.

Control zone transfers   Not every server needs a zone database copy. The master server has the original, and if you maintain a secondary server, it will occasionally need a copy (look back at zone transfers if you need a refresher on what triggers a zone transfer).

To restrict access, start in the `named.conf` configuration file and globally turn *off* all zone transfers via the option `allow-transfer {"none";}`. Within each zone configuration file in the zone directive, turn on any needed zone transfers by again using the `allow-transfer` setting, listing allowed servers (or using an `acl`). Remember that a zone setting will override any global options that you set in the `named.conf` file. This allows you to finely control each zone and allow zone transfers only to those servers that need them (secondary servers).

Besides the basic things to do to ensure that your name servers or internal DNS clients are protected, there are some additional important security measures. These measures are covered next.

Jailing BIND

We tend to think of jailing someone when they have done something bad, but in this case, jailing BIND adds an additional security level. The jail is called a *chroot jail*, and it prevents a process from navigating outside a specified directory (the jail).

The name *chroot jail* comes from the chroot command. This command allows you to run a shell command (or interactive shell), forcing the command to treat your specified directory as the root (/) of the Linux directory structure. In essence, you have "changed the root."

The basic steps to create the chroot jail are as follows:

1. Create a root directory structure for BIND within the Linux virtual directory structure. Typically, /chroot/named or /chroot/bind is chosen as the new root (/), but it can vary.

2. Create the appropriate subdirectories under the chroot jail directory, such as etc/, etc/bind/, home/named/, proc/, var/run/, and var/log/. The subdirectories that you need to create will be highly dependent on your distribution and BIND configuration.

3. Copy any files needed for BIND to operate properly, such as the /etc/timezone file.

4. Copy over the BIND configuration files to the chroot jail directory structure.

5. Copy any zone configuration and database files to the chroot jail directory structure.

6. Modify the BIND user account so that the home directory now points to the chroot jail directory's home subdirectory for the BIND user account.

7. Modify the chroot jail directory structure and files within so that ownership, group, and permissions match the originals. A script can prove useful here.

8. Modify startup files to mount the /proc filesystem in the chroot jail directory using the mount -o command.

9. Modify the startup files that make BIND run as a non-root user and by adding -u *BIND_user* to where BIND is invoked (/usr/sbin/named) in the script.

It's best to try this out on a non-production system using a caching-only server setup. It's such a complicated configuration that it's worthwhile to test it and work out any kinks prior to implementing a chroot jail on a current production DNS server.

 You may have additional steps to take, depending on your distribution and server configuration. For instance, if you are using the /dev/null device file or any other device files within your BIND configuration, you will need to create these device files within your chroot jail as well using the mknod command.

Fortunately, some current distributions have recognized how difficult this can be to set up. Thus, the bind-chroot package is available, and it does most of the work for you via creating the chroot jail (/var/named/chroot/) and creating hard links to the original BIND configuration files.

The basic steps for using the bind-chroot package on a current CentOS distribution are as follows:

1. Configure your BIND DNS if you have not done so already.

2. Install the bind-chroot package.

3. Run the setup shell script using super user privileges as follows:

```
# /usr/libexec/setup-named-chroot.sh /var/named/chroot on
```

4. If BIND was previously set up and running, stop and disable it:

```
# systemctl stop named
#
# systemctl disable named
#
```

5. Start and enable bind-chroot to run BIND:

```
# systemctl start named-chroot
#
# systemctl enable named-chroot
#
```

Once you have this set up, you will need to remember that your BIND files now exist in /var/named/chroot/var/named/ instead of the /var/named/ directory. Even though this is easier to set up than the other chroot jail method, it is still worthwhile to test the jailed BIND configuration on a non-production DNS server.

 Real World Scenario

Exploring Asymmetric Encryption and Hashing

Eventually, when discussing computer security, the topics of encryption and hashing arise. Both are heavily used to provide better security. However, if you don't understand them, you are liable to incorrectly implement the products and services that employ them. This often leaves holes in your systems that malicious attackers can use to their advantage.

Encryption is a process that uses a mathematical algorithm to convert plain text (text that humans and machines can read) into cipher text (text that humans and machines cannot read). Often, a key or set of keys is involved in this process. An encryption key is a piece of data required by the algorithm to complete the encryption successfully. To reverse the process (decrypt cipher text into plain text), the same mathematical algorithm is used along with any keys used in the encryption process.

Asymmetric encryption (also called private/public key encryption) uses two keys, called a key pair. A *key pair* consists of a public key and a private key. The key pair's public key is public and there is no need to keep it secret. It is used to encrypt data (along with the algorithm). The key pair's private key is kept secret, and it is used to decrypt the data. Thus, data that has been encrypted with the public key can only be decrypted with its private key. The advantage of asymmetric cryptography is heightened security.

Hashing uses a one-way mathematical algorithm, turning plain text into hashed text. You cannot reverse the process. Often it is used to provide a digital signature. A *digital signature* is data that has been run through a hash algorithm. Once it is hashed, the data is then encrypted using a private key. This encrypted hash is then appended to the original data, and it is considered a digital signature.

Using DNSSEC

Imagine if you asked someone a question, and before you got the answer, it was stolen and replaced by an incorrect answer. This can happen in the name resolution process. A resolver's DNS query is sent, but the answer gets hijacked. Instead of the correct answer, the DNS resolver receives a phony answer. The application employing the resolver uses the phony answer, and it is thus tricked into going to a malicious website. That's a scary scenario.

The BIND DNS Security Extensions (DNSSEC) can help protect your systems from these scenarios. Its primary goal is to protect DNS answers by ensuring that the answers match what is in the responding server's zone database and have not been altered in transit.

Keep in mind that DNSSEC does not protect zone transfers between primary and secondary name servers. It also doesn't handle dynamic updates.

Exploring DNSSEC

Though DNSSEC does not encrypt DNS query responses, it does use asymmetric encryption to provide digital signatures. DNSSEC uses additional DNS resource record types (beyond those covered in Table 8.2) and message header bits.

DNS messages that pass back and forth between a resolver and a name server consist of five standard parts (described fully in RFC 1035). The first of these five parts is the message header. In a DNS message header, various bits describe the message. For example, it contains a 16-bit message identification (Message ID) number and a single-bit query response (QR), which is set to 0 for a DNS query and to 1 for a response message.

A couple of important DNSSEC resource record types are the public key (DNSKEY) and the digital signature (RRSIG). The DNSSEC message header bits are AD to indicate authenticated data and CD to indicate that checking is disabled.

Before launching into DNSSEC, it's important to know a few terms associated with the BIND security extensions. Understanding these terms will help you follow how DNSSEC provides protection and comprehend the use of DNSSEC resource record types.

Validating Resolver   DNSSEC works using validating resolvers configured with trust anchors. A *validating resolver* is a DNS resolver that executes DNSSEC data validation (described soon) on the data it receives.

Trust Anchor   A *trust anchor* is a DNSKEY resource record on a validating resolver. The validating resolver uses this public key to validate a response's digital signature.

Chain of Trust   DNSSEC is based on a chain of trust. This particular chain of trust has a higher zone (such as the root . zone) digitally sign a lower zone's key (such as the .com TLD), which in turn signs a lower zone's key (such as example.com). To keep this chain valid, it is important to update periodically the digital signatures and keys.

Zone Signing Key   A *zone signing key* (ZSK) is the encryption key used to digitally sign a particular zone's resource records. The produced digital signature is stored in an RRSIG record. It is suggested that these keys be renewed on a yearly basis at minimum.

Key Signing Key   A *key signing key* (KSK) is the encryption key used to sign a particular zone's ZSK. This key is applied via the chain of trust described earlier.

DNSSEC Data Validation   This data validation process occurs when a validating resolver retraces the chain of trust and verifies an answer's authenticity. The validating resolver attempts to validate the digital signatures' chain to the original root zone. This process essentially verifies that the public key (KSK) stored in its DNSKEY resource record is valid. Once the chain of trust is validated, it can verify an answer's authenticity.

The answer's authenticity is verified using the validated public key (KSK), stored in the DNSKEY resource record, to decrypt the digital signature stored in the RRSIG resource record. The resulting hash is compared to an answer hash. If they match, nothing has been modified in transit and all is well.

If both the chain of trust and the answer's authenticity are successfully validated, the DNS response is proved trustworthy. If the data does not successfully validate, a SERVFAIL response is given by the validating resolver.

This is a rather complicated and difficult topic, and you may feel a little overwhelmed. Thankfully, the certification objectives require you to have only a general awareness of DNSSEC and its basic tools.

Using the chain of trust, DNSSEC digitally signs all of a zone's resource records. This adds an additional layer of security. BIND 9 is DNSSEC-capable, and it typically comes with some security extensions set up by default.

Here is a snipped named.conf example from a CentOS system. Various DNSSEC settings are shown:

```
# cat /etc/named.conf
[...]
    dnssec-enable yes;
```

```
    dnssec-validation yes;
[...]
#
```

The dnssec-enable directive is set to yes, which you may think means that DNSSEC is being used. However, that is not the case. Set to yes, this means that a security service is being used that could be DNSSEC or even TSIG (covered later in this chapter).

The dnssec-validation directive is also set to yes. This indicates that a name server that uses DNS cache will attempt to perform DNSSEC data validation. However, unless a trusted-keys or managed-keys grouping (clause) statement is included, this does not occur.

 While the DNSSEC process is all well and good, a problem can exist in it. Because of the chain of trust, the DNSSEC data validation will not work if any of your higher zones are not digitally signed. To deal with this particular issue, the DNSSEC Lookaside Validation (DLV) process was invented. It allows DNSSEC to provide a trust anchor, even if higher zones are not signed. You are encouraged to use this as only a temporary solution, if needed. Find out more at the dlv.isc.org/doc site.

Keys are typically either declared in the named.conf file or stored in a separate file, which is pointed to by the bindkeys-file directive within the name.conf file. To declare a key, you can use either the trusted-keys or managed-keys clause.

The difference between the two clauses is that trusted-keys has to be manually updated. If a key expires in your trusted-keys declaration, your DNS name server is unable to perform the data validation process successfully until the key is updated. With a managed-keys clause, an initializing key is used to load a managed key database. Once keys are in place, they are automatically updated as needed (RFC 5011).

Here is an example on a CentOS system's BIND default installation. Within the named .conf file, the bindkeys-file directive points to a DLV key file, as shown snipped here:

```
# cat /etc/named.conf
[...]
    /* Path to ISC DLV key */
    bindkeys-file "/etc/named.iscdlv.key";
[...]
#
```

Looking at the DLV key file, you can find the managed-keys grouping, as shown here using the grep command:

```
# grep managed /etc/named.iscdlv.key
managed-keys {
#
```

A DLV key is important to have as a temporary solution. Digging further into the previous `named.conf` file, a root key is found, as shown here:

```
# cat /etc/named.conf
[...]
include "/etc/named.root.key";
#
```

This included file also has a `managed-keys` grouping, as shown snipped here:

```
# cat /etc/named.root.key
managed-keys {
    # DNSKEY for the root zone.
    # Updates are published on root-dnssec-announce@icann.org
    . initial-key 257 3 8
"AwEAAagAIKlVZrpC6Ia7gEzahOR+9W29euxhJhVVLOyQbSEW0O8gcCjF
[...]
QxA+UklihzO=";
};
#
```

In this particular example, since the root zone has been signed and a root key is provided in the `managed-keys` grouping, there is no longer a need to keep the DLV key. You can simply comment it out in the `named.conf` file.

If your distribution does not provide BIND DNSSEC trusted keys, you can obtain them from www.isc.org/downloads/bind/bind-keys. The ISC has a `bind.keys` file that you can download via FTP, which has both a root key and a DLV key (if you are temporarily using the DLV solution).

You can test whether your name server is using DNSSEC via the `dig` command on your loopback address. You are looking for two flags: ad (Authenticated answer) and do (DNSSEC Okay). Here is a snipped example:

```
# dig +dnssec 127.0.0.1 edu. ns | grep flags
;; flags: qr rd ra ad; [...]
; EDNS: version: 0, flags: do; udp: 512
;; flags: qr rd ra ad; [...]
; EDNS: version: 0, flags: do; udp: 512
#
```

Because the preceding example has those two flags, DNSSEC authoritative information is available to your server. Another way to test this is to search for the SERVFAIL response, as shown here:

```
# dig +dnssec 127.0.0.1 edu. ns | grep SERVFAIL
#
```

If you *do not* receive a SERVFAIL response to the dig query using the +dnssec option, DNSSEC is working.

Signing Your Zone

The following general steps are used for signing a zone that you manage. Keep in mind that the actual steps you need to take depend on your currently installed BIND version as well as your name server's distribution.

1. Create a directory to hold your zone key.
2. Set proper permissions on the zone key directory.
3. Generate zone keys.
4. Add any needed key directives to the named.conf file.
5. Sign your zone automatically via reloading the zone's configuration files or sign it manually.
6. Verify the signature.
7. Notify the parent zone.

Because these steps and their details can vary greatly depending on your particular situation, it's recommended that you visit www.isc.org. The DNSSEC for BIND Quick Reference Guide can help get you started setting up DNSSEC and signing any managed zones. It also makes a good study sheet for certification purposes.

Generally speaking, at some point, you will employ the dnssec-keygen utility. To generate a zone key, you will pass three options: -a *Encryption_algorithm*, -b *keysize*, and -n ZONE. The *Encryption_algorithm* and associated keysizes that you can use are listed in the man pages. The -n ZONE option is required to create a DNSSEC zone key.

With no additional options, a zone signing key is generated. If you need a key signing key, add the -f KSK option. Here is an example of generating a zone signing key, split into two command lines for clarity:

```
# dnssec-keygen -a RSASHA512 -b 2048 -n ZONE \
> -r /dev/urandom example.com.
Generating key pair.......+++ ...................................+++
Kexample.com.+010+63698
#
```

Notice that at the command's end you must pass the zone's name, followed by a dot (.). Be aware that this utility will take a *long time* to run, especially if you do not use the -r /dev/ urandom option. It's best to tack on an & and run it in the background.

 The dnssec-keygen utility allows a -r option, as was used in the preceding example. This option allows you to specify a randomness or entropy source. If one is not specified, the dnssec-keygen utility can take a very long time to complete its operation, because it is gathering entropy. You can specify /dev/urandom, /dev/random, or keyboard (but you'll have to type on the keyboard for a long time) to speed up the process. Though debated, /dev/urandom is typically the best choice.

The dnssec-keygen utility creates two files. One file holds the private zone key (ending in .private), while the other holds the public zone key (ending in .key). Once these are created, move these files to the appropriate directory for the zone keys. The files created from the preceding example are shown here in a single-column format:

```
# ls -1 Kexample.com.*
Kexample.com.+010+63698.key
Kexample.com.+010+63698.private
#
```

If you do not set up automatic signing via the auto-dnssec and inline-signing directives in your named.conf file, you will need to load your keys manually into BIND using the rndc loadkeys *zone* command. Also, you will need to sign your zone manually using the dnssec-signzone command.

Not all of the DNSSEC utilities may be needed in current distributions. However, if you have an older DNS name server or do not use automatic signing, they may prove useful. Here is a DNSSEC utilities list:

```
# man -k dnssec-
dnssec-checkds (8)—A DNSSEC delegation consistency checking tool.
dnssec-coverage (8)—checks future DNSKEY coverage for a zone
dnssec-dsfromkey (8)—DNSSEC DS RR generation tool
dnssec-keyfromlabel (8)—DNSSEC key generation tool
dnssec-keygen (8)—DNSSEC key generation tool
dnssec-revoke (8)—Set the REVOKED bit on a DNSSEC key
dnssec-settime (8)—Set the key timing metadata for a DNSSEC key
dnssec-signzone (8)—DNSSEC zone signing tool
dnssec-verify (8)—DNSSEC zone verification tool
#
```

DNSSEC does provide a solid extra layer of protection, but it does not protect zone transfers or dynamic updates. Fortunately, another DNS security utility can help, and it is covered next.

Connecting via TSIG

BIND allows the use of *Transaction Signature (TSIG)*, which signs DNS messages with a digital signature. This provides point-to-point authentication as well as message integrity checking. Via TSIG, any DNS messages that have been altered in transit are revealed. This helps prevent malicious attacks against certain DNS communications.

TSIG can be used for these purposes:

- DNS zone change notification operation (NOTIFY) messages
- Dynamic updates
- Recursive Name Server query communication
- Zone transfers between primary and secondary name servers

Before making any configuration file changes to use TSIG, you'll need to generate a key file on your primary name server. In this case, you'll use the dnssec-keygen utility but employ different options. Here is an example on a CentOS distribution split onto two lines for clarity:

```
# dnssec-keygen -a HMAC-SHA512 -b 512 -n HOST \
> -r /dev/urandom texample
Ktexample.+165+10948
#
```

You'll notice a few changes from generating a DNSSEC key. For a TSIG key, the -a option specifies the HMAC-SHA512 key algorithm, along with the biggest key possible for this algorithm, -b 512. The -n option is set to HOST.

The other change is the key name. You can use just about any key name, and there is no key name standard. However, the key name must be unique for the DNS servers that will be using it. In the preceding example, the key name texample is used.

WARNING   Though it's available for generating TSIG keys via the dnssec-keygen utility, it is not advisable to use the HMAC-MD5 algorithm. It is no longer considered secure.

Two key files are generated by this process as shown here, but you need only the file with the .private extension.

```
# ls -1 Ktexample.*
Ktexample.+165+10948.key
Ktexample.+165+10948.private
#
```

The .private key file contains the needed private key. Here the texample key's .private key file is displayed:

```
# cat Ktexample.+165+10948.private
Private-key-format: v1.3
Algorithm: 165 (HMAC_SHA512)
Key:
PDYUe5i9PeA5PN/u5hoxQGL2qPcUy0sf1+FXy0PtDG5ccKACW3sWI
hvCp76r43o9l4XfN6tL+6d7oa4zw+9+QA==
Bits: AAA=
Created: 20160405022334
Publish: 20160405022334
Activate: 20160405022334
#
```

The next step is to create a primary server key configuration file for use in the BIND configuration files. Typically, these key configuration files are stored in the same directory as zone databases. Here a key configuration file is created for the `texample` key on a CentOS system:

```
# cat /var/named/texample.key
/* TSIG Key */
key "texample" {
  algorithm HMAC-SHA152;
  secret
"PDYUe5i9PeA5PN/u5hoxQGL2qPcUy0sf1+FXy0PtDG5ccKACW3sWI
hvCp76r43o9l4XfN6tL+6d7oa4zw+9+QA==";
};
#
```

In the key configuration file, the key directive sets the key's name. The `algorithm` directive denotes what encryption algorithm was used when the key was generated. Be sure to use the exact same algorithm name that you used with the `dnssec-keygen -a` option. Finally, the `secret` directive is followed by the private key within double quotation marks. As always with BIND configuration files, watch your curly bracket and semicolon placements.

 It's not advisable to write down the key and try to hand type it into the key configuration file. You can easily introduce typographical errors into the key. Instead, cut and paste or copy the key into the key configuration file.

Now that the key configuration file is completed, you can modify the primary server's `named.conf` file to include the key file. Here is a snipped example including the `texample` key configuration file on a CentOS system:

```
# cat /etc/named.conf
[...]
```

```
include "/var/named/texample.key";
#
```

You will also need to copy the key configuration file over to any servers (typically a secondary server) that will be using this TSIG key for communication. After the key configuration file is copied over and placed in the zone directory, it will need to be included into that server's named.conf, as was done on the primary server.

> **WARNING**   Unlike DNSSEC's asymmetric encryption and digital signatures, TSIG uses symmetric encryption via a secret private key shared among the communicating servers. Thus, it is very important to protect your generated TSIG keys.

How the TSIG key will be used for specific communication events (as well as your distribution and BIND version) can vary the rest of the needed steps. Looking only at zone transfers between primary and secondary servers, on the primary server you also will need to modify directives that determine who is allowed to transfer zones. For example, within the secondary server's zone configuration file, change the allow-transfer { *acl*;} directive to something like this:

```
allow-transfer { key "texample"; };
```

Essentially, you are replacing an access control list (acl) with a named key. Zone transfers will be allowed only for those holding this key.

On the secondary server (assuming you already have the key configuration file copied and included in the named.conf file), you will need to modify the key configuration file and add something like this to its bottom:

```
server primary-server-ip-address{
 keys { texample; };
};
```

At this point, you can reload the BIND configuration files on both the primary and secondary name servers using rndc or whatever utility your particular distribution uses. Test out a zone transfer, and if problems occur, review your DNS logs and use the various DNS troubleshooting methods.

> **NOTE**   TSIG uses timestamps to prevent messages from being reused (a malicious attacker may try to reuse messages). Therefore, if your servers do not have precise time, you may encounter errors using TSIG for DNS communications. Consider implementing the Network Time Protocol (NTP) daemon to provide precise server time.

Employing DANE

DANE, which stands for DNS-based Authentication of Named Entities, is an additional security measure that you can employ. It is described in detail in RFC 6698 and further clarified in RFC 7791. To understand how DANE adds security, you must first understand the security problem it helps to eliminate.

Secure TCP communications between a client and a web server are often done via the Transport Layer Security (TLS) protocol (which was called Secure Sockets Layer, or SSL, in years past). When this protocol is employed, part of its securing communications process involves a certificate. This certificate is trusted because typically another party, called a *trusted public certificate authority (CA)*, has issued and signed the certificate. Once the certificate is accepted, a key is provided to use for encrypting the TCP traffic between the client and the web server.

The problem lies in the trusted public CA model. Instead of just one or two CAs, there are hundreds. In addition, *any* CA can issue a certificate for *any* domain name. Lots of CAs, all capable of issuing signed certificates for any web server, make the trust model weak.

Unfortunately, as predicted, some CAs have been compromised and false replacement certificates have been issued. A client application, such as a web browser, accepting a compromised certificate can allow a compromised encryption key to be installed. In turn, a malicious person can use the compromised key to decrypt and read encrypted TCP traffic. This breaks the original trust granted to the CAs.

DANE attempts to correct the CA problem. It associates the web server's official and correct certificate or public key (or the trusted certificate-issuing authority) with the web server's domain name using a DNS query. For DANE to work properly, this DNS query is secured via DNSSEC. This association is called a *certificate association*. The certificate association data is stored in a DNS resource record, called a TLSA record.

According to RFC 7671, TLSA is not an acronym. However, for certification purposes, you can remember its purpose by thinking of it as the Transport Layer Security Authority (TLSA).

If you want to employ DANE, you must first pick the system that will be responsible for maintaining a TLSA record within the chosen DNS zone. This system is called the *TLSA publisher*. The chosen DNS zone must first employ DNSSEC (described earlier) and, in certain cases, have a validated DNSSEC chain of trust (also called a *trust anchor*) established.

To understand how a TLSA resource records works, it is important to understand what kinds of data a digital certificate may contain. The certificates discussed here will contain at least the issuer name to whom the certificate was issued, an expiration date, and a digital signature.

The TLSA portion of a resource record has this basic syntax: *certificate_usage selector matching_type content*. The following items explain the TLSA resource record fields:

certificate_usage   This field is set to a single digit (0–3) and specifies the particular association that must match during the TLS securing communications process. Its setting also determines whether a trust anchor must be pre-established.

A 0 indicates that the record specifies an authorized and trusted public CA. This certificate usage is often called a *CA constraint*, because it limits which CA can be used to issue certificates for a given service on a host. A trust anchor must be pre-established. Because this particular usage type offers no additional security, it is not recommended.

The number 1 specifies a trusted certificate or its public key. This certificate usage is often called a *service certificate constraint*, because it limits which certificate can be used by a given service on a host. A trust anchor must be pre-established. Because this particular usage type offers no additional security, it is not recommended.

A 2 indicates that the record specifies a new and non-public CA certificate or its public key. Typically, this usage is employed if you are acting as your own CA. A trust anchor does not need to be pre-established, because you are establishing one. Thus, this certificate usage is often called a *trust anchor assertion*, because it allows a new trust anchor to be specified. This particular usage type *does* offer additional security.

The number 3 specifies a server certificate (or public key), issued by the BIND administrator. It allows you to bypass a third-party CA, and it is often called a *domain-issued certificate*. This particular usage type also offers additional security.

selector   The `selector` field is set either to 0 or 1. A 0 indicates this record is for a digital certificate. A 1 in the `selector` field designates the record is using a public key instead.

matching_type   The `matching_type` field is set to 0, 1, or 2. A 0 indicates that content (CA, certificate, or public key data following this field) is not hashed. The number 1 indicates that the content was hashed by the SHA-256 hash algorithm, and a 2 specifies that the content was hashed by the SHA-512 algorithm. It is recommended to use the same hash algorithm that was used in the certificate's digital signature.

The entire resource record for a TLSA record contains a few additional items. Here is a snipped example of a TLSA resource record:

```
_443._tcp.www.example.com. IN TLSA (
    2 1 2 f6c4b71c216a50292b2f74e3fe51d48c
    [...])
```

In the preceding example, the 443._tcp. indicates that TCP port 443 (HTTPS) is being used for the www.example.com. server. The IN indicates that a record's class is Internet, and the TLSA designation designates this record as a TLSA record. Within the parentheses are the certificate usage (2), selector (1), matching type (2), and finally the snipped hashed content.

Once all of the appropriate fields are added, a TLSA record contains the needed certificate association data. TLSA resource records are placed within the TLSA publisher's appropriate DNS zone files.

Obviously, DNS security is a rather complicated topic, much like DNS itself. The information provided here will help you get started securing your DNS servers. The better you research and work toward a secure DNS server configuration, the easier it will be to keep out malicious attackers. Just remember to stay current on DNS security topics as well as implement new security protections.

Summary

The DNS network protocol is a complicated system that provides name resolution using a distributed database (Domain Name Space) to accomplish its task. The BIND package is popular on Linux for providing DNS services. Setting up DNS via BIND can be a complicated process. It involves modifying BIND configuration files, creating and maintaining zone configurations and databases, and implementing DNS server security. Hopefully, this chapter has started you on the right path for success.

Exam Essentials

Explain how to install and configure BIND.   On current Red Hat–based distributions, you need to install the bind and bindutils packages, and on current Ubuntu distributions, you need to install bind9 and bind9utils. The main configuration file for BIND is named.conf, and it is located in either the /etc/ or the /etc/bind/ directory, depending on your distribution. The named.conf file has various items such as comments, global options, logging directives, and zone configuration information, and it pulls in additional configuration settings from other files using include statements. DNS zones are configured via zone configuration information, which may be stored in separate files from the named.conf file (and pulled in via include statements) or entered directly into the named.conf file. Zone authoritative information comes in the form of resource records, which are stored in zone databases, also called *zone files*.

Describe how to set up a caching-only DNS server.   A caching-only DNS server, sometimes called a resolver, is a name server that receives its information from a primary (or secondary) server and caches the information locally in order to provide fast name resolutions for additional DNS queries. The named.conf file on this server must be modified. It's wise to create an access control list (acl) directive to list IP addresses of any servers allowed to query this name server's cache. The allow-query directive can be set either to the acl name or an IP address list of any servers allowed to query this name server's cache. You must also set the recursion directive to yes if it is currently set to no. The listen-on setting may need to be modified as well. Once the configuration settings are in place, test the named .conf file using the named-checkconf utility. If the utility returns no errors, either restart BIND or reload the configuration files using the system's initialization daemon, the kill command, or the rndc utility.

Describe how to troubleshoot BIND.   Besides viewing BIND logs, you can use four primary troubleshooting utilities: host, dig, nslookup, and rndc. The host tool performs basic DNS name resolutions. The dig utility is very flexible. By default, it queries the name servers in the /etc/resolv.conf file, but you can direct a dig query to a different name server by adding @*IP address* or @*server name* to the command. With the +trace option, you should see a progression from root zone servers to the TLD servers and finally name servers that can provide an authoritative answer to the dig query. The once-deprecated nslookup utility is unique in that it performs DNS lookups in either an interactive or a non-interactive mode. The rndc utility is designed specifically for BIND DNS, and it has multiple troubleshooting options that include displaying the DNS server's status, writing server stats to a file, changing the debugging level, and so on. (You can also stop BIND or reload its configuration files using rndc.)

Summarize implementing basic BIND security.   Important topics in securing BIND include keeping the BIND software up to date, running the BIND daemon as a non-root user, hiding BIND data such as BIND version information from external DNS clients, and not providing other major services (such as Apache or CUPS) on your DNS name server(s). You can also make BIND configuration modifications to include different views for external and internal clients, eliminate dynamic updates, globally turn off zone transfers (turning them on only for zones that need them), and split any DNS servers that provide multiple DNS functions. You can also protect your DNS server by implementing a chroot jail, using DNSSEC, protecting transactions by using TSIG, and employing DANE. Most important, you need to stay knowledgeable personally about the various malicious attacks that can happen against BIND-implemented DNS and modify your BIND configuration to mitigate them.

Review Questions

You can find the answers in the Appendix.

1. The .edu domain is considered which domain type? (Choose the best answer.)

   A. Root domain

   B. TLD

   C. First-level domain

   D. ICANN

   E. Second-level domain

2. Domain Name Space is broken into different zones. Which of the following could be one of those zones? (Choose all that apply.)

   A. The hint zone

   B. A first-level domain and all of its subdomains

   C. A first-level domain and a portion of its subdomains

   D. A root server

   E. The root zone

3. Which of the following server combinations could be the minimum two name servers required for a zone? (Choose all that apply.)

   A. Primary server and secondary server

   B. Secondary server and forwarding server

   C. Primary server and forwarding server

   D. Secondary server and caching server

   E. Primary server and caching server

4. A program or library routine that creates a DNS query, checks its own cache for the answer, and if it doesn't find it there, sends the query to another name server, is called what? (Choose the best answer.)

   A. Name server

   B. Cache

   C. Name resolution

   D. Resolver

   E. Zone

5. Which of the following software provides either full or partial DNS protocol implementation? (Choose all that apply.)

   A. BIND

   B. dnsmasq

   C. pdnsd

    D. Bundy

    E. PowerDNS

6. The BIND daemon is which program in the /usr/sbin/ directory? (Choose the best answer.)

    A. bind9

    B. bind

    C. named

    D. named.conf

    E. bindutils

7. Which of the following are legitimate groupings (clauses) in the BIND's primary configuration file, named.conf? (Choose all that apply.)

    A. options

    B. logging

    C. include

    D. named-checkconf

    E. comments

8. When setting up a local DNS caching-only server, which directives should be set and or modified in the named.conf file? (Choose all that apply.)

    A. acl

    B. allow-query

    C. logging

    D. listen-on

    E. recursion yes

9. Ignoring distribution differences and assuming you have the appropriate privileges, which of the following commands will stop the BIND service? (Choose all that apply.)

    A. rndc flush

    B. service bind9 stop

    C. kill -s SIGTERM *BIND_PID*

    D. rndc stop

    E. systemctl stop named

10. A logging category directive determines what? (Choose the best answer.)

    A. Where DNS messages are to be logged

    B. The DNS message types to be logged

    C. How to restart BIND to load logging

    D. How DNS messages are filtered

    E. The DNS channel log sizes

11. Which of the following are legal zone type directives? (Choose all that apply.)

    A. master

    B. secondary

    C. hint

    D. delegation

    E. root

12. Which of the following are legal zone statement classes? (Choose all that apply.)

    A. CH

    B. DN

    C. HS

    D. IN

    E. IS

13. Why might authoritative zone information be copied from the primary name server's zone databases over to the secondary name server (called a zone transfer)? (Choose all that apply.)

    A. The primary server's BIND daemon has restarted.

    B. The secondary server's BIND daemon has started up.

    C. The rndc utility was used on the secondary server, and a manual zone data refresh was requested.

    D. The secondary server's zone data's refresh time has expired.

    E. The secondary server's BIND daemon was stopped, and its configuration files were removed.

14. The default zone databases are typically stored in which directories? (Choose the two best answers.)

    A. /etc/named/ directory

    B. /var/bind/ directory

    C. /var/named/ directory

    D. /etc/bind9/ directory

    E. /etc/bind/ directory

15. A zone database has resource records of various types. One such record identifies the authority zone's start and includes the zone's authoritative data. Which one of the following is this resource record type? (Choose the best answer.)

    A. CNAME

    B. A

    C. PTR

    D. NS

    E. SOA

16. Which of the following best describes a Reverse Zone? (Choose the best answer.)

   A. A record used in zone delegation, which provides a child zone's master name server's IP address

   B. The process of copying over authoritative zone information to a name server

   C. A special zone that provides a mapping from an IP address to an FQDN

   D. A zone directive typically located in the `named.conf` file, which has a `type hint` setting

   E. A Domain Name Space portion, which delineates what a name server has authority over

17. Which of the following are methods for securing your DNS services? (Choose all that apply.)

   A. Run only BIND services on the server.

   B. Run the BIND daemon as a non-root user.

   C. Implement a Dual Horizon server.

   D. Update your BIND software yearly.

   E. Hide BIND version information.

18. When setting up a chroot jail, the new root directory is typically which directory? (Choose two answers.)

   A. `/etc/bind/`

   B. `/etc/named/`

   C. `/var/bind/`

   D. `/chroot/named/`

   E. `/chroot/bind/`

19. In the BIND DNSSEC security extension, the encryption key used to digitally sign a particular zone's resource records is called what? (Choose the best answer.)

   A. Digital signature

   B. Key signing key

   C. Zone signing key

   D. Chain of trust

   E. DNSKEY

20. Which utility is used to create either TSIG or DNSSEC keys? (Choose the best answer.)

   A. `dnssec-keygen`

   B. `dnssec-signzone`

   C. `dnssec-dsfromkey`

   D. `dnssec-tsig-keygen`

   E. `tsig-keygen`

Chapter

9

Offering Web Services

THE FOLLOWING EXAM OBJECTIVES ARE COVERED IN THIS CHAPTER:

✓ **208.1 Basic Apache configuration**

✓ **208.2 Apache configuration for HTTPS**

✓ **208.3 Implementing Squid as a caching proxy**

✓ **208.4 Implementing Nginx as a web server and a reverse proxy**

The most popular use of Linux in the server environment is as a web server. Linux web servers dominate the Internet, and they are also very popular for hosting corporate intranet applications. Everything from serving static web pages to hosting dynamic web applications often runs faster and more efficiently on a Linux server platform.

This chapter looks at how to configure your Linux system to support different types of web server environments. First, it takes a look at just what a web server is and what software is required to convert your Linux server into a web server. Next, the chapter examines how to install and configure the Apache software package, which is the most popular web server in use today. Because the Apache software is so versatile, it can be somewhat confusing to set up. The chapter walks you through just what is needed to get your website up and running. After that, it covers how to implement the Squid proxy web server. Using a proxy web server helps out in environments that may need to cache web page access to save network bandwidth and increase performance. Finally, the chapter takes a look at the nginx web server, an up-and-coming web server product that's gaining in popularity thanks to some interesting new features.

What Is a Web Server?

Before we explore how to install and use a web server in Linux, let's first look at just why we need a web server and how they work. This section discusses the basics of what web servers are all about and the protocols that are required to run them.

Web Server Basics

The power behind the Internet is the free and open transfer of information. In the early days of the Internet, though, access to data files on remote systems required having a user login account as well as using complicated file transfer programs. To help with the open and speedy sharing of data, a new method of sharing files needed to be developed.

Enter the *Hypertext Transfer Protocol (HTTP)*. HTTP was developed to help out with the easy transfer of data anonymously between systems. For public data that doesn't need to be protected, HTTP allows a client to connect to a server anonymously, retrieve data files, and then disconnect. This process has greatly helped speed up retrieving data from the remote systems connected to the Internet, and it is what has made the Internet a popular place for sharing data.

However, anonymously moving text documents around still had its disadvantages. It was still cumbersome trying to find out what data was stored in which text files, and what text files needed to be retrieved from which servers. To solve that problem, a method of linking related data files together needed to be developed, and a new standard needed to be created.

The *Hypertext Markup Language (HTML)* provided just the interface needed to facilitate easy retrieval of information from multiple data files located on multiple servers. HTML allows authors to create documents that automatically link to other documents using hyperlinks. *Hyperlinks* reference remote files by specifying the server name and a path where to find the file. Authors just need to embed hyperlinks into their standard text documents to make it easy for readers to move from one document to another.

Another feature of HTML is the ability to format data presented within a text file. Word processing documents provide formatting of data (such as using different fonts and font styles) by embedding binary data inside the document. Unfortunately, you can't do that with text documents. Instead, HTML uses text tags to identify text formatting. The HTML standard defines tags for most standard page formatting needs, such as identifying headings, separating paragraphs, and applying simple font features such as boldfacing or italicizing text.

With the development of HTML for formatting text, all that was needed was an application that could access HTML documents and display them using the specified formatting. This is where *client browsers* and *web servers* came in. Browsers connect to a specified remote web server on a standard TCP port, retrieve the specified data file, and then apply the embedded HTML formatting tags to the data content in the file to display the document as intended by the author. The browser handles embedded hyperlinks by automatically going to the specified URL when the site visitor clicks the link.

The HTTP Standard

The developers who created HTTP decided to use a text-based client/server protocol to provide an easy way to transfer data between the server and clients. Because HTTP is text based, all commands are sent by the client in text, and all server responses are returned in text. Figure 9.1 shows a basic session between a client browser and a web server to retrieve a web page file.

FIGURE 9.1   Basic HTTP session

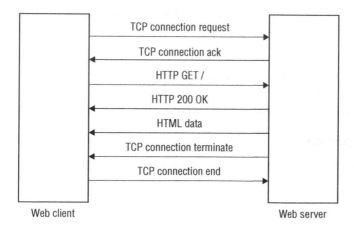

The browser sends an HTTP request to the web server, requesting a specific resource on the server. In turn, the web server returns a specially formatted HTTP response along with the data file. It helps to know the basic requests and responses, especially if you need to troubleshoot issues with a web connection. The following sections walk you through the basics of HTTP for both client requests and server responses.

Client Requests

Once an HTTP connection is established with a remote server, the client must send requests upon which the server can act. HTTP requests consist of a keyword, optionally followed by additional information that the server may need to process the request (such as the name of a file to return). Table 9.1 shows the standard HTTP client request keywords that are available.

TABLE 9.1   HTTP client requests

Request	Description
CONNECT	Convert the connection into a tunnel, usually for security.
DELETE	Delete the specified resource.
GET	Request the specified resource.
HEAD	Request the title of the specified resource.
OPTIONS	Retrieve the HTTP requests that the server supports.
PATCH	Apply a modification to a resource.
POST	Send specified data to the server for processing.
PUT	Store specified data at a specified location.
TRACE	Send the received request back to the client.

As shown in Figure 9.1, when you ask to view a web page from your client browser, the browser sends an HTTP GET request to the server, specifying the web page filename. The server then responds with a response code along with the requested data. If the client doesn't specify a filename in the GET request, most servers have a default file with which to respond.

Server Responses

With HTTP, the web server must respond to each client request received. If the client sends a request that the server can't process, the server must send some type of error code back to the client indicating that something went wrong.

The first part of the server response is a status code and text that the client uses to determine whether the submitted request was successful. The format of the HTTP response uses a three-digit status code followed by optional text message that the browser can display. The three-digit codes are broken down into five categories:

- 1xx—Informational messages
- 2xx—Success
- 3xx—Redirection
- 4xx—Client error
- 5xx—Server error

The three-digit status code is crucial to knowing just what happened with the response. There are lots of status codes defined in the HTTP standards, providing some detailed information on the status of client requests. Table 9.2 shows the standard HTTP server response codes defined.

TABLE 9.2   Common HTTP server response status codes

Status code	Text message
100	Continue
101	Switch Protocols
102	Processing Request
200	OK
201	Created
202	Accepted
206	Partial Content
207	Multi-Status
208	Already Reported
226	IM Used
300	Multiple Choices
301	Moved Permanently
302	Found

TABLE 9.2   Common HTTP server response status codes *(continued)*

Status code	Text message
303	See Other
304	Not Modified
305	Use Proxy
306	Switch Proxy
307	Temporary Redirect
308	Permanent Redirect
400	Bad Request
401	Unauthorized
402	Payment Required
403	Forbidden
404	Not Found
405	Method Not Allowed
406	Not Acceptable
407	Proxy Authentication Required
408	Request Timeout
409	Conflict
410	Gone
411	Length Required
412	Precondition Failed
413	Payload Too Large
414	URI Too Long
415	Unsupported Media Type

Status code	Text message
416	Range Not Satisfiable
417	Expectation Failed
418	I'm a Teapot
421	Misdirected Request
422	Unprocessable Entity
423	Locked
424	Failed Dependency
426	Upgrade Required
428	Precondition Required
429	Too Many Requests
431	Request Header Fields Too Large
451	Unavailable for Legal Reasons
500	Internal Server Error
501	Not Implemented
502	Bad Gateway
503	Service Unavailable
504	Gateway Timeout
505	HTTP Version Not Supported
506	Variant Also Negotiates
507	Insufficient Storage
508	Loop Detected
510	Not Extended
511	Network Authentication Required

As you can see from Table 9.2, a web server can return many possible responses. It's the client's job to parse the response and determine the next action to take.

If the response indicates that the request was successful, the server will follow the response with the data from the request, such as the contents of an HTML file. The client must then display the requested file, applying the HTML formatting tags to the data.

Secure HTTP

As mentioned, by default HTTP uses a text-based request/response method. While that helps simplify the communication between the client and the server, it doesn't provide any type of security to protect the communication. For applications that require security, instead of using a different protocol, web servers use encryption to encrypt the standard HTTP network traffic.

HTTP Secure (HTTPS) uses shared key encryption to encrypt the traffic sent across the network between the client and the server. It uses the standard HTTP client requests and server responses, but it encrypts the requests and responses at the network level to help prevent network snooping.

To encrypt the communication stream, the client and server must agree on an encryption protocol and pass an encryption key. In the past, the *Secure Sockets Layer (SSL)* protocol was used to encrypt the data, but because of its limitations, the *Transport Layer Security (TLS)* protocol is becoming more popular.

With either encryption protocol, before the secure communication can start, the client and server must pass a shared encryption key that both can use. HTTP uses the public/private key method for encryption. The server contains a private key that only it has. It passes a public key to each client that wants to communicate with the server. It's the client's responsibility to validate that the public key the server passes is valid and that the server is authentic. That's done using a *digital certificate*. A server requests that a well-known *certificate authority (CA)* digitally sign the certificate, validating the authenticity of the server. The client browser software trusts the CA and, in turn, trusts the public key to use for communication. Figure 9.2 demonstrates this process.

FIGURE 9.2   The HTTPS communication process

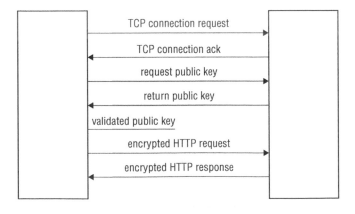

TCP connection request

TCP connection ack

request public key

return public key

validated public key

encrypted HTTP request

encrypted HTTP response

In HTTPS, the client first establishes an unencrypted connection to the web server using a special TCP port (443). The server accepts the connection, and then it negotiates a common encryption protocol that both the server and client support. Once that is determined, the server sends the public key as part of a signed certificate. The client contacts the CA to validate the certificate and, if accepted, trusts the public key and uses it for encrypting traffic to the server.

The CA is vital to this process. The browser must trust that the CA validates the web server, and it vouches that the web pages are safe to view. All commercial browsers have a list of trusted CAs, which are frequently updated using patches to the browser software.

Linux Web Servers

Many different types of web server software packages are available for the Linux platform. Fortunately, the LPIC-2 exam focuses on only three web server platforms commonly used in the Linux environment:

- Apache
- Squid
- Nginx

This section provides some background on each server and how to use it in your network environment.

Apache

By far the most popular web server on the Internet today is the *Apache* web server application. It is an open source project, maintained by the Apache Software Foundation. Since it's open source, it is available free of charge for any purpose, both commercial and private, and it now is commonly included in most Linux distribution repositories, making it easy to install.

Over the years, the Apache web server project has pioneered many new features that define just what web servers should support:

Loadable Dynamic Modules The ability to activate and deactivate features on the fly as the web server is running.

Scalable Multisession Support The ability to handle easily multiple client requests at the same time is crucial for modern web servers.

Limiting Concurrent Connections While multiuser support is crucial, so is the ability to limit the number of clients that can connect at the same time to help prevent system overload.

Bandwidth Throttling The ability to regulate the output from the web server to prevent overloading the network, even if the system can handle more connections.

Web Caching (Also Called Web Proxy)   The ability to store web pages requested by multiple clients and read additional requests from the cache rather than from the original data source.

Load Balancing (Also Called Reverse Proxy)   The ability to act as a single point of connection for clients and then redirect requests to multiple backend servers for processing.

Common Gateway Interface   The ability to forward web page content to internal server programs, commonly used for processing embedded scripting code.

Virtual Hosting   The ability to host multiple domains on a single web server.

User-Based Web Page Hosting   Allows individual users on the system to host their own web pages.

With Apache, all of these features, plus a lot more, are easily enabled or disabled using simple text-based configuration files.

One confusing issue with the Apache web server is that currently two separate versions are supported. The 1.3.x version thread supports older installations of the Apache web server. It's mostly maintained to support bug fixes and security patches for legacy systems. New Apache web server installations should use the 2.x version thread. Most Linux distributions differentiate the two versions by calling the 2.x version by the name *Apache2*. The LPIC-2 exam (and thus this chapter) focuses on the Apache2 version features.

Squid

The *Squid* web server performs not as much as a stand-alone web server but as a *web proxy* server. A web proxy server intercepts HTTP requests from multiple clients on a network before they leave the network. It then resends the requests directly to the remote destination, waits for the response, and then forwards the response back to the client. While this may seem counterproductive, there are two benefits of this process:

- The web proxy server can filter client requests to block those that the network administrators deem inappropriate.

- The web proxy server can cache the remote server responses. If another client makes the same request, the web proxy server can return the cached data instead of having to re-download the data from the remote server. This can both speed up web page performance and save network bandwidth.

Figure 9.3 shows a basic diagram of how this process works.

The Squid web proxy server has become the de facto web proxy server used in Linux environments. Most Linux distributions include it in the standard software repository, making it easy to install and set up.

FIGURE 9.3   The Squid web proxy server

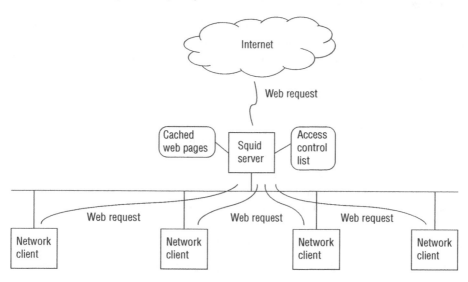

Nginx

While it too can operate as a standard web server, the *nginx* (pronounced "engine-X") web server is better known as a *reverse proxy* server. As you can probably guess, a reverse proxy server does the opposite of what a web proxy server does. Instead of processing requests from multiple clients to a single web server, a reverse proxy server processes requests from a single client to multiple web servers. This technique is also known as *load balancing*.

A load balancing server receives HTTP requests from clients and sends them to a specific server in a pool of common web servers for processing. Each web server in the pool contains the same data and can process the same HTTP requests. The load balancing process helps distribute the client load on multiple web servers in a high-traffic environment, helping prevent overloading and slow performance.

The remainder of this chapter walks you through how to install and set up each of these web servers in your Linux environment.

The Apache Web Server

With the overall popularity of the Apache web server, most Linux distributions have installation packages that make setting up a basic Apache web server easy. The difficult part comes if you need to customize special features. This section walks you through both the installation of a basic Apache web server setup and how to dig into the Apache configuration files to help you customize your web environment.

Installing an Apache Server

As mentioned, most Linux server distributions include the Apache web server software as easy-to-install software packages. For example, in Debian-based Linux distributions, the Apache web server package is called apache2. You install the basic Apache server using a single package:

```
$ sudo apt-get install apache2
```

This installs the latest version of the Apache 2.x web server supported by the Linux distribution. Once you install the Apache server in Debian-based systems, the installation package automatically configures the server to start at boot time and serve data files from the /var/www/html folder on the server.

After the Apache server is running, you can open a browser and connect to your Linux server. Figure 9.4 shows the default index.html file that is created for Ubuntu.

FIGURE 9.4   The default Apache web page for Ubuntu

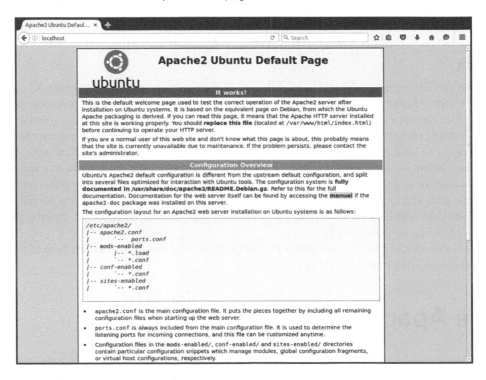

For Red Hat–based Linux distributions, the Apache package is called httpd. (This is because the name of the Apache server program is httpd.) You can use the standard yum package installer to install it:

```
# yum install httpd
```

While not specified in the filename, this is the Apache 2.x version of the server. Unlike Debian-based Linux distributions, the Red Hat package doesn't automatically start the Apache web server, nor does it start it at boot time. To do that, you'll need to use the `systemctl` command:

```
# systemctl start httpd
# systemctl enable httpd
```

Often you'll see the Apache web server referred to as `httpd`, which is the name of the executable program. To avoid confusion, some Linux distributions rename the executable file to apache2.

The Red Hat–based distributions also serve data files from the /var/www/html folder by default. Figure 9.5 shows the default index.html file that is created for CentOS.

FIGURE 9.5   The default Apache web page for CentOS

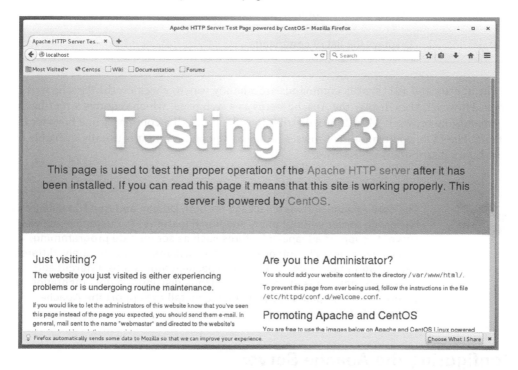

You can start, stop, restart, and check the status of the Apache program using the apache2ctl utility (some Red Hat–based distributions, such as CentOS, use apachectl even for the 2.x versions). Table 9.3 shows the commands that you can use with apache2ctl.

TABLE 9.3   The apache2ctl utility commands

Command	Description
start	Starts the Apache server
stop	Stops the Apache server, terminating any active connections
restart	Sends a SIGHUP signal to the Apache server to restart it, closing any existing connections
fullstatus	Displays a full status report from the Apache server
status	Displays a short status report from the Apache server
graceful	Restarts the Apache server, but existing connections are not terminated
graceful-stop	Stops the Apache server, but existing connections are not terminated
configtest	Parses the configuration files and reports any syntax errors
help	Displays the list of commands

The status and fullstatus commands are a handy way to check on the Apache web server. However, they display the Apache status as a web page, which requires a text-based command-line browser. Most Linux distributions don't install a command-line browser by default. The Lynx command-line browser is the most popular, and it is usually available in most Linux distribution repositories.

The core Apache software package for both Debian and Red Hat installs a basic web server without many additional features. To customize the web server to support advanced features such as server-side programming, you'll have to install additional software packages. Unfortunately, different Linux distributions bundle different Apache features into different software packages. Consult your specific Linux distribution documentation to determine which packages you need to install to support the Apache features that you want to use.

Configuring the Apache Server

A great feature of the Apache web server is that it uses simple text-based configuration files to manage the behavior of the server. The configuration file controls every feature of the server, giving you complete control over just how the Apache web server operates.

Unfortunately, though, there isn't a standard location or filename for the Apache configuration file. The main locations and files that you'll need to remember are listed here:

/etc/apache/apache.conf—Apache 1.3.x installation for Debian-based distributions

/etc/apache2/apache2.conf—Apache2 installation for Debian-based distributions

/etc/httpd/conf/httpd.conf—Apache 1.3.x and 2.x installation for most Red Hat–based distributions

/etc/httpd/conf/httpd2.conf—Apache 2.x installation for some distributions

Another confusing issue that you'll most likely run into is that not all of the Apache configuration settings are necessarily stored in one configuration file. Often, Linux distributions move configuration settings for separate features into their own configuration files and use the INCLUDE directive in the main configuration file to include them in the configuration. You will need to consult the documentation for your specific Linux distribution on how the Apache configuration files are arranged.

The following sections walk you through some of the different configuration settings that you'll run into in standard Apache configurations.

Basic Setup

When you look inside an Apache configuration file the first time, you'll see many lines that start with a pound sign (#). The pound sign denotes a comment line, allowing you to embed comments within the configuration file.

You define actual configuration settings using a directive keyword and then optionally a value for the setting, such as this:

```
DocumentRoot "/var/www/html"
```

This directive sets the default folder for the Apache server to the /var/www/html folder on the Linux server. As you peruse the configuration file, you'll see lots of directives setting basic features for the server. Table 9.4 shows the main settings in which you'll be interested.

TABLE 9.4   Common Apache configuration directives

Directive	Description
Listen	The TCP port (and optional IP address) to listen for client requests
User	The user account used to start the Apache server daemon
Group	The group account used to start the Apache server daemon
ServerAdmin	Email address of the server administrator

TABLE 9.4   Common Apache configuration directives *(continued)*

Directive	Description
ServerName	The domain name of the server.
ServerRoot	The location of the base configuration files.
DocumentRoot	The location of the default data folder.
DirectoryIndex	The default file served when a client requests an index of a directory.
ErrorDocument	The file to serve when a specific error type occurs.
ErrorLog	The log file location to use for logging error messages.
LogFormat	The format of each log file entry.
AccessFileName	The file that lists restrictions on web page files in a folder.
Include	Includes configuration settings defined in an external file.
StartServers	The number of servers to start to handle concurrent requests.
MaxClients	The maximum number of servers to handle concurrent requests.
MinSpareServers	The minimum number of extra servers to have running.
MaxSpareServers	The maximum number of extra servers to have running.
LoadModule	Load and enable the specified feature module into the server.

By default, settings that you define in the main configuration area are called *global settings*. They apply to the main Apache web server when it starts.

You can also define *conditional settings*, which apply only when specific conditions are met, such as if an environment variable is defined.

You define conditional settings as a block of directives. The block uses the following format:

```
<IfDefine variable>
    Directive
</IfDefine>
```

The <IfDefine> marker defines the start of the block, and the </IfDefine> marker defines the end of the block. The Apache server processes only the directives listed in the block if the variable is set.

Likewise, you can use *module settings* that apply only when specific modules are loaded. The <IfModule> condition specifies directives that are processed only when a specified module is loaded using the LoadModule directive.

Finally, you can use *directory settings*, which apply only to specific directories on the server. The <Directory> condition specifies the directives that apply only to the directory path specified in the setting:

```
<Directory /var/www/html/mydata>
  Directive
</Directory>
```

The directives specified in this block apply only when clients attempt to access files stored in that folder.

Apache Logs

The Apache web server creates two types of log files by default:

- Error logs
- Access logs

As you can probably guess, the *error log* keeps track of any errors that occur while the Apache web server is running. The location of the error log is defined using the ErrorDocument directive in the configuration file. Usually, the error log is located in the /var/log/apache2/error.log file in Debian-based Linux distributions and the /var/log/httpd/error_log file in Red Hat–based Linux distributions. (Note the underscore instead of the period in the filename.)

You can customize the format for entries in the error log using the LogFormat directive in the configuration file. By default, error log entries look like this:

```
[Sat Apr 16 14:58:47.516853 2016] [auth_digest:notice] [pid 4067] AH01757:
generating secret for digest authentication …
[Sat Apr 16 14:58:47.517883 2016] [lbmethod_heartbeat:notice] [pid 4067]
AH02282: No slotmem from mod_heartmonitor
[Sat Apr 16 14:58:47.599436 2016] [mpm_prefork:notice] [pid 4067] AH00163:
Apache/2.4.6 (CentOS) configured—resuming normal operations
[Sat Apr 16 14:58:47.599640 2016] [core:notice] [pid 4067] AH00094: Command
line: '/usr/sbin/httpd -D FOREGROUND'
```

Notice that the entries in the error log aren't necessarily all errors. In this example, the Apache web server is documenting notices that appear when it starts up.

The *access log* is normally located in the same folder as the error log, and it is called either access.log (for Debian-based distributions) or access_log (for Red Hat–based distributions). It documents all requests made by clients. By default, the access log entries look like this:

```
::1-- [23/Apr/2016:14:58:54 -0400] "GET / HTTP/1.1" 403 4897 "-"
"Mozilla/5.0 (X11; Linux x86_64; rv:38.0) Gecko/20100101 Firefox/38.0"
```

```
::1-- [23/Apr/2016:14:58:54 -0400] "GET /noindex/css/bootstrap.min.css
HTTP/1.1" 200 19341 "http://localhost/" "Mozilla/5.0 (X11; Linux x86_64;
 rv:38.0) Gecko/20100101 Firefox/38.0"
::1-- [23/Apr/2016:14:58:54 -0400] "GET /noindex/css/open-sans.css
 HTTP/1.1" 200 5081 "http://localhost/" "Mozilla/5.0 (X11; Linux x86_64;
 rv:38.0) Gecko/20100101 Firefox/38.0"
::1-- [23/Apr/2016:14:58:54 -0400] "GET /images/apache_pb.gif HTTP/1.1"
 200 2326 "http://localhost/" "Mozilla/5.0 (X11; Linux x86_64; rv:38.0)
 Gecko/20100101 Firefox/38.0"
::1-- [23/Apr/2016:14:58:54 -0400] "GET /images/poweredby.png HTTP/1.1"
 200 3956 "http://localhost/" "Mozilla/5.0 (X11; Linux x86_64; rv:38.0)
 Gecko/20100101 Firefox/38.0"
```

The access log not only documents the file request, but it can also document the browser type of the client, the OS of the client, and the IP address. (This example uses IPv6 addressing of `::1` for the localhost.) You can customize the output using the `LogFormat` directive as well.

User Web Hosting

The default configuration for most Linux distribution Apache servers is to provide one location for hosting files (called the *DocumentRoot*). The `DocumentRoot` directive defines this location, and for both Debian and Red Hat–based distributions it is set by default to the /var/www/html folder. Any files or folders that you want to make available to web clients are normally placed under that folder structure.

The Apache web server also provides a feature that allows each individual user on the Linux system to host their own files. To enable this feature, add the `UserDir` directive to the global configuration settings. The `UserDir` directive specifies the name of the folder in each user's `HOME` folder where they can host files. The most common setting is

```
UserDir public_html
```

To access files in the user's `public_html` folder, you must specify the username in the URL. For example, to access the file /home/rich/public_html/test.html, you'd use the URL http://localhost/~rich/test.html.

To allow access to files in your `public_html` folder, you must grant read and execute privileges to the user or group account that runs the Apache web server. Not only will that user or group need read and execute privileges to the `public_html` folder, but it will also require these privileges for the user's `HOME` folder as well. This can make things somewhat complicated for protecting other files in the user's `HOME` folder.

Virtual Web Hosting

The basic configuration for an Apache web server assumes that the host is serving files for a single server, namely, the server name or IP address on which the Apache software is running. However, Apache also allows you to host web pages for multiple domain names or IP addresses on a single physical server. This is ideal for businesses that support multiple customers, such as Internet service providers.

The ability to host multiple web environments on a single physical server is called *virtual web hosting*. There are two ways to implement virtual web hosting in Apache:

- Name-based virtual hosting
- IP-based virtual hosting

With *name-based virtual hosting*, the physical server has multiple hostnames that point to its IP address in the DNS system (see Chapter 8, "Directing DNS"). You then must configure the Apache web server to use separate directories based on the hostname that the client uses in the URL request to connect. You can do that by using the `NameVirtualHost` directive and separate `<VirtualHost>` blocks, one for each virtual host:

```
NameVirtualHost 192.168.1.77

<VirtualHost 192.168.1.77>
    ServerName www.myhost1.com
    DocumentRoot /var/www/html/host1
</VirtualHost>

<VirtualHost 192.168.1.77>
    ServerName www.myhost2.com
    DocumentRoot /var/www/html/host2
</VirtualHost>
```

The `NameVirtualHost` directive defines the IP address on which the server listens. Then you must create a separate `<VirtualHost>` block to define the IP address and use the `ServerName` directive to define the hostname that the client uses in the request. Each separate hostname points to a different DocumentRoot area by specifying separate `DocumentRoot` directives.

With *IP-based virtual hosting*, the server must listen for incoming requests on multiple IP addresses. Each IP address is assigned a different hostname in the DNS system. Again, with IP-based virtual hosting, you must define multiple IP addresses on the server either by having separate physical network cards in the server or by defining multiple IP addresses for the same network interface using the `ifconfig` network command.

After you configure your Linux server to support multiple IP addresses, you must configure the Apache web server to listen to each IP address using multiple `Listen` directives.

After that, just define separate `<VirtualHost>` blocks to define the hostname and DocumentRoot area for each IP address:

```
Listen 192.168.1.77:80
Listen 192.168.1.78:80
<VirtualHost www.myhost1.com>
    Servername www.myhost1.com
    DocumentRoot /var/www/html/myhost1
</VirtualHost>
<VirtualHost www.myhost2.com>
    Servername www.myhost2.com
    DocumentRoot /var/www/html/myhost2
</VirtualHost>
```

One advantage to IP-based virtual hosting is that you can have two separate Apache programs running at the same time, each one listening on a different IP address. Each Apache program can have a separate configuration, making it easier to separate out settings for each server.

Access Restriction

While the original intention of web servers was to provide easy access to public data, there are times when it would be handy to provide restricted access to data, such as a corporate intranet application. The Apache web server provides a few different methods for implementing authentication, forcing clients to log in before granting access to documents based on the provided authentication.

Apache provides authentication features using separate loadable modules. The LPIC-2 exam specifies the mod_auth and mod_auth_basic modules, which provided authentication using a text-based file that lists user accounts and encrypted passwords. However, that module has been replaced as of Apache 2.1 with other more advanced modules. The more common authentication modules in newer versions of Apache are these:

mod_authn_file—Uses a text-based file to list user accounts and encrypted passwords for access (the direct replacement for mod_auth)

mod_authn_anon—Uses a list of usernames but no passwords to restrict access

mod_authn_db—Uses a Berkeley database format file to list user accounts and passwords to restrict access

mod_authn_dbm—Uses a Unix dbm-formatted database file to list user accounts and passwords to restrict access

mod_authnz_ldap—Uses an LDAP network database for user authentication

mod_authnz_mysql—Uses a MySQL database for user authentication

mod_access—Uses a list of IP address, hostnames, or domains to restrict access

mod_access_compat—Uses the client's hostname or IP address to restrict access

mod_authz_host—Uses the client's hostname or IP address to restrict access

The mod_auth method (now called mod_authn_file) uses a text-based user file that's created using the htpasswd utility in Apache. To add a new user account to the authentication user file, specify the file using the -c option; then specify the user account to add as follows:

```
# htpasswd -c /var/www/html/passwords rich
New password:
Re-type new password:
Adding password for user rich
#
```

Once you create the user file, you must reference it in the Apache configuration file to use for authentication. There are two approaches to doing that.

One method is to add the authentication configuration settings in the <Directory> section for the block that you need to protect in the main Apache configuration file:

```
<Directory /var/www/html>
    AuthName "Restricted Area"
    AuthType Basic
    AuthUserFile /var/www/html/passwords
    Require valid-user
    DocumentRoot /var/www/html
</Directory>
```

You need a few different directives to tell Apache about the authentication protection. The AuthName directive provides the title of the login dialog box that appears when it asks for the userid and password. The AuthUserFile directive points to the password file created using the htpasswd utility. When a user attempts to access a file in that folder, the browser will produce a login dialog box, as shown in Figure 9.6.

FIGURE 9.6   Basic web page authentication

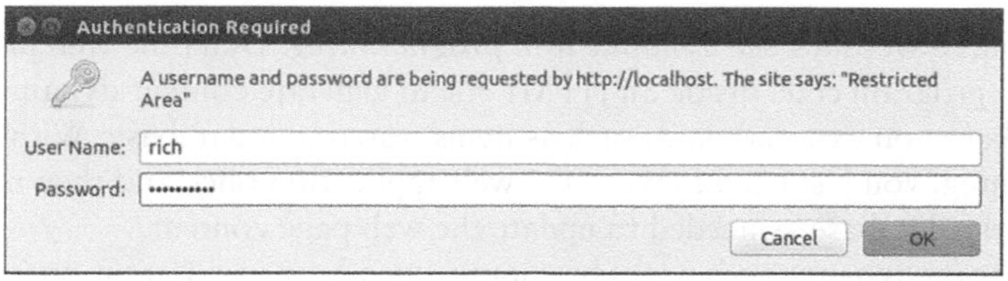

The other method to provide basic authentication is to use a special filename called .htaccess in the folder that you need to protect. The .htaccess file contains the same authentication directives that you used in the main configuration file. To tell Apache to

use the .htaccess file, the <Directory> block must contain the AllowOverride directive. Using the .htaccess file decentralizes the authentication configurations instead of placing them all in the main configuration file.

 There's also an AuthGroupFile directive that allows you to bundle user accounts into groups. You can then grant the entire group access to specific areas on the web server.

The mod_access authentication method is another popular way to restrict access to web pages. Instead of using a userid/password challenge, it allows you to restrict pages based on the IP address of the clients. It uses simple Deny and Allow directives to list individual IP addresses or network addresses to deny or allow access. Here's an example of using that method:

```
<Directory /var/www/html>
    Order Deny,Allow
    Deny from All
    Allow from 192.168.1.0/255.255.255.0
    DocumentRoot /var/www/html
</Directory>
```

The Order directive determines which rule set is checked first. In this example, you first set it to deny (block) all clients but then allow only clients that are on the 192.168.1.0 subnet.

Hosting Dynamic Web Applications

In the old days, all content provided in web pages was static. To update the information on your website, you had to open the appropriate HTML file manually, enter the changes to the content, and then save the new version. In these days of constantly changing content, that just doesn't work. It would be impossible for a large online store to have programmers making manual changes to web pages for each new product that comes in.

Instead, modern websites use *dynamic web programming*. Dynamic web programming uses embedded program code inside an HTML file to generate content dynamically. Often, the content is based on external data, such as items stored in a database. With dynamic web programming, you just need to write the web application once and then modify the data stored in the database as needed to update the web page content.

Apache supports dynamic web pages by supporting a host of different programming languages. There are, however, two different ways that Apache does that. The following sections describe each of these methods and show how to implement them in your Apache web server.

The Common Gateway Interface

The simple way for the Apache web server to process program code is to pass it off to another program to process. The Apache server acts as a gateway to the main program interpreter. This feature in Apache is thus called the *Common Gateway Interface (CGI)*.

The CGI feature uses the filename extension to detect when a web page file has embedded code, and then it passes the file off to an external program language interpreter based on the filename extension. The interpreter then processes the code, and it passes any output from the interpreter back to the Apache web server to send to the client as content. The output must be standard HTML code for the client to process it as a web page.

The programming languages that you can use with CGI are limited only by the languages that are installed on your Linux system. Because of the text nature of HTML pages, CGI applications commonly use scripting languages, such as Perl, Python, and Bash shell scripts. However, there are CGI interfaces for more advanced languages, such as C and C++.

To configure Apache to pass code to an external interpreter, you must first have the CGI feature installed in your Apache setup. For Debian-based Linux distributions, running Perl scripts means installing the `libapache2-mod-perl2` module. For Red Hat–based distributions, it's the `perl-CGI` module.

After you install the appropriate module, you must make some changes to the Apache configuration file. You'll need to add the `ScriptAlias` directive to point to the folder that can contain scripts and the `AddHandler` directive to tell Apache which filenames to process with CGI:

```
ScriptAlias /cgi-bin/ /var/www/cgi-bin
AddHandler cgi-script .cgi .pl
```

These lines allow you to place Perl scripts in the `/var/www/cgi-bin` folder. The scripts must end with the `.pl` file extension for the Apache server to process them properly. Also, the scripts must start with a line that invokes the required language interpreter:

```
#!/usr/bin/perl
```

This tells the bash shell to invoke the Perl interpreter to process the script.

Programming Modules

A faster way of handling embedded program scripts in web pages is to use installable modules. Apache includes modules for most popular web programming languages, such as these:

- `mod_perl`
- `mod_php`
- `mod_python`
- `mod_ruby`

The tricky part of using Apache programming modules is finding them in the Linux distribution. In Red Hat–based distributions, the PHP module package is just called `php`, while the Perl module package is called mod_perl. For Debian, you'll need the php5 and libapache2-mod-php5 packages for PHP and the libapache2-mod-perl2 package for Perl.

The nice thing about using the module packages is that they usually do all of the configuration work for you. For example, after installing the PHP module, you should see some new lines in your Apache configuration file:

```
LoadModule php5_module modules.libphp5.so
AddHandler php5-script .php
AddType application/x-httpd-php .php
DirectoryIndex index.html index.php
```

The AddHandler directive tells the Apache server that the PHP module should redirect files ending with the .php file extension to the PHP server process.

> **WARNING**   Adding program processing to the Apache web server does open your server to additional attack entry points. Be careful when adding these features. For CGI, make sure that you restrict scripts to a specific folder and monitor the scripts placed in that folder for unauthorized activity. For program modules such as PHP and Perl, you have to be more careful, because any document served on the server can contain embedded program code.

Creating a Secure Web Server

Protecting data transmitted across the Internet has become a high priority for most corporations. Using HTTPS for any type of transaction that involves personal information is a must.

The Apache web server supports HTTPS sessions, but it requires quite a bit of work. You must have a private/public key pair to use for the encryption plus have a signed certificate to pass your public key to clients. Creating an HTTPS server with Apache involves six steps:

1. Install the Apache SSL module (or install an Apache package that has it built in).
2. Create a public/private key.
3. Create a Certificate Signing Request (CSR).
4. Have the CSR signed by a trusted CA to create a certificate.
5. Install the certificate and key files in your Apache setup.
6. Configure Apache to use the certificate.

The following sections walk you through each of these steps in getting your Apache web server to use HTTPS.

Install SSL

To use SSL encryption on your Linux system, you'll first need to ensure that the mod_ssl Apache module is installed. Some Linux distributions provide a completely separate Apache installation package that has SSL built in, but usually you can install the standard Apache package and the mod_ssl package.

Besides SSL support for Apache, you'll need the OpenSSL software package installed. The OpenSSL package is a popular open source software package that provides SSL encryption capabilities for many network applications.

For Debian-based distributions, the mod_ssl module is normally installed as part of the Apache2 basic installation. For Red Hat–based distributions, you'll need to install the mod_ssl package separately using yum.

The openssl package may or may not already be installed on your Linux distribution. If it is not, you can install it using apt-get or yum.

> The SSL configuration file and certificate files are normally installed in the /etc/ssl folder. However, some Linux distributions use the /etc/pki folder.

Create an Encryption Key

Once you have OpenSSL installed, you can create the *encryption key* used to encrypt the SSL traffic. The openssl command to do that looks like this:

```
$ openssl genrsa -des3 -out server.key 2048
Generating RSA private key, 2048 bit long modulus
.....................................................................
+++..........+++
e is 65537 (0x10001)
Enter pass phrase for server.key:
Verifying–Enter pass phrase for server.key:
$
```

The command creates a 2048-bit RSA key using 3DES encryption and stores it in the server.key file in the current folder.

> The passphrase that you set for the key is very important. You will need to enter it every time the key is used. If you forget the passphrase, you won't be able to use the private key anymore. A drawback to this is that you will need to enter the passphrase each time the Apache server starts at boot up. To avoid that, you can remove the passphrase after you create the key using this command:
>
> ```
> $ openssl rsa -in server.key -out newserver.key
> ```

Create a Certificate Signing Request

The next step is to create a *Certificate Signing Request (CSR)* with the private key that you just created. The CSR contains your key so that the CA can authenticate it and create a certificate that contains your public key. Again, thanks to the openssl utility, this is a simple process:

```
$ openssl req -new -key server.key -out newreq.pem
Enter pass phrase for server.key:
You are about to be asked to enter information that will be incorporated
into your certificate request.
What you are about to enter is what is called a Distinguished Name or a DN.
There are quite a few fields but you can leave some blank
For some fields there will be a default value,
If you enter '.', the field will be left blank.
---
Country Name (2 letter code) [AU]:US
State or Province Name (full name) [Some-State]:Illinois
Locality Name (eg, city) []:Chicago
Organization Name (eg, company) [Internet Widgits Pty Ltd]:Rich Blum
Organizational Unit Name (eg, section) []:
Common Name (e.g. server FQDN or YOUR name) []:Rich Blum
Email Address []:

Please enter the following 'extra' attributes
to be sent with your certificate request
A challenge password []:
An optional company name []:
$
```

You must enter data identifying you (or your company) in the CSR. The Common Name is used to identify either you or your server. The name of the output file is important. In the next step, the CA signing tool will look for the newreq.pem file.

Sign the CSR

A CA validates that the key enclosed in the CSR is trustworthy. Because of that, commercial CA companies usually charge a fee to perform a simple check on you or your company, validating that you are who you say you are. The benefit of that, though, is that they produce a certificate file that your customers know is valid and thus are happy to use your website. Most browsers incorporate certificates for the big-name CA companies so that they trust certificates signed by them. If the CA you use isn't trusted, the browser will produce an ugly warning message to your website visitors, possibly scaring them away from your website.

However, for testing purposes, you don't necessarily need to use a commercial CA to sign your CSR. Instead, you can sign your own CSR, which in essence means that you're validating yourself. You'll just need to validate your certificate in your browser when you connect to your website. This is called a *self-signed certificate.*

To create a self-signed certificate, use the openssl utility. The command line to create a CA is somewhat complicated, but fortunately the OpenSSL package includes a Perl script called CA.pl that walks you through the process.

First, you need to establish yourself as a CA:

```
$ /usr/lib/ssl/misc/CA.pl -newca
CA certificate filename (or enter to create)

Making CA certificate …
Generating a 2048 bit RSA private key
..............................................................................
...................................................+++
..............................................................................
..................................................+++
writing new private key to './demoCA/private/cakey.pem'
Enter PEM pass phrase:
Verifying—Enter PEM pass phrase:
—-
You are about to be asked to enter information that will be incorporated
into your certificate request.
What you are about to enter is what is called a Distinguished Name or a DN.
There are quite a few fields but you can leave some blank
For some fields there will be a default value,
If you enter '.', the field will be left blank.
—-
Country Name (2 letter code) [AU]:US
State or Province Name (full name) [Some-State]:Illinois
Locality Name (eg, city) []:Chicago
Organization Name (eg, company) [Internet Widgits Pty Ltd]:Rich Blum
Organizational Unit Name (eg, section) []:
Common Name (e.g. server FQDN or YOUR name) []:Rich Blum
Email Address []:

Please enter the following 'extra' attributes
to be sent with your certificate request
A challenge password []:
An optional company name []:
Using configuration from /usr/lib/ssl/openssl.cnf
Enter pass phrase for ./demoCA/private/cakey.pem:
Check that the request matches the signature
Signature ok
```

```
Certificate Details:
        Serial Number: 10204964800000470641 (0x8d9f516ad964ae71)
        Validity
            Not Before: Apr 25 19:20:59 2016 GMT
            Not After: Apr 25 19:20:59 2019 GMT
        Subject:
            countryName              = US
            stateOrProvinceName      = Illinois
            organizationName         = Rich Blum
            commonName               = Rich Blum
        X509v3 extensions:
            X509v3 Subject Key Identifier:
                8C:4E:C9:7A:66:2A:11:49:FF:4F:35:08:55:65:19:05:F5:44:91:4E
            X509v3 Authority Key Identifier:

keyid:8C:4E:C9:7A:66:2A:11:49:FF:4F:35:08:55:65:19:05:F5:44:91:4E

            X509v3 Basic Constraints:
                CA:TRUE
Certificate is to be certified until Apr 25 19:20:59 2019 GMT (1095 days)

Write out database with 1 new entries
Data Base Updated
$
```

Congratulations, now you're a CA! The next step is to use your new CA abilities to sign the CSR that you created earlier. Make sure that you're in the same folder as the newreq.pem file that you created earlier, and use this command:

```
$ /usr/lib/ssl/misc/CA.pl -signreq
Using configuration from /usr/lib/ssl/openssl.cnf
Enter pass phrase for ./demoCA/private/cakey.pem:
Check that the request matches the signature
Signature ok
Certificate Details:
        Serial Number: 10204964800000470642 (0x8d9f516ad964ae72)
        Validity
            Not Before: Apr 25 19:37:23 2016 GMT
            Not After: Apr 25 19:37:23 2017 GMT
        Subject:
            countryName              = US
            stateOrProvinceName      = Illinois
```

```
            localityName              = Chicago
            organizationName          = Rich Blum
            commonName                = Rich Blum
        X509v3 extensions:
            X509v3 Basic Constraints:
                CA:FALSE
            Netscape Comment:
                OpenSSL Generated Certificate
            X509v3 Subject Key Identifier:
                5C:3A:50:3B:DF:14:18:23:DC:EE:49:B9:43:DF:D2:4B:43:72:E2:9F
            X509v3 Authority Key Identifier:

keyid:8C:4E:C9:7A:66:2A:11:49:FF:4F:35:08:55:65:19:05:F5:44:91:4E


Certificate is to be certified until Apr 25 19:37:23 2017 GMT (365 days)
Sign the certificate? [y/n]:y

1 out of 1 certificate requests certified, commit? [y/n]y
Write out database with 1 new entries
Data Base Updated
Signed certificate is in newcert.pem
$
```

The signed certificate is now stored in the newcert.pem file in your folder. It contains the public key along with the self-signed CA certificate validating it.

Now you have the key file (server.key) and the signed certificate file (newcert.pem) that you need to implement SSL on your Apache web server.

Install the Key and Certificate

To use the key and certificate files in Apache, you'll want to place them in a secure location on your server that's readable by the Apache user account. It's usually a good idea to create a separate folder in the Apache configuration folder area to store the key and certificate files:

```
$ sudo mkdir /etc/apache2/certs
$ sudo cp server.key /etc/apache/certs
$ sudo cp newcert.pem /etc/apache/certs
```

Now that the key and certificate files are in place, the last step is to configure the Apache web server to use them.

Configure Apache to Use SSL

You're almost there—just a few more things to finish up. You'll need to point the VirtualHost block to the new key and certificate as well as enable SSL on the server itself.

First, look in the Apache configuration files for the Listen directive, and make sure that you have a separate line to listen on TCP port 443 for encrypted SSL connections:

```
Listen 443
```

Next, look for the <VirtualHost> block that defines the area that you want to protect with encrypted communication. In that block, add these new directives:

```
SSLEngine On
SSLCertificateFile    /etc/apache2/certs/newcert.pem
SSLCertificateKeyFile    /etc/apache2/certs/server.key
```

Save the new configuration files, and then stop and restart the Apache web server.

 Many Linux distributions automatically make these entries in Apache configuration files when you install the mod_ssl module. For Ubuntu, these entries are in the default-ssl.conf configuration file.

Now when you attempt to connect to the website using an https:// URL, you should get a warning from your browser about the self-signed certificate, as shown in Figure 9.7.

FIGURE 9.7   The self-signed certificate warning

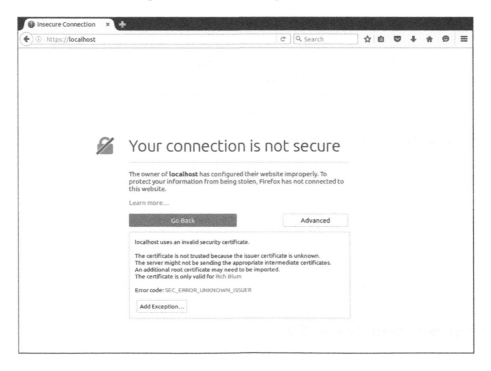

Select the option to accept the self-signed certificate. You'll then be passed to the web page. You can use the browser Certificate Manager to view your self-signed certificate, as shown in Figure 9.8.

FIGURE 9.8   Viewing the self-signed certificate in Firefox

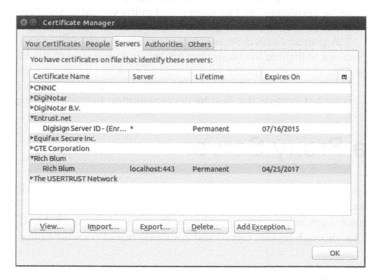

This is the basic setup to implement SSL in your Apache environment. There are, however, some additional SSL directives used in Apache that can help you customize the setup and that you may see on the LPIC-2 exam:

- `SSLCACertificateFile`—Points to a file that contains the CA certificate for validating client certificates

- `SSLCACertificatePath`—Points to a folder that contains the CA certificate for validating client certificates

- `SSLCertificateChainFile`—Points to a file that contains multiple concatenated CA certificates for validating client certificates

- `SSLProtocol`—Defines which version of SSL (or TLS) the server supports

- `SSLCipherSuite`—Defines one or more encryption protocols the server supports

- `ServerTokens`—Controls whether the server sends information about the OS in the server response sent to clients

- `ServerSignature`—Controls whether the server sends a short footer message on server-generated documents

- `TraceEnable`—Defines whether the server honors the `HTTP TRACE` command to debug sessions

The LPIC-2 exam topics note that you should be aware of an oddity when using SSL with name-based virtual hosting. When you create a CSR for a real CA, the Common Name entry should be the fully qualified domain name (FQDN) for your server. If you're using name-based virtual hosting, though, a single server can support multiple virtual hostnames, so the same certificate can't be used for all of the virtual hosts. You can use some tricks to get around this problem. One such solution is an extension to the SSL protocol called *Server Name Indication (SNI)*. SNI allows the network client to include the requested hostname in the start of the SSL handshake. This allows the Apache server to determine the correct certificate to use for the connection. If you need to implement SSL in a virtual hosting environment, consult the Apache documentation for detailed instructions.

Using a Proxy Server

The Squid web proxy server can be a useful tool in controlling bandwidth utilization for outbound Internet connections, as well as serving as a tool for restricting access to unauthorized web pages (such as preventing employees from watching YouTube all day long). This section walks through how to install and configure Squid on your Linux server.

Installing Squid

The Squid package has become popular enough that most Linux distributions now include it in their standard software repositories. You can load Squid in both Debian-based and Red Hat–based Linux distributions by installing the Squid package. The current version of Squid is 3.x, but the Squid package will install the latest version that's been approved by your distribution maintainers.

For Debian-based Linux distributions, the squid package automatically starts the Squid server. You can use the ps command to check to see if it's running:

```
$ ps ax | grep squid
 3734 ?        Ss     0:00 /usr/sbin/squid3 -N -YC -f /etc/squid3/squid.conf
 3743 ?        Ss     0:00 (logfile-daemon) /var/log/squid3/access.log
 3789 pts/0    S+     0:00 grep—color=auto squid
$
```

For Red Hat–based Linux distributions, you'll need to start the Squid server manually as well as set it to start at boot time:

```
# systemctl start squid
# ps ax | grep squid
 4209 ?        Ss     0:00 /usr/sbin/squid -f /etc/squid/squid.conf
 4214 ?        S      0:00 (squid-1) -f /etc/squid/squid.conf
```

```
4218 ?        S      0:00 (logfile-daemon) /var/log/squid/access.log
4328 pts/0    S+     0:00 grep--color=auto squid
# systemctl enable squid
Created symlink from /etc/systemd/system/multi-user.target.wants/squid.service
to /usr/lib/systemd/system/squid.service.
#
```

Unfortunately, unlike Apache, when you install Squid, it doesn't really do much of anything using the default configuration. It will listen to TCP port 3128 for incoming proxy requests, but it will just forward them out to the remote server without caching any of the returned content. You must change the default settings in the Squid configuration file to be able to use it effectively on your network.

Configuring Squid

The Squid configuration files are stored in the /etc/squid3 folder for Debian-based distributions and the /etc/squid folder for Red Hat–based distributions. The main configuration is the squid.conf file; however, similar to Apache, Squid supports the include directive, which allows you to store configuration settings in other files too. It's not uncommon to see several different configuration files in the Squid configuration folder.

The configuration file uses several different types of directives to control the behavior of the Squid server. The Squid server is very versatile and highly customizable, but there are a few basic configuration settings about which you'll need to be aware:

acl—Defines an access control list (ACL) to group similar entities for managing access

auth_param—Specifies a program to use to authenticate users

cache_dir—Specifies a folder on the hard drive to use to cache web requests, along with the amount of space to allocate for caching and the number of subdirectories to allow

http_access—Specifies a rule for allowing or denying access for an ACL group

http_port—Specifies the TCP port to which the Squid server listens for incoming connections

redirect_program—Specifies an external program to which you can redirect all web requests

The following sections show you how to use the directives to configure Squid to perform the web proxy features.

Web Cache

The basic use of Squid is as a web proxy server to cache outbound web requests for multiple clients on a network. To set up your Squid server to do that, you'll need to have two configuration directives:

```
http_port 3128
cache_dir ufs /var/spool/squid3 100 16 256
```

The http_port directive defines the TCP port to which clients must point their browsers. The cache_dir directive defines where and how Squid will store the cached web files. The first parameter defines the filesystem type (the *ufs* type that can be used for standard Linux filesystems). The second parameter defines where the cached files are stored. This can be either a folder name (as shown here in this Debian-based example), or it can be a partition name.

After that, the first number defines the total disk space (in MB) that Squid can use for caching. The second number defines the number of top-level folders that Squid can create in that folder, and the third number defines the maximum number of second-level folders that it can create. To speed up performance, Squid tries to place as few cache files in each folder as possible; thus, the more folders you allow, the better the performance you should experience.

Web Access Control

The other feature for which Squid is often used is controlling access to remote websites. It does this by allowing you to define an access control list and then apply the ACL to a blocking rule.

You define an ACL by using the acl directive:

```
acl ourhosts src 192.168.2.0/255.255.255.0
```

The acl directive first defines a name for the ACL. It then defines the type of ACL. There are several different ACL types to use:

src—A list of source IP addresses

dst—A list of destination IP addresses

port—A list of TCP ports

srcdomain—A list of source domain names

dstdomain—A list of destination domain names

time—A list of days or time-of-day

proto—A list of protocols

browser—A list of browser types

You can restrict or allow connections based on a source address or a destination address. This example defines the ACL for source addresses on our local subnet.

After you define the ACL, you use the http_access directive to define the rule that applies to the ACL:

```
http_access allow ourhosts
http_access deny all
```

These rules allow access to any client whose IP address matches the ourhosts ACL, but it denies access to anyone else.

The combination of ACLs and rules is a powerful tool in Squid. While it may take some time getting used to, once you have it mastered, you can fine-tune access for just about anything in your system, for example:

```
acl socialmedia dstdomain www.facebook.com www.twitter.com
acl lunch MTWHF 12:00-13:00
http_access allow socialmedia lunch
http_access deny socialmedia
```

The first ACL directive defines destination domains, while the second ACL directive defines a period of time (Monday, Tuesday, Wednesday, Thursday, and Friday, from 12 noon to 1 p.m.). The http_access directive applies the ACL to allow the rule, so access to these websites is allowed during that time frame. Attempting to access those hosts at any other time is denied.

WARNING   One of the more confusing parts of the Squid configuration is the default action taken by the server. The server takes the opposite action of the last http_access rule in the configuration as the default action. Thus, if the last rule defined is an allow, the default action is to block (deny) access. Likewise, if the last rule defined is a deny, the default action is to allow access. Be careful when adding new rules to your configuration files.

Client Authentication

The Squid server also allows you to set up an authentication method to force clients to authenticate and then apply ACL rules to individual clients based on their authentication. The auth_param directive defines the authentication method the Squid server should use to authenticate the clients.

The auth_param directive is somewhat confusing because you use the same directive to define multiple settings for the authentication method. For example, you may see a group of entries like this:

```
auth_param basic /usr/lib/squid/pam_auth
auth_param basic children 5 startup=5 idle=1
auth_param basic realm Squid proxy-caching web server
auth_param basic credentialsttl 2 hours
```

This tells Squid to use the system PAM authentication method to authenticate clients along with a few parameters to define how to handle authentications.

After defining the authentication type, you can apply authentication to the rules you want:

```
acl ourhosts proxy_auth REQUIRED
```

This applies authentication to the previously defined ourhosts ACL. Anyone on the local network must authenticate to the proxy server before it will pass web requests.

Squid supports many of the standard types of network authentication, and the setup does get somewhat complicated. If you need to implement authentication on your Squid server, consult the complete Squid documentation files.

Configuring Clients

After you have the Squid proxy server up and running on your network, you'll need to configure each client workstation to use it. That's normally handled in the setup for each browser. The browser should have a section for defining a web proxy server. Figure 9.9 shows where this is located in the Firefox version 38 browser.

FIGURE 9.9   The web proxy settings in Firefox

After making the entries, close the window to save them. Now your browsing is controlled by the ACL entries in the Squid configuration file. If you attempt to access a website that is denied by an ACL, you'll get a 403 error message, as shown in Figure 9.10.

Squid even allows you to customize the error page that's returned when a website is blocked, giving you complete control over what the clients see and experience.

To force your network clients to use the web proxy, you must block direct access to all websites from your network. That usually requires firewall or router settings to be made on your network.

FIGURE 9.10   The response from Squid for a denied website

The Nginx Server

While the Apache web server is by far the most popular web server running on the Internet, it's starting to get some competition from a new player. The nginx web server has made some great strides in popularity, because it's used for some very high profile commercial websites.

One of the benefits of nginx is that it doesn't use separate program threads to handle each client as Apache does. Instead, it uses an asynchronous architecture that allows it to spawn client threads within the main program as needed. This helps reduce the memory footprint required for each client that connects to the web server, and thus the same server can handle more clients.

Another benefit of nginx is its ability to work as a reverse proxy server. This allows you to place a main nginx server at the front end of your network and place your application servers behind a firewall, protected from the Internet. Your website visitors connect to the nginx server on the frontend, and it forwards the requests to the backend servers.

This section walks you through the basics of setting up an nginx server and how to use it as a basic reverse proxy server.

Installing Nginx

Because it's relatively new, many Linux distributions don't include the nginx software in their main software repositories. Fortunately, the Debian-based Linux distributions do, so installing it is easy:

```
$ sudo apt-get install nginx
```

This installs nginx and automatically starts it on your server.

Because nginx works as a normal web server, it will start on TCP port 80, the default HTTP network port. If you already have the Apache web server installed on your system, you'll need to stop it while testing nginx and then stop nginx if you want to restart the Apache web server. Alternatively, you can configure them to listen on different TCP ports so that they can both run simultaneously.

For Red Hat–based Linux distributions, the nginx software package is in the Extra Packages for Enterprise Linux (EPEL) repository. To access that repository, you first must configure it in your yum settings. Fortunately, there's a software package that does that for you:

```
$ sudo yum install epel-release
$ sudo yum install nginx
```

The Red Hat installation doesn't start nginx automatically, so you'll need to use the systemctl command to do that. (Again, remember to make sure that the Apache web server isn't already running on the default HTTP port.)

```
$ sudo systemctl start nginx
$ sudo systemctl enable nginx
```

When you've successfully installed nginx, you can test out the default web settings by opening your browser and going to the server address, as shown in Figure 9.11.

FIGURE 9.11 The nginx default web page

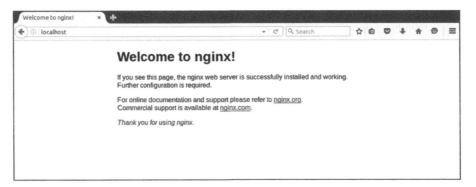

Configuring Nginx

As you would expect, the configuration files for nginx are stored in the /etc/nginx folder. The nginx.conf file is the main configuration file, but as with the Apache web server, nginx uses the include directive to allow configuration settings to be defined in external files.

For Debian-based distributions, the main website directives are defined in the /etc/nginx/ sites-enabled/default file.

The nginx configuration has many of the same features as the Apache web server, so looking at the basic configuration, you'll probably be able to pick out most of the settings:

```
server {
        listen 80 default_server;
        listen [::]:80 default_server ipv6only=on;

        root /usr/share/nginx/html;
        index index.html index.htm;

        # Make site accessible from http://localhost/
        server_name localhost;

        location / {
            try_files $uri $uri/ =404;
        }
}
```

The server section defines the basic settings for the server. The listen directives define the TCP ports and network addresses to listen for incoming connections. The root directive defines the DocumentRoot folder for the server. The index directive lists the default files for which the server should look when a client requests a directory in the URL.

The location directive defines settings unique for specific locations on the server. The entry shown in this example defines the error message that should be returned when a file is not found in the root directory.

The beauty of nginx is in the location section. In there, you can define proxy addresses for multiple backend web servers on which to implement the reverse proxy feature. Thanks to this feature, the nginx web server is gaining in popularity and may very soon become the de facto web server for Linux.

EXERCISE 9.1

Testing a Web Server

This exercise demonstrates how to test a web server using the Telnet command-line command. This allows you to submit HTTP requests to the server and see the HTTP response codes that it returns. To do that, follow these steps:

1. Log in as root, or acquire root privileges by using su or use sudo with each of the commands in this activity.

2. Ensure that you have the Apache web server installed. Open a command prompt; then type **sudo apt-get install apache2** to install the Apache web server package

on your Debian-based system or type **sudo yum install httpd** to install Apache on your Red Hat–based system. You won't see any objects added to the menu when this program is installed.

3. For Red Hat–based systems, start the Apache web server by typing **sudo systemctl start httpd**.

4. Test the Apache web server by typing **telnet localhost 80** at a command line. (You may have to also install the Telnet package on your system.) If your system has the Apache web server running, you should be greeted by the Telnet banner, but nothing from the Apache web server, because it's waiting for your request.

5. Request the default web page from the server by typing **GET /** and press the Enter key to submit the request.

6. The Apache web server will return an HTTP status code if there is an error, or it will return the HTML code contained in the index.html file from the /var/www/html folder.

7. Now test attempting to retrieve an invalid web page. Connect to the Apache web server by typing **telnet localhost 80** at a command line. At the prompt, type **GET /badfile.html** and then press the Enter key. You should receive a 404 status code, indicating that the requested file was not found. You may also see some HTML code for a generic error message web page that the browser would display informing you that it could not find the file on the system.

8. Exit from the command prompt to return to your desktop.

Summary

Web servers are the heart of the Internet, and Linux is the main server platform used for supporting them. Many different web server software packages are available for Linux, but the LPIC-2 exam focuses on just three of them.

The Apache web server is the oldest and most popular web server package. It is highly customizable, and it has defined many of the features expected from web servers. Most Linux distributions include the Apache2 server in their software repositories, so installing a basic Apache web server is easy. The Apache server supports additional features using modules, which you can load when the server is started. You have to find the separate modules in the packages for your specific Linux distribution.

Adding features to the Apache web server is as easy as changing configuration settings. You use the UserDir directive to allow users to create their own websites on the server, separate from each other. You use the VirtualHost directives to host web pages for multiple domains on the same physical server. You can also implement client authentication on your website, requiring clients to log in to access content. The Apache server also provides for secure transactions by using HTTPS and encrypting network traffic between the client and the server.

The Squid web server is best known as a web proxy server. A web proxy server intercepts web page requests from multiple clients and forwards them to the remote servers. It can then cache the responses so that future requests for the same page can be returned from the cached data instead of resending new requests. Squid also allows you to restrict what websites clients can access. You just create ACL lists and apply them to access rules.

The nginx web server is relatively new to the web server game, but it is a powerful player already. It can support larger client bases on the same physical hardware than Apache can, making it ideal for high-traffic environments. It also has made a name for itself in the reverse web proxy world. A reverse web proxy sits in front of multiple backend application servers and provides load balancing for clients.

Exam Essentials

Describe the Apache 2.x configuration environment.   Unfortunately, there is wide discrepancy between Linux distributions on installing the Apache software. Debian-based distributions use the /etc/apache2 folder to store configuration files, while Red Hat–based distributions use the /etc/httpd/conf folder. The same is true for the main configuration filename. Debian-based distributions use apache2.conf, while Red Hat–based distributions use httpd.conf. Inside the main configuration file, Apache allows you to use the include directive to reference external configuration files. Most Linux distributions utilize this to provide configuration settings for additional features in separate files.

Describe the Apache 2.x log files.   The Apache server generates two types of log files: an access log that tracks requests submitted to the server and an error log that tracks server errors. These files are normally called access.log (or access_log in Red Hat–based distributions) and error.log (or error_log in Red Hat–based distributions). The log files and their location can be changed in the Apache configuration file, but they are normally located within the /var/log folder structure.

Explain how individual users can host their own web pages.   The Apache server uses the UserDir directive to provide a location for individual system users to host their own web pages. The UserDir directive specifies the name of a folder that each user can create in their own HOME folder. The Apache web server will provide access to that folder to clients.

Explain virtual hosting and how to use either name-based or IP-based virtual hosting.   The virtual hosting feature allows a single physical server to support websites for multiple domains or IP addresses. Name-based virtual hosting uses the NameVirtualHost directive to redirect the client request based on the hostname in the URL to a separate <VirtualHost> block in the configuration file. You can define separate DocumentRoot locations for each virtual host. IP-based virtual hosting uses separate IP addresses, either with multiple network cards or by using IP aliases on the same network card. Each <VirtualHost> block defines the DocumentRoot area used for each separate IP address.

Describe how to implement access restriction on a website.   The Apache web server uses the mod_auth module (or its more modern replacements) to implement authentication methods on the web server. You can use the mod_auth_basic module to utilize a text file that contains user accounts and encrypted passwords. Use the htpasswd Apache utility to create entries in this file for each user who requires access. The AuthUserFile directive for each <Directory> block that needs to be protected points to the authentication file that contains the users who are allowed access to that area. You can also use the AuthGroupFile directive to create user groups. Alternatively, you can use IP-based authentication with the mod_access module. The Deny and Allow directives can define what IP addresses or networks should have access to the directory.

What are dynamic web applications, and how are they implemented?   Dynamic web applications use embedded program code in a web page to update dynamically the content using external data, such as data stored in a database. The Apache web server must recognize that there's embedded code in the file and ensure that the code is processed. In the Common Gateway Interface (CGI) method, the Apache web server passes the code file to an external program (such as the Perl or Python interpreters) to process the embedded code and returns the results to the client. Alternatively, you can use program modules such as mod_perl or mod_php to allow the Apache web server to process embedded code directly.

Describe how to implement an SSL web server.   The Apache web server allows you to use a public/private key method for encrypting network traffic between the server and the client. You must first generate an encryption key using the OpenSSL software. You can then embed the public key in a certificate that will be passed to clients. For clients to trust your certificate, it must be signed by a trusted certificate authority (CA). The OpenSSL software allows you to create a Certificate Signing Request (CSR), which you can pass to a commercial CA for signing. The CSR must be signed by a certificate authority (CA), validating that the server is valid and that clients can trust it. For testing, you can use the OpenSSL program to create your own CA and self-sign your own certificates. However, these certificates won't be trusted by clients by default and will produce ugly error messages. Once you have your server key and certificate files, you use the SSLEngine, SSLCertificateKeyFile, and SSLCertificateFile to define the location of the files and to define which areas on the web server are allowed to use SSL.

Describe a web proxy server.   A web proxy server receives HTTP requests from multiple clients on a network and submits them to the remote web servers. It then caches the responses before returning them to the clients. Future requests for the same web pages are served from the cached versions, decreasing network bandwidth requirements. Another feature of web proxy servers is that they can be configured to restrict access to specific websites or from specific clients. The Squid web proxy server allows you to define access control lists (ACLs) that define what is being controlled and rules that define whether to block or allow the ACL traffic.

What is the nginx server, and what makes it so special?   The nginx web server is a new way of serving web pages. Instead of using multiple threads to serve pages, it uses asynchronous events within the same program, saving memory for each client request. This allows the physical server to support more clients than an Apache environment. The nginx server can also be configured as a reverse proxy server, also known as a load balancer. It can process a request from a client and redirect it to a server contained in a pool of servers.

Review Questions

You can find the answers in the Appendix.

1. What protocol defines how a web server responds to client requests?
   A. HTML
   B. SSL
   C. HTTP
   D. TLS

2. What standard defines how a client formats the content contained in a web page?
   A. HTML
   B. SSL
   C. HTTP
   D. TLS

3. What HTTP server response code indicates that the file requested by the client was not found?
   A. 200
   B. 403
   C. 500
   D. 404

4. What utility allows you to stop the Apache web server gracefully?
   A. systemctl
   B. apache2ctl
   C. httpd
   D. apache2

5. What utility allows you to test an Apache web server configuration before actually starting the server?
   A. systemctl
   B. apache2ctl
   C. httpd
   D. apache2

6. What directive defines the location on the server that will be shared with clients?
   A. DocumentRoot
   B. ServerRoot
   C. Listen
   D. DirectoryIndex

7. What configuration feature allows you to apply directives to specific folders in the filesystem?

   A. `<VirtualHost>`

   B. `<IfDefined>`

   C. `<Directory>`

   D. `<IfModule>`

8. What configuration directive defines what information appears in the Apache log file?

   A. `ErrorLog`

   B. `LogFormat`

   C. `ErrorDocument`

   D. `DocumentRoot`

9. Which Apache log file contains information about what web page requests were made by clients?

   A. `error.log`

   B. `apache2.conf`

   C. `access.log`

   D. `httpd.conf`

10. What directive should you use to allow system users to create their own web folders?

    A. `AuthUserFile`

    B. `UserDir`

    C. `DocumentRoot`

    D. `LoadModule`

11. In name-based virtual hosting, what directive defines the domain name used?

    A. `DocumentRoot`

    B. `NameVirtualHost`

    C. `<VirtualHost>`

    D. `ServerName`

12. In IP-based virtual hosting, what directive defines the different IP addresses for the server to listen on?

    A. `Listen`

    B. `<VirtualHost>`

    C. `NameVirtualHost`

    D. `DocumentRoot`

13. What Apache utility program allows you to create text userid/password files?

    A. `httpd`

    B. `htpasswd`

    C. `apache2`

    D. `mod_auth`

14. What directive points to the userid/password file that controls access?

   A. `AuthType`

   B. `AuthName`

   C. `AuthUserFile`

   D. `Order`

15. What dynamic web programming method allows the Apache server to utilize an external program interpreter?

   A. CGI

   B. `mod_perl`

   C. `mod_auth`

   D. `mod_php`

16. What directive tells the Apache server to redirect .php files to the PHP server process?

   A. `LoadModule`

   B. `AddHandler`

   C. `DocumentRoot`

   D. `DirectoryIndex`

17. What directive tells the Apache server the location of the SSL certificate?

   A. `DirectoryIndex`

   B. `SSLCertificateKeyFile`

   C. `SSLEngine`

   D. `SSLCertificateFile`

18. What does a web proxy server do? (Select two.)

   A. Caches web requests from multiple clients

   B. Redirects requests from one client to multiple servers

   C. Restricts what websites clients can access

   D. Restricts what files a server can serve

19. What directive does Squid use to define client authentication settings?

   A. `mod_auth`

   B. `auth_param`

   C. `acl`

   D. `http_access`

20. What section in the nginx configuration file defines the basic server settings?

   A. `location`

   B. `server`

   C. `root`

   D. `listen`

Chapter 10

Sharing Files

THE FOLLOWING EXAM OBJECTIVES ARE COVERED IN THIS CHAPTER:

✓ **209.1 Samba Server Configuration**

✓ **209.2 NFS Server Configuration**

✓ **212.2 Managing FTP Servers**

There are many reasons why you may need to share files, such as a collaborative work project. While file sharing on a single system is rather easy, sharing files across different systems can be tricky, especially in mixed system environments. In this chapter, we'll explore three methods that allow you to simplify sharing files across different systems: Samba, NFS, and FTP.

Looking at Samba

Few computing environments are homogeneous. Often, you have a mix of systems, such as Linux servers and Windows computers. In these cases, it's helpful to have a file-sharing method that can deal with these mixed-system network environments. Samba allows file sharing to be accomplished in these environments, and it is especially useful because it can handle Windows Active Directory and NetBIOS atmospheres.

Understanding Samba

Samba gets its name from the *Service Message Block (SMB)* protocol, upon which it is based. Samba is an open-source SMB implementation. Using this protocol, you can allow access to a server's files and/or printers in order to share them among various computers. The various computers, even if they run different operating systems, can access these shared files and/or printers (if they implement the SMB protocol.)

Around the mid-1990s, Microsoft created an SMB protocol-based software package and named it the *Common Internet File System (CIFS)*. Though Microsoft's current SMB protocol software is very different from the original CIFS, you will still see it commonly referred to as CIFS or *SMB/CIFS*. In fact, in the man pages, Samba is referred to as a "Windows SMB/CIFS fileserver for UNIX."

Over time, Samba has changed from a simple file-sharing program into one that can provide additional functions, such as allowing a Windows/Linux user to have a single home directory for both systems; act as an Active Directory member server; map Windows users to Linux users for authentication/authorization; and so on. The focus here is primarily on sharing files and printers.

Samba is maintained by the Samba Team, and their primary website is located at www
.samba.org. Current Samba versions are at 4.4.x and above.

A great deal of Samba documentation is available. If you have Samba installed, besides
the locally installed man pages, typically the /usr/share/doc/samba-*version*/ directory
or the /usr/share/doc/samba*/ directories (depending on your distribution) have current
documentation as well. You can also find Samba documentation at wiki.samba.org. If you
are seeking older Samba documentation, such as Samba version 3 documentation, visit the
www.samba.org/samba/docs/man/ web page.

 WARNING   Some Samba documentation is rather out of date. Because of constant
malicious attacks on Samba, be sure to verify with second or even third
sources prior to making changes to your Samba configuration files.

Before deciding what Samba packages to install, you need to know a few terms
and the difference between a Samba server and a Samba client. A *Samba server* offers
various files and/or printers for use. A *Samba client* accesses and uses the files and/or
printers.

A *shared file* is really a shared directory tree. In other words, on a Samba server, a directory is created and shared. Any files and/or subdirectories within that directory are also
shared. These shared directories can be mounted and their files accessed by Samba clients.
A Samba server's shared files and printers are called *shares* or *Samba shares*.

Three daemons may be involved in providing Samba services. These daemons are described
here:

Samba Daemon   The Samba daemon, smbd, is used on the Samba server. It manages
offered SMB shares, provides share locking, handles user authentication, and so on. It is
controlled by the smb service.

NetBIOS Message Block Daemon   The nmbd daemon handles NetBIOS name service
requests. The Network Basic Input/Output System (NetBIOS), which is really now called
NetBIOS over TCP/IP, is an older protocol that was used on Microsoft systems for items
such as name resolution. For Microsoft operating systems newer than Windows Server
2000 and Windows XP, NetBIOS over TCP is handled via SMB. Therefore, unless you
have some legacy Windows Samba clients on your network, there is no need to employ this
daemon.

Name Service Switch Daemon   The winbindd daemon *binds* together and manages
connections between a Linux system and a Windows domain controller. It can employ
the Name Service Switch (NSS) and Pluggable Authentication Modules (PAM) (covered
in Chapter 11) to deal with authentication and authorization. Thus, Windows Active
Directory (AD) users are treated as Linux users via this daemon. The winbindd daemon
also acts as a Windows Internet Name Service (WINS) for older NetBIOS systems by
providing a mapping of systems' names to IP addresses. It is controlled by the winbind
service.

If you are unfamiliar with Windows Active Directory, some terms in this chapter may cause confusion. A *domain controller* is a server that manages the Active Directory service. Active Directory (AD) is a directory service, which maintains a network resource map. This network resource map considers every mapped item, such as files, printers, users, and groups, as an object. Object attributes, which are also maintained, include information such as what permissions are needed to access the object. Thus, a particular Windows user (an object with attributes) can only access other mapped objects (such as a file) if the user has the permission level to do so.

Configuring Samba

How you configure Samba depends on the Samba service(s) you wish to employ on a particular system. If you are configuring a Samba server that will be offering file shares, more work is required than setting up a Samba client that will be using those shares. This section takes you through some common configuration scenarios.

Installing Samba on Linux

There are several Samba packages available. Each has its own purpose in a Samba environment. The various packages are sometimes referred to as the *Samba Suite*.

Unfortunately, Samba packages can differ greatly among the various distributions. For example, you'll typically have the Samba client package preinstalled, but its name may be samba-client or smbclient, depending on your distribution.

While you may use an older Samba version, Samba version 4.1 and below are no longer supported. No Samba security patches are provided for unsupported versions. Security problems, such as the 2016 Badlock bug, make unsupported Samba systems vulnerable. Consider moving to a supported Samba version. See www.samba.org for details.

Generally, for a Red Hat–based distribution, you'll find that the Samba packages listed in Table 10.1 are either preinstalled or available to install. This is a general list, so be sure to review your distribution's documentation concerning Samba.

TABLE 10.1   Red Hat distribution Samba packages

Package Name	Description
cifs-utils	Samba client utilities for managing shares
libsmbclient	Samba client libraries
libwbclient	Samba client winbindd libraries
samba	Samba server functions

Package Name	Description
samba-client	Samba client functions
samba-client-libs	Samba client libraries
samba-common	Samba server and client configuration and documentation files
samba-common-libs	Samba server and client libraries
samba-common-tools	Samba server and client commands
samba-libs	Samba server and client libraries
samba-winbind	Samba winbindd functions and commands
samba-winbind-clients	Samba winbindd client additional commands

Typically for a Debian-based distribution, such as Ubuntu, you'll find the Samba packages listed in Table 10.2 are either preinstalled or available to install. Notice that some of the packages have the same name and function as those listed in Table 10.1, but others are completely different. This is not an exhaustive list, so be sure to review your distribution's documentation concerning Samba packages.

TABLE 10.2 Debian distribution Samba packages

Package Name	Description
cifs-utils	Samba client utilities for managing shares
libsmbclient	Samba client libraries
samba	Samba server functions
samba-common	Samba server and client configuration and documentation files
samba-common-bin	Samba server and client commands
samba-libs	Samba server and client libraries
smbclient	Samba client functions
winbind	Samba winbindd functions

If you are simply using your system as a Samba client, the samba-client or smbclient package (depending on your distribution) is typically installed by default, so you may only need to install the `cifs-utils` package. However, you will have to perform some configurations, which are covered later in this chapter.

If you are setting up a Samba server, most likely you will need to, at a minimum, install the samba package. Here is a snipped example of installing the package on a CentOS system:

```
# yum install samba
Loaded plugins: fastestmirror, langpacks
[...]
Installed:
  samba.x86_64 0:4.2.10-6.el7_2

Dependency Updated:
  libsmbclient.x86_64 0:4.2.10-6.el7_2
  libwbclient.x86_64 0:4.2.10-6.el7_2
  samba-client.x86_64 0:4.2.10-6.el7_2
  samba-client-libs.x86_64 0:4.2.10-6.el7_2
  samba-common.noarch 0:4.2.10-6.el7_2
  samba-common-libs.x86_64 0:4.2.10-6.el7_2
  samba-common-tools.x86_64 0:4.2.10-6.el7_2
  samba-libs.x86_64 0:4.2.10-6.el7_2

Complete!
#
```

Once you have the Samba server package installed and its dependencies installed or updated, you can start the configuration process. However, before configuring a Samba server file share, it's a good idea to review briefly the various directories and utilities used by Samba.

Exploring Samba Directories and Files

Besides the documentation directory (described earlier), there are three primary Samba directories where various Samba files are located. One of these directories is where Samba stores its log files: the `/var/log/samba/` directory.

Samba also uses the `/var/lib/samba/` directory and its subdirectories for storing things such as Samba user databases. For example, Samba user account information can be kept in either the `smbpasswd`, `tdbsam`, or `ldapsam` databases, which are typically located in this directory.

For smaller Samba implementations (less than 250 users), the `tdbsam` user database is recommended. Larger implementations should use the `ldapsam` user database with Active Directory or Lightweight Directory Access Protocol (LDAP). The `smbpasswd` database is set to be deprecated and should only be used for backward compatibility with older Samba implementations.

Samba configuration files are stored within the /etc/samba/ directory. The primary Samba configuration file is /etc/samba/smb.conf.

 Older Samba versions used the /etc/, /etc/smb/, or /etc/samba.d/ directories for storing configuration files. In earlier Samba versions, the primary configuration file was the /etc/smb.conf file. Be aware that some distributions still use these.

The /etc/samba/smb.conf file is typically provided whether you are setting up a Samba client or a Samba server. Before configuring Samba via its smb.conf file, a brief overview of Samba utilities is in order.

Exploring Samba Utilities

Samba has several utilities that can assist in testing configurations, troubleshooting Samba problems, as well as managing Samba share access. In Table 10.3, the primary Samba administration utilities are listed and briefly described.

TABLE 10.3 Samba administration utilities

Name	Description
mount.cifs	Mounts a Samba share on a client.
net	Administers a Samba server and remote servers. It is similar to the Windows/DOS net utility.
nmblookup	Looks up NetBIOS information, such as workgroup names, and provides IP addresses for the names.
pdbedit	Manages any of the Samba user databases. The user databases include ldapsam, smbpasswd, and tdbsam.
rpcclient	Executes Samba client Microsoft Remote Procedure Call functions.
smbcacls	Displays or modifies Samba file share access control lists.
smbclient	Connects, lists shares, and allows FTP-like services for a file share.
smbcontrol	Manages the Samba smbd daemon.
smbmount	Mounts a Samba share on a client. Replaced on most distributions by the mount.cifs command.
smbpasswd	Manages the Samba smbpasswd or tdbsam database.
smbspool	Sends files to a Samba printer share.

TABLE 10.3   Samba administration utilities *(continued)*

Name	Description
smbstatus	Displays current Samba server connections.
smbtar	Creates Samba file share backups to a regular file or tape device. Performs restores as well.
testparm	Tests the smb.conf configuration file's syntax.
wbinfo	Displays Samba winbindd daemon information.

The samba-tool is another Samba utility that deserves mentioning. Though documented as the "main Samba administration tool," it is not installed on all distributions with the provided Samba packages. The samba-tool is typically used when configuring the Samba server as an Active Directory controller. It also proves useful for managing DNS on the Samba server, when it is acting as such a controller.

Note that not all distributions may have all of the utilities listed. Also, the utilities you use will often depend on configuration settings in the smb.conf file.

Configuring a Samba Server File Share

After you have installed the appropriate Samba server package(s) on your Linux system, you can start to configure a Samba server file share. In this section, configuring a file share to be used by another Linux client is covered (though many of the steps are similar to configuring a file share for a Windows client). The basic steps are as follows:

1. Create a share file (directory tree).
2. Modify the smb.conf file as needed.
3. Check the smb.conf file's syntax.
4. If needed, add a local system Samba client user account and give the account a password.
5. If needed, add a Samba login account to the appropriate database.
6. Check the Samba login account.
7. Start the Samba daemon.
8. Check the Samba share(s) being offered.
9. Set the Samba daemon to start at server boot time.
10. Modify the firewall as needed. (Firewalls are covered in Chapter 12.)

Creating a share file (directory) is no different than creating a regular Linux system directory. In general, the best location is in the /srv/ directory. In the example here, the /srv/ssharea/ directory is created:

```
# mkdir /srv/ssharea
#
```

```
# ls -d /srv/ssharea
/srv/ssharea
#
```

The next step, modifying the Samba configuration file, /etc/samba/smb.conf, is more complex. This file has many settings that manage and direct Samba's overall operation as well as individual shares.

This Samba configuration file has been modified on a CentOS system to provide a file share. Only the file's global, [global], settings section is displayed here:

```
# cat smb.conf
#============= Global Settings ==========================
#
[global]
     workgroup = FIREFLYGROUP
     server string = Samba Server Version %v
     interfaces = enp0s*
     hosts allow = 192.168.56.0/24
#
#---------------- Logging Options -----------------
#
     log file = /var/log/samba/log.%m
     max log size = 50
#
#------------- Standalone Server Options -------------
#
     security = user
     passdb backend = tdbsam
#
# [...]
```

Within the smb.conf file, anything after a semicolon (;) or a hash (#) is ignored (as are blank lines). Typically, comments are placed after a hash and currently unused directives are placed after semicolons.

The Samba configuration file is broken up into various sections. Each section is designated by a name placed between square brackets. These section names are not case sensitive. The [global] section, shown in the previous example, contains directives that determine how the Samba server will conduct networking, logging, name resolution, and so on.

 Directives are not case sensitive. Also, when setting a directive in the smb.conf file, any spaces before or after the equal sign (=) are ignored. Samba treats each line (a line ends in a newline character) as an individual record. However, you can continue a record onto a second line by placing a backslash (\) at the end of the record's first line.

A few significant global directives, including the ones shown in the previous example, are described in Table 10.4. You can find more global directives in the man pages or in previously listed Samba documentation locations.

TABLE 10.4 Samba configuration file global directives

Name	Description
workgroup	Designates the Samba group (workgroup) in which this server belongs. It is not an FQDN. If the Samba server is part of a Windows workgroup or domain, typically the workgroup name is set to the Windows workgroup/domain name.
server string	Describes this Samba server, and it can include any string as well as variable substitutions.
netbios name	Sets the Samba server's NetBIOS name, which may be needed in a Linux/Windows mixed network environment but typically only if legacy Windows systems are involved.
realm	Designates the Kerberos realm in which an Active Directory controller and this Samba server participate. The realm name must be in all capital letters.
interfaces	Designates the Samba server's network interfaces to be used to provide the service. If not specified, all broadcast-capable interfaces are used. Interface directives can be interface names (including wildcards), IP addresses, broadcast/mask pair, and so on.
hosts allow	Sets host systems allowed to access these services. Hosts are designated via an IP address (CIDR addressing for subnets is allowed) or host name, and the list is comma, space, or tab delimited.
hosts deny	Sets host systems denied access to these services. Syntax is the same as the hosts allow directive's syntax.
disable netbios	Toggles NetBIOS support on the Samba server. Set to no by default. You can set it to yes if needed to disable NetBIOS support in order to stop the nmbd daemon from launching (on some distributions) or hide the Samba server from Windows systems using browsing.
smb ports	Specifies which ports the Samba server listens on for SMB traffic.
wins support	Toggles Windows Internet Name Service (WINS) on the Samba server. Set to no by default. You can set it to yes if needed for NetBIOS implementation.
log file	Designates the Samba log file (debug file). The directive can include variable substitutions, which allow a separate log file to be created for each Samba client.

Name	Description
log level	Sets the debugging level to filter Samba log file messages. By default, the level is set to 0, which means that logging is turned off. To turn on logging, the allowable range is 1 (brief logging) to 10 (ample logging), with the level typically set to 2 or 3. Log levels can be set for individual debug classes, such as smb:3 and auth:7 as well.
max log size	Specifies the maximum log file size in kilobytes. By default, the size is set to 0, which indicates there is no size limit.
security	Designates the security level (mode) that determines how clients are authenticated. It can be set to ads, domain, server, share, or user.
passdb backend	Specifies the account information database (backend) to use. It can be set to ldapsam, smbpasswd, or tdbsam (default).
smb encrypt	Designates if clients are allowed or required to use SMB encryption. It can be set to auto, mandatory, or disabled, and it can be set as a share directive instead of a global directive. By default, it is set to auto and encryption is allowed. It is recommended to set it to mandatory.

In the preceding smb.conf global section example, you may have noticed the %v in the server string directive as well as the %m in the log file setting. These are called *variable substitutions*, and they allow directives set to strings to include variables. For example, the %v variable is the Samba software's current version on this particular server. The %m variable is the Samba client's NetBIOS name (if available). A variable substitution list can be found in the man pages as well as many other global directives. Type **man smb.conf** at the command line to review the smb.conf man pages.

WARNING   If your Samba server is in a mixed environment of Windows and Linux systems, it's important to set the workgroup directive correctly. *Workgroup* is a Microsoft term, and it is applied to local area network systems with a peer relationship. For Microsoft systems, there is a difference between a domain (a workgroup with security features added) and a workgroup. For Samba's workgroup directive name, there is no difference between a Microsoft workgroup name and a domain name. However, it is important to set the workgroup directive to the *Windows* workgroup or domain name (traditionally all uppercase letters) and not a FQDN. Otherwise, your Windows systems will not be able to find the Samba service in their Network Neighborhood.

In the smb.conf file, there are also sections that are not global but instead set directives for the various offered shares and other purposes. Each section begins with a section name, which is not case sensitive, in square brackets. The most common section names are shown in Table 10.5.

TABLE 10.5   Samba configuration file section names

Name	Description
[global]	Contains globally applied directives that determine how the Samba server will conduct networking, logging, name resolution, and so on.
[*share-name*]	Holds directives applied to a particular Samba share.
[homes]	Contains directives that create a Samba file share as a client is trying to access that share, instead of creating the Samba file share beforehand. This is typically used for providing clients' home directory shares, without having to create a Samba share for each client's home directory ahead of time.
[netlogin]	Provides directives necessary for the Samba server, when it is acting as a domain controller (responds to security authentication requests).
[printers]	Contains directives that create a Samba printer share as a client is trying to access that share, instead of creating the Samba printer share beforehand. This is typically used for providing access to all of a Samba server's printer queues without having to create a Samba share for each printer ahead of time.
[profiles]	Holds directives for roaming user profiles. Offered in domain server environments, a roaming user profile allows a user's various settings and data to be available to them, no matter what computer within the environment the user logs into.

Returning to the steps for configuring a Samba server file share, the next Samba configuration file modification involves adding directives in smb.conf for the file share itself. Here a snipped CentOS system's configuration file's share definition settings section is displayed:

```
# cat /etc/samba/smb.conf
[...]
#==================== Share Definitions =====================
#
[ssharea]
    comment = Server Share A
    browseable = yes
    path = /srv/ssharea
    public = no
    writable = yes
[...]
#
```

In the example, the share name is ssharea, and there are five directives set for it. Several directives can be used here, and Table 10.6 lists the more common ones.

TABLE 10.6 Samba configuration file share directives

Name	Description
comment	Describes the Samba share. This text description is displayed when a client queries the Samba server to see what shares are available.
browseable	Determines whether or not this share is seen in an available shares list. By default, it is set to yes. The directive can also be spelled browsable.
valid users	Designates users and/or groups allowed to log in to this service. Users and/or groups are entered as a comma-separated list, and group names must be preceded by an at (@) sign. If not set, then all users can log in to this service.
invalid users	Designates users and/or groups *not* allowed to log in to this service. List syntax is the same as for the valid users directive.
path	Sets the file share's absolute directory reference.
public	Toggles whether or not passwords are required to access this service. By default, public is set to no and passwords are required. The guest ok directive is a synonym for the public directive.
guest only	Toggles whether or not only guest connections are allowed for this service. By default, guest only is set to no and other connections besides guest connections are allowed. This directive is ignored if the public directive is set to no. The only guest directive is a synonym for the guest only directive.
group	Sets the group name assigned as the default primary group for users connecting to this service. This is typically used for project collaboration purposes. The group name can be preceded with a + to indicate only the listed group's current members will be assigned this default primary group and other users will retain their normal default primary group. The force group directive is a synonym for the group directive.
writable	Determines whether or not write access is granted to this share. By default, writable is set to no and write access is denied. The read only directive is an antonym for the writable directive.
write list	Designates users and/or groups that are granted read and write access to this share. These users are granted write access no matter how the writable directive is set. List syntax is the same as for the valid users directive.

As you can see, there are many interesting ways to set up a Samba file share. Be aware that several additional file share–specific directives exist. View Samba configuration file documentation at one of the Samba documentation locations if you wish to see all of these various directives.

NOTE   In the preceding smb.conf file's ssharea section, the valid users directive is not used. This is acceptable while setting up and testing out your Samba file share. After the testing phase, it is recommended that you add any users (who are allowed access to this share) to a Samba file share group. When you have the group configured, add valid users = @*group-name* to your Samba configuration file.

Once you have completed modifying the Samba configuration file for setting up a Samba file share, it is recommended to test the smb.conf file's syntax. This is easily done with the testparm command, as shown snipped here:

```
# testparm
Load smb config files from /etc/samba/smb.conf
[...]
Processing section "[ssharea]"
Processing section "[printers]"
Loaded services file OK.
Server role: ROLE_STANDALONE

Press enter to see a dump of your service definitions

# Global parameters
[global]
    workgroup = FIREFLYGROUP
    server string = Samba Server Version %v
    interfaces = enp0s*
    security = USER
    log file = /var/log/samba/log.%m
    max log size = 50
    idmap config *: backend = tdb
    hosts allow = 192.168.56.0/24


[ssharea]
    comment = Server Share A
    path = /srv/ssharea
    read only = No
 [...]
#
```

If the testparm command returns an OK, as shown in the preceding example's line Loaded services file OK, your smb.conf file's syntax is correct. Of course, this does not guarantee that your configuration is correct, but it is step in the right direction.

> The testparm command will not show everything that you have set in your smb.conf. For example, in the preceding example, the browseable directive is not shown. Also, the testparm command may use directive name synonyms or antonyms. For example, though the writable directive is used in the smb.conf file, the testparm command displays its antonym, read only.

The next step in setting up the Samba file share is to give any client users a local Linux user account and password on the Samba server if not already provided. For example purposes only, one client user is set up:

```
# useradd Malcolm
#
# passwd Malcolm
Changing password for user Malcolm.
New password:
Retype new password:
passwd: all authentication tokens updated successfully.
#
```

> Your steps may differ here, depending on the security level (mode) you set in the Samba configuration file. Security modes are covered in more detail later in this chapter.

Once a local Linux user account and password are created (if needed), the following step is used to set up a Samba user account in the appropriate database. Because in the configuration file's global directives the security directive was set to user, a corresponding user account will need to exist in either the smbpasswd user database (on older Samba implementations) or in the tdbsam user database.

Continuing with the example Samba file share on the Samba server, the one client user is added to the tdbsam user database using the smbpasswd command, as shown here:

```
# smbpasswd -a Malcolm
New SMB password:
Retype new SMB password:
Added user Malcolm.
#
```

Users can change their own Samba passwords using the smbpasswd command, similar to how they can change their login passwords using the passwd command.

Before proceeding in the configuration process, it's a good idea to double-check the recently added user account(s). In this step, the pdbedit command will be employed. This command can help manage any of the backend user databases. In this example, any user accounts are displayed using a short listing (-L):

```
# pdbedit -L
Malcolm:1004:
#
```

You can get a lot more information from the pdbedit command concerning user accounts. Just tack on the verbose option (-v).

Due to potential differences in usernames, it may be important to set up a username map. This topic is covered later in this chapter.

Now that the client user(s) is set up, the next step is to start up the Samba service. The method used will depend on your distribution. Here on a CentOS distribution, the Samba service is started and checked using the systemctl command:

```
# systemctl start smb
#
# systemctl status smb
• smb.service–Samba SMB Daemon
[...]
   Active: active (running) since [...]
[...]
   Status: "smbd: ready to serve connections..."
[...]
#
```

After the Samba service is running, it's recommended to verify the file shares being offered. You can accomplish this step by employing the smbclient command and logging into the Samba service using the client user's account and password. This is done on the Samba server, as shown snipped here:

```
# smbclient -L //localhost -U Malcolm
Enter Malcolm's password:
Domain=[FIREFLYGROUP] [...]
    Sharename       Type        Comment
    ---------       ----        -------
    ssharea         Disk        Server Share A
[...]
#
```

Because the smbclient command is used on the Samba server, the server is designated by the //localhost specification. The -L option asks for an offered share list and the -U option states which user account is to be used to log in to the service and obtain this information. It may be a little confusing that you must log in to the Samba service to obtain this information. However, this is a requirement that even the super user cannot override (if an account is not set up within Samba), as shown here:

```
# smbclient -L //localhost
Enter root's password:
session setup failed: NT_STATUS_LOGON_FAILURE
#
```

A few more steps are required to complete the Samba server's file share. First, ensure that the Samba service will start at system boot time. The method to use depends on your particular distribution. Here is a snipped example of doing this on a CentOS system:

```
# systemctl enable smb
Created symlink from [...]
#
```

 Depending on your distribution, you may need to configure SELinux booleans to allow Samba to function properly. Though doing so is beyond this book's scope, you can temporarily disengage SELinux for Samba testing purposes. Check SELinux's status via the sestatus command and super user privileges. If its status is enabled, then you can disable it by editing the /etc/selinux/config file and changing SELINUX=enabled to SELINUX=disabled. Reboot your system and recheck the SELinux status using the sestatus command.

The last step is to modify your Samba server's firewall in order to allow Samba to function properly with clients. Though firewall details are covered in Chapter 12, you should be aware of the various ports that Samba may use. Which ones are used depends on your Samba configuration. Table 10.7 gives a brief Samba port description.

TABLE 10.7   Samba ports

Number	Protocols	Description
53	TCP, UDP	Internal DNS only
88	TCP, UDP	Kerberos
135	TCP	End point resolution

TABLE 10.7 Samba ports *(continued)*

Number	Protocols	Description
137	TCP, UDP	NetBIOS name service
138	TCP, UDP	NetBIOS datagram service
139	TCP, UDP	NetBIOS session service
389	TCP, UDP	Lightweight Directory Access Protocol (LDAP)
445	TCP	SMB over TCP
464	TCP, UDP	Kerberos kpasswd
636	TCP	LDAP over SSL (LDAPS)
901	TCP, UDP	Samba Web Administration Tool (SWAT)
1024 - 5000	TCP	Dynamic RPC service ports
3268	TCP	Microsoft Global catalog
3269	TCP	Microsoft Global catalog over SSL
5353	TCP, UDP	Multicast DNS

Simply because Samba *may* use a particular port does not mean that Samba *will* use that port. It's a good idea to see which ports Samba is attempting to use prior to modifying your firewall instead of just opening up the firewall for all of the potential ports. Here is an example on a CentOS system of determining the Samba server's smbd daemon's process ID and using the ss command to list any ports on which the daemon is listening:

```
# systemctl status smb | grep PID
 Main PID: 6869 (smbd)
#
# ss -utlpn | grep 6869
tcp LISTEN 0  50   *:139   *:*  users:(("smbd",pid=6869,fd=38))
tcp LISTEN 0  50   *:445   *:*  users:(("smbd",pid=6869,fd=37))
tcp LISTEN 0  50 :::139 :::*  users:(("smbd",pid=6869,fd=36))
tcp LISTEN 0  50 :::445 :::*  users:(("smbd",pid=6869,fd=35))
#
```

The options to use with the ss command are as follows:

u (display UDP sockets)

t (display TCP sockets)

l (display only listening sockets)

p (show process using socket)

n (display the socket's port number)

In the preceding example, ports 139 and 445 are being used by the Samba server daemon. If you are running the NetBIOS message block daemon (nmbd) or the name service switch daemon (winbindd), you will need to check the ports for their PIDs listening as well.

 If you are following along in this chapter with setting up a Samba server file share, you can temporarily lower your firewall. Using super user privileges, enter **iptables -F** at the command line.

Configuring a Samba Client File Share Access

After you have a Samba server file share available, you can start to configure the client side. The basic steps for configuring a Samba client file share on a Linux system are as follows:

1. Install or update the Samba client package, and install any additional needed utilities.
2. Add a local user account if needed.
3. Log into the Samba service from the Samba client system.
4. Create a mount point for the share directory.
5. Temporarily mount the share.
6. Test the mounted share.
7. Add a mount command to the Samba client's /etc/fstab file.
8. Create a user credentials file on the Samba client.
9. Lock down the user credentials file.
10. Test the /etc/fstab file.
11. If needed, set the Samba client service (and any other needed Samba services) to start at system boot.

More than likely, the Samba client package is already installed on your Linux Samba client system. However, you might need to check for client package updates and install additional utilities, as shown in this snipped example on an Ubuntu system:

```
$ sudo apt-get install samba-client cifs-utils
[sudo] password for christine:
[...]
Note, selecting 'smbclient' instead of 'samba-client'
smbclient is already the newest version.
```

```
Suggested packages:
  winbind
The following NEW packages will be installed:
  cifs-utils keyutils
0 upgraded, 2 newly installed, 0 to remove and 0 not upgraded.
Need to get 120 kB of archives.
[...]
$
```

Notice in the preceding example that the wrong package name (samba-client) was used, but the Ubuntu system self-corrected it to the correct package name (smbclient). Recall that package names may be different on the various distributions. Not all distributions will self-correct, so it is important to get the correct package name.

Once you have the needed packages upgraded or installed, you can proceed to the next step of adding a local user account. This account should have the same UID on the client system as it does on the Samba server system. Here is an example of adding a Samba client user on an Ubuntu system:

```
$ sudo useradd --uid 1004 -m -d /home/Malcolm Malcolm
$
$ sudo passwd Malcolm
[...]
$
```

Once the local Samba client account is created, use the smbclient command to log in to the Samba service and view the share(s) offered by the Samba server, as shown snipped here:

```
$ smbclient -L //192.168.56.102/ssharea -U Malcolm
Enter Malcolm's password:
Domain=[FIREFLYGROUP] [...]

    Sharename       Type        Comment
    ---------       ----        -------
    ssharea         Disk        Server Share A
[...]
$
```

If you get a connection refused message, it could be that the Samba server's firewall has not been properly configured. If SELinux is enabled on the Samba server, it may be improperly configured for Samba client access to shares.

Notice that this time the Samba server's IP address was used in the smbclient command. You could alternatively use its hostname or NetBIOS name, depending on your Samba and network configuration.

The smbclient command allows FTP-style access to a share. To use this access style, simply remove the -L option as shown snipped here:

```
$ smbclient //192.168.56.102/ssharea -U Malcolm
Enter Malcolm's password:
Domain=[FIREFLYGROUP] [...]
smb: \> help
?               allinfo       altname         archive  [...]
blocksize       cancel        case_sensitive  cd       [...]
chown           close         del             dir      [...]
echo            exit          get             getfacl  [...]
hardlink        help          history         iosize   [...]
link            lock          lowercase       ls       [...]
[...]
showconnect     tcon          tdis            tid      [...]
..              !
smb: \> exit
```

Notice that a help command is available within the smbclient utility, allowing you to see all of the various commands available for use concerning this share.

The next step in this process is to create a mount point for the file share. In this case, a subdirectory of the user's home directory will be created, as shown here:

```
$ sudo mkdir /home/Malcom/csharea
[sudo] password for christine:
$
$ sudo chown Malcolm:Malcolm /home/Malcom/csharea
$
```

Now attempt to mount the Samba server share locally. The mount command is used, but some important options must be included: username and noperm. An example, which has been broken onto multiple lines for clarity, is shown here:

```
$ sudo mount -o username=Malcolm,noperm \
> //192.168.56.102/ssharea csharea
Password for Malcolm@//192.168.56.102/ssharea:
$
$ touch csharea/Inara.dat
$
$ ls -l csharea
total 0
-rw-r--r-- 1 Malcolm Malcolm 0 Apr 14 02:37 Inara.dat
```

```
$
$ rm -i csharea/Inara.dat
rm: remove regular empty file 'csharea/Inara.dat'? y
$
```

 NOTE If you were mounting a Windows file share, you would use the mount.cifs utility instead of the mount command.

Once the file share is mounted, it can be used like a regular mounted filesystem. However, whether you can write to the file share depends on the share's configuration. Recall that this share is writable, because the writable directive was set to yes in the Samba server's smb.conf file.

You can also check your mounted file share using the mount command. In this snipped example, notice that the file share is mounted as a cifs filesystem type:

```
$ mount
/dev/sda1 on / type ext4 (rw,errors=remount-ro)
[...]
//192.168.56.102/ssharea on /home/Malcolm/csharea type cifs (rw)
$
```

If desired, you can have the share automatically mounted at system boot time via the /etc/fstab file. First, make a backup copy and add a new line to the filesystem table. An example is shown here on an Ubuntu system:

```
$ sudo cp /etc/fstab /etc/fstab.bck
[sudo] password for christine:
$
$ sudo nano /etc/fstab
$
$ grep ssharea /etc/fstab
//192.168.56.102/ssharea /home/Malcolm/csharea cifs
credentials=/etc/samba/Malcolm,noperm,uid=1004 0 0
$
```

Note that the /etc/fstab record is shown wrapped onto two lines, but it is a single line in the file. The share name in the preceding example uses an IP address. This is OK for testing purposes, but it's best to use a domain name, NetBIOS name, or whatever is appropriate for your Samba configuration. The mount point is /home/Malcolm/cshare. The filesystem type is set to cifs. There are also several options: credentials, noperm, and uid. The credentials option points to a Samba credentials file, which is needed for logging into the Samba service. This file is created next.

When dealing with Microsoft shares, consider adding `iocharset=utf-8` to the mount options. This option can help with the various types of filename mangling that occur when dealing with mixed environments.

After you have the /etc/fstab file updated, the next step is to create the user credentials file on the Samba client. This file must have the same filename as the /etc/fstab credentials entry. It contains the username and password for logging into the Samba service, as shown here:

```
$ sudo nano /etc/samba/Malcolm
$
$ sudo cat /etc/samba/Malcolm
username=Malcolm
password=Serenity_2005
$
```

Because the credentials file contains a plaintext password, it must be locked down. First, the file should be owned by the root user. It also should only allow file owner read access. If either of these items is missing, it must be set as shown here:

```
$ ls -l /etc/samba/Malcolm
-rw-r--r-- 1 root root 36 Apr 20 14:28 /etc/samba/Malcolm
$
$ sudo chmod 0400 /etc/samba/Malcolm
$
$ ls -l /etc/samba/Malcolm
-r-------- 1 root root 36 Apr 20 14:28 /etc/samba/Malcolm
$
```

In the preceding example, the root user does own the credentials file, so there was no need to employ the chown command. However, the permissions were too wide open, so the chmod command was used to set the file to file owner read only.

Now that the /etc/fstab file has been updated, the credentials file has been created, and it has been locked down, you can test the share mount. Here is a snipped successful test example on an Ubuntu system via using the mount -a command:

```
$ sudo mount -a
$
$ mount
/dev/sda1 on / type ext4 (rw,errors=remount-ro)
[...]
//192.168.56.102/ssharea on /home/Malcolm/csharea type cifs (rw)
$
```

You can also use a few other commands, such as df, to see if the file share is automatically mounted, as shown here:

```
$ df -h
Filesystem               [...] Mounted on
[...]
//192.168.56.102/ssharea  [...] /home/Malcolm/csharea
$
$ su — Malcolm
Password:
$
$ touch csharea/test_drive.dat
$
$ ls csharea
test_drive.dat
$
$ exit
logout
$
```

The file share mounted without any problems, and the user Malcolm can write files to the share. After you have this all in order, the last step is to ensure that the Samba client service will start at system boot, if it's not already set up.

> If you will be allowing writable share access, consider setting up a Samba group (for example, SambaWrite) on both the Samba server and client Linux systems. Use the chgrp command to set this group as the server share directory's group, remove rw other permissions, and add (if needed) rwx group permissions. Modify your Samba server's configuration file (smb.conf), add valid users = @*group-name* to the share's configuration, and restart the server. Be sure to add any share users to this group. This will help provide a little more security to the share configuration.

Configuring a Username Map

Depending on your particular Samba environment, you may have a situation where Samba server and client usernames are different. This scenario tends to happen most often when Windows systems are involved. In these cases, you will need to set up a *username map*.

On the Samba server, add a global directive in the smb.conf file using the following syntax:

```
username map = /path/map-file-name
```

The */path/* is typically /etc/samba/, but the *map-file-name* varies. The map file may be called username.map, username.txt, smbusers, and so on.

Within the map file, for each username, use the following syntax:

server_username = client_username

Here is a username map example, which maps Linux Samba server usernames to Windows clients' usernames:

```
# cat /etc/samba/username.map
[...]
rblum = RichardBlum
cbresnahan = ChristineBresnahan
kryan = "Kevin E Ryan"
gschwartz = GarySchwartz
[...]
```

Notice that quotation marks were used around the Windows username Kevin E Ryan. These were needed because this Windows username has spaces in it (which are allowed on Windows systems). There are other special characters that you can employ within the map file. See the username map directive information in the smb.conf man pages for details.

> Keep in mind that each username must have the same password if needed by the authentication process. There is no password map.

Configuring Security Levels

In the SMB protocol, a *security level* is either at the *user level* or at the *share level*. Samba implements share-level security using only one method. However, for user-level security implementation, there are four methods available. The method chosen dictates how the Samba client user authenticates with the Samba server to access offered shares.

Using the share-level security, a Samba server focuses not on usernames but instead on passwords. Each share has one or more passwords. The Samba server accepts the share password for share access authentication. Once authenticated, the user has access to that particular share.

> The share-level security is deprecated. It is recommended that you *not* use this particular security level due to various known security issues as well as Microsoft Samba clients having potential problems with this level.

The user-level security, used in the earlier configuration examples, authenticates user share access via usernames and their associated passwords. This is the preferred security level.

The different security-level implementation methods are called *security modes*. Thus, the mode defines the security level used. The security mode is set in the Samba configuration file's [global] section, and it can be set to a mode listed in Table 10.8.

TABLE 10.8 Samba security modes

Mode	Description
ads	This mode sets user-level security. The mode allows the Samba server to join an Active Directory as a member. Authentication via Kerberos can be used. However, the additional directives realm and password server must also typically be set in the Samba configuration file's [global] section. This is the typical mode set for Samba implementations greater than 250 users.
domain	This mode sets user-level security. Similar to user mode, except that user authentication is handled by a domain controller using the older NT protocols. The workgroup directive must be set to the network's domain name.
server	This mode sets user-level security. Similar to user mode, except that user authentication is handled by a remote server, which can be another Samba server or a Windows NT server. The additional directive password server must also typically be set in the Samba configuration file's [global] section. Considered a security risk, its use is no longer recommended.
share	This mode sets share-level security. Each Samba share has one or more passwords, and the server accepts the share password for share access authentication. Deprecated.
user	This mode sets user-level security. Username and passwords are required by the Samba server to log in to the service. Corresponding client user accounts must exist on the server and within the tdbsam user database (smbpasswd user database on older Samba implementations). This is the typical mode set for Samba implementations under 250 users.

Configuring Samba as an Active Directory Member

More than likely, you will operate in a mixed environment at some point. If you want to share files and already have an Active Directory controller established, setting up your Linux Samba server to be an Active Directory member can be useful. This topic is more about Samba security and access to the various Samba shares and less about share configuration.

There are a few things to keep in mind in this section. First, this is different than setting up Samba to be an Active Directory controller, which you can do, but the steps are very different. It is also assumed that your Active Directory controller is a Windows system. In addition, it's important to check your distribution's documentation, current Samba documentation, and your various Windows systems' documentation. Because of the variety of environments involved as well as Samba changes due to security issues, those documentation sources will be your best help.

Usually, *prior* to setting up your Samba server to offer file or printer shares, the server is first integrated as an Active Directory member. The typical basic steps to accomplish this on the Linux Samba server are as follows:

1. Install or update the Samba server package and install any additional needed utilities.

2. Configure Active Directory DNS name server entries, if needed.

3. Set up the Network Time Protocol (NTP).

4. Check for the proper Active Directory controller name to IP address resolution on the Samba server, and correct it in /etc/hosts or DNS, if needed.

5. Modify the Samba server's smb.conf file as needed.

6. Join the Samba server as a member of the Active Directory controller.

7. Set up the Samba server to retrieve domain user and group data from the winbindd daemon.

8. Start the winbindd daemon.

Additional details for some steps are elaborated here:

Step 2   Often, your Active Directory controller will be acting as a DNS server. (DNS was covered in Chapter 8.) If this is true in your mixed environment, you will need to modify the appropriate file to point DNS queries to the Active Directory controller. On older distributions, this is the /etc/resolv.conf file. Most current distributions reconfigure the /etc/resolv.conf file upon boot, so to set the DNS name server persistently, you need to modify other files. (This topic was covered in Chapter 8.) See your distribution's documentation to determine the appropriate file(s) to modify.

> Make sure that your Samba services are not running on your Samba server while you are proceeding through these steps. You will start up the services later.

Step 3   Because of various security issues, accurate server time is critical for being an Active Directory member. Therefore, it is best to set up the Network Time Protocol (NTP) on your Linux Samba server prior to it becoming an Active Directory member. Linux NTP implementation was covered in the LPIC-1 certification.

Step 5   You need to consider several smb.conf directive settings in the [global] section in this scenario. Which directives you set depend on your particular mixed environment. For example, consider setting or modifying the netbios name, security, workgroup, and realm (all covered earlier in this chapter) directives.

> As tempting as it is, it is not recommended to copy a Linux Samba server Active Directory member's smb.conf file off the Internet and paste it onto your Samba server. Too many important security compromises can occur. You should fully understand the necessary configuration settings needed prior to integrating your Samba server into an Active Directory environment.

A Windows Active Directory controller uses security identifiers (SIDs) to identify users. In the Samba environment, identity mapping (IDMAP) determines how Windows security identifiers are mapped to Linux UIDs and GIDs. The `idmap config` directive controls this mapping. The directive settings are sometimes called *winbind idmap backends*. You may also need to add this directive to the `smb.conf` file's `[global]` section for integrating your Linux Samba server into an Active Directory environment.

> Setting the `idmap config` directive is rather complex. Also, various potential additional directives may be required depending on how this particular directive is set. See the Samba documentation for details.

Step 6   The net utility was originally created to mimic the Microsoft utility of the same name. It has many powerful options to manage your Samba environment. Using super user privileges, the basic syntax for becoming an Active Directory member (or joining a domain) is

```
net mode join -U administrator-username
```

The *administrator-username* is the Active Directory (or domain) administrator's account name. The *mode* is either ads (Active Directory) or rpc (domain). Depending on the configuration, you may be required to supply the administrator account's password.

> Do not use the `samba-tool` utility to join the Active Directory as a member. If you do so, your Samba shares may not operate correctly.

Step 7   In order to set up the Samba server to retrieve Active Directory user and group data from the `winbindd` daemon, you modify the `/etc/nsswitch.conf` configuration file and add the following records:

```
passwd: files winbind
group:  files winbind
```

If you want the Samba server's `/etc/passwd` and `/etc/group` files to be searched for user accounts and group information *before* attempting to retrieve its data from the `winbindd` daemon, a slight modification is needed. Replace `files` with `compat` in the `/etc/nsswitch.conf` records.

> You can test the Samba server's Active Directory membership after performing the previous steps and starting the `winbindd` daemon. The `wbinfo` command will help with this. Use `wbinfo -u` with super user privileges to see if the Samba server can display Active Directory users and `wbinfo -g` to see the groups. If you can display this data, all is well. If you cannot, see this chapter's troubleshooting section to assist you in determining the problem as well as Samba documentation on Active Directory membership.

Configuring a Samba Server Printer Share

Sharing printers among Linux and Windows systems is best done using the Internet Printing Protocol (IPP), and this method has been available for many years. However, you may have a legacy system or unusual environment that requires you instead to use Samba to share printers.

Assuming that you already have users set up for a file share, adding a printer share is relatively easy. First, you will need to modify the Samba server configuration file. This Samba server's configuration file has been modified on a CentOS system to share its printers. Only the file's [printers] settings section is displayed here:

```
# cat smb.conf
[...]
#=================== Share Definitions ====================
#
[...]
[printers]
    comment = All Printers
    path = /var/spool/samba
    browseable = no
    guest ok = no
    writable = no
    printable = yes
#
```

The [printers] section directives are fairly simple. You can set directives for all of the printers loaded on your Samba server (typically from the /etc/cups/printers.conf file). The path directive sets a spool directory. The default setting should be fine. If you decide to change it, be sure that the new directory has world write access and the sticky bit is set on it.

With the printable directive set to yes, clients can submit spool files on the path directory. If the writable directive is set to no, non-printing write access is blocked.

After modifying your smb.conf file, be sure to restart the Samba service to have the modifications take effect.

You will need at least one printer queue on your Samba server. Configuring and managing printers is covered in the LPIC-1 certification. In this example, the local Samba server queue is paused (cupsdisable) to hold any incoming client jobs (for testing purposes), and the offered printer share is checked using the smbclient command:

```
# lpstat -a
SShare_PrinterA accepting requests since [...]
#
```

```
# cupsdisable SShare_PrinterA
#
# smbclient -L //localhost -U Malcolm
Enter Malcolm's password:
Domain=[FIREFLYGROUP] [...]

    Sharename       Type        Comment
    ---------       ----        -------
    ssharea         Disk        Server Share A
[...]
    SShare_PrinterA Printer     Samba Share Printer A
[...]
#
```

You can see that the SShare_PrinterA printer is available via the Samba service. Once you have your Samba server printer share checked, you can set up any number of Windows or Linux clients to use it.

Configuring a Samba Client's Printer Share Access

If you have completed all of the work for setting up a file share, and the Samba server is offering a printer share, you only need to check the service. Here the smbclient command is employed to check the offered shares on an Ubuntu Samba client:

```
$ smbclient -L //192.168.56.102 -U Malcolm
Enter Malcolm's password:
Domain=[FIREFLYGROUP] [...]

    Sharename       Type        Comment
    ---------       ----        -------
    ssharea         Disk        Server Share A
[...]
    SShare_PrinterA Printer     Samba Share Printer A
[...]
$
```

Now that the printer share has been checked, you can again use the smbclient command to send a print job to the share. In this example on an Ubuntu Samba client system, the smbclient command is broken up onto two lines for clarity:

```
$ smbclient //192.168.56.102/SShare_PrinterA \
> -U Malcolm -c "print myfile.dat"
Enter Malcolm's password:
Domain=[FIREFLYGROUP] [...]
putting file myfile.dat as myfile.dat [...]
$
```

The -c option allows a command string to be sent. Multiple commands can be sent as long as they are separated by a semicolon (;). Alternatively, you can enter into the FTP-style service provided by smbclient and enter the command(s) at the prompt.

Looking on the CentOS Samba server side, the paused printer queue is holding the job sent from the Ubuntu Samba client:

```
# lpstat SShare_PrinterA
SShare_PrinterA-1       malcolm                 2048 [...]
#
```

Once you have everything set up and tested for the printer share, be sure to unpause the Samba server's printer queue using the cupsenable command.

Troubleshooting Samba

There are many potential pitfalls when setting up and managing your Samba server and/or clients. Therefore, it's a good idea to have a standard troubleshooting map in order to address issues quickly as they arise.

The following items can help you get your Samba service back in order quickly:

Use the testparm utility.   One of the most important steps that you can take to avoid problems is to check your Samba configuration file's syntax after *every* modification. The testparm utility, demonstrated earlier, makes this task easy. Doing this quick step may save you hours of frustration later over a simple typographical error.

Make sure the daemon is running.   When Samba problems occur, the next simple task is to check to see if the needed server daemons are running. There are potentially three daemons that need to be employed. At a minimum, the smbd daemon (smb service) *must* be running on the Samba server. Whether the nmbd and the winbindd daemons need to be running depends on your mixed environment.

Perform a basic Samba share check.   On the Samba server, you can see what shares are being offered via the smbclient -L command (with the -U option and appropriate parameter if needed). If you get a response from the command but do not see particular shares, you will need to review your server's smb.conf file settings.

Employ the correct workgroup setting.   If you are in a mixed environment, recall that you must use the Windows workgroup/domain name; otherwise, Windows systems cannot find the Samba service. Traditionally, it is set to all uppercase letters. Review the workgroup directive setting within your Samba server's smb.conf file to ensure that it is correct.

Perform basic network diagnostics.   Sometimes the Samba clients simply cannot reach the Samba services because of network issues. Perform a few basic network diagnostics. Try to ping (or ping6, if you are using IPv6) a Samba client from the Samba server and vice versa. Employ the traceroute (or traceroute6) command. On the Samba server, install and use the nmap program to see what ports are open inside and outside the firewall.

Review the log files.   The various Samba server log files are typically located in the /var/ log/samba/ directory. Peruse the various files for problem clues. If you don't have the log files broken up by client, you may want to do this in your smb.conf file as follows:

```
log file = /var/log/samba/log.%m
```

The %m will substitute to either a NetBIOS name or an IP address for each client, depending on your particular configuration. Either way, it will give you finer control over the logs and allow faster problem isolation for particular Samba clients.

Increase the logging debug level.   By default, the log level directive is set to 0, which means that logging is turned *off*. You can use the directive in your Samba configuration file to turn on and/or increase the logging level. Level 1 is the lowest and Level 10 is the highest. You can also increase the logging level for particular debug classes, such as smb: 10, if desired.

An older but interesting method is changing the logging debug level on the fly. This employs the kill command, a signal, and the Samba server daemon's PID. To increase the logging level by *one* level, using super user privileges, send the SIGUSR1 signal to the Samba server daemon via its PID (*smbd-PID*):

```
kill SIGUSR1 smbd-PID
```

You can also *lower* the logging debug level (make it less verbose) by one level on the fly. This method sends the SIGUSR2 signal to the Samba server daemon:

```
kill SIGUSR2 smbd-PID
```

Check basic Samba status.   The smbstatus command (if available on your distribution) lists the current SMB connections to the Samba server. You can increase displayed information via the -d (debug) option. A -d 10 is verbose, whereas a -d 1 is less so.

The net utility has many powerful options that allow you not only to manage your Samba environment but to troubleshoot problems as well. There are three parameters that you pass to the net command to pinpoint your environment: ads (for an Active Directory environment), rad (for the older Windows 9x and Windows NT3 environments), or rpc (for the older Windows NT4 and Windows 2000 environments). For example, if you are in an Active Directory environment, you could issue the command **net ads info** to obtain details about a remote Active Directory controller.

Several other utilities may help you troubleshoot a particular problem. Look back at the various Samba tools listed in Table 10.3.

Look up NetBIOS information.   The nmblookup utility is helpful when you are in a legacy mixed environment. As long as you are using the nmbd daemon and it is running, the utility will use NetBIOS over TCP to look up NetBIOS names. For example, on the Samba server, you can issue the command **nmblookup -A *server-IP-address*** to display information, such as the Samba workgroup name to which this system belongs. You can also get the same information along with the system's hostname:

```
nmblookup -S server-hostname
```

Determine if the Samba client system(s) cannot receive or respond to a Samba server query message via the -d1 "*" option. Also, attempt to find the Master Browser (a Microsoft term that denotes the primary computer in a workgroup that keeps track of which systems are attached to the non-domain LAN), using the -M *workgroup-name* option. Failures here indicate a potential network configuration problem, such as an incorrect subnet mask setting.

Another useful troubleshooting nmblookup command option is the -B *client-IP-address* "*" option. If a failure is returned, then the Samba client is not seeing client queries, which may indicate a Samba misconfiguration or potentially a firewall issue.

Review user/group settings.   If your Samba problem is isolated to a particular Samba user or group, review the various security settings for that user/group. Depending on your configuration, these settings are potentially stored in multiple locations, such as the /etc/passwd file on both the server and the client and the Samba user databases.

For the Samba user databases, the easiest checking method is via the pdbedit command. The pdbedit utility can manage and display information concerning various Samba user databases, such as ldap and smbpasswd. To see a quick list of every account, enter **pdbedit -L**, using super user privileges at the command line. For information regarding a particular account, tack on -u *username* to the pdbedit -L command's end.

If you are in a mixed environment, check the Windows account settings. Also, don't forget your username map file if you have employed that tool. If your Samba server is an Active Directory member, use the wbinfo -u and wbinfo -g commands to see if the winbindd daemon can obtain usernames and groups data.

If you still cannot isolate the problem's cause, you can also employ the help of others via online forums. There are many Samba forums, as well as various distribution forums, where you can ask for help.

 Real World Scenario

Using NetBIOS

In a mixed Windows and Linux environment, where legacy Windows systems (prior to Windows 2000) are used, it may be necessary to employ the NetBIOS protocol. Currently, the NetBIOS protocol is implemented as NetBIOS over TCP/IP, and it provides features such as name resolution and shares for systems without DNS. The NetBIOS protocol is managed via the nmbd daemon.

Legacy Windows systems (prior to Windows 2000) connect to Samba shares using the NetBIOS protocol and the Samba server's port 139. After Windows 2000, Windows systems can connect to Samba shares using both the NetBIOS protocol (port 139) and TCP/IP protocol (port 445).

Unfortunately, NetBIOS has been documented as rather vulnerable to malicious attacks. The root cause of any Samba problems that you are encountering could be tied to such an attack. If you do not have legacy Windows systems, do *not* enable NetBIOS or run the nmbd daemon. Also, be sure to disable the nmbd daemon from starting at system boot time.

If you *must* run NetBIOS, be sure that you are also running the winbindd daemon to provide correct NetBIOS system names to IP address translations. Also, keep your Samba shares within a local network and use a firewall to block access to that network. Seriously consider upgrading your Windows systems or implementing a different method for sharing files and printers. NetBIOS vulnerabilities have been documented since at least 2005.

A Samba server offers many features that are especially helpful in mixed-system network environments. However, if you don't need all of the features that a Samba server offers, a simpler approach is to use NFS.

Looking at NFS

While NFS lacks features for mixed environments, it does provide enhanced performance for sharing files. It's a better alternative for non-mixed networks.

Understanding NFS

Covered briefly in Chapter 4, the acronym NFS stands for Network File System. *NFS* is a protocol that allows client systems to access and use NFS server-offered filesystems over a network as local filesystems.

The NFS protocol has changed over time. There are three versions, which you will often see referenced in documentation and configuration files. They are as follows:

NFSv2   Defined around 1989, this older NFS version uses only UDP. Because UDP is a connectionless protocol with no guarantee of delivery, you could experience data loss as filesystem data is transported over the network. This NFS version also uses signed 32-bit files, which adversely limits a file's maximum allowable size. It also has serious performance issues and should be avoided if possible.

NFSv3   This popular NFS version, defined in 1995, can use either UPD or TCP. It also allows asynchronous writes and other optimized operations, such as weak cache consistency. While *weak cache* sounds bad, it is not. Weak cache consistency is the ability to detect changes to data quickly (when data has been modified by others, such as another NFS client). Via additional passed data attribute information, it can be determined if file data held in its cache is stale. The caching speeds up data access, while the weak cache consistency keeps the data fresh. This NFS version also uses 64-bit files.

However, NFSv3 still has problems and weaknesses. For example, there are several network ports involved in NFSv3. If an NFS client and NFS server can only connect over a WAN and their individual LAN networks are protected by firewalls, the firewall must allow access for those multiple network ports. Another example is NFSv3's use of the Network Lock Manager (NLM) protocol (which helps prevent data corruption) via ancillary methods, which slows performance.

NFSv4   The default on many current distributions, this NFS version was originally defined in 2000 under the Internet Engineering Task Force (IETF)'s direction. NFSv4 was redefined in 2015. It provides all NFSv3's features as well as support for Kerberos authentication (v3 authenticates via usernames) and uses TCP for transport (though it offers UDP for backward compatibility purposes). It also consolidates NFSv3's multiple ports into one well-known port, 2049. Instead of using ancillary NLM methods, NFSv4 has built-in file-locking management features, which improve performance. An NFSv4 client views the NFSv4 server's exports as a *single* filesystem (NFSv4 pseudo-filesystem). Overall, NFSv4 provides superior performance, enhanced security, better scalability, improved internationalization (via UTF-8), and so on.

 The LPIC-2 certification objectives focus on NFSv3. Therefore, most of this section's information is based on NFSv3.

NFSv3 software uses the Remote Procedure Call (RPC) protocol. The *RPC* protocol allows a program to be ignorant of network details but still request services from another system within that network. For NFSv3, RPC handles mounting the NFS filesystem, lock management, and quota.

The filesystem an NFS server offers is called either an *export* or a *share*. However, the processing of making an NFS share available is only called *exporting*.

To implement NFS services, your distribution's Linux kernel must support NFS. This is because NFS is a combination of kernel-level functions and daemons.

Depending on your NFS configuration and version, there are potentially several daemons or kernel services involved in providing NFS shares. The various NFS daemons and Linux kernel services are described in Table 10.9.

TABLE 10.9   NFS daemons and kernel services

Name	Alias	Description
idmapd	rpc.idmapd	This daemon maps user and group IDs into names and vice versa based on settings in the /etc/idmapd.conf file. This daemon is required on both NFS servers and clients and is not used in NFSv3 or lower.

TABLE 10.9 NFS daemons and kernel services *(continued)*

Name	Alias	Description
lockd	rpc.lockd	Broken up into a daemon and a kernel service, the daemon starts the NLM protocol service in Linux kernels (only for kernels that don't start the NLM service automatically). The daemon service name is nfslock. The kernel service provides NFS file locking. This kernel service is required on both NFS servers and clients, and it is not used in NFSv4.
mountd	rpc.mountd	A daemon that handles NFS client mount requests on the NFS server side.
nfsd	rpc.nfsd	Broken up into a daemon and a kernel service, the daemon handles the user-level NFS service portion of file access and data streaming. In NFSv4, it is not required to work with RPC, because it handles the needed RPC services, such as file locking.
portmapper	rpcbind	This daemon maps RPC services to the various RPC ports (also called *registering*). In addition, it sets up the connection for a client-requested RPC service. This daemon is required to run on both NFS servers and clients. Access can be controlled via TCP Wrappers. Not needed in NFSv4 but provided for backward-compatibility purposes.
rquotad	rpc.rquotad	Manages user quotas on NFS exports and includes the ability to view current quota settings. This daemon is required to run on both NFS servers and clients. It is not used in NFSv4, except for backward-compatibility purposes.
statd	rpc.statd	The Network Status Monitor (NSM) daemon that works with the lockd kernel service to provide NLM protocol file locking. This daemon is started by the nfslock service (lockd daemon), and it is not used in NFSv4, except for backward-compatibility purposes.

Documentation is always important. However, as you look through Table 10.9, you can see how confusing the various daemon and kernel service names can be. Choosing which NFS version to use can be difficult. Therefore, with NFS, it is vital to review NFS documentation prior to NFS implementation.

WARNING The rquotad daemon has a known vulnerability, which could allow a malicious user to execute random commands. This NFSv3 service is typically started within the system startup scripts. It would be wise to disable it.

For NFS documentation, if you have NFS installed, typically the /usr/share/doc/nfs*/ directories have current documentation as well as the locally installed man pages. You can also find Linux NFS documentation at the developer site's wiki at http://linux-nfs.org. If you are seeking older NFS documentation, visit the old NFS developers' site at http://nfs.sourceforge.net/.

Configuring NFS

Because NFS is feature-rich and multiple-version file-sharing software, configuring an NFS server for your needs can be tricky. It's important to determine your site's requirements first, prior to configuration. These requirements will assist as you determine what configuration options to choose.

Installing NFS Server on Linux

Several NFS packages are available. Which package(s) you need to install depends on your distribution, its version, the NFS version you are trying to implement, as well as whether you are installing packages for an NFS server or a client.

Generally, for a Red Hat–based distribution, you'll find the NFS packages listed in Table 10.10 either preinstalled or available to install. This is a general list, so be sure to review your distribution's documentation concerning NFS.

TABLE 10.10   Red Hat distribution NFS packages

Package Name	Description
nfs-utils	NFS server daemon and utilities for server and client, such as the showmount command.
nfs-utils-lib	Support libraries required by nfs-utils utilities. Only needed on older distributions.
rpcbind	Provides RPC services required by NFSv3.
portmap	Older RPC services package that is replaced by the rpcbind package on current distributions.

Typically for a Debian-based distribution, such as Ubuntu, you'll find the NFS packages listed in Table 10.11 are either preinstalled or available to install. This is not an exhaustive list, so be sure to review your distribution's documentation concerning NFS packages.

TABLE 10.11   Debian distribution NFS packages

Package Name	Description
nfs-kernel-server	NFS server daemon.
nfs-common	NFS server and client support files and utilities, such as the showmount command.
rpcbind	Provides RPC services required by NFSv3.
portmap	Older package that is replaced by the rpcbind package on current distributions.

For example purposes, an NFS server will be set up on a CentOS system and an NFS client on an Ubuntu system. Here is a snipped example of installing the needed NFS server package on the CentOS system:

```
# yum install nfs-utils
[...]
---> Package nfs-utils.x86_64 [...] will be installed
[...]
Installed:
  nfs-utils.x86_64 [...]

Complete!
#
# rpm -qa | grep rpcbind
rpcbind-[...].x86_64
#
```

Notice in the preceding example that the rpcbind package, which is needed to provide NFSv3 required RPC services, is already installed.

For the Ubuntu NFS client, only the nfs-common package needs to be installed. Here is the snipped installation process:

```
$ sudo apt-get install nfs-common
[sudo] password for christine:
[...
The following extra packages will be installed:
  libgssglue1 libnfsidmap2 libtirpc1 rpcbind
[...]
[...]
Removing any system startup links for /etc/init.d/rpcbind ...
```

```
rpcbind start/running, process 4222
[...]
Creating config file /etc/idmapd.conf with new version

Creating config file /etc/default/nfs-common with new version
Adding system user 'statd' (UID 117) ...
Adding new user 'statd' (UID 117) with group 'nogroup' ...
Not creating home directory '/var/lib/nfs'.
statd start/running, process 4455
gssd stop/pre-start, process 4489
idmapd start/running, process 4543
[...]
$
```

Notice in the preceding example that the rpcbind package was also installed in this process. Even though in this situation the NFS client is prepared to use NFSv4, it still provides rpcbind for backward compatibility.

Exploring NFS Directories and Files

Several NFS files and directories are involved in the export configuration, and being aware of them makes the export management process easier. The primary files and directories are listed in Table 10.12.

TABLE 10.12   NFS files and directories

Name	Description
/etc/exports	The main NFS export configuration file. Also called the *NFS server export table*. Used on the NFS server only.
/etc/exports.d/	The directory may contain extra export configuration files. The files must have the .exports file extension to be recognized by NFS.
/etc/nfsmount.conf	The NFS mount options configuration file. Used on the NFS client only.
/etc/sysconfig/nfs	Red Hat–based distributions' primary NFS configuration file. Used on the NFS server and client.
/etc/default/nfs-kernel-server	Debian-based distributions' primary NFS configuration file. Used on the NFS server only.
/etc/default/nfs-common	Debian-based distributions' primary NFS configuration file. Used on the NFS client only.
/proc/fs/nfs/exports	Contains current exports and the individual client (not subnets) using them.

TABLE 10.12 NFS files and directories *(continued)*

Name	Description
/var/lib/nfs/xtab	Contains the same data as /proc/fs/nfs/exports, but it is *not* maintained by the kernel and is used only when /proc is not mounted.
/var/lib/nfs/etab	Contains current exports available for client systems. Used on the NFS server only.
/var/lib/nfs/rmtab	Contains current exports and client systems that have them currently mounted. Used on the NFS server only.

In addition to the items listed in Table 10.12, the /proc/filesystems, /etc/fstab, /etc/mtab, and /proc/mounts can also be involved with NFS. These files were covered in Chapter 4.

Exploring the */etc/exports* File

The /etc/exports file is where you configure your NFS server's shares. Each record represents a single export, and the typical record is formatted as follows:

export_directory client-designation (directives)

The *export_directory* is the NFS server share (directory tree) being exported. Typical share directory locations include /var/ and /srv/. For example, you can set the *export_directory* to /var/nfsshare.

The *client-designation* sets the client(s) that can access this export. It can take one of many formats, as shown in Table 10.13.

TABLE 10.13 The /etc/exports client(s) designation

Type	Description
Single Host	A single client system can be entered via IPv4 or IPv6 address (though IPv6 must be in square brackets), a host name, or an FQDN.
Netgroups	An NIS netgroup is designated by @*group_name*.
Multiple systems	The asterisk (*) or question mark (?) wildcard can be used with a hostname or an FQDN to designated multiple systems. However, with an FQDN, an asterisk wildcard can only be used between the dots (.). For example, *.c.org will include b.c.org in the system series but will *not* include a.b.c.org. Wildcards should not be used with IP addresses because of potentially unpredictable results.

Type	Description
IP networks	An IP network is designated by *IP_Address*/*netmask*. For IPv4 addresses, the *netmask* can be either by class-based format or CIDR. For IPv6 addresses, use an adjacent netmask length and do not put the netmask within the square brackets.

Some *directives* have odd names and need additional explanation. The primary /etc/ exports file directives are listed in Table 10.14, along with a brief description.

TABLE 10.14   The /etc/exports file directives

Directive	Description
ro	Sets the filesystem export as read-only.
rw	Allows reads of and writes to the filesystem export.
async	Export *is not* first checked to see if write cache buffers have been flushed to disk before reading data. Increases performance of read-only (ro) exports but also data corruption risks due to unclean server restarts after a crash.
sync	Export *is* first checked to see if write cache buffers have been flushed to disk (and if not, waits for the data to be committed) before reading or writing data. Important for read/write (rw) exports.
all_squash	All export client users (including root) are treated as anonymous users.
no_root_squash	Allows the client root user account to access the NFS export using super user privileges.
root_squash	Maps the client root user account to an unprivileged user account (typically the nfsnobody account).
fsid	Identifies filesystem export by UUID or device number. In NFSv4, can be set to root or 0, which indicates that this particular filesystem is the root of all exported filesystems.
anongid	Assigns specified GID to anonymous group clients, and it is typically used where it is desired for all client requests to appear to be from one user.
anonuid	Assigns specified UID to anonymous user clients, and it is typically used where it is desired for all client requests to appear to be from one user.

TABLE 10.14   The /etc/exports file directives *(continued)*

Directive	Description
subtree_check	Enables subtree checking, where permissions are checked on higher-level directories.
no_subtree_check	Disables subtree checking. May improve export reliability in some situations.

You can see all of the directives associated with the /etc/exports file by typing **man exports** at the command line.

You can quickly check to see if your default /etc/exports configuration file is configured to use NFSv4. Just look for the fsid option settings. If one of them is set to root or 0, you know it is configured for NFSv4 by default.

Exploring NFS Utilities

The various NFS utilities can help you in the NFS export creation, management, and troubleshooting activities. The utilities to use and which ones are available on your system will depend on the system's distribution and the NFS version. The primary utilities that you will use are listed in Table 10.15.

TABLE 10.15   NFS utilities

Utility	Description
exportfs	Manages and displays information concerning shares.
mount.nfs	Mounts a designated NFS export on an NFS client.
mountstats	Displays NFS client per-mount statistics from the /proc/self/mountstats file.
nfsiostat	Displays NFS client per-mount I/O statistics from the /proc/self/mountstats file.
nfsstat	Displays NFS client and server activity statistics from the /proc/net/rpc/nfsd, /proc/net/rpc/nfs, and /proc/mounts files.
rpcinfo	Displays RPC service information.
showmount	Displays NFS server information, such as its state and NFS clients mounting its provided exports. Can be used remotely.
umount.nfs	Unmounts designated NFS export on NFS client.

The rpcinfo utility can be helpful in certain situations. It allows you to display various RPC service information, such as what ports are involved, as shown snipped here on a CentOS NFS server:

```
# rpcinfo -p
   program vers proto   port  service
    100000    4   tcp    111  portmapper
[...]
    100000    4   udp    111  portmapper
[...]
    100005    1   tcp  20048  mountd
    100024    1   tcp  47711  status
[...]
    100003    4   tcp   2049  nfs
    100227    3   tcp   2049  nfs_acl
    100003    3   udp   2049  nfs
    100003    4   udp   2049  nfs
[...]
    100021    4   udp  57070  nlockmgr
[...]
    100021    4   tcp  42140  nlockmgr
#
```

The exportfs utility deserves some special attention too. It is responsible for reading the /etc/exports file when the NFS service starts (and for NFSv3 and lower, mounting the shares via mountd). In addition, exportfs is a handy command to use for testing and managing exports.

Used with no options, the exportfs command displays all of the current exports. Table 10.16 shows the options that you may employ on a regular basis for modified command behavior.

TABLE 10.16   The exportfs utility options

Option	Description
-a	Exports (or unexports if used with -u) all configured shares in the /etc/exports file.
-i	Ignores /etc/exports configured shares and uses command-line options for configuring shares instead.
-o	Exports designated share configured via the command line.
-r	Re-exports (refreshes) all configured shares in the /etc/exports file via rebuilding the /etc/lib/nfs/xtab file. Useful for loading /etc/exports configuration changes.

TABLE 10.16   The exportfs utility options *(continued)*

Option	Description
-u	Unexports a designated exported share.
-v	Provides verbose information while conducting operations.

See the exportfs command's man pages for additional options. Keep in mind that any references to /etc/exports also include shares configured in /etc/exports.d/*.exports files, if used on your NFS server.

Disabling NFSv4

The certification objectives focus on NFSv3, so if you are using a current distribution, you may need to turn off NFSv4 functionality in order to use NFSv3. Here are some ways to accomplish this task.

For Red Hat–based distributions on an NFS server and any client systems, edit the /etc/sysconfig/nfs configuration file. If listed within the file, change NFS4_Support from yes to no. If that option is not listed in the file, add the following file line:

```
RPCNFSDARGS='--no-nfs-version 4'
```

If the RPCNFSDARGS setting pre-exists in the configuration file, tack on the --no-nfs-version 4 argument to the other listed options. Keep in mind that if you are using an older Red Hat–based distribution, NFSv4 may not be implemented already.

For a Debian-based distribution's NFS server, edit the /etc/default/nfs-kernel-server file. Tack on the --no-nfs-version 4 option to the RPCMOUNTDOPTS directive or RPCNFSDCOUNT directive. Which directive is used depends on the distribution's age.

When you mount the NFS export, you may need to include the mount option, vers=3, to use NFSv3. This won't disable NFSv4 but instead forces the client to use an NFSv3 connection.

Once you have finished studying, it would be wise to reenable NFSv4. It provides many enhancements, as covered previously in this chapter.

Configuring a Temporary NFS Export

To create a temporary NFS export or test an NFS export before making it permanent, there are several steps to take. The steps that you need to use will depend on your distribution as well as the NFS version you are employing. The basic steps for temporarily configuring a share on an NFS server are as follows:

1. Install or update NFS server software.
2. Start the needed NFS services.
3. Create an NFS server directory for the share.
4. Export the directory share using the exportfs command.

5. Check the offered export on the NFS server.

6. Modify the firewall as needed.

7. When the client is finished using the temporary share, unexport it.

   The basic steps for using the share on an NFS client are as follows:

1. Install or update NFS client software.

2. Create an NFS client directory to mount the share.

3. Modify the firewall as needed.

4. Mount the NFS share.

5. Test the mounted NFS share.

6. Copy files as needed.

7. Unmount the NFS share on the client.

   As an example, the following section steps you through creating a share on a CentOS NFS server and using that share on an Ubuntu NFS client. Since the NFS server and client installation process was already covered in this chapter, it will not be repeated here.

   To start the needed services, use your NFS server distribution's method. For this CentOS NFS server example, the systemctl command is used to start the nfs and rpcbind services:

```
# systemctl start nfs rpcbind
#
```

 Depending on your distribution, you may need to configure SELinux booleans to allow the NFS server to export shares. Though doing so is beyond this book's scope, you can temporarily disengage SELinux for NFS testing purposes. This was covered earlier in the Samba section.

Next, if one is not already created, create an NFS server directory. An example is shown here along with the creation of a sample file:

```
# mkdir /srv/nfs_share_temp
#
# echo "Hello World" >> /srv/nfs_share_temp/file.dat
#
# cat /srv/nfs_share_temp/file.dat
Hello World
#
# ls -l /srv/nfs_share_temp
total 4
-rw-r--r-- 1 root root 12 Apr 28 17:01 file.dat
#
```

Next, the exportfs utility is employed to export the NFS share temporarily. The basic syntax for using exportfs for this task is

exportfs *client-IP-address*:/*share-directory*

The *client-IP-address* is the IP address of the NFS client system that will mount this temporary export. If you use the wrong IP address, an access denied by server message will occur when attempting to mount the share on the NFS client.

Continuing with the example, the NFS client's IP address is 192.168.56.101. On the NFS server, this exportfs command is used to export the share:

```
# exportfs  192.168.56.101:/srv/nfs_share_temp
#
```

Once the share is exported, it is wise to perform a few basic checks. The showmount command and exportfs utility can help. Here are examples of using these commands on the CentOS NFS server to check the exported share:

```
# showmount -e
Export list for localhost.localdomain:
/srv/nfs_share_temp 192.168.56.101
#
# showmount -e 127.0.0.1
Export list for 127.0.0.1:
/srv/nfs_share_temp 192.168.56.101
#
# exportfs -v
/srv/nfs_share_temp
        192.168.56.101(ro,wdelay,root_squash,no_subtree_check,
sec=sys,ro,secure,root_squash,no_all_squash)
#
# cat /var/lib/nfs/etab
/srv/nfs_share_temp    192.168.56.101(ro,sync,wdelay,hide,nocrossmnt,secure,
root_squash,no_all_squash,no_subtree_check,secure_locks,
acl,no_pnfs,anonuid=65534,anongid=65534,sec=sys,ro,secure,
root_squash,no_all_squash)
#
```

Notice that exportfs -v provides the default options set, even though no options were specified in the exportfs command when exporting the share. Also note that you can view export information from the /var/lib/nfs/etab file on this particular distribution.

If you want to specify options for temporary NFS exports, use the exportfs -o (*options*) command.

The last step in setting up a temporary NFS share on the server-side is to modify the firewall. Firewalls are covered in Chapter 12.

If you are trying out these steps at home on a non-production system, you can temporarily lower your firewall using super user privileges and entering **iptables -F** at the command line.

On the NFS client, the first step is to install or update any needed NFS client software and start any NFS client services needed. After that is completed, create a directory to mount the share, similar to the example on an Ubuntu system here:

```
$ mkdir /home/christine/NFSTemp
$
```

Once you have the mount point created, you can check the offered share using showmount and the NFS server's IP address as demonstrated:

```
$ showmount -e 192.168.56.102
Export list for 192.168.56.102:
/srv/nfs_share_temp 192.168.56.101
$
```

Now you are ready to mount the NFS exported share. This is done with the mount .nfs (or mount -t nfs) command, super user privileges, and an additional mount option. The Ubuntu NFS client mount command example is broken onto multiple lines for clarity:

```
$ sudo mount.nfs -o vers=3 \
> 192.168.56.102:/srv/nfs_share_temp NFSTemp
[sudo] password for christine:
$
```

The -o vers=3 option was used to force NFSv3 use. This may not be needed on older distributions.

You can check that the export is mounted via the mount -t nfs command.

Once the export is mounted, you can use it as if it were a locally mounted filesystem:

```
$ ls NFSTemp
file.dat
$
$ cat NFSTemp/file.dat
```

```
Hello World
$
$ touch NFSTemp/newfile.dat
touch: cannot touch 'NFSTemp/newfile.dat': Read-only file system
$
$ cp NFSTemp/file.dat file.dat
$
$ cat file.dat
Hello World
$
```

Because the share was created on the NFS server as a read-only share, the touch command does not work. However, the files pre-existing on the share are successfully copied to another local client directory.

On the NFS server, you can see information concerning this remotely mounted export by viewing the /var/lib/nfs/rmtab file. Here is an example on a CentOS NFS server:

```
# cat /var/lib/nfs/rmtab
192.168.56.101:/srv/nfs_share_temp:0x00000001
#
```

Once you are finished with the temporary export, simply unmount the share on the NFS client. Be sure to do this step prior to removing the temporary share on the NFS server. In the example, the Ubuntu NFS client system is first unmounted:

```
$ sudo umount NFSTemp
[sudo] password for christine:
$
```

Now that the NFS client has unmounted the export, the NFS server can remove (unexport) the temporary share. In the example, the CentOS NFS server system unexports the share via the exportfs command and the -u option as shown here:

```
# exportfs -u 192.168.56.101:/srv/nfs_share_temp
#
# exportfs -v
#
# showmount -e
Export list for localhost.localdomain:
#
```

Once you unexport a share, it's a good idea to use the showmount -e and/or the exportfs -v commands to verify that the export has been removed.

Configuring a Permanent NFS Export

The basic steps for configuring a permanent NFS export vary only slightly from creating a temporary one. On the NFS server, they are as follows:

1. Install or update NFS server software.
2. Start the needed NFS services.
3. Create an NFS server directory for the share.
4. Configure the NFS share within the /etc/exports configuration file.
5. Export the directory share using the exportfs command.
6. Check the offered export on the NFS server.
7. Modify the firewall as needed.
8. Ensure that the needed NFS services start at server boot time.

The basic steps for configuring the permanent share on an NFS client are as follows:

1. Install or update NFS client software.
2. Create an NFS client directory to mount the share.
3. Modify the firewall as needed.
4. Test by temporarily mounting the NFS export.
5. Modify the /etc/fstab to include the NFS share.
6. Mount the NFS share.
7. Test the mounted NFS share.
8. Ensure that the needed NFS services start at server boot time.

As an example, the following section steps through creating a permanent share on a CentOS NFS server and using the share on an Ubuntu NFS client. Any steps covered in creating a temporary NFS share that are applicable to this process will not be repeated here.

On the CentOS NFS server directory, /srv/nfs_share_perm/ was created to export. Permissions were modified on the directory first, and afterward the /etc/exports file had two records added to it. Each record in the /etc/exports file had to be displayed on two lines each because of their size, as shown here:

```
# chmod 777 /srv/nfs_perm
#
# cat /etc/exports
/srv/nfs_share_perm
192.168.56.101(rw,sync,no_root_squash,no_all_squash)
/srv/nfs_share_perm
192.168.56.*(ro,async,no_root_squash,no_all_squash)
#
```

Records are not set up per share but instead are set up *per client*. Therefore, you can have different options for different clients accessing the same share.

In the preceding example, the first record sets up a share for the NFS client machine at 192.168.56.101. The second record sets up a share for any NFS client system whose IPv4 address starts with 192.168.56. A wildcard (*) is used to accomplish this. Because the individual NFS client machine (at 192.168.56.101) is listed first, the first record's options will be applied to it. All other systems in the 192.168.56.* group will have the second /etc/exports record's options applied. The only difference in the two records' options is that the first is read/write (rw), while the second is read-only (ro).

It is critical to have *no spaces* between the NFS client machine name or IP address and the options list. A single space can result in undesired granted access.

Once changes have been made to the /etc/exports file, its contents need to be loaded into the NFS service. This is accomplished via the exportfs utility, as shown snipped here:

```
# exportfs -r
#
# showmount -e
Export list for localhost.localdomain:
/srv/nfs_share_perm 192.168.56.*
#
# exportfs -v
/srv/nfs_share_perm
      192.168.56.101(rw,[...]
/srv/nfs_share_perm
      192.168.56.*(ro,[...]
#
```

Notice that the showmount -e command shows only the last record for the /srv/nfs_share_perm share. In addition, the showmount -e command will *not* work for an NFSv4 server. The exportfs -v shows both (and it will work for an NFSv4 server). You can see the advantage of using the exportfs command instead of the showmount command.

Some NFS administrators use the exportfs -ra command to load /etc/exports modifications instead of the exportfs -r command.

On the NFS client system, once the mount point directory is created, you can mount the export. Here the export is mounted temporarily and some tests are run before modifying the /etc/fstab file:

```
$ mkdir NFSPerm
$
$ sudo mount.nfs -o vers=3 \
```

```
> 192.168.56.102:/srv/nfs_share_perm NFSPerm
[sudo] password for christine:
$
$ ls NFSPerm
$
$ touch NFSPerm/new_file.dat
$
$ ls -l NFSPerm
total 0
-rw-rw-r-- 1 christine christine 0 Apr 28 23:52 new_file.dat
$
```

Notice that the export is read/write, so the NFS client is accessing the correct share record, which was provided by the first record in the NFS server's /etc/exports file.

You can also view the mounted export using both the mount and df commands. The results are shown snipped here:

```
$ mount -t nfs
192.168.56.102:/srv/nfs_share_perm on /home/christine/NFSPerm
type nfs (rw,vers=3,addr=192.168.56.102)
$
$ df -h
Filesystem                        Size  [...]
[...]
192.168.56.102:/srv/nfs_share_perm  6.7G  [...]
$
```

An additional helpful utility in these cases is the mountstats command. It provides a great deal of information. Here the command is shown in action, snipped:

```
$ sudo mountstats /home/christine/NFSPerm
Stats for 192.168.56.102:/srv/nfs_share_perm mounted on
/home/christine/NFSPerm:
  NFS mount options:
[...]
  NFS server capabilities:
[...]
  NFS security flavor: 1  pseudoflavor: 0

NFS byte counts:
[...]
RPC statistics:
[...]
LOOKUP:
[...]
```

```
ACCESS:
[...]
$
$ sudo mountstats NFSPerm
Statistics for mount point NFSPerm not found
```

Notice that the mountstats command works only with absolute directory references. When a relative directory reference is used, it returns a not found error.

After mounting the export temporarily and testing it, the export should be unmounted (via umount) and the /etc/fstab file backed up and updated. Here is a record example that you may want to include in a /etc/fstab for a permanent NFS share (the record is displayed on two lines because of listing size limits, though the record in the file is on only one line):

```
$ cat /etc/fstab
[...]
# NFS file share
#
192.168.56.102:/srv/nfs_share_perm /home/christine/NFSPerm nfs
intr,nfsvers=3,tcp 0 0

$
$ sudo mount -a
$
```

It's a good idea to use the mount -a command to ensure that you have correct syntax in the /etc/fstab file. You can also use the mount -t nfs and df -h commands again to ensure that the export is properly mounted as well.

Only three mount options are used in the /etc/fstab preceding example, but there are several more possible options. The various and common mount options you can use with NFS shares within the /etc/fstab are shown in Table 10.17.

TABLE 10.17 NFS export fstab options

Option	Description
intr	Sets NFS client requests to be interrupted when the NFS server crashes or cannot be reached.
nfsvers=*number*	Defines the NFS version to use. The *number* can be 2, 3, or 4.
tcp	Sets the NFS share to be mounted using TCP. Typically used for read/write exports.
udp	Directs the NFS share to be mounted using UDP. Typically used for read-only exports.

Option	Description
port=*number*	Sets the NFS server port number to use. Can be set to 0 in order to force the NFS server's rpcbind to respond with the port number to use.
noacl	Turns off ACL processing. This is often used with older distributions or NFS versions.
nolock	Turns off file locking. This is often used with older NFS versions.
noexec	Turns off binary execution on mounted shares. Typically used for mounting shares from NFS servers with incompatible binaries.
nosuid	Turns off SUID/SGID on mounted shares.

You'll notice that a few options are directly related to security. There are a few other security measures you can implement, and they are covered in the next section.

When automatically mounting NFS exports via the /etc/fstab configuration file, the system may experience performance problems. In these cases, it is better to use AutoFS, which was covered in chapter 4.

Once an export is mounted on an NFS client, you can check the NFS client mount on the NFS server too. On this CentOS NFS server, two commands are used, as shown here:

```
# cat /var/lib/nfs/rmtab
192.168.56.101:/srv/nfs_share_perm:0x00000001
#
# showmount -a
All mount points on localhost.localdomain:
192.168.56.101:/srv/nfs_share_perm
#
```

After all this work, don't forget to enable your NFS services at boot time. The method to use depends on your NFS server and client's distribution.

Securing NFS

NFSv4 brings many new security features with it. Data exchanged between the NFS server and client is encrypted, TCP is the default protocol, and Kerberos can be used for authentication as well as encryption.

NFSv3 and lower use two methods to provide security. One is via the share records within the /etc/exports file. Each share record lists what system or group of systems can access a particular share via the client(s) designation (see Table 10.14). The other method involves the NFS client stating the remote user's UID and GID and enforces file permissions accordingly (called AUTH_SYS or AUTH_UNIX). Both methods can be easily overcome by a malicious user.

Securing NFSv3

If for some reason you have to use NFSv3, you need to do several things to improve its security. A few of these items may also be worthwhile on an NFSv4 configuration as well.

Use TCP.   Traditionally, NFS has used UDP, which is a connectionless protocol with no guarantee of delivery. This can allow data loss because filesystem data is transported over the network, and it is potentially insecure. UDP is easier to spoof. In other words, a malicious user could craft mount requests to look like they were coming from an authorized NFS client.

From the client side, you can force the use of TCP via the mount options used (see Table 10.17). From the server side, consider using AutoFS (covered in Chapter 4), instead of allowing clients to mount exports, and specify TCP in its mount options. Also on the server side, you can modify the NFS daemon's (nfsd or rpc.nfsd) run option to reject any UDP connections from NFS clients. Use the -U or --no-udp option when starting the daemon to enable this feature.

Limit wildcard use.   If feasible, limit the wildcard's use in the /etc/exports share records for NFS clients. Records that contain wildcards in their IP addresses, such as 192.168.56.*, potentially allow share access for systems that should not have such access. It is better to list the individual systems' IP addresses and provide access per share and per IP address.

Squash remote root access.   If no_root_squash is set on a share within the /etc/exports file, an NFS client root user can connect to the NFS server share with root privileges. It is better to set root_squash on shares. In this case, a remote root user is assigned and treated as either the user nfsnobody or nobody (depending on your distribution). The directive is so named because it squashes the remote root account's access to that of a lowly user account.

Squash everyone.   And since you are squashing remote root account access, go ahead and consider squashing everyone. Set the all_squash directive on a share record within the /etc/exports file. This way every remote account is set to that of a lowly nfsnobody or nobody user account.

Manage access to ports.   You can manage access to particular NFS server network ports using a firewall. (Firewalls are covered in Chapter 12.) The primary service ports to manage are used by rpcbind, mountd, and nfsd. Review the /etc/sysconfig/nfs, /etc/default/nfs-common, or /etc/default/nfs-kernel-server file (depending on your distribution) for additional configured ports to manage. Also, rpcinfo -p and nmap 127.0.0.1 will display ports in use (but not just by NFS), if you need a quick audit. Note that the nmap utility is not typically installed by default, but it is provided by the nmap package.

You may be able to use Kerberos and the RPCSEC_GSS protocol for authentication and traffic encryption purposes in NFSv3. Kerberos provides a network-based authentication process using symmetric (single-key) encryption and a trusted third-party Key Distribution Center (KDC). Details for this are beyond this book's scope. Find out more by reviewing your distribution's documentation on Kerberos and NFS.

These items will help to lock down your NFSv3 exports. Another method, using TCP Wrappers, is covered next.

Employing TCP Wrappers

TCP Wrappers allow you to provide access control to particular network services. Services must have TCP Wrapper support in order to use the access control they provide. The libwrap library provides TCP Wrapper support, and you can check for it as shown here:

```
# which rpcbind
/sbin/rpcbind
#
# ldd /sbin/rpcbind | grep libwrap
    libwrap.so.0 => /lib64/libwrap.so.0 (0x00007f59a302e000)
#
# which rpc.nfsd
/sbin/rpc.nfsd
#
# ldd /sbin/rpc.nfsd | grep libwrap
#
```

As shown in the preceding example, the rpc.nfsd does not have TCP Wrapper support, but rpcbind does. Therefore, you can use TCP Wrappers for access control with rpcbind.

This access control is accomplished via two files: /etc/hosts.allow and /etc/hosts .deny. They are checked in a particular order, which is important to understand.

When a remote client requests access, the hosts.allow file is checked *first*. If the remote client's address is listed, access is allowed and no further TCP Wrapper checks are made.

If the remote client's address is not listed in host.allow, the host.deny file is checked. If the remote client's address is listed in host.deny, access is denied. If it is not listed, access is allowed.

The record format in both files is the same:

rpcbind: *client-list*

The *client-list* is a comma-separated list. Each client in the *client-list* can be identified via client hostnames, IP addresses, and special patterns or wildcards that identify clients. Therefore, following the earlier example, in the /etc/hosts.allow file, the following record allowing the NFS client (at IPv4 address 192.168.56.101) and an additional NFS client (at IPv4 address 192.168.56.106) would look like this:

rpcbind: 192.168.56.101,192.168.56.106

> Once you've made changes to the /etc/hosts.allow and/or /etc/hosts .deny file, you don't need to restart the NFS server or services. It automatically takes effect.

A good general rule is to make your hosts.deny file as restrictive as possible (rpcbind:ALL). Afterward, add only the NFS clients (and other clients that need rpcbind) to the hosts.allow file (rpcbind: *address-list*).

Troubleshooting NFS

Because of its various versions and the different daemons and kernel services involved, employing NFS can result in problems that are difficult to solve. Therefore, it's a good idea to have a standard troubleshooting map in order to address problems quickly as they arise. The following items can help you get to the NFS service interruption's root cause:

Check the /etc/exports file.   One of the most important steps that you can take to avoid problems is to check your NFS server's /etc/exports configuration file's syntax after *every* modification. Unfortunately, there is no utility that makes this task easy, so this will cause you some extra work. However, doing this step may save you hours of frustration later over a simple typographical error or extra record space.

Verify that the proper NFS daemons are running.   When NFS problems occur, check if the needed NFS server daemons are running. There are several daemons that you may need on your NFS server, which are listed in Table 10.9. Which ones you need depend on the NFS version you are running as well as what distribution your NFS server is using. At a minimum, the nfsd or rpc.nfsd daemon *must* be running on the NFS server.

Review the NFS ports.   On the NFS server, use the rpcinfo -p command to view the various NFS services' ports. You should see at a minimum the portmapper, mountd, and nfs services listening on the listed ports. If not, you may need to restart your NFS server daemons.

Perform basic NFS export checks.   On the NFS server, you can see what exports are being offered via the exportfs -v and/or the showmount -e command (with the -U option and appropriate parameter if needed). If you do not see a particular export, review your server's /etc/exports share records. If you receive an RPC: Program Not Registered message, either your /etc/exports file is empty or it has not been loaded. Try running the exportfs -ra command using super user privileges.

Employ basic network diagnostics.   Sometimes the NFS clients simply cannot reach the NFS server's shares because of network issues. Perform a few basic network diagnostics. Try to ping (or ping6, if you are using IPv6) an NFS client from the NFS server and vice versa. Employ the `traceroute` (or `traceroute6`) command. On the NFS server, install and use the `nmap` program to see what ports are open inside and outside the firewall.

Review the log file.   The NFS server logs messages to the `/var/log/messages` file. You can easily grep for NFS messages and filter it down if needed. A snipped example here demonstrates looking for NFS messages and searching for unmatched host messages within the results:

```
# grep nfs /var/log/messages* | grep unmatched
[...]
/var/log/messages-[...] rpc.mountd[1598]:
refused mount request from 192.168.56.101 for
/srv/nfs_share_temp (/srv/nfs_share_temp):unmatched host
#
```

Check the NFS client view.   On the NFS *client*, see what exports are being offered via `showmount -e` and the NFS server's IP address. If you receive a `no route to host` message or something similar, the NFS server may be down or the server's firewall may be blocking the query. A `connection refused` message or something similar indicates the NFS server's rpcbind service may not be running. If you receive an `RPC: Program not registered` message, the NFS service is not running or no shares have been exported.

Check the NFS export options.   If you cannot mount the export on the NFS client, check export's options via either the NFS server's `/etc/exports` file or the `/proc/mounts` file. For example, you cannot mount a read-only share as read/write. You can find even more option details in the NFS server's `/proc/fs/nfs/exports` file and the `/var/lib/nfs/etab` file.

If you have been able to mount the export, but it is not behaving as expected, view all of the export's options and settings by looking in the NFS client's `/proc/mounts` file. You can also view all of the clients currently using a particular export by viewing the `/var/lib/nfs/rmtab` file on the NFS server.

Several NFS utilities may also help you troubleshoot a particular problem. Look back to the various NFS utilities listed in Table 10.15.

If you still cannot isolate the problem's cause, you can also employ the help of others via online forums. There are many Linux NFS forums as well as various distribution forums where you can ask for help.

NFS exports are helpful where performance and security are needed. However, if don't want to mount a share for your file sharing, an FTP server may be in order.

Looking at FTP Servers

Typically, FTP is used when mounting a share permanently or temporarily is not desired or workable and transfer speed is an issue. It is ideal for situations where files are shared for download purposes only, such as when an instructor on a local lab LAN is sharing binaries with newbie Linux students.

Understanding FTP

File Transfer Protocol (FTP) has been around for a long time. It is a simple network protocol for sharing files between systems. It is primarily used to share public documents over a network.

When you connect to an FTP service, its authentication process may require you to give it a valid username and password. Once you are authenticated, depending on the FTP service's configuration, you can essentially look around and download (or upload) files.

 WARNING   If you are using account and password information to log into an FTP service, be aware that they are typically not encrypted. This means anyone using a network sniffer application, such as Wireshark, will see your FTP server username and password in the clear. It is better to use Secure FTP (SFTP), which encrypts FTP via OpenSSH.

It's more common for an FTP service to be set up for anonymous access and only allow file downloads. With *anonymous FTP access*, instead of an individually assigned username, a general username, such as anonymous or ftp, is used. There may be no password required or a request for your email address as the password (though the email address is not verified).

Understanding Passive and Active Connections

It's important to know that FTP l uses two *operating modes*: passive and active. The mode used determines how a connection is established. Passive mode has fewer problems (as covered shortly), so it is the more popular of the two.

FTP also uses two TCP ports: the *data port* and the *command port*. The command port is used for sending commands and handling command responses. The data port is used for transporting file data.

In *active mode*, both the FTP server and client are active in establishing the connections. Also, the FTP server uses port 20 as its data port and port 21 as its command port. The basic active mode connection steps are as follows:

1. The FTP client picks and opens a random unprivileged port C (where C is >1024) to serve as its command port in order to send and receive commands.

2. The FTP client picks and opens another random unprivileged port D (where D is C+1) to serve as its data port and begins to listen for FTP server data.

3. The FTP client uses its command port (port C) to inform the FTP server via the server's command port (port 21) that it is listening for data on its data port (port D).

4. The FTP server uses its command port (port 21) to acknowledge the request, which is sent to the FTP client's command port (port C).

5. The FTP server uses its data port (port 20) to connect to the FTP client's data port (port D).

Thus, in active mode, the FTP client establishes the command connection, but the FTP server establishes the data connection. The server's active role can cause problems with certain network configurations because of firewalls. The FTP client's firewall may see the FTP server data port connection attempt (step 5) as potentially malicious (an external system trying to connect with an internal system) and block the attempt. For example, if you have a local FTP client trying to connect to a FTP server across the Internet using active mode, your LAN firewalls most likely will block this.

Because of this issue, the FTP passive mode was created. In *passive mode*, the FTP server is passive, and only the FTP client is active in establishing the connections. Also, the FTP server uses port 20 as its data port but a random unprivileged port as its command port. The basic passive mode connection steps are as follows:

1. The FTP client picks and opens two random unprivileged ports: port C to serve as its command port and port D to serve as its data port.

2. The FTP client uses its command port (port C) to inform the FTP server via the server's command port (port 21) that it is establishing a *passive* connection.

3. The FTP server picks and opens a random unprivileged port SD (where SD is > 1024) as its data port to send/receive the FTP client's data.

4. The FTP server uses its command port (port 21) to inform the FTP client via the client's command port (port C) that it is listening for data on its data port (port SD).

5. The FTP client uses its data port (port D) to connect to the FTP server's data port (port SD).

There are pros and cons to both passive and active FTP modes. Generally, passive mode is used by FTP servers that are servicing many WAN FTP client systems. However, if you employ this mode on an FTP server, it is important to configure your server's firewall properly and consider making it an FTP-only server to help prevent malicious attacks.

Looking at FTP Servers and Clients

FTP services are available through various packages. Linux FTP servers mentioned in the certification objectives are listed here:

Very Secure FTP   Very Secure FTP (vsftpd) is open-source Unix and Linux FTP server software whose primary focuses are on security, performance, and stability. It supports non-anonymous and anonymous FTP server access as well as PAM authentication. This popular FTP server software has been the default FTP daemon in many distributions for several years, though it typically must be manually installed. The project web page is security.appspot.com/vsftpd.html.

Pure-FTPd   Pure-FTPd (pure-ftpd) is an open-source cross-platform FTP server software whose primary focuses are on security, efficiency, and ease of use. Its security features include built-in chroot emulation, virtual accounts, and optional support for SSL/TLS encryption. The software is installed from source or a special repository if offered by your distribution. The project web page is www.pureftpd.org.

ProFTPD   ProFTPD is open source and somewhat cross platform. (It can run on Windows via Cygwin.) This FTP server software is full of features, including several security attributes. For example, you can block scripted FTP clients, which are typically maliciously trying to find and exploit poorly configured anonymous FTP sites. Though feature rich, it is not overly difficult to configure. It has a single primary configuration file, /etc/proftpd/ proftpd.conf, and has an Apache-like configuration. By default, there is a command-line interface, but several third-party GUI interfaces are available. The project web page is www.proftpd.org.

There are also many FTP client applications. The one you choose will depend on how you are using FTP and your security needs.

Web Browsers   You can use just about any web browser, such as Mozilla Firefox or Google Chrome, to connect to an FTP server. In the address bar, type in **ftp://** followed by the FTP server's FQDN or IP address. An anonymous connection is made if you do not include a username and password. By clicking the presented links, you can either download files or traverse the listed directories.

GUI Applications   Several free FTP client GUI applications are available, such as the popular open-source cross-platform FileZilla software. Once it's installed, you enter the FTP server's FQDN and your username and password information. Afterward, the connection is initiated via menu options or key sequences. A rich GUI interface offers the ability to drag and drop files to download/upload. The FileZilla project web page is filezilla-project.org.

Command-Line Utilities   There are also command-line FTP client utilities available to install and use (depending on your distribution). The ftp utility is a standard basic FTP client, whereas the lftp utility is a refined FTP client that provides more features, such as the ability to transfer files in parallel. Most current distributions include these two utilities in their repositories.

The FTP server and FTP client packages you choose depend heavily on your particular file transfer needs. Keep in mind that if you are using FTP primarily for copying files back and forth over the network, it may make more sense to use something like the ssh or scp utilities (covered in Chapter 12).

Configuring *vsftpd*

Typically, the Very Secure FTP (vsftpd) software is not installed by default. Fortunately, the package name is the same across most distributions: vsftpd. Here is a snipped example of installing it on an Ubuntu system:

```
$ sudo apt-get install vsftpd
[sudo] password for christine:
[...]
The following NEW packages will be installed:
  vsftpd
```

```
[...]
vsftpd start/running, process 3084
[...]
$
$ dpkg -s vsftpd
Package: vsftpd
Status: install ok installed
[...]
$
```

If you have vsftpd installed, there is a man page for it. In addition, the /usr/share/doc/vsftpd-*version*/ directory or the /usr/share/doc/vsftpd/ directory (depending on your distribution) has current documentation.

> You can have vsftpd start at system boot time or be controlled by a super server, such as xinetd.

The primary configuration file, vsftpd.conf, is located in either the /etc/ directory or the /etc/vsftpd/ directory (depending on your distribution). It is fairly well internally documented, but there is also a vsftpd.conf man page if needed.

> Some distributions' vsftpd works right "out of the box" with no further configuration, except for a few firewall modifications, required. It is generally a good idea to review your FTP settings instead of simply deploying it. If you don't, you may open up your FTP server to malicious attacks.

There are many directives in the vsftpd primary configuration file. A few of the more basic ones are listed in Table 10.18.

TABLE 10.18   vsftpd FTP server configuration directives

Directive	Description
anon_mkdir_write_enable	Determines whether the anonymous user can create directories. If set to YES, for this to work properly, the write_enable directive must also be set to YES, and write permission on the parent directory must be enabled for the anonymous user account. This boolean is set to NO by default.
anon_other_write_enable	Sets whether the anonymous user will be permitted to perform file operations such as file deletion and renaming. This boolean is set to NO by default.

TABLE 10.18 vsftpd FTP server configuration directives *(continued)*

Directive	Description
anon_root	Determines the directory the anonymous user changes into after an FTP server login. If this directive is not set, the directory used is the anonymous account's (see ftp_username) home directory defined in the /etc/passwd file. This string value has no default value.
anon_world_readable_only	Sets whether the anonymous user can see and download files that are world readable. This way, some files owned by the anonymous account (see ftp_username) can be protected from anonymous FTP server users. This boolean is set to YES by default.
anon_upload_enable	Determines whether an anonymous user can upload files to the FTP server. If set to YES, for this to work properly, the write_enable directive must also be set to YES, and write permission on the upload location's parent directory must be enabled for the anonymous user account. This boolean is set to NO by default.
anonymous_enable	Sets whether the anonymous user account is used for FTP server access. If only anonymous user access is desired, this directive should be set to YES and the local_enable directive should be set to NO. This boolean is set to YES by default.
chown_uploads	Determines whether all anonymous uploaded files have their ownership changed to a specified username (see chown_username). This boolean is set to NO by default.
chown_username	Sets the username for ownership of all anonymous uploaded files. If set, for this to work properly, the chown_uploads directive must be set to YES. This string has no default value.
chroot_local_user	Determines whether to place local users accessing the FTP service into a chroot jail using their home directory as the new root directory. This boolean is set to NO by default. (Chroot jails were covered in Chapter 8.)
chroot_list_enable	Sets whether a list of local users is placed in a chroot jail using their home directory as the new root directory. If set to YES and chroot_local_user is set to YES, this activates a list (see chroot_list_file) of users *not* to be placed in a chroot jail. If set to YES and chroot_local_user is set to NO, this activates a list of users *to be* placed into a chroot jail. If set to YES, for this to work properly, the chroot_list_file directive must be set. This boolean is set to NO by default.

Directive	Description
chroot_list_file	Designates the file containing the list of users to be or not to be placed in a chroot jail using their home directory as the new root directory. If set, for this to work properly, the chroot_list_enable directive must be set to YES. This directive's default value is distribution dependent.
ftp_username	Sets the anonymous account username to be used for anonymous logins. This directive's default value is ftp.
listen	Determines whether the vsftpd runs in a stand-alone mode and is started via an initialization service (YES) or it is managed via the xinetd daemon (NO). Either way, it listens only for IPv4 communication. This boolean is set to NO by default.
listen_ipv6	Determines whether the vsftpd runs in a stand-alone mode and is started via an initialization service (YES) or is managed via the xinetd daemon (NO). Either way, it listens only for IPv6 communication. This boolean is set to NO by default.
local_enable	Sets whether or not local logins to the FTP service are permitted. If set to YES, user accounts listed in /etc/passwd (also called non-anonymous) may be used to log in to the FTP service. This boolean is set to NO by default.
log_ftp_protocol	Determines whether all FTP queries and answers are logged. This boolean is set to NO by default.
userlist_enable	Sets whether a username list file is loaded and checked against when a user attempts a login. If set to YES, any user in the username list file is denied access before a password attempt. Also if set to YES, for this to work properly, the userlist_file directive must be set to a username list file. This boolean is set to NO by default.
userlist_file	Designates the file containing the username list to be denied access upon a login attempt. This directive's default value is distribution dependent.
write_enable	Sets whether any FTP user can issue commands to modify the filesystem, such as uploading files or deleting files. This boolean is set to NO by default.

Many vsftpd.conf file directives are interdependent. Also, whether you use a particular directive, or a set of them, depends on what you are trying to accomplish. If you want to view all of the various vftpd.conf directives, you can do so via its man page.

Depending on your distribution, you may need to configure SELinux booleans on an FTP server to allow access. Though doing so is beyond this book's scope, you can temporarily disengage SELinux for FTP server-testing purposes. This was covered earlier in the Samba section.

Accessing with Username and Password

Setting up a vsftpd FTP server that accepts usernames and passwords for accessing files is fairly simple. As an example, an FTP server will be set up on an Ubuntu system, and the FTP client will log in from a CentOS system.

First, within the vsftpd.conf file, check the directives. The local_enable directive should be set to YES, as shown snipped here:

```
$ grep enable /etc/vsftpd.conf | grep -v '#'
anonymous_enable=NO
local_enable=YES
[...]
$
```

If you need to make any changes to the vsftpd.conf, make a backup copy first. (This is always a good idea.) When you have completed your changes, restart the service as follows:

```
$ sudo service vsftpd restart
vsftpd stop/waiting
vsftpd start/running, process 5392
$
```

Next, an FTP user account is added. Here a user Kaylee has an account and password added to the FTP server Ubuntu system:

```
$ sudo useradd -d /home/Kaylee -m Kaylee
$
$ sudo passwd Kaylee
Enter new UNIX password:
Retype new UNIX password:
passwd: password updated successfully
$
```

Since this user is an FTP user and should not be granted full login access to the system, the account's default shell is changed to /usr/sbin/nologin (on some distributions this shell is /sbin/nologin):

```
$ sudo usermod -s /usr/sbin/nologin Kaylee
$
```

This Ubuntu FTP server has PAM authentication implemented. The pam_username directive is the clue. If it is set, most likely your system is using PAM, as shown here:

```
$ grep pam_service_name /etc/vsftpd.conf
pam_service_name=vsftpd
$
```

PAM is covered in Chapter 11. However, you can look in the /etc/pam.d/ directory for the vsftpd file (the filename will be the pam_service_name setting) for the following line or something similar:

```
auth    required    pam_shells.so
```

The preceding PAM record indicates that the /etc/shells file must contain the FTP user's default shell. Since, on this server, the FTP users are assigned /usr/sbin/nologin, the shell needs to be included in the file, and it is, as shown here:

```
$ cat /etc/shells
# /etc/shells: valid login shells
/bin/sh
/bin/dash
/bin/bash
/bin/rbash
/usr/sbin/nologin
$
```

Once the FTP user login configuration is set up, it's a good idea to test it on the FTP server prior to trying it from a remote system, as shown here:

```
$ ls -l /home/Kaylee
total 12
-rw-r--r-- 1 Kaylee Kaylee    0 May  4 18:47 mynumbers.txt
$
$ ftp 192.168.56.102
Connected to 192.168.56.102.
220 (vsFTPd 3.0.2)
Name (192.168.56.102:christine): Kaylee
331 Please specify the password.
Password:
230 Login successful.
Remote system type is UNIX.
Using binary mode to transfer files.
ftp> pwd
257 "/home/Kaylee"
```

```
ftp> ls
200 PORT command successful. Consider using PASV.
150 Here comes the directory listing.
-rw-r--r--  1 1008   1008    0 May 04 18:47 mynumbers.txt
226 Directory send OK.
ftp>
ftp> exit
221 Goodbye.
$
```

In the preceding example, the `ftp` command (not installed by default on all distributions) is used to test the FTP user access. It works perfectly. Notice that within the `ftp` utility, many of the similar Bash shell commands work.

Once a successful test is conducted on the FTP server itself, it's a good idea to test the FTP username/password access from a remote FTP client system. This ensures that access is working as expected.

If you are following along in this chapter with setting up FTP access, you can temporarily lower your firewall if needed. Using super user privileges, enter `iptables -F` at the command line. Firewalls are covered in Chapter 12.

For this example, the test is being conducted on a CentOS FTP client, and the `lftp` utility is used for the test. First, install the `lftp` utility using super user privileges as shown here:

```
# yum install lftp
[...]
Complete!
#
```

Now the FTP server is accessed. With the `lftp` utility, you can pass the username with the -u option and also include the FTP server's IP address or hostname, as shown here:

```
$ ls mynumbers.txt
ls: cannot access mynumbers.txt: No such file or directory
$
$ lftp -u Kaylee 192.168.56.102
Password:
lftp Kaylee@192.168.56.102:~> pwd
ftp://Kaylee@192.168.56.102
lftp Kaylee@192.168.56.102:~> ls
-rw-r--r-- 1 1008   1008    0 May 04 18:47 mynumbers.txt
```

```
lftp Kaylee@192.168.56.102:~>
lftp Kaylee@192.168.56.102:~> get mynumbers.txt -o mynumbers.txt
lftp Kaylee@192.168.56.102:~>
lftp Kaylee@192.168.56.102:~> exit
$
$ ls -l mynumbers.txt
-rw-rw-r-- 1 chris chris 0 May  4 14:47 mynumbers.txt
$
```

This works perfectly. Notice that the get command was used to download the mynumbers.txt file to the local machine.

Controlling Access via TCP Wrappers

You can also control access to the vsftpd FTP service via TCP Wrappers. You can see that the ability to use TCP Wrappers is included in vsftpd, as shown snipped here on this Ubuntu system:

```
$ which vsftpd
/usr/sbin/vsftpd
$
$ ldd /usr/sbin/vsftpd | grep libwrap
    libwrap.so.0 => /lib/x86_64-linux-gnu[...]
$
```

TCP Wrappers were covered earlier in this chapter. They work just the same for vsftpd as they do for NFS. However, you do have to substitute vsftpd for rpcbind in TCP Wrapper file records.

Accessing with Anonymous for Downloads

A popular method of accessing FTP servers for file downloads is via an anonymous account. This is a handy setup for situations where you need to distribute public files to a great many users. Continuing with the previous example, an FTP server will be set up on an Ubuntu system to accept only anonymous connections.

The vsftpd.conf file is modified, so local users accounts are disabled (local_enable=NO). Also, anonymous_enable is modified and set to YES, and the service is restarted, as shown snipped here:

```
$ grep enable /etc/vsftpd.conf | grep -v '#'
anonymous_enable=YES
local_enable=NO
[...]
$
$ sudo service vsftpd restart
```

```
vsftpd stop/waiting
vsftpd start/running, process 6434
$
```

If the ftp_username directive is not set within the vsftpd.conf file, it will default to the ftp username (see Table 10.18). On this Ubuntu FTP server, the directive is not set, and the /etc/password file is searched for the ftp user account record:

```
$ grep ftp_username /etc/vsftpd.conf
$
$ grep ftp /etc/passwd
ftp:x:118:126:ftp daemon,,,:/srv/ftp:/bin/false
$
```

Typically, by default, the FTP servers offer files from either the /var/ftp/ or /srv/ftp/ directories, depending on your distribution. In the preceding example, the ftp user record shows the home directory is /srv/ftp/, which indicates that this is the default directory where files are offered.

A few test files are created in the FTP directory, as shown in the following example. This will assist the various anonymous FTP access tests to be conducted.

```
$ ls /srv/ftp
$
$ sudo touch /srv/ftp/Hello.dat
$
$ sudo touch /srv/ftp/World.dat
$
$ ls /srv/ftp
Hello.dat  World.dat
$
```

Once the test files are created, a test can be conducted on the FTP server prior to trying it from a remote system. It works successfully, as shown here:

```
$ ftp 192.168.56.102
Connected to 192.168.56.102.
220 (vsFTPd 3.0.2)
Name (192.168.56.102:christine): anonymous
331 Please specify the password.
Password:
230 Login successful.
Remote system type is UNIX.
Using binary mode to transfer files.
ftp>
```

```
ftp> pwd
257 "/"
ftp>
ftp> ls
200 PORT command successful. Consider using PASV.
150 Here comes the directory listing.
-rw-r--r--   1 0    0              0 May 04 20:11 Hello.dat
-rw-r--r--   1 0    0              0 May 04 20:11 World.dat
226 Directory send OK.
ftp>
ftp> exit
221 Goodbye.
$
```

Notice in the preceding example that anonymous was entered for the username. The password entered can be anything, but traditionally it is the user's email address.

Now a test can be conducted on a remote system. Again, a remote CentOS system is used as the FTP client, as shown here:

```
$ lftp -u anonymous 192.168.56.102
Password:
lftp anonymous@192.168.56.102:~> pwd
ftp://anonymous@192.168.56.102
lftp anonymous@192.168.56.102:~> ls
-rw-r--r--   1 0        0              0 May 04 20:11 Hello.dat
-rw-r--r--   1 0        0              0 May 04 20:11 World.dat
lftp anonymous@192.168.56.102:/>
lftp anonymous@192.168.56.102:/> get Hello.dat -o Hello.txt
lftp anonymous@192.168.56.102:/>
lftp anonymous@192.168.56.102:/> get World.dat -o World.txt
lftp anonymous@192.168.56.102:/>
lftp anonymous@192.168.56.102:/> put Hello.txt -o Hello.txt
put: Access failed: 550 Permission denied. (Hello.txt)
lftp anonymous@192.168.56.102:/>
lftp anonymous@192.168.56.102:/> exit
$
```

Notice in the preceding example that the two files on the FTP server were easily downloaded. However, when the anonymous user attempted to upload a file, permission was denied. How to configure an FTP server for anonymous uploads is covered shortly.

This FTP server can be accessed using anonymous access from a Windows system as well, using a web browser, such as Mozilla Firefox, or a GUI application, such as FileZilla. In Figure 10.1, the FTP server's files are accessed from a Windows system using Mozilla Firefox.

FIGURE 10.1   Accessing an FTP server with Firefox

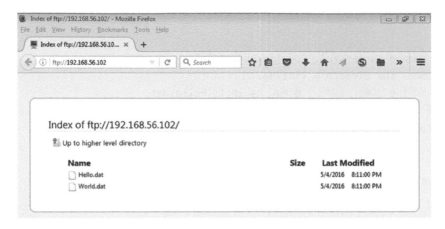

Accessing with Anonymous for Uploads

If you would like to allow anonymous FTP users to upload files, you will need to make a few FTP configuration file changes and create a new directory. Using the earlier Ubuntu FTP server example, you need to uncomment three directives in order for anonymous uploads to be allowed, as shown snipped here:

```
$ grep write_enable /etc/vsftpd.conf
#write_enable=YES
[...]
$
$ grep anon_ /etc/vsftpd.conf
#anon_upload_enable=YES
#anon_mkdir_write_enable=YES
$
```

After removing the hash mark (#) from the directive records, the vsftpd service is restarted to have them take effect:

```
$ sudo nano /etc/vsftpd.conf
[sudo] password for christine:
$
$ grep write_enable /etc/vsftpd.conf
write_enable=YES
[...]
$
$ grep anon_ /etc/vsftpd.conf
```

```
anon_upload_enable=YES
anon_mkdir_write_enable=YES
$
$ sudo service vsftpd restart
vsftpd stop/waiting
vsftpd start/running, process 6981
$
```

For enabling anonymous uploads, a special directory should be created for uploaded files. Since the example Ubuntu system's FTP directory is /srv/ftp/, a subdirectory will be created for file uploads, as shown here:

```
$ sudo mkdir /srv/ftp/upload
$
$ sudo chown ftp:ftp /srv/ftp/upload
$
$ sudo chmod 775 /srv/ftp/upload
$
$ ls -ld /srv/ftp/upload
drwxrwxr-x 2 ftp ftp 4096 May  4 21:48 /srv/ftp/upload
$
```

After creating an upload subdirectory, the file owner and group should be set to the ftp_username directive's username. In the example, the username is ftp. Also, chmod is used to modify the /srv/ftp/upload/ directory permissions as needed.

Once the directives are modified and the upload subdirectory is created with appropriate permissions and ownership, files can be uploaded via anonymous. Using the example CentOS FTP client and the lftp command, a simple file is successfully uploaded to the FTP server:

```
$ ls *.txt
Hello.txt  mynumbers.txt  World.txt
$
$ lftp -u anonymous 192.168.56.102
Password:
lftp anonymous@192.168.56.102:~> ls
-rw-r--r--    1 0         0               0 May 04 20:11 Hello.dat
-rw-r--r--    1 0         0               0 May 04 20:11 World.dat
drwxrwxr-x    2 118       126          4096 May 04 21:48 upload
lftp anonymous@192.168.56.102:/>
lftp anonymous@192.168.56.102:/> put Hello.txt -o Hello.txt
put: Access failed: 553 Could not create file. (Hello.txt)
lftp anonymous@192.168.56.102:/>
```

```
lftp anonymous@192.168.56.102:/> cd upload
cd ok, cwd=/upload
lftp anonymous@192.168.56.102:/upload> ls
lftp anonymous@192.168.56.102:/upload>
lftp anonymous@192.168.56.102:/upload> put Hello.txt -o Hello.txt
lftp anonymous@192.168.56.102:/upload>
lftp anonymous@192.168.56.102:/upload> ls
-rw-------    1 118      126            0 May 04 21:50 Hello.txt
lftp anonymous@192.168.56.102:/upload>
lftp anonymous@192.168.56.102:/upload> exit
$
```

Notice in the preceding example that the first attempt to upload the file failed. This is because anonymous logs into the /srv/ftp/ directory and uploads are not permitted there. Once the cd upload command is issued and the anonymous user's present working directory is /srv/ftp/upload/, a file is easily uploaded using the put command. A check on the Ubuntu FTP server side confirms the upload was successful:

```
$ ls /srv/ftp/upload
Hello.txt
$
$ ls -l /srv/ftp/upload
total 0
-rw------- 1 ftp ftp 0 May  4 21:50 Hello.txt
$
```

Notice that the uploaded file is owned by the ftp user and belongs to the ftp group as well. If you need uploaded files to be owned by a different user, modify the chown_uploads and chown_username directives in the FTP configuration file.

> **NOTE**   Once you have your FTP configuration completed, don't forget to enable the vsftpd service to start at boot.

Configuring Pure-FTPd

Pure-FTPd is rather easy to configure, and it comes with many features ready to go "out of the box." The most difficult part can be installing the software. You can download the source code from this site, www.pureftpd.org/project/pure-ftpd/download, and install from source code (covered in Chapter 2.)

Some distributions, however, provide Pure-FTPd via a special repository. On CentOS, the pure-ftpd package is available in an Extra Packages for Enterprise Linux (EPEL) repository. You should check to see if this repository has been enabled on your system by using super user privileges and issuing the following command:

```
# yum --enablerepo=epel info pure-ftpd
Loaded plugins: fastestmirror, langpacks

Error getting repository data for epel, repository not found
#
```

If you get detailed package information on the pure-ftpd package, then the epel repository is enabled. However, if you get an error similar to the preceding example error, there are a few more steps that you need to take before you can perform an installation.

To enable the epel repository for a CentOS or other Red Hat–based distribution, go to the dl.fedoraproject.org/pub/epel/7/x86_64/e/ website and record the current version of the epel-release*.rpm package. In the following snipped example, the wget command is used to download the current package, but you can use other methods:

```
# wget http://dl.fedoraproject.org[...]epel-release[...].rpm
[...]
Resolving dl.fedoraproject.org (dl.fedoraproject.org)...
[...]
#
# ls *.rpm
epel-release-7-6.noarch.rpm
#
```

Once the epel repository package is downloaded, it is installed using super user privileges and the rpm command, as shown in this snipped listing here:

```
# rpm -ivh epel-release-7-6.noarch.rpm
[...]
Updating / installing...
   1:epel-release-7-6
            ################################ [100%]
#
```

After all that work, you can now install the pure-ftpd package using yum and super user privileges. A snipped example on a CentOS system is shown here:

```
# yum --enablerepo=epel install pure-ftpd
[...]
Installing:
 pure-ftpd               x86_64         [...]
Installing for dependencies:
```

```
postgresql-libs      x86_64        [...]
[...]
Complete!
#
```

 On Ubuntu, the pure-ftpd package is in the standard repositories. Just type **sudo apt-get install pure-ftpd** to install Pure-FTPd.

The pure-ftpd daemon has a man page that will allow you to do some research. However, the Pure-FTPd project has extensive documentation at www.pureftpd.org.

Looking at Command-Line Options

The Pure-FTPd daemon, pure-fptd, can be run from the command line and has many useful options. To see all the available options, type **pure-ftpd --help** at the command line.

A few of these options deserve some special attention. Therefore, Table 10.19 lists them.

TABLE 10.19   pure-ftpd command-line options

Short Option	Long Option	Description
-4	--ipv4only	Listen only for IPv4 traffic connections.
-6	--ipv6only	Listen only for IPv6 traffic connections.
-A	--chrooteveryone	Perform chroot for all clients except the root user.
-a *gid*	--trustedgid *gid*	Do not chroot clients in GID *gid*.
-B	--daemonize	Start the service in the background.
-C *num*	--maxclientsperip *num*	Accept only up to num concurrent clients per IP address.
-c *num*	--maxclientsnumber *num*	Accept only up to num concurrent clients. Defaults to 50.
-d	--verboselog	Turn on command logging. Use the option twice to turn on response logging as well.
-e	--anonymousonly	Allow only anonymous users.
-E	--noanonymous	Do not allow anonymous users, but do allow individual username/password authentication.

Short Option	Long Option	Description
-h	--help	Obtain help information.
-I *time*	--maxidletime *time*	Set maximum idle *time* minutes before forced client logout. Default is 15 minutes.
-i	--anonymouscantupload	Disallow anonymous uploads.
-k *num*	--maxdiskusagepct *num*	Disallow additional uploads when partition is greater than *num* percent full.
-M	--anonymouscancreatedirs	Allow anonymous users to create directories.
-r	--autorename	Force uploaded files with same name as a current file to be renamed.
-U *umask*	--umask *umask*	Set the default umask for uploaded files.
-u *uid*	--minuid *uid*	Disallow users with a UID below *uid* to log into the FTP server. Typically used for low UIDs (administrative accounts).
-V *ipaddr*	--trustedip *ipaddr*	Only allow non-anonymous access from this *ipaddr* IP address.
-Z	--customerproof	Block common FTP client mistakes.

Pure-FTPd can also be controlled via its configuration files, though few changes are typically needed. The following sections step you through various FTP server access methods.

Accessing with Username or Anonymous

The primary Pure-FTPd configuration files and locations are different, depending on your distribution. You may find configuration files in the /etc/pure-ftpd/ or /etc/default/ directory or within a /etc/pure-ftpd/ subdirectory.

Following the CentOS example, the primary configuration file is /etc/pure-ftpd/ pure-ftpd.conf. However, to access the FTP server and upload files using anonymous, no changes to the default configuration file are necessary. Here the service is started and tested on the CentOS FTP server:

```
# service pure-ftpd start
Redirecting to /bin/systemctl start  pure-ftpd.service
#
# touch /var/ftp/test.dat
```

```
#
# ls /var/ftp
test.dat
#
# lftp 192.168.56.101
lftp 192.168.56.101:~> ls
drwxr-xr-x    2 0     0              21 May  5 17:35 .
drwxr-xr-x    2 0     0              21 May  5 17:35 ..
-rw-r--r--    1 0     0               0 May  5 17:35 test.dat
lftp 192.168.56.101:/> get test.dat -o copy_test.dat
lftp 192.168.56.101:/> exit
#
# ls copy*.dat
copy_test.dat
#
```

On CentOS, the default directory for the ftp user is /var/ftp/. Therefore, a file in the proceeding example was created within that directory. The lftp command was used to test anonymous access and download the file. It works successfully and requires no pure-ftpd configuration file changes.

To check username/password access, a file was created in the /home/chris/ directory. Again, there were no problems accessing in this manner and downloading a file.

```
# touch /home/chris/reg_user_test.dat
#
# ls /home/chris/reg_user_test.dat
/home/chris/reg_user_test.dat
#
# lftp -u chris 192.168.56.101
Password:
lftp chris@192.168.56.101:~> ls reg_user_test.dat
-rw-r--r--    1 0     0               0 May  5 17:37 reg_user_test.dat
lftp chris@192.168.56.101:/>
lftp chris@192.168.56.101:/> get reg_user_test.dat -o my_test.dat
lftp chris@192.168.56.101:/> exit
#
# ls my_test.dat
my_test.dat
#
```

If you want to use Pure-FTPd for anonymous uploads and downloads, you will have to make some configuration file changes as well as create a special directory.

Here is the code for creation of an upload directory, including adding a test file to the directory:

```
# mkdir /var/ftp/upload
#
# chown ftp:ftp /var/ftp/upload
#
# chmod 755 /var/ftp/upload
#
# touch /var/ftp/upload/myfile.txt
#
```

Setting up an upload directory is no different than how it was accomplished for use with the vsftpd FTP server. Once the upload directory is configured, a change to the configuration file is needed, as shown here:

```
# grep AnonymousCantUpload /etc/pure-ftpd/pure-ftpd.conf
AnonymousCantUpload         yes
#
# nano /etc/pure-ftpd/pure-ftpd.conf
#
# grep AnonymousCantUpload /etc/pure-ftpd/pure-ftpd.conf
AnonymousCantUpload         no
#
# systemctl restart pure-ftpd
#
```

The AnonymousCantUpload directive must be changed from a yes to a no setting. Once the modification is completed, the pure-ftpd service is restarted, effectively reloading the modified configuration file.

The anonymous upload tests were conducted on an Ubuntu system acting as the FTP client. The ftp command was used, which has slightly different internal commands, as shown snipped here:

```
$ touch Hello.txt
$
$ ftp 192.168.56.101
Connected to 192.168.56.101.
220---------- Welcome to Pure-FTPd [privsep] [TLS]----------
[...]
Name (192.168.56.101:christine): anonymous
230 Anonymous user logged in
Remote system type is UNIX.
```

```
Using binary mode to transfer files.
ftp>
ftp> ls
200 PORT command successful
150 Connecting to port 46424
drwxr-xr-x    3 0      0              34 May  5 18:00 .
drwxr-xr-x    3 0      0              34 May  5 18:00 ..
-rw----r--    1 0      0               0 May  5 17:35 test.dat
drwxr-xr-x    2 14     50             23 May  5 18:18 upload
226-Options: -a -l
226 4 matches total
ftp>
ftp> get test.dat test.dat
local: test.dat remote: test.dat
200 PORT command successful
150 Connecting to port 36338
226 File successfully transferred
ftp>
ftp> cd upload
250 OK. Current directory is /upload
ftp>
ftp> ls
200 PORT command successful
150 Connecting to port 56887
drwxr-xr-x    2 14     50             23 May  5 18:18 .
drwxr-xr-x    3 0      0              34 May  5 18:00 ..
-rw-r--r--    1 14     50              0 May  5 18:13 myfile.txt
226-Options: -a -l
226 3 matches total
ftp>
ftp> put Hello.txt Hello.txt
local: Hello.txt remote: Hello.txt
200 PORT command successful
150 Connecting to port 36660
226 File successfully transferred
ftp>
ftp> ls
200 PORT command successful
150 Connecting to port 52853
drwxr-xr-x    2 14     50             39 May  5 18:20 .
drwxr-xr-x    3 0      0              34 May  5 18:00 ..
```

```
-rw-r--r--    1 14    50              0 May  5 18:20 Hello.txt
-rw-r--r--    1 14    50              0 May  5 18:13 myfile.txt
226-Options: -a -l
226 4 matches total
ftp> exit
221-Goodbye. You uploaded 0 and downloaded 0 kbytes.
221 Logout.
$
```

The anonymous user from the Ubuntu FTP client was able to download the /var/ftp/test.dat file. Also, the user was able to upload a file, Hello.txt, to the /var/ftp/upload/ directory.

 Once you have your FTP configuration completed, don't forget to enable the pure-ftpd service to start at boot.

Summary

Sharing files between homogeneous or mixed-system network environments can be done using Samba, NFS, or FTP servers. Which one you use depends on many factors, such as network environment, security needs, and desired file transfer rates. Typically, a mixed environment where Linux and Windows systems exist demands a Samba server. In non-mixed environments, where it is desired to mount filesystems remotely, an NFS server can be useful. In an environment that may also be mixed where mounting remote shares is not desired, an FTP server works well. You may even have situations where all these various file-sharing servers are employed. Hopefully, this chapter has helped you understand file servers and provide you with insights into which ones may meet your particular file server requirements.

Exam Essentials

Describe Samba configuration file directives.   The primary Samba configuration file is smb.conf, and it may reside in various locations depending on your distribution. Typical locations are the /etc/samba/ directory or for older distributions, the /etc/, /etc/smb/, or /etc/samba.d/ directory.

The Samba configuration file directives control how the Samba server operates. The workgroup directive is an important one in a mixed Windows and Linux network environment, because it designates the Samba group (workgroup) and is typically set to the

Windows workgroup/domain name. In legacy mixed-network environments, the netbios name directive is necessary and sets the Samba server's NetBIOS name. The security directive designates the security level (mode) to either a user-level or share-level mode, and it determines how clients are authenticated. For troubleshooting purposes, the log level directive is important, because it sets the debugging level to filter Samba log file messages. By default, the level is set to 0, which means that logging is turned off. Samba log files are traditionally stored in the /var/log/samba/ directory.

Summarize the various Samba daemons.   While not every Samba daemon is used in every Samba environment, it is important to know the various daemons as well as whether they are used in mixed Linux and Windows network environments and with legacy systems. The Samba daemon, smbd, is always used on the Samba server. It manages offered SMB shares, provides share locking, handles user authentication, and so on. The nmbd daemon handles NetBIOS name service requests, and it is used in mixed legacy environments. The winbindd daemon *binds* together and manages connections between a Linux system and a Windows domain controller. It is used in mixed current and mixed legacy environments.

Explain the various NFS mount options.   When creating a /etc/fstab record for permanently mounting an NFS filesystem, it is important to include the correct options. Setting the tcp option forces the NFS share to be mounted with TCP and is important for avoiding data loss on read/write exports. The udp option forces the NFS share to be mounted with UDP, which can improve performance for read-only exports. The nfsvers option sets whether NFS version 2, 3, or 4 is used for mounting and managing the export. NFS version 2 should absolutely not be used any longer, and it is wise to no longer use NFS version 3 either because of potential security issues. To allow an NFS client request to be interrupted and avoid hanging when an NFS server crashes or cannot be reached, the intr mount option is used. The noexec mount option turns off binary execution on mounted exports, which is typically used when mounting an export where the systems (NFS server and NFS client) may have incompatible binaries stored on the share.

Summarize various vsftpd.conf directives.   The vsftpd.conf file is the primary Very Secure FTP configuration file. Within it are various directives, which may need to be modified depending on the FTP server's requirements. The anonymous_enable directive is the primary directive for enabling (if set to YES) or disabling (if set to NO) anonymous user access. The local_enable directive determines whether local usernames (from the FTP server's /etc/passwd file) and passwords (from the FTP server's /etc/shadow file) are needed to access the server. The various chroot* directives determine whether FTP clients have chroot applied to them and, if so, how it is applied. The listen (for IPv4 only) and listen_ipv6 (for IPv6 only) directives determine whether vsftpd runs in a stand-alone mode and is started via an initialization service (YES) or it is managed via the xinetd daemon (NO). The ftp_username directive sets the anonymous account username to be used for anonymous logins. If not set, the default action is to use the ftp username.

Review Questions

You can find the answers in the Appendix.

1. In which of the following directories would you typically find Samba log files? (Choose the best answer.)

    A. /etc/smb/

    B. /etc/samba/

    C. /var/log/samba/

    D. /var/lib/samba/

    E. /etc/samba.d/

2. Which of the following Linux daemons may be used in providing Samba services? (Choose all that apply.)

    A. smbd

    B. cupsd

    C. winbind

    D. nmbd

    E. cifsd

3. To set up a Samba share, you need to modify the main Samba configuration file. Which of the following is this file? (Choose the best answer.)

    A. smb.conf

    B. samba.conf

    C. mount.cifs

    D. /etc/samba.d

    E. smbcontrol

4. Once you have modified the main Samba configuration file, what should you do next? (Choose the best answer.)

    A. Reload the configuration file into the Samba server daemon on the Samba server.

    B. Reboot the Samba server.

    C. Test the Samba configuration syntax with smbstatus.

    D. Test the Samba configuration syntax with testparm.

    E. Create a directory or set up a printer queue to share.

5. For setting up Samba in a mixed environment of Windows and Linux systems, it is essential to set the _____ directive to the Windows workgroup or domain name and not an FQDN. (Choose the best answer.)

    A. domain name

    B. adgroup

    C. windows group

    D. workgroup name

    E. workgroup

6. For the Samba `passdb backend` directive, which of the following are legal settings? (Choose all that apply.)

    A. tdbsam

    B. ads

    C. smbpasswd

    D. ldapsam

    E. domain

7. Which section in the `smb.conf` file might you find a file share defined? (Choose the best answer.)

    A. [global]

    B. [netlogins]

    C. [myshare]

    D. [printers]

    E. [profiles]

8. Which of the following Samba directives can be used to set whether passwords are required to access this file share service? (Choose the best answer.)

    A. public

    B. browseable

    C. guest only

    D. writable

    E. read only

9. Assuming appropriate access is granted, the _____ command allows FTP-style access to a Samba share. (Choose the best answer.)

    A. pdbedit

    B. smbclient

    C. smbpasswd

    D. rpcclient

    E. ftp

10. Which of the following items might assist you in troubleshooting a problem with a Samba client accessing a Samba share? (Choose all that apply.)

    A. Turn on logging by setting the `log level` directive in the `smb.conf` file to a number higher than 0 but lower than 10.

    B. See what shares are being offered via the `smbclient -L` command (with the `-U` option and appropriate parameter if needed) on the Samba server.

   C. Perform a few basic network diagnostics between the Samba server and client systems.

   D. Test the Samba configuration syntax with `testparm`.

   E. Determine if the needed Server daemons are running on the Samba server.

11. The NFS service that manages NFS client mount requests on the NFS server is which of the following? (Choose the best answer.)

   A. `portmapper`

   B. `rpc.lockd`

   C. `rpcbind`

   D. `statd`

   E. `mountd`

12. NFS export configuration files are typically located where? (Choose all that apply.)

   A. `/etc/`

   B. `/etc/exports/`

   C. `/etc/exports.d/`

   D. `/proc/fs/nfs/`

   E. `/var/lib/nfs/`

13. Which of the following are typical NFS share directory locations? (Choose all that apply.)

   A. `/`

   B. `/etc/`

   C. `/proc/`

   D. `/srv/`

   E. `/var/`

14. Which of the following `/etc/exports` directives would be important for trying to create a read-only share's configuration record? (Choose all that apply.)

   A. `ro`

   B. `rw`

   C. `async`

   D. `sync`

   E. `subtree_check`

15. Which of the following NFS utilities would show NFS share information specifically? (Choose all that apply.)

   A. `exportfs`

   B. `mount.nfs`

   C. `rpcinfo`

   D. `showmount`

   E. `smbstatus`

16. When using the `exportfs` command to display NFS share information on an NFS server, which of the following operands is the most helpful? (Choose the best answer.)

    A. -a

    B. -o

    C. -r

    D. -u

    E. -v

17. Which of the following is software that you may employ to implement an FTP server? (Choose all that apply.)

    A. ftp

    B. pure-ftpd

    C. vsftpd

    D. FileZilla

    E. lftp

18. Which of the following statements are true about FTP passive mode? (Choose all that apply.)

    A. The FTP server and FTP client are active in establishing the connections.

    B. Only the FTP server is active in establishing the connections.

    C. Only the FTP client is active in establishing the connections.

    D. A data connection and a command connection are established.

    E. The FTP server uses port 20 and port 21 in the established connections.

19. Which usernames are typically used on the FTP server for handling anonymous connections? (Choose all that apply.)

    A. anonymous

    B. vsftpd

    C. Individual usernames

    D. anon

    E. ftp

20. Which of the following directives are used in various FTP server daemons to allow anonymous uploads? (Choose all that apply.)

    A. anonymous_upload=YES

    B. write_enable=YES

    C. AnonymousCantUpload no

    D. anon_upload_enable=YES

    E. anon_mkdir_write_enable=YES

Chapter

11

Managing Network Clients

THE FOLLOWING EXAM OBJECTIVES ARE COVERED IN THIS CHAPTER:

✓ **210.1 DHCP configuration**

✓ **210.2 PAM authentication**

✓ **210.3 LDAP client usage**

✓ **210.4 Configuring an OpenLDAP server**

Managing multiple clients and applications in a network environment can be a headache for even the most experienced of Linux administrators. Fortunately, the Linux server environment supports several software packages that can help make your life much easier.

This chapter looks at some of the Linux server packages available to help you manage multiple clients on a network. First, it looks at how to manage the IP network addresses assigned to clients. Each client on the network must have a unique IP address, and trying to manage them can be a nightmare. Linux provides DHCP software that helps with that task. After that, the chapter explores how to implement the Pluggable Authentication Module (PAM) system on a Linux server. The PAM system allows multiple applications on a server to share the same authentication database so that your clients need to remember only one userid/password combination for all of the applications they use on the server. Finally, the chapter examines how to take authentication one step further on the network by utilizing the OpenLDAP implementation of the Lightweight Directory Access Protocol. With an OpenLDAP server and client software, different applications on different servers on the network can share the same authentication database.

Assigning Network Addresses

One of the most difficult jobs on a network is managing IP addresses. Each device that communicates on the network must have a unique IP address, appropriate for the subnetwork to which it is connected. If any two devices have the same IP address, problems will arise.

You have three methods for assigning IP addresses to devices on IP networks:

- Manually assigning addresses (called *static IP addresses*)
- Automatically assigning addresses (called *dynamic IP addresses*)
- Using a mixture of static and dynamic addresses

With static IP addresses you must manually assign and track IP addresses on the network. You must configure each individual network device with a unique IP address, subnet mask, and default router so that it can communicate on the network and ensure that no other device on the network has the same address.

This works fine for small networks, but it quickly becomes a nightmare for larger networks. Trying to ensure that each device on the network uses the correct IP address is nearly impossible, especially when network users have the ability to configure the IP address on their own client workstations.

Dynamic IP addresses use a central repository of addresses that are assigned automatically as network devices boot and request them. The *Dynamic Host Configuration Protocol (DHCP)* provides a standard method for clients to request an IP address from a central server and for the server to assign a unique address to each network client. This section walks you through the DHCP standard and how to implement a common Linux DHCP server package on your Linux server to offer IP addresses to clients on your local network.

The DHCP Standard

A DHCP server listens to the local network for requests from clients requiring a network IP address. As each network client boots, it sends out a broadcast message on the local network requesting an IP address. The DHCP server detects that request and then responds, assigning a unique IP address to the network device. This process is shown in Figure 11.1.

FIGURE 11.1   The DHCP process

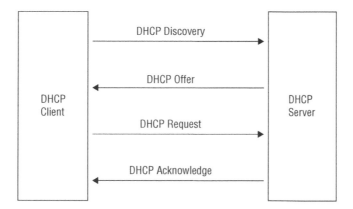

The client first broadcasts a DHCP discovery packet. In response to the discovery packet, every DHCP server on the network responds to the client with a DHCP offer packet. The client can accept only one offer, but it sends a DHCP request packet to all servers so that each knows which server the client selected to process the DHCP discovery. The selected DHCP server sends a DHCP acknowledgement packet back to the client, completing the DHCP process. When the client has finished using the network address, it can optionally send a DHCP release packet back to the server.

The DHCP standard also provides a way to send other types of configuration data to the network client, called *DHCP options*. Each DHCP option uses a standard option number to identify the type of data, along with the data value that the client uses to enhance its network configuration. Common option data types passed in DHCP options are the subnet mask, default router, and one or more DNS servers required for the client to interact with other devices both on the local network and on the Internet. Table 11.1 lists a few of the more common option numbers that are defined in the DHCP standard.

TABLE 11.1   Standard DHCP options

Code	Name
1	Subnet mask
2	Time offset
3	Default router
4	Time server
5	Name server
6	Domain name server
7	Log server
12	Hostname
50	Requested IP address
51	IP address lease time
66	TFTP server
67	Boot filename

The subnet mask, default router, and domain name server provide all of the information that the client should need to know to interact with other hosts. The other options provide additional information unique to the particular local network.

The following sections walk you through how to implement a DHCP server on your Linux server to serve your local network clients.

Linux DHCP Software

These days, you can configure many different types of devices on a network to be a DHCP server. Most routers provide this service, as well as most server-oriented operating systems, such as Windows Server, and of course, Linux servers.

The most popular Linux DHCP server package is maintained by the Internet Systems Consortium (ISC) and is called *DHCPd*. Just about all Linux server distributions include this in their software repositories, including Debian- and Red Hat–based distributions.

Once you have a DHCP server running on your network, you'll need to tell your Linux clients to use it to obtain their network addresses. This requires a DHCP client software package. There are three popular DHCP client Linux packages that you can use:

- dhcpcd
- pump
- dhclient

Most Debian- and Red Hat–based distributions use the dhclient package and even install it by default when a network card is detected during the installation process. In most Linux desktop environments, you don't need to do any network configuration at all; the installation program installs and activates the DHCP client software automatically. All you need to do is to plug in a network cable or connect to a wireless network.

Installing a Linux DHCP Server

If you need to implement a DHCP server on your local network, install the ISC DHCPd package on your Linux server. While the DHCPd program is popular enough that it is included by default in most Linux distribution repositories, unfortunately it's often called by different names in different Linux distributions. Currently, Debian-based Linux distributions call the DHCPd package isc-dhcp-server (however, older Debian-based distributions called it dhcp3-server). To install the DHCPd program, just use the standard apt-get utility:

```
$ sudo apt-get install isc-dhcp-server
```

For Red Hat–based Linux distributions, the package name is just dhcp:

```
# yum install dhcp
```

The installation creates the necessary core configuration files, along with installing the dhcpd executable file to run the DHCP server in the background on your system. You'll just need to customize the configuration files for your own network environment. The next section covers that.

Configuring a DHCP Server

After you install the DHCPd server program, you'll need to define your DHCP environment in the configuration file. For both Debian-based and Red Hat–based Linux distributions, the standard DHCPd configuration file is stored in the /etc/dhcp folder and is named dhcpd.conf. Unfortunately, you must configure quite a few options to customize the DHCP server for your network. The following sections walk through the basics that you'll need to know to get things working.

Global Options

At the start of the configuration file, you'll find global options that apply to all of the clients in the network. These are usually options that define network-wide resources, such as domain name servers, mail servers, and time servers. These option lines look like this:

```
option domain-name-servers 10.0.0.10 10.0.0.11;
option smtp-server 10.0.0.100;
option pop-server 10.0.0.100;
option nntp-server 10.0.0.101;
option time-servers 10.0.0.150;
```

You must define each type of server in a separate `option` configuration line. Fortunately, DHCPd configuration option names are somewhat self-explanatory as to what they define. For example, the `domain-name-servers` option sends a list of one or more DNS servers that the clients use to resolve hostnames. In this example, we used IP addresses to define the servers, but you can also specify the servers using standard hostnames.

Setting Subnet Ranges

After defining the global options, you'll need to define the individual subnet requirements for your network environment. Most large networks use subnetting to create multiple smaller networks inside the larger network. This helps control the broadcasts on the network, as well as makes it easier to restrict workstations to specific areas of the network.

Each subnet requires its own subnet mask and default router configuration, as well as a range of IP addresses to which clients on that network should be assigned. To group these values together for a subnet, you define a `subnet` declaration section of the `dhcpd.conf` configuration file:

```
subnet 10.1.0.0 netmask 255.255.0.0 {
    option router 10.1.0.1;
    option broadcast-address 10.1.255.255;
    range 10.1.0.10 10.1.0.200;
}
```

This configuration creates a single subnet address range, 10.1.0.0. The `router` option entry defines the default router address that each client on the subnet must use, while the `broadcast-address` option entry defines the local broadcast address for the subnet.

The range entry defines the pool of IP addresses that will be assigned to clients in the subnetwork. In this example, network client addresses start at 10.1.0.10 and go through 10.1.0.200. This setup reserves a small number of IP addresses in the subnet to be used as static IP addresses, not controlled by the DHCP server.

You can include multiple subnet sections within the configuration file to define multiple subnets on a network. If multiple subnets share the same options, you can group them together in a `shared-net` declaration, giving the network a name:

```
shared-net sales {
    option domain-name-servers 10.0.0.10;
    option time-servers 10.0.0.15;
```

```
   subnet 10.1.0.0 netmask 255.255.0.0 {
      option router 10.1.0.1;
      option broadcast-address 10.1.255.255;
      range 10.1.0.10 10.1.0.200;
   }
   subnet 10.2.0.0 netmask 255.255.0.0 {
      option router 10.2.0.1;
      option broadcast-address 10.2.255.255;
      range 10.2.0.10 10.2.0.200;
   }
}
```

The options defined within the shared-net section apply only to the subnets defined in that section.

 It can get somewhat tricky trying to track individual IP addresses as the DHCP server assigns them. Fortunately, the DHCPd package can help out some. As the server assigns IP addresses, they're logged in the /var/lib/dhcp/dhcpd.leases file. You can peek in that file to see what IP addresses are leased out and for how long. You can also use the standard arp command-line command to list IP addresses and their associated MAC addresses found on the network.

Static Hosts

Some devices on the network always need to use the same IP address, such as servers and printers. There are two ways of assigning static IP addresses to these devices:

- Manually assign the IP address, subnet mask, default router, and domain name server values.
- Create a static host entry in the DHCP server for the device.

Trying to combine static and dynamic IP addresses on the same subnetwork can get somewhat confusing, since the address information is stored in multiple locations. To solve this problem, the DHCPd package allows you to define static IP addresses for specific devices within the configuration file.

When a device that requires a static IP address requests an IP address using DHCP, the DHCPd server always assigns the device the same IP address. The benefit of this method is that now you have a single place where both static and dynamic addresses are documented, helping prevent duplicate static IP address issues.

The DHCP server configuration allows you to assign a specific IP address to a network device based on the device's network MAC address. You do that with the host section:

```
host shadrach {
   hardware ethernet 00:01:02:FE:DC:BA
```

```
   fixed-address 10.1.0.5;
   option router 10.1.0.1
   option broadcast-address 10.1.255.255
   netmask 255.255.0.0
   option host-name "shadrach";
}
```

The hardware entry defines the type of address (Ethernet), along with the MAC address of the device. If you have many static host entries for a single subnet, you can use the group statement to create a group of static IP address assignments that share the same default router, broadcast address, and subnet mask:

```
group {
   option router 10.1.0.1;
   option broadcast-address 10.1.255.255;
   netmask 255.255.0.0;
   host shadrach {
      hardware ethernet 00:01:02:FE:DC:BA
      fixed-address 10.1.0.5;
      option host-name "shadrach";
   }
   host meshach {
      hardware ethernet 00:01:02:AB:CD:EF
      fixed-address 10.1.0.6;
      option host-name "meshach";
   }
}
```

You aren't required to group the fixed-address definitions together, but it does come in handy when working with lots of static addresses. You can also define static addresses in the individual subnet sections to which they belong, which can help you keep track of which IP addresses are being used in each subnet.

BOOTP Hosts

Back in the early days of network computers when hard drives were expensive, diskless workstations became popular. A diskless workstation didn't use an internal hard drive, but instead it used a connection to a shared disk space on a server to run applications and to store files. However, without its own hard drive, a diskless workstation had no place to store its own operating system files.

Enter the *Bootstrap Protocol (BOOTP)*. With BOOTP, a diskless workstation sends out a broadcast message on the network looking for a server to send it the operating system file it can use to boot the workstation. The BOOTP server maintains different operating system files for different diskless workstations on the network.

These days, although diskless workstation aren't all that common, some network devices, such as switches and routers, still use BOOTP to load an operating system file from a remote server. This helps reduce the amount of hardware in the network device, often so that it just needs a small amount of ROM to perform its operations. This also helps make upgrading network devices a snap. All you need to do is to change one file on the BOOTP server and reboot all of your network devices.

The DHCPd package supports BOOTP devices. It can respond to BOOTP requests and then either service them directly or pass the device to another server. To enable BOOTP support on your DHCP server, you just need to add two lines to the configuration:

```
allow booting;
allow bootp;
```

Then for each individual BOOTP host you'll need to add two more lines to the host definition, one line that specifies the name of the boot file to download and another that specifies the name of the server from which to download the file:

```
host shadrach {
       hardware ethernet 00:01:02:FE:DC:BA
       fixed-address 10.1.0.5;
       option host-name "shadrach";
       filename "/mybootfile.img";
       server-name "mainhost";
       next-server "backuphost";
}
```

You can also add the `next-server` entry to specify a secondary boot server where the client can download the boot file if the primary boot server fails. If the DHCP server is also serving the boot file, you can omit the `server-name` entry.

BOOTP clients use the Trivial File Transfer Protocol (TFTP) to transfer the actual boot file data. If you want to implement BOOTP and DHCP from the same server, you'll need to install TFTP server software on your DHCP server.

DHCP Relaying

One problem with DHCP is that it uses broadcasts from the clients to find a DHCP server. If your network uses subnets, broadcasts are usually blocked at the central router, so a network client on one subnet won't be able to send requests to a DHCP server on a different subnet. That environment would require having separate DHCP servers for the network, one on each subnet.

To get around this situation, you can use *DHCP relaying*. With DHCP relaying, you incorporate a separate DHCP relay server on each subnet that relays any received DHCP

Discover packets it detects on its local network to a remote central DHCP server for processing.

For this to work, each subnet in the network will need a separate DHCP relay server. Figure 11.2 demonstrates this setup.

FIGURE 11.2 DHCP relay set up

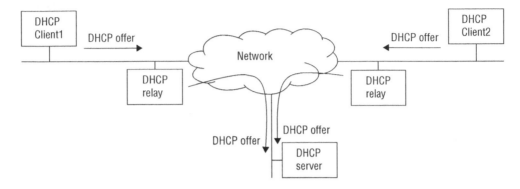

Fortunately, most routers have DHCP relaying services built in, so this setup is not as bad as it looks. You just configure each router interface to relay DHCP Discover packets to the central DHCP server.

 If your router doesn't support DHCP relay, the ISC DHCPd package does include a separate program, called dhcrelay, that you can run on any Linux client or server to act as a DHCP relay.

DHCP Log Files

The DHCPd application logs all DHCP events to the standard log file for your Linux system. For distributions that use the syslog facility, that's usually the /var/log/messages file. For systems that use the systemd journal application for logging, you'll need to use the journalctl application.

Configuring Clients

To use DHCP on a Linux client to obtain a dynamic IP address, you'll need to have one of the three Linux DHCP client packages mentioned earlier (dhcpcd, pump, or dhclient). Normally, when you install a Linux client system, the default DHCP client package for your Linux distribution is installed by default. For Debian-based and Red Hat–based distributions, this is dhclient.

If your Linux client uses a graphical desktop, there's usually a utility for enabling the DHCP setup for the network card, as shown in Figure 11.3 for an Ubuntu Linux client.

FIGURE 11.3   The DHCP settings for an Ubuntu client

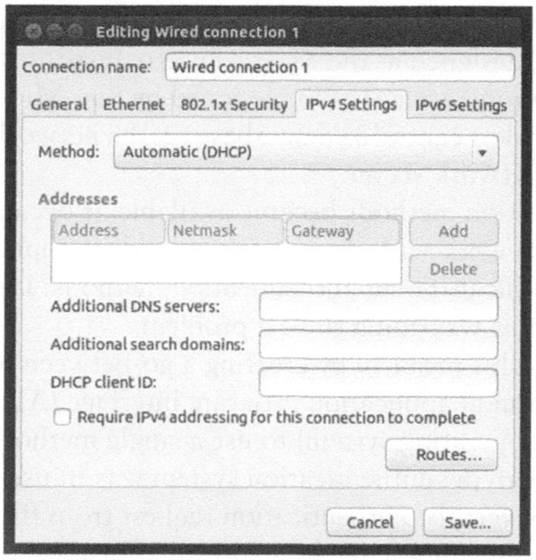

After you enable DHCP for the network interface, it will automatically request an IP address from the DHCP server each time you boot the system.

Authentication Service

These days, just about every application that's hosted on a server needs some type of authentication system to protect the application data. Each user of the application must provide some type of unique authentication information (such as a fingerprint, certificate, or userid/password combination) before being allowed to access the application. If your Linux server hosts several different applications, it can get somewhat cumbersome if each one has its own database of user accounts for authentication.

To help solve this problem, Linux provides a single interface for authentication that multiple applications on the server can use. The *Pluggable Authentication Module (PAM)* system provides a simple interface for multiple applications to interact with different authentication databases. This section walks you through what you'll need to know to implement PAM on your Linux system and how to utilize it for different applications.

PAM Basics

In the "old days," Linux systems used a single method for controlling access to the system. The /etc/passwd text file was used to track user accounts and passwords. The /etc/passwd file originally contained both the user accounts and their passwords, but as Linux administrators became more security conscious, the /etc/shadow file was added to that process to hold the passwords separate from the user account information and to help protect passwords from public view.

As systems became networked, additional authentication methods became available. Options such as *Kerberos*, designed at the Massachusetts Institute of Technology (MIT), and the *Network Information Service* (NIS), designed by Sun Microsystems (now part of Oracle Corporation), provide a centralized database on the network for authentication that could be accessed by any network server.

As additional authentication methods became available, it became harder for both Linux systems and applications to work with them. Each individual application needed to have code to work with each of the different authentication methods. It didn't take long for developers to realize that this was going to be a problem.

The PAM system solves this problem by creating a go-between for authentication functions. PAM provides a common application program interface (API) that allows applications (as well as the Linux operating system) to use a single method for authenticating users, no matter what underlying authentication system was in use on the server. The PAM system uses modules to convert the authentication request from the application into the proper format required for the underlying authentication method used. It then converts the response received from the authentication method into a standard format that applications can understand. Figure 11.4 demonstrates this process.

FIGURE 11.4 The PAM system in action

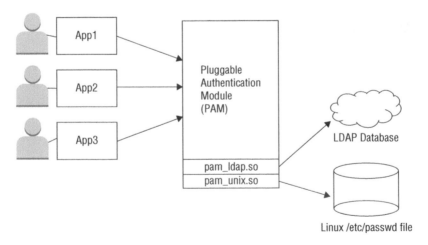

The key to PAM is the underlying authentication modules. Each module supports a single authentication method, but you can install multiple modules into a PAM installation to support multiple authentication methods. Table 11.2 shows some of the different PAM authentication modules available to use.

TABLE 11.2   PAM authentication modules

Module	Description
pam_unix.so	Uses the standard /etc/passwd and /etc/shadow files
pam_krb5.so	Uses the Kerberos 5 authentication system
pam_ldap.so	Uses a Lightweight Directory Access Protocol (LDAP) server
pam_nis.so	Uses an NIS server
pam_sss.so	Uses a System Security Services daemon (SSSD)
pam_userdb.so	Uses a standard .db database file for authentication

Besides the authentication modules, PAM provides additional library modules that have added features to help with the authentication process. These modules provide the rules that you can incorporate for user account management, such as password complexity rules or login attempt limits. Table 11.3 shows some of these modules.

TABLE 11.3   PAM library modules

Module	Description
pam_access.so	Used to provide anonymous logins for public FTP servers
pam_chroot.so	Used to create a locked down area for logins
pam_console.so	Provides a console login environment
pam_cracklib.so	Provides password strength checks
pam_deny.so	Prohibits login attempts (often used as a default)
pam_env.so	Sets or unsets environment variables
pam_lastlog.so	Provides the last login time for the user account
pam_limits.so	Enforces resource limits (such as number of open files) on accounts
pam_listfile.so	Allows or denies actions based on a list file

Just about all Linux distributions install and use PAM by default, even if they just use the standard /etc/passwd file for authentication. How individual applications use PAM is controlled by a PAM configuration file. The next section discusses how that works.

Configuring PAM

Each application that uses PAM must have a configuration setup defining which authentication module to use and how to use it. Unfortunately, there are a couple of ways that Linux distributions handle the PAM configuration system.

One method is to place all application configurations in a single /etc/pam.conf configuration file. Each line in the configuration file has the same format:

```
service type control module arguments
```

The service entry defines the application, such as the login application for console login prompts or the passwd application for changing your password.

The type entry defines what feature(s) in PAM the service needs to use. You can define four groups of *PAM feature types*:

- account—Account verification services
- auth—Authentication services
- password—Password management services
- session—External services, such as logging attempts to a file or mounting a directory

An application can define multiple feature types for an authentication, but you must use a separate configuration line to define each feature type.

The control entry defines what should happen if the authentication fails. You can define four *PAM control actions*:

- requisite—Terminate the application if authentication fails.
- required—Return a failure status if authentication fails, but continue checking other rules.
- sufficient—If the rule succeeds, the authentication process stops with a success status.
- optional—The rule is not necessary, unless it is the only rule defined for the module.

The module entry defines the PAM module library file (including the full path) to use for the authentication. Finally, the arguments entry defines any additional command-line arguments required for the module.

An example of an entry in the /etc/pam.conf file for the login program looks like this:

```
login auth required pam_unix.so
```

The login application is what authenticates users at the login command-line prompt. This rule authenticates the user login attempt using the pam_unix module, which uses the standard /etc/passwd and /etc/shadow password files. Since the control is set to required, if the authentication fails, the login program fails and the user doesn't get to the shell command prompt.

Each application can have several different lines in the configuration file, defining different rules for different situations. Because of that, things can get somewhat confusing. Fortunately, there's a better solution to configuring the PAM environment.

Using PAM Application Files

The other PAM configuration method uses a separate PAM configuration file for each application that uses PAM. In this setup, the configuration files are stored in the /etc/pam.d folder. Each application file uses the service name for the filename and omits that entry from the configuration line. Listing 11.1 shows a listing of the /etc/pam.d folder in an Ubuntu system.

Listing 11.1: The /etc/pam.d folder in Ubuntu

```
$ ls -al
total 136
drwxr-xr-x   2 root root  4096 Mar 17 00:06 .
drwxr-xr-x 140 root root 12288 May 16 21:50 ..
-rw-r--r--   1 root root   179 Jan 17  2014 accountsservice
-rw-r--r--   1 root root   384 Feb 16  2014 chfn
-rw-r--r--   1 root root    92 Feb 16  2014 chpasswd
-rw-r--r--   1 root root   581 Feb 16  2014 chsh
-rw-r--r--   1 root root  1208 Nov  2  2015 common-account
-rw-r--r--   1 root root  1249 Nov  2  2015 common-auth
-rw-r--r--   1 root root  1480 Nov  2  2015 common-password
-rw-r--r--   1 root root  1470 Nov  2  2015 common-session
-rw-r--r--   1 root root  1435 Nov  2  2015 common-session-noninteractive
-rw-r--r--   1 root root   527 Feb  9  2013 cron
-rw-r--r--   1 root root    69 Feb 14  2014 cups-daemon
-rw-r--r--   1 root root    81 Mar  7  2014 dovecot
-rw-r--r--   1 root root    56 Apr  9  2014 gnome-screensaver
-rw-r--r--   1 root root   144 Oct 30  2013 imap
-rw-r--r--   1 root root   752 Apr 13  2014 lightdm
-rw-r--r--   1 root root   510 Apr  8  2014 lightdm-autologin
-rw-r--r--   1 root root   636 Apr 13  2014 lightdm-greeter
-rw-r--r--   1 root root  4788 Feb 16  2014 login
-rw-r--r--   1 root root    92 Feb 16  2014 newusers
-rw-r--r--   1 root root   520 Jan 31  2014 other
-rw-r--r--   1 root root    92 Feb 16  2014 passwd
-rw-r--r--   1 root root   255 Feb 11  2014 polkit-1
```

```
-rw-r--r--  1 root root    145 Oct 30  2013 pop3
-rw-r--r--  1 root root    168 Jan 22  2013 ppp
-rw-r--r--  1 root root     84 Apr  1  2014 samba
-rw-r--r--  1 root root   2139 May  2  2014 sshd
-rw-r--r--  1 root root   2305 Feb 16  2014 su
-rw-r--r--  1 root root    239 Feb 10  2014 sudo
-rw-r--r--  1 root root     56 May 21  2015 unity
$
```

On this particular system, quite a few different applications are configured to use PAM for authentication. The system creates some files that can be shared between applications, such as the ones that start with common. Application configurations just include the common files that they need into their own configuration.

While the basic idea of the PAM configuration files is somewhat straightforward, in reality, PAM configuration files for an individual application can get somewhat complicated. Listing 11.2 shows the configuration file for the login application on a CentOS system.

Listing 11.2: PAM configuration file for the login application in CentOS

```
#%PAM-1.0
auth [user_unknown=ignore success=ok ignore=ignore default=bad] pam_securetty.so
auth        substack        system-auth
auth        include         postlogin
account     required        pam_nologin.so
account     include         system-auth
password    include         system-auth
# pam_selinux.so close should be the first session rule
session     required        pam_selinux.so close
session     required        pam_loginuid.so
session     optional        pam_console.so
# pam_selinux.so open should only be followed by sessions to be executed in
  the user context
session     required        pam_selinux.so open
session     required        pam_namespace.so
session     optional        pam_keyinit.so force revoke
session     include         system-auth
session     include         postlogin
session     optional        pam_ck_connector.so
```

That's a lot of rules for a simple login! The PAM system checks each rule in the order in which it appears in the configuration file. If any of the required steps fail, the login process is terminated and the user login attempt is denied.

Be very careful when working with PAM files. If you delete the wrong application file or modify the wrong rule within a file, you can lock yourself out of your own system. This is one case where it's a good idea to have a rescue LiveDVD handy before messing with any configurations.

Network Directories

Network authentication systems allow multiple servers to share the same authentication database. Much work has been done on network authentication systems, providing a single sign-on for network clients to access any application or device on a local network. Many commercial companies have made great strides in providing proprietary network authentication directories. The Microsoft Active Directory system is by far the most popular network authentication system used today.

The open source world isn't too far behind, though, creating its own network directory system. The *Lightweight Directory Access Protocol (LDAP)* was created at the University of Michigan to provide simple network authentication services to multiple applications and devices on a local network. The most popular implementation of LDAP in the Linux world is the *OpenLDAP* package. Most Linux distributions include both client and server packages for implementing LDAP in a Linux network environment.

This section walks through how to install and implement the OpenLDAP open source client and server software packages on your local Linux network. But first, let's take a look at what makes up LDAP.

LDAP Basics

Network directory services allow administrators to create a database to store information regarding network objects. These objects can be network devices (such as servers, printers, and network switches), users, and even applications. Any device on the network can access the database and retrieve information regarding the other objects defined in the database.

This has become a handy way to store usernames and passwords in a common location where any server in the network can authenticate a user and grant (or deny) access based on properties found in the database. Besides authentication, the LDAP database can also store permissions for network objects, such as which users are allowed to connect to a server or printer or run a network application. This creates a centralized database that controls everything on the network.

An LDAP database is based on the *hierarchical database design*, similar to how the DNS protocol defines domain names. A root name defines the core of the database (such as the .com in a DNS name), and additional entries build off that. The name of an object in the database relies on its interrelationship with other objects higher up in the database structure.

In the hierarchical database, objects are connected in a tree-like fashion to one another. Each LDAP tree must have a root object, with other objects connected in sequence. Objects connect to other objects by reference, similar to the DNS naming system. Figure 11.5 shows a sample LDAP database structure.

FIGURE 11.5   A sample LDAP directory tree

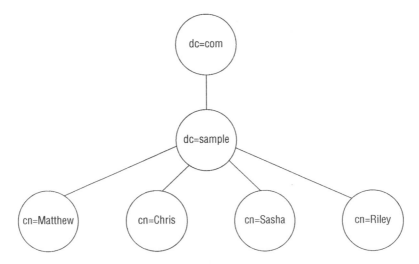

Hierarchical databases are best known for fast read times but slow write times. This method assumes that once an object is written into the database, it will be accessed many times but not updated very often. This works for most network situations where a userid is created once, and servers read the record each time the user attempts to log into the server.

The LDAP database consists of one or more *schemas*. A schema defines the objects contained in the database and how they are interrelated. Each database object is defined by an *object class* and assigned a unique *object ID*. The object class defines a template that contains a set of *attributes* that the object contains. The attributes define information about the object, such as a userid for a user object or a server name for a server object. Each attribute has a name and an associated data value. The attributes are where the real data is stored, so that's what you'll need to retrieve in your data queries.

An *LDAP tree* references objects using the standard X.500 naming convention. For example, the object

```
o="Sample, Inc.", c="US"
```

refers to the object defining the Sample, Inc. corporation located in the United States. The o and c in the X.500 name refer to attribute names associated with the object (an organization and a country).

To simplify names, many (if not most) companies have incorporated their registered domain name into their LDAP tree. This method is often implemented using the parts of the domain name for each *domain context* (dc) attribute:

```
dc="sample", dc="com"
```

Once the base objects are defined for the corporation, you can create additional objects underneath the corporation tree. You must define each individual object using a unique name in the database. In LDAP, this unique name is called the *distinguished name*, or dn. Each dn references each of the parts of the tree that describe the path to the unique location of the specific object, for example:

```
cn="rich", dc="engineering", dc="mycompany", dc="com"
```

The LDAP tree can branch out by having objects that are created to serve no other purpose but to contain other objects (such as the engineering domain context shown in this example). This helps make the database more manageable than having all of the objects at one level. Figure 11.6 demonstrates a more complicated LDAP tree structure that utilizes objects as containers for other objects.

FIGURE 11.6   A more complicated LDAP tree structure

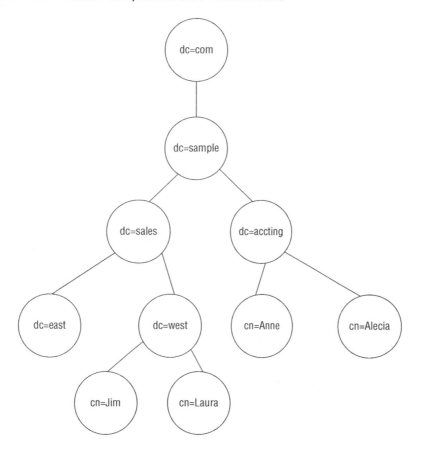

With the LDAP schema containing multiple objects, and each object containing multiple attributes, it can get pretty confusing trying to decipher just where your data is located. One standard that's become popular for defining an LDAP object is the LDAP Data Interchange Format (LDIF). The LDIF standard uses a text-based method for describing an LDAP object entry and its attributes. The format of an LDIF record looks like this:

```
dn: <distinguished name>
<attrtype>: <attrvalue>
<attrtype>: <attrvalue>

...
```

The dn line defines the distinguished name of the object. Each line after the dn defines individual attributes for the object, one attribute and value pair per line. The beauty of LDIF files is that you can easily export an entire LDAP database into an LDIF file for documentation or backup purposes. There are also utilities to import an LDIF file into an LDAP database.

The LDAP database itself can be stored on one or more servers on the network. You can use three different methods to store the LDAP database:

- The entire database on a single server (stand-alone)

- The entire database on multiple servers (replication)

- Parts of the database on multiple servers (distributed)

Each method has its own unique way of storing information and operating on the network.

An LDAP server that is operating in *stand-alone mode* stores all of the objects contained in the defined LDAP database locally. Any requests for information from the LDAP database must be directed to the single LDAP server. The stand-alone server is responsible for responding to queries for data in the local LDAP database. Any requests for data outside the defined LDAP database are not processed.

In *replicated mode* there is more than one LDAP server, each containing the entire LDAP database. Since each server contains the entire database, any request for network information can be handled by any of the LDAP servers. This method works well for organizations that may have WAN links between sites. Network clients can be configured to query the LDAP server that is local to their WAN segment without having to obtain information from a remote LDAP server.

The last method used is *distributed mode*. This can be the most complicated method to implement. In distributed mode, each server is responsible for only part of the LDAP database. No one server contains the entire LDAP database. For a client to resolve a query, it must connect to the LDAP server responsible for the section of the database that contains the information being queried. Figure 11.7 shows a simple distributed LDAP network.

FIGURE 11.7   Simple distributed LDAP server network

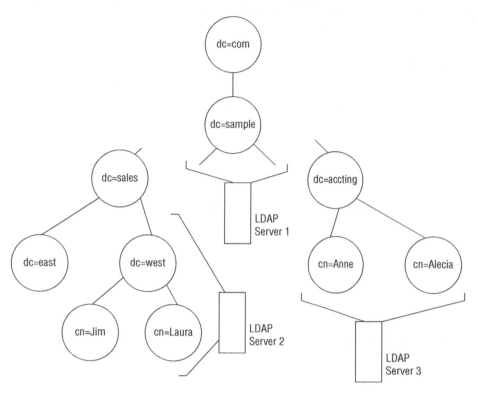

Clients wanting to retrieve information in the dc=sales, dc=sample, dc=com tree must connect to the Server 2 LDAP server. This method works well for organizations that divide their LDAP database into geographical pieces, where each location can contain objects related to the local area.

Unfortunately, distributed mode does not provide for redundancy. If any of the LDAP servers should crash, information contained in that section of the LDAP database tree will become unavailable. Some LDAP implementations now allow for replicated distributed LDAP servers to combine the best of both replicated and distributed modes.

The OpenLDAP Server

The most popular LDAP implementation for the Linux platform has been the OpenLDAP package. This package allows a Linux server to host stand-alone, replicated, or distributed LDAP databases. It also includes client software to allow the Linux server to access an LDAP database on the network. The OpenLDAP software website is located at http://www.openldap.org.

This section describes how to install the OpenLDAP software package on a Linux server. Once this has been done, you can configure OpenLDAP to support the directory tree structure required for your organization.

Installing OpenLDAP

Most Linux distributions include the OpenLDAP software as two separate packages in the software repository. One package bundles the files necessary to run an OpenLDAP server, while another package bundles just the files needed for an OpenLDAP client.

For Debian-based distributions, the packages are slapd for the server (you'll see why in the next section) and ldap-utils for the client programs:

```
$ sudo apt-get install slapd ldap-utils
```

For Red Hat–based distributions, the packages are conveniently named openldap-servers and openldap-clients:

```
# yum install openldap-servers openldap-clients
```

The OpenLDAP packages install several server and client programs, as well as the default configuration files. However, you'll need to do some customization before you can start your LDAP database.

OpenLDAP Server Programs

The OpenLDAP server package consists of several executable programs that are used to maintain the LDAP database and to respond to network queries to the database. Two main programs are used to implement the LDAP server:

- slapd
- slurpd

The *slapd* program is the heart of the OpenLDAP server. It runs as a background process to listen for LDAP requests from the network. Once an LDAP request is received, slapd processes the request based on the configured LDAP database and returns any results to the client.

The format of the slapd command line is

```
slapd [-f config_file] [-h URL] [-d debug] [-n service] [-s syslog]
[ic:ccc] [-l syslog-user] [-r dir] [-u user] [-g group]
```

As you can see, lots of command line options can be included with the slapd program, although all of them are optional. Invoking the slapd command without any options starts the LDAP server with default values for each of the options. Table 11.4 describes the different command-line options that can be used.

TABLE 11.4   *slapd* command-line options

Option	Description
-f config	Specify an alternative configuration file.
-h URL	Specify the URL that the LDAP server will bind to for LDAP requests. By default, it uses the local host IP address.
-d debug	Turn on debugging at the specified debug level.
-n service	Specify an alternate service name for logging purposes.
-s syslog	Specify the level to log statements into the logging facility.
-l syslog-user	Select the user-specified local name for the syslog facility. By default, this is LOCAL4.
-r dir	Specify a chroot directory for slapd to operate in.
-u user	Specify an alternate user name to run slapd with.
-g group	Specify an alternate group name to run slapd with.

While the command-line parameters control how the OpenLDAP server behaves in general, there is also a configuration file that controls the finer details of how the server operates.

The *slurpd* program is used when operating OpenLDAP in a replicated server environment. Its job is to connect with slapd programs running on remote LDAP slave servers and propagate any LDAP database changes. The format of the slurpd command line is

slurpd [-d debug] [-f config] [-r replog] [-t dir] [-o] [-k srvtab]

Much like the slapd program, all of the options for the slurpd program are optional. If no options are included in the command line, slurpd uses default values for each of the options. Table 11.5 describes the options available.

TABLE 11.5   *slurpd* command-line options

Option	Description
-d debug	Turns on debugging at the specified debug level
-f config	Specifies an alternate slapd.conf configuration file
-r replog	Specifies an alternate replication log file
-t dir	Specifies an alternate location to copy the replication log file while processing it

TABLE 11.5 *slurpd* command-line options *(continued)*

Option	Description
-o	Runs once and exits
-k srvtab	Specifies an alternate location of the Kerberos srvtab file, which contains keys for the replica LDAP servers

The slurpd program reads the replication log file, which identifies LDAP database changes and connects to remote LDAP servers to submit the changes to the remote replica databases. After contacting all replicas, slurpd goes to sleep for a set period. When it wakes back up, it rereads the replication log file. If it is empty, it goes back to sleep. If it contains new database updates, slurpd again connects to the remote replica databases and sends the new database updates.

Designing a Directory Schema

After installing OpenLDAP, you should spend a few minutes (or hours) designing the LDAP database tree that will be used for your organization. As mentioned, you can take any of several approaches in designing the database.

Most organizations that implement LDAP databases use their registered domain names as the top-level containers for the database. After that, you can create additional containers to hold employee objects. By creating additional containers, it will be easier for the LDAP administrator to manage the database, especially if there are many employees in your organization. Figure 11.8 demonstrates a simple LDAP database layout that can be used.

FIGURE 11.8 Sample LDAP database layout

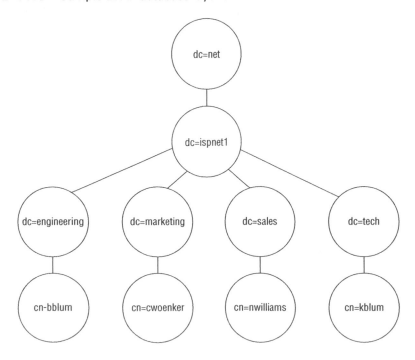

By using this layout, employee distinguished names would look like the following:

```
cn=bblum, dc=engineering, dc=ispnet1, dc=net
cn=nwilliams, dc=sales, dc=ispnet1 dc=net
cn=cwoenker, dc=marketing, dc=ispnet1, dc=net
cn=rmullen, dc=accounting, dc=ispnet1, dc=net
cn=kblum, dc=tech, dc=ispnet1, dc=net
```

You don't necessarily have to design your own database schema from scratch; the OpenLDAP software includes several standard schema templates that you can use. The schemas are included in the OpenLDAP package as LDIF files, so you can easily import them into your LDAP database structure.

The most popular generic schema is the inetOrgPerson schema, which implements a simple *white pages* schema, because it emulates the old-fashioned White Pages telephone directory, updated for the computer world. The white pages schema allows you to store simple information about people into the database, such as names, addresses, email addresses, and phone numbers.

Once you have designed a suitable LDAP database schema for your organization, you must define it in OpenLDAP. Regrettably, this is where things can get really complicated.

Implementing a Directory Schema

Unfortunately, there are two different methods for implementing the LDAP directory schema on your OpenLDAP server:

- The slapd.conf method
- The slapd-config method

The slapd.conf method uses a single text configuration file (/etc/slapd.conf) to hold the definitions for the root of the LDAP directory schema.

However, starting with version 2.3.3, OpenLDAP provides an alternative method for storing the configuration. The slapd-config method uses standard LDIF files to define configuration options. This method is gaining in popularity among Linux distributions, and it has become the default configuration method for both Debian- and Red Hat–based distributions.

The slapd-config method uses multiple LDIF files in the /etc/slapd.d folder to store configuration and database schema information. However, you don't modify any of these files directly, because OpenLDAP provides utilities to do that for you.

If your Linux distribution uses the slapd.conf method, you'll need to modify three lines in the /etc/slapd.conf configuration file to define the root of your LDAP database and an administrator account for your database:

```
suffix    "dc=ispnet1, dc=net"
rootdn    "cn=Administrator, dc=ispnet1, dc=net"
rootpw    testpasswd
```

The suffix entry defines the root of the LDAP tree structure for the organization. As mentioned, most often it's the domain name assigned to the organization (ispnet1.net for this example).

The rootdn entry defines a user account object that has full administrator privileges to the LDAP database. Often this user account object is at the root level of the organizational structure, but that doesn't have to be the case.

The rootpw entry defines the password for the root user account. Older versions of OpenLDAP defined this as a text value in the configuration file. Newer versions store this as an encrypted value. You can use the slappasswd utility that comes with OpenLDAP to generate the encrypted password value and then plug that into the slapd.conf file. When using the encrypted value, the format for the rootpw entry becomes

```
rootpw {SHA}<encrypted password>
```

The {SHA} prefix indicates that the value is encrypted.

> The rootdn user account is automatically granted full read/write permissions to the entire database. There may be situations where you'd like to grant partial permissions to a subset of the database. OpenLDAP allows you to implement *access control* by defining access rules in the configuration file. The access rules define what LDAP user accounts have what permissions to what areas of the database structure. This can come in handy if you need to split administration of the organization database among multiple admins.

OpenLDAP provides four additional server utilities:

- slapadd—Adds new objects directly to the LDAP database by reading the object definitions in LDIF files
- slapcat—Exports the LDAP database into an LDIF file
- slapindex—Re-indexes the LDAP database based on a specific attribute
- slappasswd—Generates an encrypted password from a text value

These utilities allow you to set up the directory structure on your OpenLDAP server before opening it up for clients. The slapadd utility reads an LDIF file and adds the objects defined in the file into the LDAP schema. For example, to add a new user object, you'd create the LDIF file:

```
dn: cn=rblum, dc=engineering, dc=ispnet1, dc=net
cn: Rich  Blum
givenName: Rich
sn: Blum
telephoneNumber: 312-555-1234
```

```
mail: rich@myhost.com
objectClass: inetOrgPerson
objectClass: top
```

You can define multiple objects in one LDIF file; just separate each object with a blank line. Once you have all of the objects defined, you can add them to the LDAP database with the command

```
# slapadd -l ldif.txt
```

The slapadd utility automatically inserts the objects, as defined by their distinguished names, and automatically re-indexes the LDAP database.

WARNING The slapadd utility is an easy way to mass-insert multiple objects into an existing LDAP database. However, the slapd server program must not be running when you use this utility, because it needs to lock the LDAP database while performing the inserts.

If your Linux distribution uses the slapd-config method, you define the base LDAP tree using standard LDIF files and the slapadd utility. With the slapd-config method, the core configuration file is called cn=config and is stored in the /etc/slapd.d folder. As you build additional nodes in the LDAP tree, OpenLDAP creates additional configuration files under the /etc/slapd.d folder.

With the slapd-config method, you never modify the actual configuration files; instead, you use the standard OpenLDAP utilities to add or modify nodes on the tree using LDIF files to define the operations.

Implementing LDAP Clients

The OpenLDAP client package includes several programs for interacting with an LDAP database, either on the local system or hosted elsewhere on the network:

- ldapadd—Adds objects defined in an LDIF file to the LDAP database
- ldapdelete—Removes objects from the LDAP database
- ldapmodify—Modifies attributes of existing objects in the LDAP database
- ldappasswd—Generates an encrypted value from a text value
- ldapsearch—Queries the LDAP database

The ldapadd and ldapdelete utilities are actually just links to the ldapmodify utility. When the ldapmodify utility detects that it's run as either ldapadd or ldapdelete, it assumes those specific options. Table 11.6 shows the other options that are available for the ldapmodify utility.

TABLE 11.6   The *ldapmodify* utility options

Option	Description
-a	Add new objects.
-c	Continue processing entries in the LDIF file even if there are errors.
-D dn	Use the specified dn to log into the LDAP directory.
-d debug	Specify the debug level for debugging.
-E ext	Use the specified search extensions and values.
-e ext=param	Use the specified general extensions and values.
-f file	Read the LDIF entries from the specified file.
-H uri	Use the specified URI to connect to the LDAP server.
-h host	Use the specified host to connect to the LDAP server.
-I	Enable interactive mode.
-N	Do not use reverse DNS to look up hostnames.
-n	Show what objects would be modified, but don't actually modify them.
-O security	Set the security properties of the connection.
-o opt=param	Set the specified options and values.
-P x	Use the specified LDAP protocol version (either 2 or 3).
-p port	Use the specified port to connect to the LDAP server.
-Q	Enable quiet mode.
-R realm	Use the specified realm when authorizing.
-S file	Entries that produced an error are written to the specified file.
-U authid	Use the specified authorization ID.
-v	Use verbose mode, writing output to the standard output.

Option	Description
-V	Display version information.
-W	Prompt for a password.
-w passwd	Use the specified password.
-X authxid	Use the specified dn or username when authorizing.
-x	Use simple authentication.
-Y mech	Use the specified mechanism when authorizing.
-y passfile	Read the password from the specified file.
-Z	Initiate a secure operation using Transport Layer Security (TLS).

The ldapadd utility differs from the slapadd utility in that instead of working directly with the LDAP database files, the ldapadd utility connects to the OpenLDAP server as a client and submits a request to add the new objects. Because it acts as a client, you don't need to take down the LDAP database for it to work. However, because of that, using ldapadd to insert lots of objects will be slower than using slapadd.

The core client utility is the ldapsearch command. That's what you use to query the LDAP database for information. As you would expect, LDAP queries can get somewhat complicated. The ldapsearch utility allows you to customize many things, such as the location in the LDAP database to search and the items to search for. Table 11.7 shows the command-line parameters used to help customize the search.

TABLE 11.7   The *ldapsearch* command-line parameters

Parameter	Description
-a	Specify how distinguished name aliases are handled.
-A	Retrieve attributes but not the values.
-b base	Use the specified distinguished name to start the search.
-C	Automatically follow referral links.

TABLE 11.7 The *ldapsearch* command-line parameters *(continued)*

Parameter	Description
-d debug	Set the debug level to the specified level.
-D bind	Use the specified distinguished name to log into the database.
-f file	Read the search criteria from the specified file, one search per line.
-h host	Use the specified host for the LDAP server.
-H uri	Use the specified URI to connect to the LDAP server.
-I	Enable interactive mode.
-k	Use Kerberos authentication.
-K	Bind using Kerberos but don't connect.
-l time	Specify a time limit for the search.
-L	Display results in LDIF format.
-n	Display what would be done, but don't perform the search.
-O prop	Specify the security properties.
-p port	Use the specified port to connect to the LDAP server.
-P	Specify the LDAP protocol version to use.
-Q	Enable quiet mode.
-s	Specify the scope of the search to the base dn, one dn, or sub dn.
-S addr	Sort the output based on the specified attribute.
-t	Write retrieved values to a temporary file.
-u	Include the user-friendly version of the distinguished name.
-U authid	Specify an authentication ID to log into the LDAP database.
-v	Use verbose mode.

Parameter	Description
`-w pass`	Use the specified password for simple authentication.
`-W`	Prompt for a password for simple authentication.
`-x`	Use simple authentication.
`-X authid`	Specify an authorization ID for the login.
`-Y mech`	Specify the mechanism for authentication.
`-z size`	Specify a size to limit the amount of data returned.
`-Z`	Use Transport Layer Security (TLS) for the connection.

The ldapsearch command is very versatile, but with versatility often comes complexity. Listing 11.3 demonstrates how to perform a simple search.

Listing 11.3: Searching for LDAP objects

```
$ ldapsearch -b 'dc=ispnet1, dc=net' '(objectclass=*)'
version: 2

#
# filter: (objectclass=*)
# requesting: ALL
#

# ispnet1, dc=net
dn: dc=ispnet1, dc=net
objectClass: organization
o: "ISP test network"

# Administrator, dc=ispnet1, dc=net
dn: cn=Administrator, dc=ispnet1, dc=net
objectClass: organizationalRole
cn: Administrator

# search result
search: 2
result: 0 Success
```

```
# numResponses: 3
# numEntries: 2
$
```

In the example shown in Listing 11.3, the -b option defines the base distinguished name for the start of the search. Instead of starting at the root of the database schema, you can start at any node. The second parameter defines the search criteria. This example returns all objects that match all object classes.

EXERCISE 11.1

Setting Up and Testing a DHCP Server

This exercise demonstrates how to set up a simple DHCP server on your Linux system. To do that, follow these steps:

1. Log in as root, or acquire root privileges by using su or by using sudo with each of the following commands.

2. Open a command prompt, and then type **sudo apt-get install isc-dhcp-server** to install the DHCPd package on your Debian-based system or **yum install dhcp** to install it on your Red Hat–based system. You won't see any objects added to the menu when this program is installed.

3. Edit the /etc/dhcp/dhcp.conf configuration file. Add the following option lines:

   ```
   option domain-name-servers 10.1.0.1;
   subnet 10.1.0.0 netmask 255.255.0.0 {
       option router 10.1.0.1;
       option broadcast-address 10.1.255.255;
       range 10.1.0.10 10.1.0.200;
   }
   ```

4. Save the /etc/dhcp/dhcp.conf configuration file.

5. Shut down the Linux system; then disconnect it from your normal network.

6. Connect the Linux system into a stand-alone hub or switch that isn't connected to any other networks. Restart the Linux system.

7. Go into the network settings window, and assign the workstation a static IP address of 10.1.0.5, a subnet mask of 255.255.0.0, and a default gateway of 10.1.0.1.

8. Connect another client workstation to the same network hub or switch. Make sure that the new client's network card is configured to use DHCP. It should obtain an IP address from the Linux DHCP server. You can check the IP address assigned by using the **ifconfig** command at the command prompt.

9. Use the ping utility to test connectivity between the two Linux systems to ensure network connectivity.

10. Uninstall the DHCPd package from your Linux system so that it won't try to serve IP addresses when you plug it back into your normal network.

11. Log out from the Linux system and plug it back into the normal network.

Summary

Operating a Linux server in a multiclient network environment can be a challenge, but fortunately there are some Linux programs that can help out. One of those is the ISC DHCPd program. It provides a DHCP server program that can serve IP addresses to clients on your network. It can also use DHCP options to pass along addresses for other key servers on the network to clients, such as DNS and time servers. Linux clients can use several different DHCP client programs to request an IP address from a DHCP server on the network. The dhclient program is the most commonly used DHCP client application in Linux distributions.

Authentication is another big issue in multiclient or multiserver environments. The Linux PAM system provides an easy way to implement different authentication methods for different applications. The PAM system uses either a configuration file or a set of configuration files stored in a configuration folder to define how each application on the Linux system authenticates users.

For implementing a network directory on your network, you can use the OpenLDAP application. The OpenLDAP software provides both an LDAP server and LDAP client utilities that can interact with the LDAP server. The LDAP server maintains network objects in a hierarchical directory structure that can be easily queried.

Exam Essentials

Describe how DHCP is configured and used on a Linux server.   Most Linux distributions use the DHCPd application to provide DHCP server services. The DHCPd application uses the dhcpd program to listen for DHCP requests from clients and offers dynamic IP addresses. The DHCPd application stores the configuration settings in the /etc/dhcp/ dhcpd.conf file. You must define the range of dynamically assigned IP addresses within the configuration file to assign to clients as they request addresses.

Describe how to obtain a dynamic IP address on a Linux desktop.   Three different applications can be used as a DHCP client in Linux: dhcpcd, pump, and dhclient. Most Debian- and Red Hat–based distributions use the dhclient application and install it automatically if a network card is detected during installation. Normally, the dhclient application is activated automatically, and it will request an IP address from the network. You can use the graphical Network Manager program to make any changes to the setup.

Explain how multiple applications can share the same authentication method.   The Pluggable Authentication Module (PAM) system provides a single API for applications to use to authenticate users. Any application that supports PAM can share the same authentication database, such as the /etc/passwd users file, along with the /etc/shadow passwords file. The pam.conf configuration file, stored in the /etc folder, defines which applications can use which authentication methods. Because PAM application configurations can get somewhat lengthy, it allows you to split up each application configuration into separate files, each located in the /etc/pam.d folder.

Summarize how the System Security Services Daemon (SSSD) works.   The SSSD allows authentication using network-based directory servers, such as Microsoft Active Directory and Linux OpenLDAP directories. This provides a method for users to log into multiple Linux and Windows devices on a network using the same userid/password information. It plugs into PAM.

Explain the two ways to configure OpenLDAP.   The OpenLDAP program currently supports two methods for configuring an LDAP environment. The slapd.conf method uses a single text configuration file, located at /etc/ldap.conf. It defines the root of the LDAP directory tree, as well as an administrator account used for full access to the tree. The slapd-config method uses LDIF files to define the base LDAP directory tree and the administrator account. The base directory is stored in the cn=config file in the /etc/slapd.d folder. You must use the slapadd utility to process the file and start the LDAP tree.

Describe the OpenLDAP client utilities.   The OpenLDAP client package contains several command-line utilities for interacting with an LDAP server. The ldapsearch utility provides a way to query the LDAP server quickly for information on objects in the directory. The ldapadd and ldapdelete utilities allow you to add and remove objects from the LDAP tree. The ldappasswd utility allows you to easily change the password assigned to the LDAP account you logged in with.

Review Questions

You can find the answers in the Appendix.

1. What does the DHCPd application use for its configuration file?
   A. /etc/dhcpd.d/
   B. /etc/dhcp/dhcpd.conf
   C. isc-dhcp-server
   D. /etc/services

2. What DHCPd option setting do you use to define the default router for network clients?
   A. smtp-server
   B. broadcast-address
   C. router
   D. range

3. What DHCPd configuration option setting do you use to define the pool of IP addresses to assign to network clients?
   A. smtp-server
   B. broadcast-address
   C. router
   D. range

4. What file do you use to track IP addresses currently assigned by DHCPd?
   A. /var/lib/dhcp/dhcpd.leases
   B. /etc/dhcp/dhcpd.conf
   C. /etc/dhcp/dhcpd.leases
   D. /var/lib/dhcp/dhcpd.conf

5. What DHCPd configuration setting defines the MAC address of a device so that you can assign it a static IP address?
   A. range
   B. fixed-address
   C. host-name
   D. hardware

6. What DHCP configuration feature bundles settings assigned to a specific client?
   A. host
   B. group
   C. range
   D. fixed-address

7. What DHCP option number defines the subnet mask assigned to a client?

   A. 1

   B. 3

   C. 5

   D. 6

8. Which PAM module supports using the standard /etc/passwd and /etc/shadow files for authentication?

   A. pam_ldap.so

   B. pam_userdb.so

   C. pam_unix.so

   D. pam_sss.so

9. Which PAM module supports using a network directory to authenticate users?

   A. pam_unix.so

   B. pam_ldap.so

   C. pam_userdb.so

   D. pam_access.so

10. Which PAM module provides restrictions on user passwords.

    A. pam_limits.so

    B. pam_unix.so

    C. pam_cracklib.so

    D. pam_userdb.so

11. When using a single configuration file for PAM, where is it located?

    A. /etc/pam.d

    B. /etc/pam.conf

    C. /etc/pam.d/pam.conf

    D. /etc/pamd.conf

12. What folder does PAM use to store multiple application configuration files?

    A. /etc/pam.d

    B. /etc/pam.conf

    C. /etc/pam.d/pam.conf

    D. /etc/pamd.conf

13. Which PAM control entry terminates the application if the authentication fails?

    A. sufficient

    B. required

    C. requisite

    D. optional

14. Which PAM feature type logs authentication attempts to a log file?

   A. account

   B. session

   C. password

   D. auth

15. What part of the LDAP database defines a template for a set of attributes that can be assigned to an object?

   A. The object ID

   B. The schema

   C. The LDAP tree

   D. The object class

16. What part of the LDAP database defines the information stored for an object?

   A. Attributes

   B. Object class

   C. Object ID

   D. Schema

17. What is the unique name assigned to each object in the LDAP database called?

   A. Object ID

   B. Attribute

   C. Object class

   D. Distinguished name

18. What OpenLDAP program runs as the main LDAP server, listening for LDAP client requests?

   A. slurpd

   B. slapd

   C. slapadd

   D. slapindex

19. What LDAP server program allows you to add new objects to the LDAP database?

   A. ldapadd

   B. slapindex

   C. slapadd

   D. ldapmodify

20. What LDAP client application allows you to add new objects to the LDAP database?

   A. slapadd

   B. ldapadd

   C. ldapmodify

   D. slapindex

Chapter

12

Setting Up System Security

THE FOLLOWING EXAM OBJECTIVES ARE COVERED IN THIS CHAPTER:

✓ **212.1 Configuring a router**

✓ **212.3 Secure shell (SSH)**

✓ **212.4 Security tasks**

✓ **212.5 OpenVPN**

Security is an important component of the Linux system administrator's job. It's imperative that you have proper security procedures in place to protect the data on your server.

This chapter looks at some different security techniques designed to help protect your Linux system and the data it contains. First, we'll look at how to protect your Linux system from network attacks. While networks provide a world of resources for Linux servers, they also provide an avenue for attackers to reach your system. We'll explore how to block attackers by using the power of Linux to inspect the network traffic and watch for problems. Following that, we'll look at how you can use secure communications to connect remotely to your Linux system safely. A few different applications are available for protecting your data while it's on the network, and we'll look at the two most popular ones. Finally, we'll discuss how to keep current with security topics in the Linux world. Every day new exploits appear, and it's crucial for the Linux administrator to keep up with what's going on.

Server Network Security

Local networks allow you to interconnect Linux servers and clients to make accessing data simple and cost effective. While this is a great benefit to the system users, it comes at a great risk. Connecting your Linux system to any type of network opens the door to attackers. Taking that one step further, connecting the local network to the Internet opens even more doors. Now attackers from around the world can attempt to break into your Linux systems.

If you have your Linux system on any type of network, you must take extra precautions to protect it. This section walks you through some of the tools that you have available to help out with protecting your system.

Port Scanning

Linux network applications must continually monitor the network interface, watching for clients requesting access to the application. Connecting remotely to a network application requires a combination of a network protocol and a software port number to define a communications channel uniquely on the server.

For the network protocol, the two most commonly used protocols are TCP, used for connections that must be reliable, and UDP, usually used for connections that move lots of data quickly but, can afford to lose a packet or two now and then.

Each protocol also uses port numbers so that each application knows when a client is trying to connect to it. Standard port numbers are assigned to applications, such as TCP port 25 for email servers or TCP port 23 for Telnet sessions. When the Linux server sees a client connect to TCP port 25, it knows to pass that traffic to the email server program. The /etc/services file documents the different standard application ports and protocols supported by the Linux system.

The more ports that are open on a Linux system, the more opportunities there are for attackers to attack the system (called *attack vectors*). The key to network security is to reduce the number of available attack vectors on your Linux system. Removing unused network applications helps reduce the number of open ports on the server, thus reducing the number of attack vectors. For example, if your Linux server has the Apache web server installed but not in use, this provides an unnecessary connection path to the server. If you don't happen to keep up with the Apache server software patches, an attacker can use a known vulnerability to access your system.

To reduce the attack vectors, you need a way to determine what ports are listening for incoming network traffic on your system. This section walks you through the different ways that you can monitor what ports are open on your Linux system.

Telnet

In the old days of Linux, the Telnet application was the only way to connect remotely to a Linux system on the network. However, because it uses plain text to pass data between the client and the server, it quickly became a security risk and is no longer used for that purpose.

However, the Telnet application provides a quick-and-easy way to test TCP network ports on a Linux system, seeing what application is listening on the port. To do that, you just include the port number as the second parameter in the telnet command line:

```
$ telnet localhost 25
Trying 127.0.0.1...
Connected to localhost.
Escape character is '^]'.
220 ubuntu02 ESMTP Postfix (Ubuntu)
```

This example shows using the telnet command to connect to TCP port 25 (the standard port for SMTP email servers) on the server. Notice that there's a plaintext response from the email server application, which indicates that, indeed, something is listening on that port. The response from the network application provides a header identifying exactly what application (Postfix) is using that network port and even what operating system (Ubuntu) the server is running. That's exactly the type of information attackers are looking for.

netstat

While the `telnet` command is a quick way to check out a single port, trying to do that for all of the available ports (from 1 to 65,535) would be somewhat time consuming. If you need to check the status of multiple ports on your local system, use the `netstat` command.

The `netstat` command is very versatile, but with versatility comes complexity. Numerous command-line options are available in `netstat` that allow you to customize just what information it returns. For example, to display only ports that are listening for incoming TCP packets, you'd use the following:

```
$ netstat --tcp --listening
Active Internet connections (only servers)
Proto Recv-Q Send-Q Local Address           Foreign Address         State
tcp        0      0 ubuntu02:domain         *:*                     LISTEN
tcp        0      0 localhost:ipp           *:*                     LISTEN
tcp        0      0 localhost:smtp          *:*                     LISTEN
tcp        0      0 *:http                  *:*                     LISTEN
tcp6       0      0 ip6-localhost:ipp       [::]:*                  LISTEN
tcp6       0      0 [::]:3128               [::]:*                  LISTEN
tcp6       0      0 ip6-localhost:smtp      [::]:*                  LISTEN
tcp6       0      0 [::]:http               [::]:*                  LISTEN
$
```

The name after the local address is the port name as defined in the /etc/services file. If the port number isn't defined in the /etc/services file, it appears as the number.

Another great feature of the `netstat` command is that it can also display current open network connections to your Linux system:

```
$ netstat --tcp
Active Internet connections (w/o servers)
Proto Recv-Q Send-Q Local Address          Foreign Address        State
tcp        0      0 10.0.2.15:48964        hanger.canonical.c:http TIME_WAIT
tcp        0      0 10.0.2.15:59411        strix.canonical.co:http TIME_WAIT
tcp        0      0 10.0.2.15:48963        hanger.canonical.c:http TIME_WAIT
tcp6       1      0 ip6-localhost:57291    ip6-localhost:ipp       CLOSE_WAIT
$
```

This example shows an Ubuntu system connecting to the Canonical software repository, checking for software updates. With the `netstat` tool, you can snoop on any network connection to your system.

nc

Netcat (nc) is an application that provides both client and server network services. It is often used to create a simple data transfer between two systems (thus the *cat* part of the name, like the cat command-line command). Just start netcat on one system as a server and on the other system as a client connecting to the server.

Moreover, netcat is also a valuable network troubleshooting tool. The -z option provides port-scanning capabilities, allowing you to scan multiple ports looking for an open port. By default, the -z option returns an exit status of 0 if at least one of the ports is listening for network traffic. To be able to see which port is active, add the -v option:

```
$ nc -vz localhost 20-30
nc: connect to localhost port 20 (tcp) failed: Connection refused
nc: connect to localhost port 21 (tcp) failed: Connection refused
nc: connect to localhost port 22 (tcp) failed: Connection refused
nc: connect to localhost port 23 (tcp) failed: Connection refused
nc: connect to localhost port 24 (tcp) failed: Connection refused
Connection to localhost 25 port [tcp/smtp] succeeded!
nc: connect to localhost port 26 (tcp) failed: Connection refused
nc: connect to localhost port 27 (tcp) failed: Connection refused
nc: connect to localhost port 28 (tcp) failed: Connection refused
nc: connect to localhost port 29 (tcp) failed: Connection refused
nc: connect to localhost port 30 (tcp) failed: Connection refused
$
```

The benefit of netcat is that you can specify any host to connect with, making it easy to check for open ports on any host on your network.

WARNING Two versions of the netcat command are used in Linux, so be careful. The OpenBSD version supports the -z option, while the version that installs as part of the nmap package doesn't. It appears that Red Hat–based versions use the nmap version, so you'll need to install the OpenBSD version manually to use the port-scanning feature.

nmap

The nmap command was specifically developed as a network port-scanning application. It can scan multiple remote network servers, documenting all of the ports and protocols that they support.

Not only does the nmap command perform standard TCP and UDP connections, but it also tries spoofing other known network attacks, such as half-open connections, proxy attacks, ping sweeps, SYN packet sweeps, and null scans.

To start a scan of TCP ports on a server, use the -sT option. Add the -p option to specify the port range:

```
$ nmap -sT -p 1-65535 localhost

Starting Nmap 6.40 (http://nmap.org) at 2016-07-19 19:22 EDT
```

```
Nmap scan report for localhost (127.0.0.1)
Host is up (0.00021s latency).
Not shown: 65530 closed ports
PORT        STATE  SERVICE
25/tcp      open   smtp
80/tcp      open   http
631/tcp     open   ipp
3128/tcp    open   squid-http
42117/tcp open    unknown

Nmap done: 1 IP address (1 host up) scanned in 1.66 seconds
$
```

This command scans all of the TCP ports from 1 to 65,535 on the localhost system. The output of the nmap command is a report showing just which ports in that range are open, listening for client connections, and what service name is assigned to those ports in the /etc/services file. You can do the same for the UDP ports:

```
$ nmap -sU -p 630-640 localhost
You requested a scan type which requires root privileges.
QUITTING!
$
$ sudo nmap -sU -p 630-640 localhost

Starting Nmap 6.40 (http://nmap.org) at 2016-07-20 09:30 EDT
Nmap scan report for localhost (127.0.0.1)
Host is up (0.000060s latency).
PORT        STATE        SERVICE
630/udp closed          rda
631/udp open|filtered ipp
632/udp closed          bmpp
633/udp closed          unknown
634/udp closed          ginad
635/udp closed          mount
636/udp closed          ldaps
637/udp closed          lanserver
638/udp closed          unknown
639/udp closed          msdp
640/udp closed          pcnfs

Nmap done: 1 IP address (1 host up) scanned in 3.45 seconds
$
```

Note that you must have root administrative privileges on the system to run the nmap command against some network ports, such as the UDP ports requested in this example.

Another interesting feature of the nmap command is that not only can it detect open network ports, but it also has some intelligence built in to help identify the operating system of the remote system. By detecting the open applications and how they respond to requests, nmap creates a fingerprint of the remote system and can often determine what operating system it is and what applications it's running. You can do that using the –A option:

```
$ sudo nmap -A localhost

Starting Nmap 6.40 (http://nmap.org) at 2016-07-20 09:33 EDT
Nmap scan report for localhost (127.0.0.1)
Host is up (0.00011s latency).
Not shown: 996 closed ports
PORT     STATE SERVICE    VERSION
25/tcp   open  smtp       Postfix smtpd
|_smtp-commands: ubuntu02, PIPELINING, SIZE 10240000, VRFY, ETRN, STARTTLS,
ENHANCEDSTATUSCODES, 8BITMIME, DSN,
| ssl-cert: Subject: commonName=ubuntu.gateway.pace.com
| Not valid before: 2015-02-14T21:46:46+00:00
|_Not valid after:  2025-02-11T21:46:46+00:00
|_ssl-date: 2079-04-25T11:29:40+00:00; +62y278d21h55m40s from local time.
80/tcp   open  http       nginx 1.4.6 (Ubuntu)
|_http-methods: No Allow or Public header in OPTIONS response (status code 405)
|_http-title: Welcome to nginx!
631/tcp  open  ipp        CUPS 1.7
| http-methods: Potentially risky methods: PUT
|_See http://nmap.org/nsedoc/scripts/http-methods.html
| http-robots.txt: 1 disallowed entry
|_/
|_http-title: Home—CUPS 1.7.2
3128/tcp open  http-proxy Squid http proxy 3.3.8
|_http-methods: No Allow or Public header in OPTIONS response (status code 400)
| http-open-proxy: Potentially OPEN proxy.
|_Methods supported:  GET HEAD
|_http-title: ERROR: The requested URL could not be retrieved
No exact OS matches for host (If you know what OS is running on it, see http://
nmap.org/submit/).
TCP/IP fingerprint:
OS:SCAN(V=6.40%E=4%D=7/20%OT=25%CT=1%CU=35620%PV=N%DS=0%DC=L%G=Y%TM=578F7DC
OS:9%P=x86_64-pc-linux-gnu)SEQ(SP=FF%GCD=1%ISR=10A%TI=Z%CI=I%TS=8)OPS(O1=MF
OS:FD7ST11NW7%O2=MFFD7ST11NW7%O3=MFFD7NNT11NW7%O4=MFFD7ST11NW7%O5=MFFD7ST11
```

```
OS:NW7%O6=MFFD7ST11)WIN(W1=AAAA%W2=AAAA%W3=AAAA%W4=AAAA%W5=AAAA%W6=AAAA)ECN
OS:(R=Y%DF=Y%T=40%W=AAAA%O=MFFD7NNSNW7%CC=Y%Q=)T1(R=Y%DF=Y%T=40%S=O%A=S+%F=
OS:AS%RD=0%Q=)T2(R=N)T3(R=N)T4(R=Y%DF=Y%T=40%W=0%S=A%A=Z%F=R%O=%RD=0%Q=)T5(
OS:R=Y%DF=Y%T=40%W=0%S=Z%A=S+%F=AR%O=%RD=0%Q=)T6(R=Y%DF=Y%T=40%W=0%S=A%A=Z%
OS:F=R%O=%RD=0%Q=)T7(R=Y%DF=Y%T=40%W=0%S=Z%A=S+%F=AR%O=%RD=0%Q=)U1(R=Y%DF=N
OS:%T=40%IPL=164%UN=0%RIPL=G%RID=G%RIPCK=G%RUCK=G%RUD=G)IE(R=Y%DFI=N%T=40%C
OS:D=S)

Network Distance: 0 hops
Service Info: Host:  ubuntu02; OS: Linux; CPE: cpe:/o:linux:linux_kernel

OS and Service detection performed. Please report any incorrect results at
http://nmap.org/submit/.
Nmap done: 1 IP address (1 host up) scanned in 54.01 seconds
$
```

The nmap command correctly identifies the system as a Linux operating system, and it even points out some potential security issues with the listening applications! This is a great tool to have in your network troubleshooting toolkit.

The nmap command performs a somewhat intrusive scan of the remote system, and it can trigger any intrusion detection system (IDS) installed on the server into thinking that the system is under attack (more on that in the "Intrusion Detection Systems" section later in this chapter). Because of that, if you're working in an environment with lots of different servers run by different administration groups, it's always a good idea to warn administrators before running nmap against their servers.

OpenVAS

The *Open Vulnerability Assessment System (OpenVAS)* is an open source project that combines several services and tools into a single application that can detect vulnerabilities on your Linux system. One of the great features of OpenVAS is that it's not a static system: it receives updates of *network vulnerability tests (NVT)* on a daily basis, providing up-to-date testing of known attack vectors against systems. The NVTs simulate known attack vectors on your system. You can check out the current list of vulnerabilities that OpenVAS monitors on their website, www.openvas.org.

For Debian-based systems, the OpenVAS software is included in the default software repository as package openvas-server. Unfortunately, Red Hat–based systems don't include OpenVAS by default.

You can install OpenVAS on a Red Hat–based distribution by using a repository sponsored by Atomicorp. You'll need to add that repository to your trusted repositories first, and then you can install the openvas package using yum:

```
$ wget -q -O - http://www.atomicorp.com/installers/atomic |sh
$ sudo yum install openvas
```

After you install OpenVAS, you'll need to run the openvas-setup script. That script performs several operations for you:

- Updates the vulnerability definitions

- Creates an administrator account

- Generates default configuration files in the /etc/openvas folder

- Installs the OpenVAS server application in the system startup files

After the setup script completes, you can connect to the OpenVAS web interface using the URL http://localhost:9392. Log in as the admin user account using the password that you created during the setup process. Figure 12.1 shows the opening OpenVAS web page.

FIGURE 12.1   The OpenVAS main web page

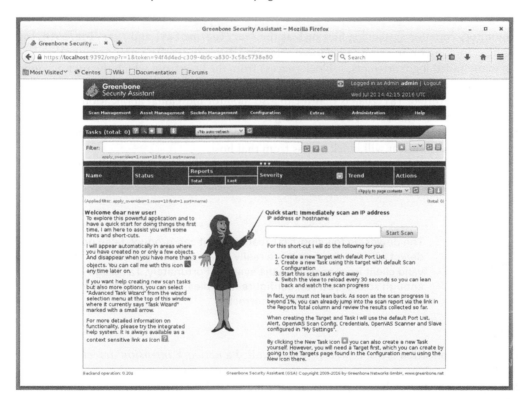

The OpenVAS tool is supported by Greenbone Networks, which created the web interface. Don't be confused by the branding that appears on the main page; it's still the OpenVAS interface. From here you can manage all of the features of OpenVAS, such as what hosts to scan and how often to scan them. Once OpenVAS performs a vulnerability scan on a host, you can view the result reports from the web interface.

Intrusion Detection Systems

While monitoring possible attack vectors is useful, it doesn't prevent attackers from trying to break into your system using the existing valid applications that your server must support. It helps to have software that monitors the network and applications running on the system, looking for suspicious behavior. These applications are called *intrusion detection systems (IDSs)*. An IDS application can't stop attackers, but it can warn you as soon as it detects something happening.

This section discusses two of the more popular IDS applications in Linux, fail2ban and Snort.

fail2ban

The fail2ban program monitors system logs, looking for repeated failures from the same host. If it detects a problem, fail2ban can block the IP address of the offending host from accessing your system.

The fail2ban program monitors both system and application logs looking for problems. It monitors common system log files such as the /var/log/pwdfail and /var/log/auth.log log files, looking for multiple failed login attempts. When it detects a user account that has too many failed login attempts, it blocks access from the host from which the user account was attempting to log in.

A great feature of fail2ban is that it can also monitor individual application log files, such as the /var/log/apache/error.log log file for the Apache web server. Just as with the system log files, if fail2ban detects too many connection attempts or errors coming from the same remote host, it will block access from that host.

The fail2ban configuration is stored in the /etc/fail2ban/jail.conf file. It defines the applications to monitor, where their log files are located, and what actions to take if it detects a problem.

 The downside to using fail2ban is that it can produce false positives that detect a problem when there really isn't one. This can cause it to block a valid client from accessing the system. Fortunately, fail2ban is robust enough so that you can configure it to release the block after a set time to allow the client to reconnect correctly.

Snort

The Snort application is a special type of IDS called a *network intrusion detection system (NIDS)*. It doesn't monitor activity on the server, but instead it monitors the network traffic coming into the server. It then performs real-time analysis of the traffic, looking for attacks.

The key to Snort is where you place the Snort server on your network. If you just plug your Snort server into a standard network switch like any other server, you'll be somewhat disappointed with the results you get. Snort can work only on the packets that it sees, and the network switch will limit those packets to only packets destined for the Snort server.

To get the full benefit of Snort, connect the Snort server to the network in a location that sees all of the network traffic coming into and out from your local network, as shown in Figure 12.2.

FIGURE 12.2   Placing the Snort server on your network

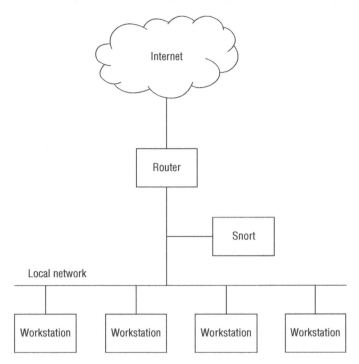

When the Snort server is placed in a location that sees all of the network traffic, it can monitor your entire local network for intrusion attempts.

> Many network switches support the span feature, which allows you to set a port to mirror another port on the switch. Using this feature, you can tap into the port that connects your local network to the router, monitoring all inbound and outbound network traffic without having to physically tap into the network connection.

Snort supports three different modes:

Sniffer: Snort just dumps network packets to the terminal display.

Packet logger: Snort logs all packets to a log file.

NIDS: Snort doesn't store detailed packet data but only reports on detected intrusion attempts.

Snort is a very popular package, and it is included in the software repositories of most Linux distributions. Installing Snort is usually easy using either apt-get or yum.

After you install Snort, you'll need to set the configuration to determine what to monitor and define rules that determine how to handle the network events Snort looks for. The main configuration file is named snort.conf, and it is stored in the /etc/snort folder. It defines several variables that customize how Snort works, as well as rules to define how Snort handles network events.

The HOME_NET variable defines the network addresses to monitor. The default value of any allows Snort to monitor all local network addresses. Likewise, the EXTERNAL_NET variable defines which external hosts to monitor.

Snort rules have a specific format:

```
action protocol address direction address options
```

The action entry determines what Snort should do when the rule is met by a network packet. Common action values are alert, which sends a message, and log, which enters the event into a log file, normally stored in the /var/log/snort folder.

The address entries specify the source and destination addresses and are entered as either an IP address and port (address:port) or by using the value any to cover all addresses or ports. You can specify a range of IP addresses by including a subnet mask in CIDR address format, such as 192.168.1.0/24.

The direction entry defines which address is the source address and which address is the destination address. You use symbols for that, -> or <-for unidirectional traffic monitoring or <> for bidirectional traffic monitoring. An example of a Snort rule is

```
alert icmp any any -> 192.168.1.0/24 any (msg: "ICMP traffic detected")
```

This rule monitors the 192.168.1.0 subnet for any incoming ICMP packets originating from any outside network. If an ICMP packet is detected, Snort sends an alert message.

Managing Snort rules can be somewhat complicated. To help with that process there's a separate package called PulledPork. It allows you to download predefined rules from a common library and install them.

If you have a server dedicated to running Snort, you'll need to add the snort program to the system startup scripts so that it starts automatically. If you just want to run Snort occasionally on your system, you can also run the snort command directly from the command line:

```
# snort
Running in packet dump mode

        —== Initializing Snort ==—
Initializing Output Plugins!
pcap DAQ configured to passive.
Acquiring network traffic from "enp0s3".
Decoding Ethernet

        —== Initialization Complete ==—
```

```
 ,,_      -*> Snort! <*-
o" )~     Version 2.9.6.1 GRE (Build 56)
 ''''     By Martin Roesch & The Snort Team: http://www.snort.org/snort/snort-team
          Copyright (C) 2014 Cisco and/or its affiliates. All rights reserved.
          Copyright (C) 1998-2013 Sourcefire, Inc., et al.
          Using libpcap version 1.5.3
          Using PCRE version: 8.32 2012-11-30
          Using ZLIB version: 1.2.7

Commencing packet processing (pid=26642)
07/20-11:33:45.832940 10.0.2.15:38839 -> 107.170.224.8:123
UDP TTL:64 TOS:0x0 ID:20268 IpLen:20 DgmLen:76 DF
Len: 48
=+=+=+=+=+=+=+=+=+=+=+=+=+=+=+=+=+=+=+=+=+=+=+=+=+=+=+=+=+=+=+=+=+=+=+=+=+=+

07/20-11:33:45.918301 107.170.224.8:123 -> 10.0.2.15:38839
UDP TTL:64 TOS:0x0 ID:35379 IpLen:20 DgmLen:76
Len: 48
=+=+=+=+=+=+=+=+=+=+=+=+=+=+=+=+=+=+=+=+=+=+=+=+=+=+=+=+=+=+=+=+=+=+=+=+=+=+
```

Notice in the snort command output that part of the Snort copyright is owned by the Cisco Corporation. The Snort application itself is open source software, but Cisco owns the copyright to the Snort pig logo. You're still free to use Snort for all of your NIDS needs.

External Network Security

Having your Linux server connected to just a local network for in-house clients to access isn't usually all that much of a security risk. At least you have control over what people and systems connect to it. However, once you connect your local network to other external networks, things change. Now you must be aware of unknown people and systems trying to access your system from unknown remote locations.

When you have to connect your local network to the Internet, some tools are available to help you protect against attackers. This section walks through some of these tools.

Private Network Addresses and NAT

One way to protect your local network from outside intruders is to utilize *private network addresses*. A private network address is an IP or IPv6 address that can only be accessed from devices connected to the local network. Private network addresses can't be routed to outside networks, so outside attackers can't gain access to your systems.

The IPv4 address specification as created by the Internet Assigned Numbers Authority (IANA) reserved three separate address ranges for private network addresses:

- 10.0.0.0 through 10.255.255.255
- 172.16.0.0 through 172.31.255.255
- 192.168.0.0 through 192.168.255.255

If you use any of these network ranges for your local network, hosts on external networks can't directly route network traffic to your local hosts.

The IPv6 standard goes one step further in defining private network addresses. The IPv6 standard defines *link local addresses*. When IPv6 is enabled on a Linux system, a link local address is automatically assigned when the system boots up. That way, IPv6 hosts can communicate with one another without requiring any manual configuration of network addresses.

IPv6 defines a standard range of network addresses for the link local addresses. The IPv6 link local address starts with the value fe80 and usually contains the MAC address of the system as part of the host address to ensure that each system has a unique link local address on the network.

While using private network addresses helps prevent attackers from getting inside your local network, the downside is that no remote systems can send packets back to clients on your network, including servers with which you want to communicate. This prevents your local network clients from connecting to any outside resource. To get around that problem, you utilize *Network Address Translation (NAT)*.

NAT is a method of translating the private network address of all of the clients on your local network into a public network address for use on the Internet. All of your network clients appear as a single host address to the rest of the Internet. Because of that, the NAT server must have some intelligence built in so that it knows which incoming packets are destined for which local client. Figure 12.3 shows an example of how NAT would look for a local network.

FIGURE 12.3   Using NAT for a local network

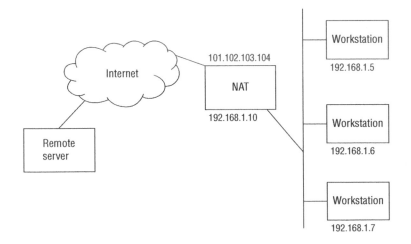

Hosts on the internal network use the NAT server as the default router. Any packets destined for external networks are sent to the NAT server.

External servers needing to communicate back to internal servers use the NAT server's external public network address as the destination. The NAT server maintains a dynamic table that maps all of the active network connections from local clients to remote systems on the Internet, so it knows which private IP address to forward the incoming packet to. Now all of your local network clients can interact with remote hosts, but remote hosts can't initiate connections into your local clients, thus providing a great balance of security and functionality.

Sometimes when using NAT, you do need to allow external hosts to connect to an application running on a server on the local network. Most NAT devices allow you to use *port redirection*, which accepts external network traffic as a proxy for the internal host and then forwards that traffic directly to the internal server. Be careful when using this feature, though, because opening your internal hosts to clients on the Internet can be a dangerous thing.

Firewalls

Another technique for blocking unwanted network traffic to your local network is the use of a *firewall*. A firewall sits between the network router and the local network and uses rules that you define to determine which network traffic to allow into the network and which traffic to block. This is illustrated in Figure 12.4.

FIGURE 12.4   Using a firewall on a local network

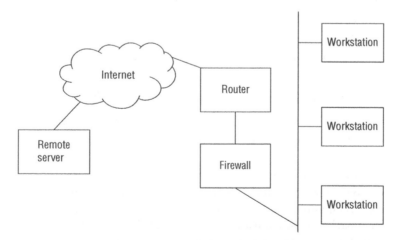

These days, many Linux administrators take this idea one step further. Besides having a network firewall, they also create a firewall directly on each Linux server. This allows them to have control over exactly what network traffic the server allows and what traffic it blocks. The next section explains just how to do that on your Linux server.

Using *iptables*

Linux uses a series of internal kernel processes called *chains* to process network packets that enter the system. The chains determine the path each packet takes as it enters the Linux system and works its way to the appropriate application or as an application sends packets back out to the network to remote clients. Figure 12.5 shows the different chains involved with processing network packets on a Linux system.

FIGURE 12.5   The Linux packet processing chain

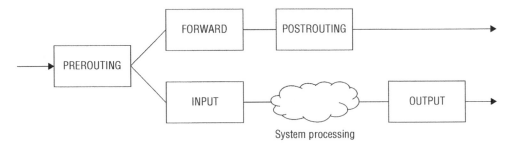

As shown in Figure 12.5, five separate chains process packets:

PREROUTING handles packets before the routing decision process.

INPUT handles packets destined for the local system.

FORWARD handles packets being forwarded to a remote system.

POSTROUTING handles packets being sent to remote systems, after the forward filter.

OUTPUT handles packets output from the local system.

Each chain contains tables that define rules for handling the packets. There are three types of tables:

FILTER applies rules to allow or block packets from exiting the chain.

MANGLE applies rules to change features of the packets before they exit the chain.

NAT applies rules to change the addresses of the packets before they exit the chain.

As you can probably guess, implementing NAT requires using the NAT table to alter the address of packets in the OUTPUT chain. Implementing a firewall is a little trickier, because you can apply filter tables to the INPUT, OUTPUT, and FORWARD chains in the process. This gives you multiple locations in the process to block packets.

All of the system packet-handling features are performed internally in the Linux kernel program. Unfortunately, you can't just set a configuration file to define the rules used to filter packets on the system. Instead, you need to interact directly with the kernel.

The tool that you use to alter the internal kernel chains and filters is the `iptables` command. It interacts with the internal kernel chains and tables, allowing you to alter how the Linux kernel processes packets.

Because of the complexity of the chains and tables, using the `iptables` command can get somewhat complex. Table 12.1 shows the command-line options that are available.

TABLE 12.1 The `iptables` basic command-line options

Option	Description
-A chain rule	Add a new rule to the specified chain.
-D chain rule	Delete a rule from the specified chain.
-F [chain]	Remove all rules for the specified chain or all chains if none is specified.
-I chain index rule	Insert a new rule into the specified chain at the specified index location.
-L [chain]	List the rules in the specified chain or all chains if not specified.
-P chain target	Define the default policy for the specified chain.
-R chain index rule	Replace the rule at the specified index location.
-S [chain]	List the rules in detail of the specified chain or all chains if not specified.
-t *table*	Specify the table the rule applies to.

Here's an example of displaying all the current rules applied to all chains on the system:

```
$ sudo iptables -L
[sudo] password for rich:
Chain INPUT (policy ACCEPT)
target     prot opt source              destination

Chain FORWARD (policy ACCEPT)
target     prot opt source              destination

Chain OUTPUT (policy ACCEPT)
target     prot opt source              destination
$
```

Notice that to access the kernel information from `iptables`, you must have root privileges on your system. The listing shows that no rules defined are for each chain.

However, each chain has a *policy* value. The policy entry defines how packets are handled by default for the chain when no rules apply to the packet. There are several different policy values; the most commonly used ones are these:

ACCEPT: Pass the packet along to the next chain.

DROP: Don't pass the packet to the next chain.

LOG: Log the packet and pass it to the next chain.

REJECT: Don't pass the packet, and send a reject notice to the sender.

If you want to block all packets leaving your Linux system, you would just change the default OUTPUT chain to a DROP policy:

```
$ sudo iptables -t filter -P OUTPUT DROP
$ sudo iptables -L
Chain INPUT (policy ACCEPT)
target     prot opt source               destination


Chain FORWARD (policy ACCEPT)
target     prot opt source               destination


Chain OUTPUT (policy DROP)
target     prot opt source               destination
$
```

Now if you try to send packets out the network, the application will get an error message:

```
$ ping 192.168.1.254
PING 192.168.1.254 (192.168.1.254) 56(84) bytes of data.
ping: sendmsg: Operation not permitted
ping: sendmsg: Operation not permitted
ping: sendmsg: Operation not permitted
^C
-- 192.168.1.254 ping statistics--
3 packets transmitted, 0 received, 100% packet loss, time 2006ms

$
```

The ping command returns a failure message because it can't send packets on to the network. To return things back to normal, just change the default policy back to ACCEPT:

```
$ sudo iptables -t filter -P OUTPUT ACCEPT
$ ping 192.168.1.254
PING 192.168.1.254 (192.168.1.254) 56(84) bytes of data.
64 bytes from 192.168.1.254: icmp_seq=1 ttl=63 time=1.95 ms
64 bytes from 192.168.1.254: icmp_seq=2 ttl=63 time=7.56 ms
```

```
^C
-- 192.168.1.254 ping statistics--
2 packets transmitted, 2 received, 0% packet loss, time 1004ms
rtt min/avg/max/mdev = 1.951/4.759/7.567/2.808 ms
$
```

To change chain rules, you need to use some additional command-line options in the iptables command, as shown in Table 12.2.

TABLE 12.2 Rule options for the iptables command

Option	Description
-d address	The destination address
-g chain	Jump to a new chain
-i name	The input interface
-j target	The action to take
-o name	The output interface
-p protocol	Matches a specific protocol, such as tcp, upd, or icmp
-s address	The source address

The -j option defines the action, which mirrors the policy values of ACCEPT, DROP, LOG, and REJECT. Here's an example of a simple rule:

```
$ sudo iptables -A INPUT -s 10.0.1.25 -j REJECT
$ sudo iptables -L
Chain INPUT (policy ACCEPT)
target     prot opt source              destination
REJECT     all — 10.0.1.25              anywhere              reject-with
icmp-port-unreachable

Chain FORWARD (policy ACCEPT)
target     prot opt source              destination

Chain OUTPUT (policy ACCEPT)
target     prot opt source              destination
$
```

The command added a rule to the INPUT chain rejecting all packets coming from the remote host 10.0.1.25. Listing the contents of the chain now shows that indeed a new rule exists on the system.

 Often you need to block only a single port instead of an entire destination address. To do that, use the –p option to specify the protocol and then the --sport or --dport option to specify either a source port or destination port.

The downside to modifying the kernel chain rules is that the new rules aren't persistent. When you reboot your Linux system, the new rules that you added will be gone and the chains will be back to their default configuration. You can save any existing rules that you define using the iptables-save command:

```
$ sudo iptables-save > myrules.txt
$ cat myrules.txt
# Generated by iptables-save v1.4.21 on Wed Jul 20 20:28:44 2016
*filter
:INPUT ACCEPT [3:316]
:FORWARD ACCEPT [0:0]
:OUTPUT ACCEPT [3:260]
-A INPUT -s 10.0.1.25/32 -j REJECT—reject-with icmp-port-unreachable
COMMIT
# Completed on Wed Jul 20 20:28:44 2016
$
```

Then you can restore the rules using the iptables-restore command:

```
$ sudo iptables -F INPUT
$ sudo iptables -L INPUT
Chain INPUT (policy ACCEPT)
target     prot opt source                destination
$ sudo iptables-restore < myrules.txt
$ sudo iptables -L INPUT
Chain INPUT (policy ACCEPT)
target     prot opt source                destination
REJECT     all — 10.0.1.25                anywhere               reject-with icmp-
port-unreachable
$
```

After clearing out the rules for the INPUT chain using the –F option, we restored the rules using the iptables-restore command. Notice that you must use the redirect operator to redirect the saved rules file to the command.

 You can also create a shell script file that contains the individual iptables commands to create the rules and then run that script automatically as part of the startup process.

The `iptables` command applies only to the IPv4 packet-handling features in the Linux kernel. As you can probably guess, there are IPv6 packet-handling features as well in the kernel. To manipulate the chains in that process, you use the `ip6tables` command.

Routing in Linux

One thing that we haven't talked about is the packet-forwarding feature in Linux. The FORWARD chain allows Linux to forward packets to a remote host, but that feature must be enabled in the kernel. To enable that feature, just set the `ip_forward` entry for IPv4 or the `forwarding` entry for IPv6. You can do that with the `sysctl` command:

```
$ sudo sysctl -w net.ipv4.ip_forward=1
$ sudo sysctl -w net.ipv6.conf.all.forwarding=1
```

You can check the current kernel values by using the `cat` command in the `/proc` filesystem entries:

```
$ cat /proc/sys/net/ipv4/ip_forward
1
$ cat /proc/sys/net/ipv6/conf/all/forwarding
1
$
```

Once those kernel values are set, your Linux system will be able to forward traffic from one network interface to another network interface. If there are multiple network interfaces on the Linux system, it must know which interface to use to send traffic to remote hosts. To do that, Linux maintains a *routing table*.

The routing table notes which network interface should be used to send packets to specific remote hosts. The table is populated by both past experience from sending packets and from information obtained from other network routers. Linux implements the *Router Information Protocol (RIP)*, which provides a way for network routers to advertise the networks that they support. As the Linux system receives RIP packets, it updates the router table. Linux uses the `routed` program to listen for RIP packets and update the router table. As new routes are discovered by the `routed` program, they are automatically added to the route table. You can view the new routes using the `route` command.

Connecting Securely to a Server

In the old days of Linux, connecting to a remote Linux server was as easy as just using the `telnet` command and listing the IP address or hostname of the remote server. Unfortunately, those days are over.

With the increased awareness of security issues, it's no longer recommended to use the text-based `telnet` application to connect to remote servers. Instead, a more secure method must be used.

This section discusses the two most popular methods used to connect to remote Linux servers using a secure connection: OpenSSH and OpenVPN.

OpenSSH

The most popular package used in Linux to provide quick, secure connections to Linux servers is *OpenSSH*. The OpenSSH package uses the *Secure Shell (SSH)* protocol to establish an encrypted connection between two network devices.

This section walks you through the parts of the OpenSSH package and demonstrates how to use OpenSSH to connect to a remote Linux server.

The OpenSSH Files

Just about all Linux distributions include the OpenSSH application in the default software repository. You can use `apt-get` or `yum` to install it. The OpenSSH package consists of a few different files that are installed:

- The sshd server program
- The ssh client program
- The sshd_conf server configuration file
- The ssh_conf client configuration file
- Several certificate files required for encryption

The configuration and certificate files are all stored in the /etc/ssh folder. Usually, the installation process also generates a host certificate to identify the host uniquely in SSH connections.

WARNING   Notice that the OpenSSH package provides both the server, sshd, and the client, ssh, applications. Because of the similarity of the two programs, it's easy to get things confused. The same also applies to their prospective configuration files, sshd_conf and ssh_conf. Be careful when working with the applications and configuration files.

OpenSSH Configuration

Usually both the OpenSSH server and client programs work fine as is after installation. However, there may be some situations where you'd like to customize just how they behave.

The /etc/ssh/sshd_conf configuration file defines server options in the format

```
option value
```

The `option` entry is the name of an option to set, and `value` is the value assigned to that option. Table 12.3 lists the more common options that you may need to change on your OpenSSH server.

TABLE 12.3 Common OpenSSH server configuration options

Option	Description
Protocol	Specify the encryption protocol level. Level 2 is preferred and more secure.
PasswordAuthentication	Allow authentication using text passwords.
PubkeyAuthentication	Allow authentication using certificates.
AllowUsers	Allow the specified list of users to log in using SSH.
DenyUsers	Block the specified list of users from logging in using SSH.
PermitRootLogin	Allow the root user account to log in using SSH.
X11Forwarding	Allow remote X servers to run X client applications using tunneling.
AllowTcpForwarding	The server will accept tunneled protocols.

Most of these options take a simple yes or no value to enable or disable the feature. The AllowUsers and DenyUsers options use a space-separated list of user account names on the system to determine which users to allow or block access to the server.

The default sshd_conf configuration file contains lots of other options, which are documented in comments within the file. Take some time to go through each option to determine if it is something that would be beneficial in your network environment. After you make any configuration changes, you need to restart the OpenSSH server for them to take effect.

Using OpenSSH

With the OpenSSH server running, you can connect to it using the ssh client program. To log into the remote server using the same user account that you use on the client, just specify the remote server hostname or IP address:

```
rich@ubuntu02 ~$ ssh 192.168.1.77
```

This command will attempt to log into the remote host 192.168.1.77 with the userid rich. If the user account is set for password authentication, you will get prompted for your password on the remote system. If the user account is set up for certificate authentication, you'll be presented immediately with a command prompt on the remote system.

The first time you connect to a remote host, you'll be prompted to accept its certificate into your client key store. This provides a way to validate remote hosts to ensure that your session is not getting hijacked by an attacker's system.

If you need to log in as a different user account, just specify it on the command line using the ampersand sign, like an email address:

```
barbara@ubuntu02 ~$ ssh rich@192.168.1.77
```

The OpenSSH package also includes a handy utility for quickly copying files between systems. The scp command uses SSH to encrypt the transfer of the files between the two systems. To transfer a file from your local system to a remote system use

```
$ scp myfile.txt rich@192.168.1.77:/home/rich/Documents/myfile.txt
```

To transfer a file from the remote system to your local system use

```
$ scp rich@192.168.1.77:/home/rich/Documents/myfile.txt myfile.txt
```

A handy feature of scp is the ability to copy files between two remote servers:

```
$ scp rich@192.168.1.77:myfile.txt rich@192.168.1.78:myfile.txt
```

Another common use of OpenSSH is to provide a tunnel for graphical X11 sessions. The X11 protocol allows you to run applications on a server but send the graphical windows across the network back to your workstation (in X11 lingo, the system sending the window is actually the client, and the system receiving the window is the server, which is somewhat backwards from what you'd expect). Unfortunately, the X11 protocol sends the graphical window and its data unencrypted.

To secure a remote X11 session, you can tunnel it through an SSH connection. To do that, the client side of the X11 connection must run the OpenSSH server, and the server side of the X11 connection must connect as an OpenSSH client.

For the server side, ensure that the X11Forwarding configuration option in the sshd_conf file is set to yes, and for the client side, ensure that the ForwardX11 option in the ssh_conf file is set to yes.

Once that is complete, use the ssh program to connect from your workstation to the remote server and then launch your X11 application. The graphical window will automatically transfer via the SSH connection back to your workstation, which will display the window.

Using Client Certificates

SSH supports public/private key pair authentication. To log into an SSH session using a certificate instead of a password, you just need to create a public/private key pair on your client and then export the public key to the server.

To generate a public/private key pair, you use the ssh-keygen command, included in the OpenSSH package:

```
$ ssh-keygen -q -t rsa -f ~/.ssh/id_rsa -C '' -N ''
```

This command generates the private and public keys using the RSA encryption. The private key will be named id_rsa, while the public key will be named id_rsa.pub.

Copy the id_rsa.pub file to the remote server. The key contents must be copied into the ~/.ssh/authorized_keys file for your user account on the remote server. You can do that using the cat command:

```
$ cat id_rsa.pub >> ~/.ssh/authorized_keys
```

The double greater-than sign appends the text to the existing authorized_keys file. If you log into the same server from multiple clients, just generate a key pair for each client and append the public key to the authorized_keys file.

Once you've copied the public key to the server, you can use the ssh command to log in. This time you won't be prompted for a password; you'll just go directly to the command prompt for the remote server.

OpenVPN

The OpenSSH package is great for securely connecting a client to a server session or for performing quick secure connections between two clients. But what if you need to connect two systems on separate networks for a long-term period? Linux has a solution for that too.

A *virtual private network (VPN)* establishes a secure encrypted tunnel between two devices on separate networks with a public network between them, as shown in Figure 12.6.

FIGURE 12.6   Using a VPN to connect two remote systems

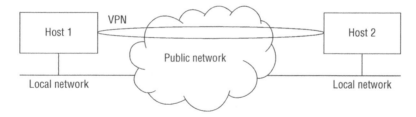

The encrypted tunnel acts as a separate private network, allowing you to pass any type of network between the two systems securely. A few different VPN applications are available in Linux, but the LPIC-2 exam focuses on the *OpenVPN* package (www.openvpn.net). The OpenVPN package creates an encrypted tunnel between two remote Linux systems. The Linux systems can then route any type of network traffic destined for the network to which the remote system is connected. Most Linux distributions include the OpenVPN package in their standard software repositories.

In a strange set of terminology, even though the connection is peer-to-peer, OpenVPN calls one end of the connection the server and the other the client. In point-to-point connections, it doesn't matter which end is called the server. However, if you implement a multi-point VPN between several sites, one site must be called the server and the others, clients.

Installing and Configuring OpenVPN

The OpenVPN package is available in both the Debian and Red Hat software repositories, so you can use the standard software installation programs to install the package:

```
$ sudo apt-get install openvpn
```

```
# yum install openvpn
```

OpenVPN allows you to change option settings, either by storing them in a configuration file or by specifying them on the command line when you run the openvpn command. When you specify the options on the command line, you must precede the options with a double dash (--). When you specify the options in the configuration file, you need to use two separate configuration files:

- /etc/openvpn/server.conf for the server
- /etc/openvpn/client.conf for the client

The option settings are shown in Table 12.4.

TABLE 12.4   The openvpn configuration options

Option	Description
config	Specify additional configuration files to use to store options
dev	Specify the virtual network device name for the VPN tunnel
nobind	Create the tunnel without a local network address or port
ifconfig	Set the IP addresses of the local and remote VPN tunnel endpoints
secret	Specify a static key encryption file

OpenVPN supports two types of encryption methods for creating the tunnel:

Static key encryption: Both the server and client use the same encryption key file.

Public key encryption: The server and client both generate private and public keys and then share the public key with the remote system.

To use the public key encryption, you need to use a certificate authority (CA) to sign the private and public keys. It uses the OpenSSL engine to generate those, as demonstrated in Chapter 9, "Offering Web Services." OpenVPN includes several scripts to help generate the required certificates and keys:

vars: Creates the certificate signing request (CSR) to create a CA certificate from settings in the /etc/openvpn/vars file

build-ca: Creates the CA certificate

build-key-server: Creates the public and private key pair for the server

build-key: Creates the public and private key pair for the client

build-dh: Computes a large prime number used for the encryption process

When you run the scripts to build the server and client keys, you'll be asked lots of questions about the system name for the keys. Each system in the VPN requires a unique common name to establish the connections.

After you run these scripts, the key files will be generated and placed in the /etc/openvpn/ keys folder. You must move the client keys to the appropriate client systems using a secure method, such as by copying them using scp or by copying them to a USB drive and then manually copying them to the remote system.

The static key encryption method is much simpler. Since both the server and client share the same static key, you don't need to generate separate sets of keys. Instead, you can use the openvpn command to generate a single secret key:

```
$ openvpn—genkey—secret secret.key
```

This generates the secret.key file, which is used by both the server and the client. If you must copy the key to a remote client, be careful that you do that securely.

With the keys generated, you're ready to start configuring the VPN connection. For the server configuration, you'll use something like this:

```
dev tun
ifconfig 192.168.1.10 10.0.1.1
keepalive 10 60
ping-timer-rem
persist-tun
persist-key
secret secret.key
```

The ifconfig line sets the local and remote IP addresses or hostnames used for the VPN endpoints. This creates device tun0 as the VPN network interface.

For the client.conf configuration file used on the client system, the configuration file would look something like this:

```
remote vpnserver.example.net
dev tun
ifconfig 10.0.1.1 192.168.1.10
keepalive 10 60
ping-timer-rem
persist-tun
persist-key
secret secret.key
```

Once you have the configuration process complete, you're ready to use OpenVPN to communicate securely between systems.

Using OpenVPN

To establish the secure VPN connection, on the server, enter the command

```
$ sudo openvpn server.conf
```

Then, on the client, enter the command

```
$ sudo openvpn client.conf
```

That's all that is required! The client should attempt to establish a connection with the server. If successful, you'll see the `tun0` device created. You can look at its statistics by using the `ifconfig` command to ensure that data is traversing the connection.

Security Resources

Installing and using encryption software and intrusion detection software goes a long way in protecting the data on your Linux system. However, security is a fluid process, and new vulnerabilities appear every day. As a conscientious Linux administrator, you should do your best to keep up with the latest security issues and fixes.

The easiest way to do that is to follow one or more of the major security websites. They provide up-to-date information on the latest attacks and vulnerabilities. This section walks you through some of the security websites referenced in the LPIC-2 exam to give you an idea of what they are.

US-CERT

The United States Computer Emergency Readiness Team (US-CERT) is part of the U.S. Department of Homeland Security, and it leads the nation's efforts to coordinate cybersecurity sharing and manage cyber risks to the nation.

The team was created by the U.S. Congress in 2000 and was originally called the Federal Computer Incident Response Center (FedCIRC). In 2003, it was moved to the Department of Homeland Security and renamed US-CERT.

The US-CERT maintains a website (`www.us-cert.gov`), and a news feed to which anyone can subscribe. Both publish four types of information:

Weekly vulnerability bulletins summarize new vulnerabilities documented in the U.S. National Vulnerability Database (NVD) as well as information on how to patch the vulnerabilities.

Technical alerts provide information about vulnerabilities, incidents, and trends as soon as they're detected.

Current activity entries contain a concise description of an issue and associated actions administrators can take.

Tips detail issues with broad appeal to US-CERT constituents.

The US-CERT technical alerts news feed is an excellent way of staying up to date with all of the latest issues facing Linux system administrators.

SANS Institute

The SANS Institute is a private U.S. company that specializes in cyber security training and certification. As part of this mission, it also supports cyber security research and posts its findings in information security research papers for public viewing. While not necessarily up to date, the research papers do provide very useful information on how vulnerabilities work and ways to prevent them from happening on your system.

Bugtraq

The Bugtraq mailing list is a component of the SecurityFocus website (www.securityfocus .com) sponsored by Symantec. What makes it unique is that it is a "full disclosure" listing of vulnerabilities—not only does it report known vulnerabilities, but it also reports on how attackers are exploiting them to gain access to systems. Their opinion is that by publishing a full disclosure of known vulnerabilities, vendors will be more proactive in fixing issues when they occur.

EXERCISE 12.1

Setting Up and Testing a Firewall

This exercise demonstrates how to use the iptables utility to create a firewall on your Linux system:

1. Log in as root, or acquire root privileges by using su or by using sudo with each of the commands in the following steps.

2. Display the current iptables rules and policies. Open a command prompt, and then type **sudo iptables -L**. Enter your password if prompted. Note if the rules are empty or if your system is currently blocking any network traffic.

3. Open a second command-prompt window, and use the nc command to start a server, listening on TCP port 1234. Type the command **nc -l 1234**.

4. Back in the original command prompt window, use the nc command to connect to the server. Type the command **nc 127.0.0.1 1234**.

5. Enter text in the client window, and press the Enter key to send it to the server. You should see the text appear in the second command-prompt window. Press Ctrl+C to stop the session.

6. Create a firewall rule to block TCP traffic on port 1234. Type the command **sudo iptables -A OUTPUT -p tcp --dport 1234 -j DROP**.

7. Check the new rule by typing the command **sudo iptables -L**.

8. Go to the second command-prompt window, and restart the server by typing the command **nc -l 1234**.

9. Back in the original command-prompt window, connect to the server by typing the command **nc 127.0.0.1 1234**.

10. Type text at the client window, and press the Enter key to send it. Nothing should happen on the server. The new iptables rule has blocked the network traffic. Press Ctrl+C to exit the nc client.

11. Clear out the rule by typing the command **sudo iptables -F OUTPUT**.

12. Start the client by typing the command **nc 127.0.0.1 1234**.

13. Type text in the client window, and press the Enter key to send it. Now you should see the text appear in the server window.

Summary

Operating a Linux system in a network environment can be a challenge. You must protect your system from attacks by both internal and external attackers. Linux provides a few tools that you can use to help monitor and prevent network attackers. Several different tools are available to help monitor the Linux system for open network ports. You can use the telnet command to check individual TCP ports or the nc and nmap commands to check a range of TCP or UDP ports. The OpenVAS tool provides a web-based frontend to several vulnerability scanners.

Intrusion detection systems (IDS) can monitor your system and inform you when suspicious activity occurs. The fail2ban program can monitor both system and application log files and determine when an attack is occurring and then notify you of the attack. The Snort application provides network intrusion detection system (NIDS) features by monitoring network traffic and looking for suspicious behavior.

Linux also provides a couple of ways for you to connect securely to remote servers. The OpenSSH program provides a secure shell connection to a remote server, as well as the ability to copy files securely between servers. The OpenVPN program creates a secure private tunnel between two Linux systems, which allows you to route any type of network traffic across the private tunnel to get to the other end.

Finally, quite a few security resources can provide important up-to-date information on vulnerabilities. The US-CERT group is operated by the Department of Homeland Security, and it posts up-to-date releases on known vulnerabilities and attack methods. The SANS Institute doesn't provide real-time reports, but instead it publishes useful research papers that help shed light on the inner workings of vulnerabilities to help you understand them more. The Bugtraq mailing list from SecurityFocus provides full disclosure of any vulnerability, giving you a sneak peek at just what types of program code are being compromised by attackers.

Exam Essentials

Describe how an IPv4 private address or IPv6 link local address can help make a Linux system more secure. IPv4 private addresses and IPv6 link local addresses work only on the local network. External hosts can't route traffic to private or link local network addresses. You can create NAT on the local network to allow outbound traffic from the private addresses or link local addresses to outside networks.

Explain how to create a firewall using the iptables command. The Linux kernel processes network packets using five chains: PREROUTING, INPUT, FORWARD, POSTROUTING, and OUTPUT. There are also three tables that control what you can do to the packets: FILTER, MANGLE, and NAT. You can define rules and default policies in each table to determine how packets are handled. The iptables command updates the rules and default policies in the kernel. Unfortunately, these updates are not retained when the kernel is rebooted, so it's necessary to save the rule and policy changes to a file and run it at boot time to update the tables and chains.

Describe how SSH allows you to log into a remote system without using a password. OpenSSH allows you to log into a remote system using a public and private key pair. You use ssh-keygen to generate both a private and public key on your system. You then copy the public key to the remote server and append it to the authorized_keys file in your .ssh folder. When you attempt to log into the remote server, Open SSH matches the private key on your system to the public key on the server and allows the session if they match.

Explain the difference between the sshd and ssh applications. The sshd OpenSSH application is an SSH server that listens for incoming connections. The ssh OpenSSH application is an SSH client that can connect to a remote SSH server to start a secure shell.

Summarize how to manage login attempts with the sshd application. The sshd OpenSSH application uses the /etc/ssh/sshd_config configuration file to define how to process login attempts. The PasswordAuthentication option allows clients to use passwords when connecting. The PubkeyAuthentication option allows them to use certificates. You can restrict which users can log in using SSH with the AllowUser and DenyUser options. The PermitRootLogin option determines if the root user account is allowed to log in using SSH.

Explain an intrusion detection system. An intrusion detection system (IDS) monitors the system or network and detects when an attack is attempted. It compares events to predefined rules that define bad behavior, such as too many login attempts or too many network connection attempts. The IDS can be configured to notify the administrator when an attack attempt is detected.

Describe two types of IDS packages used in Linux.   The `fail2ban` IDS package monitors both system and application error logs, looking for anomalies. You can define rules to tell `fail2ban` what to look for (such as three failed login attempts in a row) and what action to take when that rule is matched (such as disable access to the client's IP address). The Snort IDS package is a network IDS (NIDS) application. It monitors network traffic on the network and can detect attacks based on their network footprint. As with `fail2ban`, you can configure rules in Snort on what type of events to monitor and what actions to take when an event is detected.

Explain how port redirection works.   When external clients need to access an application on a server located in a private network, you can use port redirection to allow that. The NAT server on the network accepts incoming network traffic as a proxy server and then forwards the traffic to the server on the private network address. This should be used sparingly, though, because it opens internal servers to external clients.

Describe how to communicate securely between two public networks.   When a client on one public network needs to communicate securely to a server on another public network, you can establish an encrypted tunnel between the two devices using a virtual private network (VPN). The OpenVPN software package lets you create a secure VPN between two or more devices located on separate networks. Once the VPN is created, it appears as a network interface on the end points, and any application can send network traffic to the remote end point securely.

Review Questions

You can find the answers in the Appendix.

1. What do you call a vulnerability that allows an attacker to gain access to a system?

   A. Attack vector

   B. Open port

   C. Open application

   D. Unsecure communication

2. What file contains a list of standard application ports?

   A. `/etc/ssh/sshd_conf`

   B. `/etc/openvpn`

   C. `/etc/services`

   D. `/proc/sys/net/ipv4`

3. How can you use the `telnet` command to detect an open port?

   A. `telnet` *port address*

   B. `telnet` *address port*

   C. `telnet` *address:port*

   D. The `telnet` command only connects to port 23.

4. Which command can display a list of TCP ports that are listening for incoming connections on a local server?

   A. `telnet`

   B. `iptables`

   C. `ssh`

   D. `netstat`

5. Which option of the `netcat` command allows it to scan multiple ports?

   A. `-v`

   B. `-z`

   C. `-l`

   D. `-6`

6. Which `nmap` option specifies that it should determine the fingerprint of the remote system?

   A. `-A`

   B. `-sT`

   C. `-sU`

   D. `-p`

7. What OpenVAS feature allows it to simulate different vulnerability attacks on the system it scans?

A. National Vulnerability Database (NVD)

B. Software Repository

C. Network Vulnerability Tests (NVT)

D. Web interface

8. What type of software can warn you of an active attack on your system?

A. Port scanner

B. Network Vulnerability Test (NVT)

C. Virtual private network (VPN)

D. Intrusion detection system (IDS)

9. What file contains the `fail2ban` rules?

A. `fail2ban.conf`

B. `jail.conf`

C. `pwdfail`

D. `error.log`

10. Which application is a network intrusion detection system (NIDS)?

A. Snort

B. OpenVPN

C. OpenSSH

D. OpenVAS

11. Which Snort mode dumps packets to the display for viewing?

A. Logging mode

B. NIDS mode

C. Sniffer mode

D. Command-line mode

12. What does the `HOME_NET` variable define in the Snort configuration?

A. The remote addresses to monitor

B. The address of the local host

C. The local addresses to monitor

D. The default configuration folder

13. Which rule address format tells Snort only to look for packets going from the 10.0.0.1 address to the 10.0.0.2 address?

A. `10.0.0.1 <- 10.0.0.2`

B. `10.0.0.2 -> 10.0.0.1`

C. `10.0.0.1 <> 10.0.0.2`

D. `10.0.0.1 -> 10.0.0.2`

14. How many private network address ranges does IPv4 support?

  A. Two

  B. Three

  C. Four

  D. None

15. What value do IPv6 link local addresses start with?

  A. fe80

  B. ff02

  C. ff05

  D. aabb

16. What system allows you to connect clients on a private network address to outside servers?

  A. SSH

  B. Telnet

  C. NAT

  D. IDS

17. What Linux command do you use to create firewall rules on the system?

  A. nc

  B. iptables

  C. netstat

  D. nmap

18. Which iptables option adds a new rule to a chain?

  A. -L

  B. -F

  C. -A

  D. -j

19. Which iptables policy is used to send a return packet back to the source indicating that the packet was dropped?

  A. REJECT

  B. DROP

  C. ACCEPT

  D. LOG

20. Which iptables option defines the default policy for a chain?

  A. -P

  B. -j

  C. -L

  D. -F

Appendix

Answers to Review Questions

Chapter 1: Starting a System

1. A. The workstation firmware looks for the bootloader program to load an operating system. The init and telinit programs (options B and E) are used to change the runlevel of a running Linux system, so they aren't useful until after the Linux system has started. The Windows operating system only starts after a Windows bootloader program runs, so option C is incorrect. The mount program is a Linux tool for attaching a partition to the virtual directory, which isn't available until after the Linux system starts, so option D is also incorrect.

2. B. The workstation firmware looks at the first sector of the first hard drive to load the bootloader program. This is called the Master Boot Record, so option B is correct. The bootloader program itself can use the chainloader feature to look for another bootloader in a boot partition, but the firmware can't do that, so option D is incorrect. Option A specifies the configuration folder used to store the GRUB configuration file and the kernel image file, but the actual GRUB bootloader program can't be stored there. Option C specifies the common log file folder, but that doesn't contain the GRUB bootloader program. Option E also specifies a common Linux configuration file directory, but it's not used to store the GRUB bootloader program that the firmware can access.

3. D. The kernel ring buffer, which you can view by typing **dmesg**, contains boot messages from the kernel; thus option D is correct. The fsck program (option A) fixes corrupt partitions, and the mount program (option C) is used to attach partitions to the virtual directory, so neither of those is correct. Option B, the init program, is used to start programs from the kernel, not display boot messages, so it also is incorrect. Option E, the chkconfig program, is used to display the runlevels assigned to individual programs in the startup scripts and is not related to the boot messages, so it too is incorrect.

4. C. Most Linux distributions store boot log files in the /var/log folder. The /etc folder is most often used for storing system and application configuration files, not boot logs, so option A is incorrect. Some Unix systems use the /var/messages folder for storing log files, but Linux has not adopted this standard, so option B is also incorrect. The /boot folder contains the GRUB configuration files along with the image files necessary to boot the system, but it's not where Linux stores boot logs and is thus incorrect. The /proc folder is unique in that the Linux kernel dynamically stores information about the system there, but it doesn't store boot log information there.

5. A, B, C, D, E. The BIOS firmware can look in multiple locations for a bootloader program. Normally, it looks at the internal hard drive installed on the system; however, if none is found, it can search other places. Most workstations allow you to boot from an external hard drive or from a DVD drive. Modern workstations now also provide the option to boot from a USB memory stick inserted into a USB port on the workstation. Finally, many workstations provide the PXE boot option, which allows the workstation to boot remotely from a network server.

6. A. The Master Boot Record (MBR) is located in only one place—on the first sector of the first hard drive on the workstation. Thus option A is the only correct answer. The boot partition in any hard drive may contain a bootloader, but it is not the MBR, which is run first

by the firmware; thus option B is incorrect. The other locations are not valid for the MBR, so options C, D, and E are all incorrect.

7. D. The ESP is stored in the /boot/efi directory on Linux systems. The UEFI firmware always looks for the /boot/efi directory for bootloader programs, so option D is correct. The /etc directory is used to store application and system configuration files, not boot-loader programs, so option B is incorrect. The /var folder is used to store variable files such as log files, not bootable files, so option C is incorrect. Option E, the /boot/grub file, is used in GRUB Legacy and GRUB2 to store the bootloader configuration files, as well as the kernel image files. However, it is not used to store the bootloader files themselves, so option E is incorrect.

8. E. The UEFI specification doesn't require a specific extension for UEFI bootloader files; however, it has become somewhat common in Linux to use the .efi file extension to iden-tify them; thus option E is correct. Option A and option D specify file extensions used to identify GRUB2 (option A) and GRUB Legacy (option D) configuration files, not UEFI bootloader files, so they are both incorrect. Option C specifies the .lst file extension, which is also used for GRUB Legacy configuration files, so it too is incorrect. The .uefi file extension is not used in Linux, so option B is incorrect.

9. B. The Linux Loader (LILO) bootloader program was the first bootloader used in Linux, so option B is correct. The GRUB Legacy bootloader, despite its name, wasn't the first boot-loader but the second bootloader commonly used in Linux. The GRUB2 bootloader was a later improvement over the GRUB Legacy bootloader, so options A and C are incorrect. Option D, the SYSLINUX bootloader, provided features for use with Microsoft FAT parti-tions so that you can boot Linux from a USB memory stick, but it was a later creation and not the first Linux bootloader. Option E, ISOLINUX, was also a later bootloader, which lets you boot Linux from a CD or DVD drive.

10. A. The GRUB Legacy configuration files are stored in the /boot/grub directory, so option A is correct. Option B, the /boot/efi directory, is used to store UEFI bootloader programs, not GRUB configuration files, so it is incorrect. Option C, the /etc directory, stores many application and system configuration files but not the GRUB Legacy configuration files. The /var directory stores variable files, such as log files, but not configuration files, so option D is incorrect. Likewise, Linux uses the /proc directory to provide dynamic kernel runtime data and not configuration files.

11. B, C. The GRUB2 bootloader stores configuration files in both the /boot/grub direc-tory and the /etc/grub.d directory, so options B and C are correct. Linux uses the /proc directory to provide dynamic kernel runtime data and not configuration files, so option A is incorrect. Option D, /boot/efi, stores UEFI bootloader program files, not GRUB2 con-figuration files, so it is also incorrect. Option E, /var, is used to store variable files, such as log files, and not configuration files, so it is incorrect.

12. C. The grub-mkconfig command combines the configurations defined in the /etc/ default/grub file and all of the files in the /etc/grub.d folder into a single grub.cfg configuration file. The chkconfig command (option A) is used to check and change run-levels for programs, so it is incorrect. Likewise, the update-rc.d command (option B) is also used to change runlevels for programs on Debian systems, so it too is incorrect. The grub-install program is used by the GRUB Legacy bootloader to install the bootloader in the MBR or a boot partition, but it isn't used to generate the GRUB2 configuration files and is thus incorrect. Option E is the init program, which starts background programs from init scripts on the Linux system and is an incorrect answer for this question.

13. D. The kernel starts the init program, which in turn uses the init scripts to start and stop other programs based on the default system runlevel, so option D is correct. The GRUB2 program is a bootloader, which is started by the workstation firmware, not the kernel, so option A is incorrect. Option B, the systemctl program, is used to control programs in the systemd startup method, but it isn't started by the kernel, so it is incorrect. Option C, the telinit program, can be used to change the current runlevel, but it isn't used by the kernel to start programs, so it too is incorrect. Option E, the BIOS, is the workstation firmware that begins the startup process, so it can't be started by the kernel.

14. B. The /etc/inittab file contains the initdefault setting, which defines the default runlevel for the Linux system. The /etc/init.d and /etc/rc.d folders contain the startup scripts used by the init program to start and stop programs, but they don't define the default runlevel, so options A and D are incorrect. Option C, the /etc/grub.d directory, and option E, the /boot/grub.cfg file, both contain the configuration settings for the GRUB2 bootloader, but they don't control the default runlevel.

15. E. Debian-based systems use runlevel 2 to start all of the applications necessary for multiuser activity on the system, so option E is correct. Option A, runlevel 0, shuts the system down, and option C, runlevel 6, reboots the system, so neither of these can support running applications. Option B, runlevel 1, indicates single-user mode, and it is not typically used in desktop and server environments but rather in troubleshooting and maintenance modes. Option D, runlevel 5, is used by Red Hat–based Linux distributions as the default runlevel for graphical workstations, but it is not used by Debian-based systems.

16. A, D. Both the init and telinit commands are used to change the current runlevel on a Linux system, so both options A and D are correct. The chkconfig command is used to change the start and stop runlevels of an individual program but not for the running system, so option B is incorrect. Likewise, the update-rc.d command is used in Debian-based systems to change the start and stop runlevels for an individual program but not the running system. Option E, the dmesg command, displays the boot messages and does not influence the runlevel for the system, so it is incorrect.

17. A. The chkconfig command displays the status of the program at the seven different runlevels, so it is the correct answer. The update-rc.d command in option D is used to control the runlevels in which a program starts and stops, but it doesn't display the status of the runlevels and is thus incorrect. The init (option B) and telinit (option E) commands can change the runlevel of the entire system, but they don't display the runlevels associated with an individual program, so they are incorrect. Option C, the dmesg command, isn't related to runlevels; rather it just shows the most recent boot messages for the system.

18. B. Debian-based systems use the update-rc.d command to change the runlevels assigned to individual programs. They generally don't use the chkconfig program, although that is used by Red Hat–based systems, so option A is incorrect. The init (option C) and telinit (option D) programs are used to alter the runlevel of the entire system, but they can't be

used to change the runlevels for individual programs. The dmesg program (option E) is incorrect because it only displays the boot messages and can't alter runlevels.

19. C. The fsck program can perform a filesystem check and repair multiple types of filesystems on partitions. You should use it on any partition that can't be mounted due to errors. The mount program (option A) is used to append a partition to a virtual directory; it can't correct a partition that contains errors (and will usually refuse to mount them). The umount command (option B) is also incorrect. It is used to remove a mounted partition from the virtual directory. Options D (the init command) and E (the telinit command) are used to change the current runlevel of the Linux system and not for fixing corrupted disk drives.

20. A. The mount command lets you specify both the partition and the location in the virtual directory where you want to append the partition files and folders. The files and folders contained in the partition then appear at that location in the virtual directory. The umount command (option B) is used to remove a mounted partition. Option C, the fsck command, is used to fix a hard drive that is corrupted and can't be mounted; it doesn't actually mount the drive itself. The dmesg command in option D is used to view boot messages for the system, which may tell you where a hard drive is appended to the virtual directory, but it doesn't actually do the appending. Option E, the init command, controls the runlevel of the Linux system and doesn't directly handle mounting hard drives to the virtual directory.

Chapter 2: Maintaining the System

1. B, E. Option B, the write command, and option E, the wall command, will allow a message to be sent to any tty terminals with write access allowed. Option A is incorrect, because the mesg command checks whether write access to the terminal is allowed, and it also can set the access. Option C, the echo command, simply displays whatever follows it to the current terminal's standard output. Option D, if implemented on your system, allows the user to send and read email, not terminal messages.

2. C. The --no-wall option allows a shutdown to proceed with no wall messages to the terminal users. Only the super user issuing the command will receive a message. Option A is incorrect, because the -c option cancels a shutdown. Option B is also incorrect, because the -k option does not bring down the system but disables logins and sends out shutdown messages. The --wall option shown in option D is made up.

3. A. Option A is the best choice. By editing the /etc/issue file, the legal notification will display to anyone before attempting to log into the system via a terminal. It would also be worthwhile to put the notice in the /etc/issue.net file for users connecting over the network, as well as in a login banner, if you have GUI users. Option B is not a good choice, because the notice would not be displayed until *after* a user is logged into the system. Option C is also not a good choice, because it would send a one-time-only message only to GUI users. Option D is not a good choice, because the ~./bashrc file is a login environment script.

4. D. Currently, SSDs can be expensive, but if you have the money, they provide the fastest media for backups. Option A, magnetic tapes, is one of the slowest choices for backups.

Optical discs, option B, have limited capacity, so you have to change them out more often, and they are also slower than SSDs. Hard disk drives, option C, are faster than tape but slower than SSDs. Finally, with option E, you cannot tell what media type is network attached; therefore it is not the best answer.

5. B, C. An incremental backup, option B, is a copy of all data that has been added or modified since the last backup. Therefore, it doesn't matter whether the last backup was a full one or not; the SSD can contain this backup type. Also, the differential backup, option C, is a copy of all data that has been added or modified since the last full backup. Since the last backup was a full backup, it's possible that the SSD contains this backup type. Option A doesn't work, because a full backup copies all data.

6. A, B. The /bin/ directory, option A, contains utility programs that will be needed in a full system restore situation, so they should be included in the backup. The /home/ directory, option B, typically has system user files. They should also be included in the backup. Option C, /run/, and option D, /tmp/, both contain temporary data and do not need to be included in any data backups.

7. A, B, D. Amanda, Duplicity, and Bacula are all GUI and/or web-based backup solutions that you can employ to assist in system backups. Option C, Nagios, and option E, connectd, are both utilities used in resource monitoring.

8. B, C, E. The options that cause tar to use gzip compression when creating a tarball include the --gzip option, which is a long-style option; the -z option, which is a short-style option; and the z option, which is an old-style option. The -g (option A) and g (option D) are used by tar for incremental backups, not compression.

9. E. The snapshot file can have any name you desire and can be located anywhere within the filesystem, however, it needs the .snar file extension to indicate that it is a tar archive snapshot file. Option A, .tar, indicates that the file is a tar archive file. Option B, .tgz, indicates that the file is a tarball compressed with gzip. Options C and D, .tar.snap and .snap, are made-up file extensions.

10. A, B, C, D. The --compare and --diff (options A and B) are long-style options of -d (option C). These three options compare a tar archive file's members with external files and list the differences. Option D, the -W option (long style is --verify), automatically verifies a tar archive as soon as it is created. However, it cannot be used with tarballs, only tar archives. Option E, -J, is a tar option that causes the tar command to employ xz compression.

11. A, C. The /dev/st0 (SCSI) and /dev/ht1 (PATA) tape device files are for automatically rewinding tape devices. Options B, D, and E all point to non-rewinding tape devices as indicated by the leading n in their device filename, /dev/n*.

12. C. The mt program allows you to control a tape and determine its current status. The tar (option A) and star (option B) utilities can use tapes as a storage medium but do not control them. The rsync (option D) utility is a backup program, but it cannot be used with magnetic tapes, much less control them. Option E, the dd command, can also be used as a backup utility, but it does not control tapes.

13. D. Option D uses the proper rsync syntax for sending a backup over to the remote ServerA host using encryption via OpenSSH. Option A is simply using rsync to send a backup to a removable media device, indicated by /run/media/ServerA. In option B, the Project file is simply copied to another file, called ServerA. In option C, the filenames are flipped-flopped, so that the ServerA file is copied to a new file, Project. In option E, the file is copied to a remote host, ServerA. However, OpenSSH is not used. The rsync daemon is used instead, and therefore the transfer is not encrypted.

14. A, E. The dd command can be used for creating a low-level copy of a hard drive. It can also be used to zero-out a drive by employing the /dev/zero file. The dd command is not popular for daily incremental backups (option B), because it can easily corrupt a mounted drive. Therefore, option C is also incorrect. The dd command is not used for managing tapes (option D).

15. A, B. The README and INSTALL files typically can provide you with additional installation instructions, including items such as what other packages are needed to complete the installation successfully. The COPYING file (option C) often holds software license information. The RELEASE-NOTES (option D) and NEWS (option E) typically contain features and bug fixes that have been included in the latest program version.

16. B. The configure utility is really a script that checks your system for various program dependencies and a compiler. It also creates or updates the Makefile with the Makefile.in file's contents and what it finds on your system. Option C, the make command, takes the information in the Makefile and uses it to compile the source code into binary. Option D, the make install command, moves the program files to their necessary locations in the directory structure. The cp command (option E) just copies files. You may use it to copy the program installation file's tarball from one place to another. Option A, the INSTALL file, typically can provide additional installation instructions.

17. A, D, E. The free (option A) and vmstat (option E) commands provide information primarily about system memory usage. The top (option D) command, while providing other resource statistics, also provides memory usage data. The mpstat (option B) command provides network statistic information, while the mtr (option C) command provides a dynamic display of network routing data.

18. D. The sar 2 20 command will display CPU usage information 20 times and space it 2 seconds apart. The uptime command (options A and B) does not accept parameters, and therefore it would display CPU data only one time. In option C, the sar command parameters are backward. In this case, it would display CPU information 2 times and space it 20 seconds apart.

19. A, C, D. MRTG, collectd, and Nagios are all resource-monitoring solutions that can be employed on your Linux system. Duplicity (option B) can also be employed on your Linux system, but it is used for backing up data, not monitoring resource usage.

20. B, C. Memory for idle processes can be swapped out from RAM to a special partition called swap space, swap, or virtual memory. Therefore, options B and C are correct. Memory is divided up into chunks called pages (option A), not sheets. Swapping is the memory management technique where idle processes' memory is swapped out to swap. The processes do not trade memory (option D). Finally, the psmap tool is primarily for mapping processes (option E). The best tools for viewing memory statistics are tools like free, sar, and vmstat.

Chapter 3: Mastering the Kernel

1. B. The kernel manages the system memory in Linux, so answer B is correct. The GNU utilities provide programs that mimic common Unix programs for file and data manipulation, but they don't manage the system memory, so answer A is incorrect. The graphical desktop manages the graphical environment on the display but not memory, so answer C is incorrect. Application software doesn't manage the system memory, so answer D is incorrect.

2. A. Swap space is the area on the hard drive that's used to store memory pages in the virtual memory, so answer A is correct. Physical memory is the memory locations stored in the actual RAM on the system, so answer D is incorrect. Virtual memory is the combination of both RAM memory and hard disk memory, so answer B is incorrect. The filesystem stores data on the disk, not memory locations, so answer C is incorrect.

3. C. Linux uses modules to load device drivers into the kernel, so answer C is correct. DLL files are used to load device drivers in the Microsoft Windows world, but they aren't used in Linux, so answer A is incorrect. Virtual memory expands the physical memory used by the Linux system by utilizing a swap space on the hard drive, but it doesn't help with loading device drivers, so answer B is incorrect. The bootloader loads the kernel software into memory, but it doesn't load device drivers into the kernel, so answer D is incorrect.

4. A. Compiling the kernel source code produces a binary file that's loaded into memory, so answer A is correct. The kernel source code files can't be loaded into memory, so answer D is incorrect. Likewise, the source code patch files can't be loaded into memory, so answer C is also incorrect. Modules are loaded into the kernel after the system boots, so they aren't used directly to boot the Linux system, so answer B is incorrect.

5. A. The Linux kernel developers release patches to upgrade source code easily from one version to the next version, so answer A is correct. Modules are used to load device driver software into the kernel, so answer B is incorrect. Binary files are used to load the kernel into memory to run, so answer C is incorrect. Development releases are full source code software releases and are not used to upgrade an existing kernel, so answer D is incorrect.

6. D. The config target produces questions on the Linux console that you must answer to determine the configuration settings for the kernel, thus answer D is correct. The xconfig target produces a graphical menu system, which isn't text-based, so answer A is incorrect. The mrproper and clean targets are used to remove previous configuration settings, not create new configuration settings, so answers B and C are incorrect.

7. C. The gconfig target uses the GNOME desktop library to produce a graphical menu to determine the configuration settings, so answer C is correct. The config target uses text questions to determine the configuration settings, so answer A is incorrect. The mrproper and clean targets remove previous configuration settings, they do not create new settings, so answers B and D are incorrect.

8. B. The `mrproper` target removes all old configuration settings and object files from the source code folders, allowing you to start with a new configuration, thus answer B is correct. The `gconfig` and `bzImage` targets are used to create a new configuration file but don't remove any previous object files, so answers A and C are incorrect. The `oldconfig` target uses the old configuration file, but it doesn't remove any old object files, so answer D is incorrect.

9. A. The `zImage` and `bzImage` targets create a compressed kernel binary file from the source code, so answer A is correct. The `kernel` target is invalid, and it will produce an error message, so answer B is incorrect. The `config` target creates a configuration file, but it doesn't compile the kernel binary file, so answer C is incorrect. The `clean` target removes any previous configuration settings but doesn't compile the kernel binary file, so answer D is incorrect.

10. C. Debian-based systems use the `mkinitramfs` program to create the initial RAM disk used at boot time, so answer C is correct. The `mkinitrd` program is used by Red Hat–based systems, but it is not available on Debian-based systems, so answer A is incorrect. There is no `make` target to create an initial RAM disk, so answers B and D are incorrect.

11. D. To list all of the installed modules in the running kernel, you use the `lsmod` command, so answer D is correct. The `modinfo` command only lists module information for a single module—it doesn't list all of the installed modules, so answer A is incorrect. The `insmod` and `rmmod` commands are used to insert and remove modules, respectively, so answers B and C are incorrect.

12. C. The `insmod` command allows you to insert a module, but you must know the module filename, so answer A is incorrect. The `modprobe` command allows you to insert a module based on the module name, so answer C is correct. You use the `rmmod` command to remove a module and the `lsmod` command to list all modules, so answers B and D are incorrect.

13. A. The `lsusb` command lists all of the USB devices connected to the Linux system, so answer A is correct. The `lspci` command lists PCI cards but not USB devices, so answer B is incorrect. The `lsmod` command lists modules loaded, which may show some of the USB devices installed, but if any USB device drivers were compiled into the kernel, it won't list all of the USB devices, so answer C is incorrect. The `lsdev` command displays information about hardware device I/O ports and interrupts but for all devices, not just the USB devices, so answer D is incorrect.

14. D. The verbose option of the `lsusb` command displays detailed information about the USB devices, so answer D, `-v`, is correct. The `-d` option only displays USB devices with a specific vendor ID, so answer A is incorrect. The `-s` option only displays USB devices connected to a specific bus, so answer B is incorrect. The `-t` option displays information in a tree format, so you can see device dependencies but not detailed information about the devices, so answer C is incorrect.

15. B. Hotplug devices, such as USB devices, allow you to connect the device while the system is running, so answer B is correct. Coldplug devices can be connected only while the system is powered off, so answer A is incorrect. Both PCI and PCIe boards can be inserted only while the system is powered off, so answers C and D are both incorrect.

16. B. The udev device manager system uses the udevd program to listen to kernel event messages and load the appropriate modules for inserted hardware based on rules, so answer B is correct. The lsusb command only lists installed modules, so answer A is incorrect. The modprobe and insmod commands can only install modules manually; they can't automatically detect new devices, so answers C and D are incorrect.

17. D. The /etc/udev/udev.conf configuration file defines settings that control how the udevd program operates, thus answer D is correct. The /lib/modules folder is used to store module files, not configuration files, so answer A is incorrect. The /boot folder is used to store the kernel binary file but not the udevd configurations, so answer B is incorrect. The /etc/udev/rules.d folder stores udevd rules but not the configuration settings, so answer C is incorrect.

18. B. Rules for the udevd program are stored in the /etc/udev/rules.d folder, so answer B is correct. The /etc/udev/udevd.conf file contains configuration settings for controlling the udevd program, not rules, so answer A is incorrect. The /boot folder is used to store the kernel binary file, not udevd rules, so answer C is incorrect. The /lib/modules folder is used to store kernel module files, not configuration files, so answer D is incorrect.

19. C. The /proc filesystem is created by the kernel automatically to allow you to read and write kernel settings and view kernel performance statistics, so answer C is correct. The /usr/src/linux folder is used to store the kernel source code files, so answer D is incorrect. Answers A and B are folders that aren't valid in the Linux system, so they are both incorrect.

20. A. The sysctl command allows you to change kernel settings at any time, so answer A is correct. The lsmod and lsdev commands allow you to view the kernel modules and device information, respectively, so answers B and D are incorrect. The modprobe command allows you to insert and remove modules but not change any of the module settings, so answer C is incorrect.

Chapter 4: Managing the Filesystem

1. A, C, E. Answers A, C, and E all contain legitimate mkfs command variations, which format the /dev/sdd2 partition into an ext2 filesystem. Option B uses an invalid filesystem type, extended2, and therefore is incorrect. There is no mke2fs.ext2 command, so option D is also incorrect.

2. A. The /proc/filesystems file, option A, contains a list of all of the filesystems supported by your system. The /etc/mtab and /proc/mounts files show currently mounted filesystems. While these are supported filesystems, they are not all of the supported filesystems, and therefore options B and C are incorrect. Option D is incorrect, because the /proc/swaps file contains information concerning your system's swap space. Option E is also a wrong answer, because the /proc/cpuinfo file contains information concerning your system's processors.

3. E. The mount command with the proper options and parameters will temporarily attach the filesystem to the Linux virtual directory structure. Therefore, option E is the best answer. The mkfs command is for high-level formatting and not attaching a filesystem, and therefore option A is incorrect. Option B is a bad answer, because even though you can use the e2label command to determine a filesystem's label, which you might use in the mount command, it does not attach a filesystem. Option C is also a bad answer, because AutoFS has to be configured before it will automatically attach a network-based file. The /etc/ fstab file is for persistently attached filesystems, so if you added an entry for the filesystem in this file, it would not be temporarily attached. Therefore, option D is not the best answer.

4. C. The number shown in the question is a filesystem UUID number. The -U option is used with the mount command to identify a filesystem via its UUID number. Therefore, option C is correct. The -o is for specifying filesystem mount options, so option A is incorrect. Option B is wrong, because the -L option is used to identify a filesystem to be mounted by its label. The -a option, used with the mount command, will cause any filesystem listed in the /etc/fstab file that is not currently mounted to be mounted. Therefore, option D is incorrect. The mount command -n option will mount a filesystem but not update the /etc/ mtab file, and thus option E is the wrong answer.

5. D. Option D is correct, because the sync command allows you to flush the filesystem buffers, which essentially forces the data commitment process to take place immediately. Option A's unmount is not a command (umount is the correct spelling of the unmount command), and it is therefore not correct. Options B and C are incorrect, because the fuser and lsof commands are for assisting you in determining who is using a filesystem when you are unsuccessfully attempting to unmount it. The dmesg command displays the kernel ring buffer, which may be helpful in determining attached USB flash drive names but not in flushing filesystem buffers. Therefore, option E is incorrect.

6. A, B, D. The six fields for each /etc/fstab entry include name (partition, volume, UUID, and so on), mount point, filesystem type, mount options, dump option, and filesystem check (fsck) priority. Therefore, options A, B, and D are correct. Option C is incorrect, because the dump utility, not the cpio utility, is indicated in the /etc/fstab file. Option E is wrong, because filesystems that are mounted via the AutoFS service should have no entries within the /etc/fstab file.

7. B. The blkid command, when used with super user privileges, displays various block device attributes, including a device's UUID. Therefore, option B is correct. Option A's findmnt command displays all of the mounted filesystems in a tree format, but it does not display device UUIDs, so it is incorrect. The e2label utility shows a filesystem's label, not its UUID, so it is also incorrect. Option D is wrong because the findfs command finds filesystems, but you must already know either its label or its UUID, and only the device name is shown. Finally, option E is wrong because, although the mount command shows you the currently mounted filesystems, their UUID is not displayed.

8. A, B, E. Options A, B, and E are correct, because RAID 0, RAID 1, and RAID 10 configurations can be implemented on a btrfs filesystem. Options C and D are incorrect, because RAID 5 and RAID 6 configurations cannot be implemented on a btrfs filesystem...yet.

9. C, D, E. El Torito, Joliet, and Rock Ridge are all ISO9660 standard extensions for use with optical media. Therefore, options C, D, and E are correct. Option A is incorrect, because Universal Disk Format (UDF) is a cross-platform specification standard primarily for

DVDs, not an ISO9660 extension. Option B is also wrong, because btrfs is a filesystem, not an optical media standard.

10. C. The `mkisofs` command will allow you to create an ISO image, so option C is correct. The `mkfs` command is for making filesystems, and there is no `-t iso` option, so options A and B are wrong. Option D's `cdrecord` allows you to record an ISO image onto optical media but not create the image, so it is incorrect. Finally, option E is incorrect, because it is the start of the command to allow you to temporarily mount optical media with an ISO9660 filesystem but not create an ISO image.

11. B. Option B is correct, because the `mkswap` command is used to perform the preparations necessary to ready a partition to be used as swap space. Option A is incorrect, because there is no `-t swapon` option for the `mkfs` command. Option C is also incorrect. Although you can use this command to activate the swap space on `/dev/sde3`, it is not the command used to prepare the swap space. Option D is wrong, because the `swapoff` command deactivates the designated swap space. The `swapon -s` command is useful for displaying current swap statistics but not for preparing swap space, so option E is also incorrect.

12. A, B, C. Options A, B, and C are all map types that you may find in the AutoFS master map file, `/etc/auto.master`. Option D's SMART refers to Self-Monitoring Analysis and Reporting Technology devices, not AutoFS map types. Therefore, option D is incorrect. Option E is incorrect, because a road map is used for navigating your way while driving or walking, and it is not a known AutoFS map type.

13. E. The `/etc/sysconfig/autofs` file, shown in option E, is a correct configuration file to modify. Depending on your distribution, the file's name might be `/etc/default/autofs`. Option A's file is a direct map file and is therefore incorrect. Options B and D show two possible indirect map type files and are also incorrect. In option C, an old AutoFS script file, `/etc/autofs.net`, that may be found on older distributions is shown but is also incorrect.

14. C. The eCryptfs filesystem is a pseudo-filesystem that is layered on top of another filesystem, and it provides file-by-file encryption. Thus, option C is correct. Both options B and D show encrypted filesystems, but they are not considered layered filesystems, so they are incorrect. Option A's XFS filesystem is not encrypted, and neither is option E's btrfs filesystem, so they are also incorrect.

15. D. The `uuidgen` utility is used for producing new UUID numbers that can be assigned to filesystems. It does not adjust any filesystem, and therefore option D is the correct answer. Commands in options A, B, C, and E all adjust extended filesystems and are therefore incorrect answers.

16. E. Option E's `tune2fs` command can use the generated UUID and change the filesystem's UUID, so it is the correct answer. Commands in options A, B, and C also adjust extended filesystems but not the UUID number and are therefore incorrect answers. The `blkid` command in option D can display a device's UUID but not change it, so it is also an incorrect answer.

17. E. Because the XFS filesystems (btrfs too) have their own repair utilities and do not operate in the same fashion as extended filesystems, the `fsck.xfs` utility does nothing. Therefore,

option E is correct. For extended filesystems, you may see the actions in options A through D occur, depending on your command options and actions prior to running the command. However, in this case, options A through D are incorrect.

18. D. Option D, btrfs restore, is the most powerful command for restoring the btrfs filesystem data, and it is the best choice. Options A and C also can help, but they are not as powerful as option D, so they are not the correct answers. The btrfs commands in options B and E do not do repairs or restores, so those answers are also incorrect.

19. A. Option A is correct, because the xfs_check utility checks an XFS filesystem's consistency but does no repairs. It is typically no longer included in many distributions, but you can use the xfs_repair -n command in its place. Option B's xfsdump creates a backup of the filesystem's data and attributes but does no checking, so it is incorrect. The xfs_info command displays and checks filesystem information, but it does not look for filesystem inconsistency, so option C is wrong. Option D's xfs_metadump only copies the filesystem's metadata to a file, so it is also wrong. Finally, the xfsrestore command restores a filesystem's data and attributes from a backup dump, so option E is incorrect.

20. B. Option B's command will show you a quick drive summary health status, including whether or not it has passed the overall health self-assessment test. Therefore, option B is correct. The commands in options A and E will conduct tests but will not show the results, so they are incorrect. Option C's command will display information concerning the drive, such as whether or not it supports SMART and whether or not SMART is enabled. It is also incorrect. The command in option D will provide you with the drive's health information, but it displays all of the information, not just a summary, so it is also an incorrect choice.

Chapter 5: Administering Advanced Storage Devices

1. B, C, D, E. Answers B, C, D, and E are all considered fault tolerant because of their structures. Only RAID 0 is not fault tolerant, because it uses disk striping. Thus, option A is the only incorrect choice.

2. E. RAID 6 is also called disk striping with double parity, and so option E is the correct answer. RAID 0 is called disk striping, so option A is incorrect. Option B is incorrect, because RAID 1 is also called disk mirroring. Option C is also wrong due to RAID 10 being called disk mirroring and striping. RAID 5 is called disk striping with parity (not double parity), and therefore option D is also incorrect.

3. A. The /proc/mdstat file will indicate if that RAID level is supported, and thus software RAID is potentially supported, so option A is correct. Option B is incorrect because /dev/md0 is a device file representing a RAID array. The filesystem table, /etc/fstab, may have a record for mounting a RAID array at boot, but it is not the indicator being sought, and therefore option C is also incorrect. Option D is wrong because /etc/mdadm/mdadm.conf is a RAID configuration file, not a status file. Finally, option E's /dev/mapper is the directory holding LVM and RAID Device Mapper files, and it is also not a status file indicating software RAID support, so it is an incorrect choice.

4. C. Option C, delete mode, is a made-up mdadm command mode and therefore is the correct choice. Option A's grow mode is a legitimate mode, which grows, shrinks, or reshapes a RAID array. Option B's `--follow` is an option to indicate follow mode, which monitors md drives, and if an event or alert occurs, performs a designated action. The `--manage` in option D is an option to indicate manage mode. In manage mode, the mdadm utility can manage RAID array members, such as adding a new spare drive to a RAID array. Option E's miscellaneous mode is a mode for RAID array operations that do not fall into any other mode category, such as deleting a drive's superblock.

5. D. Option D is correct, because the `-C` option chooses the create mode, so a RAID array can be created. The `--create` option does too. Option A chooses the grow mode, option B chooses the follow/monitor mode, and option E chooses the miscellaneous mode. While these are legitimate modes, they do not create RAID arrays and are thus incorrect choices. Option C's answer is made up and therefore also incorrect.

6. D. Current RAID array status can be found in option D's /proc/mdstat file, and it is therefore the correct answer. Options A and B are incorrect because mdadm.conf is a RAID configuration file, not a status file, which can be stored in either the /etc/ or the /etc/mdadm/ directory, depending on the distribution. The /etc/fstab file does not hold RAID status, and so option C is wrong. Finally, the /etc/sysctl.conf file is a configuration file for the sysctl command, and it is therefore an incorrect choice.

7. B. Option B is the best answer, because any RAID array that the drive may belong to will be displayed using these mdadm options. Option A is close, but if the /dev/sdc1 drive is not a member of the /dev/md0 RAID array, then you won't know which RAID array has its membership. Therefore, option A is incorrect. Option C is also close and yet incorrect, because again if the /dev/sdc1 drive is not a member of the /dev/md0 RAID array, then you won't know which RAID array has its membership. Option D is incorrect, because it only shows various options available in monitor mode. Since option B is correct, option E is incorrect.

8. A, D. Options A and D are correct, because you must first stop a RAID array and then delete the superblocks on each of the array's drives. There is no need to delete the drives' data, so option E is incorrect. In addition, you neither need to shrink the RAID array nor monitor it in order to delete it, so options B and C are both incorrect.

9. E. The hdparm utility can view, test, and, if needed, modify various PATA, ATAPI, SATA, and SCSI drive settings. Therefore, option E is correct. However, it can only handle SCSI devices that support SCSI-ATA command Translation (SAT), and only some hdparm options can be used on them.

10. E. If no option is included along with the sdparm command, it will show all of the common mode parameters for a designated device. Therefore, option E is correct. Option A will show all of the recognized file information for the device type, option C will display the device's VPD pages in hex, and option D will display the hex code associated with each of those VPD pages. Therefore, those options are all incorrect. Option B is a correct option,

but the correct option parameters include stop, sync, start, and load but not show. Thus, option B is also incorrect.

11. C. Option C is correct, because the IQN designates both the iSCSI target server as well as an iSCSI disk it is offering. A WWID is the same as a WWN, and while they may uniquely identify an iSCSI disk, they do not identify an iSCSI target, so options A and B are incorrect. A LUN can also uniquely identify an iSCSI disk, but it does not identify an iSCSI target, so option D is also incorrect. Option E is a command that you can use to create a unique iSCSI number, so it is incorrect as well.

12. C, D. During the discovery process, two records are created by the iscsiadm tool: a discovered node record stored in the /var/lib/iscsi/nodes database file (option C) and the target server's IP address record stored in the /var/lib/iscsi/send_targets file (option D). Therefore, options C and D are correct. Option A is the iscsiadm tool's configuration file, so it is incorrect. Option B is the scsi_id command's directory location, so it also is incorrect. Option E is a made-up file, so it is a wrong choice.

13. B, D. Both RAID and logical volume management or Logical Volume Manager (LVM) allow multiple partitions to be grouped together and used as a single partition for formatting, mounting on the Linux virtual directory structure, storing data, and so on. Thus, options B and D are correct. PATA is drive interface technology, so option A is incorrect. Option C is incorrect, because iSCSI is a storage network transport protocol, which makes a target server's iSCSI disk appear as a locally attached disk, but no grouping is involved. Finally, option E's storage fabric is an incorrect choice, because it is any hardware that connects SAN storage devices to systems.

14. A. Option A is correct, because a physical volume (PV) is a designated unused disk partition (or whole drive) to be used by LVM. A volume group (VG) has PVs in its storage pool and feeds logical volumes (LVs), which consist of storage space chunks (logical extents). Therefore, options B and C are incorrect. Option D's SATA is incorrect, because SATA is a drive interface technology. Option E is incorrect, because a backstore is a data accessing method that points and allows access to a physical storage medium in a storage fabric SAN.

15. C. The PE block size is actually set during the process of adding a PV to a VG. Therefore, option C is the correct answer, because it is not true. Options A, B, D, and E are all correct statements concerning PEs and are therefore incorrect choices.

16. B. Option B is true, because logical extents (LEs) are mapped to VG physical extents. Option A is not true, because LVs are made up of logical extents (LEs), and therefore it is an incorrect choice. Option C is not true, because the mapping provides a way to access the data, not block the data. Therefore, option C is a wrong choice. Option D is incorrect, because LE mapping does not occur during PV designation. Finally, option E is incorrect, because option B is true.

17. D. Option D is the correct answer, because the pvcreate utility can designate a partition as a PV. The pvdisplay utility displays PV attributes. Option B is incorrect, because vgcreate adds a single PV or more to a VG pool. Option C is incorrect, because lvcreate either creates an LV from a VG pool or creates snapshots. Option E is also incorrect, because the pvscan utility lists all of the various PVs on a system.

18. D. Option D is the correct answer, because the vgdisplay utility displays a VG's attributes, and vg01 is a VG. Option A is incorrect, because pvdisplay displays PV attributes. Option B is incorrect, because vgcreate adds a single PV or more to a VG pool. Option C is incorrect, because the pvscan utility lists all of the various PVs on a system and vg01 is a VG. Option E is also incorrect, because lvdisplay displays an LV's attributes.

19. A, C. Options A and C are true and therefore correct. Option B is not true and is incorrect, because an LV snapshot has both read and write access. Option D is incorrect, because the original data is not copied to a LV snapshot. Option E is also not true, because LV snapshots are created with the lvcreate command.

20. A. Option A is correct, because the lvrename command allows an LV's name to be changed. Option B is incorrect, because the lvremove deletes a LV. The lvconvert utility changes an LV's layout, and therefore option C is an incorrect answer. Option D's lvs is incorrect, because it displays information about LVs on a system. Finally, option E is incorrect because lvmchange is an obsolete command.

Chapter 6: Navigating Network Services

1. B. The Wi-Fi Protected Access encryption protocol protects access to wireless access points. The wireless network operates at the physical network layer, so option B is correct. The network layer uses addressing protocols, such as IP, to send data between systems on the network, but it doesn't interact with the wireless signal, so answer A is incorrect. The transport layer uses ports to direct network traffic to specific applications running at the application layer so options C and D are both incorrect.

2. D. The netmask value determines the network portion of the IP address, which identifies to which network the system is connected. Thus, option D is correct. The default router is another IP address on the network, but it doesn't indicate the network portion of the address, so it can't be used to determine the network address, and option B is incorrect. The IP address by itself doesn't define the network address without the netmask, so option A is incorrect. The hostname doesn't indicate the network address, so option C is incorrect. The DNS server maps hostnames to IP addresses, but if you only know the IP address, you still won't know the network portion of the address, so option E is incorrect.

3. A. The netmask value sets the network portion of the IP address to 1s and the host portion of the IP address to 0s. Thus, the netmask value must have consecutive 1s in the address at the start of the value. Option A, 255.255.255.0, indicates that the first 24 bits of the address are 1s, so it represents a proper netmask value, and it is the correct option. In option B, the 1s values aren't consecutive, so it is not a proper netmask value and is thus incorrect. Option C shows a network address but not the netmask address, while option D shows a host address but not the netmask address, so those are both incorrect. Option E shows an address that uses consecutive 1s values, but they are at the end of the address and not at the beginning, so it is incorrect.

4. E. An IP address consists of the network address and a unique host address, so option E is correct. The host address and router address won't indicate the network address, so option A is incorrect. Using the netmask and host address won't reveal the network address, so option B is incorrect. Likewise, the netmask and router addresses determine the network address, but not the host address of the system, so option C is incorrect. The hostname is not part of the IP address, so option D is also incorrect.

5. C. IP version 6 uses 128 bits separated into eight groups of four hexadecimal values, so option C is correct. The original IP version 4 addresses use 32 bits, but not IPv6, so option A is incorrect. Many IPv6 networks use a 64-bit network address and a 64-bit host address, but the full IPv6 address is 128 bits, so option B is incorrect. Currently, there isn't an IP version that uses either 256 or 8 bits, so options D and E are incorrect.

6. A. The default router is used to send packets from the local network to remote networks, so to communicate with a remote host you need to define the default router address, making option A correct. The netmask only defines the local network; it doesn't define what to do with packets for remote hosts, so option B is incorrect. The hostname and IP address only define features of the local host, so options C and D are incorrect, while the DNS server defines how to retrieve the IP address of a host based on its domain name, so option E is incorrect.

7. E. The DNS server maps the hostname to an IP address, so you must have a DNS server defined in your network configuration to be able to use hostnames in your applications. Thus, option E is correct. The default router only defines how to send packets to remote hosts; it doesn't map the hostname to the IP address, so option A is incorrect. The netmask value defines the local network but not how to map hostnames to IP addresses, so option B is incorrect. The hostname and IP address define features of the local host, so options C and D are incorrect.

8. B. The Dynamic Host Configuration Protocol (DHCP) is used to assign dynamic IP addresses to client workstations on a network, so option B is correct. The default router can't assign addresses to devices, so option A is incorrect. The ARP table maps the hardware address of the network card to IP addresses, but it doesn't assign the IP addresses, so option C is incorrect. The netmask value determines the network address but not the IP address of the host, so option D is incorrect. The `ifconfig` command can set the static IP address of the host, but it doesn't automatically assign the IP address, so option E is incorrect.

9. B. The loopback address is a special address assigned to the loopback interface, which allows local applications to communicate with each other, making option B the correct answer. Dynamic and static IP addresses are assigned to network interfaces, which interact with remote systems, not local applications, so options A and C are incorrect. The hostname identifies the local host for remote connections, not for local applications, so option D is incorrect. The MAC address identifies the network card hardware address, but it isn't used by local applications, so option E is incorrect.

10. A. TCP guarantees packet delivery between applications, so option A is correct. UDP is faster, but it doesn't guarantee packet delivery, so option B is incorrect. ICMP is used to send control messages between applications, but they are not guaranteed, so option C is incorrect. DNS and DHCP are not transport layer protocols, so options D and E are incorrect.

11. B. HTTP connections use TCP port 80, and to listen on TCP port 80 you would use the −l 80 option for the nc command, making option B the correct format. Option A shows the nc command to connect to the web server running on host 192.168.1.77, so it's incorrect. Option E listens on TCP port 22, so it's incorrect. Options C and D are not in the proper format for the nc command, so they are both incorrect.

12. A. Red Hat–based systems use separate files to store the IP address and router information. Those files are stored in the /etc/sysconfig/network-scripts folder, making option A correct. Option B is where Debian-based systems store the interfaces file, which contains the network configuration settings. The ifcfg-eth0 is a file used to store the configuration, not a folder, so option C is incorrect. The ifconfig and iwconfig are commands and not folders, so options D and E are incorrect.

13. B. Option B is the correct format to set a dynamic IP address for the interface. The Debian system uses the iface setting to set features for an interface, so options C and E are incorrect. Option A sets a static IP address for the interface and not a dynamic address, so it's incorrect. Option D sets a link local IPv6 address and not a dynamic IP address, so it's incorrect.

14. B. The DNS servers are listed in the /etc/resolv.conf configuration file using the name-server setting, so option B is correct. Options A, C, and E list files that are used in the tcp_wrappers program, not the DNS system, so they are all incorrect. Option D specifies the file used to define most network settings in a Debian-based system, but the DNS servers are not specified in that file, so it is incorrect.

15. A. The ifconfig command must specify the network interface, the IP address, and then the netmask option before the netmask address. You can use the up or down option to place the network card in an active or inactive state by default, but it's not required. Option A is the only option that uses the correct values in the correct order. Option C is close, but it fails to specify the network interface. Option B is not in the correct format, and options D and E fail to list the necessary configuration settings.

16. A. The iwlist command displays all of the available wireless network access points detected by the wireless network card, so option A is correct. The iwconfig command configures the network card to connect to a specific access point, but it doesn't list all of the detected access points, making option B incorrect. Option C specifies the ifconfig command, which is used to assign an IP address to a wireless network card, but it doesn't list the access points. The ip command specified in option D likewise can be used to set the IP address of the card, but it doesn't list the access points. Option E, the arp command, maps hardware addresses to IP addresses so that you can find duplicate IP addresses on your network, but it doesn't list the wireless access points.

17. D. The SSID value defines the access point name, and it is set using the essid option in the iwconfig command, making option D the correct answer. The key specifies the encryption key required to connect to the access point but not the access point name, making option A incorrect. The netmask and address values aren't set by the iwconfig command, so options B and C are incorrect. The channel defines the radio frequency the access point uses, not the access point name, so option E is also incorrect.

18. E. The `ip` command allows you both to display and to set the IP address, netmask, and default router values for a network interface, so option E is correct. The `ifconfig` command can set the IP address and netmask values but not the default router. The `iwconfig` command is used to set the wireless access point settings, and the `router` command is used to set the default router but not the IP address or `netmask` values. The `ifup` command only activates the network interface; it can't set the address values.

19. C. The `ping` command sends ICMP packets to a specified remote host and waits for a response, making option C the correct answer. The `netstat` command displays statistics about the network interface, so it's incorrect. The `nmap` command can scan remote hosts for open ports, but it doesn't send ICMP packets, making option B incorrect. The `nc` command allows you to simulate a server or client with TCP or UDP connections, but it doesn't handle ICMP packets, making option D incorrect. The `tcpdump` program captures network packets but doesn't send them, so option E is also incorrect.

20. B. The `tcpdump` command captures packets from the network interface and displays them or saves them in a file, so option B is correct. The `netstat` command only displays statistics about the network interface; it doesn't capture packets, so option D is incorrect. The `dig` command is used to find DNS information about networks, the `ping` command sends ICMP packets to remote hosts, and the `nc` command sends or receives packets to simulate a client and server, so options A, C, and E are all incorrect.

Chapter 7: Organizing Email Services

1. B. The Postfix package installs the configuration files in the `/etc/postfix` directory, so option B is correct. The `/var/spool/postfix` directory contains the email processing directories and files but not the configuration files, so answer A is incorrect. The `/var/spool/mail` directory contains local user mailboxes but not configuration files, so answer C is incorrect. The `/var/log` directory contains log files but not configuration files, so answer D is incorrect. The `/etc/mail` directory is not part of the Postfix setup, so answer E is incorrect.

2. C. The `master` process in Postfix controls which Postfix programs are started for processing messages, so option C is correct. The `qmgr`, `pickup`, `cleanup`, and `smtp` processes handle email messages in the mail queue but don't control the other processes, so options A, B, D, and E are all incorrect.

3. A. The `master.cf` configuration file contains settings that define when the Postfix processes start and stop, so option A is correct. The `main.cf` configuration file controls how Postfix handles email messages but not the individual processes, so option B is incorrect. The `install.cf` configuration file controls what features Postfix installs and enables, but it doesn't control the individual processes, so option C is incorrect. The `/var/spool/postfix` and `/var/log/maillog` options are not Postfix configuration files, so they are both incorrect.

4. D. The `main.cf` configuration file contains settings that control how Postfix processes email messages, so option D is correct. The `master.cf` configuration file contains settings that control how Postfix manages processes but not how it processes email messages, so option A is incorrect. The `sendmail.cf` configuration file is used by sendmail, not Postfix, so option B is incorrect. The `/etc/aliases` file contains alias names and local user mailbox names for forwarding email messages, but it doesn't control how Postfix processes the email messages, so option C is incorrect. The `/var/log/maillog` file contains log entries from Postfix; it is not a configuration file, so option E is incorrect.

5. B. The `/var/spool/postfix` directory contains subdirectories where Postfix stores messages as they are being processed, so option B is correct. The `/var/spool/mail` directory contains mailbox files for storing delivered email but not as the messages are processed, so option A is incorrect. The `/etc/postfix` directory contains the Postfix configuration files but not messages as they're processed, so option C is incorrect. The `/etc/mail` directory is not used by Postfix, so option D is incorrect.

6. E. The `mailq` command shows the number of email messages waiting in the mail queue to be delivered, so option E is correct. The `master`, `pickup`, and `smtp` programs are part of the Postfix email process and aren't used from the command line, so options B, C, and D are incorrect. The `newaliases` command creates a new alias database file from a text alias file, but it doesn't display the number of messages in the mail queue, so option A is incorrect.

7. A. The `newaliases` command converts the text alias entries to the aliases database file for processing, so option A is correct. The `master`, `pickup`, and `smtp` commands are part of the Postfix email processing system, but they don't process aliases, so options B, C, and D are all incorrect. The `mailq` command displays the number of email messages waiting in the queue to be sent, so option E is incorrect.

8. A. The `/etc/aliases` file contains alias names and the local user accounts to which they point. The `newaliases` command reads this file to generate the binary aliases database used by Postfix when delivering messages, so option A is correct. The `master.cf`, `main.cf`, and `install.cf` files are Postfix configuration files, but they don't specify alias mappings, so options B, C, and D are incorrect.

9. B. Postfix writes system messages to the `/var/log/maillog` file by default, so option B is correct. The `/var/spool/mail` file is where Postfix stores mbox-style mail messages, so option A is incorrect. The `/var/spool/postfix` directory is where Postfix stores messages as it processes them, so option C is incorrect. The `/var/log/messages` file is where the kernel stores system messages, but that is not used by Postfix, so option D is incorrect.

10. C. Each user on the system can create personalized recipes and store them in the `.procmailrc` file in their `$HOME` directory, so option C is correct. The `/etc/postfix` directory is not part of the procmail setup, so option A is incorrect. The `/etc/procmailrc` file defines recipes applied to all email messages for all user accounts, so option B is incorrect. The `/etc/aliases` file defines alias mappings to local user accounts, not procmail recipes, so option D is incorrect. The `.procmailrc` file must be located in the user's `$HOME` directory so that they can access it; since the `/users` folder doesn't relate to a specific user account, option E is incorrect.

11. B. Procmail applies the recipes defined in the `/etc/procmailrc` file to all incoming email messages, so option B is correct. Procmail applies the `$HOME/.procmailrc` file only to incoming messages for the specific user account, so option C is incorrect. Options A, D, and E are not valid locations for procmail recipes.

12. C. The :0 c recipe matches against all incoming email messages, and the c option copies the messages to the specified directory, so option C is correct.

13. B. The procmail program is the only one listed that is an MDA program used for processing incoming email messages, so option B is the only correct answer.

14. A. The mailbox_command setting defines a program to which Postfix sends all incoming local email messages, so option A is correct. The mydestination setting defines addresses for which Postfix will accept incoming email messages, so option B is incorrect. The myhost setting defines the hostname of the local server, so option C is incorrect. The relayhost setting defines a host to which to send all outbound email messages, so option D is incorrect.

15. D. The mbox mailbox style stores all messages for a user in a single file, either in the /var/spool/mail directory or the user's $HOME directory, so option D is correct. Sendmail, Courier, and exim are application names and not mailbox styles, so options A, B, and E are incorrect. The maildir style of mailboxes uses a directory to store email messages, so option C is incorrect.

16. C. The maildir mailbox style creates separate files for each email message stored in a common folder, so option C is correct. Sendmail, Courier, and exim are application names and not mailbox styles, so options A, B, and E are incorrect. The mbox mailbox style uses a single file to store all messages for a user, so option D is incorrect.

17. C. The Courier program uses the /etc/courier folder to store the configuration files that define how it operates, so option C is correct. The /var/spool/mail and /var/spool/postfix folders store mail messages, not configuration files, so options A and B are incorrect. The /var/log directory stores log files and not configuration files, so option E is incorrect. Courier doesn't use the /etc/mail directory, so option D is incorrect.

18. A. The MAXDAEMONS setting determines how many copies of the Courier program can run at the same time, which controls how many clients can connect, so option A is correct. The MAILDIRPATH setting defines the location of the mailbox directory, so option B is incorrect. The ADDRESS setting defines the interface(s) to listen for incoming connections, so option C is incorrect. The MAXPERIP setting defines the number of connections from a single client but not the total number of clients that can connect, so option D is incorrect. The PORT setting defines the TCP port to listen to for incoming connections, so option E is incorrect.

19. A,D. Some Linux distributions store the Dovecot configuration settings in the dovecot.conf configuration file, while some create multiple files under the /etc/dovecot directory, so options A and D are both correct. Dovecot doesn't use any of the Postfix files or folders, so options B, C, and E are all incorrect.

20. B. The mechanisms setting lists the authentication methods that the server supports, so option B is correct. The mail_location setting defines the mailbox location, so option A is incorrect. The listen setting defines the TCP port Dovecot listens to for incoming client connections, so option C is incorrect. The login_max_connections settings define how many users can connect at the same time, so option D is incorrect. The protocols setting defines what email protocols the server supports, so option E is incorrect.

Chapter 8: Directing DNS

1. B. Option B is correct, because the .edu domain is a Top-Level Domain (TLD), like .gov or .us. The root domain, option A, can be represented by a single dot (.), and on the DNS database tree structure it is a level below the TLDs. Therefore, option A is incorrect. A first-level domain is a TLD subdomain, so option C is wrong. ICANN, option D, is incorrect, because ICANN is the organization responsible for selecting TLD managers. Option E is also wrong, because a second-level domain would be two levels above a TLD on the DNS database tree structure.

2. A, B, C, E. A root server is a server that helps to manage the root zone, so option D is wrong. Options B and C are correct, because a zone can be either a first-level domain and all of its subdomains or a first-level domain and a portion of its subdomains. A zone can be the root zone, which is a special zone managed by root servers, and it encompasses the root domain, so option E is correct. Option A is also correct, because the hint zone is another name for the root zone.

3. A, C, E. Options A, C, and E all fit the requirement of two servers per zone, because one of the servers must be a primary (master) server and one of the following: secondary server, caching server, or forwarding server. Options B and D are real server types but are missing the primary server from their configuration, so these options are incorrect.

4. D. Option D is the correct choice, because a resolver is a program or library routine that creates a DNS query, checks its own cache for the answer, and if it doesn't find it there, sends the query to another name server. Option A is incorrect, because a name server is not a program or library but a server that either has the name resolution data to answer a DNS query or contains a resolver to get the answer. Cache is a location typically checked for a DNS query's answer, and it is not a program or library routine, so option B is wrong. Option C is incorrect, because name resolution is the process of translating an FQDN into an IP address (DNS query and answer). Finally, option E is also incorrect, because a zone is a Domain Name Space portion and not a program or library routine.

5. A, B, C, D, E. Options A, B, C, D, and E are *all* considered software that provides either full or partial DNS protocol implementation. Option D is the tricky one, because it was originally named BIND 10, and it has been renamed Bundy, which is maintained by the Bundy-Project instead of ICANN.

6. C. Option C is correct, because /usr/sbin/named is the BIND daemon. Option A is incorrect, but bind9 is the name of the BIND package on Ubuntu distributions. Option B is wrong, but bind is the name of the BIND package on CentOS distributions. The named.conf file is a BIND configuration file, not the BIND daemon, so option D is wrong. Option E is incorrect, because bindutils is the name of the BIND utilities package on CentOS distributions, not the BIND daemon.

7. A, B, C, E. Options A, B, C, and E are all legitimate groupings (clauses) in the BIND's primary configuration file, named.conf. Option D is a utility, which will allow you to check the named.conf file for proper syntax, and it is the only incorrect choice.

8. A, B, D, E. Options A, B, D, and E all need to be set and/or modified when setting up a local DNS caching-only server. Option A's acl directive lets you create an access control list of hosts allowed to use this caching-only server. Option B's allow-query can use the defined acl to allow the designated host to query this caching-only server. Option D's listen-on directive sets the port to listen on as well as the acl to listen to for DNS queries coming from the allowed hosts. Option E's recursion yes is modified, if needed, so that allowed hosts may use this caching-only server. Option C is incorrect, because you don't have to have BIND logging set in order to use a DNS caching-only server (though it would be a good idea to set this directive as well).

9. B, C, D, E. Options B, C, D, and E all are methods for stopping the BIND service. Of course, the methods that will work for your particular server depend on what distribution is on the server. Option A is incorrect, because rndc flush flushes all of the server's caches but does not stop the BIND service.

10. B. Option B is correct, because a category directive defines DNS message types to be logged. The channel directive defines where DNS messages are to be logged (option A) and how DNS messages are filtered (option D), so options A and D are incorrect. Option C's "How to restart BIND to load logging" has nothing to do with the category directive, so it is a wrong answer. Also, DNS channel log sizes are not set by the category directive, so option E is also incorrect.

11. A, C. Options A and C are correct. The type master directive indicates that this is a zone's primary name server, and the type hint directive specifies that this is the hint or root zone, which is a list of current root name servers. Option B is wrong, because the type directive, which indicates that this is a zone's secondary name server, is type slave and not type secondary. Option D is incorrect, because to indicate that this zone is to enforce a root zone's delegation-only status, the type delegation-only directive should be used. Finally, option E is incorrect, because there is no type root directive.

12. A, C, D. Options A, C, and D are correct. A zone statement class can be either IN (Internet), CH (Chaosnet network protocol), or HS (Hesiod network software). Options B and E are made-up zone statement classes, so they are incorrect.

13. B, C, D. Options B, C, and D are correct. In these cases, a zone transfer will occur. Option A is incorrect, because a zone transfer is not initiated by the primary server's BIND daemon restarting. Option E is also incorrect, because this option essentially shuts down and removes the BIND service on the secondary server.

14. C, E. You'll typically find your default zone databases located in either the /var/named/ directory or the /etc/bind/ directory, depending on your server's distribution. Therefore, options C and E are correct. The other directories are made up, so options A, B, and D are incorrect.

15. E. Option E is correct, because the SOA (start of authority) is the zone resource record type that identifies an authority zone's start and includes the zone's authoritative data. The CNAME (canonical name) record type maps an alias name to a host name, so option A is incorrect. Option B's A record type is a host address record for IPv4 addresses. A PTR record type points to another domain name space location and is typically used in reverse lookups,

so option C is wrong. Option D's NS record type specifies the zone's authoritative name server, so it is incorrect.

16. C. Option C is correct, because a Reverse Zone is a special zone that provides a mapping from an IP address to an FQDN (the reverse of regular DNS mappings). Option A is wrong, because it describes a glue record. Option B is a zone transfer, so it is an incorrect answer. Option D is wrong, because it describes a Hint Zone, and option E is also incorrect because it is the definition of a zone.

17. A, B, C, E. Options A, B, C, and E are correct. Only option D is incorrect. Updating BIND software is not tied to a calendar. Because of constant malicious attack threats, BIND software should be updated as soon as a new version is available.

18. D, E. When setting up a chroot jail, either /chroot/named (option D) or /chroot/bind (option E) is typically used as the new root (/) directory, depending on your distribution. The other directories may also be used in the BIND configuration, but they are not used as the new root (/) directory in a chroot jail. Therefore, options A, B, and C are incorrect.

19. C. The zone signing key (ZSK) is the encryption key used to digitally sign a particular zone's resource records, so option C is correct. Option A's digital signature is produced when the ZSK is used to sign the zone's resource records, so option A is incorrect. A key signing key (KSK) is the encryption key used to sign a particular zone's ZSK, so option B is wrong. In option D, the chain of trust has a higher zone's key sign a lower zone's key, creating a trusted chain with a trust anchor, so it is an incorrect choice. Finally, option E's DNSKEY is where the KSK is stored, so it also is an incorrect choice.

20. A. Option A's dnssec-keygen utility can produce either TSIG or DNSSEC keys, depending on the options used, so it is the correct choice. The dnssec-signzone utility is used on systems that have the TSIG keys generated but do not set up automatic signing via the auto-dnssec and inline-signing directives in the named.conf file, to sign the zone manually. Therefore, option B is wrong. The dnssec-dsfromkey utility is used to create a record for the parent zone in the chain of trust, so option C is also wrong. Options D and E contain made-up utilities, so they are incorrect choices.

Chapter 9: Offering Web Services

1. C. HTTP defines the client requests and server responses required to transfer a data file from a web server, so option C is correct. HTML (option A) defines the format of a web document but not the transfer protocol. SSL (option B) and TLS (option D) define encryption protocols, and they aren't used in the actual file transfer protocol, so both are incorrect.

2. A. The HTML standard defines formatting rules for creating web pages, so option A is correct. HTTP (option C) defines the protocol used to transfer the document from the web server to the client browser but not how to format the document itself, so option C is incorrect. SSL and TLS are encryption protocols and don't format any content in the actual data, so options B and D are incorrect.

3. D. The 404 response code in HTTP indicates that the file requested by the client was not found on the web server, so option D is correct. The 200 status code (option A) indicates that the request was successful, so option A is incorrect. The 403 status code indicates that the client does not have permission to retrieve the requested file, so option B is incorrect. The 500 status code indicates that there is a server problem preventing the file from being downloaded, so option C is incorrect.

4. B. The apache2ctl utility allows you to issue a graceful shutdown request to the Apache web server, preserving any existing connections to the server, so option B is correct. The systemctl is used by some Linux distributions to stop or start processes, but it doesn't shut down the Apache web server gracefully, so option A is incorrect. The httpd and apache2 programs are the actual web server and don't have options to stop the server gracefully, so options C and D are incorrect.

5. B. The apache2ctl utility can also parse the Apache configuration files and note any syntax issues, so option B is correct. The systemctl utility is used by some Linux distributions to stop or start processes, but it doesn't parse configuration files, so option A is incorrect. The httpd and apache2 programs are the main Apache web server, and they don't have the option to parse the configuration files, so options C and D are incorrect.

6. A. The DocumentRoot directive defines the folder from which the web server allows clients to request files, so option A is correct. The ServerRoot directive defines the location of the configuration files for the server, so option B is incorrect. The Listen directive defines the IP addresses and ports the Apache server uses to listen for incoming requests, so option C is incorrect. The DirectoryIndex directive defines the default files to look for when a client requests a folder name instead of a filename, so option D is incorrect.

7. C. The <Directory> feature allows you to create a block of directives that apply to a specific folder location, so option C is correct. The <VirtualHost> feature allows you to create a block of directives that apply to a specific virtual host but not a directory, so option A is incorrect. The <IfDefined> feature allows you to create a block of directives to apply only when an environment variable is defined but not apply it only to a specific directory, so option B is incorrect. The <IfModule> feature allows you to create a block of directives to apply only when a module is loaded but not apply it to a specific directory, so option D is incorrect.

8. B. The LogFormat directive defines the format of the log file entries, allowing you to decide what information is stored in the log file, thus option B is correct. The ErrorLog directive defines where the error logs are located but not what they contain, so option A is incorrect. The ErrorDocument directive defines how error messages sent to the clients are defined but not how the error logs are formatted, so option C is incorrect. The DocumentRoot directive defines the folder from which to serve files but not the format of the error log, so option D is incorrect.

9. C. The access.log file logs all client requests to the web server, so option C is correct. The error.log file contains only errors, not valid requests, so option A is incorrect. The apache2.conf and httpd.conf files are configuration files for the Apache web server, not log files, so options B and D are both incorrect.

10. B. The `UserDir` directive defines the folder name that users can create in their HOME folders to offer files on the web server, so option B is correct. The `AuthUserFile` defines the location of a user authentication file, so option A is incorrect. The `DocumentRoot` directive defines the server folder to offer to web clients, not the name of individual user folders, so option C is incorrect. The `LoadModule` directive loads feature modules into the Apache server; it doesn't specify the location of the user web files folder, so option D is incorrect.

11. D. The `ServerName` directive defines the domain name in each virtual host block, so option D is correct. The `DocumentRoot` directive defines a folder and not a domain name, so option A is incorrect. The `NameVirtualHost` directive defines the IP address of the physical server, not the domain names to accept, so option B is incorrect. The `<VirtualHost>` block defines all of the directives for the virtual host, not just the domain name, so option C is incorrect.

12. A. The `Listen` directive defines the IP address and port the Apache server uses to accept incoming client requests, so option A is correct. The `<VirtualHost>` feature allows you to create a block of directives for the virtual host, but it doesn't define the IP addresses, so option B is incorrect. The `NameVirtualHost` directive defines the common IP address for name-based virtual hosts, but it isn't used for IP-based virtual hosting, so option C is incorrect. The `DocumentRoot` directive defines a folder and not an IP address, so option D is incorrect.

13. B. The `htpasswd` utility creates a text file with a userid and encrypted password that can be used for authentication, so option B is correct. The `httpd` and `apache2` programs are names for the main Apache web server program and don't generate text files, so options A and C are incorrect. The `mod_auth` is a module used to implement authentication on the Apache server, but it doesn't create the userid/password file, so option D is incorrect.

14. C. The `AuthUserFile` directive defines the location of the userid/password file used for user authentication, so option C is correct. The `AuthType` directive defines the type of authentication used but not the location of the authentication file, so option A is incorrect. The `AuthName` directive defines the text used to query the client for authentication but not the location of the authentication file, so option B is incorrect. The `Order` directive defines a network restriction and not an authentication restriction, so option D is incorrect.

15. A. The Common Gateway Interface (CGI) allows the Apache web server to pass files to an external program interpreter to process embedded program code, so option A is correct. `mod_perl` and `mod_php` are names for modules that incorporate internal program processing; they don't pass the code to an external program, so both options B and D are incorrect. The `mod_auth` module is for authentication and not programming, so option C is incorrect.

16. B. The `AddHandler` directive defines how the Apache web server should handle files based on their file extensions. It is used to redirect files to specific processes, such as code interpreters, so option B is correct. The `LoadModule` directive installs a module but doesn't redirect files to separate processes, so option A is incorrect. The `DocumentRoot` directive defines the folder on the server from which files are served but not how to process them, so option C is incorrect. The `DirectoryIndex` directive defines what files should be used by default when a client requests a directory but not how to process them, so option D is incorrect.

17. D. The `SSLCertificateFile` directive defines the location of the signed server certificate file that should be used for SSL sessions, so option D is correct. The `DirectoryIndex` directive defines the default files to serve when a client requests a directory, so option A is incorrect. The `SSLCertificateKeyFile` directive defines the encryption key file, not the certificate file, so option B is incorrect. The `SSLEngine` directive defines when the server should allow SSL connections but not the location of the certificate file, so option C is incorrect.

18. A, C. A web proxy server caches web requests from multiple clients so that future requests can be served from the cache. It also can restrict the websites clients are allowed to view. That makes options A and C correct. Option B defines the role of a reverse proxy server, not a standard web proxy server, so it is incorrect. Option D defines the role of the `DocumentRoot` directive, a web proxy server doesn't restrict the files that a server can serve, so option D is incorrect.

19. B. The `auth_param` directive defines authentication settings used to authenticate clients, so option B is correct. `mod_auth` is an Apache web server module and not a Squid directive, so option A is incorrect. The `acl` directive is used to define access groups, so option C is incorrect, and the `http_access` directive is used to define access rules, so it too is incorrect.

20. B. The `server` section in the nginx configuration file defines the directives that apply to the entire server, so option B is correct. The `location` section defines directives that apply to a specific folder location, not the entire server, so option A is incorrect. The `root` directive defines the DocumentRoot location on the web server, so it is incorrect, and the `listen` directive defines the IP addresses and ports the server uses to listen for incoming client requests, so it too is incorrect.

Chapter 10: Sharing Files

1. C. Option C is correct, because the `/var/log/samba/` directory is where you would typically find Samba log files. The `/etc/smb/` directory (option A), `/etc/samba/` directory (option B), and `/etc/samba.d/` directory (option E) are all incorrect, because these are (or were) directories for storing Samba configuration files. Option D is also incorrect, because the `/var/lib/samba/` directory is used for storing things such as Samba user databases, not log files.

2. A, B, D. Option A is correct, because it is the daemon used on a Samba server to implement the SMB protocol. Option B is a tricky one, but it is also correct. The CUPS daemon, cupsd, can be used with the Samba server daemon to provide Samba print shares. Option D is also correct, because if you have legacy Windows systems within your network and need Samba services, NetBIOS over TCP via the nmbd daemon must be used. Option C is also a tricky one, because the actual daemon name for the Name Service Switch daemon is winbindd and not winbind, so option C is wrong. Option E is a made-up daemon name and therefore is incorrect.

3. A. Option A is correct, because the `smb.conf` is the main Samba configuration file. Option B is made-up and is therefore a wrong choice. Option C, `mount.cifs`, is a command that allows you to mount a Samba share on a client system and is an incorrect choice. Option D is also incorrect, because /etc/samba.d is a directory (typically not used anymore) for storing Samba configuration files. Option E's smbcontrol is a command for managing the Samba smbd daemon and is also an incorrect answer.

4. D. Option D is correct, because after modifying the main Samba configuration file, you should next check the file's syntax, and the testparm command will do that. You should not reload the configuration file into a Samba server daemon until you have checked the configuration file's syntax, and therefore option A is wrong. Option B is wrong, because there is no need to reboot the Samba server daemon. The smbstatus command displays current Samba server connections but does not check the Samba configuration file's syntax, so option C is wrong. Option E is also incorrect, because creating a directory or setting up a printer queue to share is not the next needed step.

5. E. Option E is correct, because the correct directive is workgroup and it needs to be set to the Windows group or domain name for setting up Samba in a mixed Windows and Linux environment. The other options are wrong because they are incorrect or made-up directive names.

6. A, C, D. Options A, C, and D are correct, because they are legal settings for the passdb backend directive, and they are the various Samba user account information databases typically located in the /var/lib/samba/ directory. Options B and E are incorrect, because they are legal settings for the Samba security directive and not the passdb backend directive.

7. C. Option C is the best answer, because file shares are typically found under a share name, such as [myshare]. Option A is incorrect, because the [global] section is for globally applied directives that determine how the Samba server will conduct networking, logging, name resolution, and so on. The [netlogins] section, option B, is incorrect, because this section is for providing directives needed for when the Samba server is acting as a domain controller. Option D's [printers] is incorrect, because this section is for defining printer shares. Option E is also wrong, because the [profiles] section holds directives needed for roaming user profiles.

8. A. Option A is correct, because the public directive can be set to no (passwords required) or yes (passwords not required). The browseable directive (option B) is incorrect, because it determines whether a share is seen in an available shares list. Option C is a wrong choice, because the guest only directive sets whether only guest connections are allowed for this service. The writable directive in option D is an antonym for the read only directive in option E, and they are both incorrect choices because they determine whether write access is granted to a share.

9. B. Option B is correct, because the smbclient allows FTP-style access to a Samba share (as long as the appropriate access is granted). The pdbedit command (option A) is incorrect, because it does not provide access to a Samba share but instead manages any of the Samba user databases. Option C is wrong, because the smbpasswd command manages either the Samba smbpasswd or tdbsam database but provides no share access. The rpcclient command in option D is incorrect, because this command executes Samba client Microsoft

RPC functions. Option E is an incorrect choice, because the `ftp` command is an older command that provides access to FTP servers, not Samba shares.

10. A, B, C, D, E. All the answers are correct, because they are all potential troubleshooting items if a Samba client is unable to access a Samba share. Of course, you may find and fix the root problem cause before needing to complete all the various items.

11. E. Option E, `mountd`, is correct because this daemon manages any NFS client mount requests that come into the NFS server. Option A, `portmapper`, and option C, `rpcbind`, are the same daemon (just different names), but they are not the correct answer, because this daemon registers RPC services to the various RPC ports, among other things. Option B, `rpc.lockd`, is incorrect because it is the kernel service that provides NFS file locking. The `statd` daemon, option D, is a wrong choice, because this daemon works with the `lockd` kernel service to provide NLM protocol file locking.

12. A, C. Option A is correct, because the primary NFS configuration file is `/etc/exports`. Option C is also correct, because the `/etc/exports.d/` directory may contain extra export configuration files with an `.exports` file extension name. Option B is a made-up directory name, so it is an incorrect choice. The `/proc/fs/nfs/` directory houses the `exports` file, which contains current exports and the individual clients using them, so option D is a wrong choice. Finally, option E is incorrect, because the `/var/lib/nfs/` directory stores the `xtab`, `etab`, and `rmtab` files, which contain various NFS export information.

13. D, E. Options D and E are correct. On current distributions, system administrators typically use these filesystem locations to create subdirectories, which serve as NFS exports (shares). Options A and B are wrong, because you should never share either the NFS server's root directory (/) or its `/etc/` directory. The `/proc/` directory, option C, is also incorrect, because it is illogical to share this directory, which houses process information.

14. A, C. Options A and C are the best answers. The `ro` directive sets the share as read-only and the `async` directive increases performance of read-only (`ro`) exports. The `rw` directive sets the share as read/write, so option B is incorrect. The `sync` directive is best used with read/write shares, so option D is also incorrect. Option E's `subtree_check` enables permission checking on higher-level directories and is not directly tied to a read-only share.

15. A, D. Options A and D are correct, because both the `exportfs` and the `showmount` utilities display NFS share information. Option B's `mount.nfs` utility is used for mounting an NFS share from an NFS client, so it is a wrong choice. The `rpcinfo` command (option C) displays RPC service information, and though the information may be related to NFS shares, it is not NFS share information. Therefore, it is an incorrect choice. The `smbstatus` command in Option E is used for displaying current Samba server connections and not NFS shares, so it also is an incorrect choice.

16. E. Option E is correct, because the `exportfs -v` uses the utility's verbose mode and displays all the various NFS shares being offered with detailed information concerning them. The `-a` (option A) is incorrect, because it is used to export all configured shares in the `/etc/exports` file. Option B's `-o` is also wrong, because it is used to export a share configured on the command line. The `-r` operand (option C) re-exports configured shares, so it is a wrong choice. Finally, the -u operand in option D unexports an NFS share, so it is also an incorrect choice.

17. B, C. The pure-ftpd daemon is from the Pure-FTPd FTP server package, so option B is correct. The vsftpd daemon is the Very Secure FTP server, so option C is also correct. FileZilla (option D) is a GUI-based FTP client, so it is an incorrect choice. Options A and E (ftp and lftp) are command-line FTP clients, so they are wrong choices as well.

18. C, D. For a passive FTP connection, only the FTP client is active in establishing the connections, so option C is a correct choice and options A and B are wrong. A data connection and a command connection are established for *both* active and passive modes, so option D is correct. Option E is wrong, because only in active mode does the FTP server use ports 20 and 21. In passive mode, the FTP server uses port 20 as its data port but a *random* unprivileged port as its command port.

19. A, E. Option A is correct, because often the username accepted upon an FTP client connection is anonymous. Option E is also correct, because the user and group for typical FTP client connections is ftp and for vsftpd is set via the ftp_username directive. Option B is incorrect, because it is a FTP server daemon. Individual usernames are not typically used for anonymous FTP connections, so option C is wrong. Option D is also incorrect, because it is a made-up username.

20. B, C, D, E. Options B, D, and E are correct, because these three directives are needed by vsftpd for files to be uploaded by anonymous. Option C is also correct, because this directive is needed by pure-ftpd for files to be uploaded by anonymous. Option A is a wrong choice, because it is a made-up directive.

Chapter 11: Managing Network Clients

1. B. The DHCPd application stores its configuration in the /etc/dhcp/dhcpd.conf text file, so option B is correct. Some applications use a folder to store multiple configuration files, but DHCPd doesn't do that, so option A is incorrect. The isc-dhcp-server is the name of the Debian software package, not the configuration file, so option C is incorrect. The /etc/services file contains a list of valid TCP and UDP ports defined for the server, not the DHCPd configuration file, so option D is incorrect.

2. C. The router option defines the default router assigned to network clients, so option C is correct. The smtp-server option defines a default mail server for clients, so option A is incorrect. The broadcast-address option defines the address used to send broadcasts on the network, so that is incorrect. The range option defines the pool of IP addresses assigned to clients in the network, so that is also incorrect.

3. D. The range option setting defines a range of IP addresses from which the DHCP server can assign an IP address to network clients, thus option D is correct. The smtp-server option defines a default mail server, so option A is incorrect. The broadcast-address option defines the address used to send local broadcast messages on the network, so option B is

incorrect. The router option is used to define a default router for the network, so option C is incorrect.

4. A. IP addresses assigned to network clients are called leases, and the file used to track currently leased IP addresses is the dhcpd.leases file, stored in the /var/lib/dhcp folder, thus option A is correct. The /etc/dhcp/dhcpd.conf file is the standard configuration file for DHCPd, but it doesn't store the current IP address lease information, so option B is incorrect. The dhcpd.leases file is not stored in the /etc/dhcp folder, so option C is incorrect. IP address leases are not stored in the dhcpd.conf configuration file, so option D is also incorrect.

5. D. The hardware setting defines the Ethernet address (MAC) of a client to assign it a static IP address, so option D is correct. The range setting defines a pool of IP addresses to assign to network clients, not a static IP address, so option A is incorrect. The fixed-address setting defines a fixed IP address to assign to a client but doesn't define the client's MAC address, so option B is incorrect. The host-name option defines the local hostname to assign to the client, but not the MAC address, so option C is incorrect.

6. A. The host feature allows you to bundle multiple configuration settings and options together to assign to a specific device on the network, so option A is correct. The group feature is similar, but it bundles options and settings for multiple hosts on the network, so option B is incorrect. The range setting defines a pool of IP addresses assigned to all clients, not a specific client, so option C is incorrect. The fixed-address setting defines a fixed IP address to assign to a specific client, but it doesn't bundle multiple configuration settings and options together for the client, so option D is incorrect.

7. A. DHCP option 1 defines the subnet mask assigned to the network client, so option A is correct. DHCP option 3 defines the default router, so option B is incorrect. DHCP option 5 defines the name server for the network, so option C is incorrect, and DHCP option 6 defines the domain server for the network, so option D is incorrect.

8. C. The pam_unix.so module uses the standard Linux /etc/passwd and /etc/shadow files to authenticate users, so option C is correct. The pam_ldap.so module uses an LDAP network directory to authenticate uses, so option A is incorrect. The pam_userdb.so module uses a database to authenticate user accounts, so option B is incorrect, and the pam_sss.so module uses the System Security Services Daemon (SSSD) method to authenticate users on remote directories, not the local /etc/passwd and /etc/shadow files, so option D is incorrect.

9. B. The pam_ldap.so module uses an LDAP server to authenticate users using a network directory, so option B is correct. The pam_unix.so module authenticates users using the standard /etc/passwd file, so option A is incorrect. The pam_userdb.so module authenticates users using a local database file, so option C is incorrect. The pam_access.so module provides anonymous logins for FTP servers; it doesn't authenticate users with a network directory, so option D is incorrect.

10. C. The pam_cracklib.so module provides checks for weak passwords, so option C is correct. The pam_limits.so module provides resource limits, such as number of files open or CPU time, but it doesn't restrict passwords, so option A is incorrect. The pam_unix.so

module just performs standard authentication using the /etc/passwd file; it doesn't monitor the user passwords, so option B is incorrect. The pam_userdb.so module authenticates users against a local database, but it also doesn't enforce any password restrictions, so option D is incorrect.

11. B. The PAM application uses the pam.conf configuration file, stored in the /etc/ folder, so option B is correct. Option A, /etc/pam.d, is a folder, not a single configuration file, so option A is incorrect. The /etc/pam.d/pam.conf location mixes the single file and multiple file methods together and doesn't exist in the PAM setup, so option C is incorrect. The /etc/pamd.conf file doesn't exist in the PAM setup, so option D is incorrect.

12. A. The PAM application uses the /etc/pam.d folder to store individual application configuration files, so option A is correct. When using separate application configuration files, PAM doesn't use the pam.conf file, so options B and C are incorrect. The pamd.conf file doesn't exist in the PAM set up, so option D is incorrect.

13. C. The requisite control entry terminates the authentication process if the authentication fails. No other entries in the configuration are checked. Thus, option C is correct. The sufficient entry passes the authentication if the check succeeds, but it doesn't terminate the authentication if it fails, so option A is incorrect. The required entry only indicates a failure status if the authentication fails, but it allows the authentication process to check other entries, so option B is incorrect. The optional entry doesn't block further entries if it fails, so option D is also incorrect.

14. B. The session feature type allows you to define a log file where PAM will log authentication attempts, so option B is correct. The account feature type only verifies the account; it doesn't log the transaction, so option A is incorrect. Likewise, the auth feature type only provides authentication services; it doesn't log them, so option D is also incorrect. The password feature type provides password management features but also doesn't log the transactions, so option C is incorrect.

15. D. The object class defines a template that provides a set of attributes assigned to an object in the LDAP database, so option D is correct. The object ID uniquely identifies each object, but it doesn't provide a template of attributes, so option A is incorrect. The schema defines the structure of the database, but it isn't used as a template for objects, so option B is incorrect. The LDAP tree encompasses the actual objects contained in the LDAP database, not just a template for new objects, so option C is incorrect.

16. A. The attributes define the data values associated with an object in the LDAP database, so option A is correct. The object class defines a template of attributes that is applied to an object but not the actual attribute values themselves, so option B is incorrect. The object ID is a unique value assigned to each object, but it doesn't include any information about the object, so option C is incorrect. The schema defines the objects in the database and how they are interrelated, but it doesn't define the actual information about individual objects, so option D is incorrect.

17. D. Each object must have a unique distinguished name that references the location of the object in the LDAP tree as well as the object name, thus option D is correct. The object ID value for each object is unique, but it isn't a name that you can reference, so option A is

incorrect. The attributes of objects aren't unique, so option B is incorrect. The object class defines a template that is applied to all similar objects in the LDAP tree, so it too is not unique, and option C is incorrect.

18. B. The main application program for the OpenLDAP server is slapd, so option B is correct. The slurpd program is used only when replicating LDAP servers, so option A is incorrect. The slapadd program is used to add new objects to the LDAP database; it isn't the main LDAP server program, so option C is incorrect. The slapindex program allows you to re-index the LDAP database, but it too isn't the main LDAP server program, so option D is incorrect.

19. C. The slapadd command-line program allows you to update the LDAP database with new objects, so option C is correct. The ldapadd and ldapmodify programs are client applications and not server applications, so options A and D are incorrect. The slapindex program only re-indexes the existing objects in the LDAP database; it can't add new objects, so option B is incorrect.

20. B. The ldapadd program allows you to add new objects into the LDAP database from a client, so option B is correct. The slapadd program also allows you to add new objects, but only from the server, since it interacts directly with the LDAP files, so option A is incorrect. The ldapmodify program is a client program, but it can only modify existing LDAP objects, not add new ones, so option C is incorrect. The slapindex program is a server program that re-indexes the existing objects in the LDAP database, so option D is incorrect.

Chapter 12: Setting Up System Security

1. A. An attack vector is any path that allows an attacker to gain access to a system. Since a vulnerability allows access to a system, it's an attack vector; thus option A is correct. The other three options just describe other types of vulnerabilities, so options B, C, and D are incorrect.

2. C. The /etc/services file contains a mapping of port numbers to applications, so option C is correct. The /etc/ssh/sshd_conf file is the configuration for the OpenSSH server, the /etc/openvpn folder contains configuration files for the OpenVPN application, and the /proc/sys/net/ipv4 folder contains settings for the IPv4 stack in the kernel, so options A, B, and D are all incorrect.

3. B. The second parameter of the telnet command specifies the TCP port to connect to, so option B is correct. Options A and C show incorrect formats for the telnet command, so they are incorrect. Option D is incorrect, because you can specify any TCP port number for the second parameter.

4. D. The netstat command can display all of the ports that are open, listening for incoming network connections, so option D is correct. The telnet command can connect to only one port at a time, so option A is incorrect. The iptables command works with the kernel packet processing features and not network ports, so option B is incorrect. The ssh command can connect only to port 22, so option C is incorrect.

5. B. The −z option specifies a list of ports or a port range that the netcat command should scan looking for listening ports, so option B is correct. The −v option provides more verbose output, so option A is incorrect. The −l option tells netcat to listen for incoming connections, so option C is incorrect. The −6 option tells netcat to use IPv6 addresses, so option D is also incorrect.

6. A. The −A option tells nmap to perform a fingerprint analysis of the remote system, so option A is correct. The −sT option scans all TCP ports, while the −sU option scans all UDP ports, so options B and C are incorrect. The −p option specifies a port range to scan, so option D is also incorrect.

7. C. The Network Vulnerability Tests (NVT) simulate known attacks against systems, and they are downloaded as part of OpenVAS, so option C is correct. The National Vulnerability Database (NVD) is maintained by US-CERT to define vulnerabilities but not use them to simulate the vulnerabilities, so option A is incorrect. The distribution Software Repository doesn't store vulnerabilities, so option B is incorrect. The web interface allows you to interact with OpenVAS, but it doesn't simulate vulnerabilities, so option D is incorrect.

8. D. An intrusion detection system (IDS) can monitor system and network events, looking for triggers that indicate an active attack is occurring, so option D is correct. Port scanners can tell you of open attack vectors, but they can't tell you when an attack is happening, so option A is incorrect. The Network Vulnerability Test (NVT) simulates attacks, but it doesn't warn you of current attacks, so option B is incorrect. The VPN allows you to establish a secure connection between two remote hosts, but it doesn't warn you of an attack, so option C is incorrect.

9. B. The jail.conf file, located in the /etc/fail2ban folder, contains the rule definitions that determine what events fail2ban should monitor.

10. A. The Snort application monitors the network looking for active attacks, so option A is correct. The OpenVPN package provides an encrypted tunnel between two public networks to provide a secure environment, but it doesn't act as an NIDS, so option B is incorrect. The OpenSSH application provides a secure channel between a client and server, but it doesn't monitor packets on the network, so option C is incorrect. The OpenVAS application is a vulnerability tool, but it doesn't monitor network packets by itself, so option D is incorrect.

11. C. The sniffer mode of Snort displays a brief description of each packet received, so option C is correct. Option A is the logging mode, which logs packets to a file instead of displaying them, so option A is incorrect. The NIDS mode only reports vulnerability events, so option B is incorrect. By default, the Snort command-line mode doesn't display the packets, so option D is also incorrect.

12. C. The HOME_NET variable defines the local addresses for Snort to monitor, so option C is correct. The EXTERNAL_NET variable defines remote addresses, so option A is incorrect. Snort doesn't need to define local addresses or point to the configuration folder name, so options B and D are both incorrect.

13. D. The arrow indicates the traffic flow, so 10.0.0.1 -> 10.0.0.2 defines the traffic flow we are looking for, and option D is correct. The <- indicator shows that the traffic is coming from the .2 address to the .1 address, which is wrong, so option A is incorrect.

Option B also shows the traffic going the wrong way, so option B is incorrect. Option C uses the <> bidirectional operator, so it too is incorrect.

14. B. The IPv4 specifications use the 10.0.0.0 through 10.255.255.255, 172.16.0.0 through 172.31.255.255, and 192.168.0.0 through 192.168.255.255 network address ranges; thus option B is correct. Options A, C, and D all have the incorrect number of address ranges, so they are all incorrect.

15. A. The `fe80` value identifies the starting address for link local addresses in IPv6. The remainder of the address is usually derived from the Ethernet MAC address to ensure it's unique on the network. The `ff02` value is the multicast address for routers, and `ff05` is the multicast address for DHCP servers, so option C is incorrect. The `aabb` value isn't a reserved number in IPv6, so option D is incorrect.

16. C. Network Address Translation (NAT) allows a client on a private network address to have its address translated to a public address before leaving the network, so option C is correct. SSH provides an encrypted network connection, so option A is incorrect. The `tel-net` command provides plaintext communication, so option B is incorrect. The IDS software detects attackers; it doesn't provide connection support, so option D is incorrect.

17. B. The `iptables` command allows you to manipulate the rules defined in the kernel chains and tables to filter the network traffic, so option B is correct. The `nc` command provides only network communication, so option A is incorrect. The `netstat` and `nmap` commands allow you to view only network port status, so options C and D are both incorrect.

18. C. The `-A` option is used to add new rules to a chain or table, so option C is correct. The `-L` option lists the existing rules, so option A is incorrect. The `-F` option flushes the rules cache, so option B is incorrect. The `-j` option specifies a default action; it does not add a new rule, so option D is incorrect.

19. A. The REJECT policy drops the packet but sends an ICMP message back to the source IP address indicating the failure; thus option A is correct. The DROP policy drops the packet silently, so option B is incorrect. The ACCEPT and LOG policies accept all packets, while the LOG policy stores packet information in a log file, so options C and D are incorrect.

20. A. The `-P` option defines the chain and policy to use as the default. The `-j` option defines the action for a rule, so option B is incorrect. The `-L` option only lists chains and tables; it doesn't modify them, so option C is incorrect. The `-F` option flushes all rules out from the chain, so option D is incorrect.

Index

D

E

F

G

O

Comprehensive Online Learning Environment

Register on Sybex.com to gain access to the comprehensive online interactive learning environment and test bank to help you study for your LPIC-2 certification.

The online test bank includes:

- **Assessment Test** to help you focus your study to specific objectives
- **Chapter Tests** to reinforce what you learned
- **Practice Exams** to test your knowledge of the material
- **Digital Flashcards** to reinforce your learning and provide last-minute test prep before the exam
- **Searchable Glossary** gives you instant access to the key terms you'll need to know for the exam

Go to http://www.wiley.com/go/sybextestprep **to register and gain access to this comprehensive study tool package.**

Printed and bound by CPI Group (UK) Ltd, Croydon, CR0 4YY

27/10/2024

14580184-0005